Choosing to change

Extending access, choice and mobility in higher education

The report of the HEQC CAT Development Project

The mission of the Higher Education Quality Council (HEQC) is to contribute to the maintenance and improvement of quality, at all levels, in institutions of higher education in the United Kingdom. HEQC is a company limited by guarantee and is funded by subscriptions from individual universities and colleges of higher education. The services it provides for these institutions cover:

- quality assurance, including the regular auditing of institutions' quality processes;

- quality enhancement, including the dissemination of good practice;

- acting as a national voice on quality issues in higher education.

The Council also advises the Secretaries of State for Education, Scotland and Wales on applications from institutions for degree awarding powers.

ISBN 1 85824 150 2

Published by Higher Education Quality Council

344-354 Gray's Inn Road

London WC1X 8BP

Tel: 071-837 2223

Fax: 071-278 1676

Cover: Slapstick Design Partnership (071-600 0205)
Origination: Davies Communications (071-482 4596)
Printing: WBC Ltd, Bridgend (0656-668836)

Preface

This report is the outcome of a project commissioned and funded by the Department for Education, the Employment Department, the former Council for National Academic Awards (CNAA) and the Higher Education Quality Council (HEQC).

The work of the project has been undertaken by a team led by Professor David Robertson (Project Director) at Liverpool John Moores University with a Project Management Group established by HEQC's Credit and Access Advisory Group.

The views expressed in this report are those of the author, Professor David Robertson, and are not necessarily endorsed by HEQC or the sponsoring departments.

The Council wishes to place on public record its thanks to Professor Robertson and the project team and also to the large number of people in higher education and elsewhere who have contributed in many and various ways to the development of this report. Particular thanks go to the members of the HEQC Credit and Access Advisory Group under the chairmanship of Professor Peter Toyne, and to the members of the Project Management Group under the chairmanship of Mr Richard Lewis.

The HEQC will be consulting with higher education institutions and other key parties and will report on the outcomes to the sponsors. The Council looks forward to the continuing discussion.

Roger Brown
Chief Executive

Foreword

The investigative programme began in November 1992 and, with the preparation of the final report, it has been completed in under 18 months. The scale and complexity of the investigation proved greater than initially anticipated and the final report reflects this. Expressions of interest have been overwhelming and expectations have needed restraint. There is now so much activity in the development of credit systems that in a short time further changes may overtake us. This report will have served its purpose if it has made a modest contribution to that process. For the report itself, its conclusions are limited by the time to do them justice. Further research and extensive consultation on a number of matters will be necessary.

From the investigation it is clear that we are near to establishing in the United Kingdom the critical mass necessary for the development of a *credit culture*. However the shift from meritocratic to democratic participation in higher (and further) education will require perseverance. Government, institutions, national bodies and the beneficiaries of higher education have much to gain from a sector which commands public support and respect by educating large numbers of individuals to the limits of their potential. It is a prize which the development of credit systems can help to bring within our reach.

I cannot leave these matters without recording my debt to the hundreds of colleagues in universities and colleges who have contributed to this work and wished it success. I am particularly grateful to members of the Project Advisory Groups who gave their time and experience freely, and to my team of consultants who gave generous advice and support on a wide range of matters. I would wish to offer the most generous tribute to the investigative team: Gareth Parry, Norman Evans, Professor Anne Hilton, Dr Rob Allen, Geoff Layer, Stephen Adam and Professor Peter Scott for their inventiveness, patience and much-needed support throughout the long research programme. Their efforts have been central to the preparation of this report.

I acknowledge specific assistance from a number of other colleagues. Firstly, my appreciation is due to: Dr Edwin Kerr and Dr Derek Pollard, for their commitment to credit systems in higher education and for guidance on matters too numerous to mention; to David Browning, Geoff Stanton, Tony Tait and Peter Wilson for innovation and perseverance with credit systems in further education; to Malcolm Christie and Dr Adrian Seville for clarifying certain aspects of the new funding proposals; to Alan Tuckett, for helpful comments on a number of points; to Dr Ron Barnett and Professor Tony Becher for providing a thoughtful note on the impact of these proposals for the character of British higher education; and to the Vice-Chancellors and Principals, Dr John Ashworth, Professor Laing Barden, Dr John Daniel, Professor David Johns, Professor Philip Love, Professor Leslie Wagner and Professor Roger Waterhouse, busy people who found time to advise and support this work. Secondly, I have a special debt to pay my colleagues in Liverpool: Teresa Bergin (MerOCF), Dr Liz Haslam, Dr Steve Jackson, Dr Terry Jeves, Phoebe Lambert, Dr Phil Margham, Anne Richardson, Rod Tyrer and Dr Jim Wrightson, who helped build the Integrated Credit Scheme at Liverpool John Moores University, and the Merseyside Open College Federation, which have provided me over the years with experience in the development and management of modular credit systems. Without their help, this report would not have been written, although errors of judgement or fact are mine alone.

In conclusion, I must record my thanks to my University for allowing me the opportunity to undertake this research, and specifically to Professor Peter Toyne and members of the HEQC Credit and Access Advisory Group, and to Richard Lewis and members of the Project Management Sub-Group for their encouragement and kindness during the investigation. Furthermore, I am grateful for the support I received from the funding partners, Dr Roger Brown and the staff of HEQC, Ros Seyd (Employment Department) and Anthony Woollard (DFE) who always made themselves available to provide the guidance I needed at critical moments in the preparation process. I hope they feel their efforts have been repaid by the publication of this report which I am now pleased to submit for their attention.

David Robertson, Project Director   Liverpool, 6 April 1994

Contents

Tables and figures

Part One

I. *Introduction*

1.   This report reviews progress to date and makes recommendations on the further development of credit accumulation and transfer within higher education and beyond. It has been commissioned and funded by the Higher Education Quality Council, the Department for Education and the Employment Department.

2.   The Higher Education Quality Council appointed a Project Director to lead an investigation and a research team was assembled by November 1992. The initial explorations were completed within a year and a final report from the Project Director followed thereafter.

3.   The Project was assisted by a Steering Committee, the Credit and Access Advisory Group, which met four times; interim progress was considered by a symposium of project members and associates. Representatives of institutions, funding councils, national agencies, government departments, employers and professional bodies were members of the Steering Committee and attended the symposium. Details concerning the Steering Committee and the symposium may be found in Annex A to this report.

4.   The investigative programme was organised into eight sub-projects, each with a Project Officer assisted by an Advisory Group. The advisory groups met on more than fifty occasions, usually in London: at the Senate House of the University of London, at the National Council for Vocational Qualifications, and at the Higher Education Quality Council. Various other meetings were also arranged in Scotland, Wales and Northern Ireland.

5.   This report brings together the work of the sub-projects, results of commissioned surveys, archive material, written submissions, statistical data, unpublished materials and other documentary sources collected during the investigation.

6.   The Project Director and members of the research team visited over 35 institutions of higher education across the United Kingdom; conducted over 200 individual interviews, many with Vice-Chancellors, Registrars and other senior institutional staff; received over 100 written submissions, of which 40 were from professional bodies; conducted four extensive surveys involving almost 400 respondents; and invited the views of national agencies, including employer bodies, with an interest in higher education.

Structure of the report

Part 1   Background to the report, identifying its terms of reference, methodologies and scope

Part 2   The context of the report: assessing the policies of stakeholders in higher education; considering the response within higher education and beyond; and reviewing progress to date

Part 3   Recommendations and proposals: outlining the conclusions of the investigation, and offering options for further development

Part 4   A resource database: identifying bibliographic and documentary sources relevant to the project and to future research and development

Part 5   Annexes: identifying membership of committees and advisory groups; recording consultants, respondents, sources of information, including universities, national agencies, professional bodies and employers

Appendices: including contributory reports, tables and other documentary materials

7.   The objectives of this report are derived from the outcomes of the *Learning without walls* conference held at the University of Oxford in February 1991.

Statement by the Minister for Higher Education

The Government has long recognised the potential offered by credit accumulation and transfer. Our commitment to the promotion of these principles was emphasised in the 1987 White Paper on Higher Education. Progress has perhaps been rather slower than the early enthusiasts might have liked or expected. With the present expansion comes the need to take stock of where we are, reflect on some of the current obstacles to further progress and identify desirable developments. "CAT" needs to be a term understood by all prospective students. We will need a general strategy for ensuring that credit accumulation and transfer become basic features of our further and higher education system.

Alan Howarth, MP, Minister of State for Higher Education, February 1991

Speaking to that conference, the Minister for Higher Education provided guidance for the Project in his statement outlined above. In response, the Oxford conference proposed that the universities and colleges should establish a 'Task Force' jointly with government departments and other bodies, with the authority to prepare an agenda for action to nurture and promote the wider use of credit accumulation and transfer within the United Kingdom. The 'Task Force' was also asked to recommend policies and practice which would encourage the wider use of credit accumulation and transfer in education, employment, and by professional bodies.

8.   The opportunity for establishing a Task Force, subsequently renamed the CATS Development Project, arose with the establish-

ment in May 1992 by the bodies representing the institutions (CVCP, CDP, SCOP and CSCFC) of the Higher Education Quality Council (HEQC). The HEQC seeks to maintain and improve the quality of higher education provision in institutions throughout the United Kingdom, thereby assuring the public, the funding councils and the Government of the continuing excellence of higher education. One of the Council's functions is to assure the quality of more flexible patterns of student learning, including arrangements for credit accumulation and transfer.

Terms of reference

- to investigate, propose and negotiate principles for the award and transfer of credit between different providers within higher education and beyond

- to ensure that adequate provision is made for assuring the quality of transferable credits

- to identify funding and other obstacles to the development of a system of transferable credits as a core feature of higher education

- to consider how higher education should respond to the development of transferable credits in other sectors of education, particularly within post-16 and further education

- to consider how transferable credits can be more effectively marketed with students, employers and institutions

- to co-ordinate aims and programmes of credit transfer with international developments

---

Project specifications

- to conduct research into matters associated with the development, management, implementation and promotion of credit systems

- to explore the potential of credit systems for fundamental change in order to establish credit-based learning as a basic feature of higher and further education consonant with national policy commitments to widen access and extend individual student choice

- to make proposals to the HEQC for further action in a number of areas, including:

  the establishment of a national credit framework

  quality assurance arrangements

  institutional management systems

  resource management arrangements

  student guidance

  international exchange

  the impact of credit systems upon academic values and institutional cultures

- to explore the means by which student mobility and exchange may be facilitated within and between higher education institutions, with further education colleges, between higher education and employment, and internationally

---

Further specifications

9.   The Higher Education Quality Council further specified that the investigation should address a wide range of related matters. The research team were therefore invited to explore current developments and make suitable recommendations for further progress.

10.   The Council went on to request that the Project should attempt to produce a constituency of support for further progress amongst institutions and other parties to higher education. A final report was required which would make recommendations:

- to ensure the maximum support of the national policy community for final proposals;

- to inform the work of the Higher Education Quality Council in the discharge of its responsibilities to the universities and colleges;

- to set an agenda for further work.

11.   These terms of reference and detailed specifications set ambitious and comprehensive objectives for the Project. As we explore further in subsequent sections of this report, the immediate and long-term impact of recommendations is likely to depend in significant measure upon the circumstances obtaining in higher and further education over the next few years. We cannot emphasise too frequently our view that the apparent fluctuations in policy affecting the sectors should not distract from the long-term obligation of institutions to find ways of managing learning opportunities for a much greater number of students. Many believe that credit accumulation and transfer arrangements are likely to play a prominent part in shaping the future character of higher education by improving the quality of the student learning experience, enhancing employment opportunities and contributing to the efficient use of resources, institutionally and nationally. We have directed our efforts to understanding how this might be possible.

III. *Methodological aspects*

Introduction

12.	The investigative work of the project has been conducted in order to supply final recommendations which command wide support. Care has been taken to represent the diversity of practice and opinion across a range of institutions and national bodies, reflecting the views of those in senior institutional positions as well as those more directly engaged in practical initiatives in the field. We have attempted to recognise the unevenness of understanding of some of the issues involved by offering, wherever possible, full analysis of the ideas and practices which form the basis of current activity in credit accumulation and transfer. In a number of places, we offer new thinking on some familiar practices.

13.	We have received ideas and opinions on future developments from individuals, institutions and national agencies. These have been offered freely and openly. We have been overwhelmed by the volume of information that colleagues have provided, much of it unpublished material which has been placed in the public domain for the first time. We are grateful for this generosity and judge it to be testimony to the interest and enthusiasm of individuals for successful further progress in credit accumulation and transfer. From this platform, the report has sought to build a comprehensive assessment of current practice and a realistic prospectus for future action.

Principles of conduct

14.	The investigative project has been conducted according to a number of guiding principles. These have helped to shape the methodological instruments deployed throughout the work, ensuring that the investigation would:

- achieve close alignment with developments within the wider environment of higher education, being aware of relevant policy developments;

- review current practice across the United Kingdom, including antecedent conditions, to provide an assessment of progress to date;

- receive opinion and information openly, inviting particularly the views of employers, professional bodies and students;

- address the development of credit accumulation and transfer as part of the process of quality assurance and quality improvement in higher education;

- establish the principles and the practical steps for the promotion of further developments, building wherever possible on existing strengths;

- build a constituency of support for the recommendations of the report.

15.	The investigation adopted a variety of methodological procedures. Case studies of institutions and consortia were used extensively. Four surveys were conducted to seek opinion on matters of quality assurance, a national credit framework and international credit transfer arrangements. Documentation was assembled on current and antecedent practice. Individual interviews provided valuable insights into different perspectives on the potential of credit systems. The Advisory Groups provided a professional network within which ideas and different perspectives could be worked through. Many of these ideas were further cross-checked in professional seminars and conferences. Finally, the recommendations and proposals were considered and revised by a team of senior academic consultants.

Information sources

16.　The Project was able to assemble evidence from a wide range of sources. Information was gathered from extensive personal and documentary contributions, outlined below.

Information sources

- policy documents from government departments, national agencies, professional institutions, employer bodies and other organisations contributing to developments in higher education and beyond;

- archive materials from the records of the CNAA, NAB, UFC, PCFC;

- the results of consultations with Vice-Chancellors, Chief Executives of national bodies, senior civil servants and individuals with influence in higher education policy-making;

- case study materials from various institutions and consortia;

- the results of responses to the surveys undertaken within the project, including major surveys of opinion from professional bodies, and on the features of a national credit framework;

- the outcomes of surveys undertaken as part of other complementary research investigations;

- the comments received from the Project Advisory Groups;

- written submissions from national bodies and individuals on general and specific aspects of the investigative programme, including substantial previously unpublished documentary material;

- official statistical data from relevant sources (USR, FESR, PCAS/UCCA, ECCTIS, Hansard and government publications, and from the work of research institutes.

Methodological constraints

17.　Although there is substantial information relevant to the general development of credit accumulation and transfer, specific information sources vary in reliability and scope. The research was constrained by the fact that, despite the obvious investment throughout the United Kingdom over the past two decades in the development of credit systems and modular programmes, the higher and further education sectors have yet to reach a settlement on basic principles, structures and organising concepts. Moreover, progress on student flexibility and mobility has yet to achieve the prominence which would encourage higher education agencies to monitor and report on the range of individual and institutional practices. Accordingly, we were constrained by a number of related factors.

Differences within the United Kingdom

18.　We have sought to reflect as far as possible the activities and developments throughout the whole of higher education and beyond. However, it has to be recognised that there are different systems operating within the United Kingdom, particularly in Scotland, which have made it difficult for the investigation to capture as much of the variety of practice as we would have wished. The report attempts to give as accurate an impression of developments elsewhere in the United Kingdom but has inevitably relied for much of its evidence on practice in England and Wales. A number of visits were made to universities in Scotland and colleagues were represented on advisory groups. Findings have been included wherever possible but there remain in the Scottish system of post-secondary and higher education distinctive features to which some of our conclusions and recommendations may not apply with the same force. The report has not been able adequately to explore the aspects of Scottish institutions beyond the universities. Moreover, we have not been able to address differences of approach between the various funding councils in their treatment of student choice and mobility. We understand that SHEFC has been able to make more progress in developing methodologies to account for this than may have yet been possible in England or Wales. For progress in Northern Ireland, we have been able to visit some institutions in higher and further education to consult on the state of development but the report may not reflect all the dissimilarities of sector organisation in Northern Ireland as colleagues would wish.

Contested concepts and problems

19.   Terminology and concepts with which to describe student and institutional behaviour appear to be at best in the process of formation. Even the most basic concepts remain contested; principles and practices which pass as commonplace in some quarters remain largely unfamiliar or disputed elsewhere. This unevenness of interpretation and perception gives rise to concerns about how best to capture the range of practices that cluster under the canopy of the term 'CATS'. This is particularly noticeable in the gap that appears to have developed between those who have been immersed in the developments leading to credit-based and modular systems, seeing them as innovative instruments in the repositioning of higher education for democratic participation, and those who see such developments as relatively marginal, and possibly transient, devices for coping with short-term resource distress.

20.   Given these differences, we spent some time trying to establish whether there was an agreed framework of questions and a shared definition of problems. Responses to these matters varied according to how institutions and national bodies believed they could cope with increased participation in higher education. Some institutions believed that they would be able to respond with minor adjustments to prevailing arrangements; others maintained that a more fundamental reappraisal of priorities would be essential. Universities and colleges which took the latter position were more likely to have addressed the further development of credit-based learning. This usually involved a more direct exposure to the range of opportunities open to them and an assessment of their implications. In these conditions, institutions will tend to have developed more sophisticated approaches to the academic and educational potential of credit

systems, leading to a more thoughtful engagement with concepts and principles.

21.   Although arrangements for credit accumulation and transfer take many different forms, institutions generally accept the importance and centrality of student flexibility and mobility whilst remaining unclear about how far they are prepared to facilitate either. For example, three earlier surveys of institutional behaviour (Taylor, 1990; Davidson, 1992; Harvey, 1992) comment on the practice, or intentions, of universities and colleges with respect to the development of credit–based systems and modularity. The data from these surveys suggests high levels of engagement with both developments, yet the surveys do not define conceptually what is meant by 'CATS' or 'modularity', nor how institutions may interpret the terms. In 1990, Taylor reported to the Open University that he estimated 33% of Polytechnics had CAT schemes, with a further 33% under active development. He estimated that very few ex-UFC universities possessed schemes. Two years later however, Harvey reported that 86% of institutions in the United Kingdom now offer a 'CAT Scheme' yet he accepts that no attempt was made to explore how institutions understood the term.

22.   Similarly, a survey for the CVCP (Davidson, 1992) treats the concept of CATS and modularity unproblematically, inviting ex-UFC institutions to describe their intentions but proposing no categories by which to classify arrangements. Accordingly, of 54 ex-UFC universities, 27 were 'adopting the CNAA or SCOTCAT credit rating scheme', of which 19 had 'signed agreements with the CNAA scheme'. On modularity, 40 ex-UFC universities either had established, or were establishing, or had agreed in principle to establish, modular schemes. The extent of internal or external mobility and choice is not discussed. These surveys, while invaluable in many ways, draw attention to the differences of interpretation within higher education about the meaning of basic concepts. They leave open the prospect that institutions may satisfy themselves by describing their arrangements as 'CATS' or 'modularity', but offer no further challenge to the reality of institutional practice.

23. Other analysis is however beginning to occur. Important work is currently being undertaken into the conceptual basis of credit systems, associated with the efforts of the Further Education Unit (FEU) to sponsor a post-secondary credit framework. This work is being developed in response to the FEU publication *A Basis for Credit?* Yet very few colleagues in higher education appear to be familiar with these discussions. We are convinced that an engagement by colleagues in higher education with the ideas being generated by the FEU would significantly assist universities and colleges to build on the earlier work of the CNAA, the Open University, ECCTIS and others. It would enable higher education to strengthen the conceptual and educational basis of their own credit arrangements. Later in this report, we have attempted to introduce some clarity into these matters by drawing upon earlier work (Theodossin, 1986; Squires, 1986; and various CNAA publications) and combining it with the work of the FEU.

Availability of statistical data

24. There is also a lack of reliable statistical data which adequately describes relevant patterns of student behaviour. Information exists which identifies the volume of students exiting with some interim and sub-degree qualifications; other information can be identified which records the volume of transfer from further to higher education, via 'franchising' and other means. Some institutions, and notably the Open University, report the numbers applying with claims for academic credit with advanced standing for experiential learning. From existing data sources, such as the volume of enquiries to ECCTIS or to the former CNAA CATS Registry, we have been able to infer the potential for mobility and transfer but we have not been able to identify data which reliably records inter-institutional transfer, or internal institutional mobility, or mobility between 'off-campus' and institutional programmes.

25. The official statistics agencies, Universities' Statistical Record (USR) and Further Education Statistical Record (FESR), have not yet found it useful to report on patterns of student mobility and choice. Data is not assembled directly for this purpose, although reports are prepared on student 'non-completion' rates from which limited evidence of student transfer may be obtained. Moreover, the Funding Councils do not require information to be provided specifically on mobility and choice. This information would not necessarily be relevant to the purpose of the Funding Councils, although the Polytechnics and Colleges Funding Council (PCFC) did collect data on students enrolled on modular programmes. Some limited inferences can be made from this information. Furthermore, few institutions appear to be in a position to capture data and report on those patterns of student behaviour which describe student choices, changes of decision, mobility or transfer. Also, institutional consortia do not generally supply data on student mobility. The paucity of data is particularly apparent for the behaviour of part-time students. This category of students may be treated as a useful test of the maximum mobility potential for all students. They are more likely to move between institutions, or to interrupt their studies, or to transfer with prior credit, yet little reliable data exists with which to explore these variables.

26. We were therefore forced to accept that data sources invariably reflect the extent to which institutions and agencies believe the collection of information will be useful. The case for a comprehensive data collection system which is sensitive to patterns of student mobility does not appear to have been made. Given the limited development of credit-based systems at present, this may be understandable. Yet, if policy is to be accurately informed of the extent of student flexibility and mobility, the usefulness of such data cannot be underestimated. Steps will need to be taken to encourage institutions to establish information systems which are capable of reporting on patterns of student mobility. It is possible that Funding Councils will need to play a supportive role in this.

Policy fluidity and the negotiation of policy options

27. For both the reasons identified above, we have been sceptical from the start of the investigation of the prospects for arriving at

conclusions by weight of empirical evidence alone. We accepted that decisions would be more convincing if they were well-informed, but we believed that the quality of the information may be as readily revealed through the expression of informed opinion as through empirical assessment based on scarce data. Preferences would in some measure reflect the different positions adopted by institutions and agencies, and their rate of progress towards their individual goals. Accordingly, we attached importance to the comments of our informants and correspondents, particularly from Vice-Chancellors, Chief Executives and similar colleagues, as well as those actively engaged with the implementation of initiatives.

28. We have to admit frankly that the Project has been affected to some extent by recent modifications in Government policy towards the sector. This has had the effect, latterly, of disturbing the confidence of some colleagues and institutions in their commitment to further developments. They argue that Government policy does not appear to have stabilised sufficiently and therefore they prefer to retain their options until events unfold more clearly, perhaps in the long term. Amongst this group of more cautious and sceptical institutions, some appear anyway to have decided to emphasise traditional strengths; therefore they plan only limited engagement with credit transfer arrangements. In other institutions where provisional developments are being undertaken, their permanence has yet to be secured or they are still narrowly based. Such institutions remain equivocal about the extent to which credit systems and modularity offer convincing solutions to their preferred position in higher education and beyond. We were therefore constrained by the limited active engagement amongst some institutions with many of the central propositions underpinning the development of credit accumulation and transfer arrangements.

29. On the other hand, a significant number of institutions continue to take the long view, accepting that expanded participation has become a permanent feature of modern higher education, and recognise that student mobility and flexibility will be central features of any future higher education landscape. For these institutions, recent modifications to Government policy appear to act as irritants to forward planning, but do not yet appear to have disturbed the long term commitment to the development of credit-based systems. Indeed, in a small minority of cases, it is held that recent changes to Government policy will assist the further development of credit accumulation and transfer systems by placing greater emphasis on variable modes of attendance, individual and credit-led student financing, and on structural flexibility.

Mode of operation

30. The reliability of the evidence gathered in support of the recommendations has been assured by the extensive scope of the investigation and by a careful choice of project participants. The investigative team was composed of academic colleagues with well-established experience in their respective fields. They were chosen from both ex-UFC and ex-PCFC institutions. Additional experience and judgement was provided by the choice of senior consultants to advise on issues of strategic importance. Efforts were made through discussions with consultants to ensure the maximum possible alignment of thinking with key national agencies: the CVCP, COSHEP and SCOP, funding councils, employers (including the CBI and TECs) and professional bodies, NCVQ, BTEC, FEU, ECCTIS, and the National Union of Students. (A list of the project team and consultants is included in Appendix 1 to this report.)

31. The conduct of the *CATS Development Project* was undertaken both through extensive personal research by the project Director and also through the sub-projects. These were conducted by members of the project team and supported by an advisory group. The role of the Project Advisory Groups was crucial in providing a platform of informed opinion and experienced advice against which ideas and proposals were debated. Colleagues were invited to participate in the work of the advisory groups on the basis of their academic (or administrative) experience. They were chosen to reflect both the range of opinion, practice and experience, and the different

systems of higher and post-secondary education throughout the United Kingdom. (A list of membership of Project Advisory Groups is included in Appendix 1 to this report).

32.   The Project Advisory Groups constituted a significant network of expertise, drawing together in over 50 separate meetings 70 experienced representatives of higher education, further education and national agencies. Attendance at advisory group meetings rarely fell below 80%, a testimony to individual commitment and the importance which institutions and agencies have attached to the work of the project. Colleagues who were directly involved in the groups have commented favourably on the understanding they have gained of different dimensions to the development of student mobility and flexibility.

33.   The advisory groups were free to modify their investigative strategy, advising the project officers on methodological approaches and data sources. They invited papers, presentations and other documentary inputs. Individual members were able to present such materials as they thought appropriate, much of it reflecting the positions of their institutions and agencies. Various interim reports were endorsed by the relevant advisory groups, and the conclusions have assisted the Project Director in defining the proposals and observations contained herein.

34.   Beyond the work of the Project Advisory Groups, the Project Director was able to gain access to wide-ranging additional sources of information and opinion. The contributions of the sub-projects provided essential advice and assistance to the Project Director in developing the general character and focus of this final report. In this way, it proved possible to establish a comprehensive overview of the entire project, providing the means by which the various sources of evidence and interim reports have been co-ordinated into an overall report. This final report represents the amalgamation of all the inputs into the project, from various sources including the advisory groups and the research team, based upon the principles, methodologies and modes of operation outlined above.

Introduction

35. We have considered the general environment currently affecting universities and colleges. Circumstances continue to change in response to Government policies, but we have tried to take the long view. This has required us to make assumptions about the continuity of policy objectives towards the sector where manageable and affordable long-term growth features more prominently than medium-term policies for contraction. In preparing this report, we have therefore assumed that the development of credit accumulation and transfer is likely to be attractive to institutions which see it as a credible means of responding to the changing long-term conditions of higher and further education.

Priorities of the investigation

36. The investigation set out to explore what additional benefits credit systems might bestow upon the learning experiences of students consonant with the maintenance of quality, institutional academic autonomy and diversity of purpose. This approach implies a more comprehensive treatment of credit systems than may hitherto have been the case. We accept that credit accumulation and transfer arrangements have often been applied to more tightly-focused areas of higher education, addressing the interests of specific groups of learners in higher education (see Table 1).

37. Whilst we are sure that the development of credit accumulation and transfer arrangements will continue to improve access to learning for these students, we believe it is important that future policy should be informed by the *comprehensive* application of credit-based learning. Thus, we took the opportunity to investigate the applicability of credit systems to *all* students in higher education.

Table 1:
Student groups conventionally regarded as benefiting from 'CATS'

- employees: seeking academic credit for professional or in-company training, continuing education and professional development; students in this group may experience job relocation as part of their career development;

- adult returners: claiming academic credit for experiential learning, where such learning may be previously certificated learning, or increasing as formally constructed portfolio-based learning including work-based learning from paid or unpaid work;

- women returners: specifically women subject to deferred or interrupted participation in higher education often for family reasons, for whom transferrable credit would be helpful;

- part-time students: including the above categories, who may see advantages in a credit system in order to gain credit for learning achievement, deploying it towards qualifications over time and at different institutions;

- continuing education students: where decisions on a formal academic programme of study leading to a qualification may need to be deferred without loss of recognition for formal learning achievement; these students may be on courses in extra-mural departments, on Associate Student schemes, or undertaking vocational short course programmes;

- 'independent' students: typically full-time students wishing to make more autonomous choices of academic programme, not formally offered by their university or college, but on whose behalf the institution provides for individually negotiated programmes.

38.	Many institutions now frequently accept an elision of certain recent developments: increased participation, wider access, the structural modifications of modularity and semesterisation, the recognition of 'off-campus' learning, changes to learning technology, and the development of learning opportunities which are more responsive to labour market needs. The term 'CAT' is often used to capture some of the means by which universities and colleges have sought to address issues of flexibility, student choice, and academic programme renewal. At the same time, institutions have been concerned to establish comprehensive quality assurance arrangements, seeking to reconcile these academic developments with improved accountability, effectiveness and an enhanced student learning experience.

39.	We accept that not all institutions are yet persuaded by the merits of these developments, nor are they uniformly able to implement the changes contingent on them. Institutions will continue to conduct their affairs according to their preferred priorities and the rate of development across the sector will reflect this. Nevertheless, we believe that arrangements for the promotion of credit accumulation and credit transfer can be usefully adopted for the management of all student learning arrangements. Therefore, we have focused upon those arrangements which extend learning opportunities in higher education to the largest number of eligible students, offering them choice and flexibility in the construction of learning programmes, and leading to successful achievement with the prospect of useful employment.

Organising assumptions

40.	In our explorations we have found it helpful to be guided by certain basic assumptions. They have helped to focus our work on what we believe is a fair reflection of policies and aspirations in higher and further education. These assumptions are:

Policy towards higher and further education displays continuity over time

41.	We have been interested to identify a long-term continuity of policy over the past thirty years since the Robbins Report. This is explored in more detail in a later section. The key feature is a gradual move towards a more participative further and higher education. There have been frequent setbacks to the momentum over the period, noticeably during the revenue crises of the early 1980s and 1990s, but in the long term, certain policies seem to persist:

- *universities and colleges have remained academically autonomous*

- *institutions have been expected to meet diverse needs, regionally as well as nationally*

- *higher education has not been formally structured hierarchically although different missions will remain evident*

- *entry to higher education will continue to be available in increasing numbers to those able to benefit from it*

42.	These principles and policies are important for the further extension of credit transfer. They confirm that there will not be a 'system' of higher education, but they encourage the prospect of successful collaboration between diverse institutions. This would enable students to pass more readily within and between institutional programmes according to their needs. In turn, this raises questions of mutual respect between institutions and the mutual recognition of the quality of academic programmes. These policy objectives are reflected in the changes to higher and further education proposed by the White Papers *Higher education: meeting the challenge* (1987), *Higher education: a new framework* (1991) and *Education and training for the 21st century* (1991). However, if effective collaboration, mutual recognition and credit transfer are to take place, this raises other questions concerning a regional policy for the sectors.

Considerations of efficiency, effectiveness and accountability will continue to define dispositions towards higher education

43.   Investment in higher education is likely to be attended by a much closer inspection of the use of public resources. Measures which assist the achievement of value-for-money will be supported in advance of those which imply net additional resources. We believe the development of credit systems may have an important role to play. To assess the implications for the further development of credit systems, we have used conventional definitions of efficiency and effectiveness: *efficiency* is the ratio of outputs to inputs, and *effectiveness* measures the extent to which outputs meet objectives. *Accountability* is the process by which efficient and effective performance may be established.

44.   Considerations of efficiency and effectiveness are reflected in certain policy objectives for higher education:

- *an improvement in the aspirations and achievements of people of all ages, encouraging more prospective students to orientate their ambitions towards lifelong education and training;*

- *a commitment to the further expansion of student numbers in the medium- and longer-term;*

- *support for the principle of democratic participation, widening access to higher and further education for traditionally under-represented groups.*

45.   Credit systems may be usefully judged against the proposition that they help to improve the efficiency of higher education by attracting a wider range of students with previously untapped potential. They assist the effectiveness of higher education by accepting that learning may be recognised in all its forms, by mitigating the consequences of non-completion and 'failure', and by facilitating greater flexibility in student choice and curriculum design. The effect is to make higher education more relevant to individual life-career needs.

Increased participation involves the recognition that 'more means different'.

46.   The commitment to expanded participation has been supported by employers, and is largely welcomed by universities and colleges. Current projections, taking into account recent downward modifications, suggest that student numbers (including Open University students) will continue to rise twofold, from 698,000 in 1985 through 975,000 in 1991 to 1,440,000 by the end of the century. Many of these students will be studying part-time, independently, or outside formal institutional settings. Support from the general public and prospective students may be inferred from the enthusiasm with which newly-available places in universities and colleges have been rapidly occupied.

47.   We have been largely sceptical of those claims which suggest that extended participation can be met with the same instruments that have applied to the management of elite provision. We have worked with the propositions of Sir Christopher Ball that 'more means different' and 'learning pays' in creating a Learning Society, accepting the assessment that certain 'differences' will become commonplace in higher education. This implies that attention will need to be paid to the condition of higher education within and beyond the University.

> Yesterday's courses are unlikely to be the most appropriate for tomorrow's world. Industrialists and business people are very clear that their support for the expansion of higher education does not mean they just want more of the same. Higher education is being challenged to think again about the nature of a good general education – the competence and capabilities expected of the finest barristers and journalists, of outstanding civil servants and statesmen.
>
> *Sir Christopher Ball,*
> *'More means different' (1990, VI, 6.2)*

We have therefore assumed that:

- *the student cohort of an expanded higher education will be drawn from a broader social and educational range;*

- *students will require access to different types of academic programme, with greater choice and flexibility, including greater mobility between institutions;*

- *students will learn in different ways, including the use of open learning and multi-media technologies;*

- *students will need to be better prepared for labour market placement, being able to demonstrate improved personal effectiveness and provide evidence of successful learning achievement.*

The needs of the economy and labour market opportunities will continue to influence the propensity to invest in higher education

48.   National priorities will continue to be influenced by the needs of the economy, its international competitiveness and the distribution of labour market opportunities. Increased participation in higher education, yielding an increased supply of graduates and other qualified students, will be measured by the extent to which student career aspirations and employers' needs are fulfilled. We have explored how credit systems might influence:

- *the means by which a twofold increase in the supply of qualified leavers can be adequately prepared for future labour market needs;*

- *modifications to the curriculum of higher education to accommodate a broader range of learning needs for a more flexible employment environment;*

- *a closer association and parity of esteem between academic and vocational elements of higher education, improving employment prospects for students;*

- *the specification of learning achievement in higher education for students and employers, possibly through the use of learning outcome*

statements, records of achievement and credit transcripts.

49.   We have taken the opportunity to examine the case for the further extension of structural flexibilities in higher education, such as modularisation and semesterisation. In particular we have been interested to note how these developments can assist the creation of an achievement-led curriculum which improves the individual competitive advantage of students in pursuing labour market opportunities. The Enterprise in Higher Education initiative has been influential in this respect. Additionally, credit systems may assist employers and professional bodies in authenticating the quality of employee learning.

Respect for the academic autonomy of institutions and a diversity of provision will continue to define policy towards higher education

50.   Institutional academic autonomy and the diversity of institutional provision are distinctive features of higher education in the United Kingdom which the development of credit systems does not prejudice. Following Ernest Boyer (1993), we have tried to distinguish various generic aspects of higher education, expecting that institutions will give different emphasis to each of them:

- discovery of knowledge: the research and scholarship function;

- integration of knowledge: the development of interdisciplinarity and disciplinary convergence;

- application of knowledge: the service provided to the wider community, including employers;

- transmission of knowledge: the teaching function, including the development of skills.

51.   This typology suggests that credit systems may have the greatest advantage in the enhancement of the integration, application and transmission of knowledge. In this, we associate ourselves with

a comment from the Robbins Report (1963) that could readily apply to the development of credit systems:

'…although the extent to which each principle is realised in the various types of institution will vary, there is room for a speck of each in all. The system as a whole must be judged deficient unless it provides adequately for all of them.'

52.   Although we do not deal directly with the function of research in this report, universities and colleges which define their purpose largely in terms of research may wish to engage with the development of credit systems in a different manner. We believe that credit transfer arrangements and inter-institutional co-operation at the postgraduate level will become increasingly relevant. Overall, we believe that increased student choice, at both undergraduate and postgraduate levels, may act to promote closer co-operation between disciplines and institutions, assisting the development of new subject clusters in response to student demand. We also believe that the teaching of academic and practical skills may be improved by the flexibilities offered by credit systems.

Quality assurance is a central concern of higher education institutions

53.   The quality of higher education in the United Kingdom has hitherto been predicated upon claims to excellence, founded on forms of learning experience delivered to a well-prepared minority of students. Expanded participation raises questions about how the quality of higher education can be maintained. Improvements in efficiency and effectiveness do not necessarily imply improvements in quality. Some concerns have been expressed, by the former CNAA and in HMI reports, that efforts to accommodate greater numbers of students through innovative or unfamiliar learning arrangements may need particular attention. We have been able to focus on a number of aspects of this problem. We have considered those arrangements which broaden the definitions and location of higher education learning achievement, paying particular attention to the quality assurance of 'off-campus' or work-based learning, to the accreditation of in-company and professional training, and to 'franchising' arrangements.

54.   Furthermore, we have tried to comment on aspects of the design of academic programmes which encourage greater student choice. Specifically, the increase in modular programmes with the possibility of greater elective choice has been identified as a source of concern by those who remain influenced by the need for structured academic coherence and progression. Those who have expressed an interest in these matters include employer representatives and graduate recruiters, and professional bodies, who wish to ensure the quality of graduate supply.

55.   Our work on quality assurance has been informed by a number of assumptions:

- *the arrangements necessary to ensure the quality of diverse and flexible learning opportunities should be the property of academically autonomous individual institutions;*

- *it is legitimate to attribute higher education outcomes to achievements gained from 'off-campus' or external learning programmes, including those achievements derived from employee training, work experience or similar activities;*

- *increased student choice, flexibility and mobility, within and between learning environments, are consistent with quality higher education;*

- *the outcomes of learning achievement are as important for the assurance of quality as the process of learning.*

56.   In common with many others, we have struggled with the concept of 'quality'. We have worked with a definition of quality combining value-for-money and fitness-for-purpose with more subjective dimensions of development and change. With generalised access, the challenge has been to establish the conditions of quality assurance in circumstances requiring innovation, flexibility and individual choice. If we were pressed for a definition of

quality, it would contain some of the attributes outlined below:

> - effective access: learning opportunities available to the greatest number, consistent with the achievement of defined outcomes, in which promises of greater access are matched by the delivery of effective learning opportunities;
>
> - efficient use of resources: arrangements for the deployment of resources aligned as closely as possible to the learning needs of students;
>
> - systematic flexibility: structures allowing the greatest display of informed student choice;
>
> - pooled autonomy: arrangements promoting collaboration between institutions for the improvement of efficient access and systematic flexibility;
>
> - effective outcomes: ensuring that students are able to achieve optimum success leading to desired career opportunities.

57.   This treatment of quality has allowed us to offer contributions on the structure of academic programmes and the student learning experience; make proposals for the enhancement of student aspiration and achievement; suggest fresh thinking in the efficient and effective management of resources within and between institutions; and comment on the cultural impact of change for institutions. We have done so because credit systems appear to offer a means of improving quality assurance by lending visibility to the processes and outcomes of learning, thereby delivering greater accountability for higher education practices and achievements.

Co-operation between higher and further education is necessary to establish for students better progression and achievement

58.   The investigation has addressed the development of credit systems principally from the perspective of higher education. However we have been careful to recognise that credit transfer arrangements are increasingly relevant to students seeking transfer from programmes in further education. Current policy suggests that the two sectors share many objectives: improved student aspiration and achievement; better institutional accountability; greater labour market sensitivity; enhanced student choice of academic, vocational and combined programmes; and reliable quality assurance.

59.   Cross-sectoral developments make it essential that initiatives for the promotion of credit systems in higher education be considered alongside those in further education. Three developments in particular are important:

> ### Table 2
>
> - the work of the National Council for Vocational Qualifications (NCVQ) in promoting a modular and credit-based approach to vocational programmes;
>
> - the proposals of the Further Education Unit (FEU) for a comprehensive credit framework for further and higher education;
>
> - the activities of the National Open College Network (NOCN) in sponsoring cross-sectoral credit transfer between further, higher and adult education.

60.   These initiatives will be considered in later discussion but it is important to record at this stage that we believe they have significant consequences for higher education. Their initial development has tended to be within post-16 and adult education, but the long-term objectives of the three agencies is to achieve close collaboration with higher education for the formation of a national credit framework. The purpose of such a framework would be to facilitate achievement and progression, *vertically* throughout post-secondary and higher education and *horizontally* between academic and vocational programmes. The work of the three agencies has yet to be given sustained exposure within universities and colleges and we believe this should be corrected in the future.

61.   We have taken the negotiated alignment of qualification structures in higher education and those proposed by the NCVQ as an important focus of the project. Moreover, we have explored the academic and educational predicates which form the basis of proposals emerging from the FEU and NOCN and considered their impact on the further development of credit systems in higher education. There are important consequences for the ways in which the future development of Access courses, 'franchising' and other similar developments can articulate with credit systems arising in higher education.

62.   Our work in this area has been organised around some assumptions which reflect our assessment of the significance of current developments:

- *a 'ladder of progression' between further and higher education, embracing academic and vocational programmes and qualifications, would be best achieved through a national credit framework;*

- *proposals leading to the formation of a national credit framework need to be presented in terms relevant to academic and educational matters, identifying their importance for quality assurance.*

63.   We are aware that some concern has been expressed that closer co-operation through a common credit framework might imply a more general convergence of higher and further education. We would wish to make it clear that our concern is solely with the mobility, progression and achievement of students, and the arrangements which promote them. We do not seek to move ahead of policy by commenting on matters which concern the specific objectives of further or higher education, or the structural relationships with which they are achieved.

The development of systems to support informed student choice and mobility is a priority for higher education

64.   The guidance and information service offered to students within a flexible learning environment is widely recognised as central to the successful development of frameworks for student mobility and progression. Yet there is little evidence that higher education institutions have afforded it the priority it deserves. This is despite the efforts to create a national information service, recognised in 1979 by the establishment of the Educational Counselling and Credit Transfer Information Service (ECCTIS). Subsequent initiatives have sought to complement this service. The National Educational Guidance Initiative has focused attention on the co-ordination of pre-entry information, and recent Government policy has addressed the future role of the local authority Careers Service. In addition, the TEC/LECs have continued to support their Training Access Points (TAPs) as a source of information on education and training opportunities.

65.   Despite these stimuli, many students still enter higher education poorly informed of their learning opportunities, taking decisions which they may wish to modify, and inadequately served by the conventional sources of information. Too often, in our opinion, these are designed for recruitment rather than for independent guidance.

66.   We have noted that significant aspects of the management of choice and flexibility remain contested by academic colleagues. Responsibility for the provision of educational guidance is often poorly defined; the freedom of students to construct programmes, or to exercise elective choice, is often hedged around with constraints of an academic or an administrative kind. Some of these restrictions will be necessary, but others appear to flow from a reluctance to accept the consequences of student choice for the conventions of subject disciplines. We discuss many of these matters elsewhere in this report, but of one thing we are certain: effective student mobility and choice are dependent on the existence of an independent professional education guidance service.

67.   To inform our discussion of these matters, we have focused our work on some basic assumptions:

- *the quality assurance of arrangements for student mobility and choice is significantly dependent on the demonstration of effective educational guidance;*

- *institutions need to distinguish their recruitment information strategies from their guidance strategies;*

- *universities and colleges do not yet address student guidance arrangements at an appropriate strategic level;*

- *national information and guidance arrangements, where adequate or in need of modification, would benefit from some strategic co-ordination.*

Credit systems may assist the development of more rational financial and resource distribution arrangements

68.   We have been significantly exercised by the prospect that credit systems may be usefully developed as resource management instruments, as well as for the promotion of academic choice and flexibility. Measures which provide rational and equitable formulae for the distribution of institutional and personal resources are likely to be widely attractive if their feasibility can be demonstrated. We have taken care to avoid an overzealous engagement with the theoretical potential of credit systems as agents of resource management and have concentrated instead on the practical aspects as far as possible. It must be said, however, that higher education appears to have less experience of the consequences of internal market management and 'consumer' choice than some other public service organisations. Thus much of our investigation was concerned to understand what steps might need to be taken if a tariff-based resource formula were introduced.

69.   We have concentrated on two aspects of the problem. Firstly, we considered the credit-based formulae that might be commendable to funding councils and institutions. Secondly, we addressed the financial arrangements that might facilitate greater student mobility and flexibility. These arrangements concern the regulations and procedures governing individual student entitlements to grants and fees, the scheduling of their payment, and the requirements of attendance for fixed periods at particular institutions.

70.   These matters have been given added importance by the continuing debate over various aspects of the funding of expanded participation and the formulae for resource distribution. The CVCP has commissioned work on proposals for future funding arrangements; the HEFCE has proposed new arrangements for the funding of continuing education and is consulting on wider application of such formulae to part-time students; SHEFC in Scotland and FEFC in England & Wales have made proposals encouraging a credit-based methodology for higher and further education funding respectively; the Flowers Report and the Irvine Report on the reform of the academic year have considered new arrangements for both students and institutions; and the CBI has supported the Training Credits Scheme.

71.   We believe it is timely to consider further how credit-based formulae might assist the promotion of credit systems for institutions and credit transfer for students. We have been guided by a belief that there is support for:

- *more equitable and neutral instruments for resource distribution;*

- *the erosion of distinctions between full-time and part-time student categories, modes of attendance which become problematic under conditions of student flexibility;*

- *the need to consider the regulatory basis of student financial support in the light of greater flexibility;*

- *a further consideration of the proposition that students might be vested with a proportion of responsibility for the costs of their higher education in return for greater flexibility and choice;*

- *an exploration of the consequences and impact of internal market mechanisms on the character and arrangements of higher education, emphasising the role of the student-as-consumer in such transactions.*

National systems for credit transfer need to be developed in the context of international student mobility

72.   Many of the developments in credit-based learning in the United Kingdom have been influenced by developments in other countries, particularly the United States. Trans-Atlantic student exchanges have been commonplace for a number of years. Increasingly attention has begun to turn to our European relationships, stimulated by an increase in student mobility and exchange through the ERASMUS programme, and through institutional participation in the ECTS pilot programme. Globally, credit systems are beginning to be adopted in many other countries throughout Asia, Australasia and, to a lesser extent, Africa.

73.   We have sought to document these developments and identify the problems of managing international student mobility. We recognise the importance many students will attach to the prospects for easier international transfer and exchange. With this in mind, we have assumed that:

- *there will be growing student demand for international transfer and exchange;*

- *the growth in demand will place considerable strain upon the ability of nations to meet students' aspirations, either academically or financially;*

- *problems of compatibility between national systems, standards and conventions will continue to frustrate effective transfer;*

- *for the United Kingdom, there will be particular problems resulting from the net inward flow of prospective students, and from the poor second language skills of our exchange students.*

The further development of credit systems will be most securely achieved with the development of a 'credit culture'

74.   Our work has set out to capture some of the significance for higher and further education of the comprehensive application of credit systems. In our judgement, the impact is likely to be as great on the cultural and normative dimensions of academic life as it is on administrative and structural arrangements. We wish to stimulate academic discussion of the values which lie behind the introduction of credit accumulation and transfer arrangements. These values reflect the emphasis given to the individual student in determining learning needs and this may have consequences for the balance of institutional and professional power in higher education and beyond. We acknowledge that definitions of what constitutes 'higher education' may need to be revised in the light of increased participation and extended learning opportunities.

75.   We discuss more extensively what is meant by a 'credit culture' later in this report. By way of introduction it may be helpful to make one initial distinction. Credit systems have developed to the extent that it may now be useful to talk of 'first' and 'second generation' developments. In using this distinction, we are seeking to describe the progress that has been made over the past decade in the development and operation of academic credit systems. We make no assumption about a preferred state of development, nor do we seek to prescribe the progress of individual institutions. Instead we have worked with some distinctions:

Table 3

- first generation credit systems designed as arrangements to address the needs of relatively small, often marginal groups of students, who may make 'idiosyncratic' demands on institutional arrangements;

- second generation credit systems designed to address the needs of all students, conflating credit and modularity in ways which seek to modify structures and relationships in higher education to produce flexibility and choice for the benefit of all institutional members.

---

76.   This is not a precise distinction and elsewhere we elaborate on aspects of it. However, we are attempting to capture one

essential difference: either universities and colleges address developments piecemeal and marginally, limiting their impact upon institutional arrangements, both culturally and structurally; or they embrace the development of credit systems comprehensively and recognise their consequences for fundamental change. It is quite conceivable to us that institutions may choose either course. The response will be determined by the extent to which an institution is persuaded by events that it must change. We would be unhappy however if, in embarking on a particular route, institutions were not given the opportunity to become aware of the consequences of a particular strategy, based on the experience of others. Choosing to change may be the most important challenge for higher and further education in the coming years, but it will need to be informed choice and advantageous change, for institutions and students alike.

Credit systems and modularity are necessary but not sufficient conditions for the achievement of student flexibility and choice

77.   We include this final assertion as a warning to ourselves. It would be easy for an investigation conducted by colleagues closely associated with developments in credit

and modularity to lack a sense of proportion. It has long been claimed by critics of these initiatives that their proponents are driven by a zeal which claims the moral high ground and denies critique. We do not wish to deny our own enthusiasm for the benefits to students, academics and others of the further extension of modularity and credit-based learning. However, this needs to be pursued with even greater enthusiasm for sensible and objective research.

78.   We have therefore tried to conduct our investigation with an appropriate critical and constructive rationalism. We have been aware from earlier experience, confirmed by the investigation, that of themselves credit systems and modularity change nothing necessarily; they are tools which can be used for various purposes. Our task has been therefore to explore the extent to which these tools do indeed improve opportunities for choice and flexibility, what other options might exist to achieve the same ends, and what other changes might need to take place to supplement the development of useful instruments for this purpose. In the final analysis, the scope of the Project and of this report reflects the tensions between scholarly scepticism and the desire to encourage acceptable policy development.

Part Two

V. *Policy environment*

Introduction

79.   The development of credit accumulation and transfer arrangements has been taking place over the past few years in a relatively supportive policy environment. We have considered it important to place our investigative work in this context, understanding how the emerging policy framework for higher and further education has influenced the further development of credit systems. Several factors appear to be significant:

Table 4: Policy support

- a longstanding policy objective to encourage greater flexibility and mobility in higher and further education, reaffirmed more recently by ministerial statements and by White Paper proposals;

- encouragement from both the DFE, Employment Department and the DTI to develop a more flexible range of learning opportunities in higher and further education;

- the establishment of National Education and Training Targets, the continuing work of the NCVQ, and assessments of future labour market opportunities;

- numerous policy statements, including those from learned societies, employers, professional bodies and student organisations, commenting on the future shape of higher and further education;

- the progress already under way throughout institutions in higher and further education.

---

80.   Academic credit transfer has been a policy objective for higher education for the past thirty years. Both the Robbins Report on higher education (1963) and the Russell Report on adult education (1973) affirmed the importance to students and to national efficiency of the cumulative transfer of academic credit.The 1972 White Paper, *Education: a framework for expansion* also encouraged the development of courses based on 'units' which would earn credit towards various qualifications. Establishing national arrangements for the transfer of academic credit has been accepted in principle, but practical proposals have emerged more slowly. In 1977, in an effort to make progress, the Department of Education and Science (DES) commissioned a feasibility study (Toyne Report, 1979) which led to the development of the Educational Counselling and Credit Transfer Information Service (ECCTIS). Since then, progress has proceeded fitfully until recent years when the pace has noticeably quickened. We review progress on credit transfer in higher and further education more extensively in Chapter VI.

81.   For the purposes of this discussion we have looked at support for the development of credit systems amongst the main stakeholders in higher education, beyond the institutions themselves. It is clear that there has been widespread support from employers, professional bodies, government departments and lately from students' organisations, for the development of greater flexibility and choice in higher and further education. A significant majority of policy papers and reports in this area make explicit reference to the advantages of modular course structures and the desirability of credit accumulation and transfer arrangements. We have taken most of our references from within the United Kingdom. Had we chosen to include comment from various reports of the Organisation for Economic Co-operation and Development (OECD), the European Commission (EC) or the World Bank, the message would have been the same.

Ministerial support: 1983-93

82.   Support for credit accumulation and
        transfer arrangements has often been
provided in ministerial statements from relevant
government departments.

Table 5:
Occasions of ministerial support

- 1984: Minister of State (HE)
  commended transbinary
  collaboration for credit transfer,
  inviting the CNAA to act as a
  catalyst for initiatives.

- 1986: Minister of State (HE)
  announced support for CNAA
  proposal for a credit accumulation
  and transfer scheme.

- 1988: Minister of State (HE) called for
  wider access and commended the
  extension of credit accumulation
  and transfer, noting *inter alia* the
  contribution of Open College
  Federations to both developments.

- 1990: Secretary of State for
  Employment emphasised the
  importance of higher education in
  economic terms, pointing out its role
  in improving national skills and calling
  for increasing flexibility and
  responsiveness from higher
  education in its engagement with
  students and employers. He stressed
  the role to be played by the NCVQ in
  contributing to a national vocational
  framework.

- In 1991, Minister of State (HE), Alan
  Howarth MP, gave the most
  sustained encouragement yet to the
  development of credit accumulation
  and transfer.

- In 1991, celebrating five years of the
  CNAA CAT scheme, Secretary of
  State for Education, Kenneth Clarke
  MP, paid tribute to its pioneering
  work in moving forward the ideas
  and principles of credit
  accumulation and transfer.

For the individual, I believe there is great
incentive to embark on a programme of
study that allows credits towards a
qualification to be gained over time, and
not necessarily in the same part of the
country... 'CATS' will help to demolish the
myth that higher education is something
you do when you leave school, or not at
all... Services (in higher education) should
be determined by the user rather than the
provider. Credit accumulation and
transfer are growth areas for consumer
power.

*Alan Howarth MP, Minister of State for Higher
Education, 'Learning without walls' conference,
University of Oxford, February 1991.*

Policy and the White Papers

83.   Ministerial support has been
        complemented by sustained commit-
ment reflected in the various White Papers from
the DFE since 1987. This has added considerably
to the impetus behind the introduction of greater
choice and flexibility in higher education. These
policies have encouraged greater access to
higher education, stimulate increased
participation in science and engineering,
established government commitment to rising
levels of achievement, urged higher education
into closer association with business and
national economic priorities, and stressed
continuing expectations of value for money.

Higher education: meeting the challenge

84.   The White Paper, *Higher education:
        meeting the challenge* (1987), commented
specifically on matters directly related to the
further development of credit accumulation and
transfer and the changes contingent on this.
Identifying three routes of progression from
further to higher education: *academic* (via 'A'
levels) , *vocational* (via NVQ/SVQs and similar)
and *access* (via specially defined Access courses),
the White Paper went on to comment on the
development of credit transfer schemes:

*'The Government welcomes such initiatives,
particularly attempts to work with employers to
integrate their in-house training courses and
development schemes into broader based programmes
of professional development.'* (2.23)

Higher education: a new framework

85.   By 1991, *Higher education: a new framework* was able to move the discussion forward. With increased participation and discernible progress towards greater institutional responsiveness, the White Paper commented:

> As higher proportions of both young and more mature people enter higher education through academic and vocational routes, it will be important for institutions to review the content and structure of their courses and the way in which they are provided. More flexible patterns of teaching and learning are already being widely introduced and the Government welcomes this... The Government sees scope both for more extensive use of credit accumulation and transfer and for providing courses on a more intensive basis, making more effective use of buildings and equipment...
>
> *Higher education: a new framework (1991: 16)*

86.   The immediate outcomes of these observations were the Pearce Report (1993) on premises costs followed by the Flowers Report (1993) on the reform of the academic year. We can only speculate on the influence exercised on these policies and reports by the outcomes of HMI visits to the United States in 1988-89 (see Table 6).

Education and training for the 21st century

87.   The two White Papers on higher education were complemented by the publication in 1991 of *Education and training for the 21st century*, a White Paper (in two volumes) on the development of post-secondary and further education. It offered similar objectives:

88.   The White Paper called for the development of modular NVQ/SVQs and GNVQs, the creation of incentives to reach higher levels of training, and equality of esteem between academic and vocational qualifications with *'clearer and more accessible paths between them'* (1.5). Taken together, the three White Papers set the future direction of higher and

further education in which the further development of arrangements for credit transfer feature prominently.

> Young people and adults need a clear framework of qualifications to measure their success in education and training. We need to build up a modern system of academic and vocational qualifications which are equally valued. They must both set high standards and offer ladders of opportunity after 16 and throughout working life, building on achievements of school.
>
> *Education and training for the 21st century (1991)*

The outcomes of the White Papers

89.   The White Papers also commented on quality assurance, accountability and efficiency. We believe it is important to understand the consequences of this emphasis for the further development of credit transfer arrangements. Government views were set out in the 1987 White Paper:

'The Government attaches no less importance than previously to its policy of maintaining and raising standards. It believes that increased participation in higher education need not be at the expense of academic excellence; indeed the stimulus of change should help to sharpen awareness of the different types of achievement that properly form part of the output of higher education.' (2.15)

90.   On efficiency and quality, it stated:

*'The Government is concerned both with the efficiency of individual institutions and with that of the national system of higher education as a whole... **It is about helping institutions and individuals to achieve more of what they should achieve with the money that is available** (3.23) ... Academic standards and the quality of teaching in higher education need to be judged by reference mainly to students' achievements... Essential data on performance in each institution should be published so that its record can be evaluated by the funding agencies, governing bodies, and employers.'* (3.30)

Table 6: Policy development and the reports of HMI 1989-91

Aspects of education in the United States of America

During 1988 and 1989, the Department of Education and Science conducted a number of investigations of different national systems of education. These included visits by HMI to Denmark, France, Germany, Japan, and the Netherlands. By far the most extensive series of visits was arranged for the United States. The subsequent reports made proposals for the further consideration of various aspects of post–secondary and higher education in the USA which, HMI concluded, had consequences for the development of further and higher education in the United Kingdom. The outcomes of these reports are summarised here.

Report	Terms of reference	Selected conclusions
Aspects of Higher Education in the United States of America (1989)	*The examination of aspects of higher education in the United States to highlight issues which might inform thinking in the United Kingdom, relating to: standards; finance; governance and the management of institutions; unit costs; participation levels; access and wastage; tuition fees; student loans; curricula; and research*	*Institutions are responsible for own standards, subject to five-year review; no national standards for institutions or degree qualifications; curriculum more broadly-based, leading to 'impressive maturation and sense of responsibility' but lower specialist attainment by age 21; access, diversity and modular programmes are distinctive features, encouraging greater participation and mixed-mode attendance; financial constraints force students to move in and out of study; credit system assists students to retain learning achievement; loans ubiquitous but complex*
Vocational and Continuing Education (1990)	*The examination of aspects of vocational and continuing education in the United States to highlight issues which might inform thinking in England and Wales relating to: standards; access; credit transfer; unit costs; participation levels; links between institutions and their communities; tuition fees; student loans; curricula; and course validation*	*Community colleges bridge further and higher education; offer two-year degrees and facilitate credit transfer to four-year universities, often via articulation agreements (cf franchise arrangements); some two-year degrees constitute high quality vocational qualifications; credit transfer assisted by core curriculum and universally recognised transcript*
Quality and its Assurance in Higher Education (1991)	*The examination of quality and its assurance in higher education in the United States to highlight issues which might inform thinking in the United Kingdom relating to: quality assessment;, quality and funding; quality and student choice; quality control and institutional effectiveness; and quality assurance and institutional accreditation*	*Self-regulation with financial incentives to enhance quality; peer review and low central costs; assurance to meet minimum standards; fitness for purpose is central to process as institutions are assessed against own objectives; funding follows accredited status; greater student awareness of institutional quality; shift from inputs to outputs in quality assurance, in response to needs of users of higher education*
Indicators in Educational Monitoring (1991)	*The examination of the use of performance indicators to monitor, evaluate and manage educational reforms in schools, colleges and universities in the United States, assessing the indicators at state and national level, and drawing conclusions about the potential for the use of similar indicators in the United Kingdom*	*Indicator analysis linked to institutional mission statement; use of targets and benchmarks to monitor progress; use of indicators to link resources to student outcomes, rewarding excellence and repairing poor performance; used to inform local community, state and national government; benefits to management in identifying progress towards targets*

91.   The 1991 White Paper followed by inviting universities and colleges to describe their arrangements for the continued assurance of quality in the light of the dissolution of the CNAA. It is the widely held view that the higher education institutions are best placed to assure the quality of their programmes, and thereby demonstrate their accountability to government, students and employers. The institutions therefore responded by establishing the Higher Education Quality Council (HEQC) to be responsible for the quality assurance and quality improvement of academic programmes. These responsibilities embrace the further development of credit systems and access course recognition, a particularly important function in circumstances where students are being invited to become more closely involved in the construction of their personal learning programmes.

92.   In a statement more recently (1993), the current Minister for Higher Education has elaborated:

'Accountability demands some effort and may demand some sacrifice of professional pride… the day of the unaccountable professional is over… I believe we are seeing the emergence of a new and healthier kind of pride amongst those professionals who recognise that they are not omniscient, or accountable only to their own conscience or culture, and must be called to account by others for what they provide…'

We believe that this observation is particularly pertinent under conditions of greater student choice. The general application of credit systems to student programmes, and the consequent improvement in the visibility of outcomes, may assist institutions in improving the quality of higher education and in meeting calls for greater institutional accountability. This is likely to require a strengthening of the relationship between the HEQC, NCVQ, BTEC, SCOTVEC, employers, professional bodies and student representatives.

Policy: the view of employers

93.   There is such disparity of function, focus and need amongst employers that

---

Sources of information

- the *Employment Department* has been concerned to support developments in higher and further education;

- the *Department of Trade and Industry* has published five reports on higher education since 1990, proposing closer co-operation with industry;

- the *Council for Industry and Higher Education* (CIHE) has published a further six reports, including several case studies;

- the *Confederation of British Industry* (CBI) has published two influential reports on post-secondary education and training since 1989;

- the *Association of Graduate Recruiters* (AGR) has recently issued a report on graduate supply and employer needs for the next decade;

- *Training and Enterprise Councils* some of which have expressed a position on flexibility and mobility;

- *individual employers* such as British Petroleum, Grand Metropolitan, Glaxo, Ford, IBM, British Telecom, Allied-Lyons and many others have made formal commitments to closer association with higher and further education.

---

it is difficult to establish representative views. Attention must inevitably be paid to views expressed by the relevant government departments and through representative employer agencies. In terms of policies on higher and further education, views from these sources are more easily available:

The Employment Department

94.   In a statement offering strategic guidance to the Training and Enterprise Councils, *1990s: the skills decade,* the Secretary of State for Employment identified a number of features relevant to the development of a credit framework:

- an education system relevant to every level of working life;

- a national system of work-related qualifications;

- increased employer commitment to education and training;

- increased motivation of individuals for self-development and self-investment;

- action to be taken at the local level, the meeting point of customer and supplier.

95. In its written submission to the *Learning without walls* conference, the Higher Education Branch of the Employment Department elaborated further (see below). Its contribution went on to suggest that, on the evidence available to it so far, the organisation of learning through flexible academic credit systems provided: enhanced clarity and coherence of study programmes; greater entry flexibility; increased learner flexibility, encouraging students to vary their mode of attendance, pace of learning and subject combinations; and the linkage of credit for learning at work to more widely accepted systems of academic credit. The Employment Department also identified an agenda for further development and research. Items included:

- a specification of what learning outcomes are being accredited in higher education;

- a comparison of the outcomes from academic programmes with those from higher level NVQ/SVQs;

- a definition of what constitutes evidence for assessment of academic programmes in higher education;

- the balance between the flexibility bestowed by credit accumulation and transfer arrangements and the requirements of professional bodies.

96. The strategy of the Department with respect to education and training has been to provide support for an extensive range of research and development programmes within universities and colleges. Since 1987, the Department has sponsored the Enterprise in Higher Education programme (1988-); projects to increase access to higher education; to establish closer links between higher education institutions and employers; and to explore the assessment of learning outcomes (1988-92); projects to integrate work-based learning in academic programmes in higher education (1990-); projects: to explore closer links between the outcomes of higher education academic programmes and those of higher level NVQ/SVQ programmes, to encourage the further development of accredited work-based learning, and to define and operate educational guidance in higher education (1993-); and a research programme to investigate various conceptual aspects of the nature of higher education.

97. Two reports have been published, summarising the work of the Department in these areas: *The skills link* (1990) and *Learning through work* (1992). It has also supported work by UDACE which sought to establish the basic accreditable elements common to undergraduate programmes. This resulted in the publication: *Learning outcomes in higher education* (the Otter Report, 1992).

98. The Department has also recognised the importance of its work for the management of higher education institutions (see the reference below), taking a realistic approach to the problems of managing fundamental change. It has also commented

> Credit accumulation and transfer systems, in higher education and elsewhere, offer flexible and cost effective ways towards qualifications. They are an important part of moves towards increased participation in education, training, and in particular higher education. By offering qualifications they serve to increase the accessibility of learning to a range of people; and by offering credit for learning acquired elsewhere than in higher education institutions they acknowledge that learning at all levels takes place through individuals' experience.
>
> *Employment Department, HE Branch (1991)*

positively on the capacity of credit-based learning to deliver achievement consistent with high quality. In its submission to the *Learning without walls* conference, the Department also commented:

'CATS may be seen both as a form of quality assurance and as a means of offering certificated learning in achievable amounts. Valid certification is itself a motivator of individual investment.'

> 'CATS' has immense potential... to draw together the common experience of learning, at work and through life, with the more stylised learning offered within higher education modules or courses. As such it will be a major force towards opening higher learning for all. (But) this focus on strengthening the role and responsibilities of individuals for their own learning raises questions of the structure and development of the institutions themselves. Is 'CATS' to become an institution's norm or is it to remain an unusual learning route? Will departmental structures, both academic managerial and financial, accommodate easily to students who are no longer easy to identify with the department or the subject? The full implementation of 'CATS' will require those issues to be tackled.
>
> *Employment Department, HE Branch (1991)*

Department of Trade and Industry

99.   Principally concerned with providing advice and support to companies, the DTI has published five reports jointly with the Council for Industry and Higher Education on collaboration between business and higher education. These reports comment on strategies for the recruitment of graduates, and on the organisation and management of institutions for closer company liaison. Two reports are particularly helpful for our purposes. *Policy and strategy for higher education* (1990) and *Continuing education and training* (1990) both confirm the importance the DTI and companies attach to flexibility and personal effectiveness in graduates and other qualified leavers. The reports emphasise the motivational consequences on employees of continuing professional development, particularly where this attracts credit towards higher education qualifications.

Council for Industry and Higher Education

100.   The Council for Industry and Higher Education (CIHE) is an independent association of eleven Vice-Chancellors and senior representatives of universities and colleges with 26 Chief Executives of several large 'blue chip' companies in the United Kingdom. Since its inception in 1986 it has represented to government the joint thinking of industry and higher education. It has consistently reflected the support of its members for a more flexible and open system of higher education, seeking to maintain the rapid growth in the numbers of mature and part-time students. Support for the development of a comprehensive credit system has featured prominently in the Council's proposals.

101.   The Council has commissioned several studies in higher and further education and published a number of reports. It has argued that students must be equipped to be versatile and adaptable to changing work demands, claiming that an insistence on 'rigour' and 'standards' should not be used to inhibit the development in the United Kingdom of a bigger and more open system of higher education. It has consistently supported proposals for a two-year standard higher education qualification.

102.   The CIHE has maintained a clear commitment towards the type of higher education learning environment it believes will best suit students and employers. In *Towards a partnership* (1987), it stated:

'Employees will develop best and most relevantly when what they learn at college is interwoven with training programmes and experience at work. This should encourage universities in restructuring their own courses into discrete blocks ('modularisation') so that students can move through their careers, assembling credits in their workplace and at college.' (6.7)

103.   This report went on to commend the CNAA's credit transfer arrangements, commenting that *'similar experiments among universities will be welcome'*. By 1988, the Council felt able to report with confidence the responses from companies (as below):

> Firms spoke of their concern about the lack of a national system of portable credits: this is a major obstacle to employees' taking full advantage of all the sources on offer. We believe that clear encouragement from industry for a national system of transferable credits (in which all HE institutions ought to take part) will spur the growth of such a system.
>
> *Towards a partnership: the company response, Council for Industry and Higher Education, 1988*

104.   After publishing in 1990 eight case studies of collaborative partnerships between universities and industry, the Council released a major report on higher education policy, *Investing in diversity* (1992). It stated:

'Those charged with overseeing the "quality" of higher education should seek employers' views not only on the skills they immediately need but on the long-term demands of employment, including flexibility and adaptability, which students must be prepared to meet… Courses and teaching methods must above all be chosen so as to inspire students with a passionate curiosity to continue learning through life.' (Ex Summ 2)

105.   Amongst its various proposals for policy development in higher education, which included recommendations for investment in science and engineering, and the development of a financial strategy for higher education, *Investing in diversity* also proposed:

'To ask all academic departments to make explicit how their courses provide, inter alia, both training in skills and a broad preparation for forty years of working life and continued adaption and training.' (1.2)

106.   It also renewed Council's support for the further promotion of credit accumulation and transfer, commenting in favour of a national credit framework and the continuing work of the NCVQ:

'To encourage continuing development of people in employment, we need ladders to allow smooth progression between institutions… Co-operation between universities and colleges should be a policy

objective. (2.6) The Professional Institutions need encouragement in reviewing how to bring their accreditation procedures within a single common framework.' (Ex Summ)

107.   Overall, the Council for Industry and Higher Education has emphasised consistently the support of large employers for a system of education and training which delivers flexibility and variety within a framework of excellence.

Confederation of British Industry

108.   The CBI has directed most of its attention towards education policy for the 16-19 age group, believing that reform of this sector is crucial for national skills regeneration. A policy statement on higher education is about to be produced (CBI, 1994) and its observations to the 1980 Select Committee on Education, Science and Arts remain broadly representative:

'We are convinced that there should be more regard for courses orientated generally towards vocational aims as a basis for the provision of higher education courses in the future… We would like to see somewhat greater weight attached to the personal qualities, such as motivation, ability for original thought and the ability to get at and solve problems.'

109.   It has published two influential reports: *Towards a skills revolution* (1989) and *Routes for success* (1993), both of which contain proposals relevant to the development of credit systems in higher and further education. The policy objectives of the CBI's education and training strategy were described in the first report:

- motivating people to learn within a coherent education and training framework

- creating an individual focus through personal profiles

- giving individuals buying power in a new education and training market by offering transferable skills and qualifications.

Table 7: National targets for education and training

Foundation learning

- by 1997, 80% of young people to reach NVQ2 (or equivalent);

- training and education to NVQ3 (or equivalent) to be available to all young people;

- by 2000, 50% of young people to reach NVQ3 (or equivalent);

- education and training provision to develop self-reliance, flexibility and breadth.

Lifelong learning

- by 1996, all employers should take part in training or development activities;

- by 1996, 50% of the work-force to be aiming for NVQs or units towards them;

- by 2000, 50% of the work-force to be qualified to at least NVQ3 (or equivalent);

- by 1996, 50% of medium to large organisations (200 or more employees) to be 'Investors in People'.

110.　To support these objectives, the CBI recommended in 1991 the creation of formal National Targets for Education and Training (see Table 7), continued support for the NCVQ and the development of a broad post-16 curriculum emphasising a range of core skills. In its subsequent report, *Routes for Success*, the CBI commented: 'As firms must anticipate change, they need employees with a breadth of ability. This means having core transferable skills. It involves recognising the limits of knowledge and an awareness of what is unknown. Detailed expertise in one narrow area will no longer be enough; broad occupational competence is now required... The more adaptable, responsible and creative each employee, the more effective the organisation.' (3,4)

111.　Although the National Targets for Education and Training (NTETs) make only indirect reference to the role of higher education, they do imply a more intensive commitment to lifelong education and training by employers than ever before. For example, to meet the target of qualifying 50% of larger organisations as '*Investors in People*', then the number of awards will need to rise from 74 organisations (1992) to over 6,000 organisations by 1996. It follows therefore that, if these lifelong learning targets are to be met, the number of employees seeking to access continuing professional development should rise steeply. Higher education may have a prominent role to play with further education in the achievement of a system of accreditation and qualification for these prospective learners. A national credit framework may prove influential in encouraging investment in employee training.

112.　The CBI has offered two further contributions which may be directly relevant to higher education developments. Firstly, in *Towards a skills revolution*, the CBI promoted the concept of 'careership'. The report explained the concept as follows:

'Careership should generate more interest in and demand for learning, give attainment more overt recognition, improve the quality and the content of education and training provision and provide incentives for its take up. It should provide a single framework to guide and structure the development of foundation skills (from 14 to 19) and a basis for continuous learning and training throughout working life.' (33)

113.　Secondly, in *Routes for success*, the CBI proposed a system of post-16 training credits, enabling students to become direct purchasers of education and training needs. The CBI has maintained that this system, universally applied to 16 year-olds, would create financial incentives for people to train and would challenge producer-led definitions of learner needs.

114.　To date, there has been a muted response to the proposals for a universal system of training credits. The Further Education Funding Council in particular has not been persuaded of the advantages for financial control. Yet the concept of 'careership' and the application of a universal system of (education and) training credits do open up the potential of 'credits' both as financial units of account and as units of (academic or vocational) learning achievement. Both ideas may be worth exploring further.

Association of Graduate Recruiters

115.   The Association of Graduate Recruiters (AGR) represents the views of employers who recruit significant numbers of graduates. Its assessment of current labour market demands may be taken as proxy for the judgements of those employers who may come over time to recruit significant numbers of graduates and other higher education leavers in an expanded labour market (see Table 8). In 1993 the AGR published its conclusions on the future employment needs of its members. *Roles for graduates in the 21st century* addressed the changes that are being experienced by major employers and the consequences for graduate employment.

116.   Of the changes in the workplace for which prospective graduate employees would need to be prepared, the AGR named: firstly, a more diversified range of jobs for graduate entry; secondly, greater flexibility of skills, including good communications skills and the ability to organise and contribute to teams; thirdly, the earlier assumption of responsibility roles; and finally, greater expectation of continuing personal development within 'learning organisations'. This view

Table 8: Projected employment change by occupation 1991-2000		
General	**Occupational group**	**% change**
Managerial	Corporate managers and administrators	+ 31
	Managers/proprietors in agriculture and services	+ 17
Professional	Science and engineering professions	+ 31
	Health professions	+ 24
	Teaching professions	+ 22
	Other professional occupations	+ 40
Associated professional	Science and engineering associated professions	+ 20
	Health associated professions	+ 13
	Other associated professional occupations	+ 28
Non-manual	Protective service occupations	+ 16
	Personal service occupations	+ 16
	Buyers, brokers and sales representatives	+ 6
	Other sales occupations	+ 10
	Clerical occupations	+ 2
	Secretarial occupations	+ 4
Skilled and semi-skilled manual	Skilled construction trades	+ 7
	Skilled engineering trades	- 8
	Other skilled trades	- 17
	Industrial plant and machine operatives	- 21
	Drivers and mobile machine operatives	- 5
	Other occupations in agriculture	- 18
	Other elementary occupations	- 5
	All occupations	+ 7

Institute for Employment Research, University of Warwick

> ## Table 9: What employers want from students
>
> - effective communication skills
>
> - leadership qualities
>
> - problem-solving skills
>
> - personal skills:
>
>   self-discipline
>
>   organisation
>
>   decision making
>
> - teamwork skills
>
> - information technology

coincides closely with the preferences of employers recorded by the Association of Graduate Careers Advisory Services (AGCAS) in their report, *What do graduates do?* (1993). When employers hire graduates, they seek senior management potential; the qualities they seek are outlined in Table 9. Above all, employers appear to want students leaving higher education to possess basic core skills beyond academic subject knowledge.

117.   To assist employers in achieving their objectives, the AGR report recommended the further development of credit-based learning and modular systems, supported by adequate student guidance and a culture of lifelong learning. Above all, employers want to preserve quality outcomes from higher education consonant with the development of innovation, personal initiative and problem-solving. As the AGR report commented:

'The restrictive view of "appropriate" jobs for graduates is considerably out of line with the actual choices open to them, both at the outset and throughout their careers. Obsolete beliefs are limiting the constructive growth of a wide range of good choices… (We) strongly encourage the growth of "employment-friendly" cultures in higher education: better integration, more co-operation and mutual understanding.'

Training and Enterprise Councils

118.   Training and Enterprise Councils (TECs) and their Scottish equivalents (Local Enterprise Councils, LECs) occupy a key position in the development of education and training opportunities in higher and further education. The involvement of employers in regional educational developments makes the observations of TEC/LECs particularly influential for initiatives between the sectors. Accordingly, we have been impressed by the statement on credit accumulation and transfer issued in 1993 by the Chief Executives of the co-ordinated London TECs. Calling for the adoption of a 'CAT Manifesto', the Education Policy Group of the London TECs places the development of a credit framework for London at the core of their education, training and employment objectives, stating in unequivocal terms:

> Credit accumulation and transfer is an idea whose time has come… TECs have an important role to play, both in progressing CAT more quickly than might otherwise be the cae, and in settling the CAT agenda which might otherwise be dominated by concerns that have lower priority for TECs.
>
> *Joint policy statement of the Chief Executives of the London Training and Enterprise Councils (1993)*

119.   This position is reflected to a greater or lesser extent by many TEC/LECs across the country. Credit accumulation and transfer is seen by many of them as an ideal vehicle for achieving a coherent response to disparate objectives, amongst which are the achievement of parity of esteem between academic and vocational learning, an increase in cross-sectoral learning opportunities, improvements in achievement and progression, and the prospect of developing a student-centred formula for resource management.

Policy and professional bodies

120.   For the purposes of this report, we have included in the category 'professional body' those agencies, institutions and

<table>
<tr><td colspan="2" align="center">**Table 10: Corporate employers and credit systems: two cases**</td></tr>
<tr><td>**Allied-Lyons Retailing**</td><td>**Ford (UK) Motor Company**</td></tr>
<tr><td>

The company has committed itself to an extensive programme of management development in both professional and strategic expertise. It has close links with the University of Bradford, Manchester Metropolitan University and the University of Greenwich for accredited programmes in Management and International Studies, Retail Sales and Marketing, and Management for the Brewing Industry respectively.

'We now expect our younger managers to achieve full professional standards in their major discipline whether this be in brewing, marketing, engineering, or any of the other key functions in the company.'
Roy Moss, Deputy Chairman.

'We use accreditation of our internal courses to ensure that the levels of teaching and student attainment are to a high externally recognised standard and provide successful students with tangible recognition of their success. The opportunity to gain high level academic credits has been welcomed by our managers. As we have companies in many locations, both in the UK and abroad, the transferability of credits is of considerable importance. We therefore look to universities to accept credits from other universities. As employers we welcome the intellectual rigour required in attaining academic credits; we also believe we can contribute in a practical way to the development of standards in higher education.'

Dr David Frean, Management Development Executive.

Source: Correspondence with Professor David Robertson

</td><td>

The company is involved at many levels in employee development and training, most notably in the EDAP programme. In higher level education and training, the company has formed close working relationships with both Anglia Polytechnic University and the University of East London. The ASSET programme at the former is a well-established example of the accreditation of prior and work-based learning from experience is a prominent feature of the company's education policy.

'Many engineers who have not been able to take advantage of a degree course in the past are also discouraged from trying later in their careers. Having to start at the beginning of a course and studying subjects on which they are the acknowledged local 'experts' is a large disincentive. With the advent of modular course structures, it now becomes possible to accredit the knowledge and experience, gained over many years of engineering, to a standard equivalent to that studied within a degree module. An individual could in certain circumstances reduce a four year part-time degree to two years with the appropriate accreditation. This is not an easy option. All claims for exemption must be supported by evidence. Accumulating and collating the evidence and matching it to the outline learning objectives of a degree module requires tenacity, vision and an appreciation of the educational and technical development process.'

Geoffrey Johnsish, Education & Training Central Office.

Source: Correspondence with Professor David Robertson

</td></tr>
</table>

associations which set professional standards and regulate the practice of members. This allows us to comment on the views both of regulatory supra-agencies, such as the Engineering Council or the United Kingdom Central Council for Nursing, Midwifery and Health Visiting which are not themselves professional bodies, and the individual institutes, such as the Institute of Electrical Engineers, the Royal Pharmaceutical Society, the Institute of Physics or the Chartered Institute of Public Finance and Accountancy.

121.   It is generally assumed that the requirement of professional bodies to regulate and monitor the maintenance of professional standards presents an impediment to the expression of greater student choice and mobility. Many academic staff, when planning

to reshape their courses in modular and credit-bearing form, anticipate the reservations of professional bodies and restrict flexibility accordingly. We were able to discuss these matters with over forty professional bodies and regulating authorities. This extensive consultation provides the basis for discussions later in this report but we have provided a summary of policies towards student choice and mobility in Table 11. In developing this summary, we have been helped by the earlier surveys undertaken by Squires (1986) into attitudes towards modularisation, and by Vaughan (1991) into the views of professional bodies on credit-bearing Continuing Professional Development (CPD). The conclusions of our work are largely consistent with earlier findings, with one important exception. Many professional bodies appear to

Table 11: Professional bodies and their policies towards student choice and mobility

	Commitment to flexibility, student choice and mobility	Consideration of the labour market effect of increased access
Accountancy and Finance	Strongly supports the principle of CATS (CIB); Basic philosophy of CATS is excellent. Students find the idea attractive. It works most effectively between FE and HE (CIB in Scotland); happy with modularisation and extended choice (ACCA); but fairly minimal at present (CIPFA)	Widening of access is welcome and keen to see trend continue (CIPFA); increased access cannot be allowed to reduce credibility of qualifications (ACCA); increased availability of graduates has led to greater recruitment selectivity… quality of those emerging with first degrees is sufficient (CII)
Business and Management	Modularisation is tolerable as long as compet-encies are covered.Universities appear to have more difficulty with flexibility than the Institute (IPM); acceptable only if outcomes establish competence.Welcomes initiatives to extend man-agement skills across the curriculum (IMan); Happy to work with a flexible curriculum (IAM)	Irresponsible to produce qualified graduates in profession where the market cannot absorb them. Students are advised to research the market for professional skills to inform subject choice (IPM); it is likely that personal effectiveness will assume increasing significance,integrating management skills with other disciplines (IMan)
Construction	Modularisation is handled through individual negotiation with institutions (RIBA); move to centre rather than course accreditation may be seen as recognition of desirability of flexibility… but concern for discontinuity if modularisation is carried to its extreme (RICS); moving away from the validation of courses to validation of a series of modules across the UK (IH)	Increasing numbers can lead to worries about employment opportunities (RIBA); surveying education is good education and we play down the vocational opportunities… Larger numbers may lead to a wider spectrum of graduates with no expectation of a reduction in quality of recruitment (RICS); we do not engage in manpower planning (RTPI); majority of students are part-time and employed (IH)
Engineering	Basic core of pre-requisite subjects,with flexibility in supporting elements (IEE); problem with CATS is to ensure common standards and avoid reptition of learning… 60% subjects in modular courses (ICE); modularisation may dismantle barriers between initial education and CPD (IEEIE); no problem with modularisation and student choice if content of modules is readily discernible (IQA)	Entry standards are the business of universities… more concerned with exit standards… linked where possible to NVQs (IQA); the accreditation process encourages 'more of the same'… however an ongoing review within the profession may lead to a broadening of attitudes (IEE); no lowering of standards for CEng and more graduates will become IEng (ICE)
Health Care, Dentistry and Medicine	Welcomes the approach to a more flexible curriculum (UKCC). Modular programmes are widely accepted in Nursing (ENB); universities may proceed with modularisation subject to approval (CSP); has seen no reason so far to limit modularity and extended student choice (CollRad); has recommended development of more flexible curricula in medicine for some years (GMC); choice may have a role in basic dental science components but is regarded as inappropriate in the clinical stages (GDC)	Balance between fitness-for-purpose and academic standards must be maintained and will become an increasing challenge in a climate of decreasing employment (UKCC); need to consider NVQs (ENB); students are funded by health authority bursaries, determining training places (CSP); the supply of doctors, dentists and pharmacists is constrained by *numerus clausus*
Law	Doubts whether a free 'pick-and-mix' system could ever produce a graduate with a coherent knowledge of law… seeks to lay down foundations of law for qualifying degrees (Law Society)	Undergraduate legal education is excellent in its own right and need not lead to employment within the profession… new emphasis on acquisition of skills will help (Law Society)
Science	If the core curriculum is covered, we have no objection to optional modules (IEHO); we wish to encourage greater breadth and flexibility in the higher education curriculum (IPhys)	We remain strongly committed to wider access and the use of GNVQs (IPhys); the Institute is currently reviewing its requirements for practical training in the light of local authority shortages (IEHO)

be more relaxed about prospects for modularisation and credit transfer than has hitherto been the case; indeed some appear to have changed their position in the last year or so.

122.   It is clearly difficult to generalise effectively on the policy positions of diverse professional bodies. They are differentiated by statutory obligations, *numerus clausus,* history, size and labour market position. They are internally differentiated by status, grade and occupational function. Moreover they may be distinguished by their emphasis on initial training, undergraduate or post-graduate education, and/or continuing professional development. Finally, professional bodies may be differentiated by the extent to which they describe themselves as customers or accreditors of higher education; only those in the former category appear to seek an extensive engagement with credit systems.

General policy developments

123.   Despite their heterogeneity, professional bodies appear to have made relatively steady progress towards a reconciliation with the changes currently underway in higher education. This accepted, it must be said that the scale of commitment is very uneven. Many professional bodies remain highly cautious of the implications for their responsibilities of modifications to higher education structures, quality assurance arrangements, the role of the NCVQ and the impact of increased participation. We have been able to identify a number of policies which professional bodies hold in common.

124.   **Autonomy in accreditation:** professional bodies uniformly wish to preserve their autonomy in the discharge of responsibilities towards the maintenance of high standards. The majority are happy to do this in partnership, wherever possible, with higher education institutions but the responsibility is not something which many bodies feel able to delegate. Some professional institutions are however moving towards the accreditation of centres rather than courses (for example, the Royal Institute of Chartered Surveyors is adopting this policy). This would suggest a readiness in some quarters to accept a greater

degree of freedom in programme design with more emphasis consequently on qualified outputs.

125.   **Modularisation:** many professional bodies appear more prepared to accept the consequences of modularity now than was evident in earlier studies (eg Squires, 1986). Having said this, there is uniform acceptance of the need to describe the core credit acceptable to the professional body. Choice is seen as a function of any optional or elective programme, which in some cases may be permitted up to 40% of the total programme.

126.   **Flexibility and student choice:** some professional bodies remain apprehensive of modularity based on 'pick-and-mix' or 'cafeteria' styles of programme construction. Despite the fact that we can find no evidence of any such style of course organisation anywhere in the United Kingdom (nor are we aware of it in the United States for that matter), the stereotype continues to act as a source of consternation for certain professional bodies. Further work will need to be undertaken by universities and colleges, probably through the HEQC, to create a basis of confidence within these bodies in the quality of modular programmes.

127.   **Credit systems:** there is widespread support for the development of credit systems and modularity, particularly amongst the professions allied to medicine, social work, and the caring professions generally (for example, CCETSW, UKCC, ENB). This commitment is sustained by the acceptance under appropriate conditions of the accreditation of prior experiential learning (APEL) and credit for work-based or practice-based learning, as well as by the promotion of professional and institutional consortia.

128.   **Credit transfer and student mobility:** there is significant unease over prospects for student mobility and credit transfer *between* higher education institutions. Some of the health and caring professions appear to be exempt from this apprehension, but otherwise it does appear to reflect a general scepticism towards the view that students might transfer credit from one programme to another

Table 12: The engineering profession: a policy case study

Engineering futures; ed Gareth Parry; **Engineering Council, RSA and Training Agency, 1990**	**Conference recommendations:** preliminary programmes should be available at work as well as in post-compulsory education; first year courses in higher education should be common to all engineering disciplines and organised on a modular and flexible basis to account for the diverse education backgrounds of young and older entrants; undergraduate engineering should be pursued through a common core curriculum with later specialisation within the degree and through continuing education and training; attention should be given to a framework of awards to ensure that engineering courses meet the needs of industry for chartered and incorporated engineers.
Investing in talent: the use and development of science and engineering graduates; Andrea Spurling; **Council for Industry and Higher Education, 1992**	A number of new programmes have been developed in collaboration with companies, sometimes using regional consortia; sponsored students and staff move back and forth between employers and higher education… students are increasingly attracted to institutions which allow them to combine academic study in engineering with the chance to improve language, business and personal skills. Employers are generally satisfied with the purely technical aspects of graduates' skills. Whether they work in industry or commerce, graduates will need ability in team-working, interpersonal and communication skills, and evidence of initiative and creativity. (3.27-3.28)
National system for CPD in engineering: a framework for action; **Engineering Council 1993**	**Recommendations to higher education:** design courses to meet needs of individuals and business in the most effective way; innovate by using a variety of learning methods, including flexible and modular programmes; wherever possible, give credit for CPD and provide opportunities for credit accumulation and transfer; place CPD information in relevant directories and databases; provide quality CPD by working to standards approved by the Engineering Council.
A review of engineering formation: discussion document; **Engineering Council 1993**	**Pathways to Engineering Professional Practice:** The Engineering Council is committed to diversity, flexibility and quality in the provision of engineering education and training. These features would be expressed through the complementary concepts of Foundation Learning and a lifetime of continuing professional development. The former would provide the breadth and depth of learning and the capability needed to exploit subsequent opportunities for specialism, updating and career change. The latter would provide a flexible and responsive set of pathways to continued professional competence. **Standards and Routes to Registration (SARTOR):** The criteria for registration published by the Engineering Council are based on the concept of competence but with standards implicit in 'routes' rather than precise definitions. The Engineering Council recognises that formally derived employment-led standards of competence can provide objective criteria for assessment and that vocational qualifications can provide evidence which may be used for registration, alongside other criteria concerning professional conduct, ethics and commitment to continued competence. **Quality and Accreditation:** The accreditation environment is changing in both education and industry, particularly with emphasis on quality assurance, the advent of outcomes-based qualifications and an increased range of bodies required to assess, audit or accredit. The Engineering Council is committed to partnership between the Council, funding councils, TECs, NCVQ, the Engineering institutions and other bodies to create simplified and cost-effective systems. It would support the concept of a single, joint engineering-wide accreditation body for educational courses.
Investing in talent: a view from employers; **Council for Industry and Higher Education, 1992**	"It is because the teaching is drab that drab people go into engineering… You have all the benchwork and it's utterly boring. You're learning by rote. You don't get a chance to become worldly, take part in student politics, or meet in the bar for deep and meaningful discussions and so forth." "The main defect, which still afflicts a new generation of graduates, was the failure to inspire." "I would love to see Engineering courses change so that it becomes a three year general engineering-with-management type course, with an optional bolt-on year at the end for the really heavy theoretical stuff… They build in all this heavy engineering theory all the way through the course which is pretty unattractive for people who want an engineering degree to be a degree as a stepping stone to a whole range of jobs."

without loss of coherence and academic integrity. Many professional bodies seem to be more secure in the quality of student choices within an individual institution, but this confidence does not extend to the construction of programmes from more than a single institution.

129.   **Credit consortia:** smaller professional bodies, and those regulating social work and some health professions, support the idea of institutional and subject-based consortia. CCETSW has formally promoted inter-institutional collaboration through training partnerships and some Regional Health Authorities would wish to consider the same. The College of Radiographers has convened a small association, the Federation of Radiography Education Departments (FRED), to explore credit transfer between approved programmes.

130.   **Continuing professional development:** there is general support for the applicability of credit-bearing and flexible learning arrangements to continuing professional development programmes. The Engineering Council has been particularly active in its support for this type of development and the recent *Review of engineering formation* (1993) confirms this (see also Table 12). Some of the individual institutions of the Council have less well-formed views and appear less convinced. This confirms the view of an earlier study (Vaughan, 1991) which indicated that 45% of professional bodies had negotiated credit-bearing CPD with universities and 81% expected activity to increase.

131.   **Competence and skills outcomes:** there has been an apparent growth of awareness in the importance of achievement in the assessment of accreditable courses. Professional bodies now widely talk of their reliance upon competence as a basis for judging professional achievement. This is the case particularly in the fields of business and management and in some of the professions associated with construction. Clearly the work of the NCVQ has had some impact upon the thinking of professional bodies, although we have noticed some apprehension towards the

NCVQ amongst many individual respondents. We attribute this to a lack of clarity amongst some professional bodies at this stage of development over their preferred relationship with the NCVQ.

132.   **International mobility:** we have not explored this matter directly with professional bodies but some have chosen to comment, indicating that this dimension is important for them. The position of the Engineering profession may be taken as indicative. The Engineering Council has been part of initiatives internationally and in Europe to promote mutual recognition of Engineering qualifications. This has been pursued through the FEANI initiative in Europe and via the Washington Accord elsewhere. The Engineering Council reports slow progress in reconciling national differences but emphasises the importance of persistent effort.

The student perspective

133.   The views of students on changes in higher education have been well-expressed in the *Student Charter* published by the National Union of Students in 1993. In this document, the NUS make imaginative commitments to radical changes in higher education, supporting modularisation, credit systems and the introduction of what we have chosen to describe as credit-based resourcing. Indeed the NUS proposals for reform are as fundamental in their implications for change as any that have emerged from other sources.

134.   Some of these aspects are supported by the draft proposals in the *Charter for higher education,* published by the Department for Education as a consultation document in 1993. Although by no means as radical or extensive as the proposals of the NUS, the *Charter for higher education* does formally establish limited student rights in respect of increased choice and flexibility. Commenting on the right to know in advance how courses are to be taught and assessed, the draft document states:

'Universities and colleges will… increasingly encourage more flexible patterns of study and easier

access for students... (Where they) operate "credit accumulation and transfer", students may have greater choice over what they study. They may be able to transfer between courses and between universities and colleges without repeating work or levels of study.'

A trade union perspective

135.   Support for educational developments contingent upon credit systems is most apparent amongst the professional associations and trade unions representing staff in higher and further education. However, support remains qualified by concerns over the consequences of these changes for the quality of professional life and by perceptions of the motivations which lie behind the promotion of specific developments (for example, the creation of a third semester). We offer below the views of the association currently representing the largest number of academic staff in further and higher education, the University and College Lecturers' Union, NATFHE which itself has formed a close association with the Association of University Teachers (AUT) in the last two years.

136.   We have not been able to establish the extent of support for the developments associated with this report amongst trade unions generally. We are aware that the TUC and its constituent associations place great

importance on strategies for comprehensive education and training, but we could not discover specific commitments to student flexibility, choice and mobility. This may give cause for further consultations in the future.

Conclusions

137.   We are quite clear that support for the further development of credit accumulation and transfer, largely within a modular context, is genuine and substantial amongst the 'external' stake-holders in higher and further education. Not only do they give implicit support to such developments, but explicit support is clear from the evidence of published policies. In many ways, the language of credit accumulation and credit transfer has been adopted more widely in certain quarters outside higher education than within it. Having said that, we would like to make it equally clear that stakeholders see themselves generally as the 'consumers' of higher education outputs. They are mainly concerned with the quality and

proficiency of graduate supply. How universities assure high quality outputs is still regarded as the proper business of the institutions concerned. This latter point should not be taken as an indication that employers, professional bodies and government departments will accept without comment the decisions of universities and colleges. Whilst we have not detected in our investigations any desire for an adversarial relationship with institutions, we have been made aware by all the groups concerned that they would largely welcome greater flexibility and diversity of skills from future graduates and other qualified leavers. The message to us has been so insistent and consistent on this matter that we pass it on with the appropriate emphasis.

Government policy

138.	We are able to confirm our initial assumptions on the general consistency of Government policy. The rhythms of the long-wave of policy remain undisturbed by occasional ripples of short-term setbacks. We add to this conviction in the following chapter. All government departments concerned with higher (and further) education, principally DFE, ED, and DTI, encourage similar developments. All are committed to assisting greater individual student choice and personal effectiveness as a means of improving the quality of student achievement and its impact on national economic performance.

139.	We have not been able to confirm it so readily, but we have detected a frustration in certain quarters that universities and colleges appear to be slow to respond to the persistent encouragement from employers, some professional bodies and students themselves to modify and modernise the curriculum and liberalise access to learning opportunities. This frustration is compounded by a generous acceptance of the excellence of much British higher education, extending to a reluctance to compromise the academic autonomy of institutions by direct intervention in their affairs. We have taken these indications of impatience seriously and have offered some constructive proposals for closer co-operation with external stakeholders, which we discuss in Chapter X. In passing on these observations, we

would not wish to contribute to a further defensiveness or retrenchment amongst institutions, but rather to affirm the willingness of government departments, as we perceive it, to assist higher education in managing appropriate change.

140.	On the other hand, there is considerable frustration within universities and colleges at what are perceived to be inconsistencies in policy towards the sector. This is making it difficult to conduct the management of change, central to which process is the willing co-operation of members of the academic community. Accordingly, **we recommend** that government departments continue to reinforce their policy objectives by reference to the continuity of policy over time. We believe that institutions and their staff would welcome clear statements from relevant departments which confirm the importance Government attaches to extending curriculum breadth, student choice and flexible academic programmes throughout higher education in order to improve the personal effectiveness of students for future employment. We believe that funding councils may have an important role to play in this, and **we recommend** that funding councils encourage institutions, both to develop more flexible arrangements for student choice, and to monitor the achievements in this respect.

Professional bodies

141.	We have detected positive and encouraging indications from many professional bodies. The growth of their awareness of credit accumulation and transfer has been extensive in the last few years. The vast majority of professional bodies are now actively engaged in the negotiation of credit-based learning arrangements of one form or another. The accreditation of continuing professional development remains the most familiar source of activity, whilst the modularisation of professionally-accredited courses has grown considerably. We are so encouraged by the responses in certain quarters that we believe professional bodies need not be seen by academic staff as major impediments to the further development of modularisation and credit-based learning.

142. On the other hand, we cannot leave this matter without advising on some less encouraging aspects. Our consultations indicated that some professional bodies continue to entertain misgivings about the quality assurance of flexible learning arrangements. This is particularly apparent in the case of inter-institutional credit transfer, both between higher education institutions and as a consequence of 'franchising' arrangements. We have not been able to determine whether the misgivings are any more strongly held by professional bodies than by many academics. We suspect not. The concerns arise from the potential inadequacy of the match between the original student programme and the chosen destination programme. Professional bodies, being concerned with the maintenance of consistent standards, feel more confident that they can guarantee these under conditions of student stability rather than mobility.

143. Moreover, we have detected a reluctance in certain quarters to countenance any reorganisation of curriculum opportunities which would lead to a learning and assessment regime different from that experienced by the majority of professional members. It would be easy to be dispirited by this, because it speaks of an assumption that what was good enough in the past remains appropriate today. We have been encouraged to find that the exposure of these membership opinions has been volunteered by those professional bodies which are at the forefront of efforts to address the matter. Some professional bodies are beginning to commission their own investigation of new learning and assessment regimes in order to inform their membership. Again, **we recommend** that the HEQC should seek to play a supportive role.

144. **We recommend** the time has come for a systematic engagement between universities, colleges and professional bodies to discuss the long-term character of the higher education curriculum, establishing the tolerances acceptable to all parties and determining shared strategic objectives. Professional bodies should be drawn more closely into partnership with higher education institutions on matters associated with the development of academic structures, learning and assessment methods, qualifications and employment opportunities. **We recommend** that the HEQC, acting on behalf of the representative bodies of the institutions, should arrange this dialogue.

145. In return, **we recommend** that, as part of the process of dialogue and in preparation for formal participation, professional bodies should be invited to identify their preferred positions with respect to student choice, credit transfer and modifications to the academic programmes in higher education. We have been less satisfied that all professional bodies have given as much attention as they themselves would wish to the consequences of mass participation and mass graduation. We would encourage all professional bodies to develop policies on the following aspects:

- the development of modularity and credit systems with respect to undergraduate, postgraduate, post-experience and continuing professional development;

- the quality assurance of programmes in the context of increased student choice, attending to admissions and assessment policies, the accreditation of prior and experiential learning, the construction of student programmes, and the character of qualifications;

- the preferred working relationship with universities and colleges in the future, commenting on policies for institutional accreditation on the one hand, and on the other, offering advice on the important of inter-institutional collaboration and consortia arrangements;

- the development of relationships with the NCVQ, commenting on the accreditation of programmes at higher levels;

- the response of professional institutions to increased graduation, commenting on the prospects for professional membership of academically qualified students, and their prospects for successful employment.

Employers and their representative bodies

146.   Employers, and particularly representatives from large companies, are generally more aware than may be commonly assumed of the advantages of accredited continuing professional development; some are increasingly persuaded by the internal modifications which result from modularisation, especially where this improves personal effectiveness. This is particularly true for larger employers where they have reached accreditation agreements with universities and colleges, reflected in the growth of university-company partnerships of many kinds. There appears to be some uncertainty amongst some employers about how they might go about reaching these agreements (see the DTI reports in earlier discussion). On balance, larger companies seem to be reasonably well-informed about the potential of accredited arrangements with institutions, but may have difficulty in identifying suitable partners. Small and medium-sized companies may well have to depend on the enterprise and commitment of their local institutions of higher education if they are to make satisfactory arrangements for accreditation partnerships.

147.   We have been impressed by the constancy of commitment towards student flexibility and choice which has been demonstrated by the Council for Industry and Higher Education, and we have wondered how best this might be translated into productive gain amongst institutions and companies. For reasons similar to those outlined above for professional bodies, we think it is timely to pursue an active dialogue with employers and their representatives. **We recommend** that this dialogue be formally started as soon as possible between the representative bodies of the HEQC, the CIHE, CBI and representatives of TECs and LECs to consider an agreed strategy for further work. We believe there is much to be done to consolidate the relationships that have formed successfully and to disseminate the lessons therefrom. We believe that individual company examples, such as those of British Telecom, Allied-Lyons, IBM, Ford, or the Rover Group, could serve as good models around which to organise further work. The HEQC could again act as a catalyst but **we recommend** that

representative bodies of employers take an active role in convening an appropriate forum for dialogue.

148.   However, we have detected in the response from some TEC/LECs that they would like a more active engagement with strategic developments in higher education. We welcome this and we have been disappointed to discover that by no means all TEC/LECs have yet defined a policy of interaction with the sector. The decision of the joint London TECs to issue a 'CATS Manifesto' seems to us to be an ideal example of the practice. If TEC/LECs were to define their strategy towards higher education, having defined it towards further education, then a foundation for further co-operation would be established. This would benefit the smaller and medium-sized companies in any region and produce accreditation partnerships to assist the fulfilment of National Targets for Education and Training or *Investors in People* commitments. **We recommend** that TEC/LECs develop policy statements on their preferred engagement with higher education, commenting in particular on aspects concerning improved student choice, mobility, the needs of employers and prospects for suitable employment.

Students

149.   In common with many others, we have been impressed by the policy positions adopted recently by the National Union of Students. It is clear that student representative bodies do not represent any significant source of apprehension towards greater choice and flexibility. Their main concern appears to be the environment, rather than the specific character, of their learning experience. However, it has proved difficult to obtain general opinion from the student body and we believe this provides an opportunity for further work. It is most timely, as higher education goes through a period of transition towards a more generalised modular experience, for further research to be undertaken into the student perceptions and experience of greater flexibility and choice. If this research occurs now, it may be possible to capture opinion from a generation of students able to compare different styles of learning experience within their time as a student.

150. We would like to know more about whether structural modifications genuinely open up access to more diverse learning opportunities, or whether they merely re-form conventional programmes. Where conscious efforts have been made to deliver access to wider opportunities, through Enterprise in Higher Education initiatives, through work-based learning internships and similar, or through generalised elective programmes, it would be helpful to know how students respond to these opportunities and under what limitations and constraints. **We recommend** further research in this area, not in order to fuel the debate on whether to modularise or not, but to establish objectively if modular and credit-based learning experiences do indeed facilitate the acquisition of the range of personal skills which students and employers deem necessary.

Recommendations and guidance for future policy

On future policy development

To Government

1. **We recommend** that Government departments should reinforce their policy objectives, giving confidence to universities and colleges by emphasising the continuity of policy on access, student choice and mobility over time.

To funding councils

2. **We recommend** that funding councils should encourage institutions, both to develop more flexible arrangements for student choice, and to monitor achievements and progress in this respect.

On dialogue between higher education, professional bodies and employers

To Higher Education Quality Council

3. The time has come for a systematic engagement between universities, colleges and professional bodies to discuss the long-term character of the higher education curriculum, establishing the tolerances acceptable to all parties and determining shared strategic objectives. **We recommend** that HEQC, acting on behalf of the representative bodies of the institutions, should consider an early arrangement of this dialogue.

4. **We recommend** that HEQC should play a supportive role in assisting professional bodies and employers to increase confidence in the consequences of student choice and mobility arising from the modular and credit-based systems.

5. **We recommend** that consultations should begin as soon as possible between the representative bodies of the HEQC, the CIHE, CBI and representatives of TECs and LECs to agree a strategy for further work in respect of closer co-operation between higher education and employers on matters concerned with student choice and flexibility, its consequences for personal effectiveness in employment, and prospects for employment in a future labour market.

To professional bodies

6.   **We recommend** that, in preparation for the process of consultation with universities and colleges, professional bodies should identify their policy positions with respect to:

- the development of modularity and credit systems in higher education with reference to undergraduate, postgraduate, post-experience and continuing professional development programmes;

- the quality assurance of programmes in the context of increased student choice and mobility, attending to admissions policy, assessment criteria, the accreditation of prior and experiential learning, the construction of student programmes, the character of qualifications and the development of relationships with the NCVQ, commenting on prospects for its accreditation of programmes at higher levels;

- the preferred working relationship with universities and colleges in the future, commenting, on the one hand, on policies for institutional accreditation, and on the other, offering views on institutional collaboration and consortia;

- the response of professional institutions to increased graduation, commenting on the prospects for professional membership of academically qualified students, and for successful employment.

To employers and their representative bodies

7.   **We recommend** that representative bodies of employers, including the CBI and the CIHE, should take an active role in convening an appropriate forum for dialogue with higher education institutions in order to clarify mutual objectives in the management of student learning opportunities and the needs of employers. **We recommend** that TEC/LECs should develop policy statements on their strategies for higher education, commenting on aspects concerning improved student choice and mobility, the needs of employers and prospects for suitable employment.

On further work

To the research community

8.   **We recommend** that further research is required into the scale of increased flexibility, and into the consequences of increased student choice and mobility for the achievement of academic objectives and successful employment.

VI.

Review of progress

Introduction

151.   In the previous chapter, we argued that the general policy environment beyond higher education has become quite receptive to the further development of credit systems. We now turn to the progress made within higher education itself. As the following discussion will show, there has been no lack of support *in principle* from universities and colleges for an extension of flexibility, choice and mobility for students. Progress within some institutions has been quite noticeable. Within many others however it has been much slower and this has given an impression of tardiness for the sector as a whole.

152.   We have attempted to provide a review which emphasises examples of positive progress amongst institutions whilst pointing out the impediments to comprehensive change. In common with our observations elsewhere in this report, this review treats as a continuum the development of modularisation and credit-based learning arrangements, both internal and external to institutions. Moreover, it addresses developments in higher education alongside those in adult and further education, without which it would not be possible to obtain an overall assessment of progress. Finally, it seeks to show how those policy developments, which have emerged largely from within higher education itself, have influenced institutional practice.

Antecedent influences 1963-73

153.   It has become a convention, in describing the development of modularity and credit transfer, to honour the influence of Scottish higher education upon the American course-credit system during the 19th century, and thereafter the influence of the American higher education system upon the rest of the United Kingdom since the 1960s. We have no desire to depart from this convention.

The Scottish Ordinary MA does indeed display many of the features of choice, flexibility and breadth that distinguish the general undergraduate education in America. Indeed, our observations during the investigation confirm that there remains in the traditional Scottish university degree structure a greater choice and flexibility than might be found amongst the programmes of the former polytechnics and central institutions. This is particularly evident in arrangements at the University of Stirling. We join with those who, for many years, have asserted the strengths of the Scottish system over the English model in the promotion of participation and flexibility. However, we have not dwelt on these matters, which have been more appropriately addressed by historical analysis of the developments of national systems, and which have in any case been considered by policy-makers in the past. Instead, we begin our analysis of progress with the Robbins Report, which had the opportunity to propose changes but chose to retain distinctive Scottish and English systems.

The Robbins Report, 1963

154.   We make no apology, if one were ever needed, for referring in more detail to the Robbins Report. Its influence on the general character of higher education over the past thirty years is such that any review of progress must recognise its formative role in higher education policy. The report is well known for confirming, or setting in motion, many of the developments which we now accept as commonplace – the commitment to academic freedom and institutional autonomy, the expansion of student numbers, the creation of new universities, the establishment of the CNAA with degree-awarding powers, and proposals for student finance and institutional management. The observations of the report on curriculum structure, student flexibility and credit transfer have received perhaps less attention over the years than they deserve.

155. In the extracts selected in the accompanying table (see Table 13), we have sought to indicate just how the vision Robbins offered is consistent with the further development of student choice and flexibility. Yet the effects of the report in this respect were relatively limited at the time. Some of the new universities of the 1960s took notice of Robbins' support for new styles of course. Keele introduced the four-year interdisciplinary degree in conscious imitation of the broader Scottish degrees; Sussex pioneered similar three-year programmes; and East Anglia developed an early course-unit system. Elsewhere, the ancient and 'redbrick' universities remained unmoved, secure in the case of Cambridge perhaps that its Tripos system provided adequate choice and breadth for its undergraduates, and in the case of other universities that their graduates were not disadvantaged by more specialised programmes. Indeed, Robbins readily admitted that the restricted school curriculum and desire to ensure progression to research remained crucial bulwarks against significant change to university courses, noting that *the specialised sixth form, like the British honours degree, is the exception in the world and not the rule'*.

156. In the medium term, the Robbins Report appears to have been more successful. It gave encouragement to the development of 'new types of institution' and new styles of course structure. By the early 1970s, some of the new polytechnics began to take up the challenge offered by their relative freedom under the CNAA to experiment with modularisation and new types of qualification. The pursuit of the 'Robbins principle' led many academic innovators of the time in efforts to extend access through the development of the Diploma of Higher Education supported by modular structures and combined studies programmes. We comment on this later.

157. We can add only modestly to the assessment of the long-term benefits of this well-received report. In terms of its support for access, choice and flexibility, it was consistent in supporting these features as integral to the fabric and character of higher education. The report is radical for its time in asserting the *general* advantages of curriculum breadth, deferred student choice, and credit

transfer, not just for part-time or continuing education students, but for all students. As for so much else, the Robbins Report provides the platform for modularisation, credit transfer and curriculum innovation upon which institutions have built steadily.

Table 13:
The Robbins Report, 1963

On credit transfer

There should be no freezing of institutions into established hierarchies; on the contrary there should be recognition and encouragement of excellence wherever it exists. If it is true that certain differences of level and function must be expected to persist among institutions, it is also true that such a structure can only be morally acceptable if there are opportunities for the transfer of a student from one institution to another when this is appropriate to his or her intellectual attainments and educational needs. We attach great importance to this. (37,38)

On the structure of courses

A higher proportion should be receiving a broader education for their first degree. We regard such change as a necessary condition of any large expansion of universities. Greatly increased numbers will create the opportunity to develop broader courses on a new and exciting scale, and we recommend that universities should make such development one of their primary aims. A more general education has begun to influence policy, and there have been many interesting attempts to provide broad courses... yet the results have been comparatively meagre. (262-263)

On student choice

We welcome the arrangements that exist in some universities to allow the student to postpone his choice of special study until the end of the first year. It should be an important principle of policy to arrange as much (financial) flexibility as possible. The lack of it can mean frustration for the students who initially made the wrong choice and even eventual failure to complete the course successfully. (271)

158.	On the other hand, the Robbins Report was more cautious and, at times, quite defensive. Anticipating that calls for greater curriculum breadth might meet with opposition from academics seeking to defend standards, Robbins commented, in a metaphor from another age: *'We are not urging greater breadth in order to temper the wind to the shorn lambs'*, going on to argue the case in terms of personal growth and economic benefit. Moreover, the references to credit transfer can be read as patrician support for the mobility of able students from colleges of education or technical colleges up to the university. Furthermore, Robbins appeared to adopt an ambivalent attitude to academic solutions drawn from America. The report both compliments the American college system, with its emphasis upon choice, flexibility and access, but recoils from acceptance of the 'college-credit' system which makes this possible. This may be explained by a desire to work with the grain of British 'exceptionalism'. Perhaps the case could not be easily made at the time for significant modifications to conventional patterns of university course structures, in advance of the achievement of increased participation. In the event, the Robbins Report encourages the development of all the features of a more open and student-driven higher education without provoking counter-reaction. In that sense, it was a highly skilful report, the consequences of which remain with us today.

Open University, 1969-

159.	The second most significance influence on the development of modularisation and credit transfer has been in our judgement the establishment in 1969 of the Open University. We cannot do justice to its original and effective contribution to the general development of British higher education. It should be sufficient to record that the Open University was the first higher education institution comprehensively to embrace modular academic structures, credit accumulation and transfer, the accreditation of prior learning, the award of interim certificates and qualifications, the use of multi-media learning technologies, the provision of extensive student guidance and support systems, and the issuing of transcripts as records of achievement. Furthermore, the admiration it has attracted

internationally requires no supplement here.

160.	It may not be entirely correct to say that the Open University was the first higher education institution to promote open access. Perhaps institutions such as Birkbeck College, or Ruskin College, can claim that. However it is true to say that the Open University has successfully promoted open access on a scale unprecedented in British higher education, and it has raised participation rates for part-time students to levels previously unseen.

161.	The radicalism of the Open University has also been tempered with a certain degree of conservatism. The modular structure of the course units has been designed around learning blocks that are much larger than those expected from most modular programmes. At 1/8th of an honours degree, the credit-unit is larger than anything experienced in America (1/120th), or for that matter on most modular programmes in the United Kingdom. The effect has been to limit the internal choice and flexibility of students, lending a more conventional character to the style of Open University degrees.

162.	This apart, the Open University has continued to pursue its ambitions, outlined in 1971: *'as a national institution, we hope by the award of general credit exemption to act as a catalyst for a general increase in the transferability of credit'*. It has even produced its own (unplanned) progeny. The Open College Federations owe their origins from the late 1970s and 1980s to efforts to imitate the principles (if not the technology) of the Open University in adult and further education. Their contribution to the further development of credit systems is examined later, but without the example of the Open University to inspire them, it is doubtful whether they would have gained such support amongst academic staff in colleges and adult institutes.

163.	The recent decision to bring the Open University into the unified body of universities is a most important step forward. It is a final recognition, if this were needed, that the work of the Open University is indisputably part of the mainstream of British higher education, and that its students enjoy a prestigious learning experience, organised by credit and managed flexibly. Specifically, those students who find the Open University is able to meet their needs, may also find that other institutions, under resource constraints or other market pressure, will begin to adopt similar strategies for credit accumulation and transfer. This is likely to assist considerably the general extension of credit systems as the means to promote increased choice and flexibility throughout British higher education.

White Paper, 1972 and Russell Report, 1973

164.   Neither the 1972 White Paper nor the Russell Report on Adult Education can be said to have had as great an influence on policy for the development of credit systems as the Robbins Report, but their contributions were significant in continuing the momentum for change. The White Paper, *Education: a framework for expansion,* made explicit reference to the development of unitised courses and credit transfer and in doing so it enabled various institutions, especially some polytechnics, to gain authority with the CNAA to move forward new modular schemes, particularly through the development of the Diploma of Higher Education. These initiatives are discussed more extensively below.

165.   The Russell Report helped to consolidate the place of the Open University as a major influence on developments in adult learning. It also drew particular attention to the importance of its credit system:

> The experience of the Open University offers useful guidance. The credit system it operates is appropriate to the circumstances in which adults study, especially if it allows for certain prior study elsewhere to count for credit. A credit structure that allows for transfer of credit has the flexibility that adult students require. (296)
>
> *Russell Report on adult education, 1973*

A culture of negotiation 1966-81

166.   If the Robbins Report and the Open University had created respectively the policy and the institutional platforms for further progress, then the task of moving forward the comprehensive development of greater flexibility and choice fell to a small number of institutions. Modularity, but not yet credit-based systems, developed initially within the Science Faculty of the University of London during the late 1960s, and then more extensively at the polytechnics of Hatfield, Middlesex, City of London, and Oxford during the early 1970s. Later in the decade, other modular combined studies programmes began to develop elsewhere. We have not pursued a detailed historical investigation of the development of modularity and credit systems, although we do not doubt that such an exercise, properly researched, would be very helpful. Only *The modular market* by Theodossin (1986) for the Further Education Staff College offers any sustained and authoritative historical assessment to date, supplemented by the more restricted but helpful surveys of Squires (1986) for the Manchester-based CONTACT consortium, and Davidson (1993) for the Universities Council for Adult Continuing Education (UCACE). We do not intend to repeat their work here, except where it supports, complements or throws a new perspective on this investigation.

Modularisation: the University of London

167.   Discussions to develop a course-unit structure began in the early 1960s in the Science faculty. By 1967, course regulations had been approved and students were admitted to the unitised system. Slowly over the next twelve years, other schools were drawn into the structure so that, by 1979, the university was largely covered by the unit system. A unit was defined as *'a third of the amount of work a student can be expected to complete in a year, that is, one-third of a student workload'.* Later variations to the regulations required that students accumulated a minimum of nine course-units for a degree, rising frequently to twelve or more as individual schools devised their own variants.

168. Theodossin has provided the most sustained analysis of the University of London scheme. His description is acerbic and at times very pessimistic. Nevertheless, his account of the development of the unit structure, supported by other assessments, leaves no doubt that the best intentions can be readily frustrated by professional and institutional inertia. He remains very sceptical that changes to the structure produced very much noticeable change for students. Admissions policy remained the same; there was little inter-school movement or module-sharing; assessment became burdensome; course regulations became fragmented into schools. On the other hand, some modest inter-disciplinarity was encouraged; joint/combined honours programmes developed; and the university did develop a central course-unit registry. Overall, the structure gave greater autonomy to teachers, but not evidently to students. It is worth quoting Theodossin fully on this point:

University of London scheme

Although several writers have attempted to explain the London modular scheme in terms of the need for rationalisation amidst a declining market, the main support for the new scheme was political: the course unit structure gave freedom to teachers in individual schools to devise and plan their own courses with a minimum of interference from central authorities. At an early stage, supporters suggested a wide range of innovatory uses: wider student choice, slower rates of study, inter-disciplinarity, economies of scale, inter-school co-operation, etc. *None of these intentions has been realised to any significant extent.* (Emphasis added.)

Ernest Theodossin, The modular market, 1986

---

169. Despite Theodossin's critique of the University of London scheme, we believe a more sympathetic treatment is appropriate, not least in respect to those who tried to implement it successfully. Our investigations suggest that the thwarted vision of the University of London scheme is more commonplace than might readily be admitted.

The University of London was not overly ambitious in its treatment of modularity, not least by standards that have come to apply in some institutions since. Modules were large course blocks; there were no term or semester restrictions on length; and individual schools retained control of admissions, student choice and assessment regulations. Yet even under these most conservative of arrangements, prospects for greater student autonomy were frustrated by the countervailing claims for course autonomy from academic staff.

170. It appears that efforts to shift the balance of power between staff and students foundered as predictably in the University of London as they have done from time to time elsewhere. We have found that the pattern of modularisation undertaken by the University of London, and the limitations of achievement encountered, represent a familiar pattern, particularly but not exclusively amongst the older (ex-UFC) universities. A relatively conservative approach to modularisation, although perceived as radical by many academics, appears to yield rather limited long-term change and is subject to the attrition of key objectives. We comment on these matters in Chapter XII.

Modularisation: the Polytechnics of Hatfield, City of London, Middlesex and Oxford; and some Colleges of Education

171. Developments in the public sector institutions of the time took a different form from those of the University of London. Although each of these early initiatives had distinctive characteristics, on which we comment shortly, certain features were held in common. Firstly, the developments were more overtly influenced by, or reflective of, styles of American course organisation. Semesters or trimesters defined the length of the module; students could combine major and minor subjects, or retain joint/combined subject programmes; some elective programmes were developed; interim awards were available via the DipHE. This latter qualification was particularly popular in certain Colleges of Education, following the James Report. On the other hand, these schemes were modular rather than credit-based in a conventional American

sense. They permitted varying degrees of flexibility in practice and they often struggled with problems of status compared with more specialist programmes.

172.	Secondly, those individuals who were responsible for leading the developments were faced with a constant struggle to maintain the momentum of change, beset by internal hostility from unconvinced academics and external scepticism from some CNAA subject boards of the time. The threat of regression from original principles became a distinguishing feature of the 1970s. In this, the CNAA played an ambiguous role, encouraging originality and diversity on the one hand, but insisting on coherence, progression and structural consistency on the other. Intellectually, it might be possible to reconcile these approaches; pragmatically and politically within the turbulent environment of institutional life, it became nearly impossible as sceptical academic colleagues used the latter principles to defend the unitary degree structures. Indeed, although the CNAA remained formally and actively supportive of modular developments throughout the decade, incorporating modularity and then credit into its regulations, tensions did break out elsewhere. There were claims that modular degrees were 'rag-bags' and involved the award of 'Green Shield' stamps. Not surprisingly, there were frequent regressions and false starts.

173.	Thirdly, as institutions began to settle for less ambitious alternatives to expressions of student choice, and as subject loyalties reasserted themselves, modularity began, in some of the institutions, to assume a mechanistic rather than an educational instrument of institutional management. Even this became problematic for institutions into the 1980s as policy towards student numbers fluctuated, and as funding bodies struggled to find methodologies to cope with what appeared to them to be unusual forms of course organisation. In fact, the lack of understanding of modular programmes amongst funding bodies has been a recurring feature of the past twenty years and has acted as a substantial disincentive to institutional innovations in this direction. Nothing would secure the further development of flexible academic arrangements more quickly than the confidence of universities that funding bodies understood, and would not disadvantage, institutions with modular and credit-based arrangements.

174.	More optimistically, the developments that began in the early 1970s in these four polytechnics have survived, flourished in some cases, and are recognisable in the new universities of Hertfordshire, Guildhall, Oxford Brookes and Middlesex. The University of Hertfordshire was the only one of the group to commit institutionally in the early 1970s to a policy of modularisation; interestingly, of the four, it is the one institution that has most fostered its specialist degrees, leading to the charge that its commitment to modularity has not outlived the enthusiasm of its initiators. On the other hand, the modular programme at Oxford Brookes University began as a very small scheme and has grown incrementally over twenty years to become one of the largest (if not the largest) integrated modular programmes in the country. It is however principally a joint honours scheme. The schemes at Guildhall University and at Middlesex University both began and remain sub-institutional schemes with considerable flexibility bestowed on students, and over the period they have both endured waves of regression. Currently policy in both institutions is leading towards an adoption of modularity (and credit) as organising features of their entire academic programmes.

175.	Having commented on the problems of regression from initial objectives, and the lessons which can be drawn from this (see further in Chapter XII), it would be unfair if we did not attend to some of the enduring benefits that have been derived from these initial developments. The legacy which future generations will most readily respect is the academic and educational enthusiasm of early innovators to produce genuine student involvement in their own learning careers. The strategies were driven by progressive attitudes towards the modernisation of higher education through increased access and greater student choice. Waterhouse (1986) has described this as the pursuit of a *culture of negotiation,* moving beyond the redefinition of course structure towards genuine student freedom. We agree and recognise this in later efforts to move these developments forward elsewhere.

176.   Beyond these ideological influences, the institutional developments of the 1970s established an organisational and operational basis which allowed institutions throughout the 1980s to learn from, imitate, modify and build upon the lessons from more experienced institutions. The development of modular and combined studies programmes during the mid-1980s at the universities, then polytechnics, of Wolverhampton, North London, Westminster (Central London), Central Lancashire, and Manchester Metropolitan were directly influenced by the coalition of modularity/DipHE/ student access. Similarly, developments in many colleges of higher education, notably at Cheltenham & Gloucester, were based on the ideas and structures of the original polytechnic schemes.

The 'Oakes' Committee, 1977 and the Toyne Report, 1979

177.   The event which drew together the work of the 1960s and 1970s was the committee convened in 1977 by Gordon Oakes, the then Minister of State for Higher Education. This occurred in response to policy analysis in the DES, which suggested the need to meet falling future demand from 18-year olds by stimulating demand from older students ('Model E' in *Higher education into the 1990s*, 1978). As a consequence, it predicted that there would be rising demand for credit transfer which, if not met and managed, would lead to a substantial wastage of resources. There were several reasons for believing this. First, the Open University had demonstrated the potential for credit recognition and credit transfer through its open access policies; secondly, the growth of modular programmes and interest in the DipHE suggested rising demand for credit transfer; thirdly, the Business Education Council (BEC) and the Technician Education Council (TEC) – later merged and hereafter referred to as BTEC – were developing modularised programmes; and finally, there was general concern about student failure and 'wastage of talent' which credit transfer might alleviate. Interested parties were brought together to consider a response.

178.   The Oakes Committee considered that the way to address the perceived problem might be to establish a comprehensive database and information source on credit transfer opportunities. It resolved that the best way forward would be to commission a study to advise on *'the necessity, feasibility and cost of establishing and running a service for recording and providing information on credits'*. The outcome of this study was the *Educational credit transfer: feasibility study* (the Toyne Report) 1979.

179.   Toyne presented a comprehensive description of the scale and potential of credit transfer activity at the time. Early in the report, he offered an explanation of credit transfer which, in a truncated form has become the much-quoted definition:

> ## Credit transfer: a definition
>
> In the context of access to higher and further education, credit transfer is an essential process whereby qualifications, part-qualifications and learning experiences are given appropriate recognition (or credit) to enable students to progress in their studies without unnecessarily having to repeat material or levels of study, to transfer from one course to another, and to gain further educational experience and qualifications without undue loss of time, thereby contributing to the maximisation of accumulated educational capital.
>
> *Peter Toyne, Educational credit transfer: feasibility study, 1979*

180.   He drew extensively on the experience of the Open University, and also on evidence of growing modular transfer, introducing into the public domain the work in further and adult education of the Open College, then an embryonic consortium in Lancashire. He treated credit transfer in three principal categories:

- credit for initial admission, with alternative qualifications;

- credit with advanced standing, including credit exemption;

- internal credit transfer within modular schemes.

181. The report was objective in identifying the limitations to progress. Toyne experienced similar problems to ourselves in trying to capture reliable data, but he was sufficiently confident to estimate that the prospective ECCTIS would receive 18,000 enquiries each year from 600 hundred institutions of higher and further education and from professional bodies. In the short-term, this proved optimistic. Moreover, Toyne found reasonable, but by no means convincing, welcome for the service. Of the 586 institutions surveyed, 33% thought they would rarely or never use the service, and a further 42% thought they might use it occasionally. In the medium-term events turned out better than this. Furthermore, and relevant to the objectives of this report, Toyne warned of potential problems with credit transfer if individual institutions were pressed to supply transfer criteria:

Problems of credit transfer

Eliciting general principles for transfer must be treated with caution. Despite the considerable support for a national information service which would help… institutions to negotiate general agreements, concern was expressed lest, in attempting to codify specific transfer requirements and practices, institutions faced with a request to state their transfer terms might have a tendency to tighten their admission requirements.

Toyne Report, 1979, (Annex 5; 13.3)

---

182. These reservations did not dissuade the DES from moving matters forward. Accepting the positive recommendations of the report, the Department subsequently established the Educational Counselling and Credit Transfer Information Service (ECCTIS), the work of which we discuss in Chapter XIII.

183. Our assessment of the Toyne Report is that its influence lies, less in the proposal to create a national information service, and more in its success in bringing together for the first time in the United Kingdom explicit reference to credit transfer in terms of internal mobility (modularity) and external general mobility (credit accumulation and transfer). We give this opinion, in no way to diminish the necessary and important role that ECCTIS has subsequently established for itself. Rather, it is apparent to us from the relatively slow beginning of ECCTIS in the early 1980s that a national information service for credit transfer may have been ahead of developments in the field. As institutions have begun to move in the late 1980s and early 1990s to adopt credit as an organising feature of their work, its time may finally have arrived. This may imply that ECCTIS was a far-sighted initiative of the DES. In one sense this is true. A flourishing credit transfer environment would certainly require a professional information service. Yet in another sense, despite Toyne's optimism on the subject which reflected the mood of the time, and despite the notable work of the Open University in this area, the potential for credit transfer has not been fully realised by events and demand has been muted. We confirm this with documentary and empirical analysis in Chapter VII.

184. We believe that the importance of the Toyne Report, and the policy analysis which initiated it, lies in the fact that it stands at the confluence of two young streams – modularity and credit transfer. By merging these tributaries into a more substantial flow, it allows the developments of the 1980s to take on a different character than may not otherwise have been possible. It introduced some new reference points to British higher education, more openly influenced by American sources. The ideas of access, experiential learning, student mobility, student guidance, and credit transcripts do not begin with this report; they were common throughout America and were being implemented by the Open University amongst others. But as ideas, they did begin to pass into the language of policy-thinking, if not yet policy-making.

185. We would make one final point in closing this particular discussion, as much for the benefit of those who welcome an understanding of the origins of their circumstances as for those who have lived through these times. The terms of reference of

the Toyne Report were tightly drawn, and its formal recommendation was relatively modest. The DES wished to know if there was sufficient support and potential demand for an affordable national information database on credit transfer opportunities. The Toyne Report confirmed this. It dealt with a world much less complex in terms of modularity and credit transfer than we find today. At the presentation of the report to the DES, participation in higher education remained at 8% of the 18-year old age group; adult participation in higher education was minimal for most institutions, and marginalised across the sector in specific institutions such as the Open University. Student choice was restricted to the modular 'experiments' of some progressive polytechnics; the BTEC modular initiatives in further education were still untested; and Open College Federations were only just emerging. Moreover, the technologies required to support a sophisticated professional service from ECCTIS had not yet emerged – for example, even word-processing was still in its infancy. Yet within five years, the CNAA had established its CATS Registry; by the end of the 1980s participation in higher education had risen to 22% of the age-group; most former polytechnics and some ex-UFC universities had embraced modularity and credit; there were over twenty credit-awarding Open College Federations, and the decade of 'Access' was established.

186.   We are sure all of this cannot be laid at the feet of the Toyne Report, but it is reasonable to say that the report represents an important step in the development of policy in these matters. It demonstrated the consistency of purpose of government departments, to which we have made repeated reference; it treated credit transfer as a function of activity in both higher and further education; and it encouraged the development of some of the necessary instruments with which to deal with the long overdue expansion of British higher education when that time came.

A culture of access, 1981-90

187.   As we now know, the 1980s became the decade of 'Access', although it did not begin in that way. This is not the place to produce a narrative of the early years of the decade, except to observe that access, expansion and greater student choice were distant objectives in a higher education sector where some universities were experiencing budget reductions of up to 40%. Inventively, these universities survived and at the University of Salford, for example, they were able to use financial calamity as a spur to launch regional educational initiatives. The Salford '2+2' arrangements with local colleges grew during these times. We begin however with an event which became for higher education in the 1980s almost as influential as a Royal Commission, lacking only formal Government support.

The Leverhulme Reports, 1981-83

188.   In the midst of this period of pessimism, leading individuals in higher education assembled with the support of the Leverhulme Trust to produce a sustained and highly influential assessment of the condition of higher education. The ten reports which were published in 1983 offered the most extensive critique yet of higher education by academics themselves. In scope the reports ranged more widely than a Royal Commission and proposed far-reaching reforms of the sector. Support for credit accumulation and transfer, modularity, wider access, an emphasis on improving student skills, the relevance of courses to the labour market, and greater student choice featured prominently. We indicate Fulton's assessment of prospects for credit transfer in Table 14. The overall tone of the reports was refreshingly free from professional defensiveness; it has been suggested that in this respect at least the reports were unrepresentative of the sector. The recommendations were radical, far-reaching and in places defiant, giving little indication of a sector beleaguered by budget reductions or complacency.

189.   The Leverhulme Reports were published on the day of the 1983 General Election, which may have deflected some of the initial attention the studies deserved. Thereafter, their effects were largely witnessed through the contributions of members of the various seminars. Of those who

Table 14: Credit transfer: the assessment of the Leverhulme Reports

Credit transfer is one of the easiest reforms to propose, and one of the hardest to implement within the standard three-year Honours degree package. The difficulties stem from its potential consequences for the curriculum and are perceived by many academics as totally insurmountable. (Yet) there is no other single reform entirely within the control of higher education institutions which could have such an effect on demand levels. Credit transfer would open up enormous possibilities for recurrent and continuing education, and make even the conventional first degree less formidable as an ambition for those without three full-time years to spare...

Credit transfer, and all that it implies for the curriculum through delayed or recurrent entry, is a powerful but double-edged weapon. If tightly controlled and rigidly interpreted, it could act as a brake on diversification by insisting on a 'gold standard'... But it could also be a means of shifting the balance in the market for educational qualifications away from the supplier and towards the consumer. A student who is essentially committed to completing a course, subject to severe penalties, even before embarking on it, has far less influence over the course content than one who can take his or her fees elsewhere if the course fails to meet expectations. Indeed it is at least arguable that it is the credit system which has really made possible the unique, consumer-orientated quality of American higher education.

Oliver Fulton, 'Access to higher education: principles and policies', Leverhulme studies into the future of higher education, 1981

Policy and the funding bodies, 1984-87

190.   An early manifestation of the influence of this 'network' was the decision by the National Advisory Body (NAB) for the polytechnics and colleges and the University Grants Committee (UGC) for the universities of the time, separately (1984) and then jointly (1987) to report on the further development of continuing education. The term 'Continuing Education' has never enjoyed a definitive linguistic identity. The two funding bodies adopted it as a portmanteau term with which to capture activities from continuing professional development and short courses through to part-time degree programmes, but there were differences of emphasis between the NAB and the UGC.

National Advisory Body report

We have adopted a wide definition of Continuing Education, to cover any form of education undertaken after an interval following the end of initial education.

University Grants Committee report

Universities should give further attention to the development of part-time modular courses, particularly at post-graduate and post-experience level, and all the institutions and validating bodies should co-operate in the development of a continuing education credit system leading to the award of recognised qualifications.

191.   It is worth a moment to comment on these different approaches because they may underline important differences in the way policy is implemented in various institutions. The NAB definition appears particularly forthright, seeking to embrace all post-initial education, but conceding that 'continuing education' may be distinguished from other forms of post-initial education by interruption or absence of continuous study. The UGC approach is much more circumspect and specific, emphasising the importance of flexibility and choice for postgraduate and post-experience students. Our interpretation of this

did not already exercise influence in authoritative positions in higher education, many went on to occupy senior posts in universities and higher education bodies in the following years. The 'Leverhulme network' provided one of the most important means by which policy in higher education, including that on credit systems, was developed and changed during the 1980s.

difference of approach is that it reflects the desire of the NAB to protect the interests of institutions within its orbit by broadening the definition of 'continuing education' as widely as possible in order to promote more comprehensive changes to the general academic environment. On the other hand, the UGC works with a more conventional and restricted treatment of 'continuing education', seeking to focus the impact of any proposals upon specifically postgraduate and post-experience continuing professional development, effectively exempting the main undergraduate programme from contingent changes.

192.   Of the two reports in 1984, the report of the NAB Continuing Education Working Party provided the more thoroughgoing analysis of problems and prospects to date. It addressed institutional attitudes, the need for improved student guidance, and more flexible and equitable financial support for students, including part-time students. The report identified the elements which it regarded as necessary for the further development of higher education: a common credit framework; modularisation of courses in which *'the content of modules must be clearly defined'*; the accreditation of prior and experiential learning; open learning; the use of credit transcripts.

193.   The NAB also called for closer co-operation between professional bodies and employers in the establishment of new arrangements, including the development of a national credit framework, but warned against the *'grandiose imposition of a credit system'*, preferring instead to recommend the adoption by all major parties of the *principle* of credit accumulation and transfer. This nervousness

> There seems little doubt that attitudes towards the introduction of schemes involving credit accumulation and credit transfer have changed markedly in recent years. Although there is obviously still some way to go in this respect, the major obstacle to the introduction of credit-based schemes now appears to relate less to institutional attitudes than to organisational practicalities and funding problems.
>
> *Report of the NAB continuing education working party*

aside, the NAB report was extremely encouraging and far-sighted. From our investigations for this report, we can confirm the importance of organisational practicalities and funding problems for the further development of credit systems, but we are less convinced by assertions concerning changes in institutional attitudes.

194.   The comments on this point appear to be over-optimistic, both in terms of experience at the time and in the light of progress. Nevertheless, we have no doubt that the report of the NAB Continuing Education Working Party, and that of the joint NAB/UGC Working Party in 1987 proved highly influential in preparing the environment in higher education for the appearance of the 1987 White Paper. Moreover, these reports further consolidated the position of credit transfer and, more generally, credit systems on the policy-making and institutional agendas. On one final point, the authors of the NAB report were frustrated. In conclusion, they stated:

'We recommend that the DES, the Welsh Office and SOED call a meeting of representatives of the major organisations to consider how a co-ordinated approach to credit accumulation and credit transfer can be promoted.'

That meeting was not arranged until 1991; it was the *Learning without walls* conference at the University of Oxford, which recommended the establishment of the 'Task Force' which supports this report.

CNAA CAT Scheme, 1985-92

195.   We cannot attempt to provide a history of the development of the CNAA CATS initiatives. Their impact is discussed in several places throughout this report. We address the role of the CNAA in the work of credit transfer and consortia (Chapter VII), in the establishment of a national credit framework (Chapter IX) and in quality assurance (Chapter X) . The contribution of the CNAA is also recognised and discussed on many other occasions in the report. Instead, we have attempted to explore the origins of the scheme in order to understand the thinking which lay behind its development, identifying where it is helpful to our general

objectives those aspects which inform current debates. In many ways, the initial discussions within the CNAA have bearing upon policy proposals in the circumstances of higher education ten years later.

196.   During the course of the investigation, we were able to gain access to archive material from the CNAA, including minutes and reports of meetings. This allowed us to understand more clearly the tone and focus of the debates at the inception of the scheme. It is clear to us that there was a close association between the objectives of the NAB and the CNAA in respect of the further development of credit-based systems, produced as much by a close involvement of the same significant individuals as by any agreed strategic alignment. This appears to have encouraged initiatives in the development of credit systems to take root in the then public sector polytechnics and colleges, causing 'credit' to be seen by many universities as a 'polytechnic activity'. We are not sure that matters could have been arranged otherwise, given the binary character of higher education at the time, and we imply no criticism whatsoever. On the other hand, if the history of these matters is to inform future developments, then the exposure of individuals in institutions and national agencies to different influences will explain in large measure the extent of their confidence and familiarity with matters associated with credit systems, modularity and other attendant features. We have in mind here the comprehension of individuals making policy in the CVCP, the funding councils and the HEQC, as well as those influencing developments in their universities and colleges.

197.   During 1984, and concurrently with the publication of the NAB and UGC reports, the CNAA proposed the establishment of arrangements which would provide: a) **an advisory service,** offering guidance on the credit worthiness of a student's past achievement; b) **a brokerage service,** negotiating a programme of studies between institutions. It was to be a five-year pilot programme *initially based in the London area,* drawing together the CNAA institutions and universities in London and the Open University. The proposal sought to establish a central Registry to accredit students and **to**

make appropriate awards. The ultimate aim was that the scheme would become nationwide in due course (which, following an encouraging number of student enquiries, was agreed a few months later).

198.   In approving the proposals, the Council noted a number of problems associated with the scheme, and a number of Council members expressed reservations:

- an external agency might not be able to make coherent awards; how would final academic standards be determined? Would the awards to students be deemed credible by other institutions?

- would students in the scheme be isolated?

- would a centralised Registry distract students from institutional enquiry and application?

- would the CNAA scheme inhibit individual institutional developments?

- current student finance regulations did not facilitate study at more than one institution, *therefore primary legislation would be needed.*

199.   Despite these observations and reservations, work began on establishing the principles which would underpin the scheme. It was generally agreed that the scheme was a conscious attempt to change the polarity of student-course relationships, giving more freedom and control to the student. Secondly, it was an attempt to promote and sustain inter-institutional collaboration and mutual recognition. Thirdly, the scheme was to be an instrument for the promotion of wider access, accepting that 'more means different' in the context of lifelong learning. Finally, and most importantly of all, it sought to establish a triangular relationship between the student, the course and employment.

200.   The CNAA expected the practical development and implementation of these principles, and of the scheme itself, to be conducted through consortia of institutions.

These would be geographically-based or subject-based, and the CNAA expected to co-ordinate good practice between them. We explore the progress and limitations of consortia in the next chapter.

201.   Further work was needed to define the technical instruments which would describe the proposed scheme. These discussions centred around the levels of progression within the scheme and, above all, the appropriate credit tariff. Agreement was reached quickly on levels; these were taken as equivalent to the years of the conventional three-year full-time undergraduate programme and a Master's level. Progress on defining a credit tariff proved more difficult. Various options were considered and rejected. Arrangements which proposed a differential weighting of credit by level were not generally supported. Proposals which worked with pragmatic arithmetical formulae were received more favourably and the most arithmetically flexible option was finally approved. It was agreed to represent the undergraduate degree as 360 credits and the Master's degree as 120 credits. At this stage, few further details were provided although these emerged over the period prior to the launch of the scheme in Spring 1986.

202.   We provide further analysis of the principles and practice of the CNAA CAT scheme in our discussion of a national credit framework in Chapter IX. For the purposes of this progress review, it will be sufficient to record that, in the five years of the formal existence of the CNAA scheme, it proved very successful in promoting the further development of credit systems in higher education, amongst institutions, employers and professional bodies. More than any other initiative to date, the scheme has influenced the climate of opinion in favour of the usefulness of credit-based learning. Its relative conservatism and pragmatism as a scheme has perhaps helped in this respect. In particular, institutions subscribing to the scheme were not required to do anything unusual; it did not threaten or challenge prevailing forms of curriculum organisation; and it did not imply modularisation or any other form of academic structure. It has always

been presented as a scheme in the process of evolution and this negotiable character allowed the scheme to absorb some of the developments that emerged during the late part of the 1980s, particularly the growth of interest in an outcomes-led curriculum. This evolutionary character may also allow the scheme to absorb other changes contingent on this report.

203.   However, the most significant achievement of the scheme lay, not in its original objective to stimulate and manage greater individual student transfer between institutions, but in its success in persuading employers and some professional bodies that the accreditation of employee training was an attractive option for them. Many institutional partnerships have developed as a consequence of the CNAA's activities in these matters. As an example, the credit arrangements and work with local employers at Sheffield Hallam University and the University of Greenwich begin with a close association with the activities of the CNAA scheme. The development of the Portsmouth-IBM scheme would be another influential example.

204.   The CNAA proved significantly less successful in responding to suggestions for a national and comprehensive credit framework. In the mid-1980s, policy proposals were forthcoming, prior to the establishment of the NCVQ, which sought to establish common arrangements to embrace academic and professional qualifications. In the discussions with interested parties which took place around this proposal, it appears that the CNAA was unable to unite a coalition of support for a form of development which would have brought together the work in quality assurance, credit transfer, student information and the oversight of qualifications covered by the CNAA, the Open University, professional bodies and the individual institutions. The higher education institutions and the NCVQ appeared to be unconvinced that there were sufficient grounds for immediate co-operation and the CNAA was pre-occupied by the proposals of the Lindop Report. By 1987, a general association of interested parties had not secured adequate support.

205. We feel this was a missed opportunity because students especially, but all interested parties, may not be best served by fragmentation and sectionalism if this can be avoided. Our investigations suggest that it is timely for arrangements to be defined which allow informed dialogue and much closer co-operation between parties involved in quality assurance and the management of qualifications in higher education and beyond. We have made this point in Chapter V and again Chapter IX and X.

206. The CNAA published during the course of its work a wide range of materials to assist institutions in their chosen developments. Amongst the collection, we have found it useful from time to time to refer to certain publications in particular: *Going modular* (1989), *Credits for change* (1989) and *Practising CATS* (1992).

207. An assessment of the contribution of the CNAA is bound to conclude positively, notwithstanding some setbacks mentioned above. The Council worked within the limitations described for it. It did not seek to impede the exercise of institutional academic autonomy and sought to negotiate credit arrangements with willing partners. To this extent, it reached credit transfer agreements with the Open University in 1977, with most other universities and colleges in the country by 1991 and with numerous corporate employers and professional bodies. The CNAA worked at the interstices of institutional life, seeking to

---

Corporate employers working with the CNAA by 1991

Abbey National	Lucas
BBC	MoD
British Airways	Nationwide
British Telecom	Rank Xerox
BP	Rolls Royce
Cable & Wireless	Rover Group
Digital	Royal Mail
GEC	Safeway
GKN	Sainsbury
Glaxo	Shell UK
IBM	Thomas Cook
ICI	Thorn EMI
ICL	United Biscuits
John Lewis	WH Smith
Littlewoods	Wimpey
Lloyds Bank	Woolwich

---

manage the mobility of students between institutions, and between work and institutional programmes. Its relative radicalism and lightness-of-touch in the development of credit-based learning may be compared with its perceived conservatism in the quality assurance of modular programmes. This may be explained by the fact that development of the former lay largely in the hands of Council officers collaborating with willing academic enthusiasts in the quality assurance of often marginal and external programmes, whereas the quality assurance of modular schemes, as core institutional programmes, was conducted by peer review, involving academic staff, some of whom may have been unpersuaded by the claims to quality and coherence of modularisation and internal mobility. Above all, the CNAA provided an arena for debate, something which is lacking in the current environment. As progress on modularity and credit transfer attracts more attention, so the debate is joined with more academic colleagues. The HEQC may well need to consider new arrangements to facilitate dialogue between colleagues.

Educational Counselling and Credit Transfer Information Service (ECCTIS)

208. Progress on the principal recommendation of the Toyne Report was initially slow. The establishment of ECCTIS as the national information service finally took place in the early 1980s, but its public visibility increased from 1986-87 onwards with the publication of its *Handbook on educational credit transfer* and other public information materials. By 1987, its course database was available on CD-ROM and with the growth of interest in credit transfer by the end of the decade, demand for its services had risen dramatically. This said, the databases have proved more popular with schools and post-16 colleges and they have not generally been exploited by higher education institutions or their students.

209. Throughout its short history, ECCTIS has attempted to define its role in supporting individual students and acting as a source of information. Developments in information technology have helped considerably and the availability of CD-ROM

disc units has enabled ECCTIS to disseminate its information more effectively. ECCTIS began with two roles: the promotion of credit transfer policies and practices; and the dissemination of these policies to interested parties. Quickly, these expanded to five principal roles: **liaison** with existing schemes; **advice** to students and others based on the liaison role; **information** on current practice; **student enquiries** on credit transfer opportunities; and **promotion** of credit transfer initiatives. We give further detailed attention to the developing contribution of ECCTIS in Chapter XIII. In terms of progress to date, we have suggested in early comment on the Toyne Report that the establishment of ECCTIS appeared to be ahead of developments in the field. Toyne, writing in the first issue of an ECCTIS information sheet, identified one of the main problems:

Until institutions become more realistic and recognise that there are genuine and compatible alternatives to their own way of doing things, credit transfer will remain a small-scale phenomenon. However, this 'loosening' of the definition of 'equivalence' is precisely what the opponents of credit transfer object to, because it leads, they claim, to the making of superficial assessments and consequently to a reduction in standards.

Peter Toyne, FACTS No 1 (1986)

210.   ECCTIS has therefore been required to wait for the changes in institutional practice and culture that would supply it with the role for which it has been designed. Meanwhile, it has successfully developed a role in the supply of information on higher education opportunities to schools and colleges.

211.   It has also maintained close links with the Open University, with the CNAA and now with the HEQC. We think these arrangements are most important and should be further consolidated. Currently ECCTIS is an independent company, supported by corporate sponsors. In Chapter XIII we offer further suggests about how the work of ECCTIS might be given greater prominence in the affairs of higher education, and how institutions might ensure this.

Learning from Experience Trust

212.   The LET exercised an influence on developments throughout the 1980s out of all proportion with its size. Enjoying no formal institutional base, and as a charitable trust with no permanent source of funding, it acted as a 'think-tank' and ginger group for the promotion of prior and experiential learning. Credit transfer has always been concerned with prior learning but it has proved most difficult in practice to establish its legitimacy within universities and colleges. The Learning from Experience Trust set as its objective the dissemination of practices common throughout the United States. In a series of forty study tours from 1981, the Trust introduced over 200 leading academics and policy-makers to American higher education in general and to experiential learning in particular. Although it is only possible to speculate on the impact and influence of these visits, it would be fair to say that most of the leading individuals in institutional developments for credit-based learning have been participants of these visits. They have helped consolidate the network of academic colleagues who are committed to the further promotion of credit systems.

213.   The Trust has also been responsible for stimulating a range of innovative developments in British higher education. With funding support from both the Employment Department and the CNAA, the Trust has organised a number of successful projects with institutions. Most of the work in the accreditation of prior and experiential learning, including the introduction of portfolio-based assessment, began as a consequence of Trust initiatives. Furthermore, the Trust has provided a centre of expertise in the accreditation of work-based learning, from health care through to engineering. Recently the Trust has been largely responsible for the promotion of work-based learning for academic credit. A successful example of their work would be the project run jointly by the University of Liverpool, Liverpool John Moores University and Chester College. This project has enabled students on non-sandwich courses to earn academic credit from personally negotiated workplace internships. The idea has been practiced for a number of years at a centre in Philadelphia and has now

been translated into British conditions. The current projects on work-based learning, funded by the Employment Department, have their origins in the stimulus provided by the Learning from Experience Trust.

Miscellaneous developments

214.   It is not possible to do justice to the many influential and imaginative individual contributions to policy development in higher education during this period. It must be said that throughout the period, despite organisational changes, the various funding councils continued to support and encourage institutional developments towards greater student choice and flexibility. This may have been more noticeable with the NAB and its successor, the Polytechnics and Colleges Funding Council (PCFC), than with the UGC and then the UFC, although by the end of the decade, the latter body had become very active in prompting developments in the established universities. Furthermore, we would like to say more about the effects of the Enterprise in Higher Education initiative on institutional progress but with so many projects still moving their way to a conclusion, it has not been possible to form a definitive view on its success. The general impression formed during the investigation has been that the EHE initiative has significantly changed the language of engagement, by placing centrally on institutional agendas the importance of modularity and credit systems as instruments to facilitate skills development in academic programmes. We remain less convinced by the enduring qualities of the initiative if institutions do not remain persuaded by the pedagogic and organisational benefits of more open and flexible structures. We will return to some of these matters in Chapter XII.

215.   One report captured effectively the mood of the moment. Fulton & Ellwood produced an important report for the Employment Department, *Admissions to higher education: policy and practice* (1989). This surveyed the institutional behaviour of a number of universities and former polytechnics and made a series of recommendations. The findings of the report confirmed the buoyancy of the period: demand was rising; institutions

Table 15: Selected reports influencing policy 1986-93

Report	Indicative comments or recommendations
Geoffrey Squires, 1986 *Modularisation*	*"Modularity and credit accumulation and transfer are intimately related. Indeed, current interest in modular courses seems to derive from an interest in credit systems rather than the other way round. Whereas in the 1970s, some writers were in favour of modularity because they believed it was a good form of curriculum per se, modularity now seems to be a means to several ends....There are two conflicting paradigms of higher education (in the United Kingdom): the 'holistic' paradigm in which higher education is irreducible, indivisible and not wholly susceptible to rational analysis; and the 'aggregative' paradigm (in which) the institution delivers and provides, rather than inducts and socialises. The limited impact of modular schemes on higher education in the last fifteen years may be due to the fact that they run counter to the holistic paradigm".*
Oliver Fulton & Susan Ellwood, 1989, *Admissions to higher education*	*"Courses and course structures should be adapted to fit the changing pool of potential applicants – including Credit Accumulation and Transfer (CAT) and Associate Student schemes, and modular structures where appropriate. Regional access consortia, direct entry procedures, intermediary diplomas, outreach and equal opportunities policies should be encouraged – with appropriate funding".*
Sir Christopher Ball, 1990, 1991, *More means different; learning pays*	*"The unhelpful distinction between education and training would dissolve into the more generous idea of learning. The sharp divide between compulsory and post–compulsory stages would be replaced by a distinction between initial and continuing learning, where the latter would be typically part–time and enjoyed alongside employment. Opportunities for late–developers and those who find motivation later in life would be generous." (1990) "The idea of a learning society offers a broad vision. It rejects privilege – the idea that it is right for birth to determine destiny. It transcends the principle of meritocracy, which selects for advancement only those judged worthy and rejects as failures those who are not. A learning society would be one in which everyone participated in education and training throughout their life. It would be a society characterised by high standards and low failure–rates. In the past we have too often allowed ourselves to believe that high standards can be attained only at the expense of high rates of failure; or that low levels of failure necessarily entail low standards. In a learning society this would not be the case." (1991)*
UDACE, 1992, *What can graduates do? Learning outcomes in higher education (Otter Report)*	*"Describing learning outcomes could be a means of stating clearly and explicitly what students know and can do as a result of higher education. Focusing on the outcomes of learning, rather than on course content or aims, could help to describe the intellectual, analytical, personal and enterprise qualities which are developed by higher education. They may make it easier to recognise that learning acquired in a range of settings can be equivalent to learning in higher education, increas(ing) the flexibility of higher education by encouraging the accreditation of prior learning and the development of credit systems. They may help students to make better informed choices about higher education, thus increasing motivation and reducing wastage, and they offer opportunities for the development of more flexible and innovative approaches to assessment."*
CSUP, 1992, *Teaching and learning in an expanding higher education system (MacFarlane Report)*	*"There is now a pressing need to increase efficiency and provide economies in the processes of teaching and learning. The new–found concern for teaching efficiency is paralleled by a need for course delivery systems that augment learning effectiveness. Many departments now find that the development of their disciplines in the last decade or two has been such that there is a real need to find innovative methods of encouraging student assimilation and retention of the core concepts upon which the exploration of more advanced concepts is predicated. Such methods may also make it easier for students to take shorter or more intensive courses...The changing context of higher education demands radical solutions... (an) imperative to develop much greater flexibility (to) free students from constraints of time and place, and even allow for more individualised feedback than could be contemplated within the traditional university teaching system."*
NIACE, 1993, *An adult higher education: a vision*	*"A coherent national credit framework will provide the underpinning for all qualifications, whether work–based or academic, at all levels from basic education to postgraduate education.The framework will make it possible to combine achievement within the academic system with credit from national vocational qualifications, and guidance will be available to assist learners to plan coherent programmes to meet their individual needs. Accreditation will be designed to recognise a wide range of achievement rather than to exclude people. Qualifications will be constructed from credits, recognising coherence, but allowing for the constant reshaping of fields of knowledge and professions."*
Royal Society, 1993, *Higher education futures*	*"Credit transfer within an institution provides valuable flexibility for students who want to study a breadth of subject areas or who want to change their choice of course. Credit transfer between institutions is more complicated and usually happens for personal reasons when students need to relocate. A modular structure provides an ideal framework for credit accumulation and credit transfer which is why modular systems are often strongly associated with both. We would urge the development of a national system of credit accumulation and credit transfer by participating institutions. Transfer between institutions relies on mutual recognition of relevant accumulated credit. The system must command the confidence of those who operate it. The transfer and recognition of earned credits is obviously easier between HEIs having reasonably similar missions."*

were changing; alternatively qualified students were being admitted. On the other hand, this was occurring more visibly in the public sector than in the established universities, and the perceived requirements of professional bodies were reinforcing the reluctance of many admissions tutors to make a radical break with familiar arrangements. Furthermore, some institutions were found to be hesitant in establishing performance indicators to assess the effectiveness of student choices. The report emphasised the importance of modularity and credit-based learning, and made a number of recommendations shown in Table 15.

216.   Within Table 15, we have also included indicative comments from a number of other recent and influential reports the outcomes of which we do not intend to address in detail. These reports show how the discussion has developed and moved on over the last few years. Squires (1986) was not particularly optimistic about the prospects for early progress on modularisation and credit systems in the four universities in Manchester that he surveyed for the CONTACT consortium. Three years later, Fulton & Ellwood were much more confident about progress, particularly in the former polytechnics, whilst Sir Christopher Ball was reshaping the policy debate towards the need to think all of these developments in a more comprehensive and ambitious manner, emphasising the importance of establishing a 'learning society'. This visionary approach is revisited in the NIACE Report (1993) and in that of the Royal Society (1993).

217.   However, the discussion is already moving on. We include reference to the Otter Report (1992) and the MacFarlane Report (1992) because, in their different ways, they demonstrate how broad the interest has become in reshaping higher education. The Otter Report is important for the question it asks: what can graduates do? If we returned to the quotation from Squires (1986) which states that, for many, higher education is "not wholly susceptible to rational analysis", we can begin to see just how challenging the question is. By the time of the Otter Report, a small number of universities had already begun to use learning objectives as curriculum design tools in credit systems. It is possible that many more will come to appreciate

their usefulness for quality assurance in the next few years. Furthermore, the MacFarlane Report for the Committee of Scottish University Principals (CSUP) takes the discussion on again, to the means by which individualised and student-centred learning may be married with new technologies and multi-media learning resources.

Institutional responses 1981-90

218.   We turn now to the impact upon institutions. For most of the decade, the main institutional developments for extended access, flexibility and choice in higher education were dominated by the polytechnics. There were exceptions, examples of which would be the commitment of the University of Lancaster in supporting the Open College of the North-West, setting the tone for other universities; the '2+2' schemes developed by the University of Salford and the University of Warwick; various forms of consortia involving established universities; and the 'Mundella' programme at the University of Sheffield, seeking to promote wider access.

219.   The polytechnics accepted the full force of the expansion and, since developments were often already underway, they proved naturally fertile grounds for the further establishment of modularity and credit-based systems. Most of the developments built on and extended the earlier strategies; we have offered a summary of developments in representative institutions of the 'second wave' in Table 16. It is not easy to generalise about a very diverse set of initiatives in these institutions, except to say that they were largely carried forward by academic colleagues with the same sense of radical educational commitment that had motivated the innovators of the early 1970s. In some cases, this earlier generation was now able to support, from senior institutional positions, a new wave of enthusiasts. In almost all cases in the polytechnics throughout the 1980s, modularity and credit systems were developed for pedagogic reasons. There may have been an organisational sub-agenda, appealing to institutional managers, but the drive for increased and wider access was the principal motivating force.

Table 16: Development of credit systems in selected universities 1985-91

(Arrangements in leading polytechnics of the period)

	Principal characteristics	Strengths and influences	Limitations and current standing
University of Northumbria at Newcastle (1985-)	*PASS (Polytechnic Associate Student Scheme) first scheme based on credit outside the OU Central unit arranging student progress. Linked with local consortium (HESIN)*	*Directly influenced by discussions around credit transfer; became role model for other Associate Student schemes particularly in non-modular institutions*	*Limited impact on institution; restricted to negotiation for individual students; dependent on other institutional changes. Still exists as institution developing modularisation*
University of Central Lancashire (1986-)	*Combined Studies programme and LINCS (Lancashire Integrated Colleges Scheme)led to institution-wide scheme; access consortium and 'franchising' coupled to internal credit-based scheme*	*Model for 'franchising'; networks; CATS programme provided platform for further institutional developments. Influenced heavily by Access movement and USA*	*Move into institution-wide scheme at time of rapid growth led to problems of overload; structure aims to prevent regression. From 94-95, modular and adoption of 30-credit year*
University of Wolverhampton (1987-)	*Extensive modular scheme, supplemented by separate CATS scheme; strong guidance support; latterly adopted an outcomes-led curriculum of which it is arguably the best developed and embedded*	*Inherited modular commitment from Middlesex and CATS from CNAA; centre of national consortia for a time; now involved in company training accreditation; good but complex outcomes approach to curriculum*	*Possible disjuncture between modularity and CATS; devolved system may lead to retention of subject-based courses. Institution retains commitment to modularity and CATS*
University of North London (1988-)	*Combined Studies modular programme, not necessarily credit-based; most definitive commitment to 'Access' of any institution, but not fully modular; committed to access networks (initially ALFA)*	*Influenced by modular developments of other London institutions; better known for initiatives specifically in Access courses, the development of which it has largely influenced*	*Ambiguous engagement with credit systems and possibly modularity. Tests proposition that access can be delivered without either. Institution currently exhibits mixed features of both*
Sheffield Hallam University (1988-)	*CATS Unit; most successful of its type; supports Combined Studies programme; now active in employee accreditation with local firms and many professional bodies; houses SYOCF consortium*	*Best example of the 'bolt-on' CATS Unit, distinct from main institutional programme. Strong on guidance for students on negotiated programmes and 'off-campus' accreditation*	*Difficulties in securing status in institution and reaching agreement for students with mainstream courses. Recently reorganised as Access and Guidance team*
University of Greenwich (1988-)	*Credit system without modularity; emphasises possibility of using credit in INSET and employee accreditation without further changes to academic programme*	*Best test of the proposition that credit can work without modularity; extensive experience in credit for prior and work-based learning; influenced by University of Northumbria initially*	*Currently reliant on test of credit systems via 'off-campus' programmes, posing little challenge to mainstream programmes. Currently assessing benefits of modularity*
Liverpool John Moores University (1989-)	*Integrated Credit Scheme (ICS); major synthesis; fusion of credit, modularity and outcomes-led curriculum; common assessment regulations; credit-led resourcing; fully institutional programme with shared credit system in local Open College Federation (MerOCF) in regional HE/FE credit network*	*Best test of the 'Big Bang' approach; use of credits and modules to improve student experience; good assessment regulations, student record system. Influenced by Oxford Brookes (modules), USA, OCFs, OU and Lancashire (credits), NCVQ (outcomes). Major institutional impact, and on FEU proposals*	*'Big Bang' arguably in advance of institutional capacity to manage; institutional reorganisation complicated authority roles; little 'off-campus' accreditation. Scheme remains institution-wide and developing, but with regressions, problems of scale and some unfulfilled potential*

220.   Of particular institutional developments which act as landmarks of the period, we can identify several. Firstly, the development of the *Polytechnic Associate Student Scheme (PASS)* at the University of Northumbria at Newcastle was significant in that it established the first arrangement overtly intended to operate in terms of a credit system. The Associate Student Scheme was widely copied by other institutions, and the specific influence of the central unit can be traced in, for example, the various 'CATS Units' of Sheffield Hallam University, Leeds Metropolitan University and the University of East London. The intention of the arrangement was to treat 'CATS' as an attribute of access, and particularly of prior learning or mature entry. In some variations of this approach, the unit became dedicated to APEL arrangements or student guidance.

221.   Secondly, some institutions placed greater emphasis upon the credit transfer of 'second-chance' students via specially designed Access courses. These arrangements took different forms, but in London and particularly at South Bank University and then at the University of North London, the institution positioned itself centrally in a network of such courses. This decision did not necessarily imply the development of formal credit-based systems, and as the networks grew in stature and experience to become Authorised Validating Agencies under the joint CVCP/CNAA arrangements of the time, some did introduce credit systems but others did not. Those networks that chose to work with credit were generally Open College Federations. One further point needs explanation: for most if not all polytechnics, Access courses were developed and delivered by the local further education college; they were rarely 'owned' by the higher education institution. The courses were linked to the local HEI with varying degrees of exclusivity, but the colleges were generally responsible for the quality assurance of their courses, albeit in partnership with the HEIs. On the other hand, some established universities developed in-house Access courses, often through their Continuing Education departments, giving rise to an important issue of policy. Currently responsibility for the quality assurance of Access courses lies with the HEQC. Despite the familiarity of these arrangements, it is not clear to us whether it is a wholly appropriate solution that an agency of higher education should assume the sole responsibility for the quality assurance of programmes designed and delivered principally in further education. We address this matter in Chapter X.

222.   Some former polytechnics took a different path in their use of credit. Beginning with the IBM accreditation arrangements with the University of Portsmouth, several institutions started to join with corporate employers in the formal accreditation of employee training. Throughout, the CNAA lent its authority to the quality assurance of such programmes. The University of Greenwich became particularly active in this area, forming well-known partnerships with the Woolwich Building Society, Allied-Lyons and the Brewers' Society and other bodies. These arrangements made use of credit systems in order to assimilate the 'off-campus' learning of employees, but they did not necessarily imply modularity. In such cases, credit systems related to learning external to the university, although in other examples such as those developed at the University of Wolverhampton, modularity and credit systems co-existed for internal and external programmes.

223.   Finally, towards the end of the decade and into the 1990s, a few former polytechnics began to synthesise various developments. The University of Central Lancashire began to draw together its commitment to access, expressed through its franchising and LINCS arrangements, with its Combined Studies programme, producing a whole-institution modular and credit-based scheme. And at Anglia Polytechnic University and the University of Derby, similar comprehensive schemes were developed.

224.   Meanwhile, at Liverpool John Moores University a yet more ambitious synthesis was attempted. This involved creating a whole-institution modular and credit-based scheme, the Integrated Credit Scheme, formally designed to incorporate the application of learning outcome statements to module

definition, appropriately modified from the competence statements of the NCVQ. Moreover, the credit system was designed as a common and shared scheme with the local Open College Federation. This produced a comprehensive regional credit framework, using a common definition of credit, which allowed students to pass from further and adult education into higher education in an uninterrupted manner. Within the university itself, students were then able to access a variety of modular pathways, including an elective programme, accumulating credits which were recorded on a credit transcript. In attempting these syntheses, neither UCL nor Liverpool JMU directed their initial energies as extensively as others to the use of credit for the recognition of 'off-campus' learning. In the case of Liverpool JMU, it was hoped that these arrangements would follow once a 'credit culture' had been established within the institution. To some extent this has begun to happen. The institution was amongst the first to engage with work-based learning for academic credit counting towards final classification, although to date it has not successfully negotiated accreditation arrangements with corporate employers.

225. The experience of those institutions which have attempted a similar synthesis is important for what it tells us about the influences acting upon developments. It suggests that institutional behaviour displays a pattern of learning over the past twenty years. For example, the Liverpool JMU Integrated Credit Scheme relied for its modular and administrative character upon the lessons learned about the schemes at Oxford Brookes University and to a lesser extent at Middlesex University. Its use of credit derived less specifically from the CNAA than from the Open College Federations of the early 1980s, although the credit system remains compatible with that proposed by the CNAA. The application of learning outcome statements was derived from the influence of the NCVQ, although the scheme has been careful not to embrace the concept of 'competence statements', believing them to be too rigid and inflexible a representation of learning achievement. Finally, the scheme was modular, but driven by credit; indeed, initial steps were taken to develop a credit-led resourcing model for internal resource

distribution. Although other universities have developed similarly since 1991, for a time the Liverpool JMU Integrated Credit Scheme was unique in combining many of the academic and organisational features of whole-institution credit systems common throughout North America.

226. The synthetic approach has indeed proved popular with some other institutions, although not all who wished to travel this route have been able to marshal the necessary physical and political resources. Moreover, not all universities which began the process have found the subsequent pace of development and change as comfortable as they would have liked. The operational and administrative arrangements have often collided with academic resistance and institutional power structures; information systems have sometimes not kept pace with the scale or pace of developments; changes in organisation structure can disrupt newly-formed arrangements; and old cultures can reassert themselves. In the thirty years or so since colleagues attempted change at the University of London, the problems of regression from original principles remain as similar and as evident as ever. We explore this further in Chapter XII.

Towards a culture of credit? 1991-

227. During the 1990s, the agenda of change towards greater flexibility in higher education has largely been set by three converging factors:

- the commitment of most older universities towards extensive modularisation, embracing in many cases an agreement to reform the structure of the academic year;

- the continuing momentum amongst the new universities towards the use of credits and/or modularity as organising concepts of institutional life, sometimes embracing the accreditation of work-based learning;

- the active interest now being shown by

funding councils and others in the potential of credit systems to provide rational resource management formulae, responsive to student choice.

Progress amongst established universities

228. We have indicated earlier that the UGC Continuing Education Working Party had joined in 1984 with its NAB equivalent to support the development of credit systems. This was further supported by the UGC's *A Strategy for Higher Education into the 1990s* which commented: '*A system needs to be developed which will allow students to accumulate credit for completed course units and to transfer those units from one institution to another, leading finally to the award of a degree or diploma.*' Furthermore, the Universities' Council for Adult Continuing Education, in its report on credit transfer (1988) suggested that: '*what is now required is a general adherence to a basic scheme **which would have no ill-effects** but which would give a basis for credit transfer between those institutions which were prepared to use it*' (emphasis added).

229. We draw attention to the point emphasised above, because we feel it is symptomatic of the caution expressed by most older universities towards changes which might erode their basic character and autonomy. During the 1990s, many older universities have moved with speed to ensure that they have available suitable instruments for managing extended choice and flexibility. Institutions have begun to modularise and introduce semester structures. Institutional examples would include the University of Nottingham, the University of Liverpool, the University of Leeds, the University of Bradford, the University of Kent at Canterbury and several others. Davidson (1993) provides further examples of universities where change is in progress.

230. These developments in the older universities have largely been driven strategically from the administrative apex of the institution. There appears to have been less academic engagement with the pedagogic advantages of internal credit transfer than has been the case in the former polytechnics. Momentum has been sustained by Vice-Chancellors, Registrars and Academic Secretaries, supported by regional profession networks. The Northern Universities' Registrars Group (NURG), the Southern Universities' Management Programme (SUMP) and the 'Southern Comfort' association of senior institutional staff have provided the forums within which older universities have sought to move in harmony. Moreover, the CVCP arranged a series of seminars for academic and administrative staff during the early 1990s, at the universities of Stirling, Bradford, Canterbury, the Open University and Nottingham. Although membership of these networks and seminars has been opened up in some cases to the new universities, it is by no means evident that developments in the older universities have been informed by lessons from the former polytechnics. It appears to us that there is substantial scope for further work to ensure the general exchange of lessons learned, if the sector as a whole is to benefit from the experience of change. We believe this is important if an appreciation of strategic differences is to assist the development of reciprocal institutional respect.

231. The older universities have largely chosen not to adopt credit directly as an organising tool in the manner of some former polytechnics, a fact confirmed by Davidson (1993) in her work for the UCACE CAT Project. Most had a formal agreement with the CNAA CAT scheme by 1991 and a large number declare that they have a functioning CAT scheme (see Table 19 later), but the use of credit systems for the accreditation of 'off-campus' learning has not yet generally developed. In the sample of universities and colleges chosen for investigation on this point, not one older university claimed it had arrangements in place for the accreditation of 'off-campus' or employee learning. In general credit transfer is regarded almost entirely as a condition of general admissions policy. Our investigation has revealed that the largest single reservation amongst established universities towards credit-based learning remains that of quality assurance.

232. There has not been very much work undertaken to explore the internal institutional dynamics of change towards choice and flexibility within the older universities.

Table 17:
Policy and strategy towards choice and flexibility in 'research' universities.

For some older universities, movement towards modularity and the introduction of credit systems is closely tied to an assessment of strategic opportunities mitigated by a reluctance to depart from inherited and familiar arrangements except under conditions of environmental shock. For such institutions flexible arrangements encouraging the expression of more extensive student choice, at entry, in- programme and by choice of terminal qualification are seen as less important than the maintenance wherever possible of a strong core of programmes dedicated to single Honours, disciplinary-based outcomes. Their assessment of their academic strengths, professional commitments, market position, student labour market opportunities and personal preferences leads them to conclude that they have few compelling reasons radically to alter the configuration of their academic programmes.

Modularity and semesterisation may be introduced in formal terms, offering benign structural and administrative modifications to assessment cycles and to the work patterns of academic staff, but with limited impact upon the choice for students. Course structures remain largely linear, with units strung together by prerequisite conditions; entry points remain restricted; course regulations remain discrete and individual; exit qualifications remain restricted and unmodified. Modularity and semesterisation commend themselves, firstly because students and academic staff see mutual advantages in easing the end-of-year assessment load, and secondly, because some academic staff have seen the added value to their research commitments of consolidating much of their teaching in one semester, freeing the second semester and vacation periods for extended research time.

Under such conditions, the introduction of modularity and credit-based systems is rarely connected directly to the development of strategies for improved access or student choice, but rather to a tactical appreciation that instruments need to be put in place as insurance against the day that the university could be forced to reposition itself down market as a consequence of loss of research focus, or changes in patterns of student demand, or some other 'shock' factor. The principal thrust of these universities is to maintain their individual positions as leading research institutions, retaining high quality academic staff who might be attracted to the specialist and disciplinary character of an academic programme which complements their own enthusiasms for specific subject-oriented research. The introduction of increased inter-disciplinary choice and greater student mobility across the academic programme is seen as a possible dilution of the specialist academic focus of subject disciplines, prejudicing the ability of the university to retain its research cadre which in turn would force the institution down market as it lost its research standing.

For universities in which income from research funds is more than 50% of total teaching funds, the potential loss of market position in research is a real threat to their identity and purposes. Being aware of the threat and prudently putting in place instruments which give a capacity to respond, such institutions are faced with a dilemma: too much progress towards flexibility and student choice may create the very change in market position which the university sought to avoid initially.

Source: Summary of interviews with Vice-Chancellors and Registrars in five 'research-focused' universities.

Duke (1993) draws extensively on his experiences at the University of Warwick, but Kelly (1990) provides a more intimate insight into the difficulties of transforming two established universities. Her study of developments at the University of Leeds and the University of Bradford tends to confirm the pessimism of Squires (1986) during his study of the various universities in the Manchester area. Academic staff in such institutions were not easily persuaded that the academic case for change had been made; they remained sceptical of the impact upon research commitments and of the benefits to students; they questioned the motives of university administrators in proposing the changes and their capacity to manage it; they perceived the changes as 'the tail wagging the dog'; they suspected that effort would be expended in pursuit of a passing fashion; and the proposals for change *'more properly belonged to educational institutions which are not associated with the highest standards of academic excellence.'* According to Kelly, the response of academic staff ranged from *'incredulity through to weariness'*.

233.   We have not taken so bleak a view of the prospects. Our investigations suggest that there is indeed considerable scepticism within all universities, but particularly within the older institutions, towards the rationale for the introduction of modular and credit-based systems. Too frequently, it is perceived as an attempt to increase the productivity of universities and materially deteriorate the conditions of professional life at a time when policy towards the sector is generally so perceived. The presentation of academic and pedagogic rationales is therefore overridden by general disbelief and charges of naivety. On the other hand, Davidson (1993) argues that many older universities are now managed by a generation of younger Vice-Chancellors who are committed to modularisation and systematic change. Their support will be crucial in confirming the permanence of many of the modifications currently being promoted through the old universities.

234.   Moreover, the strategic position of many research-focused older universities is hedged around with more subtle constraints than merely whether academic staff or Vice-Chancellors are sufficiently committed to the proposed changes. Most senior university figures are keenly aware of the options before them, and they are aware that the external environment is not determined by them. In the summary of individual interviews on this matter (Table 17), Vice-Chancellors and Academic Registrars make the point that they must be prepared for unanticipated 'environmental shock'. We suggested in our investigations that significant changes in the patterns of student maintenance could constitute one such 'shock', by encouraging students to study at their local institution. Our respondents agreed unanimously.

235.   There is one aspect of the move towards increased flexibility in which the older universities have continued to play a prominent role: the introduction of semesters and the contingent reform of the academic year. We discuss this and the Flowers/Irvine Reports

Table 18:
Course structure and the organisation of the academic year: 'old' universities

	Yes	All	Part	No			
Considering modularisation?	38			5			
Reached decision to modularise?	32	13	9	23			

	1991	1992	1993	1994	1995	96+	DK
Modularisation completed by?	4	5	7	4	1		7
Semesterisation completed by?		1	5	11	5	3	10

Influences on decisions to modularise or introduce semesters:	Very important		Important		Not Important	
* internal academic criteria?	28		11		0	
* decisions of other universities	7		28		0	
* wish to change structure of year?	6		13		16	
* changes to school year?	8		11		12	
* other (conferencing season etc)	10		7		1	

Pattern of academic year?	3 x 10 week terms	2 x 15 week reformed semesters	2 x 15 week unreformed semesters	
	11	5	17	

Preferred start of second semester?	1 Jan - mid Jan	Late Jan - early Feb	Mid-Feb+	
	5	20	9	

Source: Survey of attitudes of 'old' universities towards modularisation and the reform of the academic year, CVCP 1992

further in Chapter XII. Initial suggestions for the reform of the academic year were first formally proposed at the CNAA Telford conference in November 1991 (see Table 20 later) but had surfaced in discussions within the Northern Universities' Registrars Group at the same time. The general agreement has been to develop a model largely in common with that which has operated at the University of Stirling since 1967 and throughout the United States for many years. In 1992, the CVCP conducted a survey amongst its members of the time ('old' universities), the outcomes of which are shown in Table 18. The majority of institutions declared in favour of early progress towards a reformed academic year. Although there is not universal agreement on the need for change, the Flowers Report (1993) does strongly recommend the reformed model proposed at Telford and supported by older universities in the Northern and Southern Registrars Groups. If enough institutions commit to this, most of the others will follow.

Progress in the 'new' universities and colleges, 1991-

236.   Amongst the new universities, progress has tended to take the form, either of consolidation where developments began in the 1980s, or of institution-wide application where initiatives were localised in particular courses and combined studies programmes. A good example would be the progress being made at Middlesex University. As an institution in the 'first wave' of developments in the 1970s, the university's modular programme settled into a Combined Studies course. In the last three years, this has now expanded into a whole-institution modular and credit-based programme, with some of the support systems and styles of student catalogue that would be found routinely in the United States. The University of East London has similarly moved out from a Combined Studies programme towards a comprehensive undergraduate scheme.

237.   There has also been substantial progress in some of the colleges of higher education. At Cheltenham and Gloucester College of HE, for example, the institution has developed a whole-institution

modular scheme, following the longstanding example of Oxford Brookes University. Indeed, some of the former colleges, which were more recently designated as universities, have shown themselves capable of considerable progress and inventiveness. For example, Thames Valley University has chosen to develop its programmes through multi-media access, whilst the University of Derby has sought to produce the type of synthesis to which we referred earlier. At the University of Luton, there is progress towards a more definitive use of learning objectives, coupled with strategies for dual accreditation with NCVQ-derived programmes. We draw these examples into our frame of reference because we believe they indicate that some of the more radical developments may well begin to occur in institutions which have the greatest need to respond quickly to competitive pressure and changing student needs. It may not be too fanciful to suggest that some new initiatives in higher education development may be more usefully piloted in the very new universities which are still able to take a fresh approach to the nature of higher education.

238.   One of the more significant developments in the new universities in the 1990s has been the attention paid to the promotion of work-based learning for academic credit. This has taken many forms. It has involved the relatively straightforward award of special credit, 'P' credit, for sandwich placements, professional practice, or occasionally the year-abroad for Languages students. The credit awarded in these circumstances has generally been additional to the quantum required for an honours degree or other qualification and has not challenged prevailing assumptions about the academic integrity of the final qualification. Then, in more ambitious projects, academic credit has been awarded for the assessed work-based activity itself, allowing students exemption from designated parts of their academic programme, or substituting for a dissertation (often as part of some elective programme or similar). Finally, in the most ambitious programmes, the work placement is offered as a core part of the modular programme, with credit contributing directly to the final qualification, including its classification.

Currently the scale of these activities remains small. Accreditable workplace learning opportunities are hindered by labour market conditions, an under-developed workplace mentor system, and some caution amongst many institutions concerning the assurance of academic quality.

239.   We have already drawn attention to some institutions which are committed to the accreditation of in-company employee training. Elsewhere, Napier University has been exploring the application of learning objectives and work-based competence to academic programmes; the University of Huddersfield has made considerable progress in the use of learning outcome statements as curriculum and assessment design tools, particularly in Mathematics, Engineering and Technology and elsewhere in their academic programme. We are sure that there has been a close relationship between the many developments in these areas and the Enterprise in Higher Education initiative. The EHE programme has made it possible for institutions to release staff for development work and this can be seen in the extensive support materials that have been produced by the University of Northumbria at Newcastle, for example, and by many other universities. We are equally clear that EHE has been the facilitator, but not the cause of some of these undertakings. The accreditation of work-based learning is a natural continuation of the progress that has been made over the past few years in creating credible arrangements and procedures for the quality assurance of such learning achievement. This is now reflected in the confidence with which some universities embrace many forms of work-based experiential learning. We address its quality assurance in Chapter X.

Funding councils and progress on credits

240.   Finally, it would not be appropriate to leave this part of the review of progress without referring to the role being played by the funding councils in the further development of credit systems. It is clear to us that funding councils throughout the United Kingdom would welcome means by which a rational resource formula could be developed. The application of credit to academic programmes offers the prospect of just such a formula. Yet funding councils, at least in higher education, are careful not to promote 'solutions' which might be interpreted as an intrusion into the academic affairs of universities. We have understood this caution and throughout this report, we have been concerned to ensure that the academic case for the development of credit systems is presented as cogently and convincingly as possible. However, it has been apparent for a number of years to senior members of some universities that credit systems can act as a basis for internal resource management. In conditions in which the dividing lines between categories of student begin to blur, prospects for the use of 'credit' as a resource accounting instrument improve. We address the details of this in Chapter XI.

241.   Meanwhile, we can record that funding council interest in these matters may be traced indirectly to the NAB, and directly to the PCFC, which indicated in 1991 to the *Learning without walls* conference that it was minded to introduce a credit-based funding formula *'within two years'*. This was overtaken by events, but the HEFCE has resumed the exploration in 1993 by seeking consultation on a 'tariff arrangement' to account for part-time students in the first instance, in advance of further consultations on methodologies for full-time students in the medium-term. We very much welcome the steps that are being taken on these matters, by the HEFCE, SHEFC and the HEFCW. We are also aware of the progress that has been made in further education by the FEFC, and this is also discussed further in Chapter XI.

242.   In addition to their work of investigating suitable funding formulae, funding councils have also been active in the promotion of specific projects to assist the further development of choice and flexibility. The NAB and the PCFC supported initiatives, notably the Accelerated Degree programmes in recent years. During the 1990s, before its amalgamation with the HEFCE, the UFC also funded numerous projects in access and flexibility, most notably supporting the three-year investigative project, *CATS in the universities,* undertaken by the University of Kent at Canterbury for UCACE (Davidson

1993). The UFC was able to use the funding specially designated to support research in continuing education for these purposes. With changes to the basis of funding for Continuing Education departments in the older universities, this is no longer available to the HEFCE or SHEFC.

243. Finally, previous funding councils and the HEFCE were able to encourage the development of 'franchising' arrangements and 'Associate College' status by releasing student numbers with which universities and colleges could consolidate regional relationships. Prior to the recent change in policy, this was beginning to have the effect of stimulating the type of local networks and 'articulation agreements' that would be found throughout the United States. For the time being, these developments may be forced to proceed more slowly, but the infrastructural relationships will remain largely in place if policy moves forward again in the future.

244. During our consultations, representatives of the funding councils were keen to know how extensive the use of credit had become. We offer in Table 19 an assessment from one recent survey (Harvey and Norton, 1993). Although there are some methodological limitations to the reliability of the data, to which we have referred in Chapter III, the survey does indicate an extensive engagement with *some aspects of credit systems*. We would not wish to advise the funding councils, or other bodies, that the use of credit systems has become so extensive that it is a common or familiar feature of the student experience and institutional life. Rather, we are persuaded by our own research that academic staff in most universities and colleges are aware of the basic features of credit systems; many thousands of students on full-time and part-time programmes now earn credits formally and naturally; and the language of credit systems is understood, even if there has yet to develop a shared discourse around some fundamental features. We anticipate that within three to four years, *at the same rate of progress and assuming continued policy support*, credit-based learning will have become

Table 19: Survey of credit schemes in all universities, 1993

Questions	%	n
Currently with CAT scheme	63	48
Plans to introduce scheme within three years	21	16
No plans to introduce scheme	16	12
Current schemes compatible with 'CNAA scheme'	92	44
Planned schemes compatible with 'CNAA scheme'	70	12
Schemes adopting three levels (England, Wales & NI) or four levels (Scotland) for undergraduate work	81	39
Schemes adopting Level 0 for pre-degree work	19	9
Membership of CAT consortia	40	36
Accept credit from consortium members = yes	0	36
Current schemes accepting WBL, EBL or APEL	71	34
Maximum prior credit = 33%	5	2
Maximum prior credit = 50%	50	21
Maximum prior credit = 66.90%	45	19
Minimum attendance = 33%	20	9
Minimum attendance = 50%	22	10
Minimum attendance = other	13	6
Minimum attendance = not known	45	21
With CAT scheme and database	75	36
With CAT scheme but no database	25	12
With CAT scheme and co-ordinator	67	31
With CAT scheme but no co-ordinator	33	15
Modularisation – current, all courses	32	23
Modularisation – three years hence, all courses	59	42
Modularisation – no plans	23	16
Structure – currently 3 terms/trimesters	75	54
Structure – 3 years hence, 2 semesters	63	45
Structure – 3 semesters/4 terms	0	72
No. of modules/year – average = 3	3	1
average = 6	25	10
average = 8	20	8
average = 10	25	10
average = 12	30	11
Response rate from 88 universities	86	76

Data compiled from: Harold Harvey & Brian Norton, University of Ulster, Survey of CAT schemes in UK universities, commissioned by the Institute of Environmental Health Officers (IEHO), March 1993

commonplace in many institutions, familiar in many others, although there will be a number of institutions for whom it will not have become anything other than an instrument for the management of marginal groups of students. Harvey & Norton suggest that 16% of institutions *'have no plans to introduce a scheme'*.

245.   Our own research, supported to some extent by Davidson (1993), suggests that this may be an unduly pessimistic figure. A small minority of ancient universities and some others may not wish to move in this direction in any extensive way, but we are aware that steps are being taken within the Continuing Education department at the University of Cambridge, for example, to explore the potential of credit systems in recognising student achievement. Moreover, the Continuing Education department of the University of Oxford plans to bring forward proposals for a credit-based certificate in the near future. The examples are offered to indicate that modest efforts are underway even in the ancient institutions. Throughout the sector, credit systems may first be introduced via extra-mural and Continuing Education departments; elsewhere in other institutions, as we have shown earlier, credit systems are developing as whole-institution features. It would be a mistake to judge progress by the activities either of the traditional institutions or by the recently designated universities alone.

Developments in further education 1970-1994

246.   Developments in further education do not generally receive great exposure in higher education. Universities in the United Kingdom have tended to see secondary schools as their natural source of students. This has always been slightly different for the former polytechnics which for many years shared with further education colleges a common relationship with their local authorities. Even then, the new universities still retained a link with the 'A' level examination almost equally as strong as that maintained by the older universities. We make these observations because they are relevant to the means by which

certain aspects of educational development in higher education might take shape in the future, particularly those aspects concerning the further introduction of student choice and flexibility into the student experience of higher education. From our investigations, it is clear to us that it would not be particularly productive if the further introduction of credit systems into higher education were to take place without regard for the important and innovative work that is now taking place on these matters in the further education sector.

Higher education and further education

247.   Before we embark on a brief review of significant developments in the sector, it is necessary to anticipate some possible reservations from within higher education. The principle objection to a general consideration of further education is that it is not the business of higher education, which looks to further education simply for students. Indeed, the argument runs: universities will continue to receive a supply of more or less adequately prepared students from further education colleges as well as from secondary schools, and it would be wise to exercise an overview of developments therein from time to time. Quality control and quality assurance at the point of admission are of direct concern to institutions, and policy there will vary according to the state of the student market. Sometimes it will be necessary to create strategies for recruitment to hard-pressed areas or expansion in others, and this will determine the enthusiasm with which universities embrace initiatives such as Access courses, 'franchising', '2+2' arrangements and similar activities. Beyond this, it is claimed, further education colleges can go about their business undisturbed by the universities.

248.   A more elaborate variant of this market-focused analysis emerges from those who might be sympathetic to closer engagements with further education, believing that further education colleges may have something more to offer higher education than just a supply of students, but who fail to identify enough common purpose or shared cultural values to sustain enduring commitment. In this case, it is asserted that further education is simply different. It is less

academic than the conventional Sixth Form; it displays a greater heterogeneity of courses, qualifications, patterns of attendance and institutional missions than would ever be apparent in a higher education institution; its academic staff do not enjoy professional or curriculum autonomy, being subject to external examining bodies, the training strategies of employers and TECs, and intrusive quality inspection from various sources. In summary, these arguments suggest a case for no greater association with further education than is necessary to maintain a supply of acceptable students.

249.   We have been disappointed to hear these arguments during our investigations. It is a commonplace to observe that further education is different from higher education, and that universities are principally interested in recruiting students well-prepared in their own image. We have been more interested in the potential of further education to inform further developments in higher education. This may be possible in several areas. Firstly, further education has had more experience of managing diversity of programme and student choice than is generally the case for universities. Secondly, colleges have learned to cope with a cohort of varied learning abilities which has encouraged them to adopt more radical ways of teaching learning and assessing achievement; thirdly, further education is much more advanced and experienced in providing educational guidance and support; and finally, colleges appear to have a closer relationship with their external partners – employers and the local community, for example – than would be the case for many universities. This has encouraged colleges to be more alert to local economic and social needs as well as to employment opportunities for their students.

250.   In making these observations, we believe most certainly that higher education could benefit from a closer study of activities in further education, without prejudice to the chacteristics which make higher education distinctive. This is particularly pertinent to the further development of credit systems and modularity.

Pressure to change in further education

251.   The momentum for the development of modularity and credit systems in further education has increased noticeably over the past two or three years. This has important consequences for higher education, not least because students of the future may be arriving at university already familiar with the routines and practices of credit-based learning. The recent developments in further education have been prompted largely by the conviction that educational opportunities for students post-16 are being restricted by the unproductive separation of academic programmes from applied and vocational courses, with damaging consequences for the national skills base. This is represented most familiarly in the primacy given to GCSEs and 'A' levels as the academic route (to university) for high achievers, with more vocational training for the remaining students, provided by external assessment bodies such as the City & Guilds of London Institute (C&G), the Royal Society of Arts (RSA) and the Business and Technical Education Council (BTEC). Interest in credit systems in further education has arisen directly in response to efforts to provide points of transfer between academic and vocational programmes for young people and appropriate adult trainees. The development of General National Vocational Qualifications (GNVQs) may be seen as an attempt to provide a solution to this problem. Moreover, there have been other suggestions: the Advanced Diploma was proposed by the 1991 White Paper on Further Education; and there has been widespread support for an 18+ British equivalent to the Baccalaureate (IPPR, 1990). Both of these proposals would benefit from the unification of the different types of learning achievement that a credit system is well-placed to deliver.

BTEC, SCOTVEC and modularisation in Further Education, 1974-

252.   The progress towards a modular curriculum for 16-19 year olds in further education was led initially in England and Wales by BTEC (at the start of the initiatives in 1974, it was BEC and TEC). In Scotland, the Scottish Education Department (SED) promoted the 16-19 Action Plan which was taken up by

SCOTVEC, the Scottish Vocational Education Council. These two national bodies pursued similar, but also strikingly different approaches to the problem. The antecedent organisations of BTEC began to introduce units, modules and credits to the programmes under their authority in 1974. However it was not a unified introduction. As Theodossin (1986) records, TEC introduced a system of *units* with a series of associated levels of achievement while BEC proposed a system of *modules* closely linked around four themes with a cross-modular assignment to assure the coherence of the learning experience. When they were merged in 1983, BTEC adopted the 60-hour unit of instruction as the standard measure of unit equivalence. Over the years, BTEC programmes have retained their quasi-modular appearance but they have never fully committed to the unit-based schemes proposed in Scotland.

253.   The SCOTVEC initiatives arise from the work around the development of the Scottish Action Plan from 1979 until its introduction in 1984. From the start, it maintained a more ambitious commitment to modularisation, credit accumulation and credit transfer than anything proposed by BTEC. It sought to embrace all education and training for the 16-18 age group in a national scheme of modules defined in size by a 40-hour unit of instruction. There were **'generalist'**, **'specialist'** and **'integrative'** modules, each defined by a **'module descriptor'** which specified the level of the module; its content; the learning outcomes; and the assessment strategy. At completion, students received a **credit transcript** as a record of achievement. Moreover, it was planned that modules would be available to students through local college consortia, thereby building credit transfer into the scheme from inception. There was no doubting the assessment and enthusiasm of Theodossin (1986) at the time when he said: *'we have arrived at what is arguably the closest British equivalent of the American credit system'*.

254.   There is possibly no university in the United Kingdom, however well-advanced in these matters, that has yet exceeded the achievements of the SCOTVEC modular programme. Some universities have developed similar 'core' and 'elective' credit/modular systems and the most developed have

introduced module descriptors, learning outcome statements and credit transcripts, as we have shown earlier. It is clear therefore that both the BTEC and the SCOTVEC arrangements have had a greater effect on developments in higher education in the United Kingdom than may be apparent at first sight. This has created its own counter-reaction; in some former polytechnics, some academic staff associate modularisation with BTEC courses which are perceived to be of lower status than undergraduate academic degree programmes.

255.   The SCOTVEC initiative continued to influence related developments in England and Wales during the mid-1980s. Firstly, a small number of local authorities attempted to develop a minor variant of the SCOTVEC programme. Known as *'Mainframe'*, it sought to create a national framework of unit accreditation based initially on the training programmes of the Youth Training Scheme (YTS). Pursuing similar objectives and styles of operation to those of SCOTVEC, the *Mainframe* initiative developed a limited capability between 1986-88 but foundered for three reasons: it was too narrowly based in a limited number of local authorities; academic staff in those colleges which had experimented with the approach found the requirements of curriculum redesign too cumbersome and restrictive; and it was associated with low status training (YTS) and the professionally disputed Adult Training Strategy (ATS). However, the principal reason for the short life of the *Mainframe* programme was that it was overtaken by events. In 1986, the National Council for Vocational Qualifications (NCVQ) was set up with a mandate which enveloped that of SCOTVEC, BTEC, *Mainframe* and other similar initiatives.

256.   From 1988, SCOTVEC promoted the Advanced Courses Development Programme. Adopting the same principles of modularisation as the 16-19 Action Plan and applying them to HND and HNC awards, SCOTVEC was able to negotiate with the CNAA for an agreement on 'articulated programmes' in order to create a seamless progression from HND to undergraduate degree programmes. In the same period in England and Wales, the CNAA and BTEC were negotiating a reciprocal credit transfer agreement.

257.   There is one final Scottish development which remains relevant here. In 1992 the Scottish Office Education Department (SOED) published *Upper secondary education in Scotland* (the Howie Report). Its proposals are far-reaching and address the need to join academic and vocational pathways in a common qualifications framework based on a Certificate (SCOTCERT) and a Baccalaureate (SCOTBAC). Credit transfer is included in the proposals, as is an assessment strategy which appears to have considerable affinities with the Grade Point system used in America. The Government has yet to decide on the recommendations contained within the Howie Report, but if it declares positively as we would hope, then Scotland may have taken a further step towards the type of cross-sectoral credit transfer system which we are exploring in this report.

Open College Federations, 1981-

258.   The development of Open College Federations during the 1980s is a remarkable and influential phenomenon. The importance of these networks lies in their success in using credit as a source of quality assurance. It is this feature of their work, rather than the more visible and no less substantial commitment to access, which may have lessons for future developments in higher and further education.

259.   Open College Federations, sometimes referred to as Networks, originated with the development of the Open College of the North-West (OCNW) in 1978. This was a loose network based on the University of Lancaster, Lancashire Polytechnic and a number of further education colleges, led by Nelson & Colne College. The Toyne Report referred to its early development. Its purpose was to promote access into higher education for mature and 'second chance' students. If one is to chart the development of the 'Access movement', then OCNW will be a principal source. It prefigured the development of the Open College of South London (OCSL) which also focused primarily on access to higher education from 1983 onwards. Although both networks heavily influenced the development of Access to Higher Education courses after 1987, neither provided the model for the large number of Open College

Federations that now exist. This inspiration was provided by the Manchester Open College Federation.

260.   The Manchester development from 1981 was influenced by OCNW to the extent that it called itself an 'Open College', but MOCF developed characteristics that became more widely imitated by other networks. Its principal contribution lay in the development of a credit system based explicitly on models operating in North America, but linked more directly to quality assurance arrangements. Since MOCF was a consortium of further and higher education institutions, it did not own or offer courses itself. Instead, it invited providers to submit their programmes for accreditation (or 'validation' in the language of the CNAA). Courses would be subjected to peer assessment and claims for credit would be agreed or moderated. Thereafter students would be entitled to claim the credit for programmes and modules successfully completed. A record of the earned credits was registered in a study 'Passport'.

261.   The principal objective of MOCF was to use 'credit' to produce two solutions. Firstly, it provided the means to motivate students whose learning achievement may not have been recognised by conventional awarding bodies; this was sometimes known as the 'deep access' strategy or 'Access to Further Education'. Secondly, it offered the opportunity in further and adult education for the development of peer-centred quality assurance. It should be remembered that the involvement of academic staff in peer review quality assurance is otherwise largely absent in further and adult education. The MOCF contribution to the evolution of credit-based systems went beyond the accreditation of access to higher education courses. It quickly embraced adult basic education, large parts of community and continuing education, and by the mid-1980s, was pursuing, by means of 'dual accreditation', modularised 'A' levels, BTEC programmes, youth training courses and many others. On average, over 5,000 students per annum registered with MOCF and large numbers of academic staff would participate each year in accreditation panels, moderation and review processes.

262. It is difficult not to be impressed by the efficiency of the model created by MOCF. Working from a small central unit, with the voluntary participation of hundreds of college academic staff, MOCF managed to create, not just a major regional credit system, but also what we would now call 'quality networks'. By 1987, MOCF had been joined by two other networks which owed their existence to an imitation of the Manchester model. Both the Merseyside Open College Federation (MerOCF) and the South Yorkshire Open College Federation (SYOCF) developed similar structures, were credit-awarding and pursued identical principles to MOCF. By the end of the 1980s, the various networks in London were united in the London Open College Federation, which then adopted the credit-awarding procedures of the Northern networks. Many of the local London networks, such as the Access to Learning for Adults (ALFA) in North London and OCS in South London which we have already mentioned, had been active since the early 1980s but not necessarily in a credit-awarding form.

263. Interestingly, the first network, CNW, remained committed to access to higher education, but not to the formal use of credit, nor to the accreditation of as broad a range of programmes as the credit-awarding federations. Nevertheless, the first steps had been taken in producing a national network of credit-awarding agencies outside higher education which was committed both to access in the widest sense, and to quality assurance. The work of the networks was substantially enhanced in the late 1980s and 1990s by development activities sponsored by UDACE and subsequently taken over by the FEU. The National Open College Network was formed in 1991 and open college federations now flourish across the country. It is not possible to indicate the number of courses which are validated and accredited by OCFs, but over 50,000 students annually earn credits at various levels of further and adult education. Open College Federations remain however outside the framework of awarding bodies, with the notable exception that they do award recognised certificates for the successful completion of Access to Higher Education courses if they are Authorised Validating Agencies for this purpose. We return to this point in Chapter IX and X.

Access, credits and quality assurance

264. The development of the initial Open College Federations have their origins prior to the 1987 White Paper, although the direct stimulus to Access to Higher Education programmes, which the White Paper provided, ultimately created a more secure platform upon which OCFs could develop.

265. The need to secure the quality assurance of the rising number of Access courses led the CVCP and the CNAA of the time to bring together proposals for the formal recognition, not of Access courses themselves, but of agencies authorised to assure the quality of such courses. Open College Federations were already playing this role as part of their wider accreditation function and they were natural candidates for approval as Authorised Validating Agencies (AVAs) following the establishment of the Access Course Recognition Group (ACRG). This body was empowered to award approval to cross-sectoral networks for the quality assurance of Access courses, seeking means to ensure a common acceptance of Access course standards by receiving universities. In large measure, this has been successful and Access course recognition remains within the authority of the HEQC.

266. By no means all bodies approved for the purposes of Access course recognition were open college federations. Many others were local access consortia of one kind or another and they generally did not choose formally to work with credit in the manner of the OCFs. All bodies approved by the ACRG have subsequently formed the Standing Conference of Authorised Validating Agencies (SCAVA) which seeks to exercise co-ordination and general oversight of matters associated with their work.

267. Other national agencies occupy positions in and around the access and credit agencies. The Forum for Access Studies (FAST) has existed since the mid-1980s and seeks to provide a forum for the work of

individual Access courses and their tutors. There is a close overlap of interest and membership between FAST, SCAVA and the National Open College Network (NOCN) although each organisation would claim to represent distinctive dimensions of their commonly-held interests.

268. In the light of developments in the application of credit and quality assurance in further education which are beginning to arise from the work of the Further Education Unit, we wonder whether it is time that these various agencies were encouraged to form closer formal association. **We recommend** that the bodies themselves, together with appropriate interested parties in further education in England and Wales, including the Association for Colleges, FEFC and FEU, give consideration to how the work of open colleges federations, access consortia and similar associations can be supported in their work. The objective might be to consider how this work may be brought into a wider national context, through a national credit framework perhaps, how it should be suitably managed and resourced, and how the lessons of quality assurance can be generalised and shared more widely throughout higher and further education.

Further Education Unit: *A basis for credit?*

269. The publication in 1992 of *A basis for credit?* represented a further major step forward in the development of credit systems, not just in further education, but for national initiatives as a whole. The FEU has sought through its consultation document, and through project work associated with it over the past two years, to draw together all that is understood about the application of credit. It has attempted to examine, from first principles, how a national credit framework might be constructed, what its specifications might be, and how it could be applied with advantage to the range of programmes and qualifications in further, but also higher, education.

270. The work of the FEU has been influenced by most of the developments which we have already discussed. It has been able to assess the operation of credit systems in higher education; it has considered the experience of the open college federations; and it has sought to embrace the different approaches offered by the NCVQ. Moreover, it has been concerned to learn from the long-standing work of BTEC and SCOTVEC in the application of unit-based or modular structures, and it has been keen to address the development of credit systems in educational and curriculum terms.

271. The publication of *A basis for credit?* has been very timely and it has attracted considerable attention in further education, although it remains less well-known in universities. The reason for its timeliness can be found in policy decisions to develop closer co-operation between academic and vocational pathways in post-16 education. In short, credit systems promise to provide the 'ladders and bridges' for student mobility to enable learners to pass more freely between academic and vocational pathways. This would enable colleges to accommodate NCVQ qualifications alongside their conventional academic programmes, working over time to establish parity of esteem between them.

272. The key principles of the FEU proposals involve a close association of modules, credits and learning outcomes in which programmes are designed to establish the capacity of credit to act as a proxy for demonstrated learning achievement. Central to this process is the practice and organisation of assessment. Most of the objectives of the FEU model are familiar to universities and colleges at the forefront of these developments. Indeed most of the principles of operation have been within the systems of further and higher education for many years. What makes the FEU proposals important is that they explicitly use credit as the instrument to shape the overall framework. Although 'credit' remains an accounting device in the proposed framework, it also takes on a quality assurance dimension in ways which we explore further in Chapters VIII and IX.

273. If we were to suggest good examples of the way in which the FEU proposals are beginning to have an impact, we would direct attention to the rapid rate of increase in

participation in the Post-16 Credit Network that has been launched by the FEU. Possibly more significantly still, we would commend closer attention to the work taking place throughout Wales to create a comprehensive national credit structure based on *A basis for credit?* The activities of the Welsh *Fforwm* and the Welsh CATS Project may act as helpful models for further progress in England and its regions.

274.   On balance, we regard the work of the FEU in this area as so important for the further development of credit systems in both higher and further education that **we recommend** that appropriate measures are taken by the bodies responsible in higher education, and specifically the HEQC, to ensure that *A basis for credit?* and related publications are formally considered by universities and colleges of higher education as part of a wider consultation exercise in the development of credit systems.

National Council for Vocational Qualifications, 1986-

275.   We turn finally in this review of progress to the contribution of the NCVQ. This has been left until this stage because its work embraces the accreditation of qualifications in both further and higher education, even though the majority of its activity to date has been with lower level qualifications beyond higher education. Currently, the Council is expanding its engagement with higher level qualifications at NVQ/SVQ Level 4 and Level 5, and is in the process of consulting on the development of GNVQs at Level 4 also. In common with our earlier practice, we have not attempted to provide a full account of the work of the NCVQ. This can be found elsewhere (NCVQ, 1991).

276.   The objectives of the NCVQ have been to regularise the plethora of occupational and vocational qualifications according to common principles and standards in a way that can be easily understood by students and employers. This has committed the NCVQ to an extensive role in quality assurance specifically for employment-related qualifications. This responsibility is discharged through Industry Lead Bodies (ILBs) which set

standards and define the evidence of assessment. The authority of the Council does not extend to academic qualifications although problems may arise at higher levels in the future in determining when a programme is academic or vocational and employment-related, and what role therefore the NCVQ and/or the universities and professional bodies may play in the accreditation and quality assurance of such programmes. We consider these matters in Chapter X.

277.   Since 1991 the NCVQ has been requested by Government to develop an alternative route to NVQ/SVQs for further education. Its initial response has been to develop *General* NVQs (GNVQs) at levels below higher education, the purpose of which is to attract students who might wish greater degrees of vocationally-relevant skills than might otherwise be provided by conventional academic programmes. This has resulted in some effort being expended in the development of GNVQs at Level 3 with the purpose of encouraging further routes into higher education in addition to the academic 'A' level path. In 1993, such GNVQs were indeed retitled as *Vocational 'A' Levels* and are sometimes called 'Advanced GNVQs'.

278.   The character of the GNVQ is distinct from that of NVQs to the extent that it is neither related to a specific occupation, nor is it assessed simply in terms of operational performance. There is a greater expectation that core skills will be complemented by components of knowledge and understanding. This brings the GNVQ closer to the intellectual aspirations of academic qualifications although there remain significant differences in the styles of assessment, the nature of evidence, and in the criteria for demonstrating reliable achievement.

279.   As we will explain later in Chapter IX, both NVQs, GNVQs and their Scottish equivalents are unit-based and subscribe to a framework of credit accumulation and transfer, although we would wish to qualify our assessment of this by reference in later comments to the specificity of the NCVQ treatment of these terms. For the moment, it should be sufficient to observe that the growth of the NCVQ's work has been such that over

70,000 students are now registered for GNVQs at Level 2 and Level 3, a substantial minority of whom will aspire to transfer forward onto higher education programmes. Furthermore, a consultation exercise with universities is underway on the usefulness of GNVQs at Level 4, and the number of NVQ 4 qualifications continues to rise steadily. The CVCP has also established a working group to consider the impact of the Council's proposals for universities. We have proposals to make on GNVQ4 in Chapter IX.

Conclusions

280.   We have spent time on this review because we believe it is essential that academic colleagues, policy-makers and other interested parties, have some overview of the scale and continuity of progress to date. They deserve an opportunity to locate contextually the changes and policies that are being urged on them. We offer these observations because it has been made apparent to us during the investigation that there is a body of opinion which maintains that the development of credit systems is either a passing phase, or that it is an ideological conspiracy against the perceived virtues of existing arrangements, or that it is a series of administrative prescriptions which have little consequence for real academic life. We would be happy to join in debate on any of these points, citing evidence to refute these claims.

281.   Firstly, progress in higher and further education demonstrates unambiguous continuity of purpose in the pursuit of credit systems and a national credit framework. This is evident from policy-makers, senior institutional administrators and, where given the opportunity, from academic colleagues themselves. No model of development emerges from this review. Sometimes initiatives are encouraged from the strategic apex of institutions; on other occasions, they erupt from 'grassroots' activity. There are examples of small-scale and conceptually interesting projects and other examples of whole-institution transformations. The momentum for progress ebbs and flows between higher and further education, and between different national

systems within the United Kingdom. We do not wish to disparage the notable steps that have been taken in England by drawing attention to some remarkable and extensive progress in Scotland and latterly in Wales.

282.   Moreover, most higher education institutions now have some engagement with credit systems, either formally as credit-based academic programmes, or by derivation, as modular or quasi-modular programmes. We would not suggest that all institutions are equally or even comprehensively committed to the further development of credit systems as organising features of their work; we do not expect this for good reasons in some cases. We are convinced that, where credit systems are developing, they will remain permanent features of institutional life. The lessons of developments in the early 1970s, confirmed by institutional examples in the 'second wave' of the 1980s, suggest that there may be setbacks to original ambitions but the transformations never disappear. Once introduced, the extension of student choice acts as a powerful focus for other institutional changes. We believe this narrative is confirmed by changes in further education also. In short, progress in the development of credit systems appears to be no passing phase.

283.   Secondly, we have not been persuaded by the view that the development of credit systems, modularity and other attendant features is the product of some ideological conspiracy to which we are dupes. Commitment to credit accumulation and transfer has been sustained across the political spectrum over the years. It may be the case that different political perspectives find comfort in different aspects of the development. Those persuaded by the merits of the marketplace, the sovereign consumer, the individualisation of social and economic activity, and the erosion of professional privilege will find plenty to encourage them in the operation of credit systems. On the other hand, those who are interested to pursue greater social equity through wider access to a rare public good (higher education), or who believe that students from all backgrounds deserve an education that delivers good quality employment, or who simply wish to extend the range of benefits of

higher education more generally throughout society will also take comfort from credit systems as instruments to achieve this. We can find little to contest in the basic principles of credit systems, which are: the promotion of democratic participation in higher education to all who can benefit; the enhancement of personal skills and effectiveness; the encouragement of individual initiative, critical thinking, good judgement and self-reliance; the expectation of good quality in higher education; and the delivery to students of successful employment prospects.

284.   Thirdly, we confirm throughout the report that credit systems are effective not merely as accounting tools (the prosaic view) but as instruments for the modernisation of the curriculum and for improved quality assurance. Credit systems in the modern form cannot easily be developed separately from changes to delivery and to assessment strategies. We accept that this view may not always be welcome in quarters where this type of transformation might appear to challenge certain orthodoxies in the curriculum of higher education; under these conditions, credit systems may appear as little more than administrative superficiality. However, we have chosen to make our investigation an enquiry into the academic and educational consequences of credit-based learning, in which we believe the greater potential lies.

285.   We cannot move on without making one final observation. The scale and quality of progress over the past thirty years has been substantial but there remains much to be achieved. The Robbins Report produced proposals which were carefully sculpted to fit

the familiar forms of higher education at the time. But it gave enough encouragement to those who wished to change aspects of university life so that early initiatives in modularity and credit were sustained. Thereafter the development of these new forms of higher education has followed the 'British Way', a meander cautious and courageous by turns towards some distant vision. In this, three groups stand out. Firstly, progress would not have been possible without the persistence of a small number of individuals with the vision to maintain momentum when otherwise distracted. By their efforts at key points of influence including national conferences, both institutions, national agencies, and Government departments have sustained their support for progress (see Table 20). Secondly, other individuals, many less elevated in hierarchical terms, have given their own commitment, often in the face of opposition from colleagues and others, to carry forward the vision of a more democratic and open system of higher education. Their rewards have been in the modest transformation of institutions and in the coherence they have brought to the strategy, intellectually and operationally. Finally, a third group is perhaps the most notable of all. This group has been responsible, unprompted and often under-supported, for growing credit systems from the bottom upwards. We have in mind here the efforts of those associated with the Access movement generally and Open College Federations specifically. We could also refer to many hundreds of colleagues throughout institutional life who have been persuaded of the importance of improved student choice and flexibility and who have attempted to advance this. By their efforts, the further development of credit systems retains its original values.

Table 20: Credit systems: changing the terms of engagement

Policy and prescription from three conferences

'Lifelong learning – Britain's future' Oxford, October 1990	**'Learning without walls'** Oxford, February 1991
1. As a nation we need to improve the skills level of the workforce and raise aspirations for education and training. We need to create a higher tolerance for risk– taking in pursuit of new developments 2. The case for Continuing Education and Training is essentially an economic one: learning pays 3. Higher education should respond flexibly to the needs of learners of all ages, and to employees, in which the quality of provision should be a permanent concern 4. For Higher Education, the crucial importance of Continuing Education should not be neglected. It is time to bring Continuing Education and Training in from the cold. This requires commitment at the top	1. Funding councils should be encouraged to move rapidly to explore and develop a credit–based system of resource allocation for higher education 2. A national credit framework should be developed, seeking to articulate academic and vocational, post-secondary and higher education, embracing institutional programmes and qualifications and those developing from the NCVQ 3. A Commission, or 'Task Force', should be established, comprising representatives of the universities and colleges, government departments, employer representatives and professional bodies, the NCVQ, funding councils and other interested parties

'Practising CATS' conference

CNAA, Telford, November 1991

1. A successor body to CNAA CATS should be established to assist HEIs in developing consistent arrangements for CATS within a national framework, but its role should be facilitative and not prescriptive.

2. A National Task Force consisting of practitioners drawn from HEIs and other relevant bodies should be formed to investigate key areas of CATS in Higher Education and for the purposes of assessing its wider potential for the post–16 system.

3. A group of suitably qualified CATS practitioners should be established to consider the institutional issues of resource allocation based on credits and to assist the Higher Education funding councils in formulating an appropriate funding methodology.

4. Relevant national bodies should redesign the academic year on the basis of a reformed two–semester system.

5. A standard widely accepted definition of a 'credit' should be adopted by HEIs.

6. There should be more dialogue between CATS practitioners and the NCVQ at a national level on the articulation of NVQs and GNVQs with Higher Education awards in order to facilitate credit transfer.

7. Supportive policies at a national level, and practical arrangements at a HEI level, should be introduced in order to raise the profile of student advice, guidance and counselling.

8. Efforts should be made to develop the wider potential for credit transfer between HEIs across Europe and beyond.

Recommendations and guidance for future policy

On the further development of credit systems

To Government, funding councils, HEQC and the representative bodies of institutions

9. Whilst the progress to date has been substantial across the various sectors, it has not been so successful that we can speak of a comprehensive transformation of the culture of higher education. Credit systems, modularity and other means of increasing student choice and mobility still retain an aura of peculiarity, marginality and sometimes inferiority. **We recommend** that further attention be paid by policy makers in all interested parties and responsible bodies to the means by which credit systems and flexible learning opportunities may be presented as *normal and natural* attributes of the learning experience of full-time and part-time students, studying for all taught qualifications.

On dialogue between universities and with the

Further Education sector

To HEQC and the representative bodies of institutions

10. Increased student choice within higher education is being considerably enhanced by progress on modularisation. Yet there appears to be little communication on this subject between the new and the old universities. **We recommend** that arrangements be put in place to facilitate inter-institutional dialogue so that lessons learned from the development of modularisation and credit systems in 'new' and 'old' universities can be shared efficiently across the sector.

11. The development of credit systems has now moved far beyond higher education. Progress in further education and within the NCVQ is so apparent that additional progress will need to take this into account. Again, there appears to be some discontinuity of communication between the sectors and **we recommend** that in order to improve an understanding of the potential of credit systems and modularity in higher education, institutions should be encouraged to consider experience in further education to see if lessons may be learned from this.

On the provision of credit networks in Further Education

To FEFC, FEU, and the Association for Colleges

12. Some of the most encouraging developments in credit transfer and flexible learning have been initiated by groups of academic staff themselves. This has been a distinctive feature of the 'Access movement' generally. We have been concerned to note the relatively shallow resource base sustaining many of the agencies associated with this work. Whilst notable efforts are being made by institutions in partnership, local authorities and funding councils to provide basic support for Open College Federations, other authorised validating agencies and some other consortia, we would like to see this formalised in some way. **We recommend** that the Association for Colleges, FEFC, FEU, and other appropriate representative bodies and concerned parties join with the NOCN, SCAVA, FAST to

consider a consolidation of their work in the context of support for a range of regional accreditation agencies and quality networks in further education for the promotion of credit systems and student transfer.

On further work

To the research community

13. The review has revealed areas of practice in the development of modularity and credit in higher education about which little is known or understood. Two issues have come to our attention:

- it would be helpful to have an accurate audit of the scale of current activity. This would involve the co-operation of funding councils, HESA, UCAS and individual institutions. It would be useful to know the scale of activity generally, and the specific scale of engagement with the accreditation of (uncertificated) prior and experiential learning, work-based learning and 'off-campus' activity in general.

- we have made several references to institutional regression, by which institutions embark on a process of transformation but commonly meet setbacks. We can identify some of the cultural aspects of this problem but it would be interesting for us to know more about any organisational factors shared between institutions and how these might be addressed in future.

We recommend that the research community considers how these matters might be addressed and we encourage research councils, funding councils, individual institutions and others to supply the means to make this research possible.

VII.   *Credit transfer*

Introduction

286.   We have considered the development of credit transfer separately from the general review of progress in higher and further education because it raises specific issues to which we wish to draw attention. Indeed we are aware that a certain mythology appears to have developed around the practice of credit transfer. The considerable investment in policy development has produced widespread support for credit transfer and institutional consortia have arisen to stimulate and manage anticipated demand. Moreover, national policy has emphasised its importance for national efficiency and the effective use of sector resources. We have judged it important therefore to introduce a measure of perspective and proportion into the discussion in order to assess as accurately as possible the real scale of, and the potential for, credit transfer in higher education and beyond.

287.   Credit transfer in the United Kingdom remains heavily circumscribed by traditions, regulations and the absence of a culture of mobility and choice. This is true for higher and further education. The higher education sector, having embarked upon sustained growth and increased participation, is still too recently negotiating these changes for us to be able to claim with any certainty that former patterns of organisational behaviour or individual aspirations have modified significantly. Higher education is still seen by students and academic colleagues alike as a continuous process of three years in one institution. There have been some modifications to that stereotype, of course. The recent development of 'franchising', the growth of 'off-campus' accreditation and the steady increase in part-time study are three examples where established patterns are breaking down. This has allowed developments in further education to influence those in universities and colleges to some extent. We offer some assessment of the general scale and scope of activity in the following discussion.

288.   We have attempted to distinguish as accurately as possible the various opportunities under which credit transfer does, and could in the future, take place. We have worked with simple definitions of credit accumulation and credit transfer: the former concerning many of the familiar processes of institutional life and student progression; the latter term reflecting aspects of mobility, often between institutions but also between work and higher education. We have introduced a third term, *accumulative transfer*, to capture much of the vertical progression that takes place between and within institutions, usually involving some interruption of progress, as between qualifications, or between further and higher education. For the purposes of this review, we have not undertaken a detailed explanation of terms and categories. Comments on these matters are offered in Chapter VIII.

289.   Demand for credit transfer is difficult to assess and some scepticism is often expressed concerning its scale and character. In assessing the range of circumstances under which credit transfer might take place, we have used a more generous and comprehensive definition than would be commonly employed by many colleagues within higher education. In fact the approach to credit transfer adopted here is consistent with that adopted by the Toyne Report (1979) and the expanded ECCTIS classification, which included transfer from work-based and professional training programmes. We have extended the range of circumstances to which the term may be applied in order to introduce further clarity into our understanding of the processes involved, and in the light of subsequent developments.

290.   The popular application of the term 'credit transfer' tends to eschew references to 'accumulative transfer' and instead emphasises aspects of mobility. Likely demand

is assessed in terms of the probability that students do, or will wish to, transfer from one university to another during their period of study. Accepting that a minority of all students (but a significant proportion of Open University students) will wish to exercise rights of transfer, most informed opinion appears doubtful that demand is ever likely to be substantial.

291.   The consequences of this for the further development of *credit accumulation and transfer* are most significant. If credit accumulation is accepted as the familiar process wherein students proceed normally towards qualifications, whilst credit transfer is defined as those practices which attend to minority demands for inter-institutional transfer between universities for which there appears to be little apparent demand, then institutions and government agencies may be less readily persuaded of the need for changes to prevailing arrangements. Some universities will argue credibly that the limited demand for this type of transfer may be handled by existing admissions procedures. On the other hand, it may be possible to accept the limited demand for, and practice of, *inter-university* transfer without weakening the case for the further development of credit accumulation and transfer arrangements as instruments for the extension of access, curriculum flexibility, student choice, institutional accountability and increased effectiveness in higher education.

292.   Indeed, it may be that the terms *credit accumulation* and *credit transfer* are familiar but inexact terms for capturing the meaning of those initiatives which seek to extend student flexibility, choice and mobility. It may be more appropriate in the medium-term to work towards an elision of these terms under the rubric of an alternative reference. For example, *credit-based learning, credit systems* or some other similar term would retain for the time being a reference to the instrument of 'credit' as the means of facilitating flexibility and choice, but would allow such systems to be comprehensively developed, avoiding unproductive debates about the scale of accumulation and transfer. For the present, however, the terms remain widely in use and it is necessary to explore the scale of activity in more detail.

Scale and scope of credit transfer

293.   A classification of arrangements which might broadly define the scope of credit transfer is only possible where data is available in acceptably reliable form. Wherever possible official information and statistical data has been included; in other categories, an assessment is offered, sometimes of a speculative nature, on the capacity of arrangements to provide for credit transfer.

Voluntary and involuntary transfer

294.   Student motivations for pursuing credit transfer can be differentiated firstly according to *voluntary* and *involuntary* factors. Voluntary factors describe the extent to which a student chooses to take advantage of mobility opportunities, perhaps because a course or specific module is not attractive for whatever reason; involuntary factors describe the extent to which credit transfer is the result of circumstantial constraints on the student (eg relocation, changed personal circumstances, discontinuation or academic non-completion for whatever reason). These motivational factors may cross-cut the categories below and may lend further clarity to an understanding of the processes which influence the practice of, and potential for, credit transfer.

Regional credit transfer

295.   From our investigations, credit transfer between higher education institutions in the same regional cluster or consortium appears to be minimal. Although no reliable official data exists, circumstantial evidence and the records of consortia confirm this assessment. The South-East England Consortium (SEEC) did negotiate specific transfer arrangements in 1987-88 between, for example, Middlesex Polytechnic and City Polytechnic. Thirty students engaged in 'module-borrowing' but these arrangements have lapsed and no current student transfers are arranged. The Manchester-based CONTACT consortium records no formal transfers of students since it started operations in 1986. The SCOTCAT 'consortium' remains in the relatively early stages of development and its distinctive national identity may prove to be a stimulus for transfer. At this stage there is little

evidence of formal inter-institutional transfer demand. Clearly, some students do change universities within the same region, but this is usually perceived by institutions as a fresh application for admission. The current official data systems do not enable these types of 'informal' transfers to be monitored. The conclusion to date must be that consortia have had minimal impact as brokerage agents on the propensity of students formally to negotiate credit transfer between universities within established regional clusters.

296.   There is a further dimension to inter-university regional credit transfer that needs to be documented. Not all regional or local credit transfer need depend on the existence of formal consortia. Institutions within the same metropolitan area could choose to combine aspects of their provision for the advantage of students. We have received some anecdotal evidence, supported by some student number returns to the HEFCE, that a few examples of collaborative arrangements exist. Other examples are being planned; for example, the University of Sussex and Brighton University have established a joint planning exercise to explore arrangements for the future. However there is no evidence of substantial activity in this area yet, and there would be considerable problems of administration, information flow to students, the ownership of final qualification and general matters affecting quality assurance to negotiate if it were to become more commonplace. We comment further on the consequences of developments in this area for regional policy later in this discussion.

Inter-university credit transfer

297.   There is no official data confirming the extent of student credit transfer between universities nationally. Official statistical data would record any 'transfer' as a new course registration and the student's previous institution would not be apparent in any way. As with transfer between institutions regionally, there is circumstantial and anecdotal evidence that a small minority of students do seek institutional transfers. These examples may be picked up by individual institutional admissions offices but not currently by official statistics.

298.   There are some sources of data which may indicate some of the scale of certain kinds of inter-institutional credit transfer. Firstly, Rickwood (1993) in a survey for the West Midlands region of the Open University has estimated that there are 80 transferees per annum from the Open University in the region to other institutions. Although the Open University is not able to record reliably the destinations of 'non-returners', we have estimated from the West Midlands figure that between 500 and 1,000 students transfer each year from the Open University to other universities. The Open University believes there is an equal and opposite movement also, but cannot verify this. Many of these students transfer at the completion of their Foundation programme and are picked up as 'direct entrants' to the second year of universities in England and Wales, or the appropriate year in Scotland. Secondly, the USR and the FESR report that approximately 16% of students discontinue their undergraduate degree course, of which 8% – 10% cite 'transfer' as their reason for non-completion of their current programme. This figure does not distinguish 'internal' from 'external' transfers and the institutional destination of students transferring externally is not captured by the data fields of either the USR or FESR. A further 11% of discontinuing students cite 'interruption' as the source, indicating an intention to return when personal circumstances permit (eg after medical or maternity leave is completed).

299.   Interestingly, the academic research published on student non-completion rates (eg Johnes, Taylor and the University of Lancaster group) analyses the variables that correlate with student discontinuation but does not seem to consider the character of academic course structures as a possible variable. This is surprising when it is known that 53% of non-completing students leave within the first 15 months of their course. Although this figure can be explained by the fact that student finance regulations require that students must make a decision on course commitment by fifteen months in order to avoid penalties on future maintenance entitlement, it still leaves unanswered the questions concerning the reasons for changes in student commitment to

courses. It would be interesting to know, from micro-analytical surveys of student behaviour, whether reasons for non-completion by reason of unhappiness with initial course choice, and derivatives of this, would be mitigated by increased choice and flexibility in a broader first year programme. **We recommend** further research specifically on this matter.

300. We are therefore forced to the conclusion that, whilst some individual inter-institutional transfer does currently take place, there are no means currently available for accurately assessing the scale. Furthermore, it is impossible to distinguish between voluntary and involuntary credit transfer.

Internal transfer in universities

301. There is no official data which indicates the precise character of internal transfer within institutions. The matter is also clouded by conceptual problems. The data that exists records internal transfers between 'courses' in a institution. This implies that a student changes registration status, or that a student registers for a higher (lower) qualification than at initial entry. Such data makes little allowance for the flexible opportunities permitted by the general introduction of modular programmes, some of them specifically designed to encourage deferred choice and decision over destination qualification. Data on mixed subject or combined studies programmes is collected by both USR and the FESR but these programmes do not necessarily deliver opportunities for internal mobility. The HEFCE currently continues the practice of the PCFC in monitoring by modular programmes, but only where universities choose to record their annual returns in this form. This practice may be discontinued in the near future and we would regret this if it were not replaced by a suitable alternative arrangement. In fact, the funding councils may well be in a position to advise on alternative methodologies for reporting student behaviour following the recommendations of this report (Chapter XI).

302. Again, circumstantial evidence suggests that the demand for, and practice of, internal mobility and transfer are extensive within those academic programmes which

facilitate them. For example, the monitoring of student choice and mobility within the undergraduate modular credit scheme at Liverpool John Moores University between 1988 and 1991 indicated that initially 25% of students were retaining flexibility over their destination qualification, rising to 40% three years later as the scheme matured and students began to understand its facilities. Other universities, which operate more or less extensive elective programmes, have similar informal assessments of internal mobility, ranging up to a 25% turnover rate on initial programmes.

Inter-qualification transfer

303. Effective internal transfer from lower to higher qualifications (ie. from certificate or diploma programmes to Degree programmes) cannot be formally determined from official data. The capacity for such transfer, both internally and externally, is enormous. Transfer from BTEC programmes to university degree qualifications is potentially available to 132,000 students currently registered for HND and HNC qualifications. Moreover, there are 7,600 students registered for lower awards, CertHE and DipHE qualifications, in universities and colleges in England and Wales who, on successful completion of their programmes, could also claim credit for transfer towards degree programmes.

304. Furthermore, there are 743,000 continuing education students in (ex-UFC) universities, many currently on part-time, non award-bearing programmes, who may be attracted to the opportunities open to them as their courses achieve accredited status. Some universities may find it attractive to marshal their continuing education cohort via internal credit transfer arrangements to enable a regular throughput of part-time degree and diploma students. In the ex-PCFC universities, there are also a further 101,000 students registered on sub-degree programmes for various professional qualifications, and 12,000 students registered on INSET courses.

305. There may be a case for suggesting that, notwithstanding the distinctive characteristics of certificate and diploma programmes, students who successfully complete two full years of higher education (or

the part-time equivalent) up to second year level have demonstrated more than adequate compensation for any entry deficiencies that they may have possessed initially, and are suitable candidates for automatic transfer on application to appropriate second and third year degree programmes. This accumulative transfer potential from diploma to degree may be further compounded by claims for transfer from students with NCVQ-derived qualifications, particularly at NVQ/SVQ Levels 4 and 5, obtained perhaps via employer training programmes. Students with such qualifications may reasonably seek access to various levels of the more vocationally focused degree courses in universities, negotiating credit transfer.

Further/higher education credit transfer

306.   Transfer from further to higher education may be described as a typical case of accumulative transfer. The practice is reflective of the experience in the United States where transfer from the two-year junior colleges to the four-year senior schools (ie. universities) is the dominant form of credit transfer. The growth of student progression from further to higher education has been increasing noticeably since the late 1970s but the rate has accelerated since 1987. Over 51,000 students transfer from further to higher education in the United Kingdom via one of three routes:

- **'first route'** progression from 'A' levels to degree and diploma programmes;

- **'second route'** progression from BTEC and SCOTVEC vocationally-focused programmes and progression from NVQ/SVQs and GNVQs at Level 3;

- **'third route'** progression from Access courses; progression from 'franchised' programmes and 'Level 0' derivatives.

307.   The 1987 White Paper opened up the 'third route' of Access courses and other alternative entry mechanisms. There are now nearly 20,000 students formally registered on 600 recognised Access courses and there may be approaching 1,000 Access courses in total. The majority of students are formally accumulating academic credit through schemes validated by

Open College Networks and similar Authorised Validating Agencies. Of these, over 7,000 are recorded by UCAS as admissions to higher education although 9,000 per annum has been estimated (Davies, 1994). Perhaps the most significant development has been the growth of higher education programmes offered under licence (ie. franchised) in further education colleges. Currently there are between 8,000 and 10,000 additional students formally enrolled on franchised higher education undergraduate and diploma courses according to one estimate (Bird 1993) although the HEFCE claims to fund places for 25,000. Students are also enrolled upon higher level programmes which are traditionally located in some further education colleges.

308.   Subsequent policy initiatives to enhance entry via the 'second route' of vocational qualifications have focused attention on the development of NVQs, GNVQs and their Scottish equivalents. In 1993, 70,000 new students in further education will be committed to programmes leading to GNVQs, some expecting transfer into higher education. We estimate that demand for transfer to higher education will reach 20,000 students in the next two years at current rates of participation. There may be a supplementary figure to be derived from NVQ and GNVQ holders seeking transfer at higher levels into higher education, but no assessment of this demand is yet available.

On-campus/off-campus transfer

309.   Transfer and exchange between different 'sites' of learning have expanded significantly over the past few years. Transfer arrangements involve students earning academic credit for formal learning outside the university, in an employment or work-based setting, or via distance learning, and being able to count that credit towards higher qualifications. Arrangements may be clustered into three groups:

- **employment-based** credit transfer, where the student is employed by a company, gains credit for accredited company training and, registering with a university, accumulates this credit towards the completion of higher qualifications;

- **work-based** credit transfer, where students are formally resident at, or registered with, a university but gain credit towards their qualifications via learning from work-based placements, internships or similar arrangements;

- **distance learning** as credit transfer, where the student may be learning independently, supported by formal distance learning technologies, but may wish to claim credit towards a qualification from a university.

310.   The growth of arrangements for the accreditation of company training programmes has been significant over the past few years. The numbers involved are small currently but the company-university accreditation arrangements have given confidence that further developments are possible. Examples of such schemes would be the IBM-University of Portsmouth, the Woolwich Building Society-University of Greenwich, the Allied-Lyons-University of Bradford and the Ford ASSET- Anglia University schemes. The Ford Employee Development Assistance Programme (EDAP) would be a variant of these arrangements. The Council for Industry and Higher Education has itself published case studies of similar commendable examples (*Collaborative courses in higher education*, CIHE, 1990).

311.   The development of work-based learning for academic credit has been extensively promoted by the Employment Department initiatives since 1989. Arrangements now cover the award of academic credit for sandwich placements, professional placements and formal work-based internships. An example of the latter would be the arrangements established by Liverpool John Moores University, the University of Liverpool and Chester College for the award of academic credit for work-based learning on non-sandwich and non-vocational degree programmes.

312.   Interestingly, in research conducted for the DFE, SOED, and the Welsh Office (DFE 1993), the Centre for Higher Education Studies at the University of London Institute of Education estimated that there are nearly 4,000 providers of higher and further education in the independent sector, of which 425 are large companies and 320 are public service organisations. They estimated that 31,000 students are studying for higher education qualifications in the independent sector with a further 29,000 engaged with 'A' levels, ONDs or similar pre-entry qualifications. They provide no estimate of the numbers involved in company training accredited by a higher education institution.

Credit transfer between employers, and between professional body programmes

313.   We received written contributions from some employers, and particularly from professional bodies, which pointed to the opportunities that could arise if credit systems were to become more comprehensive. Employer-employer credit transfer would be attractive to a number of employees. Parenthesising for a moment the problems of stimulating labour market mobility, some employers would welcome in principle the idea that employees could be attracted to them bearing credit from earlier training which, together with subsequent credit for further training from the new employer, could be aggregated towards higher qualifications. The same argument applies to inter-professional body programmes. Students gaining credit for certain professional body training could with advantage have that credit counted towards qualifications awarded by another professional body in a contiguous professional field.

314.   We have not been able to identify any such arrangements at present amongst employers, and their development would depend on the successful operation of quality assurance arrangements within a national credit framework. We have received some indications that informal recognition of credit does take place between some professional bodies, particularly in Engineering and in Finance. We have not been able to explore this as we would have wished, and we believe that further work on this matter could form part of the closer partnership arrangements between the HEQC and professional bodies that we referred to in Chapter VI.

Post-graduate transfer

315.   Some limited post-graduate credit transfer does exist. The Integrated Graduate Development Schemes in Engineering and Technology have involved joint institutional co-operation. Teacher training programmes encourage certain forms of credit transfer and exchange, whilst module-sharing between local institutions takes place in a limited form. A more extensive engagement with post-graduate credit transfer could occur if the pattern of higher education provision settles into a stable and recognisable distribution of strengths. Particular universities might, under such conditions, become regional centres of postgraduate research. All universities could offer post-graduate credit, but students could find advantage in accumulating credit towards qualifications via credit transfer. Currently, such activity is limited, informal and non-documented. We can only estimate the potential.

International credit transfer

316.   These arrangements are examined in more detail in Chapter XIV. In general, it is possible to report that demand for international credit transfer appears to be rising, with no indication that prospects for its further development are becoming any easier. Three focuses for international credit transfer may be identified:

- **European transfer,** for which demand is high from British students but higher still from incoming students. Notwithstanding the pace of progress towards closer formal co-operation within the European Union, it is possible to estimate a rising tide of potential demand for general credit transfer from Britain to mainland Europe, including Eastern Europe;

- **Trans-Atlantic transfer,** of which there are long-established patterns of co-operation but for which demand remains suppressed by resource constraints and disharmonies between national systems. In one sense, however, trans-Atlantic credit transfer and exchange with the United States should come naturally to Britain if a national credit framework is developed;

- **Global transfer:** the development of credit systems in other countries outside Europe and North America remains uneven. The initial steps towards the creation of such systems have been taken in New Zealand and Australia, and early developments appear to be underway in India (amongst Engineering Institutes) and in South Africa. Elsewhere a World Bank report (Regel, 1992) reports that Singapore, Malaysia, Thailand and Senegal have introduced credit systems into their higher education institutions.

317.   Whether by formal introduction or by the adoption of new patterns of student choice, universities throughout the world can be expected to adopt variants of credit systems over the next two decades. The impact on the 'globalisation' of higher education cannot easily be assessed, but it is possible to imagine a much more expanded and electronically integrated international system of higher education, within which credit transfer of learning achievement will play a prominent part. We may need to suspend our assumptions that international credit transfer means physical relocation if a network of provision focused on multi-media, electronic and satellite technologies is established. Developments of this kind in India and Australia suggest that progress will be more rapid than we may imagine.

318.   In the summary Table 21, we offer some estimate of the total potential for credit transfer. This information does not contain data for internal mobility and transfer, which we cannot assess with any reliability. It would not be helpful to draw too many conclusions from this data as it stands, since the apparent extensive scale of potential demand is severely circumscribed in practice by admissions regulations, funded places and quality assurance matters. It is also not possible to make any reliable estimate of the demand for accredited qualifications amongst the continuing education population of the extra-mural and Continuing Education departments in the older universities. On a related issue, we

Table 21: Estimates of the potential demand for credit transfer

Source	Total volume[1]	Eligible volume p/a[2]	Estimated demand p/a[3]
HND/HNC to Degree	132,000	60,000	45,000
DipHE/CertHE to Degree	7,600	4,600	4,000
FE to HE transfer (general)	100,000	80,000	51,000[4]
Access Courses to HE	20,000	12,000	9,000[5]
'Franchise' Courses to HE	10,000	8,000	8,000
Continuing education	743,000	500,000[6]	150,000[6]
Professional qualifications	101,000	60,000	40,000[7]
Company training and independent sector	31,000[8] 16,000	10,000 7,000	10,000 5,000
Uncertificated prior learning	Substantial	1,000	1,000+[9]
Open University/Sector	Substantial	800	800[10]
Sector/Open University	Substantial	5000[10]	800
Inter-HE Transfer (f-t)	5,000	4,500	4,500[11]
Inter-mode Transfer (p-t)	445,000	350,000[12]	100,000[12]
Postgraduate Transfer	189,000	150,000	15,000[13]
International Transfer (HE)	Substantial	Substantial	Substantial
Inter-FE Transfer	Significant	Significant	Significant
(G)NVQ Transfer (Level 3+)	Substantial	Substantial	Significant[14]

Notes

1. Total eligible students in category, but excluding the principle that all students are potentially transferees
2. Estimated volume annually eligible for transfer, assuming open opportunities, often on completion of current qualification
3. Estimated annual demand, offset from eligible volume to account for non take-up of opportunities
4. UCCA/PCAS estimates for England, Wales and Scotland; degree and sub-degree
5. UCCA/PCAS estimate = 7,115 (1993) but with direct entry 9,000 is likely (Davies, 1994)
6. Estimate of CE students choosing to follow accredited programmes, and annual number seeking transfer from lower to higher level qualifications at various levels
7. Estimate of demand for HE degree-level qualifications from largely sub-degree professional awards
8. DFE estimates of volume of higher level (31,000) and pre-HE level (16,000) in 'independent' and company sector
9. Demand may exceed eligibility due to character of the claim for credit; estimate = 50 HEIs x 20 students p/a
10. Open University estimates, extrapolated from one region; sector-OU transfer = Walton Hall applications
11. Estimate = 300,000 x 15% attrition, of which 10% 'transfer' = 5,000 x 90% take-up
12. Estimate assumes any year transfer for all part-time degree and diploma students x 25% annual take-up
13. Estimate = 10% transfer demand
14. Assumes transfer from GNVQ3 to HE; and development of transfer between academic programmes and higher level NVQs and GNVQs

Sources: *DFE Statistical Bulletins, 1992-93; DFE Statistics of Education 1992-93; USR University Statistics, 1992; UCCA/PCAS Admissions Survey, 1993; Bird J (1993); Davies P (1994); project estimates*

have proposals to make in Chapter IX on the character of staged awards, sub-degree and interim qualifications.

Consortia and credit transfer

319. The promotion of credit accumulation and transfer through consortia arrangements has been assumed hitherto to be the optimum organising arrangement. The development of consortia has been an aspiration of recent policy statements. The Council for Industry and Higher Education has supported such developments and the 1987 White Paper: *Meeting the challenge* commended the further development of credit transfer initiatives, commenting:

'Credit transfer schemes provide help to extend higher education opportunities. Schemes can operate within consortia of institutions, or more widely through such means as the CNAA Credit Accumulation and Transfer Scheme. The Government welcomes such initiatives...' (2.23)

National Advisory Body and consortia

320. In 1988, the National Advisory Body published the report of its Consortia and Regional Structures Group which had been convened by the Continuing Education Standing Committee (CESC) under the chairmanship of Lord Perry. This is the only occasion of which we are aware when the implications of consortia for credit transfer have been previously considered by an authoritative source. The terms of reference of the committee required it to focus on collaborative arrangements for the extension of continuing education and training rather than on more general consortia which were developing at the time for the promotion of wider access and inter-institutional transfer. In short, the committee was influenced by the PICKUP initiatives of the period, although its observations have consequences for the discussion here.

321. The report considered four examples of consortia: training consortia designed to co-ordinate access to, and marketing of, short courses (Coventry Consortium and CONTACT

in Manchester); a Language Export (LX) Centre at Aston University; and a staff development consortium in Oxford. It identified further types of consortia which were active in the field: *subject-specific* consortia such as JUPITER which seeks to co-ordinate technology training and transfer, and *client-specific* consortia which focus on the training needs of a particular industry. The report identified 58 PICKUP consortia, of which approximately one half were committed to general training needs and ten involved a university. One consortium for credit transfer was mentioned: that operated by the University of Southampton in association with regional teacher training colleges. The report commented:

'Credit transfer is potentially very important to consortia. Such systems could help to place co-operation between member institutions on a sounder footing and make the marketing of courses easier... Some direction needs to be instilled into this field... it may well be that if a funding initiative in credit transfer is launched, consortia will be major agents of change.'

322. From our investigations, this appears to have been an over-optimistic assessment of potential, particularly for those consortia which were focused upon the provision of retraining and short course provision. Indeed the report did conclude more soberly when it observed:

'It seemed (to the committee) that consortia are supply-led rather than demand-led. Industry is not particularly interested in consortia as theoretical structures, only as sources of supply and 'consumer choice'. This carries with it the danger that unless provision has some element of planning, an absolute surplus of consortia will emerge and some will survive only by chasing grants rather than actually providing training.'

323. The distinction the report made between supply-led and demand-led consortia is most important for our discussion. It helps to distinguish between the functions of those consortia currently operating to promote the further development of credit systems. With these observations in mind, we have investigated the activities of various consortia to establish how far they have in fact been able to

justify the optimism placed in them. In particular, we have focused our attention upon the extent to which consortia provide, *in addition* to collegial professional networks, concrete evidence that they are able to promote increased student mobility with transferable credit.

Consortia: operating principles

324.	To establish whether consortia are effective in assisting the further development of credit transfer, it is necessary to consider what consortia generally attempt to achieve. The principles governing the effective operation of consortia should be as relevant to groups of institutions conspiring to promote regional commercial development as they should be for the promotion of credit transfer.

325.	The principle difficulty with the establishment and maintenance of consortia in higher education (for credit transfer or otherwise) is that they go against the grain, acting contrary to the accumulated experience of institutions habituated to the exercise of academic and professional autonomy. The establishment of *'value-adding partnerships'* has not hitherto distinguished the activities of higher education beyond the well-documented experiences of research and scholarly collaboration. Where consortia have been developed and supported, there appears to have been an attempt to assess their purpose and strategy from an early stage. Those that survive their infancy do so because a minimum energy has been generated to sustain further progress. In such conditions, institutions appear to accept that a 'pooling of autonomy' in a specifically focused arena of activity poses acceptable levels of constraint on institutional autonomy without prejudice to the rights of institutions to act separately if needs change.

326.	Moreover, the creation of consortia may be seen as a productive complement to an otherwise competitive relationship between individual institutions, although it appears questionable that such altruism ever outlives indications of competitive disadvantage. The questions which need to be addressed in the assessment of consortia are indicated in Table 22. Where consortia are able to provide successful answers over the short and medium

term, they appear to be able to find the motivation necessary for continued support. This is then further sustained in direct proportion to the extent to which the consortium meets the self-interested needs of members. This is usually provided via appropriate support services or in the availability of otherwise inaccessible professional expertise. There is a final motivation which sustains consortia, at least into the medium-term: the shared enthusiasm of colleagues working often in areas of novel development. This aspect of consortium activity is more closely aligned to the research coalitions that develop between university colleagues. Committed to finding solutions for complex problems, individuals find comfort in co-operative association. Initial developments in arrangements for credit accumulation and transfer may take on the attributes of intellectual problems for those colleagues

---

Table 22:
Problems of consortia operation

- Can the consortium provide better expertise than might be available in any single institution, and will that expertise be democratically accessible?

- Can the consortium improve the quality of delivery of a given service, producing definitive gains for those using consortium services?

- Can the services offered by a consortium be more cost-effective?

- Can the consortium extend market opportunities for a given service? If so, will all consortium members benefit adequately from an expanded market?

- Is the consortium established on a sound financial footing, capable of sustaining itself over time by commercial activity?

- Can the consortium provide effective management? Will it be able to deliver member institutions in support of arrangements and policies, and can it establish effective lines of accountability?

committed to further progress. Co-operation may be the only means by which individuals can feel that their initiatives, undertaken often in hostile and isolated circumstances, generate the respect of their professional peers.

327.   In general terms, consortia appear to fulfil two important functions: *developmental* and *brokerage* functions (see Table 23). These functions align closely with 'supply-led' and 'demand-led' orientations of consortia to which we have made reference earlier. The successful performance of these functions needs to be inspected against some significant general constraints. Whilst *development* functions may be self-sustained by the enthusiasm of active individuals, requiring little formal resource input, *brokerage* functions usually require substantial organisational commitment with revenue implications and a management and resource infrastructure. Moreover, short-term institutional coalitions can be assembled in order to bid for specifically targeted resources. Universities and colleges have gained experience of these expedient arrangements in response to initiatives from the European Community, research and funding councils, and government departments. The viability of the short-term coalition is usually in direct proportion to the scale of funds on offer. In short, many consortia develop because

---

Table 23: Functions of consortia

Development functions

Consortia may provide useful forums for key activists, thereby generating mutual confidence and respect amongst particular individuals, and the resolution of shared problems. They may help in raising the level of individual capability, and thereby the capability of institutions.

Brokerage functions

Consortia may provide services to particular groups of 'clients' - students, employers, etc - on a collaborative basis (e.g. marketing courses, contracting employers, managing student enquiries, negotiating credit transfer). As mature or tightly-focused organisations, they may be capable of specific tasks.

---

contributing members feel the need to join a professional federation; they are not necessarily driven by an objective assessment of market demand.

328.   To respond to anticipated or manifest market demand, and to provide services to client groups, longer-term arrangements are necessary. Where consortia embark on the provision of such services, they will need to have addressed some difficult issues. These flow from the consequences of attempts to provide formal services on behalf of a voluntary association, the formal standing of which has often to be negotiated:

- **Consortium ownership:** with what freedom of action and with what authority does the consortium act? Who owns the consortium and what responsibilities do members assume as a consequence of their involvement? What rights are defined for the consortium separately from its individual constituents?

- **Rules of operation:** these usually emerge from action and condense into conventions and codes of practice. However, this relative fluidity raises important issues for the authority upon which services are offered to client groups. If promises are made to client groups, as a reasonable consequence of the *raison d'etre* of the consortium, but these are not honoured or recognised by any part of a large university, it becomes directly prejudicial to the brokerage function of the consortium.

- **Central organisation:** some consortia operate with, at most, a small central service unit; the majority operate with no central organisation. Those consortia which have favoured the 'weak centre' model face problems concerning the scope and scale of the brokerage service they can offer. 'Weak centre' models which rely on personnel support principally from one institutional member appear to be less durable than those which establish 'independent' central units. There is no evidence that any consortium has persuaded its constituents of the merits of a 'strong centre' model. In keeping with contemporary management practice, and constrained by the availability of resources, this appears to be true nationally as well as regionally.

329. The successful operation of consortia seems to rely on the extent to which arrangements provide some additionality to the services and operations of individually subscribing institutions. Additionality factors will be determined more or less benignly by voluntarily associating institutions, but consortia do not appear able to define a purpose in conditions of competitive disadvantage. Moreover there is no evidence that consortia can successfully aspire, without legislation or formally pooled sovereignty, to a supra-institutional role, taking unto themselves the functions that would otherwise be discharged by individual universities and colleges. The one exception to this, examined below, might be the former Council for National Academic Awards (CNAA), a 'statutory consortium' in the sense that it held formal responsibility for the academic affairs of the former polytechnics and colleges. Its unique position in this regard allowed it to undertake significant brokerage activities for client groups, particularly in the promotion of credit accumulation and transfer for employers and professional bodies.

A review of CAT consortia

330. From the general analysis offered above, we now consider the performance of consortia operating specifically for the promotion of credit accumulation and transfer. A number of different models have been investigated (see also Table 24):

- consortia operating exclusively in **higher education nationally** (CNAA Scheme, SCOTCAT, NATCAT), in **higher education regionally** (SEEC, Northern Federation) and in **higher education locally** (CONTACT);

- consortia operating exclusively in higher education, **subject-based** (professional training consortia, CCETSW, Health Service);

- **further and higher education** consortia operating **nationally** and **locally** (NOCN and OCFs) and operating **regionally** (London Together);

- consortia operating exclusively in **further education nationally** (FEU Credit Network, Welsh Fforwm);

- consortia operating in **higher education internationally** (TEXT).

331. A number of other consortia are active from time to time, or are emergent, and may be described within the categories identified above. Amongst these, we have identified the Welsh CATS Forum (national HE), HESIN, MIDCAT and South-West CAT (regional HE), Yorkshire & Humberside Association for FHE (regional FHE) and an emergent Open College Network in Northern Ireland.

CNAA CAT scheme

332. The CNAA CAT Scheme might be loosely described as a consortium arrangement since institutions, including ex-UFC universities, could choose to subscribe to its arrangements. However, the CNAA possessed a unique advantage, irreplicable in other consortia, in that it held statutory authority for the degree-awarding powers of its member institutions, and could itself make awards. The CNAA Scheme, from its inception in 1985, offered services to prospective students (including employees) which encouraged its role as a brokerage agency. The CATS Registry was able to advise student enquirers and negotiate their progress through the programmes of institutions subscribing to the CNAA scheme. It was a most important feature of its work that the CNAA scheme was always advisory and did not seek to replace or constrain the development of individual institutional schemes.

333. In the course of its work, the CNAA unit was able to provide advice to upwards of 500 students annually, most of whom were happy subsequently to approach individual institutions. Between 50 and 100 remained directly registered with the CNAA

Table 24: Consortia and credit transfer: comparative characteristics

Consortium features	CNAA CATS	SCOTCAT	South-East England Consortium	Northern Federation	Subject Consortia	Nat. Open College Network	London Together	FEU Network	TEXT
Sector	Higher	Higher	Higher	Higher	Higher	Further and Higher	Further and Higher	Further	Higher
Activity	Development and brokerage	Development (+ brokerage?)	Development and brokerage	Development	Development (+ brokerage?)	Development	Development (+ brokerage)	Development	Development (+ brokerage?)
Student Transfer	Yes. 40–100 via central Registry or negotiated entry to institutions	Yes. Seeks to encourage transfer, but no results yet	Yes. 20–30 via negotiated entry or inter-institutional transfer	No. Doubts demand exists and has no systems for this	Yes but no clear data. Means unclear also	Yes, via national CAT agreement, but no results yet available	Yes, but likely to promote vertical transfer + employment transfer	Not principal objective at this stage. Intra-institutional transfer likely	Yes, but no evidence attributable to consortium. Means unclear
Membership	Voluntary association, subscribing to CNAA Scheme	Negotiated participation, subscribing to CNAA Scheme	Formal subscription, subscribing to CNAA Scheme or compatible	Formal subscription, no preferred scheme	Voluntary association, no preferred scheme	Voluntary association, subscribing to NOCN Scheme	Probably by voluntary association; unclear yet	Invited voluntary association, subscribing to FEU Scheme	Formal, subscribing to ECTS compatible Scheme
Institutions	Most universities and colleges of HE in England & Wales	All universities and institutions of HE in Scotland	Twenty-five universities and colleges of HE	Fifteen universities and colleges of HE; one Health Authority	Indeterminable and variable	Twenty-four Open College Federations and similar consortia	Potentially all London FE\HE institutions, and employers, TECs etc	Over 200 further education colleges in England & Wales; some TECS	Various international institutions; no formal standing in other states
Prospects	Ceased formal operation	Good, but impact emerging	Good, but transfer role unclear	Subject to internal review in 1994	Unclear; possibly very positive role	Good; continues to expand	Embryonic; will face difficulties; otherwise good	Good; demand to join very high	Unclear; possibly very positive role

CATS Registry, where their package of credits covered achievement at more than one institution. The relatively low numbers that remained centrally registered with the CNAA reflected the policy of the Council to refer onwards to institutions wherever possible students who came forward for credit transfer. Only in cases where this could not be arranged for whatever reason did students remain registered with the CNAA.

334.   The CATS Registry offered a second service, namely to adjudicate on the quality of learning being undertaken on employer courses and within the orbit of professional training. The CNAA CAT Scheme provided the initial steps towards a national credit framework by supplying a simple means of calibrating credit by educational and academic 'value' of 'off-campus' learning achievement. A committee was established to investigate and authenticate the quality of learning and to assign a credit rating against a series of levels of academic progression. The CNAA Scheme is explained in Chapter IX. In the five years or so of activity, the CNAA CATS Registry was successful in bringing into the orbit of higher education a large number of training programmes from employers and professional bodies. It was also successful in extending those activities to a significant number of institutions, offering developmental support when invited. Of those universities currently developing institutional schemes, some of them varying slightly from the CNAA scheme, all are compatible with it. Of other schemes developing through different agencies, these remain largely compatible.

335.   The CNAA CAT scheme, as a 'consortium', appears to have had more success in its developmental function than in its brokerage function. Its ability to identify and stimulate a market for credit transfer, at least for students mobile between institutions, was limited. Its most enduring achievements are likely to be seen as its success in broadening the definition of legitimate learning to achievements gained in work and professional practice, thereby encouraging credit transfer from work to university programmes, and to its success in promoting the advantages of credit systems widely throughout the United Kingdom

SCOTCAT

336.   The SCOTCAT Scheme was established in 1989 by the CNAA through its Scottish Office. It drew together the centrally funded academic institutions and the Open University in Scotland and its regulations were formally approved by the Council in 1990. By 1992 all universities and institutions of higher education in Scotland had agreed to subscribe to the arrangements proposed by the scheme. Common arrangements have been negotiated with SCOTVEC.

337.   The characteristics of the scheme have been defined largely in keeping with the CNAA CAT Scheme operating in England and Wales, modified appropriately to accommodate the structure and pattern of academic programme provision in Scottish institutions. This has involved modifications relevant to the four-year undergraduate degree awarded by Scottish universities. In common with the CNAA's arrangements for England and Wales, the focus of the SCOTCAT Scheme has been to facilitate inter-institutional student mobility, to promote work with employers and professional bodies, and to offer student guidance and academic staff development.

338.   The SCOTCAT Scheme also provided for regulations governing the central registration of students, although these arrangements are now subject to the circumstances contingent on the dissolution of the CNAA and may not be retained under subsequent arrangements. It has also been the means by which inter-institutional consultative events have been organised; conferences and seminars involving institutional representatives, employers and professional bodies have been sponsored; and interested parties have been brought together to share common experiences and resolve shared problems. Its work so far has focused upon its role as a development agency, assisting the work of institutions. There is no evidence yet that it is being required to offer particular services as a broker of inter-institutional student mobility and transfer.

339.   Currently SCOTCAT has focused its attention upon the formation of inter-institutional subject groups. Elsewhere within the 'consortium' individual institutions have

begun to develop credit transfer arrangements. Glasgow Caledonian University has emphasised the promotion of credit transfer into its part-time programmes, which were the first to be validated formally using the SCOTCAT framework. At Paisley University, we have been informed that over 1,500 students have been admitted to programmes with credit from sources outside the university.

National Association for CAT

340. The National Association for CAT (NATCAT) emerged in 1990 from the National Association of Regional Consortia for CAT (NARCCAT), a consortium of consortia representatives, largely from higher education and drawing heavily on the existence of SEEC. The original association, from 1987, was an attempt to draw together representatives from various existing and embryonic regional CAT consortia to exchange views and inform institutional and national debates in and around the further development of a national credit framework. For a time it provided a helpful forum to sustain individuals and groups who were striving to promote credit-based developments, but its work was hampered by the tenuous existence of many regional consortia, with the notable exception of SEEC. By 1990 it had become difficult to define an agenda for a consortium of consortia, and the emergence of NATCAT was an effort to move forward in a new direction.

341. NATCAT committed itself to working with institutions on a national basis, focusing particularly upon academic subject clusters. In some ways this reflected the practices that were now being requested by some professional and employer organisations, especially in the areas of health and the caring professions. Various seminars and conferences have been organised. Membership has been by voluntary subscription but it appears to be informal. An absence of resources, and changes of personal commitments, have hindered the further development of this consortium, which remains fitfully active. Its national role is now unclear.

South-East England Consortium (SEEC)

342. The South-East England Consortium is the most well-established regional consortium committed to the common pursuit of credit accumulation and transfer. It originated in 1986 as a regional response to the early work of the CNAA CATS Registry, initially drawing into association seventeen higher education institutions. These early members were all former polytechnics and colleges of higher education, but since 1990 many of the regional ex-UFC universities have been brought into membership. The consortium is sustained largely by institutional subscriptions, but also by income from conferences and similar events, contracts awarded by external funding sources, and fees from consultancy to employers, professional bodies and other agencies.

343. SEEC has always been overtly committed to the promotion of credit transfer between regional institutions, publishing in 1986 an extensive Handbook outlining a comprehensive list of all credit-bearing programmes from its contributing institutions. Accepting the basic features of the emerging CNAA CAT Scheme, SEEC offered students at this time the facility to engage in 'module borrowing', taking modules from institutions or other programmes and counting them towards their registered programme. Such programmes, potentially constructed from modules at different institutions within the consortium, were to be united through the medium of 'consortium credit', a credit system accepted by all associating institutions for the purposes of establishing common credit ratings for academic programmes. A central office was established to provide co-ordination and development, and to offer advice and information on credit-based learning opportunities throughout the consortium.

344. This initial commitment to the facilitation and promotion of inter-institutional credit transfer was predicated upon the assumptions, held similarly by the initiators of the CNAA CAT Scheme, that economic conditions would conspire to produce a much more mobile labour force and that part-time students in particular would benefit from a regional credit system based on the mutual recognition of student achievement amongst consortium institutions. In more optimistic formulations, some SEEC representatives

anticipated the possibility that the Consortium might need to become a qualification-awarding body in its own right, as students took advantage of the inter-institutional opportunities available to them.

345. In fact, the take-up of inter-institutional credit transfer opportunities through the consortium has proved to be significantly less than expected. Only thirty students engaged in the 'module-borrowing' of approximately fifty modules or half-modules. It has proved difficult to make arrangements whereby prospective students could be advised of the academic pre-requisites for modules at different institutions; it became impossible to provide adequate timetable information on the availability of modules; and reliable assessment and credit transfer arrangements have been difficult to secure. It is unclear whether these factors have suppressed demand for credit transfer, or whether there is simply limited student demand at this time or for these types of arrangements. In the event, as a brokerage agency for the promotion and management of student mobility, SEEC has had limited success.

346. Since 1988 SEEC has directed its attention more to its role as a development agency, seeking to encourage individual institutions to contribute their own initiatives towards a regional network of flexible provision. This policy objective has had more success. In particular, SEEC has sustained a programme of influential conferences, seminars, workshops and staff development events on a range of matters associated with credit-based learning. It has developed a focus prioritising the development of 'off-campus' credit-based learning, particularly emphasising the accreditation of in-company training, work-based learning and joint enterprises with TECs. It remains an important focal point for institutions seeking advice on access and credit-based developments; it maintains close liaison with ECCTIS; it sustains an influential range of working groups, assisting in the clarification of matters related to the operation of credit accumulation and transfer arrangements within its member institutions; and it continues to offer consultancy and informed advice to institutions, employers and other agencies.

347. As a voluntary association of institutions, SEEC has proved resilient and imaginative in its promotion of policies and initiatives associated with credit-based learning; its success has been founded upon its role as a development agency. In its capacity to act as a broker of student mobility, SEEC has not yet been able to identify or stimulate a market for inter-institutional credit transfer within higher education.

Northern Federation for CAT

348. The Northern Federation was established in 1992, inviting formal association by subscription from universities and colleges in the region for a two-year pilot arrangement to explore the role for a regional CATS consortium. It emerged from a looser and more informal network of institutional practitioners, concerned to ensure that momentum for credit-based developments in the region was sustained and enhanced following the termination of the CNAA and in the light of mounting institutional interest. Institutional membership is currently invited on the basis that universities and colleges must have, or must be in the process of establishing, formally recognised credit-based arrangements. This definition of eligibility for membership has been introduced to circumscribe the activities of the consortium in its pilot stage, inviting participation from those institutions which seek to use the consortium principally to resolve practical problems of implementation and operation.

349. The consortium has eschewed the promotion of inter-institutional credit transfer, believing there is insufficient evidence of demand and doubting whether a consortium is the most appropriate means of managing such activities at this stage. Currently there are fifteen universities and colleges in membership, together with one Regional Health Authority; one ex-UFC university has joined as an associate member. The consortium has organised a series of conferences and seminars on matters of current concern in credit-based learning; the conferences in particular have been open to all institutions regionally and nationally. At this stage the consortium aspires to be a development agency, informing institutional

policies and practice and inviting voluntary association on the basis of perceived need. The Northern Federation does not require adherence to a particular credit scheme and it has no plans currently to broker student inter-institutional transfer. It is committed to internal review by August 1994 by which time a decision will be made by contributing members on the basis of value-for-money whether to continue with a formal consortium or to dissolve it back into an informal network.

CONTACT

350.   CONTACT is a consortium, established in 1986 by the association of the four universities in Manchester and the Manchester Business School, the principal purpose of which has been the organisation and promotion of student opportunities in Continuing Education and Training. Largely directed to the stimulation of vocational up-dating programmes, CONTACT initially aspired to facilitate significant inter-institutional credit transfer for students seeking specific part-time, short course and other education and training opportunities. Between 1986 and 1987 it commissioned a number of reports on aspects of credit transfer, modularisation, distance learning and employer contacts, frequently drawing on international experience. In their various ways, these papers were exemplary in the extent to which they helped to inform a general understanding of the difficulties inherent in sustaining inter-institutional transfer arrangements.

351.   CONTACT has subsequently developed as an agency for the promotion and marketing of multi-institutional opportunities for continuing education and training. It has not been able to identify and sustain a market for inter-institutional student transfer; prospective students access the learning opportunities of the various universities, but with no apparent demand for credit-accumulated qualifications. CONTACT has also been unable to resolve inter-institutional differences of practice, organisation and culture. As a consortium CONTACT has been successful as a marketing and development agency, but no student has ever formally used the consortium for the purposes of credit accumulation and transfer.

Subject consortia

352.   A few institutional consortia for credit transfer have begun to develop, promoted by the need of some caring professions to organise their purchase of training requirements more efficiently. Universities have been encouraged to form subject-specific consortia, for example in Social Work or for Health Service training, within which a distribution of expertise may be defined. In principle, students may be entitled and encouraged to exploit access to the full range of learning opportunities in the designated training area, transferring credit from university to university. In practice, subject consortia are in their infancy and appear constrained by all the difficulties inherent in inter-institutional co-operation. Additionally, institutions may be operating at different levels of commitment and experience with respect to credit-based learning. This appears to compound the problems of co-operation and there is little evidence yet that there has been an increase in inter-institutional transfer generated by local subject consortia.

353.   Nevertheless, some professional bodies appear to have been persuaded that institutional consortia offer the best chance of establishing common practice. This is particularly the case for CCETSW which has actively promoted local and regional consortia to its own specifications, requiring that courses define themselves in credit-based and competence terms. The potential for credit transfer is intended to be a central feature of arrangements but we have not been able to identify this in practice to any extent. This may be because the consortia are, in many cases, in their infancy. Some other caring professions have encouraged the establishment of regional consortia in order to establish a better distribution of training resources. Ideally, student-trainees would thus be able to transfer with credit amongst institutions within local consortia.

Client-sponsored consortia

354.   A closely related form of the subject-centred consortium is the client-sponsored variety. We have not found many

examples which provide a precise model, but two developments may help identify some features. Firstly, the Ford Motor Company has sought institutional collaboration to produce learning programmes and qualifications for its employees. It has formed relationships with universities in the United Kingdom, usually near to its main plants. For some years it has been associated with the University of East London and Anglia University; now it is exploring arrangements with the University College of Swansea and Liverpool John Moores University. Whilst it is not strictly true to describe these relationships as consortia, they do indicate how such client-sponsored associations might develop.

355.   A further example is currently in the process of development. The Yorkshire Regional Health Authority, in common with many other similar bodies, wishes to provide training for its staff at many different levels of the organisation. It wishes to buy in that training from a number of providers in higher education and is looking to the Northern Federation to assist it in co-ordinating the supply of suitable programmes from universities in the region. The Health Authority is keen to make progress in credit transfer opportunities for its employees and is concerned to describe its training specifications in order to advise prospective providers. At this stage of development, the initiative is in its very early stages although the Health Authority is appointing a co-ordinator for credit transfer. Progress may be interrupted by reorganisation of the structure of the organisation but, if that can be overcome, client-sponsored arrangements may help to focus the activities of the higher education consortium.

National Open College Network (NOCN)

356.   The National Open College Network is a formally constituted association of officers and representatives from Open College Federations, formally constituted in 1990, but emerging from informal arrangements and conventions in existence since 1985. The NOCN is the national forum representing the views and aspirations of 24 contributing local federations throughout England and Wales, with progress

imminent in Northern Ireland but not in Scotland. Open College Federations are local credit consortia embracing adult, further and higher education institutions. They have been in operation in different forms since the Open College of the North West was established (1978). This initial consortium was developed principally to promote access to higher education.

357.   As we have explained earlier in Chapter VI, Manchester Open College Federation (1981) was the first to be developed explicitly to promote credit accumulation and transfer, employing credit-based learning as a means of facilitating wider access to post-16, adult and higher education. This latter model has subsequently proved to be the more influential in shaping the emergence of other credit-awarding OCFs, providing the impetus for the establishment of NOCN: Merseyside (1987), South Yorkshire (1987), London (formally amalgamated in 1989, but with antecedents throughout the city since 1984).

358.   Since 1990, and supported by the work undertaken through the Unit for the Development of Adult Continuing Education (UDACE), credit-awarding OCFs have developed throughout the country. Almost all OCFs are committed formally to the award of credit for student learning achievement, facilitating accumulation and transfer and promoting access to adult, further and higher education. A common credit tariff and system of levels, united by an outcomes-defined curriculum, characterises the operation of the OCFs associated within the NOCN. A national CAT Agreement was signed in 1991 and commits OCFs to common principles and arrangements for quality assurance, the operation of credit systems, the validation of programmes and the accreditation of learning achievement.

359.   Currently, approximately 40,000-50,000 students per annum earn credit through OCFs. The large Northern OCFs now each register 4,000-5,000 new students annually, whilst the London Open College Federation has registered over 16,000 students for credit since 1990 on over 700 individually accredited modules and courses.

360. OCFs have been supported initially by local authorities and individual colleges and universities. Increasingly amongst the larger and well-established federations, they are able to sustain a substantial part of their activities through the income generated from the services they offer in accreditation and quality assurance. From 1995, the FEFC has agreed that many of the courses accredited by OCFs will be eligible for funding support from the Council, thus increasingly the attraction of their work to contributing colleges and other institutions.

FEU Credit Network

361. The Further Education Unit has sponsored the development of a national network of post-secondary and further education colleges, committed to the exploration of issues arising from the work of the FEU in developing a comprehensive credit framework, outlined in their discussion paper: *A basis for credit?* The basis of the network is to establish the principles and operating practices of a national credit-based and modular post-16 programme, articulating with higher education and embracing academic and vocational programmes. The network is committed to shared work but does not purport to be a formal consortium. At this stage it does not seek to broker the mobility or inter-institutional transfer of students.

362. The network has currently attracted the support of over 100 participating institutions, including 94 further education colleges and fifteen TECs and a number of OCFs. Their work has been focused on the specification of the technical instruments that will underpin the framework, and the negotiation of arrangements for the alignment of various qualifications. In this the FEU network sees itself as complementary to the work of the NCVQ in its obligation to develop a vocational framework, and the FEU network has as its objective the development of a credit system that permits credit transfer and individual student mobility between academic, applied and vocational programmes. It described this system as an 'Open System' of credit transfer, which we describe in more detail in Chapter X. The FEU proposals and its

network have influenced two important developments: *London Together* and the Welsh *Fforwm* which are described below.

London Together

363. *London Together* is a consortium at an early stage of development. Revisiting the aspirations of the CNAA ten years earlier, but moving beyond them to a significant extent, *London Together* seeks to draw into a common credit-based association all the universities and higher education colleges together with the post-secondary colleges, adult education centres, Open College Networks, and local training organisations of the Greater London area (within the M25 ring). Working closely with the local TECs and major employer representatives, *London Together* is an attempt to provide a credit-based matrix of academic and vocational learning opportunities accessible to all learners post-16, supported by an integrated information and guidance framework.

364. The consortium has arisen from the perceived absence of any central body to co-ordinate the affairs and interests of London since the demise of the GLC and ILEA. In its commitment to a public-private coalition, it provides an educational analogue to the *London First* initiative, established by large employers and other bodies to improve the quality of services and boost civic pride in London. The *London Together* initiative has published a policy statement and development plan, outlining the basic principles of a credit framework for the city, and it has established a number of working groups to carry forward proposals. It will depend largely on whether it can find new solutions to the problems which have beset similar earlier consortia attempts, in London and elsewhere. These problems largely concern the tensions generated by institutional resistance to pooled sovereignty, by differences of culture and institutional status, by an absence of strategic commitment in key quarters, and by a culture of disbelief, described as an incredulity towards comprehensive innovation. The *London Together* project may be assisted by the development of a national credit framework in line with that proposed by the FEU, to which this report may make its own contribution. Its prospects for success in the long term may be

enhanced by its close association with regional employers and TECs. This is something which might be helpful to other consortia and we recommend that consortia generally should build on the experience of *London Together* to seek employer membership.

The Welsh Post-16 *Fforwm* and the Welsh HE CATS Network

365. The development of credit frameworks in Wales has been rapid over the past two years. The Welsh *Fforwm* has established, with the support of the Welsh Office, an extensive network of further education colleges which are actively implementing the basic elements of the FEU proposals in *A basis for credit?* and in a later publication, *Beyond a basis for credit*. Work is at an advanced stage of development in many colleges although inter-institutional credit transfer has not been the principle motivating force. Rather, colleges have found credit systems useful in managing diverse qualifications, increasing internal flexibility and improving quality assurance.

366. In higher education, there has been similar progress within a more loosely coupled network of institutions. Principally involving the colleges of the University of Wales, the University of Glamorgan and other higher education providers, the Welsh CATS Project is not strictly a consortium, but has sought to draw universities and others into a common framework. There has been at least one joint meeting held with the Welsh *Fforwm* in order to begin the process of drawing together a common credit system across higher and further education.

Trans-European Credit Exchange and Transfer (TEXT)

367. The establishment of TEXT represents the only attempt in the United Kingdom of which we are aware to form an international consortium. Initially drawing membership from UK institutions participating in the pilot credit transfer arrangements of the European Credit Transfer System, its membership has now broadened to include universities and technical institutions in several European countries. TEXT remains largely dominated and driven from the UK and commitment from other national partnerships usually reflects the shallow penetration of credit systems in these countries. It does however maintain close relationships with the ERASMUS Bureau in Brussels.

368. TEXT has been able to organise a number of international events, in France, Italy, Greece and Denmark. More recently it has begun to focus attention on developments in Eastern Europe. Its internal focus has been to develop subject-centred networks of fellow academic representatives, reflecting the subject-centred characteristics of the ECTS pilot arrangements. To this extent, TEXT has begun to create some useful international networks and its development role, whilst remaining modest in terms of the scale of the tasks ahead, has been influential in creating opportunities for the discussion of credit accumulation and transfer systems in at least some European institutions.

369. Its capacity to generate significant credit transfer via a brokerage role remains very limited. Students may be assisted adventitiously by individual contacts between institutional colleagues, facilitating formal bipartite exchange arrangements, but these will tend to be a by-product of the developmental networking promoted by TEXT rather than arising from any formal structures of TEXT itself.

370. It is difficult to assess what role TEXT might play in the future. The consortium is open to all institutions in the United Kingdom, yet a relatively small number choose to affiliate. This may have something to do with the perceived hierarchical arrangements that were put in place by the ECTS pilot scheme. Institutions were allocated into 'Inner Circle' and 'Outer Circle' groups, with only the five chosen institutions of the 'Inner Circle' being able to participate fully in the pilot scheme. This may have led some institutions to draw adverse conclusions about their ability to contribute effectively to this consortium. Furthermore, it is not clear how TEXT adds to the work of individual institutions which might be keen to expand in international transfer. Those universities which are already active may not

require the type of networking that TEXT provides.

371.   On the other hand, TEXT has pioneered the promotion of credit systems in Eastern Europe and acted as an ambassador for them throughout the European Union and Scandinavia. It has kept open lines of contact with the ERASMUS Bureau and provides a source of expertise and information for current developments. If TEXT did not exist, there would be no other obvious forum within which to exchange ideas on aspects of international, or more precisely European, credit transfer.

Conclusions

372.   There is an enormous potential for credit transfer in the United Kingdom, but it is manifested unevenly and circumscribed by conventions, regulations and concerns over quality assurance. The potential for credit transfer is therefore not always reflected in prevailing patterns of demand. These tend to reflect the distribution of available opportunities and, quite obviously, students will not seek where they know in advance they will not find. We have proposals to make in many of the later chapters of this report which may help create more flexible conditions for student mobility. For the purposes of these conclusions, some general recommendations are offered, with one or two specific proposals.

Credit transfer and a regional policy

373.   One of the most evident conclusions of our investigation is that there appears to be very little credit transfer between higher education institutions; only student transfer to and from the Open University appears to offer any exception to this. There is little reliable data with which to authenticate this assessment, and we make proposals to address this later. However, we are confident that the judgement is accurate, not least because those consortia which have sought to promote transfer, have themselves been unable to stimulate a market of this nature. There are several reasons for this relative immobility: students may be largely content with a sustained experience at one institution; there has never been any culture of

expectation that students could look elsewhere for learning opportunities; structural and financial regulations may impede mobility; and differences of culture and history between even the most adjacent institutions can act as barriers to greater choice. In addition, for mobile part-time students, the absence of a general acceptance of credit transfer possibilities amongst themselves and within institutions will have created further impediments.

374.   We have given some thought to whether there are any explicit advantages in actively stimulating greater inter-institutional credit transfer within higher education. One powerful argument against active intervention would be simply that if there is no natural demand from students, why artificially generate it? Furthermore, a university education should be about more than the piecemeal aggregation of learning opportunities; it is about the absorption of the culture and sensitivities of an institution of learning which might not be assisted by too mobile an engagement with the process. On the other hand, there are questions of national efficiency to be addressed. Is it appropriate that every university in a metropolitan area or region should be supported to offer a similarly comprehensive range of academic programmes? Is it efficient that funding councils should be expected to provide resources to support expensive investment in each institution according to its individual claims for development? It might be argued that one of the principal purposes of higher education is to ensure that, for the benefit of individuals and the nation as a whole, the required numbers of highly educated people are produced. Where this is achieved is of secondary importance, and the outcomes could as easily be satisfied by pooling resources and expertise as by providing them in each institution. In this model, students could be encouraged to undertake part of their (undergraduate) studies in one institution, but move on and complete them elsewhere, perhaps in the fashion of the pooled 6th forms in some local authorities. Such an arrangement in higher education might not apply to entire institutions, but could possibly apply to individual subject areas shared by institutions in the same region.

375. The consequences of this approach may not be immediately welcomed for a number of important reasons. Firstly, to achieve such a rationalisation in the distribution of resources and expertise would be to place on the funding councils a planning obligation which they would not formally invite, and which would not be volunteered by institutions keen to protect their academic autonomy. Secondly, it might imply a formal stratification of institutions in which some universities would provide initial programmes in certain areas, but more prestigious institutions would supply the more expensive final outcomes. Thirdly, quality under such conditions might be difficult to assure; inter-institutional mobility could disrupt the student experience with disadvantageous consequences; fourthly, analogous experience of joint programmes at the Master's level and elsewhere has suggested that there are problems associated with the ownership of the award of the final qualification; and fifthly, even if such credit transfer were to develop on any scale between local or regional institutions, the marginal costs of modifying administrative arrangements could outweigh the marginal gains in efficiency.

376. We accept the force of many these arguments, and recognise that neither central planning by the funding council nor a stratification of institutions is likely be welcomed in any quarter. We believe nevertheless that problems can be overcome if there is a will to proceed. For example, what would be the consequences if universities individually sought to invite the credit transfer of students from other institutions, particularly at the undergraduate level? This might require changes to university regulations in some cases, and to financial arrangements in others, but if these matters could be resolved, would a university then solicit the credit transfer of suitable students from another institution to cover a recruitment shortfall for example, or infill a particular programme or to create a stronger research cohort? Although this might create an unfamiliar and possibly uncomfortable competitive tension between otherwise neighbourly institutions, could students benefit? Would scarce resources not be more effectively targeted?

377. Despite the ambiguous benefits, we believe that further work should be undertaken to explore closer formal inter-institutional collaboration in the co-operative development of programmes for greater credit transfer. This could be undertaken by local institutions in an even-handed manner, and we have been made aware of some examples of tentative progress in this direction. **We recommend** that the representative bodies of the institutions, the funding councils and the HEQC should describe jointly and separately their policies on the further development of inter-institutional co-operation for the express purpose of facilitating student academic credit transfer, providing in each case guidance on how possible impediments may be addressed.

378. Furthermore, we believe that joint collaboration for credit transfer will be best encouraged in cases where there are definitive student interests at stake. **We recommend** further that inter-institutional pilot projects should be funded, and prospective student numbers agreed, to establish shared academic programmes, particularly at the undergraduate level, specifically designed to encourage student progression and credit transfer between local institutions of higher education.

Inter-qualification transfer in HE

379. We assess the potential demand for inter-qualification transfer to be considerable. There appears to be widespread interest in movement from diploma to degree programmes wherever that is possible. The honours degree maintains a hold on the aspirations of students which is not matched by other qualifications. However, opportunities for transfer are constrained by the availability of places, usually in the final year of the honours degree, and by reservations about the suitability of two year diplomas adequately to prepare students for progression to those programmes. However, if credit transfer is to be made meaningful within the university, between its various staged awards, then more opportunities for progression need to be made available to suitably qualified students. Ideally, we would like to encourage a more seamless progression from sub-degree to honours degree programmes

for suitably prepared students, in the manner that has begun to develop in some Scottish universities and elsewhere. We are aware of the credit transfer arrangements that were reached between the CNAA and BTEC, but it will be important to ensure that courses themselves make credit transfer a reality by harmoniously designed structures. **We recommend** that steps be taken within developing institutional modular and credit-based programmes to ensure that the maximum possible potential exists for inter-qualification progression and that students be encouraged to take advantage of this. It will require the careful design of complementary academic programmes and assessment objectives, which in turn will require close co-operation between institutions, external awarding bodies such as BTEC, with professional bodies and the HEQC to ensure that quality assurance criteria are satisfied.

Transfer between further and higher education

380.　We have been largely satisfied that arrangements are in place to cope with demand for transfer from further to higher education. General transfer occurs in large numbers and specific transfer from Access courses is becoming more familiar to many institutions. 'Franchising' arrangements remain in the early stages of development in most areas, with the notable exception of the Lancashire Integrated Colleges Scheme (LINCS), but there as everywhere else, initiatives continue to be affected by modifications to Government policy, reflected in funding council decisions on student numbers. Nevertheless, we believe that the further development of 'franchising' arrangements is most important for the promotion of credit transfer and we would encourage continued support for these initiatives. **We recommend** that higher education institutions individually and their representative bodies ensure that close relationships continue to be fostered with further education colleges through sustained 'franchising' and similar arrangements. **We recommend** further that the CVCP, COSHEP, SCOP, AFC and other relevant parties determine their preferred policy positions towards continued inter-institutional developments between further and higher education with a view to strengthening opportunities for local access and credit transfer.

381.　There is one aspect of arrangements for transfer between further and higher education which does give cause for concern. Work is now in progress to promote opportunities for access to higher education via the GNVQ qualification. Students achieving this qualification at Level 3 are being encouraged to anticipate progression to universities and colleges. Ignoring for one moment the possible impact on these aspirations of reductions in student entry numbers in the next few years, it is by no means clear whether sufficient thought has been given, either by the NCVQ or by institutions of higher education, to the extent to which students with GNVQ Level 3 qualifications will have been adequately prepared for largely unmodified academic programmes in higher education. It would be a substantial disappointment to aspiring students and to current national policy if such students were to enter higher education in significant numbers, only to fail to achieve on programmes for which they were unprepared. Moreover, it would be a frustration to strategies for broadening student choice at this level if admissions tutors, anticipating this problem, were to restrict entry to these students.

382.　We believe this matter must be addressed urgently. **We recommend** that the HEQC, NCVQ and the representative bodies of institutions begin an immediate exploration of the implications for the higher education curriculum of policies to improve opportunities for progression and subsequent successful achievement for students bearing GNVQ Level 3 qualifications. This investigation is likely to require attention at least to the character and structure of the first year programmes of higher education institutions, encouraging greater breadth and the development of core skills. It may also require further consideration of the character of the GNVQ Level 3 qualification itself. We believe failure to make swift progress on these matters could seriously prejudice the credibility and acceptability of the GNVQ3 in higher education, and will lead to disappointment and frustrated expectations for large numbers of students. We comment further on these matters in Chapter IX.

Miscellaneous forms of transfer

383.   We have been interested to note the growing opportunities for credit transfer around and outside higher education institutions. In particular, we have been surprised at the extent of higher education level work judged to be taking place in the independent sector, within large companies and public authorities. Many institutions have formed accreditation arrangements with these organisations, and we address relevant aspects of quality assurance in Chapter X. However, in common with our recommendations in Chapter VI for further research into the extent of activity in the accreditation of experiential and uncertificated learning, we believe further work needs to be undertaken in other specific areas. **We recommend** that the research community, or otherwise the representative bodies of institutions, or possibly the HEQC, investigate the extent of activity and provide examples in three areas: the number of student-employees registered with institutions for higher education credit; the scale of inter-institutional postgraduate credit transfer; and examples of any credit transfer arrangements or conventions which may exist between two or more professional bodies.

Consortia in Higher Education

384.   Consortia of different types appear to have been very effective in stimulating *developmental* activity within institutions; they appear to have had very limited impact on the *brokerage* of credit transfer between institutions of higher education, although their developmental role has assisted individual institutions to broker their own relationship with specific external clients. It is clear that the motivation to establish consortia for credit transfer has been largely *supply-led*. Institutions have taken the view that a demand for credit transfer of one form or another exists and that consortia might be the best way to manage this. From our investigations, it is not at all clear that one follows the other. Demand of various sorts does indeed exist, but consortia have not yet established their advantages over those of individual institutions for managing this. In short, consortia have struggled to date to define a demand for supply-led definitions of credit

transfer. This has consequences for quality assurance arrangements which we discuss in Chapter X.

385.   On the other hand, consortia in higher education have been very effective in raising the awareness of academic and administrative staff of the principles and practices of modularisation, credit accumulation and credit transfer (see, for example, Table 25).

Table 25:
Examples of consortium practice

South-East England Consortium Staff Development Programme 1994

Feb   Learning Outcomes: Introduction and applications

Mar   Planning for Quality Audit

Mar   Guidance, Learner Support and the Student experience within flexible credit-based systems

Apr   GNVQs and Admissions: strategy and practice .

Apr   External Examining in Modular and Credit-based systems

May   NCVQ Developments in HE

Jun   Credit-based Liberal Adult Education in the University sector

Jun   The development of APEL in Europe

Jul   Developing study skills for non-traditional students

Sep   Developments in student-centred learning

Oct   Accreditation of short courses and company training: workshop 1

Oct   Modular Structures: a practical approach

Nov   International Credit transfer

Dec   Accreditation of short courses and company training: workshop 2

SCOTCAT Network – Staff Development Programme: Spring 1994

Feb   Credit-rating within the SCOTCAT Framework

Mar   Accrediting Off-Campus Learning

Apr   Accrediting Work-based Learning

May   Further and Higher Education Credit Links

They have provided an essential forum for the dissemination of good practice and we would not wish to see this role diminished. However, this makes the role of consortia closer to that of a professional network. A consortium implies that contributing members agree to forego an element of autonomy in pursuit of collective advantages. Existing credit consortia have rarely if ever been able to achieve that. Rather, they have been sustained as relatively loosely coupled networks of professional colleagues, many of whom could not be in a position to speak for, and certainly could not expect to deliver policies for, their institutions. We are not sure arrangements could be any different.

386.   This leads us to the observation that the role and purpose of credit consortia in higher education should be more explicitly focused, promising less but delivering more. When institutions combine to form consortia for credit transfer, they should state clearly what it is they expect the consortia to achieve and how they are prepared to support the consortia in achieving agreed objectives. We would like to see the position of consortia strengthened in their contribution because we feel they have an important role to play in quality assurance and quality improvement. This will inevitably mean that consortia will have to become more accountable to their contributing members. As general guidance in the further operation of credit consortia, **we recommend** that they should formally publish their mission, operating principles and objectives, and that the HEQC should receive these statements. Wherever possible, constituent members of the consortium should give attention at an appropriately senior level of the institution to these statements, associating themselves formally, describing appropriate senior representation in the first instance, and identifying an adequate level of support for the work of the consortium, its sub-groups and events. Finally, consortia should arrange for a periodic review of activities and progress towards objectives, the outcomes of which should be made available to constituent member institutions.

387.   In return for an improvement in consortia focus, accountability and control, **we recommend** that the HEQC begins an investigation to establish whether there is a role for consortia as regional networks for quality assurance, either in general terms or as co-ordinators of subject groups. This investigation, to be conducted in close consultation with existing consortia, should consider whether such developments are consistent with the objectives and practice of the HEQC, having concern that any arrangements should be efficient and not more burdensome on institutions.

388.   **We recommend** that in general terms close working relationships should be encouraged between consortia and the HEQC in matters relevant to them. We do not believe however that this relationship should be so close as to imply oversight or supervision by the HEQC of naturally occuring consortia. It will be important to recognise that consortia have developed organically: that is, they have arisen as voluntary associations for the benefit of their members and will be dissolved by them accordingly. It would be inappropriate and unnecessary for the HEQC to seek to duplicate the work of consortia, but it would be very helpful if the HEQC were to support consortia as far as possible to act as conduits for relevant activities and developments.

Demand-led consortia in higher education

389.   We have been attracted by the idea that consortia are likely to be more useful to bodies external to higher education, employers and professional bodies particularly, if they are established to meet specific client demand. Since it has proved difficult for institutions to anticipate demand for credit transfer, **we recommend** that efforts are made by the HEQC and its representative bodies, in conjunction with professional bodies and the representative agencies of employers, to promote the prospects of credit transfer through institutional consortia based on specified client demand. We are aware of attempts in the past to respond in this way and that they proved difficult to co-ordinate. The HEQC may be able to play a constructive role here. Furthermore, **we recommend** that consortia of higher education institutions should attempt to invite membership from employers. We make this proposal in keeping with other recommendations in this report (Chapter VI

and Chapter X) which seek to give greater prominence to the needs of employers and professional bodies in defining their requirements of higher education to which institutions may respond as they see fit.

Statistics on student mobility

390. We turn finally in this review to the difficult matters surrounding the availability of reliable data with which to understand and assess the consequences of student choice and student mobility. Earlier, we suggested that more information was needed on student attitudes to course structure and opportunities for informed choice. **We recommend** that research be undertaken to explore whether incidents of student early withdrawal or non-completion of courses would be mitigated by the availability of more choice and flexibility in initial programmes and thereafter.

391. On the wider dimensions of student behaviour and patterns of mobility, **we recommend** that funding councils encourage institutions wherever possible to report student numbers in such a way that an assessment of internal student mobility may be made. We do not believe this would be particularly burdensome for some institutions currently; the information systems which have been developed to record student progress within modular schemes are usually capable of running reports which are sensitive to patterns of internal choice. For other institutions, where modular developments are less well-advanced, or which have chosen a different pathway in these matters, the funding councils and HESA will need to consult closely with institutions to establish what is possible, and what would need to be in place if this type of data could be made available. We are aware of the MAC initiatives in many universities and comment further in Chapter XII.

A personal student identification number

392. In order to assess the scale of student mobility and transfer in the general environment of higher and further education, **we recommend** the development of national arrangements for unique student identification. A personal student number would greatly assist policy-making in assessing the nature of student mobility and could have a very beneficial impact on monitoring the performance of specific cohorts. We are aware that this matter has been recommended before by the statistical agencies amongst others, but that a number of sensitivities associated with it have resulted in rejection of the idea. These reservations are real; they range from concerns over further intrusions of the State into individual life, to the problems and costs of administering such a system. We are advised that one significant practical problem lies in the fact that students will often forget, or incorrectly transcribe, their personal identification number.

393. On the other hand, the information gathered on patterns of student behaviour could be so useful for policy development in higher and further education that we believe the proposal should be revisited. The operation of a personal student number system will have no more consequences for personal liberty than the operation of national insurance or bank account number systems. Individual institutions already have unique identifier arrangements within their record systems. In order to make further progress, the representative bodies of institutions should be invited to undertake further consultations on the subject with interested parties, including the National Union of Students.

Recommendations and guidance for future policy

On transfer between and within Higher Education institutions

To HEQC, BTEC, funding councils, and the representative bodies of institutions

14 The potential for credit transfer to improve personal academic development and the efficient use of resources is considerable. **We recommend** that the representative bodies of the institutions, the funding councils and the HEQC should describe jointly and separately their policies on the further development of inter-institutional co-operation in higher education for the express purpose of facilitating student academic progression through credit transfer, providing in each case guidance on how possible impediments may be addressed.

15 Joint collaboration for credit transfer will be best encouraged in cases where definitive student interests are involved. **We recommend** that inter-institutional pilot projects should be funded, prospective student numbers agreed, and institutions invited to establish shared academic programmes, particularly at the undergraduate level, specifically designed to encourage student progression and credit transfer between local institutions of higher education.

16 Credit transfer would be greatly assisted by the easier progression of suitably prepared students between different qualifications. **We recommend** that steps be taken to exploit the flexibility bestowed by developing modular and credit-based programmes to ensure that the maximum possible potential exists for inter-qualification student progression. This will require the careful design of complementary academic programmes and assessment objectives, which in turn will require close co-operation between institutions, external awarding bodies such as BTEC, with professional bodies and the HEQC to ensure that quality assurance criteria are satisfied.

On transfer between Further and Higher Education

To HEQC, NCVQ and the representative bodies of institutions

17 To avoid the disappointment of students and the frustration of national policy objectives, **we recommend** that the HEQC, NCVQ and the representative bodies of institutions begin an immediate exploration of the implications for the higher education curriculum of policies to improve opportunities for progression and subsequent successful achievement for students bearing GNVQ Level 3 qualifications. This investigation is likely to require attention at least to the character and structure of the first year of higher education programmes and the quality assurance aspects of any modifications.

18 **We recommend** that higher education institutions individually, and the representative bodies of institutions in higher and further education, declare their preferred long-term policy towards inter-institutional developments between further and higher education with a view to strengthening local credit transfer through sustained 'franchising', Access courses and similar arrangements.

19   **We recommend** that the development of multi-exit Access courses be encouraged, but that universties and colleges give consideration to the further operation of articulation agreements with such courses as a means of formalising opportunities for Access.

On the role of consortia

To HEQC, credit consortia and individual institutions, employers and professional bodies

20   As guidance in the further operation of credit consortia, **we recommend** that they should formally publish their mission, operating principles and objectives, and that the HEQC should receive these statements. Wherever possible, members of the consortium should give attention to these statements at an appropriately senior level of the institution, associating themselves formally, describing appropriate senior representation in the first instance, and identifying an adequate level of support for the work of the consortium, its sub-groups and events. Consortia should arrange for a periodic review of progress towards objectives, the outcomes of which should be made available to constituent members.

21   **We recommend** that the HEQC establishes whether there is a role for consortia as regional networks for quality assurance, either in general terms or as co-ordinators of subject groups. This investigation should consider whether such developments are consistent with the objectives and practice of the HEQC, having concern that any arrangements should be efficient and not more burdensome on institutions than prevailing arrangements.

22   **We recommend** that the HEQC and existing consortia for credit transfer in higher education explore means for close working co-operation on matters relevant to them. The relationship should not be so close as to imply oversight by the HEQC, but it should be close enough to avoid duplication of effort and to allow the HEQC to consider consortia as appropriate vehicles for the delivery of some of its objectives.

23   **We recommend** that efforts are made by the HEQC and its representative bodies, in conjunction with professional bodies and the representative agencies of employers, to promote the prospects of credit transfer through institutional consortia based on specific client demand.

24   **We recommend** that existing consortia of higher education institutions should consider extending membership to TECs, employers and other public authorities wherever possible. We believe the practice of the *London Together* consortium is to be commended in this respect.

On statistical data for credit transfer

To funding councils and HESA

25   **We recommend** that funding councils and HESA encourage institutions wherever possible to report student numbers in such a way that an assessment of internal student mobility may be made. Information systems exist which make this possible, and the funding councils might assist institutions with further developments such as the MAC initiatives.

On a personal student identification number

To Government, HESA, the representative bodies of institutions, and the National Union of Students

26   In order to establish reliable statistical data with which to understand patterns of student mobility and choice, **we recommend** the development of national arrangements for unique student identification. A personal student number would greatly assist policy-making in assessing the nature of student mobility and could have a very beneficial impact on monitoring the performance of specific cohorts. **We recommend** that the representative bodies of institutions undertake further consultations with interested parties, including representative student bodies, to secure support for progress on this matter.

On further work

To the research community, HEQC, and the representative bodies of institutions

27   **We recommend** that the research community, or the representative bodies of institutions, or possibly the HEQC, investigate the extent of activity and provide examples in three areas: the number of student-employees registered with institutions for higher education credit; the scale of inter-institutional postgraduate credit transfer; and examples of any credit transfer arrangements or conventions which may exist between two or more professional bodies.

28   **We recommend** that research be undertaken to explore whether incidents of student early withdrawal or non-completion of courses are correlated in any way with the range of choice and flexibility in initial programmes and thereafter, and whether increases in either choice or flexibility would have any influence on student decisions in these matters.

Part Three

Part Three

VIII.   *Understanding credit*

Introduction

394.   Throughout the investigation and during the preparation of this report, we have been approached on many occasions with requests to provide some guidance on the meaning of terms and their use. Initially, we were reluctant to attempt this, for three reasons. Firstly, an exercise of this kind may be misconstrued as an attempt to impose an orthodoxy in the use of language with respect to matters which are still evolving and which remain contested conceptually. Secondly, the search for common ground may result in over-simplification. And thirdly, the undertaking may fail to capture vernacular differences or may misrepresent the interpretation of terms. We have been further disarmed by the observation of the CNAA in its publication *Going modular* (1989), which suggested:

'Although much has been learnt about the operation of modular courses in recent years, the pace and extent of current developments will ensure that much more will be learnt over the next few years. If it is ever possible to write the 'state of the art' paper on modular courses, the time for doing so is almost certainly not now.'

395.   There is perhaps an important fourth reason. Much of the discussion which follows is likely to be read with amusement by colleagues familiar with the practice of credit systems in the United States. 'Credit' is so much part of American educational culture, and so readily taken for granted in this most highly developed of credit systems, that most academic colleagues have forgotten, if they ever knew, the origins of their college-credit system. An exception is Sheldon Rothblatt, who has observed with interest the efforts by British higher education institutions and beyond to wrestle with some very simple concepts and practices in these matters. His comments on the development of the American modular system (Rothblatt 1991) repay closer attention than we have time for here. To summarise: although

Rothblatt is entirely sympathetic with the principles and practices of the American college-credit system, he remains healthily sceptical of the rationales for some of its features. It works, and it is good at what it sets out to achieve – democratic participation with choice and credit transfer – but, if one seeks evidence of the march of reason, the development of the system does not invite close inspection. As Rothblatt comments:

'The history of units (credits) is fascinating but essentially obscure. Aetiological detail is missing from the historical narrative. Over half a century the various elements of the American educational system grew together to form the everyday curricular structure so familiar today (but) a connected account does not exist. After all, it is administrative history, a tiresome account of tiny details congealing into a system. No heroic personalities combat insurmountable odds. No threats of revolution in the air. The story is humdrum.'

And he continues in more forthright vein when discussing the drawbacks of the credit system:

'As a measure of learning, the assignment of credit units on a basis of classroom contact hours is meaningless, and on the basis of student workload, arbitrary and nonsensical. Neither uniformity of input or of output is possible. Like any legal or taxation system that is unenforce-able as written, the credit-unit system will continue to produce elaborate fictions and evasions.'

396.   In fairness, it must be said that Rothblatt offers these comments as an objective and self-critical counterweight to an otherwise glowing testimonial to the American system of higher education. We include them here, not to encourage despair amongst those who have striven to introduce some clarity and purpose into these matters in the United Kingdom, but to indicate a certain self-consciousness on our part in attempting to produce a reasoned case for the further development of credit systems in the United

Kingdom against such a background. We have struggled to decide whether we are competing with a case of American 'exceptionalism', the cultural conditions of which cannot be repeated elsewhere, or whether we need to accept that the achievement of greater access, student choice and credit transfer will inevitably involve the development of imperfect instruments which are nevertheless good enough to meet the desired objectives. The trade-off between a fulfilment of greater participation in post-secondary and higher education and an intellectual precision in the development of organising principles and practices may involve a patience and a preparedness to compromise which does not always distinguish discussions on these matters.

397.   We have been made very aware during our investigations that considerable passions are being expended in various quarters to realise the entirely laudable social and educational objectives represented by the development of credit systems. So convinced are many colleagues that this provides a sensible way forward for students, academic staff and others that there may be a danger that the debate loses touch with what is possible. Understanding credit can be a fairly straightforward matter, and its application must be made simple for students and other users, but we are bound to observe that there are strongly held positions on many points. For example, the CNAA, the NCVQ and the FEU have published material informing discussions on the application of concepts, technical instruments and organising principles of credit-based systems. These publications are: *Guidelines on credit rating* (CNAA, 1992); *Guide to National Vocational Qualifications* (NCVQ, 1991); *Discussing credit* (FEU, 1993) and *Beyond 'A basis for credit?'* (FEU, 1993 draft). Each of the three agencies starts from a different point in the debate, and one of the tasks of this report is to achieve a convergence, which we attempt here and to which we attend further in Chapter IX. The task is different from that described by Rothblatt for the United States. All parties to the discussion are aware that what we are attempting in the further development of credit systems is far more than 'administrative history' for the United Kingdom. It may indeed involve a 'revolution' in the way we think about

professional responsibilities in academic life, about the rights and needs of students, and about the articulation of higher education and beyond with different social values and political currents. The scale of the task is humbling but it need not be a cause of despair.

398.   Accepting these limitations, we feel the task before us may be useful to the extent that it gives some exposure to the agreements, but also the differences and confusions, which exist in the understanding of credit systems. In an attempt to explore how terms have been used, we sought opinion from a wide representation of individuals who have been prominent in the field over the past twenty years. All their observations may not be captured here, but wherever it is possible, we give an indication of the interpretation we favour, based on an assessment of common understanding. Elsewhere in this discussion we offer some indication of what we believe to be misunderstandings and confusions. But the objective remains the same: to introduce clarity rather than conformity in order to assist shared discourse. In the end, colleagues may be guided by the observations included here, choosing to settle differences, albeit provisionally, around some common interpretations. If colleagues find this useful, then so much the better, but it is certain that the use of terms and their meaning will continue to evolve naturally.

Progress on choice and flexibility?

399.   We begin by assessing the main claims of modular and credit-based systems. They claim to deliver access, student choice, personal flexibility and mobility. There is no disagreement in published commentary, either in the United Kingdom or elsewhere in the world, that these are amongst their principal objectives. As Martin Trow (1981) has explained, of the American system:

'(We have) a system of earned and transferable "credits", a kind of academic currency that we all take for granted. Our credits make possible the extraordinary mobility of our students in three distinct dimensions: between fields of study, between institutions, and over time.'

Table 26:
Access, choice and flexibility: three views on credit and modularity

Credit systems are systems of currency: they provide the means of comparability and exchange; they offer promises of harmonisation and stability in an environment dominated by diversity and mobility. Credit is the unifying currency, linking disparate learning opportunities undertaken in a variety of educational contexts, and enabling students to aggregate learning achievements towards generally recognised awards and qualifications. In short, credit systems develop as a response to diversity, flexibility, and democratic participation in education.

(David Robertson, 1993)

Modular provision is primarily concerned with offering the student delayed and more informed choice within a given award. The scope exists, however, for a more imaginative approach, in which modules might build up to link short courses, certificate, diploma and degree awards... Modular structures facilitate the establishment of 'Associate Student'' schemes which allow individuals to study a few modules of direct interest to them, rather than an entire course, and also facilitate transfers of students between institutions.

(NAB report on continuing education, 1984)

The repeated story is of structures intended to alter attitudes and enlarge opportunities resulting in partial modification instead of transformation. The educational system has not adapted itself to modularisation. Quite the reverse: the system has either used modularisation to enhance provider power or it has relegated modularisation to the level of lower status products and resisted attempts to enhance their status... The price is generally a reduction in choice, and the result something closer in approach to the kinds of courses from which the schemes were originally intended to offer a departure.

(Ernest Theodossin, 1986)

400.   Yet as the three quotations in Table 26 reveal, opinion in the United Kingdom is divided between the optimists and, let us say, the realists – the former promoting a vision, the latter reflecting on the hallucination. From this it is clear, even to the 'optimists', that neither credit nor modularity *of themselves* deliver choice and flexibility. They are at best instruments which can be used to pursue certain policy objectives; we will discuss these later in Chapter XV. For the time being, we can confirm that the pursuit of student choice and flexibility commands widespread support in principle. It conveniently unites the radicals of the Right (markets, freedom of choice) and of the Left (democratic participation, student empower-ment) against the conservatives of the Right (elite participation and the preservation of 'standards') and of the Left (sovereignty of the academic, supremacy of the unified course, the 'student as apprentice'). In practice, develop-ments in the United Kingdom have some distance to go before they begin to resemble the conventions and arrangements common in the United States. It is by no means clear that this is the shared objective of all participants to the debate. In Chapter XV, we give some reflections upon the consequences of a more market-driven approach for higher education in the United Kingdom and Europe. In short, markets are rarely ever popular with professions and this may prove to be the case with the academic profession as well.

The language of credit

401.   The meaning of the term 'credit' should be very straightforward; in fact, no discussion causes more frustration than this. In its simplest form, the term means little more than *learning in good academic standing*, the cumulative transfer of which can take place within conventional academic arrangements. This use of the term does not imply the need for a *system of academic currency* although such a system quickly becomes necessary as demand for credit transfer increases. 'Credit' as currency allows some equivalence to be established between different learning experiences, thereby facilitating the management of credit transfer.

119

402. Once a system of currency has been established, 'credit' assumes two properties. In the first case, it can be used for *counting*: 'credit' is little more than an academic currency system which encourages students to 'trade'. They use the system to count up the amount of credit required, aggregating credits from learning units or modules until the required number has been assembled for a given qualification. This has led critics of credit systems to argue that students become more concerned with counting credits than with the coherence of the assembled programme. Theodossin (1986) has referred to this as 'the tyranny of counting' and others have dismissed the system as little more than 'academic book-keeping'. Further on in its development, 'credit' has come to be used for *accounting*. Depending on how 'credit' is defined and for what purpose it is used, it can be used as an instrument of quality assurance and accountability. This is often the case where 'credit' is defined in terms of a ratio of outputs to inputs: that is, where credit reflects in a more or less satisfactory manner the ratio of learning achievement to the learning time expended, or the workload involved, in demonstrating successful learning. This brings us to an important principle of *all* credit systems: *credit is only awarded for demonstrated learning achievement and never for attendance or experience alone.*

Definitions of credit

403. There are three approaches to the definition of credit. Because there has been no agreed definition of categories here, we offer the following terms to indicate the basis upon which 'credit' is described: *impositional, compositional* and *competence*. The difference between *impositional* and *compositional* treatments of credit is as follows: one '(super-) imposes' credit ratings upon an existing academic structure, thereby preparing the structure to receive choice-seeking students; the other 'composes' credit ratings from the elements (credit-hours) of student learning, transforming academic structures into selectable units. *Competence*-based approaches do not generally use credit ratings in this way. It is important to stress that these terms are not being used normatively in this context, although the differences of approach do have consequences for the capacity of any credit systems to apply comprehensively to all forms of learning within and without higher education.

404. *Impositional credit systems* use 'credit' to superimpose a *numerical partition* on a greater whole (ie a course) and usually employ some general concept of *workload*. This is often the expected student workload of a degree, or of a degree-year, in higher education. Sub-units of the total workload (ie. modules) are allocated a volume of credit in direct relationship to the proportion of the total workload represented by the sub-unit. In most if not all practical cases, the *credit tariff* of each sub-unit will be the same, or a multiple of the basic sub-unit. In short the credit tariff reflects the *structural* sub-divisions of the academic programme but bears no necessary relationship to either output or input factors. The CNAA CAT scheme is a good example of an *impositional* scheme, particularly when applied to the modularised programme of a university. For example, the academic structure may be sub-divided into a number of units or modules per term, semester or year. Each unit is usually treated as an equal part of the total course, with occasional multiples of the standard unit, and this is reflected by the partition of the total credit for the year or course. This approach to the allocation of credit explains why the CNAA scheme chose 360 credits to represent the honours degree (England and Wales) with a 120-credit full-time degree year. The total numerical value can be easily partitioned to accommodate most if not all modular (and non-modular) degree-based programmes in higher education.

405. *Compositional credit systems* describe 'credit' in dimensions of *notional time*. They begin with the question: how is the *unit of account*, the 'credit', to be defined? and in this way distinguish themselves from previous treatments which offer the honours degree itself as the starting point for the definition of the credit-unit. The approach to 'credit' based on the use of *notional time* begins from student learning activity. It seeks a common basis for credit in the minimum learning block available to a student, usually a *learning hour*, and from this *composes* a credit tariff for every constituent learning experience in a programme. The reference point

remains *college practice:* that is, how academic institutions conduct themselves, but rather than begin at the level of the entire course, this way of dealing with credit begins with the unit of learning time. The best example of this approach is the Carnegie *credit-hour* employed widely throughout universities and colleges in the United States. 'Credit' represents each *credit-hour per semester* that a student is engaged in supervised learning. *Supervised learning* does not necessarily mean 'class contact' but rather 'learning under the general supervision of the college' including self-directed study. Nor does it mean the actual amount of learning time a student may expend (at home or elsewhere) satisfying the requirements of the course. It is a *notional time* unit in that it represents the learning activity of any student under college conditions but not the actual learning time of any particular student. Thus a module which requires students to undertake three hours of supervised instruction per semester is a three-credit module. Since most university and college semesters in the United States involve students in up to 30 hours of *supervised learning per week* for a 15 week semester, (occasionally longer in some community colleges), students accumulate 15 'credits' each semester and a minimum of 30 credits per year towards their qualifications.

406   **A 'credit-unit' for the United Kingdom?** The nearest equivalents in the United Kingdom to this treatment of 'credit' have been the various attempts to fix a *notional time* value to the 'credit'. The absence of a common semester or term arrangement in the United Kingdom has meant it has not been possible simply to mimic the American approach to 'credit', even if this were desired. Instead, derivative solutions have been attempted. In the 1970s, BTEC began to use a 60-hour unit (with a 30-hour half-unit) to establish equivalence between its 'modules' and SCOTVEC followed in the 1980s with a 40-hour unit. In between, the Manchester Open College Federation adopted a 50-hour unit initially, and this was amended by the end of the decade to a 30-hour unit. A settlement has begun to occur around this final value. All OCFs and some universities have been using this style of credit for some time. The FEU has adopted the 30-hour unit in its proposals in *A basis for credit?* and the CNAA accepted it as the minimum accreditable

unit of learning activity, which in its scheme attracts four credits. The interesting feature about the *notional time* unit of 30 hours is not the specific value itself, but how it is variously derived, and how it can be usefully used.

407.   The 30-hour unit of credit, although formally starting with the BTEC half-unit, owes its extensive operation to those credit systems which developed outside higher education *but which wished to retain close articulation with higher education for the purposes of credit transfer*. The most widespread use of credit outside higher education has been, as we noted in Chapter VI, within Open College Federations throughout the 1980s. As these consortia developed and their engagement with Access courses grew, it became more necessary than ever to create a system of credit which was not dependent on higher education qualifications alone (ie the honours degree). But, unlike higher education, further and adult education have no standard qualification to use as a benchmark and too few students follow year-long courses to make the college year a suitable standard. It was therefore essential to find a formula for defining credit which could accredit the wide range of courses in further and adult education, permitting courses of different lengths in basic education, youth training, and Access courses, for example, to share a common unit of credit and to assist credit transfer between academic programmes in further, adult and higher education wherever possible. It needs to be remembered that work on credit in OCFs pre-dated by some years the creation of the CNAA scheme. However, even as that latter scheme developed in the late 1980s, it would have been difficult, if not impossible, to adopt partitions of a 360-credit honours degree (or even a 120-credit year) as a basis for equivalence and credit rating for a module of an Access course, or a unit in basic numeracy for example.

408.   The 30-hour credit evolved in the OCFs as the simplest means of adding a credit rating to the most varied forms of learning, and it has come as near as possible in the UK to the American *Carnegie Hour*. Firstly, the rationale for this unit of credit lay in its symmetry and simplicity. It represents the equivalent in *notional time* of an hour of 'supervised learning' per week for a 30-week college year; moreover,

it represents the standard number of supervised college hours per week for a full-time student. Both the length of the college year and the learning hours per college week are *benchmark values*. The actual college year might be longer and the learning time per week for a particular student might be greater than the 30 hours x 30 week formula implied, but for *either* reason, academic staff in further, adult and higher education could use the 30-hour unit of credit often within the context of a minimum 30-credit year. In practice, the 30-hour credit moved as close as it could to practice in higher education without compromising the usefulness of the 'credit' for progress on credit transfer in further and adult education.

409.   Secondly, the 30-hour unit was tried in every possible context, including within higher education, and it seemed to remain consistently useful in establishing equivalences between different learning at different levels, thus improving the potential for credit transfer. This has been the case from the mid-1980s when the developments associated with the NCVQ began to draw colleagues who were working with the 30-hour unit towards a recognition that it could be united with an outcomes-led curriculum. The learning outcomes statements required by the NCVQ model of curriculum design, which we discuss below, were seen as effective means of representing one side of an output-input ratio, the other side of which was represented by the *notional time* input value (30 hours). Since the late 1980s and early 1990s, much of the thinking on the nature of credit systems in the United Kingdom has centred on the ability of the 'credit', used in this way, to act as an instrument for quality assurance.

410.   **Credit as 'competence'.** Before we elaborate further on this matter, it is important to introduce the third treatment of credit in the United Kingdom. From 1986 onwards, a new approach to the treatment of credit was introduced by the NCVQ. The Council proposed to reorganise vocational qualifications in the United Kingdom with a common framework, principally to meet Government objectives for simplification and clarity of recognition by prospective trainees, students and employers. Its organising principles, following intellectual antecedents

twenty years earlier, have been based on the need to establish *agreed standards* for the fulfilment of defined occupational functions. These standards are described by nationally applicable criteria of operational performance, the evidence for the successful demonstration of which is carefully prescribed by Industry Lead Bodies (employer representatives) and monitored by authorised assessment centres. Successful performance is measured by the fulfilment of *units of competence* and 'credit' therefrom is aggregated towards the award of National Vocational Qualifications (NVQs), which represent *competence* at a certain level in a defined occupational role. Initially, NVQs have been awarded at lower levels of skill performance but increasingly, in management, construction and health, they are being awarded at levels which the NCVQ defines as commensurate with higher education. We will explain some of these matters further in Chapter IX.

411.   In the progress it has made towards the establishment of a national framework for vocational qualifications, the NCVQ has found it useful to adopt the language and practice of credit accumulation and transfer – but with a difference. Unlike either of the approaches which rely on student workload or notional learning time for the determination of a credit system, the NCVQ rejects any input-related values and emphasises the importance of output performance measures. For the NCVQ, this is quite consistent with the universally agreed principle that 'credit' is only awarded for demonstrated learning achievement. Under these conditions, the effort (workload) or time expended by learners is irrelevant to the definition of credit and its application. Therefore, in order to assure the quality of the awarded 'credit', all vocational learning experiences must be described by explicit *learning outcome statements or competence statements* which formally describe what is to be demonstrated, how it is to be demonstrated, the permissible range of conditions and what constitutes acceptable evidence of performance. The distinguishing feature of the NCVQ approach to 'credit' is the emphasis it gives to the need to provide *evidence* of successful performance. In short, *'credit' is inseparable from competence*. It does not need to be represented by numerical values, since the units of assessment

which contribute to an overall *competence* are internally sequenced within the NVQ. Credit accumulation is therefore relatively straightforward; credit transfer is more problematic. A student may transfer credit between one NVQ and another *where there are overlapping skills.* Usually though, NVQs cannot be easily compared, being referenced solely to the agreed standards of a specific occupation, and credit transfer is more difficult, if not impossible, to arrange.

412. Exactly the same principles and practices apply to GNVQs. Here the situation is complicated by the fact that GNVQs contain more elements of knowledge and conceptual understanding than would be found in an NVQ, where these elements play an 'underpinning role' to operational competence. 'Credit' is still defined in terms of the reward for successful unit achievement, which itself is time independent. In fact, the entire NCVQ learning philosophy is predicated on the assumption that *notional time* and *workload* have no more relevance to successful performance and the award of credit than does the number of driving lessons it might take a learner to pass a driving test. The only relevant matter is that the learner has achieved certain specific tasks to an agreed standard; then that learner is competent to drive, and the credit is the driving licence.

413. The intellectual predicates upon which the NCVQ is founded and according to which it conducts its work are strongly contested. This is likely to have consequences for higher education as the NCVQ seeks to extend its work in the sector. It should be sufficient to state in this summary that disquiet has been expressed from a number of quarters over some of the assumptions which the NCVQ makes about the process of learning. It has been suggested that the NCVQ has a very restricted view of learning achievement; that many intellectual and conceptual qualities do not manifest themselves simply in operational performance; that operational performance itself requires more conceptual underpinning than the NCVQ admits; that 'competence' implies too absolutist a concept of learning when much that is learnt is held provisionally and equivocally; that 'evidence' is itself subject to negotiation; and that learning outcome statements which

purport to describe competence are inevitably as imprecise and subjective as any other socially-constructed language statements. These concerns may have serious consequences, unless refuted in the light of further discussion, for the quality assurance of vocational qualifications and for the reception of NVQs and GNVQs in higher education specifically.

414. Nevertheless, the NCVQ has had a considerable and, in our view positive impact on the further development of credit systems. Without accepting the rejection by the NCVQ of input measures, both *impositional* and *compositional* approaches to credit have attempted to accommodate the use of learning outcome statements, although they are not yet used outside the NCVQ to imply 'competence'. Progress has been significantly more advanced in 'compositional' credit systems based on *notional learning time* where, as we have explained earlier, learning outcome statements are being used as a quality assurance measure to assess the relative claims for credit of different learning experiences, and in some cases to prevent *credit inflation:* that is, the over-claiming of credit for a learning experience (eg a module) a satisfactory demonstration of the learning outcomes of which does not convincingly require the claimed credit-hour learning input.

415. We evaluate the different approaches to 'credit' in the context of a national credit framework in Chapter IX. To summarise here: *impositional* schemes of credit are more wider used in higher education, where their origins in the work of the CNAA has established some familiarity in universities, colleges and amongst employers and professional bodies. The approach is held to be simple and effective in establishing credit rating on degree-related programmes without any necessary implications for course structure. On the other hand, *compositional* schemes have developed more extensively in the diverse learning environment of further and adult education, with less exposure to date in higher education in the United Kingdom. The most prominent example of this approach is that being developed by the FEU as part of its CATS Network, which in style and treatment of 'credit' draws extensively on the experiences of the Open College Federations. The third treatment of 'credit' depends almost

entirely upon the work of the NCVQ and is now well-known in further education for defining lower level vocational programmes. It has begun to surface in higher education as higher level vocational programmes are accredited in universities and colleges.

Credit accumulation and credit transfer

416.   Credit accumulation and transfer arrangements are often taken as part of the same process. Yet closer inspection suggests that *credit accumulation* is regarded less problematically than *credit transfer*. The reasons for this are straightforward. *Credit accumulation* refers to arrangements, largely internal to individual institutions, which govern how students may progress by aggregated learning achievement towards defined learning outcomes, including formal qualifications. Demand for credit accumulation can be readily inferred from the normal practice and experience of the majority of students. Credit accumulation speaks of the desire by students to progress towards designated qualifications. The majority of students will do this within the context of full-time continuous study at one institution. Even part-time students will tend to remain within one institutional setting, protracting their accumulation of academic credit over time perhaps, only a minority invoking procedures for transfer. Furthermore, credit accumulation may be managed by universities and colleges within familiar academic arrangements. In one sense, all learning towards a qualification involves the accumulation of academic credit. Where institutions elect to expand the choice and flexibility of programmes available to students, through modular programmes within which routes and pathways may be more or less prescribed, they encourage students in the accumulation of credit.

417.   Credit accumulation may also cover students 'transferring' from lower qualifications to higher qualifications, or from further education to higher education programmes. They may be justifiably said to be engaged in 'accumulating' academic credit. These forms of credit accumulation, perhaps better described as *accumulative transfer*, are more readily accepted as necessary and central

features of the pattern of higher education provision. We have tended to treat these arrangements elsewhere in this report as examples of *credit transfer* (see Chapter VII).

418.   *Credit transfer* refers to those arrangements, usually concerning students external to individual institutions, which describe the procedures and conventions for admission, often requiring some co-operative inter-institutional framework within which to operate effectively. *Credit transfer* will often involve a distinction to be drawn between *general credit* and *specific credit.* The former term describes the general capacity for transfer whilst the latter term reflects the specific amount of general credit which will be allowed against any chosen programme. This may amount to all, some or none of the general credit, depending on the nature of the programme and the relevance of the credit to it. Increasingly, *credit transfer* is being adopted to refer to patterns of internal institutional transfer, consequent on the growth of modular programmes. We have dealt extensively with dimensions of credit transfer in Chapter VII and have more to say about *general* and *specific* credit in the context of quality assurance in Chapter X.

Credit systems, credit schemes and credit frameworks and their modular equivalents

419.   Various terms are used to describe the extent to which arrangements are coupled together in some way. *Credit systems* and *modular systems* are often used as very general terms to capture the overall arrangements of a sector or an individual institution. Sometimes the terms are used interchangeably with 'schemes' and 'frameworks' and no great precision or agreement has yet been established for the proper meaning of the term. Of one thing we can be certain: *credit system* rarely implies a truly systematic and closely defined application of 'credit'; this is usually true of *modular systems* as well.

420.   A more commonly used set of terms refer to *credit schemes* and *modular schemes.* Usually these terms do imply something 'schematic' and bound by unifying regulations. In the case of *credit schemes*, these

may be institutional, or more likely sub-institutional, arrangements. In either case, the schemes will be working explicitly with 'credit' as a numerical value, and students will generally be aware of the need to earn and accumulate credits. Schemes may work within a modular or a non-modular context. An example of a modular, institutional scheme would be the *Integrated Credit Scheme* at Liverpool John Moores University; the Combined Studies degree at Sheffield Hallam University (and elsewhere) would be a good example of a sub-institutional credit scheme. This latter example would also serve as an example of a *CAT scheme*. This term often refers to schemes specifically designed to cater for a selected cohort of students. They may be designed for part-time or associate students, or full-time students seeking particular programme combinations, and they will usually be supplementary to the main programme of an institution. Therefore, when a university says it has a *'CAT scheme'*, it does not imply anything other than that some students may have the opportunity to negotiate their progress through the programmes of the institution. More often than otherwise, this will involve a relatively small group of students in an institution where 'credit' is not yet a common feature for most students. In an earlier attempt to provide some coherence to the plethora of institutional developments, Portwood (1990) offered five models of 'CAT schemes' (see Table 27). Such has been the rapid rate of development that his initial classification, whilst still useful, may have been overtaken by events. The whole-institutional arrangements now rarely call themselves 'CAT schemes' since 'credit' has become their general organising principle. In other cases, however, the *supplementary, promotional* and *developmental* models can still be discerned. The most important aspect of Portwood's typology is the emphasis he gives to the place of 'credit' in the academic control structure of the institution. Is it central or marginalised as an organising instrument? How many students, for example, would recognise its presence and understand its consequences for their learning experience?

421.   *Modular schemes* often do not use 'credit' explicitly. Even where they have been recently introduced, they tend to be modelled on older variants of *modular and credit* schemes.

Often, the 'module' and the 'credit' are co-terminous, as with the Open University arrangements. Similarly, the well-established modular schemes at Oxford Brookes University, Middlesex University, the University of Hertfordshire and the University of Stirling tend to use modules as a proxy for 'credit'. Most of the recent developments in the older

---

Table 27:
A typology of credit schemes?

1. *Embryonic models:* initial arrangements for the extension of access and greater student choice; ;may have little purchase on academic control system and facilities for negotiated programmes is limited.

2. *Supplementary models:* small scale arrangements, often linked to central 'CATS Unit', with evolutionary capacity leading to possible permeation of institutional academic control structure.

3. *Promotional models:* related to work of institution in promotion of its services to employers and similar clients through accreditation of 'off campus' learning; involved in credit transfer between workplace and higher education; specific place in academic control structure via quality assurance.

4. *Developmental models:* whole institution arrangements, but beginning with a central development unit to stimulate and negotiate progress; ultimate objective is the use of credit as an organising concept within the academic control structure.

5. *Constitutional models:* whole institution arrangements which commit the full resources and capacities of the institution to the achievement of a mission in which 'credit' features prominently as an organising concept. The academic control system of the institution becomes based on the principles of credit accumulation and transfer.

Models based on the SEEC discussion paper, Derek Portwood, 1990

universities follow this pattern. On some occasions, schemes will superimpose credit tariffs on their modules. Usually, but not always, modules in such schemes tend to be the same size. However, this will not always be the case where schemes actively use 'credit' to establish a tariff for different shaped modules or units. As with *credit schemes*, modular schemes generally possess more or less elaborate regulations, which possess greater or lesser degrees of local freedom and variation. 'Weak' schemes will tolerate a multiplicity of 'special cases' and exemptions; 'stronger' and generally more effective schemes will be able to maintain some degree of overall scheme control, but this control will invariably be qualified by the 'politics' of individual institutional circumstances.

422. *Credit frameworks* tend to be more formalised supra-institutional arrangements, although institutional or faculty frameworks can be designed which are supra-departmental equivalents. A *credit framework* generally has three features:

- *an architecture*, comprising a series of levels of progression, interim qualifications and a means of aligning a variety of qualifications, vertically and laterally within the framework;

- *articulation arrangements*, enabling progression and transfer between various levels and pathways in the framework (ie. 'ladders' and 'bridges');

- *technical instruments*, comprising a definition of credit and a definition of programmes and sub-units (modules etc); a means of relating credits with programmes and sub-units (increasingly through an outcomes-led process of credit-rating); common guidelines, or more often regulations, which define compliance with the framework. These may cover admissions, assessment and progression policies and practices, usually at an institutional level.

423. The term *credit framework* implies a notion of elective participation. Institutions and courses are usually invited,

with more or less clear policy steerage, to work within the *credit framework*. Frameworks tend to be as effective as their subscribers make them. Too many variations and 'special cases' produce weak frameworks; too much over-specificity and regulation inhibits participation and further development. *Frameworks* tend to be 'centralist', co-ordinative and integrative; they appear to work well when based on negotiated participation, but once participants are involved, general compliance becomes essential. *Modular frameworks* are largely synonymous with *credit frameworks* and with *modular schemes*, although they may not always use 'credit' explicitly. We discuss some of these aspects further in Chapter XII.

424. *Miscellaneous aspects of 'credit'*. We have established earlier that credit is only ever awarded for learning achievement. Moreover, 'credit' itself is never graded and amounts of 'credit' are not weighted by quality of performance, nor generally by their intellectual level in a programme. Modules may be graded, of course, but the grading system tends to exist separately from the award of 'credit'. We have found no examples to the contrary in higher or further education. Furthermore, fractional 'credits' are rare; the Open University 'half-credit' unit would be an exception. There does not appear to be any principled reason why fractional credits are not employed, and we conclude that colleagues reasonably accept that 'credit' is a useful tool which does not require fractional precision to fulfil its purpose. We would not rule out the need for fractional credits, at least in the short term, if this proved a useful way to overcome articulation arrangements between different sectors.

The language of modules

Modules and units

425. There has been a longstanding discussion about the relationship between credits, modules and units. We detect signs that this may now be resolving itself as the use of these terms collapses into a shared description of *modular* and *credit-based arrangements*. Squires (1986) may have been

optimistic at the time, but a few years later his observation has more force, that *current interest in modular courses, such as it is, seems to derive from an interest in credit systems rather than the other way round*. The CNAA commented similarly, in 1990:

'It is difficult to consider a scheme such as CATS or modular courses in isolation from each other. Both are concerned with a wide range of entrants, tailoring programmes of study to individual needs, breaking down a mandated programme structure and learning sequence and at the same time relating these to acceptable academic standards.'

426.   *Modules and units* have certain basic characteristics. As Theodossin (1986) and many others have observed, these are: *size and shape* – their 'width' (in continuous teaching time); their 'length' (measured in terms, semesters or year); and their 'weight' in the programme (often as 'core' or 'elective'); *arrangement* (whether taught concurrently or consecutively); and *assessment* (usually terminal, at module completion). Beyond these characteristics, modules may also exhibit other features. They may be *pre-requisite* or *co-requisite* requirements for other modules; they will be assigned a level in a framework of progression; they may have specific entry requirements; they may be shared with other programmes and therefore have mixed ability cohorts; finally, they may not be available to students at any given time if room scheduling or staff availability constrains this.

427.   For some time, there has been discussion about whether there is a difference between *modularisation* and *unitisation*. This is not a discussion that could occur in the United States, where all such segments are called 'courses'. In the United Kingdom, however, there have been two aspects to this largely unproductive debate. Firstly, *unitisation* has sometimes been employed by those for whom the term *'modularisation'* has carried overtones of unwelcome and systematic fragmentation of *courses* (in the British sense of the term). *Units* have been presented in some examples of practice as non-standardised segments, including conventional year-long elements. In other words, an institution might *unitise* by agreeing to offer students five/six

'units' a year, but not necessarily within a common term, trimester or semester structure. On the other hand, *modules* are invariably offered with a formally designated trimester or semester arrangement, often with a standard length, in which the module is almost always shorter than the length of the year. Secondly, and possibly confusingly, the NCVQ has preferred the term *'unit'*, where others might have used *'module'*, in describing the sub-units of NVQs and GNVQs. Although the NCVQ approaches the process of learning very differently, making an exact comparison impossible, the Council does expect units of the GNVQ to be of equal size, length and time (Fig. 1).

428.   There is one other dimension which is quite important. Influenced possibly by models inspired by the NCVQ, some of the work associated with the FEU's *A basis for credit?* makes an interesting distinction between *modules of delivery* and *units of assessment*. In higher education, these are invariably the same. A module is a closed segment of the overall course, the outputs from which are assessed at the completion of the module. In further education and for the NCVQ, this may not necessarily be the same at all. Several *units of assessment* may contribute to one overall *module*; or two modules may share various units of assessment (see Fig. 2). There may be relevance here for higher education, if institutions choose to take advantage of it. For example, teacher training students may need to take subjects in a specific disciplinary area. In a modular system, these subject specialisms might be delivered by specialist academics rather than lecturers in teacher training. Clearly, the specialist requirements of a student studying for a degree in a particular subject may be different from those of a student studying for a BEd. Yet they could share the same *module of delivery* in the specialist subject but be required to submit for different *units of assessment*. There are a few, but not many, examples of this in higher education and it suggests an opportunity for further work.

Modules and standardisation

429.   We have implied earlier that modularity tends towards standardisation. In many schemes and arrange-

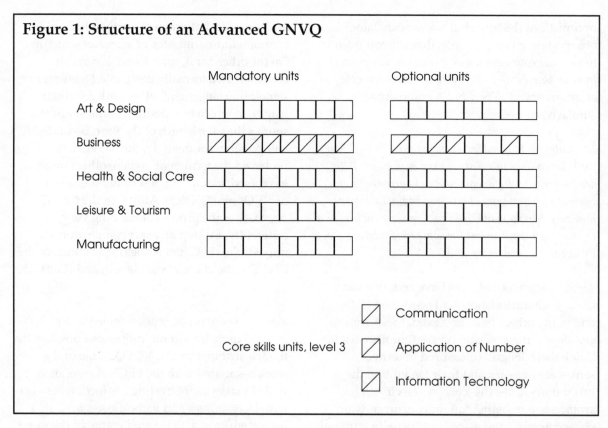

Figure 1: Structure of an Advanced GNVQ

Mandatory units / Optional units

Art & Design

Business

Health & Social Care

Leisure & Tourism

Manufacturing

Core skills units, level 3

Communication

Application of Number

Information Technology

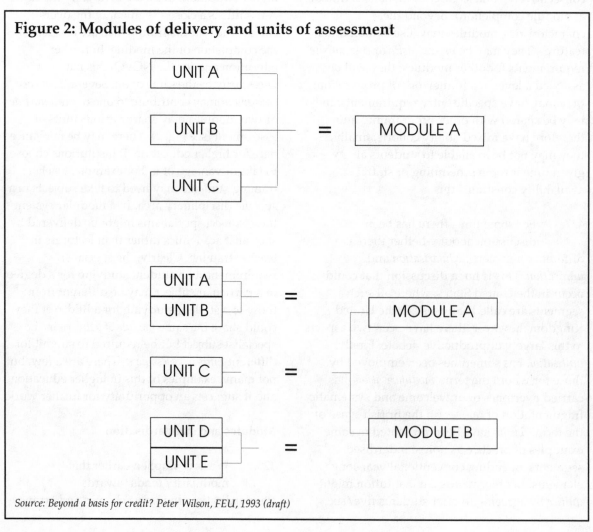

Figure 2: Modules of delivery and units of assessment

UNIT A
UNIT B   =   MODULE A
UNIT C

UNIT A
UNIT B   =
                        MODULE A
UNIT C   =

UNIT D   MODULE B
UNIT E   =

Source: Beyond a basis for credit? Peter Wilson, FEU, 1993 (draft)

ments, this appears to be true. For some institutions, the alleged administrative conveniences of standardised modules is an attractive reason for pursuing the development, accepting the 'trade-off' that it may not suit all subject disciplines equally. Accordingly, many universities attempt to create isomorphic modular structures, involving ten or twelve modules per year, regardless of the needs of different subjects. This style of homogenisation has drawn some comment, the most pertinent of which is from Waterhouse (1987): *'A restricted modular system in which all the modules must be the same size and last for the same length is a straightjacket of the sort which has given modularity a bad name.'* Academic critics of modularisation claim, with some justification in our opinion, that the patterns of subject disciplines do not necessarily lend themselves to this type of standardisation. What may be possible for Biology may not be appropriate for History or Fine Art. We observe from our investigations that the greater impetus in modularisation comes from administrative preferences for standardisation rather than from academic requirements for flexibility and variation. This is why some institutions these days believe that there is substantial merit in the application of credit to modular structures, bestowing a currency which tolerates differences of size and shape whilst retaining a measure of equivalence. We share this view.

430.   **Standardisation across the sector:** We confirm that there appears to be no prospect of a 'standard' modular pattern emerging across higher education. 'Modularised' institutions appear to be equally divided amongst those who prefer 6, 8, 10 or 12 modules. A smaller number of institutions require no fixed number of modules, because students are required to accumulate a fixed number of credits from modules with various tariffs. Although there may be advantages in administrative tidiness, we can think of no good academic or educational reason why anyone would wish to encourage a standard modular pattern across higher education; we can think of several good reasons why this would be academically most inappropriate. Moreover, standarisation in further education may be even less likely, given the range and diversity of qualifications. Only the NCVQ, in the design of

GNVQs, appear to favour a form of standardisation uncommon elsewhere, and that can be explained by the fact that the GNVQ is an award which claims to be made to uniform national standards. Local variations might complicate the assurance of these national performance criteria.

Courses, programmes and students

431.   We have been asked on occasions what colleagues mean by a *course* in the context of credit-based modular schemes. We have explained above how the term is used in the United States. In the United Kingdom, the *course* almost always refers to a structured and pre-designed learning experience, often single discipline-centred, offered by academics for students to follow. It may contain within it more or less options and choices, but its key feature is that it is designed by professional academic judgement alone, leading to a designated final qualification. A *programme* generally refers to the process from the perspective of a student. It is usually constructed by the student from the modules or units available, and may be formed initially with a specific qualification in mind. To this extent many 'programmes' are co-terminous with a 'course'. However, in modular and credit-based schemes, the potential exists for much greater individuality of programme design, initiated by students with guidance support, and authenticated subsequently by professional academic judgement. In short, *courses* tend to be '(academic) producer-led' and *programmes* tend to be '(student) consumer-led'. For NCVQ courses/programmes, they introduce a third dimension: 'employer-led' to the extent that courses are designed to standards established by employer-focused Industry Lead Bodies.

432.   Within *modular* and *credit-based* schemes, students are often described as following *routes*, or *pathways*, or occasionally these are called *'tracks'*. They may be pre-designed, or student-constructed, and they are terms which describe the passage of students across a matrix of modules and learning opportunities from (multiple) entry subjects to (multiple) exit qualifications. For example, a student may enrol on a flexible scheme to study English and History, study additional subjects

in her first year, change to major in History in the second year, but graduate with Combined Honours. Her *pathway* will have been different from that of a more conventional English/History graduate and may have included electives in Business or Media Studies or Information Technology on the way. We should add that there may be nothing novel in the use of these terms to describe student behaviour on modular schemes; such choices and 'pathways' could be available in non-modular arrangements which exploited a wider range of choices under more conventional conditions.

Semesters, trimesters and terms

433.   All modular and credit-based schemes work within one of these arrangements in such a way that the structure of the year influences the distribution of, and access to, programmes. *Terms* are too familiar to merit much attention here, but *trimesters* have been an attempt to work with the traditional pattern by dividing the year into three equal parts, often of eleven weeks. The best example of this arrangement is at Oxford Brookes University, but elsewhere its implementation as a device for securing modularisation has proved problematic. Institutions have found the teaching period prior to assessment too short; the assessment load arguably too burdensome; and the feedback and information load too cumbersome to manage successfully. There are now very few modular schemes which attempt to pursue modularisation through trimesters.

434.   More conventionally, *semesters* have been the standard alternative to *terms*, following the American practice. *Semesters* come in two forms: the *unreformed semester* and the *reformed semester*. The former has been the British way, overlaying 15-week semesters on an otherwise unreformed three-term academic year. In fact, this has not been particularly successful in the United Kingdom at supporting effective modularisation because of a disruptive inter-semester break in February, and increasingly there have been calls for its reform (Robertson, 1991; 1992; CNAA, 1992). The *reformed semester* has now emerged in proposals from the Flowers Report (HEFCE, 1993) and the Irvine Report (SHEFC, 1993), based on two 15-week semesters, the first of which would begin

in early September and be completed before Christmas. Currently many universities and colleges plan to move to the reformed arrangements in the near future, but many remain nervous that, in being the first to move without modifications to the release of 'A' level results, they may be disadvantaged in student applications. Moreover, although the benefits of the reformed arrangements are likely to be considerable to academic staff and students over time, the cultural upheaval involved in repositioning the rhythms of the year appear to be substantial in the short-term.

435.   **Third semester and extended year:** we found little conviction that a third summer semester was something that would be attractive to students or institutions in any great numbers. Some universities and colleges appear to be anticipating using this period in their planning arrangements, but only for selected summer schools. The third semester is generally perceived negatively; it is associated by academic staff particularly with a threat to professional research time and as a device for further lowering unit costs to the detriment of the student learning experience. It is not yet associated positively with either accelerated programmes or with multiple entry points and a roll-on roll-off academic year; academic staff remain sceptical of the quality of the former and the manageability of the latter.

436.   It should be noted in conclusion that we are not aware of progress towards a *reformed semester* structure in further education, and we think this should perhaps be considered. It would facilitate further and higher education progression and credit transfer, permitting the operation of more courses jointly operated. We consider this further in Chapter IX and XII.

The language of progression and achievement

Levels of achievement

437.   We have been surprised to find a very uneven commitment to the importance of *levels of achievement* in a credit framework. On the one hand, many in higher education regard

the matter as non-controversial and accept that the levels of undergraduate achievement coincide naturally with the years of the full-time honours degree; there is general acceptance of an undivided Master's level. In a few cases, there is speculation that a Part I (year 1 – foundation) and an undivided Part II (year 2 + 3 – graduation) structure might be more reflective of a real structure of intellectual progression. Colleagues who take this view also recognise that *'levels'* are relatively artificial devices for managing *student progression;* there may be a case for spending time on definitions, but little to be gained from the exercise in the end. In short, precision cannot be achieved here, so simplicity will have to suffice.

438.   On the other hand, there is a minority in higher education, joined by others in further education and the NCVQ, who believe that *levels of achievement* must be properly defined in order to lend some clarity, accountability, and quality assurance to the purpose of higher education and beyond. This opinion is driven by the argument that knowledge and skills need to be explicitly represented in outcome statements and their achievement assessed and documented. This has been successful to some extent at lower levels of attainment and therefore it should be possible at higher levels also. But this argument assumes that definitions of *levels of achievement* at lower levels have indeed been successful. These definitions 'succeed', it may be argued, because colleagues are satisfied with them for the purposes in hand rather than because of any intrinsic intellectual merit. Indeed, it has proved difficult for the NCVQ to define levels with any real degree of precision. Their definitions remain rooted in levels of supervision and control combined with references to the exercise of personal initiative and discretion. Provided all participants to the credit framework know what this means and accept it as good enough, then the *level descriptors* will be adequate for all reasonable purposes.

439.   We believe that further work could continue, and perhaps should continue amongst those for whom this is an intellectual challenge, to find *level descriptors* which describe the various levels of progression and achievement in higher education. This may become particularly important if agreements are to be reached between higher education and the NCVQ on the comparability of higher level qualifications. We are sceptical that progress on this matter will be swift or that consensual support will be achieved in the end. Furthermore the beneficial outcomes of the task are unlikely to be commensurate with the effort expended.

440.   We are reminded of two types of problem in these matters. The first is represented by the efforts to find an answer to the question: *What can graduates do?* which resulted from the Learning Outcomes In Higher Education project and the Otter Report (UDACE, 1992). Despite enormous effort, the answer remains unclear. This is not to say that we do not know what graduates can do, but rather to concede that we may lack the linguistic and conceptual apparatus with which to describe it convincingly. In the end, graduates are more or less effective in occupations where employers find them effective; this is a circular argument, but perhaps this is inevitable. The second problem concerns the 'consequences' of asking certain questions about levels of attainment. It is regarded amongst some of our respondents as a dishonesty for higher education to assume that the first year of an undergraduate degree is at an intellectual level higher than much of 'A' level, and its equivalents, in schools and colleges. If it is, they claim, then this should be inspectable in some way rather than simply asserted. The same argument applies in higher education at the boundary between undergraduate and postgraduate courses, and between post-experience and postgraduate programmes. A variant of the argument attempts to describe an undivided 'Part Two' for the honours degree. We do not deny the force of the argument but consider instead the consequences of seeking answers. It may need to be accepted that *levels of achievement* are indeed arbitrary conventions; they may be rendered less arbitrary wherever possible, but to search for the ultimate precision and fairness might cause the entire edifice of qualifications and progression to unravel in a fruitless intellectual search for the impossible.

Levels: barriers, signposts or targets?

441.   We have approached the question of *levels of achievement* from the perspective of the student: what function do they serve for

the learner? It appears that some *levels* are accepted widely as *barriers.* These define the division between further and higher education, and between undergraduate and postgraduate programmes. There are many attempts to make these barriers more permeable but no serious contestation of their legitimacy. Within these broad categories, opinion appears to accept that *levels* can act as *signposts* to students, guiding them through a progression sequence. Students seem to find this useful, allowing them to know where they stand and indicating the likelihood of success at the next 'level' up.

442.   We are aware of very little research in the United Kingdom in the area of student perceptions of progression within credit systems. One important survey for the FEU (Wisher, 1993) looked at the use of credit and progression in two Open College Federations. The conclusions from respondents in Manchester and London indicate that the greater the progression through the levels of a framework, the greater the desire to progress yet further. Aspiration for further progression rose from 22% to 60% between Level 1 and Level 4 in London and from 4% to 54% in Manchester. Students became more instrumentally orientated to achievement and less orientated to merely personal development as they became more successful. Over 53% of all students earned credits and used them as a means of progression; and 74% indicated that credits would encourage them to return to achieve at a higher level.This suggests that a framework of levels has an incentive effect, providing *targets* for students to reach further on many occasions.

The language of competence and outcomes

Competence statements and standards

443.   The search for a language with which to express levels of achievement and the specific character of individual modules has been pursued for a number of years. Work in the United States during the 1960s, reflected particularly in the writings of Mager (1965), attempted to objectify the outcomes of the

learning process and represent them as formal features of the curriculum. These became known variously as *curriculum objectives*, *learning objectives* or sometimes *terminal objectives*. Particularly when applied to vocational training, but less precisely elsewhere, they were described as *competence statements*. In the United Kingdom, limited attempts were made to find a use for this approach in curriculum design and we are aware of some efforts in this direction, reflected in the use of learning objectives statements in some Open University course units during the 1970s. However, it was not until 1986, with the growth of the NCVQ (and to a lesser degree, SCOTVEC) that the use of *competence statements* received extensive attention.

444.   As we have explained earlier, the NCVQ has been committed to a form of curriculum design which emphasises measurable outcomes and achievement to defined standards. *Competence statements* and *unit of competence* are the public expressions of objective performance criteria. In its simplest forms, *competence* is determined by whether a learner can, or cannot, *perform a specific task to an agreed standard under defined conditions.* In practice, the learning process that yields *competence* will be composed of more than operational skills. The NCVQ insists on the presence of 'underpinning' knowledge and understanding in the construction of its qualifications. Thus, any course, or more usually a unit or module, will be presented as a learning experience defined by its outcomes: ie. the extent to which the learning establishes or contributes to the achievement of *competence.*

445.   This approach to course and module specification is now more familiar in further education, where it is being used extensively to define vocational training courses in a manner also common in certain institutions in the United States, New Zealand and elsewhere. Its introduction to higher education has been slower, principally because the intellectual and conceptual basis of the approach to the curriculum remains contested. It is not possible here to offer more than a truncated version of the debate. Firstly, many academics in higher education reject the appropriateness of *competence-based* approaches

to academic programmes, and may also be sceptical of their usefulness to vocationally focused learning as well. The approach to the curriculum is held to be founded on a questionable and possibly discredited theoretical basis, grounded in behavioural theories of learning, a simplistic functionalism and a naive reliance on the precision and objectivity of language statements. Learning, they maintain, always involves more than a capacity to perform; *'what'* to do cannot easily be decoupled from *'how'* and *'why'* to do it. In the case of academic learning, its provisionality and incompleteness are essential characteristics by which students come to recognise their place in a more enduring 'conversation' with ideas and practices over time. *Competence* implies a closure of further enquiry – once a task can be demonstrated, then it must have been learned – whereas academic (and vocational) learning in

higher education needs to emphasises the equivocal and uncertain character of knowledge and understanding of the world. *Competence-based* approaches to the curriculum are therefore held to represent an intellectually unconvincing attempt to intrude pseudo-objective and mechanistic measures into the subtle and complex learning processes of higher education, with possibly damaging consequences that must be resisted.

Learning outcome statements

446.   A second smaller group of academics, whilst accepting most of these arguments, recognise that there may also be some merit in adopting an *outcomes-led* approach to both academic and vocational programmes in further and higher education. They begin by accepting that it is legitimate to

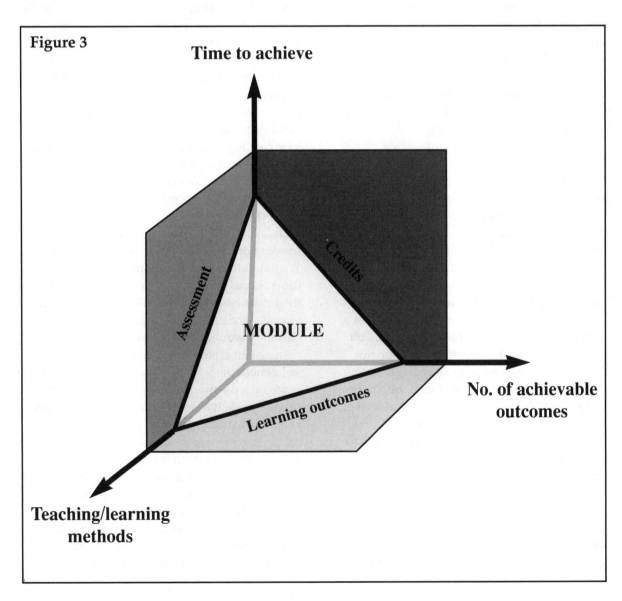

Figure 3

Time to achieve

Assessment

Credits

MODULE

Learning outcomes

No. of achievable outcomes

Teaching/learning methods

ask the question: what can a learner *do* as a consequence of any learning experience? In other words, the outcomes of learning are of legitimate public interest to students and academic staff alike. Moreover, by answering the question: *at the end of this module, a student will be able to… (what?),* considerably greater thought and precision could be introduced into the matching of learning inputs, the learning process, strategies and methodologies of assessment with stated *learning outcomes statements.* These statements might not purport to be *competence statements,* and the successful learner might not be *'competent'* in any simplistic operational sense, but the statements can themselves act as a quality assurance measure of the relationship between learning process and learning outcomes. In short, students and academic peers would have at their disposal a means of verifying explicitly whether the inputs to a particular module or course, and the associated assessment instruments, gave a fair chance that defined learning outcomes could be successfully demonstrated.

447.   Some universities have adopted this latter approach to the use of learning outcome statements. It is being used extensively at the University of Wolverhampton, Liverpool John Moores University, the University of Huddersfield and in many other institutions now as an essential part of their credit-based and modular academic programmes. It should be said that, although there has been noticeable progress in these institutions and the use of such statements are beginning to be seen as helpful curriculum design instruments, the writing of outcomes statements for particular modules at various levels has proved to be very difficult. Firstly, many academic programmes do not lend themselves readily to disaggregation into precise statements of achievement. Either the subject matter is too general or all-embracing, or the statements that can be offered are too imprecise to be helpful, or language is simply incapable of expressing the variety, subtlety or intuitive aspects of much advanced conceptual work. Even where academics are prepared to attempt the intellectual exercise, and are persuaded by the potential of using *learning outcome statements* constructively, it has proved extremely difficult to provide convincing

examples of greater objectivity and precision in the design of learning delivery and assessment. Secondly, it has proved nearly impossible adequately to define *learning outcome statements* **by level of achievement.** For example, it is by no means clear whether it is possible to use *learning outcome statements* to distinguish different levels of attainment within undergraduate degree programmes. Winter (1993) has sought to use various taxonomies to attempt this, although it is not clear whether the effort will pass a practical test.

A multi-dimensional relationship between credits, modules and learning outcomes

448.   In an effort to synthesise the advantages of *credit* (for transferability), *modules* (for flexibility) and *learning outcomes* (for accountability and quality assurance), a small number of universities to date have attempted to produce a multi-dimensional approach to the use of credit systems, representing the relationship between concepts as a feedback loop (see Fig 4): *learning outcome statements* help to define what is to be *assessed; modules* can be defined as collections of learning outcomes which are to be *delivered;* and *credits* are the means by which the equivalence of modules is established, and the successful achievement of learning outcomes is recognised and *accredited.* We have attempted to explain this as a multi-dimensional relationship (see Fig.3) in which the module exists within the co-ordinates of *credit, outcomes* and *assessment.* In short, some thinking currently would perceive the module as more than just an arbitrary and administrative segment of the whole course. Instead the *module* represents the minimum learning experience capable of delivering an intellectually coherent cluster of learning outcomes.

449.   We have been impressed by this approach to understanding the importance of credits and modules for curriculum development. It takes us away from those perspectives which see the process of modularisation simply as an administrative exercise. We are aware that some institutions

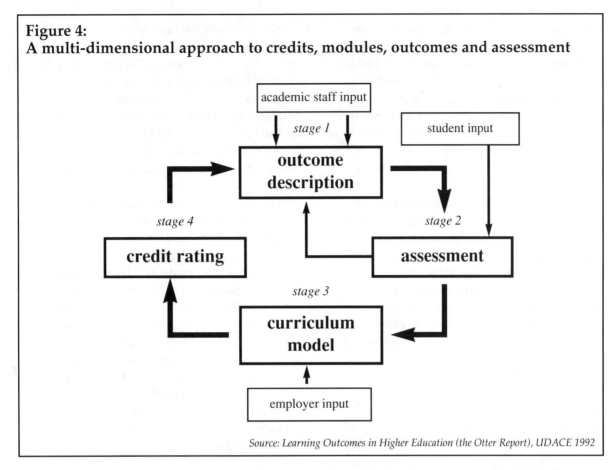

Figure 4:
A multi-dimensional approach to credits, modules, outcomes and assessment

Source: *Learning Outcomes in Higher Education (the Otter Report), UDACE 1992*

and many academic colleagues expect nothing more from the introduction of modularisation and credit-based learning than administrative convenience. On the other hand, academic colleagues have a right to expect that there should be some academic rationales for any systematic changes to curriculum structures and we believe a multi-dimensional approach to the matter might be helpful.

Conclusions

450. We said at the beginning of the chapter that we were cautious about being too prescriptive in the use of terms and concepts for matters which were still evolving. In the course of our investigations, it has become apparent that some approaches are commonly shared whilst some others are shared amongst those at the furthest edge of developments. These latter examples may be helpful as an indication of the direction of latest thinking, around which a future consensus may emerge.

451. In summary, the following observations seem to reflect a general consensus of the meaning of terms and their use. Firstly, credit systems, based on notional time or student workload and represented by a numerical currency, have far greater applicability in higher, further and adult education than arrangements based on competence or outcomes statements alone. Between these numerical systems, *impositional* schemes are more widely used in higher education, whereas *compositional* schemes appear to be more relevant to further and adult education. A solution will need to be found for the development of a national credit framework.

452. Secondly, there is general agreement amongst institutions on the definition of *credit* based on a 30-hour unit of notional learning time, although this concept of *credit* is disputed by the NCVQ. However, no alternative appears to be available which establishes a comprehensively applicable system of transferable credit currency. Thirdly, the use of competence, or learning outcome statements, is having an increasing impact upon the design of modules and the definition of assessment strategies. This is currently restricted to a small number of institutions in higher education

although it has become more widespread in further education. Moreover, *competence* as a term may not gain ready acceptance in higher education; it strikes against a value system which asserts the provisionality and the incompleteness of learning. An alternative term may be needed. Some institutions have used the concept of *capability,* but we wonder whether an appropriate alternative might be *proficiency.*

453. Next, there is evidence that credit-based arrangements are moving from small-scale schemes to whole-institution strategies. This process appears to be taking place more swiftly in the newer than in the older universities, and in many further education colleges also. Where CATS is used as a term, it appears to be retained by smaller scale and discrete arrangements for the management of specific minorities of students, often for part-time programmes or for work-based learning and 'off-campus' activities. In whole institution arrangements, the term is often replaced by *credit-based learning* or an equivalent term, and such expressions seem likely to merge into the general language of flexible and choice-centred academic programmes. Furthermore, *credit transfer* appears to be used both as an 'omnibus' term to capture most activities related to 'credit', but also as a term specifically describing inter-institutional transfer, or more commonly transfer from 'off-campus' to institutional programmes. The term is not yet widely used to describe the passage of students from further to higher education in the manner that the term is commonly used in the United States to describe the transfer of students from two-year colleges to four-year universities.

454. Fifthly, modularity and credit systems appear to be more closely related in the new universities than in the old, where modularity appears to be developing without an assumed use of a credit currency system. *Module* appears to be the more widely adopted term and modular schemes tend to be standardised with uniform modules. Where such schemes use

'credit' this is not the case, however, and there is no consensus on a standard number of modules per semester/term. Sixthly, the language of the 'course' is beginning to give way to the use of *programmes* and *routes* as alternative terms, although progress in this direction remains fitful and many institutions appear to have reached an accommodation between new modular structures and the traditional language of the course.

455. Seventh, the discourse surrounding assessment appears to be underdeveloped in much of higher education. Matters concerning assessment objectives, the definition of standards, and the relationship between learning process and outcomes are often poorly articulated, even in areas which are otherwise taking credit-based initiatives. This appears to be less obviously the case in further education. It seems to us that it would be helpful if further work were undertaken in higher education to produce a clearer definition of assessment criteria and strategies appropriate to a flexible curriculum involving greater student choice.

456. Finally, we have been impressed by multi-dimensional approaches to the use of credits, modules and learning outcomes. From our investigations, we have noticed that many institutions in higher and further education are not content to develop credit systems merely as organisational arrangements. Instead, they seek educational reasons for their appropriateness in assisting the expression of greater student choice. For this, they have begun to look at the sort of interconnections to which we have made reference in earlier discussion. If we were to advise on one single development for the better understanding of credit, **we would recommend** that institutions explore the potential of a multi-dimensional approach to provide a more comprehensive and educationally convincing rationale for the further development of credit systems than might otherwise be the case.

IX.   *A credit framework*

Introduction

457.   As we have shown in Chapter V and Chapter VI, the development of a national credit framework is strongly supported by all parties. Employers have urged its development; institutions have recognised its appeal to students; government departments have encouraged progress; and recently funding councils have begun to recognise its potential for influencing funding formulae.

458.   To explore how a national framework might be developed, what features it should exhibit and what support it would command, we consulted widely on opinion within institutions and across the various sectors. We sought the views of all agencies active in the field, surveyed participants in various conferences on the subject of credit systems, and others who have been active in their development and implementation, and studied other national systems. Throughout our investigations, respondents were asked to comment on which had the higher priority: sector-specific frameworks; academic or vocational frameworks; specific national frameworks; or a common framework for all activity. It would be fair to say that there is almost universal support for the principle of a unified credit framework, embracing sectors, nationalities and educational activities. On the other hand, there is considerable divergence of opinion on what a unified framework might look like, how it might operate and whether it could be achieved in practice. We explore some of these differences below.

459.   Two particular points of difficulty stand out. Firstly, we have referred to a national credit framework as if this were a simple matter for the United Kingdom. Yet we are fully aware of sensitivities which make the achievement of a common framework more complex. For example, progress within higher education in Scotland and further education in Wales have been more complete than in England; progress in Northern Ireland has been quite slow in general. It is quite possible that individual nations within the United Kingdom could develop frameworks which reflect their own identities and needs. Furthermore, progress within a given national context might be more rapid than that which requires participation from all parts of the kingdom. Only progress from the NCVQ has been extensive across these national boundaries, but largely in further education and there, only in vocational programmes. Accepting that national boundaries and different national systems within the United Kingdom will continue to have significant impact upon the character of any credit framework, we have chosen to reflect the common desire for a unified and comprehensive credit framework by reference to the term 'national' as the nearest adequate expression for a framework across the United Kingdom.

460.   Secondly, we have made a number of references in earlier discussion to different rates of progress and starting points in higher and further education. It would be quite conceivable that these sectors could end by completing very different frameworks, using dissimilar specifications. This may already have happened in Scotland (SCOTVEC and SCOTCAT), might be occurring in Wales, and could emerge in England as well. Although we explore options around this matter below, we have attempted in this report to represent the majority opinion that a common framework across sector boundaries should be sought.

461.   We are convinced by one aspect of this discussion. The principal purpose of any framework is to provide a common structure within which individual variations may be worked out. Whilst it is important to respect the differences of various approaches, understanding the difficulties in marrying them, it would be a substantial negation of the purpose of this report if it did not attempt to find a common workable solution. If we fail, the losers will be our students.

The demand for a credit framework

462.   We have tried to find an answer to one obvious question: do we need one common framework, or would a number of different frameworks serve just as well? In favour of the single framework, we would suggest that it has the advantage of 'tidiness' and completeness. It could be simple and simplifying to students and employers, and convenient for funding councils and other national agencies. Above all, it would rise above the artificial boundaries of nation, sector, institution or learning experience to establish an open network of opportunities for students. On the other hand, it might be 'over-tidy', losing through compromise some of the richness, specificity and focus of a framework designed for a particular purpose. Moreover, the efforts expended in the development of a common framework might not be repaid in the speed of progress which might otherwise be possible within separate frameworks. Therefore, it might be necessary to settle for different frameworks, articulated by some common arrangements for transfer.

463.   This was certainly the conclusion reached by the *Learning without walls* conference in 1991 when faced with the need to unite the CNAA and the NCVQ frameworks. However, since that time, events have moved on with the contributions of proposals from the FEU in 1992 and subsequent progress throughout further education. It might be suggested that the emergence of a third approach to credit frameworks adds weight to the argument for the loose articulation of separate frameworks rather than for a unified approach. This might be the case, were it not for the argument that it cannot be sensible for students transferring from further to higher education to move between different credit frameworks without good cause. Moreover, because they straddle the sectors, NCVQ programmes would benefit from an articulation with a common FE/HE framework rather than with two separate arrangements. In short, solutions which depend on loose articulation may still be appropriate, as we shall explore below, but an opportunity does now exist to define the principles and operation of a common set of arrangements, not least because of the widespread support for such a solution.

464.   The search for a suitable credit framework has occupied much of the development work of national agencies. It is possible to see the outlines of a comprehensive framework in the way the CNAA has sought to promote its scheme within higher education. Moreover, the NCVQ has been given the task precisely to develop a national framework for vocational qualifications, within which it has sought to realise the potential of its own unit-credit arrangements. Latterly, the FEU has taken initiatives to extend the principles of a comprehensive framework into further education in the first instance. And working in adult education, the National Open College Network (NOCN) has quietly built a national network of credit-awarding bodies to form its own credit scheme. We examine each of these arrangements in more detail below, assessing their ability to contribute to a comprehensive national credit framework.

465.   The reasons for this extensive activity are clear. By establishing a comparable relationship between different learning experiences, and by allowing students to construct units into coherent patterns for the award of qualifications, a unified credit framework fulfils substantial social and educational goals. A credit framework can extend the range of learning opportunities if it is adopted by educational providers and widely accepted by all parties, especially by students and employers. It can draw achievements into the sphere of authentic learning which might otherwise pass unrecognised, simplifying an awareness of opportunities at the same time. It can improve the quality of personal learning programmes by increasing their relevance to individual needs, blur boundaries between academic and vocational learning pathways, and improve the confidence of employers in individual student achievement. Above all, credit frameworks provide 'signposts' for students and employers alike, guiding their passage through diverse and unfamiliar educational terrain.

Principles of a credit framework

466. If the purposes of a credit framework are those suggested in discussion above, then the principles must establish sufficient agreement to secure the participation of all interested parties. A framework which seeks to impose arbitrary regulations on institutions, which is over-complex in terms of its specifications, or which is too ambitious in scope, will not succeed in attracting the coalition of support that is necessary to sustain it. On the other hand, a framework which seeks too readily to please, by accommodating every individual variation or idiosyncrasy, is unlikely to remain convincing for very long. A framework must establish sufficient structure for the sake of effective guidance, so that students and employers can see how things stand in relationship to each other, and sufficient stability so that academics and their institutions do not feel uncomfortably compromised in pursuit of complementary objectives such as the quality of teaching and research. In short, the construction of a credit framework, as with all other frameworks, is very much a question of consistency, balance and compromise.

467. An effective credit framework must achieve certain objectives. Firstly, it must be **comprehensive** and inclusive, allowing any form of learning which is achieved under any conditions to be accommodated within the framework; this comprehensiveness may be mitigated by other policy objectives, but for our purposes here, we have assumed its application to all forms of learning in higher and further education and beyond. Secondly, it must be **comprehensible** to users; it should be simple in operation and credible in its application; students and employers should know clearly what the credit framework does for them. Thirdly, it should be **coherent** and capable of monitoring itself; the framework should provide for quality assurance, and departure from its conventions should be readily apparent and subject to report. Fourthly, it should be **compatible,** both with systems operating in other countries where possible, and with the academic and educational objectives of institutions in higher and further education.

A credit framework as an open system

468. In work for the FEU leading to developments towards a credit framework for further and adult education, Wilson (1993) has introduced an interesting approach to this discussion. Borrowing from contemporary information systems analysis, Wilson suggests that the principles of a credit framework have much in common with those of an **open system.** In computer technology, and elsewhere, the development of different operating systems and technical specifications has led to the need to produce some minimum standardisation of key components whilst preserving the independence and variety of commercial products. In short, different systems need to be able to communicate by shared devices. Whilst we are wary of

---

**Table 28:
Credit framework as open system**

Principle 1: the system is open to all users

An open system of credit will have rules of operation (it will be a system) and will enable all those who wish to conform with these rules to enter (it will be open). Attempts to compel use of the system will corrupt its 'openness'. Some awarding bodies (and institutions) may choose to express their qualifications within the credit framework and others may not.

Principle 2: the system is comprehensive

A framework provides the minimum level of specifications to enable a credit system to operate, with the maximum level of accessibility to learners. As an open system, it is 'potentially' rather than actually comprehensive.

Principle 3: the system is owned by its users

No single user can 'own' the system but all who use it have an obligation to maintain its consistency and effectiveness. The strength of an open system lies in its 'weakness'. It seeks to enable rather than control participation.

Peter Wilson, 'Developing a Post-16 CAT Framework: the technical specifications', 1993

argument by analogy, and will have something to say on this particular analogy below, the principles which Wilson identifies are outlined in Table 28.

469.   These principles seem to us to be helpful and convincing. We are particularly attracted by the third principle: common ownership, because this is highly relevant for the proposals offered in this report. It is quite clear that the development of credit systems has gone well beyond the higher education sector alone. Thinking has moved on considerably since the initial discussions in the CNAA ten years ago. However useful the analogy of an 'open system' might be, there may be a danger in taking it too literally. 'Open system' does not necessarily mean that existing systems require no modifications. In the commercial market of computer technology, individual producers can remain technologically unique if they wish, but they run the risk that their products will become incompatible and obsolete. Prudent companies choose to adjust to the best available innovations, sharing basic conventions, and in this way 'industry standards' begin to develop. This is likely to be the way forward for a national credit framework. It will involve some necessary compromises on all sides if sectional conflict is to be avoided, and if we are to succeed in defining the minimum agreed specifications for a genuinely 'open system' of credit. We now have the opportunity to build on the platform established by the CNAA by incorporating some of the advantages introduced by the NCVQ and the FEU in their treatment of credit.

The scope of a credit framework

470.   If a credit framework is to be truly comprehensive and useful to students and employers, it should be applicable to both higher and further education, to academic and vocational programmes, to institutional and 'off-campus' learning, and to any form of learning achievement defined by mode of attendance, site of learning or style of delivery. This is likely to present a radical departure from present perceptions in higher education of the scope of credit systems. Experience to date has encouraged the view that credit accumulation

and credit transfer are phenomena peculiar to student flexibility and mobility in higher education. This view may be reinforced by perceptions of arrangements in the United States, and by a reasonable assessment of potential student behaviour in the United Kingdom. Certainly, the strong support from employers and professional bodies for the development of a national credit framework (outlined in Chapter V) is based largely on the assumption that it will apply principally to higher education; there appears to be complementary but separate support for the creation of a national *vocational* credit framework based on the work of the NCVQ.

471.   We have stated already in Chapter VI that it would be a substantial missed opportunity if we did not take this occasion to explore the prospects for unifying these objectives. A mandate from the sectors has been provided by successive national conferences on the subject (see Chapter VI, Table 20), and judging by the views of numerous respondents, the weight of public expectation is for a welcome and timely reconciliation of different credit systems.

472.   We emphasise these points because we are aware of some apprehension in certain quarters that a credit framework which successfully articulates higher and further education, academic and vocational programmes, and all other forms of learning achievement might be seen to compromise the distinctive objectives of either the universities or the NCVQ. Moreover, it has been suggested that such a framework might be inappropriately in advance of policy by implying a closer relationship between higher and further education than either government or institutions would wish at this stage. We are highly sensitive to these concerns, and repeat the undertaking given in Chapter IV that the development of a national credit framework has been approached entirely from the perspective of that which facilitates student flexibility and mobility, implying no necessary structural or organisational changes to the relationships between sectors or responsible agencies. With this point established, we now turn to the characteristics of the different credit systems.

Existing credit frameworks

473. The systematic development of credit frameworks in the United Kingdom began no earlier than the mid-1980s. As we have already shown in Chapter VI, both the Open University since 1969 and the Manchester Open College Federation since 1981 explicitly used credit-bearing arrangements to value learning experiences. In the former example, the arrangements remained peculiar to the Open University whilst in the latter case, the credit system did not begin to settle down until other Open College Networks joined in association towards the end of the 1980s.

474. From 1986 onwards, different arrangements have begun to take shape. The CNAA scheme started in 1986, and the NCVQ followed in the same year with proposals for a vocational framework. By 1989-90 the National Open College Network (NOCN) had begun to draw together all credit-awarding networks in further and adult education, forming national transfer and mutual recognition agreements by 1991. In that year the Further Education Unit (FEU) began work to explore the principles and technical elements that would be needed for a comprehensive credit framework for further and higher education, and as we have stated earlier, since 1992 funding councils have begun to be attracted by the prospects for formula funding.

475. In the forthcoming discussion in this section, different credit frameworks are explained and evaluated according to a number of criteria:

- **principles of operation:** how the framework sets objectives and seeks to achieve them

- **framework architecture:** how the scheme structures learning and manages progression

- **the specification of credit and other 'technical instruments':** how a system of currency and account is defined and justified

Frameworks are discussed in terms of their apparent strengths and weaknesses, drawing attention wherever possible to problems outstanding. A comparative summary is provided in Table 29.

The CNAA framework

476. We have already discussed the origins of this framework in Chapter VI, described its relevance in terms of consortia and credit transfer in Chapter VII and make observations on the lessons for new quality assurance arrangements in Chapter X. From this it is possible to conclude that the principal motivations of the CNAA framework have been initially the facilitation of inter-institutional student mobility, the encouragement of wider access through the recognition of prior achievement, and latterly, the transfer of employees between work and higher education through the accreditation of work-based learning and employee training. The framework never sought to imply modifications to intra-institutional arrangements and viewed the development of modularisation as a complementary but often separate objective for institutions.

477. The specific features of the scheme have always been fairly simple. Firstly, it has applied specifically to higher education programmes, particularly undergraduate degrees and increasingly to taught Master's programmes. The scheme has never claimed that it could be extended to learning in further education, for example, and has not been extensively tested in continuing education programmes until very recently. Secondly, the scheme has evolved slightly over the years so that its architecture, or system of levels, is now designed to require 120 credits for each of three undergraduate levels and one unified postgraduate Master's level. These levels correspond to the full-time years of the three-year honours degree or a further year for a full-time taught Master's programme. The Scottish equivalent arrangement shares the same basic architecture with allowance made for the four-year character of initial degrees in Scotland. A pre-higher education 'Level 0' has been informally introduced by some universities to account for foundation courses, some 'franchising' derivatives and occasionally

	CNAA framework	NOCN framework	NCVQ framework	FEU framework
Sector focus	*Higher: academic (+ off–campus vocational)*	*Further and Adult: academic and vocational*	*Further (+ Higher): vocational*	*Further and Adult (+ Higher): academic and vocational*
Architectural features	*Three levels (1–3) at undergraduate level (+ emerging Level 0); Master's (M) level*	*Four levels (1–4) from adult basic education to 'A' level and HE Access*	*Five levels (1–5), with the first three relevant to further education*	*Eight levels (E, 1–6, M) covering FE and HE, although still under discussion*
Specification of credit	*Unit defined as 1/360 of degree; minimum credit = 4 = 30 hours of learning; otherwise, 120 credits/year = 360 for a degree (480 Scotland) and 120 (M) for taught Master's*	*Unit = 30 hours of learning = 1 credit; applicable to various qualifications; no restrictions on credit volume by level (cf CNAA scheme)*	*Credit = unit of assessment defined by competence statements. Units accumulated to form qualified competence (NVQ). Time–based definitions rejected*	*Unit = 30 hours of learning = 1 credit; applicable to all awards, including vocational and higher education qualifications if represented by outcome statements*
Quality assurance arrangements	*Through monitoring via CNAA, and now HEQC, but principally through individual institutions. Intrinsic QA cannot be derived from use of credit*	*Through peer review within OCFs; peer review within NOCN; and monitoring by SCAVA. QA can be derived intrinsically from credit system*	*National standards set by ILBs, and assured by assessment centres under licence from NCVQ. QA intrinsic to credit system*	*Not yet resolved; likely to be through imdividual institutions, existing arrangements BUT QA is intrinsic to the credit system*
Compatibility with existing frameworks	*No, its numerical system is different from others, bench–marked against a degree and problems of adoption in further education. BUT yes, since other numerical systems are compatible (NB not NCVQ)*	*No, time–based defin- ition of credit is not accepted by NCVQ, although reconciliation discussions are taking place; BUT yes,very similar to FEU frame– work and numerical system works with CNAA (1 : 4)*	*No, formally incompatible with all numerical or time-based systems of credit; establishes different approach to credit by linking it to outcome statements and units of competence*	*Yes, seeks to incorp- orate features of other systems, including numerical and time– based unit of credit derived from outcome statements; definition of credit challenged by NCVQ, but works with CNAA (1 : 4)*
Strengths	*Pragmatic; institutional degree programmes accommodated by numerical flexibility; most widely adopted HE scheme currently*	*Tried and tested since 1981 over full range of programmes in FE, AE and in some HEIs; biggest working credit system outside HE*	*Extensively adopted by vocational programmes; quality assurance by link of credit with outcome statements*	*Builds on best features of existing schemes; unites credits, modules and outcomes; potentially adoptable by FE/HE*
Limitations	*Degree–centric; limited adoption of outcomes– led quality assurance; doubtfully applicable to non–HE programmes; benefit if developed educational rationale; otherwise, mechanistic*	*Limited exposure in HE; scheme does not generate of itself either qualifications or transfer; would benefit from incorporation within FEU proposals*	*Internally–focused definition of credit; not easily adopted by HE (nor by any academic programmes). Would benefit from alliance with time–based credit systems*	*Still at design and consultation stage; may suffer in HE from having 'FE' origins. Would benefit from extensive 'pilot' developments in both FE and HE*
Unresolved problems	*Relationship with non– HE developments (eg. level 0/Access) and NCVQ; credits for Master's (120/180?). Credit for 'off–campus' and sandwich courses or other placements*	*Alignment of four levels with those of NVQ 1–3; status of ABE work; how to achieve effective articulation between levels and with HE*	*How to articulate credit for vocational programmes with academic credit systems; character of GNVQ qualifications (especially at higher levels)*	*Negotiating operation in subscribing colleges; increasing exposure in HE; defining technical instruments, particularly levels and QA arrangements.*

Table 29: Credit frameworks: a comparison

Access courses. Thirdly, interim awards are made possible by the CNAA framework, further details of which are apparent in Table 30. Fourthly, a system of grade points is potentially available within the CNAA scheme for use in circumstances where students are mobile between institutions and where some calibration of different marking conventions might be required. Despite it, presence as an instrument within the scheme, we have been able to find few examples of active use in institutions.

478.   A comprehensive definition of the unit of credit is not provided by the CNAA scheme. One credit is simply 1/360th of an honours degree, although the CNAA has gone further in recent years and provided a more expanded definition of the minimum unit of account. Four credits has become the minimum awardable volume of credit, which is held to be equivalent to 30 hours of student effort, or one week's equivalent workload. In effect, although this minimum definition has been developed, the CNAA credit system is based on a 'top-down' partitioning of the undergraduate degree, a qualification which provides the benchmark for all interim and staged awards. If institutions have wished to use the CNAA scheme to accredit short courses, other CPD programmes, or even 'Access' and foundation courses on occasions, they have had to assess the proportion of an undergraduate (120-credit) year which the chosen course represents. This has proved satisfactory in some cases, but raises problems in those cases where the programme to be accredited bears little direct relationship with undergraduate academic courses.

479.   The strength of the CNAA framework, and the principal reason why it has made good progress in higher education, lies in its accommodating character. The principles of credit accumulation and credit transfer may challenge the values and practices of some institutions, but the architecture and specifications of the CNAA scheme do not. Universities and colleges are not required to change very much in order to work with the CNAA scheme. Modularity is not regarded as an essential prerequisite of the application of the credit framework, even if, in practice, it has been adopted by institutions as a desirable

objective in its own right. Whatever the course structure, modular or otherwise, the individual elements could be sub-divided into segments within 120 credits or 360 credits without prejudice to the academic structure thereafter. This simple and undemanding process of partition allowed any university, with any academic arrangement, to apply credit points to their courses if they wished. Thereafter, external and 'off-campus' programmes could be calibrated and given a credit-rating, enabling certain students to negotiate their entry to mainstream programmes.

480.   If the simplicity of the CNAA framework is its strength, it may also be its weakness. Its ability to accommodate any type of institutional academic arrangement may encourage institutions to feel confident that they do not compromise familiar practices when complying with its conventions. On the other hand, this flexibility and ease of association have led to the charge that institutions are merely mechanistically adding numbers to courses without offering any further opportunities for mobility. The process becomes an 'arithmetisation' of the curriculum, encouraging students to undertake 'counting games' . This can lead to 'phantom CATS' by which institutions pass up the opportunity to develop sound educational rationales for the use of credit systems as instruments to promote greater student choice, preferring instead to offer promises of credit transfer which are rarely delivered.

481.   Moreover, the simplicity and arithmetical convenience of the CNAA 120/360 credit model may belie a problem with quality assurance. If institutions are able, when sub-dividing their courses, to produce segments which carry equal volumes of credit, and since credit can be awarded only for learning achievement, it would be reasonable to assume that segments (modules, units or similar) with the same volume of credit attached to them would be of similar academic quality. Whilst they may be of similar academic *standard* (if achieved at the same level in a framework), they may not necessarily be of the same academic *quality*, if one module requires greater intellectual or other input to achieve defined learning outcomes. This problem of quality

assurance remains hidden when the academic programme is treated as a totality, as a unified course. When it is modularised, and when students begin to take advantage of this to construct different combinations, the quality assurance of the aggregated student programme becomes very much a matter of attention. Under these conditions, the CNAA framework is not able to provide assistance of itself since the unit of account, the credit, is not defined in terms either of educational inputs or demonstrable achievements outcomes.

Table 30: CNAA: CAT scheme for higher education	
Credit points and levels	
England & Wales (1986)	**Scotland (1990)**
120 Credits at Level 1	120 Credits at Level 1
120 Credits at Level 2	120 Credits at Level 2
60 Credits at Level 2 *60 Credits at Level 3*	120 Credits at Level 3
120 Credits at Level 3	120 Credits at Level 4
120 Credits at Level M	120 Credits at Level M

Qualifications and Credit Tariffs

(England and Wales)

Credit and level	Qualification	Full–time study equivalent
Level 1: 120 credits	Certificate of Higher Education	Year 1 of full–time Bachelor's degree
Level 1: 120 credits & Level 2: 120 credits	Diploma of Higher Education	Year 1 and Year 2 of full-time Bachelor's degree
At least 360 credits, including at least 60 at Level 3	Degree	Year 1, Year 2 & Year 3 of full–time Bachelor's degree
At least 360 credits, including at least 120 at Level 3	Degree (Honours)	Year 1, Year 2 & Year 3 of full–time Bachelor's degree
Not less than 35 credits at Level M	Postgraduate Certificate	15 weeks full–time of Master's degree
Not less than 70 credits at Level M	Postgraduate Diploma	25 weeks full–time of Master's degree
Not less than 120 credits at Level M	Master's Degree	48 weeks full–time of Master's degree

Council for National Academic Awards, 1992

482. This problem leads us to distinguish between the *extrinsic* and the *intrinsic* capacity of a credit framework to provide for quality assurance. The extrinsic capacity of a credit framework lies, in the case of the CNAA scheme, in its provision of external monitoring and quality assurance arrangements for the total student learning experience. This is essential for any credit framework. However, the *intrinsic* capacity of a credit framework to provide quality assurance lies in the provision it makes for assuring quality in the micro-programme, as greater student choice begins to fragment the homogeneity of the unified course. Under these conditions, if the unit of learning account, the credit, is defined as a standard measure of the student learning input required to achieve a defined learning output, then some sort of basis of equivalence, however tentative, can be established between different modules. The differences may be represented numerically, by different credit points, but the credit points represent different ratios of outputs to inputs. The most conventional means of presenting this is through the use of *notional student learning time.* We will return to this crucial point in later discussion. For the moment, it should be necessary to state that even this approach establishes only a rudimentary and imprecise means of assessing the learning equivalence of different experiences. However the use of credit is at least rooted to a modest extent in educational practice and student learning behaviour.

The framework of the National Open College Network (NOCN)

483. We have described the development of the Open College Federations which make up NOCN in Chapter VI. Their credit-awarding activities begin with the work of the Manchester Open College Federation (MOCF) in 1981 and have subsequently expanded to cover most regions and metropolitan areas of England and Wales, with development forthcoming in Northern Ireland. The principles which drove the early development of MOCF were, firstly, the desire to bring into a framework of accredited achievement all those learning activities in adult and further education which were not otherwise recognised by awarding bodies, and secondly, to use credit as a vehicle for improving the motivation of individual students by giving them direct recognition of their learning achievement. MOCF was, as other OCFs have become, committed to a strategy of *'deep access'*, seeking to accredit courses at four levels: in basic education, 'return-to-learn' and 'second-chance' programmes, pre-Access courses as well as the more familiar Access to Higher Education courses. In short, OCFs have developed 'bottom-up' and cumulative credit frameworks, attempting to assist individual student progression from level to level through improved motivation and reward for personal achievement.

484. The definition of credit used by all credit-awarding OCFs has always been time-based, determined by a notional time-unit required to achieve certain defined learning objectives. Initially MOCF employed a 50-hour unit of credit but by 1987, with the development of other OCFs based on the Manchester model, the unit size was modified. In 1987, the South Yorkshire OCF adopted a 25-hour unit and then Merseyside OCF developed a 30-hour unit. This latter alternative was developed as an attempt to provide some harmony between practice in higher education and that in further and adult education. Its deployment as a element in both the OCF and the modular credit scheme at Liverpool John Moores University has already been described in Chapter VI, and the rationale for this particular definition of credit is explained in Chapter VIII. By 1991 all OCFs across the country and within the NOCN were working with a shared credit system based on the 30-hour unit of credit, and by 1992 the FEU Framework proposals had incorporated it as well.

485. The strengths of the NOCN credit framework lie in the ability to use the unit of credit to allocate credit to any learning activity in a manner which gives a tentative basis for quality assurance in the process. Credit can only be allocated to a learning experience under these arrangements if the learning outcomes of the experience are themselves explicitly stated. Starting with the learning outcomes, a professional assessment is made of the notional time it would take a student, *under college conditions,* to achieve these outcomes. The

volume of workload in hours is divided by the unit of credit (eg 30 hours) to establish the credit tariff. Having established the credit rating of a learning experience, this claim can then be submitted for independent peer review, or to another quality assurance arrangement, when its validity and authenticity can be assessed and agreed. The credit tariff allows comparison with similarly rated modules in other areas of the curriculum, and a professional assessment of comparative practice can be developed. Attempts to engineer inflation in the allocation of credit to a learning experience can be controlled by reference to practice in adjacent areas of the curriculum, by reference to the judgement of peers, and ultimately by reference to the judgements of students and employers. In all OCFs, the allocation of a credit rating to a learning experience always *begins* the process of quality assurance. It is a claim from course designers which invites inspection, assessment and then agreement.

486. The main weaknesses of OCFs lie in their structural fragility as organisations and in their lack of purchase, at this stage in their development, on the qualifications of the further and adult education sectors. All OCFs continue to act largely outside institutions, but supported by colleges, universities and others as accreditation and quality assurance agencies. Most distinctively, and familiar to higher education, they have become the principal agents for the quality assurance of Access to Higher Education courses. With this exception, OCFs do not generally accredit qualifications. Rather, they accredit activities which currently are not otherwise accredited, and they can accredit modularised derivatives of established qualifications. They are ideally placed to manage the quality assurance of a further education sector in which students may begin to display greater mobility and exercise more extensive choice. On the other hand, they do not yet seek to become awarding bodies in their own right, although we believe this could be worthy of further exploration over time.

FEU credit framework

487. The proposals of the FEU derive directly from the experience of both the Open College Federations and the CNAA, although the influence of the former is more noticeable in the core features of the proposed framework. To this the FEU has added the lessons drawn from the NCVQ on assessment and learning outcomes. We do not need to elaborate extensively on the FEU proposals which have been addressed in Chapters VI, VII, VIII and, as an 'Open System', earlier in this chapter. It should be sufficient to say that the proposals for a credit framework attempt to provide a synthesis for various elements:

- **an architecture** of levels, based on those of the CNAA, NOCN and NCVQ;

- **a definition of credit,** based on that developed by the NOCN;

- **the use of learning outcome statements** to define modules and their assessment, influenced by the NCVQ.

488. It should be made clear that the FEU proposals offered in the consultative document *A basis for credit?* do not make any new suggestions about credit frameworks nor do they have authority over any party. They simply pull together existing ideas and represent them as a multi-dimensional package of features for application to a variety of learning programmes in further and higher education. Furthermore, the FEU, in proposing the credit framework as an 'Open System', is expressly seeking to give away ownership to the users of the framework.

489. Currently most of the development work on refinements to the proposals is taking place in further education. There is an extensive *CAT Network* established around the framework, and it has been adopted as the organising basis of the Welsh *Fforwm* and the *London Together* credit initiatives. There is a strong case to be made for some further testing of its suitability in higher education generally. We have noted already that the model has been in use successfully at Liverpool John Moores University since 1988 and is currently being developed at the University of Derby. **We recommend** exploratory work be undertaken in other universities, possibly in parallel with the CNAA scheme.

NCVQ credit framework

490.   We have spent time earlier describing the principles of the NCVQ framework and its approach to the definition of credit. The architecture of this framework can be seen from Table 31 and it is not necessary to offer extensive further commentary. However, one aspect does demand further attention.

491.   Within the NCVQ framework, credit accumulation takes place through the acquisition of units of competence, which are gained by meeting certain standard performance criteria. The accumulation of credit towards a lower qualification does not necessarily imply competence to progress towards a higher qualification. Because competence is defined largely in functional terms, success at NVQ Level 2 may not always provide a learner with a platform for success at Level 3. In practice, this may work differently since it is difficult to separate out the precise performance skills required at a given level of functional competence, but in principle at least, progression within a framework of NVQs is *non-aspirational*, by which we mean that learners are not invited to regard their performance as a precondition for necessary progression to the next level.

492.   This may be otherwise within the GNVQ framework, where the qualifications are 'occupationally-focused' rather than vocationally-specific. In these circumstances, GNVQs begin to take on some of the characteristics of academic qualifications, relying on the linear accumulation of knowledge and conceptual understanding to establish a basis for progression. We will comment further on this distinction between *aspirational* and *non-aspirational* credit frameworks later.

Credit frameworks:

towards a synthesis?

493.   As a starting point for this discussion of a common credit framework, we have provided an example of one attempt by the Royal Society to represent arrangements diagrammatically (Table 32). This approach reflects that of the NCVQ (Table 31) with some further modifications. We believe these approaches represent a useful starting point in several respects. They show the related *architecture* of different frameworks; they align interim and final qualifications; and they are comprehensive in scope. On the other hand, these diagrams might also mislead on one important matter. They tend to give the impression of vertical streams based on *academic*, *GNVQ* and *vocational* pathways, possibly encouraging the view that this is how students should behave. These diagrams do not capture the spirit of a multi-dimensional network of learning opportunities within which students might move more freely between the components of various routes and pathways. In any framework which this report commends, **we recommend** that it should be understood to imply a guided multi-directional structure for learning progression.

494.   We provide an assessment of credit frameworks in Table 33. This seeks to start the process of evaluating how existing frameworks may begin to share features in a comprehensive framework. It is interesting to observe just how much common ground there exists. Where there are differences of approach or convention, we believe these are not so great as to make further progress impossible. It is our opinion that a synthesised credit framework is within our grasp, and **we recommend** that every effort should be made, following this report and its proposals, to take the steps necessary to make this possible.

Shared features and agreements

495.   There is almost universal agreement on the *architecture* of a common framework. The structure of **levels of achievement** is generally understood to follow a pattern compatible with the NCVQ framework in further education and with the CNAA framework in higher education. There would be one additional feature: an Entry level 'E' to accommodate students earning credit in adult basic education. The term *'Level E'* is regarded as acceptably non-judgmental and non-stigmatising for students seeking basic skills in literacy, numeracy, oracy and related matters.

Table 31: NCVQ: a qualifications framework

Age	Academic		Vocational
21+	Higher Degrees		
21	Degree Year 3		NVQ Level 5
20	Degree Year 2	GNVQ Level 4	NVQ Level 4
19	Degree Year 1		
18	'A' Level	GNVQ Level 3 / Vocational 'A' Level	NVQ Level 3
17			
16	GCSE	GNVQ Level 2	NVQ Level 2
		GNVQ Level 1	NVQ Level 1
15	GCSE and Key Stage 4		
14	National Curriculum Stages		

National Council for Vocational Qualifications, 1993

Table 32: Royal Society: framework for post-compulsory education

Academic		Vocational	
PhD		NVQ Level 5	
Master's	Enhanced and Extended First Degree	Work-related Qualifications	
Degree			
Diploma of Higher Education		NVQ Level 4	Employment
Certificate of Higher Education			
Diploma of Advanced Education	*Single Framework of Academic and Vocational Education*	NVQ Level 3 / NVQ Level 2	
Certificate of Advanced Education		NVQ Level 1	
Pre-16 Education			

Royal Society, Beyond GCSE, 1991: Higher Education Futures, 1993

Thereafter, students would progress through Levels 1-3 (FE) before progressing to Levels 1-3 (HE) and Level M (Master's).

496.   We have had it presented to us that undergraduate higher education is in reality one unified level, or at worst, two levels (foundation and graduate). We have not accepted this argument and believe that, whilst the case can continue to be made intellectually, it does not significantly advance the case for student progression to pursue it. Three levels in undergraduate higher education are understood and accepted. We believe they should be retained. Similarly, we propose to retain an undivided 'M' level. The framework could be further refined by internally dividing postgraduate programmes, but this would result in infinite regressions at other levels also. We do not think it is productive to disturb these aspects of existing arrangements. We will have something else to say about the volume of credit for awards at 'Level M' in later discussion.

497.   On the balance of all the arguments, **we recommend** that the national credit framework should be made up of eight levels of achievement and progression, and qualifications should be aligned with them. These levels should be described as: *Level E; Levels 1-3 (FE); Levels 1-3 (HE); Level M.* We have not detected any welcome for a combined numerical description (eg. Levels 1-8 or some alternative) but **we recommend** that this remains an open issue for consideration at a later date if opinion changes in the light of experience.

498.   We have detected a growing awareness of the usefulness of *learning outcome statements* as curriculum design tools. This is particularly apparent in those institutions which have made the greatest progress in developing comprehensive credit systems. Such statements appear to be useful for the clarification they add to the objectives of learning, and for their capacity to assist the quality assurance of diverse learning experiences, particularly in 'off-campus' work. On the other hand, a majority of universities and colleges still prefer to work with course 'aims and objectives'. From our investigations, we very much favour the general adoption of an outcomes-led approach to curriculum design, modified to accommodate the nuances and subtleties of academic work. **We recommend** that, wherever possible, credit-based learning opportunities should be developed by using **learning outcome statements** as the basis for defining the module of learning to which a credit rating is attached. **We recommend** that further work be undertaken, at an institutional and national level, to support academic staff in these matters. As part of this process, **we recommend** that an assessment should take place of the relative merits of the terms *competence* and *proficiency* in their suitability for describing performance in vocational and academic contexts.

499.   There appears to be widespread acceptance of a definition of the **unit of credit** as *30 hours of structured learning, a minimum notional time unit for the achievement of a coherent cluster of learning outcomes.* The NCVQ will always qualify its acceptance of such a definition, but appears prepared to accept this as an attempt to achieve an accommodation with a numerical credit transfer system, without prejudice to its own specific objectives. The definition of credit outlined here has been adopted in one form or another by the CNAA, FEU, BTEC and NOCN. Each body may use the notional value differently and we explore common purpose on this matter later.

500.   There is also overwhelming support for the establishment of a common credit system across the FE/HE boundary, but there is less confidence in the prospects for early progress. The principal obstacle is the failure to agree on the simple matter of a credit currency. It is unclear from the investigation whether colleagues and institutions would be prepared to modify their hard-won arrangements in the short term in order to achieve a common credit currency across the sector boundary. Nevertheless, there is widespread support for the principle of a common system and **we recommend** that the achievement of a common credit currency within a comprehensive post-secondary and higher education should be a major objective of policy in these matters.

501.   Modularity and the development of credit systems are now so closely interwoven in practice that it has become almost theoretical to talk of their separation. This is not

Table 33: Credit frameworks: an assessment

	CNAA framework	FEU proposals	NCVQ framework
Sector and scope	Higher Education; academic programmes but with experience in credit rating of 'off-campus' learning; not responsible for development in further education	Further and Higher Education; academic and vocational programmes; potential for credit rating 'off-campus' learning but largely untested	Further and Higher Education; vocational programmes, including 'off-campus' accreditation potential, but untested in this area yet
Coverage	Most HEIs throughout United Kingdom, in an extensive or limited form; all Scottish universities subscribe to SCOTCAT; only framework which has received much exposure in the sector	Currently under development and refinement in further education colleges in England and Wales; basis for national system in Wales and for local system in London; widespread throughout all OCNs being developed by 2–3 universities currently; seeking accommodation with NCVQ	Wide range of vocational programmes throughout United Kingdom, principally in further education currently, but with expansion into higher education imminent; widespread engagement with professional body programmes in certain occupational sectors; remit to provide national vocational framework
Strengths	Simple numerical framework which accommodates most HE degree course structures; applicable to 'off-campus' learning by agreed credit rating process; simple if contestable structure of levels and interim awards	Multi-dimensional numerical framework which combines credits, learning outcomes, progression levels and assessment in curriculum modification package; widely accepted definition of credit; could apply to all forms of learning; possesses intrinsic quality assurance potential	Comprehensive standards framework, seeking to establish common criteria for achievement and performance across a variety of vocational programmes within a structure of progression levels; strong intrinsic quality assurance arrangements
Weaknesses	Does not define unit of credit; tends to be degree-centric with restrictions on its applicability to non degree-referenced programmes in HE and FE; no intrinsic quality assurance mechanisms	Possibly complex and contestable definition of credit; slightly less numerical flexibility than CNAA scheme; huge but largely untested potential; danger of becoming too technically erudite	Lack of transferability between many vocational qualifications and to academic programmes; arguably over-weighty quality assurance arrangements; premises of 'competence' intellectually challengeable and arguably inapplicable to academic programmes
Cross-sector capacity	Untested and outside initial remit; as numerical system, means could be found to accommodate non-degree and further education programmes by employing some principles from FEU proposals. Structure of levels is compatible	Planned cross-sector applicability; purposefully designed to build on established work of CNAA and NCVQ; wider testing required in higher education. Structure of levels is compatible.	Comprehensively to vocational programmes in FE and HE; no application formally to academic programmes, although some spill-over impact in use of learning outcome statements. Structure of levels is compatible.
Modifications necessary for a unified system	Accept definition of 'credit', numerical values and outcomes-led approach of FEU proposals; all other features remain the same	Accept structure of HE levels proposed by CNAA scheme; work with CNAA numerical values by defining 'credit' in units of four	Accept the application of numerical credit ratings to NVQ and GNVQ units (either FEU or CNAA); all other features remain the same

to say that all institutions are committed to both strategies. Nevertheless, throughout higher education, and increasingly throughout further education as well, the reorganisation of the curriculum into a modular form has proceeded in tandem with efforts to extend student choice. This progress would be assisted by some agreement on the shape and arrangement of the academic year. We believe that there is widespread acceptance amongst those involved in implementing credit-based and modular programmes of the need to reform the academic year along lines proposed in the Flowers and Irvine Reports (1993). Although we address these matters further in Chapter XII, **we recommend** that credit transfer within a comprehensive credit framework would be assisted by progress towards a common academic year throughout the United Kingdom, reformed in the manner of the proposals of the Flowers and Irvine reports, and that these proposals be inspected by the further education sector to examine their suitability for operation in colleges as well.

502.   Interim and staged awards are generally accepted as desirable features of any framework. This already obtains in further education and with those programmes falling under the aegis of the NCVQ. In higher education however, interim awards have tended to be less convincing qualifications when set against the honours degree. **We recommend** that a credit framework should establish strong and credible interim qualifications; we do not support the designation of interim awards without significant attention to the advantages they bestow upon prospective holders of the qualification. To this extent, it is unclear that the current arrangements for interim qualifications in higher education adequately offer students significant incentives to pursue them. We have in mind here the Certificates and Diplomas of Higher Education which were available under the CNAA, and not the specific awards offered by BTEC and others. To address this problem, we make proposals on the subject below.

503.   **We recommend** that the general character of a national credit framework should be that described in Table 34. This diagram suggests that the proposals from the FEU should be considered as the unifying seam

of the framework, drawing into alignment the qualifications of further and higher education with those of the NCVQ. This 'architecture' accepts that there will be permeable barriers at the FE/HE interface and at the boundary of undergraduate and postgraduate programmes. Elsewhere, levels will tend to act as indicators of achievement and progression. We have been unable to represent our intention that the structure should permit the greatest possible transfer between different programmes at the same level, and the fairest progression between levels. The model should be conceived of as a climbing frame rather than as a ladder.

Disputed aspects of a common framework

The currency of credit

504.   It has been clear throughout much of the discussion in this and earlier chapters that our investigation has revealed no general agreement about the credit currency that will be needed to unify different frameworks. There is no doubt that most higher education institutions which have begun to use credit as a currency in any form, however limited yet, are generally reluctant to change from the CNAA model of 120/360 credit points. Moreover, many professional bodies and employers have received credit ratings for their programmes in 'CNAA' credit points, and it could cause some disruption if they were now required to change. On the other hand, the use of credit is not yet so embedded in the culture of higher education that a simple, and largely arithmetical, modification could not be contemplated if it guaranteed the greater prize of a unified system.

505.   On the other hand, what might some higher education institutions be required to change to, in pursuit of this greater reward? The FEU proposals invite the development of a unified credit system based on the equivalent of a 30-credit (full-time) year, yielding a minimum 90-credit honours degree (England and Wales). In its simplest form this would involve dividing by 4 most existing credit ratings in higher education. If this was agreed, it would produce some

Table 34: Credit frameworks: towards a synthesis

CNAA framework		FEU framework	NCVQ framework	
CATS Level M: work equivalent to the standard required for the fulfilment of the general educational aims of a Master's programme, including an element of advanced independent work	**M**	**HE Level M:** no comment specifically but assumes consistency between HE and NCVQ	**GNVQ Level 5:** the specification has not yet been determined. One proposal suggests it would be equivalent to a course-based Master's programme	**NVQ Level 5:** competence in the application of fundamental principles and complex techniques, involving substantial personal autonomy, responsibility for the work of others, and the allocation of resources
CATS Level 3: work equivalent to the standard required for the fulfilment of the general educational aims of the 3rd year of a full-time Degree course	**6**	**HE Level 3:** no comment specifically but assumes consistency, as above		
CATS Level 2: work equivalent to the standard required for the fulfilment of the general educational aims of the 2nd year of a full-time Degree course	**5**	**HE Level 2:** no comment specifically but assumes consistency, as above	**GNVQ Level 4:** there have been initial consultations on the shape of a GNVQ 4. One current proposal is that the award should be equivalent to the first two years of a full-time degree programme, as with HND or DipHE	**NVQ Level 4:** competence in a range of complex technical or professional activities in a variety of contexts, involving substantial autonomy and responsibility, where the allocation of resources may be needed
CATS Level 1: work equivalent to the standard required for the fulfilment of the general educational aims of the 1st year of a full-time Degree course	**4**	**HE Level 1:** no comment specifically but assumes consistency, as above		
NOCN Framework **Level 4** enables students to develop the capacity for sustained study using critical and evaluative skills and understanding. Study may prepare for entry to higher education or to other professional training	**3**	**FE Level 3:** embracing 'A' levels, GNVQ and NVQ3, Access and HE 'level 0' courses, OND and academic and vocational elements of equivalent standard	**GNVQ Level 3:** the Advanced GNVQ or the 'vocational 'A' level', a GNVQ 3 is awarded for twelve units (2 'A' level equivalent) + three core skills units	**NVQ Level 3:** competence is a range of complex non-routine work activities, with some autonomy, and control and guidance of others
Level 3 enables participants to acquire or develop basic concepts and principles of enquiry. It enables them to achieve functional competence in skill areas such as languages, maths, creative and interpretative arts, and community-based applications	**2**	**FE Level 2:** embracing GCSE, GNVQ2 and NVQ2, pre-Access courses, and programmes of other awarding bodies of equivalent standard	**GNVQ Level 2:** the Intermediate GNVQ is awarded for six units + three core skills units (equivalent to 4 GCSEs at grade C and above)	**NVQ Level 2:** competence in varied work activities which may be complex and non-routine, with some personal autonomy and collaboration with others in groups
Level 2 builds on existing skills or introduces a range of new foundation skills and subjects eg craft and artistic skills, learning-to-learn skills, languages and maths, and group skills	**1**	**FE Level 1:** embracing initial general further and adult education, GNVQ1 and NVQ1, and equivalents	**GNVQ Level 1:** the Foundation GNVQ is designed for those not yet equipped to begin a GNVQ 2 course	**NVQ Level 1:** competence in a range of varied work activities, most of which may be routine or predictable
Level 1 is the foundation level for skills necessary in everyday life – reading, writing, speaking, numeracy, and practical and coping skills	**'Entry' level** Embracing most Adult Basic Education, some special needs courses, and those programmes accredited by OCNs at Level 1		**Sources:** CNAA CAT Scheme Regulations, 1991; NCVQ Guide to National Vocational Qualifications, 1991; GNVQ Information Notes, 1993; GNVQ at Higher Levels, 1994; Further Education Unit: *A basis for credit?* 1992; *Beyond a basis for credit?* 1993; UDACE: Open College Networks – current developments and practice, 1989; Manchester Open College Federation, 1984.	

National Curriculum Key Stages

'untidiness' at first, but credit is not such a precise instrument that some 'rounding' could not be tolerated. More troublesome for some institutions would be to allay the suspicion that this type of conversion could imply changes to academic structures, as institutions design programmes to 'fit' the less numerically flexible sub-divisions of 30 credits rather than 120 credits. Again, this would not be impossible if there was a will to proceed in this manner.

506.   On the other hand, we have received representations during the investigation on one important matter concerning this dispute. It has been suggested that, even if there were agreement on a 30/90 credit point model, based on the 30-hour credit, it would imply a 900-hour 'learning year' which would imply too short a period for the purposes of quality assurance. Instead, it is proposed that a gross 'learning year' of 1,200 hours would be more appropriate for higher education, and *ipso facto*, a 120-credit year is a more natural formula, yielding if one wished it, a 10-hour unit of credit.

507.   If the claims for a 30/90 credit formula are to be rejected, we do not think these arguments provide an adequate intellectual basis. Firstly, the debate between a 900-hour or a 1,200-hour 'learning year' is largely irrelevant for these purposes. It is to raise the definition of a *unit of currency* to the status of an instrument of public policy. It is important to note that funding councils define a student as full-time if she is registered to study for 21 hours or more over 18 continuous weeks in a year. This yields a minimum value of 378 hours for full-time study. Whatever value is used, it will be a more or less arbitrary 'benchmark'. Indeed it could just as readily be argued that students are expected to be 'in attendance' for 30 hours a week for 30 weeks a year, and the credit system should reflect this minimum convention. Secondly, this latter argument may even be helpful if the unit of credit were to be attractive as a unit of resource allocation, as we will discuss and commend in Chapter XI. For reasons which are too complex to explain briefly, the use of a 30-hour, 30-credit per year model does produce *credit deflation* (ie it acts as a disincentive to inflate the teaching component of any module, and acts as a 'cap' on the number of credits to be distributed throughout a year-long programme). Thirdly, the concept of a 10-hour unit of credit has the appearance of artificiality, an *ex post facto* derivation from the 120-credit year. Whilst it could be supported mechanistically for use in the credit rating of short courses and some continuing education programmes, it appears to fail a reasonable test of quality assurance: what credible cluster of learning outcome statements could be demonstrated at the level of higher education following a 10-hour learning experience? Moreover, such a unit of credit could imply a fragmentation of academic courses which would test the support of the most committed advocate of credit-based learning. And finally, the unit bestows no apparent advantages for the credit rating of programmes over those which have been established under extensive trial over a number of years by the 30-hour unit.

508.   If the 30/90 credit point system is to be rejected, it would have to be for the following reasons. Firstly, it could be claimed reasonably that, although the 30-hour unit has been tested widely in further and adult education, and in some higher education institutions, the 30/90 credit model has not been fully tried even in further education. Secondly, why should universities give up, even as a compromise, a system with which they are familiar, however imperfect it may be alleged to be, for a system which is not yet embedded in the further education colleges? Perhaps the colleges could adopt the 120/360 credit model, multiplying by 4, and compromise at that point? And thirdly, any change which was not fully accepted for convincing reasons could upset the progress which has been made so far with employers, professional bodies and within institutions.

509.   There could be a third option. Both further and higher education could compromise by adopting the credit tariff of the European Credit Transfer System (ECTS). This would be appealing on the grounds that the ultimate prize of trans-European common purpose would be greater than the struggle to find solutions to local sectional differences in the United Kingdom. We would have some sympathy with this argument if we thought that a trans-European accommodation was in sight, but as we shall argue in Chapter XIV, this is a far distant prospect. Moreover, the definition of 'credit' in the ECTS arrangements

is an even more unsatisfactory and arbitrary compromise than any other treatment of the term. Nevertheless, it could be argued that the United Kingdom should take the lead in adopting the ECTS model as its national credit scheme, thereby helping to stimulate further cross-border developments in due course.

Credit at Master's (M) level

510.　Further vexed questions concern the volume and pattern of credit to be awarded at Master's level. The CNAA scheme proposed 120 (M) credits. Disputes and variations have occurred since about whether an adequate distinction was being made between post-experience and postgraduate aspects of academic programmes beyond the undergraduate level. This problem has been provoked by the expansion of (M) level work in the Management field, with large numbers of students claiming credit for experiential learning against the credit for an MBA, for example. Although opinion remains sharply divided on the issue, we take the view that (M) level credit should only be awarded for achievement at postgraduate level, and that 120 credits under the current arrangements is adequate for this purpose. Others among us support the award of 180 (M) credits.We have something further to propose about this and a post-experience award later. Secondly, there is no clear judgement on the distinction between credit at (M) level for students on 'subject-continuous' Master's and those undertaking postgraduate programmes in a new subject area. For example, how much credit for a postgraduate award can be legitimately derived from undergraduate credit? Is credit an objective feature of the level of the module and programme, or of the individual student programme? We have not been able to find any consensus on these matters within higher education and **we recommend** that these are matters which should be further explored.

Credit at Level 0

511.　The growth of foundation courses, stimulated by interpretations of the legislation governing finance for students on 'higher education' courses, has led to the development of an HE Level 0. We are clear that in any comprehensive credit framework, the work undertaken at this level is equivalent to Level 3 (FE) and should be treated as such for the purposes of credit transfer, accepting the implications for funding. We do wish to counter any interpretation that achievement at Level 0 represents anything more than achievement on programmes at Level 3 (FE), including 'A' levels, Access courses or GNVQ 3 programmes. Accordingly, **we recommend** that the academic standing of 'Level 0' programmes be reviewed in the light of their location in a credit framework.

Credit by year or by degree?

512.　Within higher education, there has been a longstanding debate about whether a volume of credit should be awarded for a complete degree (CNAA = 360 credits) or for a year thereof (CNAA = 120 credits). This debate has produced enormously complex and intractable problems, the gist of which we produce here. Firstly, maintaining that all undergraduate degrees consist of a fixed volume of credit helps to support the view that all degrees are equal in quality and standard, at least in so far as this is reflected in the volume of achievable credit. For the CNAA this was an important consideration in the discharge of its responsibilities, because it prevented any institution from claiming that one degree was worth more credit than another 'because it was better/harder' or whatever. Moreover, 'sandwich' degrees could be held within the orbit of all other degrees, and 'P' credit was developed to cope with the year out. Problems began to arise with the accreditation of some four year degrees, and with the formal accreditation of the workplace learning during the 'sandwich' year. Was a degree now 360 credits, or 480 credits? Secondly, four year undergraduate degrees in Scotland have remained within their own circumscribed national arrangements, awarding 480 SCOTCAT credits for the completed degree. It may be reasonably asked of any comprehensive credit framework for the United Kingdom, how does it propose to deal with the fact that equivalent standards of achievement are reached after four years of undergraduate work in Scotland, but after three years in the rest of the United Kingdom?

Moreover, if this assumes common entry standards, what is happening to the nature of student progression in Scotland compared with England and Wales, and how is this to be reflected in any credit system and credit transfer arrangements? The intractability of many of these matters is so apparent that **we recommend** it would be better to operate on the basis of a 120-credit year or its equivalent, leaving issues of quality assurance to be assessed by other means.

Problems of progression: compatibility between aspirational and non-aspirational frameworks

513.   We raised this problem earlier and promised to give it further attention. The problem concerns whether different, and incompatible, objectives are being pursued by *academic* and *vocational* credit frameworks. On the one hand, academic credit frameworks seek to use credit to stimulate the recognition of personal learning achievement, motivate students to accumulate further credits, facilitate mobility whenever it is desired, and inspire students to progress from one level to another towards qualifications. They are quintessentially *aspirational* frameworks. On the other hand, vocational credit frameworks seek to motivate students no less to achieve desired goals, but they are *functional, non-aspirational* frameworks, concerned principally with performance to an agreed standard but not necessarily with a view to promoting further student progress. In short, a learner may return to study/training in years ahead in order to update skills by meeting the standards of the same level NVQ as she acquired initially some years before. Few students return in years ahead to retake their initial academic qualifications; they usually seek to move on from them. We make these observations because they raise doubts over the realistic potential for progression and credit transfer between academic, quasi-vocational and vocational programmes. Ideally, open transfer possibilities exist within a common credit framework; in practice this may be constrained by irreconcilable differences of purpose between systems which will need to be managed through closer co-operation and negotiation of principles.

Conclusions and proposals for progress and implementation

A credit framework and a unit of credit

514.   We have already discussed the general support for a *credit framework* based on an agreed series of levels, outlined in Table 34, and a definition of credit based on the *30-hour learning unit of credit*. There is a general acceptance that the architecture of levels proposed by the common framework is suitable for higher and further education, and that it will allow relationships for credit transfer with the NCVQ to develop over time. **We recommend** that the structure of levels and the defined unit of credit become the building blocks of a comprehensive national credit framework. **We recommend further** that the use of *learning outcome statements* should be adopted more widely in the design and definition of modules and courses generally.

515.   On one point, however, there will need to be further discussions. Despite the general agreement in principle on a structure of levels, further work will need to take place between higher education institutions and the NCVQ over the correct alignment of NVQ and GNVQ qualifications at higher levels. At the moment, the NCVQ has made proposals for their alignment against the first two years of an undergraduate degree (Level 4) and the final year of an honours degree and Master's (Level 5). This represents a claim for comparability which has not yet been endorsed by universities. The CVCP continues to engage in its own explorations of the implications for higher education of the NCVQ, following earlier efforts by the Committee of Directors of Polytechnics (Marks, 1991) and the NCVQ itself is currently undertaking consultations on GNVQ Level 4. To assist both parties in making further progress, **we recommend** that further exploration take place around the conceptual differences between *competence, capability* and *proficiency* as terms for the description of learning objectives in higher and further education. **We recommend** that all qualifications, academic and vocational, should be aligned with the levels of the agreed framework with the requirements for credit

accumulation towards the qualifications carefully defined. **We recommend** that a 'mapping exercise' take place to establish the extent of the development of higher level NVQs in universities and colleges. Finally, **we recommend** that further discussions should take place to determine the legitimacy of the claim of the NCVQ that Levels 4 and 5 of their qualifications are appropriately aligned with the levels of higher education qualifications, as proposed in Table 34.

Interim qualifications within the framework

516.   **We recommend** a reconsideration within higher education of the present arrangements for the designation of first cycle and interim qualifications. It has been a central principle of previous credit frameworks that they should provide intermediate qualifications as a means of stimulating initial access and subsequent progression, whilst providing staging points for students whose circumstances change for whatever reason. The CNAA scheme built on the existence of the two-year Diploma of Higher Education and introduced a one-year Certificate of Higher Education as well. In fact, as we have shown earlier in Chapter VII, support from students for these intermediate awards has been very modest indeed. Under 5,000 students enrol each year, of which over half enrol on DipHEs related to Health Service professions. In twenty years, the DipHE, and latterly the CertHE, have not found a market. On the other hand, two-year BTEC higher diplomas and certificates (HNDs and HNCs) have been more successful, registering over 60,000 students annually. As we have mentioned earlier, the NCVQ is undertaking a consultation with higher education institutions on the merits of a GNVQ Level 4 qualification which it proposes to align in a credit framework with the first two years of an undergraduate degree. Obviously, HND and HNC qualifications might be natural candidates for the receipt of a GNVQ 4 appellation, but we have wondered whether there might be other attractive possibilities for a first cycle award.

517.   We believe that one of the reasons why the DipHE has not been as successful as anticipated lies in its academic character. It is largely a two-year diminutive of the honours degree; it is in other words 'less of the same' type of qualification. It cannot compete in prestige with the three year honours degree, and therefore it is not an attractive terminal award in its own right. If it has been deployed as a vehicle to recruit specific groups of 'second chance' students, then any success in this direction may have been offset by problems of stigmatisation and inferior status. Finally, there have been few incentives, either from funding bodies or by reason of perceived added value to the student in terms of employability, for any significant numbers to seek the qualification, or for institutions to pay more than lip service to its availability within a credit framework.

518.   We believe the time has arrived to rethink the purpose of intermediate awards in higher education *in order to establish a strong and credible first cycle qualification* which would have meaning and consequence for students and their employers alike. We have looked at a number of possible alternatives in other countries. For example, the Belgian *candidat* is a comprehensive interim qualification which establishes the right to further progression for successful students. It is purposefully selective and acts as a filter for candidates seeking to move towards a degree (*licence*). The French *Diplome d'Etudes Universitaires Generales (DEUG)* is a more general interim award, complementing the more specific *Diplome d'Etudes Universitaires Scientifique et Technique (DEUST)*. The *DEUG* and the *DEUST* are credible awards in their own right and fit within the established framework of French professionally-focused higher education. The former is similar in some ways to the best known first cycle and intermediate award, the American *Associate Degree*. As a vehicle for access and increased participation, the *Associate Degree* has been highly successful. It has developed largely in the Liberal Arts and reflects the American commitment to a broadly-based general and liberal higher education. We may need to give this emphasis the sharper focus of labour market relevance to meet the needs of students currently in the United Kingdom. However, the *Associate Degree* is widely regarded as a credible qualification and it rests comfortably within a framework of comprehensive credit transfer.

519. Before we comment on the type of strong interim qualification that may be needed in the United Kingdom, we have to determine what it is for, and how it bestows advantages over existing arrangements. The first assumption that may need to be abandoned is that intermediate qualifications are designed for minorities, under-achievers or students with special circumstances. A strong and credible interim qualification would be attractive to all students, leading naturally to progression towards an honours degree, other professional qualifications and beyond. This is largely true of the *Associate Degree, DEUG* and *DEUST.* Secondly, we may also need to abandon the assumption that an intermediate award is simply a lesser version of the ultimate qualification, the honours degree. In short, this qualification will need to be distinctive in its own right.

520. Thirdly, the qualification should ideally be capable of fulfilling a number of complementary functions: it should be a credible *academic* qualification; it should be capable under certain conditions of attracting a GNVQ4 via dual accreditation; it should be accessible by students with 'A' level, BTEC, Access course and GNVQ3 qualifications; it should lead either to further academic qualifications or to further vocational and professional training programmes; and it should be amenable to intensified patterns of study.

521. Fourthly, it should be capable of delivery as two-thirds of the academic credit of an honours degree over three years (a 'vertical' Associate Degree). Fifthly, it should promise and deliver to students credibility with employers over time by offering something which other qualifications do not. And finally, we might add that certain variants of the Associate Degree should be capable of delivery in further education colleges, under appropriate conditions as well as in universities. The debate over a strong two-year award has tended to focus in the past on the establishment of a *Foundation Degree.* This is the example proposed by Ball (1990) and further supported by Schuller and many others (1991). Conventionally, the argument is favour has turned on accessibility, affordability and

progression, whilst the argument against has emphasised problems of status and social divisiveness, lack of credibility with employers, lack of demand from students, and the existence of an adequate alternative in BTEC diplomas (for a summary of this debate, see Robertson, 1992). We believe that conditions have turned again in favour of a review of these arguments. Firstly, current Government policy seeks to encourage more two-year diplomas; secondly, funding councils are urging this on institutions; thirdly, the GNVQ consultation exercise forms part of this general reassessment; fourthly, something will need to be done, possibly at the level of programmes leading to an interim award, to ensure success for greater numbers of GNVQ3 students entering higher education; and finally, a successful credit framework in higher education will need a mechanism for facilitating multi-directional transfer.

522. We are reasonably sure of one thing: no intermediate qualification can easily overcome the problem of status and social divisiveness. By definition, an interim or staged award is less prestigious than the final honours degree. However, an interim award that is available to *all* students *en route* to an honours degree, and offers them some additional distinctive advantages in itself, may be the strong intermediate qualification that we are seeking. The trade-off between status on the one hand, and access, affordability and enhanced labour market relevance on the other may be one worth making.

523. **We recommend** therefore that a strong and credible intermediate qualification should be established, with the designation of an *Associate Degree.* We commend this title, rather than any other involving 'diploma' or an alternative, because we believe this stands the best chance of survival beside the honours degree. **We recommend** that an Associate Degree should have the specifications which are outlined in Table 35. **We recommend** further that the funding councils give early consideration to providing the means by which selected universities initially be invited to develop suitable programmes to meet the specifications of the Associate Degree. This will involve the co-operation of the institutions

themselves, their representative bodies, the HEQC, NCVQ and BTEC.

524. The advantages of the development of this kind of two-year qualification are likely to have significant impact upon the ability of universities to meet the needs of both academic and occupationally-orientated students, without prejudice to the claims of students to be able to proceed forward to an honours degree. Moreover, all students potentially could have access to an intermediate qualification which establishes credit for core skills as an essential part of their programme. This will require changes to the character of first cycle higher education, involving a broadening of the programme, which will challenge the conventional single subject hegemony of some courses. Such adjustments are likely, however, to make programmes more receptive to holders of GNVQ3 awards and may be attractive to students seeking additional benefits in their search for optimum labour market placement.

525. We attach considerable importance to the modular and semester-based character of the Associate Degree, and to the prospects for a January start for some students, and a third semester. For example, a student might embark upon an honours degree programme in January via the Associate Degree 'route'. The first semester might involve largely credit for academic subject knowledge, leading to a summer semester of credit for core skills to be achieved via shared modules with groups from different subject areas or via work-based learning internships. The second year (semesters 3 and 4) could follow a largely 'academic' route or a pattern of credit leading to a GNVQ4. All students could then join a final full-time year as they wished, but already possessing an Associate Degree with core skills, and possibly a GNVQ4.

526. Of course students could proceed to an honours degree via conventional means, or achieve a GNVQ4 by a designated alternative qualification such as an HND. However, we have to concede that these arrangements do raise questions about the role, respectively, of the DipHE and BTEC

Table 35: Specification of an Associate Degree

1. It should be a full-time or part-time qualification equivalent to two years or two thirds of the credit of an honours degree, capable of being offered, by arrangement, over four continuous semesters, and ideally accessible from a September or a January start date.

2. It should be capable of supplying an appropriate balance of credit to ensure unimpeded student progression to a chosen honours degree in a third full-time year, whilst providing students with a minimum amount of credit in core skills relevant to general employment.

3. It should be an academic qualification but with the capacity to provide, under specific conditions, an appropriate balance of credit to meet the specifications for the award of a GNVQ Level 4 by dual accreditation.

4. To meet the specifications of an Associate Degree as an academic qualification, but not as a GNVQ4, the student programme should contain no less than 25% of credit for core skills.

5. To meet the specifications of an Associate Degree as an academic qualification and as a GNVQ4, the student programme should contain no less than 40%, but no more than 50% of credit for core skills.

6. The construction of Associate Degree programmes, and the balance of credit for core skills and academic knowledge between levels and years, should be spread adequately throughout the programme, but is subject to the quality assurance procedures of individual institutions and the specifications, in the case of GNVQ4, of the NCVQ.

7. Students should be able to achieve dual qualifications from the university and the NCVQ where their programmes meet the specifications.

8. It should be capable of delivery in suitable further education colleges as well as in universities.

diplomas. We have no desire in making these proposals to prejudice the place of qualifications for students, if they serve a purpose and meet a need. On the other hand, circumstances change and a greater number of students may need to be prepared for both academic and occupational success through a modest redesign of the qualifications structure of higher education. Therefore, **we recommend** that proposals for the establishment of an Associate Degree according to the specifications described earlier should be subject to consultation with relevant parties. **We recommend** that the HEQC invite comments from BTEC, NCVQ and other interested parties including awarding bodies, employers and professional bodies, whilst the representative bodies of universities invite observations from their members also.

A foundation Certificate of Higher Education

527.   It is already possible within arrangements inherited from the CNAA to award a Certificate of Higher Education. Small numbers of students currently receive this award, often as a 'fall-back' award in the event of a failure to progress. With the introduction into accredited learning of up to 500,000 students from Continuing Education departments in the near future, some thought will need to be given to improving the standing and marketability of a credible foundation award. **We recommend** therefore that attention should be paid to the design of programmes at CertHE level, equivalent to the first level of an undergraduate degree, which offer accreditation opportunities to continuing education students and others.

A post-experience award

528.   We have one final observation to make about interim qualifications at the postgraduate level. Earlier we proposed that the volume of credit for a Master's qualification should remain at CNAA 120 (FEU = 30) credits. This distinguishes credit for postgraduate achievement from that for post-experience achievement. To cover those conditions where students reasonably claim credit from experiential learning, not at postgraduate level but leading to a Master's programme, **we recommend** that a specific qualification be

defined, to be called a *Certificate in Advanced Professional Development* and worth CNAA 96-120 (FEU 24-30) credits at Level 3 (HE) and invite comments on this proposal from interested parties.

A national credit transcript

529.   **We recommend** the establishment of a national credit transcript. In our judgement, there is no other item so important for the effective operation of a comprehensive credit framework than the existence of a national, standard *credit transcript*. By this, we mean that an agreed specification should be determined for a credit transcript to which all institutions could subscribe. These specifications would identify the character and range of data to be represented on the transcript, which minimally would include the credit earned by level, programme and module, but could also include assessment data and additional qualifications, credit for core skills, institutional attendance or other relevant items. One of the elements which is impeding the further development of the ECTS is the absence of any consistent credit transcript arrangements. If this were developed in the United Kingdom, in line with proposals from the ERASMUS Bureau and informed by American experience, it would contribute considerably to the effective further development of credit-based learning. We believe that a national credit transcript would have important and beneficial consequences for quality assurance, and might improve general confidence in student credit transfer. Moreover students, employers and professional bodies would gain from the greater detail on programme performance that would be visible from an individual student credit transcript. **We recommend** therefore that HEQC organises consultations with interested parties and takes steps to ensure the further development of a national credit transcript, for higher education in the first instance, but with consequences for further education and the role of National Records of Achievement in the longer term. Such consultations will need to take account of the capacity of institutions to service an individual credit transcript. A number of institutions can already do this as part of their information systems for supporting modular and credit-based schemes. The technology exists

and is not unnecessarily burdensome, but guidance on its development will be required.

530.   It has been suggested that the development of a national credit transcript will over time prejudice the existence of the **classified honours degree.** If this is the case, we would welcome it since it would mean that employers, students and others were content with the quality of data reflected by the credit transcript.

A common currency of credit

531.   There is one final matter upon which we have expended considerable time and attention – the establishment of a common currency with which to secure the full interaction of all elements of the national framework. We have to report to our disappointment that there is no consensus on the character of the *credit currency* at this stage in the development of the framework. We have evaluated the problem from every possible direction and summarise the options as follows:

A.   **define CNAA currency as standard;** this could be successful if further education colleges accepted a modification of the FEU proposals and deemed a definition of credit as less important than the achievement of a common currency. It would imply that further education could work with a 120-credit year;

B.   **define FEU currency as standard;** this would require higher education institutions and others, minimally to divide current ratings by 4 (and round most fractional values), or maximally to operate with a different curriculum model for the use of credit. HE programmes could work either with a 30-credit year, and/or with the 30-hour unit of credit;

C.   **define ECTS currency as standard;** as a compromise, it might be attractive (and therefore necessary under certain conditions). This would require the adoption of a 60-credit year (and a 180 credit honours degree). However it would produce the worst of both worlds for higher and further education by disturbing both for the sake of a pilot scheme to which neither sector was fully committed;

D.   **define NCVQ arrangements as standard;** this could not be achieved rapidly and would be resisted in higher education, where it might not be intellectually possible nor feasible over time to define common standards and performance criteria for academic programmes. It might also imply the development of a core curriculum in higher education which universities would find unwelcome;

E.   **define articulation arrangements between different frameworks;** this would be the pragmatic solution, developing conversion factors and the like. It would imply significant and irreconcilable short-term differences between frameworks that could not be surmounted by compromise;

F.   **define no articulation arrangements, and let the passage of time sort it out;** this admits defeat in the short term, but notes that a credit currency emerged in the United States over a period of 50 to 70 years, so we might not expect more rapid progress in the United Kingdom. It also proposes a higher level of 'untidiness' than other options.

532.   To resolve this problem, we propose to eliminate certain options, recommend another, and propose a plan for progress in the short and medium term. Firstly, neither Options E or F offer stable solutions; in fact they avoid the issue altogether. They fail to face up to problems that may only return another time. They imply that relatively trivial differences present insuperable problems; and they oblige students to sort out what professional academic colleagues have not been able to do, suffering the confusions of different systems meanwhile. If Options E or F emerge in practice, it will be because of a failure to implement more obvious compromises. On this, we need to distinguish between the short-term inevitability of some articulation arrangement *as part of a process of*

convergence around an agreed currency and a medium-to-long-term acceptance that no common agreement is possible. We would counsel against placing too much store by argument by analogy. This is *not* similar to the debate over European Monetary Union. We are not dealing with many well-established systems of currency and exchange, reflecting different cultural traditions. We are dealing with relatively new and poorly established systems of academic credit which are within our powers to modify as we wish. If the inertia of our arrangements prevents some reasonable compromises, then students and employers will be justified if they react with incredulity to our collective inaction.

A currency based on competence?

533. For reasons which we have explored from time to time already, Option D cannot be recommended of itself as a solution. It will not be possible to form a professional coalition of support for a curriculum design strategy which is founded on an academically contested intellectual basis, and which could doubtfully be applied to academic programmes. The establishment of national academic standards for programmes and courses could, alone, produce a centralised intervention into the academic practices of higher education which would be universally resisted by institutions and their staff. Moreover, the NCVQ appears ready to accept the compromise that, to achieve effective credit transfer between academic and vocational programmes, some numerical currency will be necessary. This would not prejudice the standards of units falling within the aegis of the NCVQ, nor their assessment, and would not imply that the NCVQ accepted the legitimacy of time-bound prescriptions of learning achievement. On balance, we believe that higher and further education will be satisfied to work with learning outcome statements rather than competence alone.

A European compromise?

534. This leaves us with the various numerical currency systems. Option C comes into play only if there is a breakdown of agreement between Options A and B. It is very much a compromise solution, producing no convincing rationale of itself and winning little immediate commitment from either higher or further education. As we have said earlier, we would be more confident of recommending this option on its own merits if there was evidence of significant progress towards a trans-European credit transfer system. However we are unable to anticipate such significant progress in the near future that would warrant a departure from either of the other Options now under consideration. On the other hand, if a settlement on either Option A or Option B is out of reach, then the credit system of the ECTS could be the sort of compromise that many would welcome. In this case, it would need to be remembered that there is no educational rationale underpinning the system; it is purely a mechanical and arithmetic version of the CNAA currency.

CNAA credit currency as standard?

535. Could further education converge around the CNAA currency units? This would imply that everyone could either work to a 120 credit year, or could derive their credits following the FEU proposals, and then multiply by 4 to bring them in line with CNAA values. Firstly, it is clearly within the gift of any organisation or individual to multiply by 4, or any other chosen figure. If that was all a credit currency involved, then it could be easily achieved. In this case further education could be invited to work in multiples of four credits in order to align with higher education. However, we are bound to say that this implies either that credit systems are so firmly entrenched in higher education that they cannot be modified, or that higher education institutions are too obdurate to compromise on anything other than their own terms. This solution would also accept that it would no longer be possible to seek an educational or curriculum rationale for the application of credit; the practice would be reduced simply to an administrative exercise. Further education would be required to give up a method for calculating credit based on educational principles for a methodology based on pragmatism. Institutions would be required to do no more than sub-divide their courses more or less evenly in some arithmetical sequence. This could result in the atrophy of

initiatives which use learning outcome statements as a device for defining the credit rating of modules and other learning experiences. We have received widespread opinion that progress in further education is now so advanced that colleges would not be prepared to make concessions of this nature.

Convergence around the FEU proposals?

536.   If a national credit system was being designed *ab initio*, starting from first principles, we have no doubt that the FEU proposals would gain general support among those concerned with the educational basis of credit systems. Indeed, it is apparent to this investigation that wherever credit has been developed by academic colleagues themselves, working with the needs of students and their programmes, it has taken the form that is summarised in the FEU proposals. However, the centrally-designed CNAA scheme has made progress in promoting the advantages of credit transfer, at least in higher education, and we would not wish to impede that momentum. On the other hand, we have to consider the momentum that has built up in further education over the last three years. The growth of interest in credit, and the pace of change it has released in the sector, are remarkable. It is no longer true to speak of credit systems as the property of higher education alone. The fulcrum has moved to a point between higher and further education and we welcome this. We have become aware during the investigation that there is a danger of two systems of credit developing – for higher and for further education. We would regard this as a regrettable outcome and it should be avoided at this early stage if at all possible. Firstly, such a development would produce environments in some institutions where two credit systems were running side by side in different parts of their further and higher education programmes, with bewildering consequences for students and staff. Secondly, any resource management strategies, informations systems and educational guidance arrangements which looked to credit-based formulae for assistance, would be thrown into turmoil by such divergence. Thirdly, it would dramatically strain the credibility of credit systems, with possibly damaging consequences for their wider

acceptance. Fourthly, it would make the operation of a national credit transcript almost impossible. And finally, it would require the entire matter to be reopened at a later date.

An assessment and a judgement

537.   On the balance of the evidence and opinion we have received, we assess that a common comprehensive credit system can be achieved, if contributing parties are prepared to make minor modifications over time. We are less convinced that all parties will or be able to make concessions in the near future. Taking into account the different variables, the differences of opinion within the sectors and the short-term operational constraints, but noting the universal desire to achieve a common framework and currency for the benefit of students, **we recommend** that arrangements for a comprehensive credit system, with a common credit currency, converge in due course around the proposals of the FEU. This will involve the voluntary acceptance by all parties, throughout the United Kingdom and in different sectors of post-secondary and higher education, of the need to work to a standard credit currency defined by the 30-hour unit of credit and/or a minimum 30-credit full-time year (otherwise referred to earlier as the '30/90' model for higher education). This recommendation does *not* mean that universities which have begun to use the 120/360 (CNAA) model will be required to change. In these cases, and others, institutions will remain free to work with whatever arrangement suits their purpose, changing if they choose. However, it is the judgement of this report that a unified credit system should be based wherever possible upon the educational *principles* identified in the FEU proposals and universities may choose to be guided by this over time.

A process of convergence

Implementation, conversion and convergence on a common credit currency

538.   We are aware that this proposal will not be welcomed in every quarter, and that it may reopen the debate about the nature of

credit systems and the definition of credit. If this is the case, then it is likely to follow any recommendation that we could make on the subject. In some universities the prize of a unified system will not outweigh the administrative inconvenience of modifying emerging or developed arrangements. In many further education colleges, the educational advantages of working with credit will make colleagues reluctant to renounce these in favour of a less satisfactory alternative. For the NCVQ, the existence of two credit currencies will possibly impede the short-term credit transfer of students between academic and vocational programmes. For funding councils and for ECCTIS and similar services, two currency systems will make matters more difficult. If a long-term accommodation of these approaches is to be achieved, it will require the identification of a *process of convergence* which distinguishes between those universities and colleges which are able and prepared to undertake convergence and those which choose not to proceed at this stage for whatever reason.

539.   We recognise that greater confidence may need to be established in some quarters that the recommendation can meet their needs. To this end, **we recommend** the following implementation arrangements be adopted. **We recommend** that the HEQC, NCVQ, BTEC, FEU, the representative bodies of institutions in higher and further education, the funding councils and other interested parties work for the adoption of a common unit of credit currency across the regions and nations of the United Kingdom, and between sectors, in line with the recommendations of this report. **We recommend** that the HEQC actively promotes a convergence of credit currencies in higher education and beyond, and assists universities and colleges in the process of adjustment. Where universities and collegs are in the process of deciding on the matter, and/or if they are inclined to be advised by these proposals, **we recommend** that they should be invited to consider with early effect converting to, or adopting from the start, the basis for credit as indicated in this report.

540.   Where universities and colleges remain to be convinced of the merits of the proposals, and are therefore unwilling to make

an early conversion, if at all, **we recommend** that they should be invited to subscribe to an extended programme of **pilot accreditation exercises** undertaken to apply the methodologies of both the CNAA and the FEU to the credit rating of various programmes. We believe that the courses being offered by the Continuing Education departments of many universities could be a suitable testing environment for this strategy. To facilitate progress, **we recommend** close working relationships between the higher and further education sectors on the application of accreditation methodologies. University Continuing Education departments, for example, could seek the views of their local Open College Network, or through association with the national CATS Projects of both the Employment Department and the FEU, explore the relative merits of the two systems. **We recommend** that the HEQC and the FEU commission a joint evaluation study of this work to report within a year.

541.   **We recommend** that the NCVQ enter discussions with HEQC, FEU, NOCN and other interested parties to undertake pilot accreditation exercises in the credit rating of units of NVQs and GNVQs. This exercise should embrace vocational qualifications at Level 3 and above in the first instance, and should be conducted in such a way as to ensure the maintenance of national standards and to establish the potential for more flexible student credit transfer between academic and vocational programmes in higher and further education. Again, ongoing work in the projects funded by the Employment Department may assist this process.

542.   Professional bodies and employers will need an an opportunity to comment on the recommendations. In all cases of which we are aware, the credit tariff of 'off-campus' programmes which have received credit ratings through the CNAA scheme could be converted to the new arrangements by a simple divisor of 4, with no material impact on the credit-worthiness of the learning experience of individual students or accredited qualifications. **We recommend** that the HEQC publishes a parallel list of converted credit ratings for accredited programmes from professional

bodies and corporate employers, and consults with interested parties on this basis. It will be important that the HEQC is able to explain that the modifications are necessary to achieve a comprehensive national framework, and do not imply a renegotiation of the credit ratings of accredited programmes. From our discussions with professional bodies and employers, we believe that the changes will be welcomed if they produce the type of convergence between different frameworks that is necessary for the creation of a national framework.

543.   We do not expect any institution to change the way it arranges its academic programme as a consequence of these proposals. For example, we are aware that a number of universities operate with a fixed number of modules per semester or year which do not tidily subdivide into partitions of 30 credits per year. Elsewhere, GNVQ units may face a similar problem. Although the allocation of credit should be sufficiently flexible to reflect the outcomes of different modules, we recognise that many institutions will not wish to engage with a level of finesse any more extensive than an arithmetical subdivision. Under these circumstances, and for the short term, **we recommend** that half-credits be accepted as a solution to this problem for those institutions which choose to change. We do not favour the general use of half-credits because they imply a degree of precision which promises too much from a credit system and which complicate matters unnecessarily for students and others. In the short term, however, they may be a helpful compromise under limited circumstances to encourage institutions to subscribe to the common credit framework without prejudice to their chosen pattern of course organisation.

Funding councils, HESA and a credit currency

544.   **We recommend** that the Funding Councils in higher and further education, and the Higher Education Statistics Agency (HESA), consider adopting the 30-hour unit of credit as a common unit of account, reflecting a full-time student credit equivalent of 30 credits. From this, it may be possible, if desired, to define students more precisely in credits terms which reflect the number of hours

'in attendance' in further and higher education per week/year. For example, a student undertaking a programme of 20 credits would be eligible for support under the '21-hour rule' for social benefit payments. A student contracting annually for 24 credits or more (or some other agreed value) might be deemed full-time. Term or semester equivalents could easily be defined. We address further aspects of this in Chapter XI.

545.   We are aware that HESA and the HEFCE are currently recommending a base unit of credit at 3% of a full-time programme. This appears to be the nearest approximation they are able to reach between different currency systems in advance of system-wide agreement. We have not been impressed by the representation of this minimum value as 3.6 credits. This implies a greater degree of precision than may be helpful and we suggest that the minimum unit of credit should be treated as 4 (CNAA) or 1 (FEU) credit points. However, we believe that, if funding councils are prepared to move in the direction of credit-based funding as proposed in Chapter XI of this report, their views on the appropriate methodological tools may be decisive in resolving the differences in currency systems between that proposed by the FEU model and that inherited from the CNAA.

Framework articulation on a failure to agree

546.   Finally on this matter, we have had to consider the consequences of a failure to agree on a common credit currency for credit transfer, student mobility and the operational efficiency of institutions and national agencies. Whilst there is general agreement on the minimum unit of credit (a 30-hour unit), there is no such agreement on a methodology for its application in the credit rating of programmes, nor on the number of credits (four or one) which constitute the minimum unit. There is a tendency to dismiss these matters as of little importance since students and others can make the arithmetical adjustments as necessary. Indeed, the argument follows, the further and higher education sectors only need to agree on some articulation arrangements between different currencies. Provided there is a shared framework of levels for student progression,

and clear interim qualifications, then the matter of different systems of credit points becomes immaterial. We are not so sure it is this simple, for the following reasons.

547.   Firstly, the currency of credit is the element of a credit system which is most visible to students, and most used by them. Colleagues will need to be satisfied in any articulation arrangements which become necessary whether this is a sensible long-term arrangement for students and employers. If it is not, a strategy for future agreement will need to be sought by the responsible bodies. Secondly, different systems of currency will raise difficulties in securing any cross-sector co-operation at the level of funding councils, NCVQ and other agencies. It will be possible to overcome these problems but a common currency would make this unnecessary. Thirdly, educational guidance procedures will need to deal with two different credit values, causing some confusion for students and counsellors alike. Fourthly, responsible bodies and individual institutions will need to establish what they most value from a credit system – administrative convenience or an educational instrument to assist curriculum design. As systems converge, it will be important to assess which values are dominant and what losses are being incurred, if any. Finally, we have offered a process of convergence in this report. We are unable to determine how this should be moved forward, except to urge progress in individual institutions. If a convergence is genuinely to be pursued, then the representative bodies of institutions will need to seek ways of reaching appropriate and informed conclusions. In the end, this will necessarily be a matter for educational institutions alone, possibly supported by funding councils. It will never be a matter for Government.

548.   It has proved beyond the capacity of this report to secure a negotiated agreement on a common credit currency. Some universities may make accommodations to provide a shared currency but many appear unwilling to do so at this stage. Moreover, many further education colleges appear equally committed to the principles and practices which inform the proposals from the FEU. The two sectors are so close to agreement that we feel it is disappointing that we have not been able to assemble the type of coalition of support for one or the other system. Therefore, **we recommend** that in any consultation exercises on this matter, institutions be invited not to comment adversarially on either the CNAA or the FEU proposals, but to comment on what they wish a credit system to do for them and their students. We have tried to establish the first principles underpinning a credit system in this report, and this may be a starting point for further discussions. We confirm the observation made earlier in this report: where credit emerges from curriculum practice and the activities of academic colleagues, it always takes the form outlined in the FEU proposals; where credit emerges from a committee, it usually takes the form recommended by the CNAA or ECTS arrangements. We remain unclear where the balance of preference lies in the opinion of colleagues between a compliance with administratively convenient arrangements or a readiness to use credit systems to meet wider educational and curriculum objectives. We would welcome further elaboration on this point.

A national authority for quality assurance

549.   We conclude this chapter on a national credit framework with some observations on the arrangements for the oversight of qualifications, student programmes, the learning environment and their quality assurance. We are aware that there is considerable antipathy in many quarters to the existence of over-arching and all-consuming bureaucracies, pursuing questionable needs and fulfilling ill-defined purposes. We have no desire to add to such organisations. However, if one inspects current arrangements and anticipates future developments, there is an apparent absence of any systematic oversight of the quality assurance of more flexible and diverse post-secondary and higher education opportunities. For example, there are few quality assurance arrangements in further education which can address in a uniform manner the explosion of activity in modular and credit-related arrangements that has taken place in the last three years. The NCVQ plays an important role in one dimension, and the FEFC has taken up the responsibility for determining

the credit tariffs of programmes and courses which it is prepared to fund. Elsewhere, the Open College Networks play an increasingly influential role; and awarding bodies, professional bodies and others have an important stake in the processes.

550.   In higher education, the HEQC discharges its responsibilities for quality assurance and the funding councils discharge theirs for quality assessment. We do not intend to add to the weight of argument that has been brought to bear on these matters within higher education. We are concerned, further into the future, that eruptions of interest in credit-based learning, arising often from within the professional academic community itself, may not always be guided by coherent national arrangements. Moreover, the responsibility for the quality assurance of these developments is shared between so many different bodies, with different agendas, that

some co-ordination may be necessary across the sectors.

551.   We are aware that there is a view, which is worth inspecting elsewhere, that the market will sort out matters of quality. Students and employers will make up their minds about arrangements and this will act as a stimulus to quality control and quality improvement amongst institutions. If this is so, there may be no difficulty. However, in the transition to a more open marketplace in post-secondary and higher education, there may be a danger that a behavioural pattern of flexibility and choice may mature more quickly than the infrastructures capable of coping with it. In the end some arrangements for a system-wide oversight of the operation of a national credit framework may be necessary, and we draw this to the attention of interested parties. We turn in the next chapter to matters of quality assurance which affect higher education specifically.

Recommendations and guidance for future policy

On a national credit framework

To HEQC, NCVQ, FEU, BTEC, SCOTVEC, the representative bodies of institutions, Government departments and other interested parties, including professional bodies, TECs and employers

29 **We recommend** that all parties in higher and further education throughout the United Kingdom should converge around the principles of a single unified credit framework, according to the specifications advised in the report, which include agreed levels of progression and achievement by which qualifications may be aligned, procedures for the description, credit rating and assessment of modules, and a defined unit of credit.

30 **We recommend** that the HEQC, NCVQ, FEU and the representative bodies of institutions in higher and further education actively promote the specifications of the single unified credit framework and assist institutions and others to adjust to the arrangements over time. Moreover, we recommend that professional bodies and employers be consulted to explain the proposed arrangements, and that the HEQC assists this consultation process by publishing, in consultation with ECCTIS, a draft list of parallel credit ratings for professional body programmes and accredited company training.

31 **We recommend** that, where individual institutions wish further evidence of the practical possibilities of the proposals, further work should be undertaken to test the suitability of different credit systems and accreditation arrangements. Pilot dual accreditation exercises should be undertaken, using a suitable variety of programmes, perhaps in Continuing Education departments or elsewhere, and possibly drawing on the experience of accreditation work in Open College Networks. Specific pilot exercises should be undertaken in consultation and co-operation with the NCVQ to accredit NVQ and GNVQ units.

32 **We recommend** that a process of convergence be established to provide in the first instance for an articulation between different systems of credit currency, with a view to securing in the longer term a shared system of credit currency between higher and further education.

To funding councils and HESA

33 **We recommend** that funding councils in higher and further education, and HESA, give detailed consideration to the suitability of the recommended unit of credit and credit currency for adoption as the means by which a full-time student equivalent may be established. Moreover, we encourage these bodies to consider the implications of this for the management of resources and the capture of relevant institutional and student information.

On the designation of an Associate Degree, and other intermediate qualifications, within a credit framework

To HEQC, NCVQ, BTEC, representative bodies of institutions, professional bodies and others

34 **We recommend** that a new first cycle, two year intermediate qualification be established, to be called an *Associate Degree*, defined according to the specifications contained in the report. **We recommend** that further consultations take place between relevant parties on the designation of the award, and that the funding councils should invite institutions to apply for funding to develop pilot initiatives in support of this qualification.

35 **We recommend** that consideration be given to strengthening the status of the Certificate of Higher Education to meet the needs of large numbers of Continuing Education students for whom this qualification may be attractive in the first instance.

36 **We recommend** that further consideration be given to the designation of a new post-experience qualification, a *Certificate in Advanced Professional Development*, to meet the needs of those claiming credit for learning from professional or work-based experience, but where the credit may not be at postgraduate level.

37 **We recommend** that further attention be given to the development of a post-18 qualification which would allow students to bring together academic and other forms of learning into a broadly-based unified qualification, exploiting the flexibility of modular and credit-based programmes in post-16 education generally. We believe this type of broadly-based qualification will provide the best means of preparing the greatest number of students for entry to most universities in the future, and will give students the best preparation for future employment.

To funding councils and the DFE

38 **We recommend** that funding councils reconsider the academic standing and funding status of programmes described as 'Level 0', in the light of proposals in this report that such programmes would be aligned in a national credit framework with Level 3 (FE). **We recommend** that the DFE considers the implications of this for existing legislation which defines the character of higher education courses, with a view to clarification or modification of the legislation.

On a national credit transcript

To HEQC, NCVQ, BTEC, FEU, the representative bodies of institutions, professional bodies, employers, student representative bodies and Government departments

39 **We recommend** the development of a National Credit Transcript. We would encourage early consultations with interested parties on the specifications and operating circumstances of a national transcript, drawing upon institutional and international experience. We believe the development of a national credit transcript is an essential instrument for the system-wide management of student flexibility and for the effective disclosure of student achievement to employers and students themselves. We believe that the HEQC might take a lead in the first instance in making progress on this matter.

On the oversight of the operation of a national credit framework

To Government and all interested parties

40 **We recommend** that further attention should be paid to the means by which the general oversight of a national credit framework may be established. Currently, responsibility for operational oversight and the maintenance of quality assurance lies with the HEQC, NCVQ, the individual institutions, professional bodies and employers, various bodies in further education, and the funding councils in certain respects. **We recommend** that consideration of future policy options should consider whether it is sensible to promote this diversity of responsibility for a credit framework which spans sectors of education, institutions and possibly national boundaries within the United Kingdom.

On further work

To HEQC, the representative bodies of institutions and the NCVQ

41 **We recommend** that further work be undertaken to establish the extent of practice in the accreditation of NVQs in higher education and to determine the appropriate levels of alignment between higher level NVQs and GNVQs, and academic qualifications.

To the research community

42 We have been made aware of the discomfort many academic colleagues feel with the term *competence*. Equally, we have identified a growing acceptance of the legitimacy and usefulness of describing the curriculum in terms of student learning outcomes. **We recommend** that further work be encouraged to explore the most appropriate means of describing the learning outcomes of academic programmes in higher education and beyond, drawing perhaps on the concepts of *competence, capability* and *proficiency* to provide an adequate conceptual basis for the development of practice in the future.

X.   *Quality assurance*

Introduction

552.   It will be apparent from discussions in earlier chapters that considerations of quality assurance are never far from the centre of developments in credit-based learning. The growth of credit systems and modular programmes has increased the diversity of learning achievement that may be counted towards qualifications. This has been accompanied by questions concerning the quality assurance of that learning achievement. These concerns have been sharpened by the emergence in recent years of arrangements for the recognition of learning achievement gained from professional or corporate employer training programmes, and of bilateral arrangements between higher and further education institutions whereby higher education programmes are delivered under contractual licence, a practice known as 'franchising'.

553.   Different views have been expressed about the proper balance to be achieved between improved access, student choice and flexibility on the one hand, and the maintenance of appropriate standards in higher education on the other. Attention has been drawn to the means by which academic coherence and integrity may be maintained. Professional bodies and employers, as well as institutions themselves, have been interested to establish sound quality assurance arrangements to manage the variety of learning opportunities now available to students.

554.   Indeed, the objectives which underpin the quality assurance of flexible programmes, within the institution or 'off campus', involve firstly the establishment of an adequate degree of confidence in the appropriate learning processes and procedures for the credit-rating of comparable learning programmes wherever they are delivered; and secondly, the availability of relevant information about credit ratings and what they refer to, in the interests of students, institutions, employers and professional bodies.

555.   In Chapter IX, we drew attention to the need to address these matters in a comprehensive manner, accepting that arrangements for quality assurance were pertinent to developments in further as well as higher education, and in vocational as well as academic programmes. For the purposes of this report, we have confined ourselves to the immediate problems concerning higher education in the wake of the dissolution of the CNAA. This does not change our view that some serious attention needs to be paid to cross-sectoral quality assurance arrangements, which are likely to become necessary as a comprehensive credit framework matures and becomes a familiar part of the educational landscape.

The legacy of the CNAA

556.   In September 1992, as part of the process of transferring its functions to other bodies, the CNAA drew the attention of the Higher Education Quality Council and the degree-awarding institutions to a number of quality assurance matters which it believed merited further attention. The CNAA was concerned to recommend for further consideration various aspects of the maintenance of quality assurance where, in its opinion, the desire amongst institutions for growth and diversification had led the Council to believe that this had become *'too strong for the institution's own quality assurance system'*. The Council identified some areas of apprehension.

557.   **The rapid growth in modular and credit-based programmes** raised questions concerning the extent to which the academic review process might concentrate upon module delivery to the neglect of the student learning experience. Furthermore, the CNAA was concerned to draw attention to the need to ensure that quality assurance arrangements designed for conventionally structured programmes would require modification before they could be applied

to modular programmes. This would be important particularly with respect to tiered examination arrangements and to the role and responsibilities of external examiners.

558.   **The growth of teaching and learning outside the higher education campus,** particularly developments in work-based learning and in the franchising of programmes had persuaded the CNAA to recommend further consideration of the extent to which institutions had given appropriate attention to the adequacy of the higher education environment, in resource terms, and to the quality of the student experience where the learning programme was being delivered (and assessed in the first instance) by teachers who may not have been part of the course design process.

559.   **The growth in the assessment of competence** appeared to the CNAA to suggest that such assessment strategies, required by the NCVQ or by other bodies, might put at risk the development of students' knowledge, values, and understanding. In the opinion of the Council, this was to be avoided.

560.   **The development of distance learning programmes** raised questions of whether institutions were yet sufficiently experienced in understanding and providing for the special needs of distance learners, and whether they were able to provide the range of learner support that had underpinned the quality of Open University programmes. And finally, **the development of overseas programmes** had led the CNAA to identify considerable variation in quality as institutions compromised the strength of their quality assurance procedures in an effort to contain costs or gain commercial advantage.

561.   We have attempted to comment on some of these concerns, although we have taken particular notice of the request made in the White Paper (DFE,1991: 74) that arrangements should be made to replace the functions of the CNAA with respect to credit accumulation and transfer. We have therefore limited the greater part of our attention to those aspects which relate directly to the replacement of specific functions for the quality assurance of flexible learning arrangements in and beyond the university or college. To this end, we focus upon five aspects of

the quality assurance of credit-based learning:

* **quality assurance for internal credit transfer:** arrangements for the quality assurance of student mobility *within* an institutional setting, usually as a consequence of modularisation;

* **'franchising' arrangements,** where students may be registered for a higher education qualification with a university or higher education college but receive part or all of their learning experience usually in a further education college;

* **the accreditation of 'off-campus' learning:** those arrangements for the accreditation of external programmes, such as employment-based learning, including in-company and professional training, work-based learning and related forms of experiential learning. Arrangements include those negotiated with individual students, or with corporate employers and professional bodies on behalf of their employees and members;

* **arrangements for the management of individual student programmes** for those students who may be mobile between higher education institutions, where no one institution may be able to register the student for a qualification by reason of regulation, period of residence or similar circumstance;

* **the production of guidelines,** to inform the development of arrangements for modularisation, credit rating, the quality assurance of 'off-campus' accreditation, including 'franchising'. Some of these arrangements have been addressed by the CNAA in the draft *Guidelines on credit rating (1992).*

Modularisation and quality assurance

562.   Arrangements which concern the management of student choice and mobility as a consequence of modularisation

and similar developments are already being addressed by the quality audit procedures of the Higher Education Quality Council. Institutions which now operate modular programmes of one form or another will have satisfied themselves that their quality assurance arrangements are adequate to protect academic standards on their programmes. Other institutions which are considering the process may be less certain of the appropriate arrangements for quality assurance. There are important organisational and technical issues which institutions need to address for the development of effective quality assurance arrangements in this area.

563. Modular developments take two principal forms: *firstly*, the structural modification of conventional courses; or *secondly*, the integration of existing courses into a complex of individual units from which students may assemble, with greater or lesser degrees of constraint, their particular programmes. There are considerable variations of emphasis within these two models, and we discuss this further later in the report. For the purposes of our argument here, institutions which decide to use modularisation as a simple segmentation of existing courses, with minimal disturbance to their conventional academic structures, will expect to deal with matters of quality assurance through their prevailing arrangements. On the other hand, the experience of those institutions which have embarked upon an extensive restructuring of their academic programmes suggests that greater programme variety and student choice require specific modifications to existing quality assurance arrangements. Under these circumstances, institutions may well be helped by the existence of some advice and guidance on the most suitable arrangements to assure the quality of academic programmes.

Definitive guidelines on modularisation and quality assurance

564. The CNAA did produce materials in draft for the guidance of the former Polytechnics and this may be usefully revisited. The HEQC has subsequently begun to publish materials which will be helpful to institutions in the future. Its *Guidelines on quality assurance* (1993) and the briefing paper: *Checklist for quality*

assurance systems (1994) have made a useful start However the issues are extremely complex and beset by individual institutional predispositions. The development of a unified higher education sector does provide an opportunity for some new thinking on these matters. The older universities have themselves made considerable progress in recent years in the implementation of modular programmes, and they have considerable accumulated experience which is not significantly in the public domain. For example, the Northern Universities' Registrars Group has been working for the past three years on a common approach to the development and administration of modularisation. Similarly, individual ex-UFC universities, such as the University of Sussex, have produced many internal reports advising on aspects of these changes. Very little of this material has been co-ordinated, yet it provides a rich source of information and guidance. The HEQC could usefully draw together this material and, with representative informed individuals, produce a review of practice and guidance for those intending to proceed with modularisation in the future. **We recommend** that the HEQC undertake this review with a view to producing definitive guidelines on the quality assurance of modular programmes.

Modularisation as the norm

565. We would like to make one further observation. We believe that it is now timely for institutions to consider *as the norm* academic programmes which deliver greater student choice, and adjust their quality assurance arrangements accordingly. This may have long-term advantages for institutions and will avoid the current tendency to regard modular programmes as peculiar in some way. Clearly it will be possible to treat conventional and non-modular courses within such arrangements without prejudice. If this approach were to be adopted, we believe in time institutions would develop new perspectives on the quality of academic programmes. This would be reflected in a closer alignment of professional academic judgements and individual student choices, which we believe to be desirable. Moreover, quality assurance arrangements for the management of internal student mobility within institutional

programmes may be best informed by the comment of the National Advisory Body for Higher Education in the report of its Continuing Education Working Party (1984):

> '...in considering the application of requirements for coherence, progression, and integration, institutions and validating bodies should approach the question from the perspective of the individual student rather than as an observer analysing a particular course from the outside.'
>
> *(NAB, 1984, 37; emphasised in the original)*

566.	Notwithstanding the principled commitment to student-centredness expressed by the NAB Report, most institutional concerns are focused on more prosaic matters. The quality assurance of modular programmes and internal credit transfer is likely to be concerned with arrangements for the initial admission and in-programme guidance of students, the management of their programmes, the oversight of assessment practices and procedures, the standardisation of the student learning experience and the periodic review of these arrangements. Indeed, the vexed question of the role of external examiners requires some specific attention in the context of modular programmes, whilst the emphasis given to annual monitoring, compared with periodic review, may need to change in favour of the former. Furthermore, in earlier chapters, we have called for closer partnership with employers, professional bodies and the NCVQ. Their role in the future arrangements for modular courses will need specific attention, as will the place of student opinion and feedback. We recommend therefore that definitive guidelines should be produced by the HEQC to inform the development of modular programmes; these guidelines should draw upon institutional experience across the higher education sector, and they should be distinct from guidelines for the credit-rating of 'off-campus' learning.

Franchising and quality assurance

567.	The growth of franchising arrangements between higher and further education institutions has been substantial. In 1985, only the University of Central Lancashire was engaged in such activity with small numbers of students; by 1993, most universities had some exposure to franchising and a few had committed to the arrangements extensively. Bird et al (1993) estimate that there were 10,000 students on such courses in 1991 whilst the HEFCE claimed to be funding over 25,000 places in 1993, mostly at Levels 1 and 2 (HE) with 75% on part-time programmes.

568.	With the exception of an important HMI survey of higher education in further education (DES, 1991), there has been little official attention to the quality assurance of franchising arrangements. Indeed, the HMI survey drew attention to one significant matter which has increased in importance with the expansion of student numbers and bilateral agreements. Should franchising arrangements be seen as part of a general recruitment strategy, whereby universities exploit surplus capacity in further education colleges, at lower costs, to create an 'upstream' supply of students? Or should they be developed as local network arrangements for the promotion and extension of local student access? During the past few years, there have been examples of both strategies. A small number of universities have negotiated agreements with colleges nationwide, whilst others have restricted their commitments to local contracts. Moreover, these strategies have been cross-cut with differences in patterns of recruitment. Some local network agreements have involved the recruitment of students nationally, in which student places at the local further education college have taken on the character of overspill. These different strategies may be complementary, and similar issues of quality assurance may apply, but HMI were concerned to establish whether institutions entered the arrangements principally for commercial advantage or for social and educational objectives.

569.	HMI found that the vast majority (88%) of classes observed on franchised programmes were satisfactory or better. Moreover, in work for the Division of Quality Enhancement of the HEQC, Hilbourne (1993) found that higher education students in further education colleges are well supported by their tutors; discontinuation rates are no worse than for comparable students on similar courses in universities or colleges; accommodation was generally satisfactory, but learning resources including libraries were weaker. The report concluded that, on balance, *'the student experience had not on the whole been compromised'*.

570. The general practice of franchising raises new and difficult questions for quality assurance. Answers will not be so forthcoming in a period of retrenchment in student recruitment and in the absence of a co-ordinated quality assurance authority for further education. However, it may be timely to use the respite offered by current recruitment restrictions to reflect on what might be the definitive features of a preferred strategy for future bilateral arrangements of this kind. Elsewhere in this report, we have recommended much closer working relationships between higher and further education on a number of related matters. Agreements on franchising and its quality assurance may have profound consequences for the effective operation of a national credit framework.

571. **We recommend** that future consideration of the quality assurance of franchising arrangements should address the features identified in Table 36, with a view to inviting institutions and their representative bodies to associate with the outcomes of a review based on these aspects.

The quality assurance of 'off-campus' learning

572. Quality assurance for programmes delivered, or learning achieved, external to the institution raised further complex problems. We have had some difficulty in finding a term with which to describe the cluster of learning activities that now fall outside the physical environment of the university or college. In attempting to capture these activities with the term *'off-campus learning'*, we recognise that this may not be entirely satisfactory. The term might imply that all open learning or distance learning is technically 'off-campus' in that it is undertaken independently of the

Table 36: A review of the quality assurance of bilateral programmes between higher and further education: some issues

1. *Strategic Rationales:* what are the institutional objectives for bilateral arrangements?

- how do bilateral arrangements relate to the institutional Mission? How does franchising fulfil any planning objectives for the academic programme? Does it meet objectives for wider access, increased part-time student numbers, greater commitment to science and engineering, or specific regional needs?

- are bilateral arrangements part of a broader coalition of commitments and arrangements, including other FE/HE links? Are arrangements seen as overspill (for HE) or infill (for FE)?

2. *Principles of collaboration:* how is the bilateral relationship managed?

- what steps have been taken for institutional management collaboration, and at what level? What are the procedures for addressing changes of policy with respect to student numbers, or changes in financial advantage?

- with what level of discretion does the FE college act, and with what oversight? How are differences between agreements and practice monitored? How is the Memorandum of Association (or Co-operation) authorised?

3. *Quality Systems Interaction:* how far do the quality assurance arrangements of the bilateral partners interact?

institution. However, we have chosen to exclude such modes of learning on the grounds that the learning sources and materials have usually been produced directly by the higher education institution, which continues to provide support for the learner in a variety of face-to-face or remote ways. Furthermore, the term may be confused with *outreach* activities undertaken by universities and colleges in community centres, workplaces or other extra-mural circumstances. However we can think of no more suitable term with which to capture the range of student learning that is undertaken beyond the direct supervision of the higher education institution, but where the achievement remains authenticated by a university or college.

573.   The 'off-campus' nature of the learning achievement has called into question whether such learning could possibly have taken place under conditions which are likely to have led to higher education outcomes. This apprehension is reinforced by those who are sceptical that genuine higher education is possible in non-educational settings such as a commercial workplace. A yet more serious concern is that institutions could be constrained by commercial pressures and the need to diversify income sources to enter into accreditation agreements with corporate employers and others with inadequate regard for the maintenance of standards. This might be manifested in a preparedness to negotiate a commercially advantageous credit-rating agreement for the recognition of company training, thereafter pursuing less rigorously the normal processes of monitoring and review in order to preserve a commercial contract. Moreover, concerns have been expressed from the other direction. Institutions which might be keen to enter such credit-rating agreements are apprehensive that corporate employers and others could exploit a market between institutions by trading up their programmes to the 'highest bidder', an institution prepared to offer the greatest amount of credit at the highest level.

574.   We have had the opportunity to look within a sample of institutions at various arrangements for the accreditation of 'off-campus' learning; quality assurance arrangements appear to be in place. This is certainly the case for the accreditation of individual experiential learning, both certificated and uncertificated. In the limited examples of individual students who are progressing with credit for such learning, we have concluded that the standards of such learning is commensurate with that expected at

the appropriate level in higher education. Institutions would however welcome consistent guidelines to inform their future behaviour, and we address this matter below.

575.   We have detected some variations in the amount of credit awarded by different institutions for the same learning achievement. In some cases these variations are much greater than one would expect even from decisions based on individual institutional programmes. This applies to the credit-rating of learning achievement which has attracted a National Vocational Qualification (NVQ). One example was drawn to our attention by the Management Charter Initiative (MCI) and it concerned significant variations between institutions in the award of credit for a NVQ Level 4 in Management. Some institutions felt this qualification could be credit-rated against substantial elements of an MBA programme; others judged it to be worth far less credit, albeit at the Master's level; whilst one institution had allowed credit only against elements in an undergraduate Business Studies course. We have been informed of other wide variations: one further example cited the credit awarded for the Further Education Teachers Certificate. On one occasion this was counted against an undergraduate teaching degree; on another, against a Master's programme. Moreover, we have been reminded that the over-award of credit can be a recruitment device in a competitive market, although it appears to be less of a problem than the inconsistent or under-recognition of credit.

576.   We have been particularly taken with these examples because they highlight some very important and difficult issues. Firstly, the fundamental principle of the qualifications recognised by NCVQ for the award of a National Vocational Qualification is that learning is achieved against agreed and public performance standards; all NVQs Level 4 in Management assert that all qualified learners have achieved the same level of competence. Secondly, whilst vocational competence is not necessarily the same as academic proficiency, and whilst institutions are free to exercise proper professional judgement on the credit for any NVQ that may be counted towards specific academic qualifications, the quality assurance of broadly similar courses

leading to a standard academic qualification (in this case, an MBA) is not improved by the existence of significant variations in the credit allowed for a specific NVQ. Thirdly, the credibility of both academic standards and NVQ standards may be prejudiced if further attention is not given to how matters of this nature may be resolved. For example, how much credit from a Master's programme might be counted against an NVQ Level 5 qualification? Fourthly, institutions are free to be inconsistent, but this is not a convincing basis for supporting the autonomy of universities. We address some of these matters in the discussion below.

Credit transfer and mutual recognition

577.   For the individual student seeking access to institutional programmes, circumstances are frequently beset by often unspoken reservations about the authority or integrity of particular forms of learning, even when this learning may have gained credit from other institutions or national agencies. Whatever confidence individual institutions may express in their own quality assurance arrangements, they remain extensively sceptical of the standards that apply elsewhere. Solutions revolve in large measure around the principles and practice of *mutual recognition*. This concerns the extent to which individual institutions are prepared to accept the quality assurance procedures of others, accepting the transferability of credit for student learning achievement from whatever source it may be gained. Mutual recognition implies a preparedness to undertake a *'pooling of sovereignty'* in the treatment of the quality of individual student learning, agreeing that learning achievement authenticated by one institution will be acceptable to other universities and colleges.

Principles of mutual recognition

578.   Although arrangements for mutual recognition address different groups of students, there are certain common principles. Universities and colleges are expected to agree that:

- learning achievement gained within the academic programmes of one institution will be recognised for credit towards the qualifications of other institutions, enabling students to negotiate entry and credit transfer between institutional courses irrespective of academic structures, mode of attendance, style of learning achievement, or institutional regulations governing periods of residence or similar constraints;

- learning achievement gained outside the higher education institution, and subject to the quality assurance of one institution, is held to be of authentic quality and equivalent in standard to that gained from institutional academic programmes, and is eligible for negotiated credit transfer;

- professional bodies, employers and national agencies such as the NCVQ, which enter into credit rating agreements with one or more university or college can expect that the agreed credit ratings will enable their members, employees and qualified candidates to negotiate access and progression through the academic programmes of other institutions;

- information is available to students with credit for learning achievement, advising them of the conditions under which it may be deployed towards specific higher education qualifications.

579.   Mutual recognition by professional bodies raises other problems, but one additional principle can be stated: professional bodies should agree to accept for the purposes of professional qualification and eligibility for professional membership those academic programmes which they accredit and the students therefrom, including those academic programmes which include elements of properly validated 'off-campus' and experiential learning agreed between universities or colleges and corporate employers. This principle raises particularly fundamental questions for professional bodies about the discharge of their responsibilities

towards the quality assurance of professional standards. Few professional bodies are currently able to concur with this principle, and the problems associated with it are discussed below.

Problems with mutual recognition arrangements

580. The CNAA had formerly pursued the principles of mutual recognition through its relationship with the former Polytechnics. It sought to promote mutual respect for institutional standards and their quality assurance through the development of a common threshold for the award of qualifications. In principle, therefore, all higher education qualifications within the polytechnics and colleges could be said to be of the same standard and eligible for mutual recognition because they had been subject to common quality assurance arrangements approved by the CNAA.

581. To underpin this principle, and in efforts to encourage the freer movement of students, the CNAA invited its constituent institutions in England and Wales to operate a centrally designed CAT Scheme. An identical strategy was developed for Scotland with the SCOTCATS initiative. Both these schemes have subsequently been broadened to embrace universities from the ex-UFC sector. Moreover, the CNAA was happy to encourage the development of regional consortia, such as SEEC, to promote mutual respect and recognition. As we have argued earlier in Chapter VII, the establishment of effective arrangements for the mutual recognition of academic standards has proved more difficult in practice. Institutions have subscribed to common CAT schemes and regional consortia, but no significant inter-institutional credit transfer has occurred as a consequence of this. A number of factors may be identified to explain this, but significant amongst them must be the reluctance of institutions to yield a sufficient measure of their own procedures, cultures and traditions to encourage the greater mobility of students. There have been some exceptions, notably the success with which 500-800 students from the Open University are able transfer each year onto the academic programmes of other universities and colleges (see Rickwood, 1993). This may in part be explained by the visibility of the Open University curriculum (its course units are published widely) and a general familiarity with the quality of Open University students: many academic staff from other institutions have taught Open University courses at some stage in their careers. Otherwise, mutual recognition has been slow to develop and the prospects for widespread agreement on common standards for learning achievement and qualifications have not been improved by the increased diversity of the higher education sector following the end of the binary division.

582. We are not optimistic for significant early progress on this matter, and the pursuit of formal mutual recognition arrangements may not be the best way forward. Major obstacles appear to impede progress, not least the vexed question of how a common standard might be determined for the undergraduate degree. Until that is resolved, general progress on mutual recognition of standards amongst institutions is likely to be slow. Moreover, there are considerable problems of culture and status, and of organisational flexibility, to be overcome before it will be possible to speak of a more open system of inter-institutional recognition and respect.

583. Indeed it may not be helpful to regard systematic mutual recognition as *the* problem. From the perspective of the individual student, formal mutual recognition 'agreements' between institutions count for nothing if a student is unable to negotiate effective entry and credit transfer. Institutions may nod in the direction of common arrangements but in practice their procedures reflect their traditions: some universities and colleges will be more open to credit transfer than others. Moreover, institutions may in reality recognise only the quality of their peers – those other universities with similar missions, traditions, or general academic standing. Under these conditions, individually negotiated credit transfer will tend to replace formal 'agreements' as institutions make judgements about individual institutions and the students from them. This argument applies *a fortiori* to the acceptance of much 'off-campus' learning.

General and specific credit

584. This dilemma is illustrated by the debate over the usefulness of the concepts of general credit and specific credit. These terms were defined within the CNAA CAT Scheme and are explained in the draft *Guidelines on credit rating* (CNAA, 1992):

'As there is such a huge variety of HEI programmes and awards, it is not feasible to quantify (a credit rating) against the aims and objectives of every available programme. Instead CNAA assesses the extent to which (the learning activity) would satisfy the requirements for a notional rather than an actual award. A general credit represents a judgement that a particular learning activity falls within the range of higher education and indicates its quantity and level... **These credits only gain value – become specific – when they are transferred by students towards an actual programme** *leading to a higher education qualification...They will be converted into 'specific' credits by the admitting HEI'* (emphasis added).

585. Majority opinion holds that this distinction between general and specific credit is important and should be retained. The function of general credit is to act as a guide to the general standing of a learning activity, informing students of their (maximum) credit entitlement for a particular accredited learning achievement and advising institutions of the 'agreed' credit rating of that activity from which specific credit may be granted. The purpose of accrediting agencies, formerly the CNAA Credit Rating Advisory Group or some individual institutions, has been to establish the general credit-worthiness of a learning programme and commend its acceptance by all subscribing institutions. In this manner, something approaching national consistency may be achieved.

586. On the other hand, a significant minority, including some professional bodies, hold the view that it may not be particularly helpful to maintain the distinction. The function of a credit system is to assist students to gain access, make progress and achieve required learning outcomes. Since general credit does not guarantee either access or progression, the only value of credit lies in its

specific application; in this sense, all useful credit is in practice 'specific' credit. Moreover, general credit ratings can only be attributed on the basis of notional programmes and qualifications; there is no common authority or academic standard with which to maintain consistency (in contradistinction to the role and practice of the NCVQ, for example). Therefore, whenever 'agreed' general credit ratings are published, institutions may interpret these adjudications as variably as they wish. It follows from this line of argument that no obvious purpose is served by retaining a conceptual distinction between the two categories: credit is simply credit. Furthermore, investment in nationally 'agreed' credit rating exercises may have little effect in facilitating the transfer of individual students. Professional bodies, employers and individual institutions would be better placed if they negotiated case-by-case arrangements, or worked with local consortia of institutions on an agreed basis for effective credit transfer.

Quality assurance and credential evaluation

587. An assessment of this debate may be approached from two perspectives: that which addresses the requirements for quality assurance; and that which improves effectiveness for students. If *general credit* is a useful concept, it is because it acts in support of the quality assurance of learning achievement. It establishes a consensually-defined maximum credit entitlement for a learning programme which can accommodate it. The authority for the general credit rating lies, not in regulation or statute, but in the quality assurance procedures by which the credit rating was determined. Those quality assurance procedures may be the property of a national agency, consortium, or individual institution, but they can be held to bestow legitimacy on the general credit-worthiness of a learning experience.

588. Since individual institutions cannot be forced to agree to accept such credit ratings, what force do such ratings have in practice? Compliance may be achieved by consent via consortia and similar associations but we have already argued that prospects for mutual recognition from this direction are not promising. Consent may be granted formally and 'in principle', but practice at the point of

access and transfer is altogether a different matter. Individual students are usually required to re-negotiate the credit-worthiness of their learning achievement. Agreements reached by one university or college with a professional body, corporate employer or other agency are not necessarily recognised or honoured by the specific course requirements of another institution.

589.   In summary, *general* and *specific credit* may be alternatively understood as *negotiable* and *negotiated* forms of credit. The former attempts to describe the quality threshold in terms of the credit-worthiness of learning, its negotiability for entrance to a programme; the latter establishes the real currency of the achievement, its negotiated value. We have given some thought to whether a change of terminology might be appropriate, but the balance of informed opinion is strongly against this. Accordingly, we believe that future arrangements for the quality assurance of credit ratings may be properly achieved by a combination of procedures which address the **general** (*negotiable*) and **specific** (*negotiated*) forms of credit. **We recommend** that the balance of responsibility for the adjudication of credit ratings and credential evaluation should shift towards individual institutions. However, collective arrangements need to be established for the quality assurance of general credit, whilst institutionally-based procedures for credential evaluation need to be created or strengthened for the quality assurance of specific credit. Under these conditions local credential evaluation becomes the route by which most students travel in their efforts to gain access and progression. Ultimately, we hope to see an environment in which 'credit' is simply credit.

Professional bodies and mutual recognition

590.   There is a further aspect of this discussion which gives rise to considerable debate. The effective transfer of credit between institutions, or from work-based learning to academic programmes, is often made more problematic when the views of professional bodies have to be considered. Professional bodies rightly take seriously their responsibilities towards quality assurance and the maintenance of professional standards. They usually discharge these responsibilities through the accreditation of higher education courses which meet their requirements. Students who successfully complete these courses are usually eligible for membership of the relevant professional body. Recently some professional bodies and regulating authorities, particularly amongst the health care professions, social work, certain professions connected with the construction industry, and in business administration and management, have begun to adopt a more receptive approach towards student achievement gained through 'off-campus' learning. They have begun to accept that, with appropriate quality assurance, such learning can be a valuable source of credit leading to authentic academic and professional qualifications.

591.   On the other hand, many other professions have yet to be persuaded that credit for 'off-campus' and experientially-derived learning can legitimately be accumulated towards professionally acceptable qualifications. We have been interested to explore the examples of two arrangements for the accreditation of 'off-campus' learning, both of which involve different professions in Engineering. We have looked at the Partnership Scheme operated by the University of Portsmouth for a number of years, involving the accreditation of employment-based in-company training at local engineering firms. We have also considered the Ford-ASSET programme accredited by Anglia Polytechnic University. Both schemes involve the university in the formal quality assurance and accreditation of experientially-based 'off-campus' learning of company employees, leading to undergraduate qualifications in mechanical and electrical engineering. Yet successfully graduating students may not be eligible for membership of the relevant professional bodies because they have not accepted the element of 'off-campus' learning as a legitimate part of an accredited engineering course. In the case of the Ford-ASSET programme, this can mean that over 400 employee Engineers at Ford's Dagenham plant may successfully gain an Engineering degree but will be excluded from professional membership of the relevant Institute.

592.   For a number of reasons we have been interested in the case of the Engineering professions and their attitude towards academic

programmes of this type. First, the Engineering professions are often regarded by many colleagues in universities and colleges as the most obdurate in defence of familiar and conventional course arrangements. Second, this may be explained in part by the fact that these professional bodies take their responsibilities seriously towards the maintenance of public confidence in the quality of professional engineering competence. Third, they are also required to withstand considerable international scepticism about the quality of engineering students who emerge from the shorter undergraduate programmes in the United Kingdom, and elements of experientially-based learning may be held to reinforce that scepticism. Finally, there appear to be interesting differences of receptivity to the acceptance of work-based and experiential learning between the more cautious individual professional bodies and their Engineering Council.

593.   When we extend the discussion of professional bodies and their approach to mutual recognition to the development of 'franchising' arrangements, similar issues arise. For example, the Law Society has made it clear that it does not necessarily recognise in good professional standing those students graduating from law degrees, part of which may have been undertaken through a 'franchising' arrangement in a further education college. If the franchised elements of the course are not themselves accredited by the Law Society, then the subsequent graduates are not eligible for professional exemptions in the same way as qualifying students. The Law Society has been concerned that students may be misled if this is not pointed out at admission.

594.   We believe that there are very important questions here which need to be discussed further between universities and colleges on the one hand, and professional bodies on the other. If higher education institutions are to make progress on the mutual recognition of learning achievement for effective credit transfer, they are entitled to hope that professional bodies will be prepared to negotiate their position without prejudice. One of the tests of effective credit transfer will be the extent to which credit for 'off-campus' learning will be accepted by professional bodies as a legitimate

component of accredited qualifications, allowing students access to professional membership.

595.   Progress may be achieved in time if that 'off-campus' achievement gained through company training were to receive accreditation from the NCVQ, but there are likely to remain significant elements of such activity which will remain outside the scope of occupational standards but which might still be reasonably accredited as part of an academic programme. **We recommend** that the HEQC should begin the process of setting up a forum for professional bodies within which these matters may be negotiated. Moreover, **we recommend** that encouragement should be given to professional bodies to enter into pilot arrangements with accredited schemes whereby the professional outcomes of the learning process become the basis upon which a successful graduate is considered for professional membership. We believe that professional bodies, in engineering and elsewhere, will gradually establish their confidence in the type of arrangements which satisfy their standards, without prejudice to the quality assurance of professional competence.

Options for the quality assurance of 'off-campus' learning

596.   We turn now to the organisation of quality assurance for 'off-campus' learning. This discussion has been informed by the extent to which prospects for mutual recognition have changed with the creation of a unified higher education sector. We have also considered the needs of professional bodies and employers, the emerging role of the NCVQ, and the needs of students. In the light of issues raised in the foregoing discussion, we comment on some options.

Option A – a central group for credit recognition

597.   We have explored the extent to which there might be support for the creation of a body analogous to the CNAA CATS Registry. Such a national body could assume some of the functions of the CNAA with respect

to the quality assurance of 'off-campus' programmes, although it would be unable to assume the degree-awarding powers of the CNAA in cases where students were mobile between institutions (the central registration function).

598.   The case for a central body was made prior to the demise of the CNAA at the *Learning without walls* conference. In a paper to that conference (Kerr, 1991), it was noted:

'Credit ratings are now being granted for learning achieved outside educational institutions: this learning may be achieved in companies, professional bodies, private training organisations or experientially. This practice raises issues about whether these environments are comparable, and how they relate to educational institutions. Specifically some people wonder if all these organisations can really provide high quality learning cultures. There may be particular problems concerning the learning which can be provided in small and medium-sized enterprises. The variety and complexity of these matters have led to suggestions that a Central Group for Credit Recognition should be established. It would establish, maintain and publish consistent general credit ratings which would be available to all interested parties including potential users.'

599.   The functions and terms of reference of a central group could be similar to that of the former CNAA CAT Committee and its Credit Rating Advisory Group. In the case of this group, membership was drawn from universities, employers and professional bodies and it was charged to determine the credit rating of programmes submitted to it. These programmes generally included training offered by professional bodies, employers and other non-educational organisations. The Advisory Group allocated credit ratings to such programmes, which permitted universities and colleges to follow the advised ratings, and which informed students via ECCTIS of their maximum credit entitlement for particular types of prior study.

600.   This type of arrangement would have a number of advantages. It would be quite straightforward to establish such a group under the auspices of the Higher Education Quality Council. The group would have national standing and institutions may feel comfortable subscribing to its judgements. Professional bodies and employers would have a clear focus for their approaches to the sector, and they might be more confident that nationally determined credit rating would have a wider currency than might otherwise be the case. There is sufficient expertise, inherited from the CNAA and more widely, to constitute such a group. The costs of administering it would need to be carefully explored although charges might be levied for the services offered to appropriate bodies. This type of national arrangement is supported by a number of professional bodies (see Table 37). A number of larger employers also subscribe to this, particularly where they are keen to ensure access to a range of institutions throughout the United Kingdom for employees located in regional centres.

601.   There are also some disadvantages. Despite the appearance of national authority, a central group can only be advisory in these circumstances. Such a body can offer guidance to institutions but they remain free to ignore it. One of the main problems with the former CNAA arrangements was that credit ratings were determined centrally but interpreted differently at the institutional level . The existence of 'national' credit ratings did not establish general agreement over implementation amongst the former polytechnics. There is a real concern that students and employees may be made promises by a national body that are not realised at the institutional level. Furthermore, a central body can only establish a loose consensus amongst informed opinion on the *general* credit rating of a programme, since it will have no particular academic programme upon which to draw in assigning the credit tariffs. This isolation from particular institutional practice may compound the difficulties already referred to in making promises which cannot be delivered. Finally, a central body would be most effective if all institutions, employers, professional bodies and similar agencies agreed to honour its adjudications and act upon them.

602.   However, many employers prefer to negotiate with their local institutions; many professional bodies prefer to sustain

	Table 37: Professional bodies and the quality assurance of credit accumulation and transfer	
	Preferred quality assurance arrangements	**Commitment to credit transfer and prior learning**
Accountancy and finance	Difficult to justify a body mirroring the CNAA. HEQC to draw up guidelines (CII); Arrangements for mutual recognition of accreditation must be in place (CIPFA); autonomy within a credible national framework (ACCA); experience favours an 'open market' approach (CIB)	Accept APEL on a discretionary basis and will monitor any work-based component (ACCA); APEL and work-based learning are not yet components of qualifications (CII); prior learning may reduce control over admissions... but there are benefits from credit transfer (CIMA)
Business and management	Alignment of national quality assurance processes for HE with professional accreditation would be an ideal option but size of the task will act against its feasibility (IMan); if there is no co-ordination within the system people will find it inpenetrable (IPM); prefer an 'open market' option (IAM); and guard sovereignty (ICSA)	Need to consider role of NVQs as basis for achievement in higher education... transfer between academic and vocational programmes important (IMan); competence assessment route into membership gives legitimacy to APEL and work-based learning (IPM); 'off-campus' learning is inevitable but must be carefully checked for quality (IAM)
Construction	Prefer the 'open market'; the CNAA featured as a short-term external development; we do not encounter any difficulties about mutual recognition (RIBA); an 'open market' fits our accreditation system closely (RICS); 'open market' is inevitable. We place high value on specific partnerships.Role of NCVQ to be considered (IH); return to CNAA system unproductive (CIOB)	Already accept some elements of 'off-campus' learning and APEL... NVQs may have a role in this area (RTPI); little experience of APEL assessment; consortia would assist credit transfer (RICS); we are currently reconsidering our position. It is likely we will treat APEL as an alternative mode of completion of approved units. We would approve procedures but not be involved in individual cases (IH)
Engineering	Does not invite universities to offer courses for members, therefore has no policy on quality assurance mechanisms for HEQC (IEE). Should be an accord between academic levels and NVQs. Creation of a CNAA analogue might seen unattractive... but would be the best solution... If not, then the HEQC should establish a small registration authority to register arrangements (IQA)	Many professional bodies use 'experience' and 'academic' requirements for membership... some reluctance to accept experiential learning as genuine academic achievement (IQA); to complete an accredited course, it is not acceptable to progress further than the start of the second year (IEE); credit transfer internationally is monitored by the Engineering Council and the Washington Accord (ICE)
Health care, dentistry and medicine	The loss of the CNAA is seen as a disadvantage. Would prefer supra-institutional body (UKCC); favours a supra-institutional body to arrange consistency between institutions dealing with credit (ENB); the Society would not wish to support a supra-institutional body (CSP); an 'open market' is the only option (CollRad); joint CNAA arrangements were not found to be satisfactory (RPharS); GMC and GDC have statutory responsibility for quality assurance	Measures to support the legitimacy of 'practice-based learning' are strongly endorsed (UKCC); would wish to work with mutual understanding to develop 'off-campus' learning (CSP); the college is committed to APEL and 'off-campus' learning is an established fact (CollRad); credit for APEL or work–based learning is not a relevant concept since dentistry may only be undertaken by a registered dentist or as part of an approved course (GDC); innovative developments may militate against student transfer (GMC)
Law	Priority of HEQC is Audit. Concerned with quality of student experience... the relationship between the Society and institutions is at arm's length, although a partnership (Law Society)	Concerned to facilitate transfer where reasonable standards have been set... but difficulties presented by APEL, particularly in assessment... Learning which is dated is of negative value (Law Society)
Science	It would be useful to have a supra-institutional body to set standards and identify appropriate procedures (IEHO)	We welcome modularity because it allows credit for APEL... we can accept 'off-campus' learning if there is a rigorous scheme for accrediting it (IEHO)

relationships with universities in which they have confidence. It would be neither possible nor desirable to insist that these relationships be severed in the pursuit of a doubtful national consistency. Moreover many universities and colleges remain sceptical of the wisdom in developing a central analogue to the former CNAA, particularly under conditions which cannot guarantee universal acceptance and standardisation.

Option B – specialist subject groups

603.   A derivative of Option A might be an arrangement by which the HEQC, eschewing the creation of one central committee to embrace all matters, would establish or co-ordinate a number of professional subject groups. These subject groups could be convened on an ad hoc basis and charged with the credit rating of programmes within their professional area. Various candidate associations already exist and others could be convened. For example, the Association of Business Schools (ABS) could be invited to act in this capacity. Similarly, the Federation of Radiography Education Departments might be another example of the many professional academic associations that bring together colleagues and heads of department for mutual benefit.

604.   The advantages of this approach would be that the subject groups could act as 'academic lead bodies' within the HEQC in a manner analogous to the role of the Industry Lead Bodies within the NCVQ. They could agree common standards and range of practice with reference to specific courses, and they could build up mutual respect and recognition of courses to facilitate inter-institutional transfer. They would avoid the charge, which could be levelled against Option A, that no one committee can possess the breadth of expertise to cover all applications for accreditation.

605.   The disadvantages are both practical and conceptual. First, not all subject groups may need to form associations, nor would they necessarily wish to do so for this purpose. Second, if the HEQC were to convene such groups, it would require an extensive administrative infrastructure, even if groups were brought together on an ad hoc basis. Such

arrangements could again start to resemble the CNAA committee structure. Third, it is unclear how subject groups would be defined. Those such as the ABS which have arisen from perceived professional need may not be sufficiently extensive to cover all areas of demand, and those which would need to be created may not rest comfortably with the needs of different subjects. In short, the option could prove burdensome and unconvincing.

Option C – the 'centre of excellence'

606.   An alternative might be to designate one higher education institution as the centre of excellence for the accreditation of 'off-campus' programmes. Under these conditions, other universities would need to accede to the authority of one of their number in these matters. The Open University is the obvious institutional candidate for such a role. It is extensively active in the accreditation of 'off-campus' learning and has developed arrangements to promote and sustain the activity through the Open University Validation Service. Some professional bodies, the Library Association for example, are happy to use the arrangements and this is true of some employers also.

607.   There could be advantages in this model. The Open University provides an auditable set of arrangements for the quality assurance of 'off-campus' learning. The HEQC would thus be in a position to guarantee sector confidence in these arrangements over time. The allocation of credit ratings would take place directly within an academic context, against publicly visible academic programmes and qualifications. The Open University has an infrastructure in place with which to respond to demand although this would require significant supplementation if these arrangements were to be put in place.

608.   The disadvantages of this model are however numerous. Similarly with the central group, the Open University could only publish advisory ratings; and it could not expect all professional bodies and employers to accept only one source of service. Moreover, it is unlikely that other universities which have been active in this area would readily accept a

monopoly position for the Open University, not least for reasons of marginal commercial advantage. From the perspective of the OU itself, it may not be completely advantaged by this type of arrangement either. Even if it were prepared to invest further in infrastructural support for the OUVS, or if it were to receive additional resources to do so, the Open University may not have the extensive expertise within its own academic or administrative complement to offer a full service. Moreover, by establishing credit ratings in the manner proposed, the OU may be limiting the freedom of its own faculties and departments to vary advisory credit ratings, possibly placing them at a market disadvantage with other institutions. We doubt that this arrangement would ever command sufficient support.

Option D – the licence to practise

609.   A fourth alternative might be to extend the number of 'centres of excellence' to include those higher education institutions which wish to be active in the accreditation of 'off-campus' learning. The University of Greenwich, Sheffield Hallam University, and the University of Wolverhampton have been extensively engaged in the accreditation of a wide range of employer and professional body programmes for some years. Many other universities have come to formal accreditation arrangements with one or more employer or professional body, an early example of which would be the arrangement between IBM and the University of Portsmouth and a recent example might be that which has developed between Allied-Lyons and the University of Bradford.

610.   Under these arrangements, an institution might apply to the HEQC for a 'licence' to act as a centre of expertise in the accreditation of 'off-campus' programmes. The HEQC would satisfy itself that the processes by which an institution came to decisions about the credit-worthiness of a programme met the quality thresholds which it deemed appropriate for the sector. Institutions currently active in this area would be obvious candidates as centres of excellence, but it would be possible for other institutions to apply for a similar status if they chose to become active in these matters. It would be interesting to reflect further on

whether professional academic associations, such as the Association of Business Schools, could equally apply for a 'licence' to accredit. Arrangements for the award of the 'licence' might be analogous to those which have been used by the Access Course Recognition Group for the award of Authorised Validating Agency status in respect of Access courses.

611.   The advantages of this arrangement would be, first, that it would establish for the HEQC a focus for the assurance of quality by limiting in the first instance the number of institutions whose activity made them candidates. Second, it would avoid the monopoly implied by Option C and permit any institution to declare its interest in being designated as a centre of excellence, thereby establishing a market of credible agents to whom employers and professional bodies might apply for the accreditation of their programmes. Third, designated institutions could assemble, under the auspices of the HEQC or independently, to share expertise and negotiate the mutual recognition of their procedures and their credit ratings. Fourth, institutions which do not expect to engage extensively in accreditation partnerships of this nature could accept an element of 'pooled sovereignty' and adopt the credit ratings of any or all 'licensed' institutions. Over time, this style of arrangement could consolidate into a form similar to that proposed under Option A. Representatives from practising 'centres of excellence' could receive delegated authority from higher education institutions generally to form a central credit recognition group, under the HEQC, the adjudications of which would be endorsed by all other institutions.

612.   But there are manifest disadvantages. First, 'licensing' arrangements such as those developed for the quality assurance of Access courses may not be at all popular with universities and colleges which are already experienced in the accreditation of 'off-campus' learning. They may feel themselves subject to an improper or unacceptable intrusion into their academic autonomy, and may regard such arrangements as an unnecessarily cumbersome addition to the established procedures for quality audit. Second, it is not clear how any initial limit might be described to restrict the

number of applicants for a 'licence to practise'. Why should any institution be proscribed from developments in these matters? Third, there is no guarantee that an elite cartel of institutions, for this is what the model would imply, would deliver any acceptable level of consistency across the sector. Finally, there could be a danger with this model, even more apparent in Option C, that the accreditation of 'off-campus' learning is a phenomenon peculiar to certain institutions, and not really part of the mainstream. We would wish to advise against arrangements which encourage this interpretation, and therefore, for this reason and for the fact that the option is unnecessarily prescriptive and burdensome, we could not recommend it.

Option E – institutional autonomy in an 'open market'

613.   A further option would be what we have described in consultations as an 'open market' model. This arrangement proposes that there should be no restrictions on any institution freely engaging in the accreditation of 'off-campus' learning. Their procedures would be available for scrutiny via the quality audit process, and quality assurance would be guaranteed in the same manner that applied to conventional academic programmes.

614.   The advantages of this arrangement are several. First, it accepts the fact that, according to its Charter, any university or college has the right to reach accreditation agreements with whichever professional body or corporate employer it wishes. Indeed many professional bodies and corporate employers appear to welcome this variety of possible relationships. Second, bilateral arrangements are likely to increase the chances of prospective students in transferring credit to specific programmes. Third, it avoids a 'licensing' arrangement. Fourth, it does not imply that the accreditation of 'off-campus' learning is peculiar to certain institutions and may therefore encourage more universities and colleges to become active over time. Finally, it is consistent with the academic autonomy of institutions. This style of arrangement is supported by many institutions active in the field. It is also supported by most professional bodies,

although some would supplement it with an overseeing arrangement through the HEQC (see Table 38).

615.   There are nevertheless some difficulties. One important problem would be to determine how the various bilateral arrangements might be organised in some consistent manner. This could be assisted by the development of a national credit framework, which has been discussed in Chapter IX. However, a plethora of individual arrangements might produce confusion in students and could lead to a wide variation in the credit ratings of similar programmes. If this were the case, it could undermine confidence in the process. Next, whilst a majority of professional bodies supported the idea of an 'open market' arrangement and some of them are developing unique bilateral arrangements, it is not clear that all professional bodies and large corporate employers would welcome the need to negotiate individual agreements with a large number of institutions. Thirdly, an 'open market' may be attractive in principle but it could produce problems if institutions began to seek commercial competitive advantage through the award of premium credit ratings. Careful controls would need to be established to prevent any 'quality drift' which might emerge from this. On balance, however, we have argued throughout this report that institutions should accept direct responsibility for their affairs, and Option E would be consistent with this. We recommend therefore that Option E should form the basis for any arrangements in these matters.

Option F – quality networks

616.   A solution to the quality assurance of credit ratings might lie in a variant of the 'open market' option. Institutions might agreed to the development of common quality standards to facilitate credit transfer on a local or regional basis through what we will call 'quality networks'. This option would involve institutions reaching some agreement on the mutual recognition of quality assurance, standards and qualifications. This could occur in circumstances where institutions believe that there might be improved efficiency from credit transfer, or where they believe new patterns of

Table 38: Options for quality assurance in credit rating and credit transfer

	Option A Central recognition group	Option B Subject groups	Option C Centre of excellence	Option D Licence to practise	Option E Institutional autonomy	Option F Quality networks	Option G A role for the NCVQ?
Simplicity	Yes, probably the clearest of all the options to all interested parties	Yes, within subject areas, but possible confusion between different groups	Yes, one point of contact would clarify matters. (cf. Option A)	Possibly, although competition could lead to confusion initially	No, likely to be quite complex for those unfamiliar with arrangements	Possibly, for local arrangements, but potential confusion between networks (cf Option B)	Yes, for vocational programmes, but no role in academic accreditation
Efficiency	Yes, if the HEQC is able to deploy resources to this end; otherwise burdensome	No, likely to be expensive of resources and organisational time	Yes, if a unique centre were prepared, or supported, to provide the service	Possibly, since those applying to practise would have agreed resources, but cumbersome procedures	Possibly not, since every institution would need to develop individual arrangements	Possibly, although most existing networks and consortia do not have significant infrastructures	Yes, infrastructure already in place with Assessment Centres, but cumbersome Lead Body arrangements
Authority	Yes, if all interested parties agree to act according to decisions, this option would have clear authority	Yes, as with Option A, if all interested parties agreed to recognise decisions, and if co-ordinated by HEQC	Yes, but only if all institutions agreed to yield their sovereignty in these matters	Yes, by reason of an agreed 'licence', although other institutions may not be bound by decisions	No national authority unless overseen by HEQC (+NCVQ), but best means to ensure student transfer	Possibly, if contributing institutions agree to pool their independence and act in concert	Yes, clearly in the case of vocational qualifications, but no authority for academic awards
Acceptance	No. Unlikely to gain acceptance amongst institutions, except as 'weak' variant, but welcomed by some professional bodies and large employers	Possibly, although likely to lack conviction in certain subject areas, and be costly to organise	No. Unlikely to gain support from institutions. Others may not be happy with a monopoly service either	No. Unlikely to be attractive to practising institutions, although non-active institutions may be relatively neutral	Yes, it preserves local freedom to act; would be attractive to small employers and many professional bodies; but complex to others	Yes, to subscribing institutions and therefore to some employers and professional bodies. Otherwise, unclear in national terms	Yes, for employers and most professional bodies, and possible for institutions,but if effects neutral on academic autonomy.
Evaluation	Could be operated in tandem with B+F+G; more likely to work with E (+G)	Viable with A (+G) and possibly with C; more likely with E (+A)	Could work with G (+B or F) but contrary to E, thus unacceptable	Cumbersome variant of C; no advantages over A or B+F; hostile to E	Preferred solution, with minimum A, + G (and B+F as support)	Otherwise known as consortia. Could work with A + G; unclear towards E	Could only work with E + A, and with B or with C if chosen

student demand might be stimulated by closer local co-operation. This option, if developed, would have the advantage of avoiding unnecessary duplication of effort by institutions, employers or professional bodies, whilst assisting realistic opportunities for credit transfer. Moreover, if regional arrangements were to be created on this basis, they could evolve by aggregation towards the national arrangements outlined in Option A.

617.   On the other hand, as we have already noted in earlier discussion (see Chapter VII), the current operation of regional consortia does not provide much support for the view that local agreements can be achieved more readily than national agreements. It is not at all clear that universities and colleges are prepared to do anything more than comply with the minimum arrangements necessary to sustain collective arrangements. These circumstances may change if local policy is successful in producing distinctive collective agreements. We can identify three regions where, by reason of their relative homogeneity and identity as regions, the prospects for formal mutual recognition agreements might be worth further promotion – London, Scotland, and Wales. The first two regions have consortia already in place or in the process of development (*London Together* and SCOTCATS) and the third, Wales, is in the process of negotiating arrangements.

Option G – a role for the NCVQ?

618.   Reference has already been made above to arrangements analogous to those which apply in the NCVQ. In the quality assurance and accreditation of *'off-campus learning'* we believe there may be a role for the NCVQ to play, particularly where the training programmes of employers and professional bodies are concerned. The NCVQ may of course be invited to act in this capacity independently of the interests of universities and colleges. However, where the learning achievement gained from professional training or employment practice seeks to claim credit against higher education qualifications, a partnership in quality assurance and accreditation will need to be established. **We recommend** that the HEQC and the NCVQ should begin to explore this.

619.   The advantages of providing a direct role for the NCVQ would be, first, that common standards of achievement could be set which diverse learning experiences would need to meet. Secondly, all employers and professional bodies would have a common focus for quality assurance and accreditation, and students would be granted credit to a nationally approved standard. Thirdly, students gaining credit in this manner could accumulate it towards an NVQ or a GNVQ, and, subject to arrangements for the development of a national credit framework, could also negotiate its contribution towards an academic qualification from a university or college. Finally, institutions may benefit from an association with the NCVQ in the development of Assessment Centres which are required before an institution can act as an approved centre for the award of NVQs.

620.   On the other hand, by no means all learning achievement from professional training, in-company programmes or particularly from work-based internships lends itself to accreditation under the standards defined by the NCVQ. In the case of many work-based learning programmes, students are invited to use the workplace to demonstrate learning achievements which are relevant to their academic programmes rather than to occupational standards. Second, unless it was carefully managed, two forms of credit might begin to develop – 'academic' credit and 'vocational' credit. We would strongly oppose this and advise against any measures which further entrench boundaries between academically and vocationally inclined learning achievement. On balance, we do think there is a constructive role for the NCVQ and **we recommend** that this should be investigated further.

Organising quality assurance – an evaluation

621.   We have attempted to evaluate the respective merits of the various options against a number of criteria: **simplicity:** can arrangements be understood by interested parties, including students? **efficiency:** does the proposal make the best use of available

resources? **authority:** would the proposal establish adequate authority in quality assurance? **acceptance:** would the arrangements gain enough support from interested parties? A summary evaluation is contained in Table 38.

622.   It is clear that no one arrangement guarantees to meet the objectives of quality assurance and easier credit transfer within a framework of institutional academic autonomy. We have sought therefore to make recommendations which combine aspects of a number of different options with the effect that arrangements should encourage greater activity in the credit rating of 'off-campus' learning, enhanced opportunities for genuine credit transfer, yet should be as simple and straightforward as it is possible to achieve under complex constraints. We have been particularly concerned to ease the operation of such arrangements for employers and professional bodies.

Monopoly and oligopoly services

623.   We can find little justification for supporting either Option C or Option D. A monopoly service supplied by a single institution, however proficient, does not bestow any advantage in authority or simplicity over Option A – a central recognition body. Extending the practice to an oligopoly of service providers would involve the establishment of an unconvincing 'licensing' arrangement and might act as a disincentive to other institutions to become involved in the quality assurance of accreditation. We are highly sceptical of any institutional acceptance for the academic equivalent of the Assessment Centres proposed by the NCVQ for the quality assurance of its vocational standards.

A role for the NCVQ?

624.   Nevertheless, we do think there is an important role for the NCVQ (Option G), particularly in the credit rating of employment-based training and the programmes of professional bodies. Indeed we would wish to encourage employers and professional bodies to look to the standards being negotiated by the NCVQ with lead bodies in order to bring their programmes into a national vocational framework. However, we do not think that the NCVQ can act independently of higher education in these matters, particularly where such accredited programmes may seek to gain credit towards higher education qualifications. One of the great attractions to employers and professional bodies of current arrangements is that their employees and members may gain credit for their training programmes towards academic qualifications. If the NCVQ were to grant credit for such programmes, then it would need to be clear that such credit could also be counted towards academic awards where the student wished this. This implies a commitment to a closer alignment between academic and vocational credit systems (see discussions on the national credit framework in Chapter IX), and a much clearer mutual recognition of the quality assurance procedures of the NCVQ and those of universities and colleges.

625.   We would wish to advise against arrangements which might lead to the creation of two (or more) kinds of credit – 'academic' credit and 'vocational' credit, for example. In making this point, we are aware that some institutions find it useful to award 'P' credits for the work placement element in 'sandwich' courses or some professionally-qualifying programmes (such as teacher training, social work, health care, etc.) This credit is usually supplementary to the credit required for an academic qualification. We would generally wish to avoid the creation of further impediments to the mobility of students between different types of learning experience. **We recommend** therefore that the NCVQ and the HEQC begin to explore their respective obligations and priorities with respect to the quality assurance of 'off-campus' learning with a view to reaching a closer affinity of learning from work and other experiential sources with that achieved on higher education programmes. In making this proposal, we would wish to preserve the ability of institutions to define credit from work-based learning and similar activities as transferable towards higher education academic qualifications, whether or not it meets the occupational standards defined by the NCVQ.

Local practice and national authority

626.   The remaining options can be grouped around a dichotomy: either local autonomy by which institutions are left free to negotiate their own arrangements, or a central authority, with potentially little direct local influence. We are not convinced by Option A alone. This option has been attempted before by the CNAA. Whilst its aspirations to provide some commonality across the sector and a central focus for employers and professional bodies cannot be gainsaid, the CNAA arrangement was not able to provide effective agreement in practice to support common credit rating or student mobility. Nor are we convinced by Option E alone. An 'open market' may in time produce the openness and accessibility that students seek, but equally it may not. In the interim, it is likely that all parties may be confused about how to proceed, and students could become distracted by the variety of arrangements. Of itself, Option E would not guarantee quality assurance and the maintenance of standards across the sector and may well contribute to further scepticism. We have been interested by aspects of Option B – the idea of subject groups acting as *academic lead bodies'* – and believe that this idea merits further exploration by the institutions themselves. If such associations arise naturally, they may have a role to play in future. Moreover, we are interested in Option F and believe there may be some merit in the development of *'quality networks'* where institutions themselves feel they may be helpful.

627.   Taking all the variables into account, we believe the solution to future arrangements lies in a careful combination of elements from these options, emphasising the importance of individual institutional autonomy but providing some arrangements to guarantee quality assurance on a national basis. We cannot fail to recognise the importance of individual institutional responsibilities in these matters, and **we recommend** that Option E is the starting point in any future arrangements. Thereafter, **we recommend** that Option A should lead to a role for the HEQC, which should be discussed in terms of a relationship with the NCVQ. Then, **we recommend** that institutions and the HEQC should consider how best to discharge their interests through Options B and F in a manner which is most efficient and least burdensome to them.

Arrangements for quality assurance in credit transfer

628.   We believe that arrangements which facilitate effective credit transfer for individual students must take precedent over arrangements which merely establish common agreements but which do not otherwise facilitate transfer. If students are able to negotiate credit transfer with institutions of their choice, then the quality of those arrangements may be assured by the procedures of the individual institution. Our starting point is therefore the individual institution and the individual student.

Negotiating individual credit transfer

629.   Institutions will need to establish specific arrangements for the credit transfer applications of individual students. We are not persuaded that these arrangements can be met by the admissions procedures which obtain in most institutions which are understandably orientated to the admission of the majority of conventional student applicants. Specific arrangements would accept the need to work within a framework of credential evaluation and credit rating, but would acknowledge the legitimacy of diverse forms of learning achievement. The local institutional service would represent a first point of contact for students; it would also function as the institutional reference point for interactions with other institutions and with the national quality assurance arrangements proposed below.

Individual partnerships

630.   We are concerned to improve the ease with which professional bodies and corporate employers may reach agreement for the accreditation of their training programmes. As we have already noted, opinion and practice are sharply divided on whether individual partnerships are preferred to sector-wide

arrangements. No clear settlement is possible on this point. Smaller employers and many professional bodies generally prefer arrangements with individual institutions; some larger employers and other professional bodies require some national consistency, even when they may negotiate in the first instance with a single institutional partner. In this latter case, it would provide a considerable disincentive to proceed if employers or professional bodies were to be expected to negotiate institution by institution.

631.   Corporate employers and professional bodies may find it advantageous not to have general credit ratings determined by a national body with doubtful benefits for students at the point of access, but to specify clearly the scale and scope of credit transfer they wish to negotiate. This would require a more active involvement by professional bodies and employers in defining the strategies which would be appropriate for them. We believe that, under certain circumstances, they could become important initiators of closer collaboration between institutions, bringing a greater purpose and focus to the work of consortia and similar networks. For example, we have been impressed by the efforts of some regional health authorities to specify their staff training needs, describing a framework of provision which they wished to 'purchase' and inviting regional institutions to contribute to the supply of learning opportunities leading to a common qualification. Clearly a balance will need to be struck between the needs of client 'purchasers' and the quality assurance of academic programmes and qualifications, but we believe this should be possible. Professional bodies and employers could not of course be expected to instigate initiatives unaided and unguided. **We recommend** that the HEQC should play a helpful role here by assisting employers and professional bodies to create the partnerships they require.

An advisory committee on credit arrangements

632.   It would not be helpful to impede or circumscribe arrangements between individual employers or professional bodies and the institutions with which they are happy to associate. Local and regional arrangements of mutual benefit will need to be supported. However, in those cases where a sector-wide arrangement is seen to be important, the HEQC would be the natural focus for assistance in ensuring that client objectives were met. The HEQC would be able to invite institutions, by region, or subject group, or by direct specification from the professional body or employer, to negotiate independently or preferably collectively for the credit rating of their training programmes against the specific academic courses of the relevant institutions. Under these arrangements, the HEQC would act as a broker, facilitating negotiations rather than negotiating itself. **We recommend** that the HEQC establishes an Advisory Committee to act as a 'clearing house' for employer or professional body clients, indicating to them the candidate courses and institutions that might meet their needs. Individual institutions would remain free to accept or decline invitations to negotiate arrangements with corporate employers or professional bodies.

633.   **We recommend** the establishment by the HEQC of a small and expert group to begin the process of exploration with the NCVQ on common agreements for the credit rating of units of NVQs and, if appropriate, of GNVQs in higher education. We are wholly convinced that the quality and character of GNVQs at Level 4 in higher education will need to be negotiated jointly by the NCVQ and the institutions, through the HEQC. We have already referred to the frustrations experienced in the business and management fields. It is therefore important that some progress should be made quickly on a common approach for quality assurance in credit rating between institutions and the NCVQ. **We recommend** that the HEQC should begin the process of negotiation.

A quality assurance forum for professional bodies

634.   From our extensive consultations with leading professional bodies, we received a generally favourable response to our enquiry on the establishment of a regular forum

for the exchange of views between higher education and professional institutions. It was apparent from our investigation that most professional bodies would welcome the opportunity to discuss and resolve matters of strategic importance with a body representing the universities and colleges. Amongst the matters to which our attention was drawn, the reciprocal responsibilities for quality assurance featured prominently. Other matters could include discussion of the priorities for the sector, as understood by the institutions, labour market opportunities for students, government policy towards the sector and other items of mutual concern.

635.   **We recommend** the establishment of such a forum by the HEQC, in conjunction with professional bodies, although its structure and agenda would require careful management. Professional bodies were not keen to engage in a 'talking shop' but were interested to address a relevant agenda. It is also apparent to us that professional bodies are by no means a homogenous group of association. The differences that exist between them have important implications for the way in which future discussions need to be structured and focused. It may be the case that a series of interactions may need to take place, drawing upon existing collaborative arrangements such as the UK Inter-Professional Group, the Health Care Consortium, or the Engineering Council.

An annual conference on higher education and employment

636.   We believe a similar function could be performed in respect of employers. Although it is traditionally difficult to establish representative views from the diversity of employers, there is clearly a need for an environment within which higher education and employers can interact on matters of strategy and policy. We have been aware throughout the investigation that mixed signals pass between government, higher education institutions and corporate employers. Employers seem to want specifically-skilled graduates and graduates with a broad base in communication skills and personal

effectiveness. This view is also reflected in different professional bodies within the same professional area – for example, in the different attributes required from Chartered and Certified Accountants, or from Chartered and Incorporated Engineers. Government has added to these mixed signals by encouraging the output of more two-year diplomates.

637.   We have detected some unease amongst representatives of universities and colleges about just how they are expected to respond to mixed signals, whilst retaining their commitment to high quality higher education and research. This unease is being compounded by uncertainty about the long-term interaction between the supply of higher education outputs and the shape of the future labour market. Many of these issues are addressed from time to time by existing bodies. The Council for Industry and Higher Education fulfils an important role in bearing messages between government, higher education and employers. The Association of Graduate Recruiters also represents the views of some employers, and the policies of the CBI receive substantial attention in higher education policy-making. Agencies such as the National Institute for Economic and Social Research (NIESR), the Institute for Manpower Studies (IMS) and the Centre for Labour Market Studies have provided important research materials to inform policy developments. We would not wish to see any diminution of these important activities and believe their work may become more relevant in an environment dominated by mass participation and extended student choice in higher education.

638.   On the other hand, we do believe it would be useful to find a means of improving the quality of exchange between employers and higher education over matters of mutual interest. One idea would be to arrange annually, as a prestigious event, a conference specifically focused upon matters of strategy and policy for employers and higher education. We believe that it is timely for such an event to be organised in the United Kingdom. Public interest in the employment opportunities of graduates is likely to increase sharply as increased graduation leads to increased pressure on premium market placement. The current decision to stabilise levels

of participation in higher education is unlikely to ease this pressure. Parents and students are likely to ask themselves more searchingly about the extrinsic value of higher education if they are expected to meet an increasing share of the costs. Institutions and employers will therefore need to be clear about how they define a role for an expanded higher education sector, and what they expect each other to provide for the future. **We recommend** that further thought be given by interested parties, including the HEQC, CBI, CIHE and the Employment Department to the organisation of an annual HE-employer conference.

639.   The Employment Department might wish to take a lead in this, and the CIHE, CBI and AGR might be expected to play an active part. We would very much hope that bodies representing the universities and colleges, HEQC, CVCP, CSCFC, SCOP and funding councils, would also be active partners in organising such an annual event, and that participation would be attracted from senior institutional figures, including Vice-Chancellors. We believe that a useful agenda will quickly develop, based upon current changes in government policy, labour market needs and the responses of institutions. There is already a substantial base of research to inform discussions, and the Employment Department continues to fund other work in this area. We are also aware that the Economic and Social Research Council (ESRC) is currently launching a major new research programme: *The learning society: knowledge and skills for employment*. The outcomes of the various research projects within this programme are likely to influence debate in this area over the next few years.

640.   We would expect an annual conference to bring together senior representatives from government, corporate employers, professions, institutional leaders, leading researchers and national agencies in the field. In time, **we recommend** that it should become a conduit through which seminars might be organised, further research promoted, and policy development stimulated. It would certainly assist higher education in defining its purpose more clearly in terms of its effectiveness in meeting the aspirations of students and employers.

A register of credit agreements

641.   **We recommend** that the authority of the HEQC should be enhanced with respect to the monitoring and audit of 'off-campus' learning accreditation by the production of a national credit register. Individual or collective negotiations will inevitably lead to a variety of 'specific' negotiated credit ratings for a wide range of 'off-campus' programmes. These credit ratings may in large measure reflect the diversity of academic programmes. **We recommend** that the outcomes of all credit rating exercises are received, recorded and published by the HEQC, the latter probably through ECCTIS or other suitable sources, in the form of a dedicated documentary source for reference, guidance and comparison amongst institutions. We believe it is essential that universities and colleges should formally and regularly register their agreements on credit rating and credit tariffs with the HEQC. We would go further and **recommend** that, for any bilateral agreements between professional bodies, they also should be invited to register their agreements, particularly where students wish to claim credit transfer to the academic programmes of a university or college.

642.   The publication of a national credit register will also act as an important instrument of quality assurance. Individual institutional agreements on credit rating will lie in the public domain, available for comparison and useful as a basis for audit. A public document in this form may act against any tendency to engage in credit inflation for reasons of commercial or other advantage.

A credential evaluation service

643.   The publication of a Register of Credit Rating Agreements by the HEQC, via its own publications and/or via ECCTIS, will act as a source of information to students, prospective students and institutions. We are keen to encourage all institutions to engage in the accreditation of 'off-campus' learning but recognise that many institutions will prefer to be guided on common practice. If the HEQC publishes regular information on institutional credit rating agreements, this will quickly act as

a national register of credit. If student mobility increases, or if demand for credit information rises, then the need for a credit evaluation service will also increase. In a short time, the HEQC and ECCTIS will be able to offer an independent service or to support institutional credit evaluation services. **We recommend** that the HEQC takes steps to put in place, on its own authority, or jointly with another party, arrangements for a credential evaluation service, to include an evaluation of international credentials and credit claims.

A registry for students

644.	Arrangements need to be put in place for the central registry of students who may not formally be registered on an academic programme, or for a qualification, at any one university or college. We have described such students as 'extensively mobile' to try and capture their circumstances. The quality of their individual programmes and qualifications needs to be assured by appropriate means. We have noted earlier in this report that the experience of the CNAA CATS Registry suggests no great demand amongst students for a central registration which is independent of any one institution. The vast majority of mobile students were content to have their registration arranged with one particular institution for the purposes of a final qualification. Accordingly, less than 100 students were ever registered centrally with the CNAA CAT Scheme.

645.	We have been unable to assess future demand for such a service although we have shown the considerable potential for credit transfer in Chapter VII. It is unclear whether the present low level of demand for inter-institutional transfer is a reflection of the real dispositions of students, whether it reflects the relative novelty of credit transfer, or whether it is a consequence of regulatory inhibitions. Informed speculation suggests that demand could rise in response to a number of factors. Changes in the pattern of student funding and an erosion of differences by mode of attendance could increase mobility; changes in labour market conditions could have the same effect. Improved publicity for credit transfer, an emphasis on institutional regional collaboration, and a better informed student body

might also stimulate demand for a central registration function. If demand remains low, or increases only incrementally over the medium term, the pressures on any central Registry will be relatively light.

646.	The functions of a central Registry would be: to manage individual enquiries concerning credit transfer opportunities; to negotiate individual learning programmes and assure their quality; to award higher education qualifications to successful students. The HEQC is an organisation with a national infrastructure and it could undertake the first two functions. However, it is not a qualification-awarding body and would itself be unable to discharge the third function. Only universities and colleges may award higher education qualifications, and only one university – the Open University – has an infrastructure throughout the United Kingdom, based on its regional offices. We can find no suitable alternative and **we recommend** that the Open University be formally invited to offer a central registration service for students, with the authority to publicise this service to prospective students. It should also be invited to undertake the negotiation of the quality assurance of individual student programmes and to arrange the award of higher education qualifications to successful students.

647.	We believe therefore that the Open University should be invited to discharge this function, and if it is prepared to do so, it should be fully supported by the institutions and bodies associated with the HEQC. In making this proposal, **we recommend** further that some consideration should be given to the provision it might be necessary to make to ensure that the Open University has the means to provide a service of quality on behalf of all institutions.

Quality assurance and quality enhancement in the HEQC

The role of the Council

648.	The HEQC has a central role to play in the quality assurance of credit-based learning. Indeed, we believe from our investigations that matters concerning student choice and flexibility are likely to permeate the work of the Council in future. It appears timely that the Council should consider precisely how it expects to address the future character of higher education in which modular arrangements are likely to be the norm. Moreover, we predict that expressions of student choice and patterns of student mobility will change dramatically over time, with significant consequences for conventional perceptions and judgements of the preferred character of higher education. To anticipate these developments, **we recommend** that the HEQC puts in place the organisational and developmental capacity to respond through its divisional structures. This would also imply that the Council should state explicitly how it expects to be able to respond to an environment of greater student choice, identifying the impact this may have upon its quality assurance and quality enhancement activities. Furthermore, **we recommend** that the Council should give clear guidance on how it expects to develop relationships with institutions, employers, professional bodies, the NCVQ, other awarding bodies and the further education sector for the further promotion and development of quality assurance within the context of a national credit framework.

The quality audit of 'off-campus' accreditation

649.   **We recommend** that the HEQC should regard the audit of procedures for the quality assurance of 'off-campus' learning and 'franchising' arrangements as wholly contiguous with its functions in respect of the audit of internal academic programmes. We do not believe that the quality assurance of 'off-campus' learning should be regarded any differently in terms of rigour and consistency from the arrangements for institutional academic quality control. For practical purposes, the HEQC has often chosen to audit arrangements separately. This has been judged necessary to cope with the dispersed physical location of much 'off-campus' work. We are sympathetic to this problem but point out that it may create the appearance of a separation of functions, and thus a separation of procedures. **We recommend** therefore that the procedures for the quality assurance of internal and external academic programmes should be audited as a comprehensive entity and, wherever practical, in a single unified event.

Monitoring credit rating agreements

650.   **We recommend** that the HEQC should keep under review current credit rating agreements, a function that could be discharged through its *Advisory Committee on Credit Arrangements*. This committee would be required to monitor the range of credit ratings across the sector, drawing the attention of the Council to any arrangements which appear to fall outside an acceptable range. Under such circumstances, the Council may decide to invite an institution, through its quality audit function, to explain the quality assurance procedures and academic rationale for the case in question. We are aware that the fulfilment of this function will require the assent and co-operation of institutions and others, and **we recommend** that the representative bodies of institutions should commend this practice to their members. This should be a matter of self-interest for them. Under the arrangements for quality assurance which we have discussed earlier, much greater responsibility is placed upon individual institutions to make their own arrangements for credit rating. However it cannot possibly be helpful, nor compatible with effective quality assurance, for these arrangements to be kept from the public domain and we are sure institutions will agree. One further point should be emphasised. In declaring their credit rating agreements, we do *not* propose that institutions should be expected to disclose the commercial basis upon which these agreements may have been reached. That remains the proper business of the institution concerned.

Principles for the practice of 'off-campus'

651.   Any academic institution making provision for academic credit to be derived from any form of off-campus learning needs to ensure that its procedures are suitable for individual applicants and for voluntary and employing organisations and the professions. Firstly, for employing organisations and professions, procedures need to be based on a clearly articulated scheme of partnership. Partnerships established on documentary

agreements between an 'off-campus' provider and an institution need to be supported by continual and close liaison between the contributing partners. Such partnerships should clarify the means whereby the interests of individual employees as well as those of employers can be protected.

652. Secondly, all academic and administrative arrangements for 'off-campus' learning should be fully integrated with an institution's quality assurance procedures. Moreover, employing organisations and professions should be actively involved in all academic and administrative arrangements as providers of 'off-campus' learning. Thirdly, academic and administrative arrangements should include provision for the credit transfer of 'off-campus' learning for individuals from one institution to another. Fourthly, external assessors/advisors should have a prominent role in the quality assurance of 'off-campus' learning and they should be carefully selected for their understanding and experience in such matters. **We recommend** that the HEQC might compile a directory of appropriate examiners, as advised by institutions, for the benefit of those still new to these activities. Fifthly, **we recommend** that the HEQC and individual institutions consider the best means of building a national and regional cohort of trained workplace mentors. We believe this to be essential for the quality assurance of some forms of work-based learning. This initiative might be undertaken through accredited training programmes in institutions, in conjunction with the Employment Department and the TEC/LECs.

653. Next, **we recommend** that all credit ratings validated by academic institutions and accepted by employers and professions should be made public, and included in entries published by the HEQC via ECCTIS. Institutions should accept the responsibility for publicising opportunities offered through 'off-campus' learning, and employers and professional bodies for promoting internal communications, while ECCTIS should be responsible for a national information system.

654. Finally, **we recommend** that institutions should clarify with professional bodies the status and standing of degrees incorporating

provision for any form of experiential and work-based learning. This should form part of a wider attempt to help those bodies relate their concerns for quality to developments in higher education affecting curricula, academic organisation and the student body. Moreover, **we recommend** that professional bodies give consideration to the proportion of credit for work-based learning that they would be prepared to tolerate in academic programmes which they accredit.

A compact on credit

655. We have given some thought to whether greater confidence might be established in the quality assurance of 'off-campus' learning by the creation of a voluntary *Compact on credit*. If there is merit in such a proposal, it is because we are recognising that there is something essentially unfamiliar about 'off-campus' learning for which, at least in the short term, greater confidence needs to be established. This does not weaken our conviction that 'off-campus' learning has every reason to expect similar standing to institutionally-based programmes in higher education, provided the outcomes and achievements of students are consistent. Rather, it accepts the reality of circumstances which suggests that not every institution will be so readily persuaded, and an agreed Compact might help in some way.

The compact

656. Accordingly, the principles of the *Compact* apply to institutions wishing to have procedures available for individuals as well as voluntary, professional and employing organisations to have their off-campus learning considered for academic credit. In all cases arrangements are formulated and authorised so that the principles of the *Compact on credit* are met. **We recommend** that the HEQC should invite universities, colleges, employers and professional bodies engaged in providing learning opportunities on a credit accumulation basis, to agree to the general principles set out in Table 39 as a means of promoting quality, consistency and congruence between their respective learning activities.

Table 39: A compact on credit

1. procedures for accrediting, assessing, recording and monitoring 'off-campus' learning are monitored and annually reviewed through approved quality assurance systems for higher education, professional bodies and the 'off-campus' provider;

2. external advisors/assessors are appointed to the relevant quality assurance bodies;

3. procedures are established by higher education institutions (in partnership where relevant) for: enabling individuals where appropriate to have off-campus learning which has been assessed for academic credit recognised and awarded; considering applications from those wishing to transfer credit in appropriate disciplines into the institution; enabling transfer students to complete programmes of study leading to a qualification;

4. information, advice and guidance are made available for individual applicants and students/employees, including the relationship between the credit they have acquired already and what may be acceptable in the context of a particular programme.

5. the status of any qualification to be obtained needs to be established by the higher education institution/partnership and the relevant professional body;

6. all credit ratings of provision by employers and professional bodies are made public, wherever possible through the HEIs entries on the ECCTIS programme;

7. a copy of these Principles and Procedures is held by any employer or professional body working in partnership with an HEI as a complement to a Memorandum of Cooperation linked to a detailed scheme and is also available to individuals.

Guidelines for institutions

657.   We believe from the approaches made to us and from our own investigations that the negotiation and publication of guidelines on credit rating would be helpful to institutions. The HEQC has already made progress in the publication of guidelines for institutions on quality assurance. These proposals have sought to align the traditions established by the CVCP for the ex-UFC universities and those established by the CNAA for the former polytechnics. In consultation with institutions, the Council found there was a mixed reception to the development of guidelines, although a clear majority of universities and colleges welcomed them. We do not anticipate a similar mixed response from institutions in respect of guidelines on credit rating. In these circumstances, developments are still relatively unfamiliar and we believe most institutions will welcome them. Nevertheless, we believe that the methodology employed by the Institutional Guidelines Working Party of the HEQC could be repeated in this case. **We recommend** that the HEQC take measures swiftly to produce various helpful materials, which would include:

- taking existing sources of guidance as a starting point. This would involve an examination of the draft CNAA *Guidelines on credit rating* together with the recommendations from this report;

- the establishment of a small working party of the HEQC, under the chairmanship of a suitable authority, with membership drawn from experienced practitioners, with the remit to confirm, modify or thoroughly re-present the draft *Guidelines on credit rating* or an alternative set of proposals;

- the establishment of a similar group to perform the same exercise, *de novo*, for the production of other guidelines on modularity and related matters.

Implications of recommendations for the HEQC

658.   We have been asked to provide some assessment of the implications of these

proposals for the HEQC. These take two forms: implications for its role and functions in the sector, and resource implications.

659.   There can be no doubt that higher education will require an effective focus for quality assurance in the changing world of higher education. The expansion of learning opportunities and the variety of relationships of which higher education is a part give the clearest indication possible that the HEQC will continue to play a prominent role on behalf of its members in quality assurance and the enhancement of quality with respect to credit-based learning. In short, if the HEQC did not exist, we would have needed to recommend its establishment in order to carry forward many of these recommendations. If there is any doubt on this matter, compare the position of the HEQC in higher education with the absence of any single authority for quality assurance in further education.

660.   The implications for resources are also straightforward. We have taken considerable care to ensure that the expectations of the HEQC do not become so burdensome that supplementary resources are required. We judge that the specific responsibilities attributed to the Council in these matters can be discharged with a small professional team, supported by an adequate administrative infrastructure. We fully support the view that the quality assurance of credit systems lies properly within a framework defined by quality audit and quality enhancement. Therein, the conduct of duties in these matters may properly become the property of all staff of the Council, as choice and flexibility steadily permeate higher education over the next few years. Moreover, **we recommend** that many functions can be supplied to the Council by academic colleagues in institutions and through consortia, with considerable benefits to individuals.

Recommendations and guidance for future policy

On arrangements for quality assurance

To Government, HEQC, NCVQ, representative bodies of institutions, and all interested parties

43 In keeping with the principles of institutional academic autonomy, and because it is likely to favour the interests of students, **we recommend** that the balance of responsibility for arrangements for credit transfer and for the adjudication of credit ratings should lie principally with individual institutions. Accordingly, Option E in the report should form the starting point for any arrangements in these matters.

44 However, some general oversight will be necessary, and **we recommend** that there should be a facilitative and co–ordinating role for the HEQC, to be discharged in partnership with the NCVQ and quality assurance authorities in further education where appropriate.

45 Furthermore, **we recommend** that institutions of higher education and the HEQC should consider how best to discharge their interests in the quality assurance of credit transfer either through subject groups or consortia (as quality networks) in a manner which is least burdensome to institutions and the Council itself. **We recommend** therefore that the HEQC negotiates the supply of some functions from academic colleagues, to the benefit of those individuals and their institutions.

On the role of the Higher Education Quality Council

A response to greater student choice and mobility

46 Demand for credit transfer and the general exercise of student choice and mobility is likely to increase over the next few years. This will place renewed emphasis upon aspects of quality assurance. **We recommend** that the HEQC puts in place the organisational and developmental capacity to respond, stating explicitly how it expects to be able to assist institutions in these circumstances. Furthermore, **we recommend** that the Council should give clear guidance on how it expects to develop relationships with institutions, employers, professional bodies, the NCVQ, other awarding bodies and the further education sector for the ongoing promotion and development of quality assurance within the context of a national credit framework.

The quality assurance of flexible programmes

47 Choice, mobility and credit transfer affect the patterns of student behaviour on programmes internal and external to the institution. **We recommend** that protocols for the audit of quality assurance procedures should be able to treat modular structures as normal arrangements within which conventional programmes might fit. Moreover, **we recommend** that the HEQC should regard the audit of procedures for the quality assurance of 'off-campus' learning and 'franchising' arrangements as wholly contiguous with its functions in respect of the audit of internal academic programmes. The procedures for the quality assurance of internal and external academic programmes should be audited as a comprehensive entity, and wherever practical, in a single unified event.

48 **We recommend** that future consideration of the quality assurance of franchising arrangements should address the features identified in Table 36 of the report, with a view to inviting institutions and their representative bodies to support a general review of the quality assurance of franchising arrangements.

Partnerships with professional bodies

49 **We recommend** that the HEQC should begin the process of setting up a *consultative forum* for professional bodies within which matters of mutual strategic significance may be negotiated. Moreover, **we recommend** that encouragement should be given to professional bodies to enter into pilot arrangements with accredited schemes whereby the professional outcomes of the learning process become the basis upon which successful graduates may be considered for membership of professional bodies.

50 **We recommend** that institutions should clarify with professional bodies the status and standing of degrees incorporating provision for any form of experiential and work–based learning and that professional bodies should advise on the proportion of credit for work–based learning that they would be prepared to tolerate in academic programmes which they accredit.

A relationship on quality assurance with the NCVQ

51 **We recommend** that the HEQC and the NCVQ begin to explore their respective obligations and priorities with respect to the quality assurance of 'off-campus' learning, with a view to establishing that the quality of learning achievement gained from professional training or employment practice, from work-based internships and other experiential sources, is comparable with that achieved on higher education programmes.

52 **We recommend** the establishment by the HEQC of a small expert group to begin an exploration with the NCVQ of common arrangements for the credit rating of units of NVQs and, if appropriate, of GNVQs in higher education, such an expert group to consider experience in further education for this purpose.

Improving co–operation with employers

53 **We recommend** that further thought be given by interested parties, including the HEQC, CBI, CIHE and the Employment Department, to arrangements for the improvement of contact between employers and higher education on matters of mutual strategic significance. **We recommend** as one solution the organisation of an *Annual Conference on Higher Education and Employment* which in time could become a conduit through which seminars might be organised, further research promoted, and policy development stimulated for the improvement of relationships between higher education and employers.

On specific arrangements for the Higher Education Quality Council

An advisory committee on credit arrangements

54 **We recommend** that the HEQC should establish an *Advisory Committee on Credit Arrangements* to receive, review and publish the credit rating agreements between institutions and their partners amongst employers, professional bodies and other external

clients. **We recommend** that the *Advisory Committee* could play a helpful role by assisting employers and professional bodies to create the credit rating partnerships they require by acting as a 'clearing house' for employer or professional body clients, indicating to them the candidate courses and institutions that might meet their needs. Individual institutions would remain free to accept or decline invitations to negotiate arrangements with corporate employers or professional bodies.

A national credit register

55 **We recommend** that the HEQC, in conjunction with ECCTIS, establishes a national Credit Register. The outcomes of all credit rating exercises should be received, recorded and published, by the HEQC through ECCTIS or other suitable sources, in the form of a dedicated documentary source for reference, guidance and comparison amongst institutions. **We recommend** that, for any bilateral agreements between professional bodies, they also should be invited to register their agreements, particularly where prospective students may wish to claim credit transfer to the academic programmes of a university or college.

56 **We recommend** that the representative bodies of institutions commend this arrangement to their members and invite compliance for the purposes of improved quality assurance, accountability and public information.

A credential evaluation service

57 **We recommend** that the HEQC takes steps to put in place, on its own authority or jointly with another party, arrangements for a credential evaluation service, to include an evaluation of international credentials and credit claims as well as an advisory service on the academic standing of credit in the United Kingdom. Further thought might be given to whether this service could be provided on a commercial basis.

A register of external assessors for 'off-campus' learning and a mentor training programme

58 **We recommend** that the HEQC compiles a Register of Expertise and a directory of appropriate examiners, as advised by institutions, for the benefit of those institutions unfamiliar with expertise in the area of 'off-campus' learning. We recommend also that the HEQC and individual institutions consider the best means of building a national and regional cohort of trained workplace mentors. We believe this to be essential for the quality assurance of some forms of work–based learning. This initiative might be undertaken through accredited training programmes in institutions, in conjunction with the Employment Department and the TEC/LECs.

A credit compact

59 **We recommend** that the HEQC should invite universities, colleges, employers and professional bodies engaged in providing learning opportunities on a basis of credit accumulation and transfer, to agree to the general principles set out in Table 39 of the report in the form of a Credit Compact as a means of promoting quality, consistency and congruence between their respective learning activities.

Guidelines for the further development of credit systems

60 **We recommend** that the HEQC undertake a review of existing reports and materials on institutional approaches to modularisation with a view to producing, in collaboration with informed individuals and drawing upon institutional experience in universities and colleges, *definitive guidelines on the quality assurance of modular programmes.*

61 **We recommend** that definitive guidelines should be produced by the HEQC to inform the development of the credit-rating of 'off-campus' learning. We believe that the methodology employed by the Institutional Guidelines Working Party of the HEQC could be repeated in this case by taking as a starting point the draft CNAA *Guidelines on credit rating.*

On the establishment of a central student registration service

To Government, HEQC, the representative bodies of institutions, and the Open University

62 **We recommend** that the Open University be formally invited to offer a central registration service for students seeking institutional registration and credit transfer, with the authority to publicise this service to prospective students. It should also be invited to undertake the negotiation of the quality assurance of individual student programmes and to arrange the award of higher education qualifications to successful students. **We recommend** further that consideration should be given to the provision it might be necessary to make to ensure that the Open University has the means to provide a service of quality on behalf of all institutions.

XI.   *Finance and flexibility*

Introduction

661.   In the report so far, we have considered the further development of student choice and mobility principally in terms of the negotiation of opportunities within familiar academic and administrative arrangements. These arrangements may have been modified by modularisation and credit-based learning to make the exercise of choice and mobility more readily available to students. Nevertheless, the balance of power in higher education and beyond has remained largely dominated by professional academic definitions of appropriate patterns of student behaviour, whether manifested through academic programme selection or through subsequent decisions affecting mobility or continuation of study. Indeed, the model of student choice conventionally operating in the United Kingdom gives a student substantial choice in the initial selection of an institution of higher education. Thereafter, choices are heavily circumscribed by academic structures and procedures, professional judgements and administrative regulations.

662.   In order to make proposals for the enhancement of student choice and mobility through credit accumulation and transfer, we have considered two aspects of the matter. Firstly, prevailing institutional funding arrangements have been designed largely with conventional patterns of student behaviour in mind. Traditionally, the interaction between the student, a course and an institution has been fairly stable and immobile; funding methodologies have tended to reflect this. Secondly, the regulations governing student fees and maintenance payments have also been predicated upon similar traditional assumptions. Our investigations have provided an opportunity to rethink some alternative arrangements, for funding councils, institutions and students, in the light of extended participation and increased student choice.

663.   We have been somewhat hampered in our considerations by the absence in the United Kingdom of any extensive literature on the subject. Because we do not yet have experience of large scale student choice, reflected in greater mobility within and between institutions and elsewhere, the literature of institutional funding and student financing understandably gives greater attention to conventional patterns of organisational and individual behaviour. For example, one of the more influential contributions on sector financing of recent times (Williams, 1992) pays little attention to the consequences of student mobility for institutional or personal funding. Credit systems are treated as an extension of arrangements for the accreditation of prior learning or INSET courses. Helpful comments are provided on the general impact of current funding changes on institutional management structures and the development of funding council policy, but otherwise the 'market' is described as a source of differentiated funding sources (government, employers etc) rather than an arena for consumer (student) choices. This approach is also adopted in a slightly different manner by another well-respected source (Becher & Kogan, 1992). Markets are presented as the contemporary condition but are approached defensively in terms of their impact upon professional academic autonomy and institutional effectiveness. In short, there is a paucity of material in the public domain which explores the impact on higher education of markets generated by the interactions between student choice and institutional academic provision.

664.   We make these points because, in the forthcoming discussion, we have adopted a perspective unfamiliar to many in higher education in the United Kingdom who have commented on these matters in the past. We have attempted to conduct an analysis by inverting the polarity of perception. Instead of beginning from the perspective of institutional 'suppliers' looking outwards in search of

funding solutions, we have attempted to view the world from the perspective of the student-consumer, looking into the system for access, flexibility and personal relevance. We have asked ourselves the question: what would need to change in order to deliver these conditions to students? What principles would need to guide our thinking and what arrangements would need to be proposed to achieve this type of responsiveness. Later in the report, in chapter XV, we consider what the cultural consequences might be.

The principles of financing flexibility

665.   We are concerned therefore to explore how funding arrangements may assist or constrain student choice and mobility, and whether it is necessary to make proposals for their modification in the light of anticipated changes in student behaviour. We are guided by a number of principles and objectives. Firstly, we believe that wherever possible the distribution of resources in higher education should reflect the demands of 'clients' for services, including the demand of students for courses. Universities and colleges have to satisfy the requirements of many stakeholders other than students, and they do so through research and other important activities. However, students' interests define the main purpose of all institutions of higher education and we believe that their informed choices should have a greater influence over the distribution of resources across the sector and within institutions themselves. In short, resources should follow students. This is likely to require the development of funding methodologies which make this possible. Funding councils will therefore have an interest in proposing formulae which are rational, equitable and acceptable to institutions. Such formulae might complement the present contractual relationship that exists between institutions and funding councils.

666.   Secondly, student demand cannot be the sole determinant of resource allocation in higher education. It will be necessary to take into account national needs, the shape of the labour market, and the capacity of higher education to respond to changing demands over time, in determining the supply of learning opportunities. Nevertheless, it may be timely to consider the role of individual student choice in influencing sectoral and institutional decisions for the future. If the exercise of informed student choice is to be circumscribed in any way, it should be by academic and educationally-related factors alone; administrative regulations including financial arrangements should not, of themselves, further constrain the exercise of reasonable student choice within and between institutions, nor between modes of attendance ideally. Thirdly, claims that academic autonomy or professional sovereignty might be compromised by greater student choice should not impede the development of arrangements which respond more effectively to the demands of students and others.

667.   Finally, we believe that any proposals concerning these matters should have the effect of simplifying arrangements for students, improving efficiency for institutions and funding councils, contributing directly to the development of personal choice and flexibility throughout higher education, and enhancing rationality and equity in the management of resources for learning opportunities. This will involve the acceptance of changes to the character of higher education in order to bring it into line with the needs of the vast majority of potential learners. The recommendations outlined below are fundamentally important for the further modernisation of higher education in the light of sustained expanded participation.

668.   We should add that a consideration of flexibility in financial arrangements, both at the level of the individual student and at the level of the funding councils, is intimately concerned both with improved opportunities for student choice and mobility, and with better quality in higher education. On this latter point, we recognise that the sector is unlikely to benefit from net additional resources in the short term and it will therefore be essential to manage more efficiently. The quality of higher education is likely to be heavily dependent on a successful outcome to this challenge. We are therefore interested to investigate three related matters:

- how funding councils, and institutions, might adopt measures and methodologies for the more efficient and rational distribution of resources;

- how existing arrangements may be helpfully modified to assist student choice and mobility;

- how students themselves might be able directly to influence sectoral and institutional decisions over the allocation of resources.

Credit-led resource management

669.   It has been a regular feature of discussions amongst those responsible for the development of institutional credit-based schemes since the late 1980s that considerable potential might exist within the comprehensive application of credit-based learning to develop a resource management methodology which is sensitive to patterns of student choice. This could apply both to movement within the sector as a whole, but above all to patterns of academic behaviour within institutions. The purpose of this part of the investigation has been to explore whether 'credit', (as defined earlier in Chapter IX), can act as an effective and rational means of distributing resources according to student choice. If the potential can be demonstrated, then it may be possible to recommend constructive and welcome innovations to funding councils and institutions. We are aware that this raises important questions about the proper balance to be achieved between producer-led and consumer-led definitions of higher education, implying the need for a sensitive treatment of conventional academic arrangements, including that of institutional academic autonomy, but we have already made our position clear on the balance that needs to be achieved here.

670.   We cannot pass up the opportunity of exploring the capacity of credit systems to act in this manner simply because there are sensitivities involved. Moreover, an interest in student financial arrangements and an investigation of alternative resource management methodologies come together in the treatment of the *full-time equivalent student*.

This concept, familiar to educational management for decades, is predicated upon a particular image of the student in higher education. It assumes that the full-time student is the norm from which all other types of student deviate in some way. This is of course an entirely reasonable starting point, since the majority of students on conventional undergraduate and postgraduate courses in higher education are indeed full-time students (823,000 in 1992). However, this model of the 'normal' student tends to undervalue the volume of part-time qualification-seeking students in the sector (445,000 in 1992) and the number of continuing education and short cycle students (over 740,000). Student maintenance arrangements and institutional funding methodologies need to say something about these categories of student also, producing as equitable arrangements as possible for the comprehensive management of all students.

Financing expanded participation

671.   We would go further and suggest that the future development of higher education will not depend as before on the steady expansion of full-time students on continuous three year courses at a single institution. For many students this will continue to be their chosen pattern of study, but personal financial considerations are likely to disrupt aspirations in this direction. It is clear to us, and to many others, that the cost to the Exchequer of a steady expansion in student numbers is so great, at least in terms of student maintenance, that it is unlikely sufficient political support could be assembled for the requisite redistribution of national resources towards increased spending on higher education. Therefore, either full-time student expansion is constrained or alternative means are found for spreading the burden of the cost of higher education appropriately between the State and the individual. We will have more to say on this item in later discussion. For the purposes of this introduction, we make this point to support the view that students of the future may need to contemplate patterns of interrupted study in higher education as they face an obligation to generate personal resources to meet their commitments by periods of employment. We acknowledge that

this would be an unusual experience for full-time students in the United Kingdom, but it is common practice for students throughout Europe and the United States. A decline in the real value of student support may make it a reality in the United Kingdom as well.

672. We might add that it is the regular practice for part-time and continuing education students. They enjoy no significant support from the state in the pursuit of their learning objectives. They have traditionally been expected to finance their own progress through higher education, supported sometimes by employers or by bursaries and similar devices. Colleagues in higher education are therefore faced with a stark choice: either we define the arrangements for participation in higher education principally in terms of full-time attendance at a single institution, protecting the rights of one group of students, but effectively denying rights to many others; or we define arrangements more widely by including all students within the scope of financial arrangements in some appropriate way. If we choose the latter option we may be able to create an environment which is affordable and open to all who can benefit from higher education. This report is in no doubt which strategy is more commendable, and we shall be making proposals which seek to provide for extended flexible and affordable participation, even where this may have consequences for the share of costs to be borne by the individual and for the reform of existing legislation.

673. Having said that, we are aware that there are considerable sensitivities associated with changes to the distribution of resources between various deserving groups. Policy development is always exercised by the relationship between 'winners' and 'losers' in any rebalancing exercise, and the effect it will have on the successful achievement of policy objectives. Yet, when resources are limited, there will either be some 'winners' and some 'losers', or there will be no change. The challenge lies in the creation of arrangements which diminish the gradient between 'winners' and 'losers' in an acceptable manner. We believe this may be possible by producing credit-led funding formulae and more personalised forms of payment for student fees and maintenance

which provide neither disincentives at the point of access, nor obstacles for sector management.

Releasing student choice by financial means

674. One logical extension of arrangements for the extension of student choice is to provide students with personal purchasing power. Under current arrangements, full-time students enjoy the power of initial choice but little other financial leverage on institutional behaviour. Part-time students enjoy more personal purchasing power, but their leverage is frequently too marginal to matter in most institutions. The policy decision of the later 1980s to switch the financing of higher education towards a greater reliance on student fees produced no noticeable change in the ability of the individual student to do anything different about her education. The fee was paid automatically to institutions along with the recurrent funding element. This allowed institutions to become more aware of the impact of student decisions but the arrangement has little consequence for the perceptions of individual students that their decisions had impact on institutions. As long as the individual student is decoupled from the ownership of fee and maintenance payments, this is likely to remain the case.

675. Since 1992, the manipulation of the student fee element has been the single most significant instrument of control over institutional recruitment levels employed by the Government. We have attempted to establish whether this is the most appropriate instrument consonant both with the need to maintain prudent control of finances and with the desire to extend greater individual choice. In the discussion which follows, we have wondered whether some credit-based formula might be an appropriate means of determining the study pattern of students, providing an instrument for the distribution of the tuition fee element in a manner more closely related to actual costs.

Flexibility, choice and student maintenance

676. We have considered the impact on student choice and mobility of the regulatory framework governing student

maintenance and institutional attendance. These features have remained largely unmodified since the Anderson Report (1962) and the Robbins Report (1963) established the principles for the maintenance of students on full-time courses in higher education. There have of course been subsequent adjustments to the extent of support made available to students through the student maintenance grant, including the introduction of arrangements for student loans, 'access' funds and other related initiatives. We do not intend to comment on the adequacy of such arrangements for effective student maintenance. Rather, we have been concerned to establish what modifications may need to be proposed to existing regulations, including current legislation, which would be consonant with the further promotion of credit transfer and student choice. To this effect, we have considered the possible advantages and disadvantages of amending existing regulations towards this end. Furthermore, we have compared various forms of student funding in terms of their effect on credit transfer, access and student choice.

Credit systems and funding councils: towards a new resource methodology

677.	Funding councils play a pivotal role in creating the conditions both for institutional stability and for student mobility. In many ways already, funding councils have created a 'managed market' between institutional suppliers (of courses) and Government purchasers (of academic outputs, including graduates) in the form of a contract on student numbers. This has two aspects. Firstly, we join with those who reject the view that funding councils themselves can be a proxy for a competitive market (Sizer, 1992 for example). Competitive bidding may not be the best way to stimulate market responsiveness, and our argument has assumed the retention of some balance between a recurrent grant element and tuition fees. This position is also adopted by the 1991 White Paper, *Higher education: a new framework*. Secondly, it implies that funding councils would welcome the development of a

methodology which allows them to distinguish student activity at the micro-level of individual programmes, producing a potentially more sensitive methodology for the attribution of resources against costs.

Stability, steerage and turbulence in resource methodologies

678.	However theoretically attractive a funding methodology might be, for whatever ideological or operational reasons, it must pass one test. It must encourage sufficient dynamism in the system to ensure that resources are being deployed efficiently whilst, at the same time, it must assuage the concerns of those who would otherwise turn away from uncertainty. In short, a funding model which releases some elements of a competitive market cannot be so dynamic that it discourages innovation, investment and a preparedness to take risks. Government has rightly, in our opinion, taken the view that an element of recurrent grant will provide the enduring stability of the system while tuition fees will provide the leverage of the market to encourage institutional responsiveness. In the end, recurrent funding is not guaranteed; nor is student demand itself, nor the threat of institutional closure due to competitive pressure, which provides adequate incentives to restructure and modernise higher education in the United Kingdom. A balance of the three might however have the desired effect.

Credit-based resource management and progress to date

679.	The potential of a credit system to act as a more rational and transparent resource acquisition and distribution mechanism has been under exploration for the past few years. This has taken place following decisions by some universities and colleges since the late 1980s to adopt whole-institution schemes based formally on credit accumulation and transfer. Interest has focused on two related aspects, both of which arose from difficulties associated with funding methodologies and student accounting procedures of the PCFC. Firstly, work within some institutions centred upon an unease with the prevailing resource methodologies as they applied to modular programmes. The rapid and extensive development of such programmes, facilitating greater student access to individually defined programmes, began to raise questions about funding methodologies which relied largely upon homogenous courses. Sometimes these methodologies were modified only to result in formulae based upon calculations of teaching load, itself an easily manipulated quantity. As modular schemes became comprehensive, embracing many cross-disciplinary combinations and adopting credit tariffs as a means of internal institutional comparability, prevailing methodologies began to expose their vulnerability to interpretations contrary to the intentions of funding councils. Otherwise, the formulae were inadequately responsive to the development of more individually-defined learning programmes.

680.   Secondly, the development of these comprehensive modular and credit-based programmes also drew attention to the inability of existing funding methodologies to account adequately and fairly for part-time and mixed-mode programmes, and programmes which contained 'credit' for non-institutional learning (ie. APL, work-based learning, accredited vocational training, etc). Since funding councils have been obliged to fund students, rather than courses, it has seemed appropriate to those engaged in thinking about these matters to shift the emphasis of accountability for funding onto the individual student programme. This could be facilitated by the development of a credit-based or unit-based funding methodology.

681.   Some of this thinking began to emerge in 1990 and initial proposals were advanced at the *Learning without walls* conference (Oxford, February 1991). Consequently some consultations were organised by the PCFC (April 1991); these involved attempts to explore the principles to be adopted in establishing a common (credit) tariff, particularly with reference to the funding of part-time students. Some research into the problem was undertaken to explore whether a credit system could determine the specific volumes of activity of different categories of part-time students (Robertson, 1991). For example, the individual programmes of day,

day/evening, evening only attenders and 'associate' students were disaggregated by credit volume and reassembled by category. In the case in question, the results showed that the average volume of credit being undertaken by students in any part-time attendance category did not vary significantly from the 0.4 fte and 0.2 fte multipliers which were being recommended by the funding council. The survey did show however that an institution could produce substantial gains of marginal income by the judicious manipulation of part-time categories, using the conventional multipliers. This would not be possible using a credit-led formula.

682.   Support for a credit-based funding methodology was further emphasised at the CATS Conference (Telford, November 1991) and the PCFC did attempt progress with consultative proposals for a credit tariff formula. These were based on a credit unit of one-eighth of an academic year, or 15 CNAA credits. This proposal met with a very mixed response since it tended to assume that institutions were developing common modular frameworks. Furthermore, the proposed unit was both too large and too inflexible to commend itself more widely. However, had the PCFC consulted more carefully and proposed a credit-unit of 4 CNAA credits, then they would have reached the conclusions which have been outlined earlier in this report. In the event, the PCFC explorations were submerged by the review of funding methodologies consequent on the establishment of unified Higher Education Funding Councils. Following that review, the HEFCE advised initially that it would continue to monitor progress relevant to the development of credit-based funding (April 1992) and, in its Continuing Education Policy Review (March 1993), offered for discussion the principle of such a methodology. By the end of 1993, the HEFCE had concluded that a system of tariffs might indeed be the way forward, having launched a consultation exercise with selected institutions on the merits of such an arrangement for part-time programmes. In early 1994, the Council announced that it would conduct a more extensive review of prospects covering all modes of student attendance. The recommendations of this report may assist the HEFCE in its work. Elsewhere, the SHEFC has

adopted a unit-based methodology for the funding of higher education institutions in Scotland and the HEFCE funds the Open University on a student-unit basis. Each of these approaches may be seen as sharing common principles with the methodology to be recommended here.

683.   Meanwhile, progress in further education has been more remarkable. In February 1992, the FEU published *A basis for credit?* establishing the academic and educational arguments for a credit system. Later, in December 1992, the newly-established Further Education Funding Council (FEFC) published an equally influential consultative document, *Funding learning,* which outlined a number of funding options, the most salient of which could be described as a credit-based methodology. In responses to the document (April 1993), this has proved to be the most popular with further education colleges and has subsequently been adopted as the basis for future funding methodologies in the sector. In addition, the FEFC (Wales) published its own proposals which went a step beyond the proposals of the FEFC (England) by recommending the adoption of a specific unit of credit as the basis for funding. The proposed unit, which has subsequently been adopted by the further education sector throughout Wales, is that defined in *A basis for credit?* and recommended by this report. In short, it is the 30-hour, 30 credit per year model that we have already discussed extensively (see Chapters VIII and IX).

684.   The most significant contributions to the discussion offered by the developments in further education have not been concerned specifically with the principles of credit-based funding, nor with the definition of the credit unit itself. As we have demonstrated, these matters were already understood, if not yet in practice, by the time the FEFCs adopted the ideas. The novel contribution lies in the attempts by the FEFC (England) to produce a funding model which uses credit tariffs to fund the complete learning process, from pre-entry guidance, through enrolment to achievement. Indeed, it is the achievement-led funding aspect of the FEFC(E) proposals that arouses the greatest interest. Most previous thinking on these matters has concentrated on the potential of credit to fund students according to their programme, implicitly adopting enrolment registration as the only significant criterion for funding. The shift from this type of input-led funding orientation to an explicitly output and outcomes-led approach is a radical departure to which we shall turn our attention in due course.

685.   We are very aware that progress on credit-based resourcing may have been swifter in further than in higher education for very specific reasons. Firstly, the needs of funding councils have been greater; funding by credit unit offers the promise of a unified funding methodology for a complex and diverse sector. Secondly, funding councils in further education have been able to start afresh; they have inherited few existing or convincing alternative methodologies. Thirdly, academic credit systems are still in their infancy in the sector so there has been a chance to put together an entirely new and comprehensive set of arrangements, covering academic and resource management. And finally, funding councils in the sector have not had to deal with institutions whose entire history has prepared them to repel intrusions from the agencies of Government whenever possible. This latter point is most important. The principles of a credit-led funding approach for higher education, to which we turn now, must be based on a respect for the academic autonomy of institutions. Funding models will not be welcomed by universities if they imply that institutions must adopt a particular form of academic organisation to which they are not willing parties. We are very aware of this matter and proceed accordingly.

Principles informing credit-based funding proposals

686.   The following discussions have been predicated upon the prospect that all higher education provision can be brought within a credit framework sufficiently general and comprehensive to embrace traditional provision and sufficiently flexible not to inhibit non-traditional developments. Moreover, although programmes in higher education continue to be dominated by the full-time three

year degree, providing students with fairly homogenous programmes, there is now evidence that greater diversity and heterogeneity will shape provision in the future. Credit systems may be the means by which a degree of comparability can be placed upon academic programmes within higher education without prejudice to the diversity of provision, applying not just to Continuing Education or part-time students, but to students and programmes full-time and part-time, academic and vocational, on- or off-campus, in further, higher or continuing education.

687.   Accordingly, it is recognised that proposals for the reform or modification of existing arrangements will need to win respect as improvements or necessary adjustments to those arrangements, offering mechanisms and methodologies which are as far as possible continuous with present funding regimes and institutional objectives. **We recommend** that the principles upon which new funding methodologies should be based are as defined in Table 40.

688.   If the conditions above can be met, a credit-based funding methodology would provide the basis of an internal market within higher education, supplementing the quasi-market that exists between institutions and facilitating a more transparently accountable market within institutions. On the other hand, student-referenced and credit-based resource methodologies challenge inherited patterns of institutional provision, and raise issues concerning the impact of student decisions on the deployment of resources. Whilst funding councils and institutions may welcome a funding methodology which is more sensitive to patterns of student choice, permitting resource management decisions to be made in response to market information, there will be some outstanding matters of concern.

689.   Firstly, funding councils and institutions may not be convinced that student demand and informed student choice, however circumscribed, provides a better basis for the deployment of resources than informed planning. Secondly, where institutions operate systems for devolved budgetary management,

Table 40:
The principles of a credit-based funding methodology

- to provide funding councils with at least the same degree of control and influence as at present;

- to be as simple as possible, rational and transparent, with no greater room for unintended interpretation than existing funding regimes;

- to be neutral with respect to the balance of responsibilities between funding councils and institutions, and continuous with respect to relationships between Government, its departments, the funding councils and institutions;

- to contain no hidden policy implications which would force institutions to adopt a particular pattern of academic provision, nor require modifications to existing provision where this was not agreed;

- to be cost efficient and effective with no significant increases in costs to funding councils or institutions, and capable of being managed with no more than modest new investment in information systems;

- to allow institutions to distinguish between resource strategies applied by funding councils to the sector as a whole (resource *acquisition*) and resource strategies applied by institutions to the management of their funding council allocations (resource *distribution*);

- to emphasise the importance of the reporting and accounting methodologies for providing an articulation between **acquisition** (external) and **distribution** (internal) resource allocation mechanisms;

- to define a comprehensive, comprehensible and consistent unit of account: **the unit of credit,** to act as the unit of 'currency' which defines the operation of the credit system. Such a unit of account would be relatively arbitrary, and neutral with respect to policy outcomes;

- to be distinguished from proposals for modifications to student mandatory award and support systems.

devolving also the management of the student academic programme, this can lead to the development of local strategies inimical to the exercise of student choice; budget centres may tend to 'ring-fence' students as their principal sources of income, closing down their learning opportunities. Next, the transaction costs of internal markets and quasi-markets can be substantial; internal market strategies may introduce greater degrees of instability and turbulence between cost centres which imply greater sophistication in the use of appropriate management instruments.

Implications for institutions

690.   As funding policy seeks to underpin the move from producer-led domination of student choice to demand-responsive factors, the incentives to improve student choice may have profound implications for institutional management. This could imply a separation of the management of teaching resources (supply) from the management of student programmes (demand) This style of organisation would have further consequences for institutional structures, raising questions about the extent to which existing faculty and departmental structures inhibit and constrain student choice by conflating control of both supply and demand factors. Indications from the internal resource management strategies of the six universities and one college, which have contributed to our understanding of current practice, suggest unevenly developed systems of institutional devolved or delegated budgetary authority. The implications for the flow of resources reflect different patterns of student mobility and choice. No institutions in the sample could claim to have developed a resource distribution model that was fully sensitive to student choice, and the extent of student choice varied considerably as well.

691.   If a credit-based funding methodology were to commend itself to funding councils and institutions, considerable attention would need to be paid to its impact upon orientations to conventional institutional priorities. For example, how far does the tendency towards the stabilisation of income streams militate against student mobility? Moreover, further clarity may be required of how 'internal market' mechanisms can be understood in higher education; arrangements that have developed to date seem to describe relationships between suppliers (ie. between departments, faculties, 'off-campus' agencies) rather than between suppliers and consumers (ie. students).

692.   Secondly, attention will need to be given to the 'instability tolerance' that could be sustained between planned student numbers and greater student choice. No institution can tolerate the turbulence generated by relatively unpredictable patterns of student choice. Fixed cost commitments constrain the deployment of educational resources, and in any event, institutions would not expect to have to respond to short-cycle changes in student demand. This would be likely to disturb their commitment to other scholarly activities including research. On the other hand, institutions cannot shelter behind the need to preserve a broad range of academic purposes as an excuse for failing to meet the reasonable demands of students.

693.   If an internal market were to operate within an institution, there would be a need to design cost centre incentives to facilitate freer internal student mobility. In this, differential fee levels and (bid) pricing arrangements are significant constraining variables. Many institutions are developing more or less sophisticated internal trading arrangements, producing formulae for the transfer of funds from cost centre to cost centre. With differential fee levels, this means that arrangements have to be negotiated to provide incentives to cost centres in higher fee-banded subjects to release 'their' students to earn credit from low-banded subject areas. By the same measure, high fee-banded areas have to be given some reason to accept internal student transfer from low fee-banded areas rather than seek to recruit additional high fee-banded students in the main subject area. For example, what incentives might exist for an Engineering department to release 25% of their students to earn 10% of their credit by studying business administration as an elective component of their academic programme? Furthermore, what incentives might be needed to encourage a department of Biological Science to exploit the

internal market by attracting marginal students from Social Science to earn elective credits in, say, environmental management?

694.   One way might be to reduce the number of different 'cost categories' by minimising the invariable anomalies of categorisation and subject coding. Currently, the funding councils operate with eleven Academic Subject Categories to which student numbers are attributed as a basis for the allocation of the recurrent grant. Whilst these subject categories do indeed reflect something of the conventions of institutional decisions on 'natural' academic subject groupings, they also encourage institutions to create trading barriers between these categories. It would be much simpler for institutions and funding councils if these subject categories were reduced in number.

695.   Finally, for many institutions, the marginal gains (losses) incurred through internal market transactions may be insufficient to offset the benefits from marginal increases in research income or other revenue sources. In this, differences within the sector are important. Many ex-UFC institutions earn more than 50% of their income from research grants; the teaching funds (from block grant and tuition fees) are therefore not the only significant source of revenue. For ex-PCFC institutions, income from research allocations rarely rises much above 5-7% of the allocation for teaching. This material difference will be enormously influential in determining the propensity of some institutions and their departments to encourage greater student mobility.

The role of funding councils

696.   It is impossible to under-estimate the influence of the funding councils in determining the rate of progress on some of these matters. They are rightly sensitive about the care which needs to be taken in proposing arrangements which would imply some form of compliance by institutions, with perceived prejudicial academic consequences. In short, whilst funding councils appear very receptive to the sort of credit-led formulae which this report is recommending, they remain firmly committed to the view that it is not their role to

expect institutions to adopt either modular, or credit-based, or semester-based academic structures. We share this view also, and wish to make recommendations based on credit which can be applied evenly and fairly to all institutions, whether they are using, or plan to use credit or not, as the case may be.

Credit as a unit of account

697.   We have spent considerable time in this report debating the issue of 'credit', its meaning (Chapter VIII), its definition and application in a credit framework (Chapter IX) and its relevance for quality assurance (Chapter X). We do not propose to rehearse these discussions again. It is apparent however that funding councils generally would welcome the development of a credible and common unit of account with which to describe the variety of learning in higher education and beyond. This unit of account could be the means by which the allocation of fees and recurrent grant was determined on an individual student basis. Arrangements of a similar nature are already developing in further education, and a credit-based variant applies in the determination of the Australian Higher Education Contributions Scheme (HECS). Whilst the case for such a development was less pressing when the vast majority of programmes involved full-time students, the introduction of the PCFC institutions into the combined higher education sector changes that. They have brought with them many institutions where the volume of part-time students on degree and similar programmes is 30% or more of the total student body. In a small number of universities and colleges, the total passes 50%. Furthermore, the ex-UFC institutions are now faced with the encouragement to bring into accreditation the bulk of their extra-mural and Continuing Education programmes. These recruit largely part-time students. Therefore, the hegemony of the full-time student and the homogenous three year degree course has been challenged by these new developments.

698.   We have maintained throughout that a credit system offers an effective means of coping with this diversity from the perspective of the funding councils. We also believe that it will help the Higher Education

Statistics Agency (HESA) in its work. However, a credit system will assist no one if it does not carry the assent of institutions in the sector. To achieve common support, the proposed credit-based formula must ensure certain things. Firstly, it must be applicable to all types of academic programme and all categories of student without prejudice respectively to their structure or status. This means that institutions registering predominantly full-time students on single honours degree programmes should be as comfortable with the arrangements as any other more differentiated institution.

699.   Secondly, and paradoxically perhaps, institutions which do subscribe to credit-based systems should not be disadvantaged compared with those which do not. This could occur if credit-based funding arrangements encouraged such institutions to use the flexibility and capability of their academic programmes to disaggregate student behaviour in such a way that funding council had a clearer picture of real student behaviour than would be possible in other institutions. For example, it would be anomalous if a flexible and credit-based university were disadvantaged in funding terms because it was capable of showing, by credit volume and subject category, that an Engineering student spent, say, 25% of his time in 'low-cost' teaching activities compared with the 100% 'high-cost' activities that might be claimed by another, less transparent, institution. Formula safeguards would need to be built into any arrangements to take account of this possibility.

700.   **We recommend** therefore that the funding councils adopt as the minimum unit of account the 30-hour unit of credit proposed in the report. As we have said earlier, this unit of account is equal to one 30 hour learning week, or equivalent to one hour of learning per week for a 30-week 'college year'. This arrangement yields a full-time equivalent student 30 credits. The HEFCE has already signalled its support for the principle of this unit in its discussion document on the funding of Continuing Education (January 1994). For institutions preferring to work with the CNAA values for the time being, this minimum unit would represent four credits; otherwise, it would represent one credit.

701.   We would make one last, and highly relevant, comment in support of this recommendation. This report has maintained throughout that the unit of credit based on a 30-hour unit and a 30-credit year is its preferred model and is used by a small number of universities. However, it acknowledges that most universities, where they are using credit, currently use the CNAA 120-credit model. Whilst funding councils will not wish to impose a solution to this dilemma on institutions, they may need to determine which model best suits their purposes. To this extent, we advise in the following manner. The 30-hour unit of credit, as proposed, is made up of two elements: an objective quantity of teaching time (X) and a subjective element of professionally assessed learning time (Y). Each credit, or credit multiple, can have any balance of X to Y. Modules or courses involving largely taught work will have, say 70% X and 30% Y. On the other hand, open learning programmes may have 5% X and 95% Y. **It does not matter to the suitability of the credit for funding purposes what ratio an institution chooses to apply** as a consequence of its academic arrangements. In fact this approach to credit tends to favour downward pressure on teaching time (X) since there is no incentive to increase the ratio of X to Y as no funding gain follows. This formula is significantly different in this respect from all previous formulae which have given (inadvertent) incentives to the upward movement of teaching time. On the other hand, the CNAA 120-model offers no means of establishing the appropriate balance of teaching or learning inputs to a learning experience, and it will tend to produce undifferentiated and homogenous modular structures. These may succeed, by their relative symmetry, in disguising the real teaching and learning inputs in a series of different learning experiences, and thus encourage the manipulation of credit values in a distorting manner. For these reasons, we believe the 30-hour credit unit is the preferred instrument for producing a rational and fair resource methodology and we recommend it strongly. We accept however that the argument is more complex than we have been able to describe in these comments, and the funding council will need to consult more widely amongst informed opinion before it is in a position to give final advice.

Output-related funding: credit for achievement

702. We have been very interested in the proposals of the FEFC to link part of the funding of students to their achievement. In this respect, higher and further education have escaped fairly lightly over the years. Few other services so obviously receive payment from public funds for the provision of a service no matter how successful in advance of demonstrated outcomes. Currently, institutions are contracted to recruit students to meet the supply of an agreed number of places. Providing for an element of output-led funding would be an attempt to link funding to performance in a way which would avoid loading the total funding allocation onto the enrolment process. A funding methodology which sought to achieve such an objective would require the existence of a credit-based formula. Students would contract at entry for a fixed quantum of credit; their progress and achievement would be determined by the quantum of credit successfully earned.

703. However, such an approach would raise difficult questions over definitions of student 'exit' and 'achievement'. Such terms might be misplaced in an environment encouraging flexibility and mobility. For example, when might a student be said to have 'achieved'? At the end of a semester or year? At the end of a 'course'? In a transfer environment, which institution would 'own' final student achievement? Would a measure of added-value be more appropriate than merely an assessment of final achievement? Indeed there may be sensitive issues of quality assurance to address if institutions, in any effort to protect scarce resources, ensure that their pass rate improves. The complexity of issues associated with the determination of achievement, and its appropriateness as an equitable basis for funding, would seem to pose problems for the applicability of this option to higher education. Nevertheless, **we recommend** that further discussions take place between funding councils and institutions with a view to linking funding in some measure to student achievement, in addition to student enrolment, through credit-based formulae.

The abolition of funding distinctions by mode of attendance

704. In a credit system, the distinction between full-time/sandwich and part-time can give way to a funding methodology by individual student programme (ie. by credit-based learning contract). Under this model, students might be engaged on *intensive* (ie relatively continuous) or *extensive* (ie relatively discontinuous) programmes, and these could be described for monitoring purposes by disaggregating individual programmes by credit over time. For the purposes of funding council allocations, institutions might contract to award an agreed quantum of credit, the internal distribution of which would be constrained only by programme level and subject category. **We recommend** that the categories of mode of attendance be replaced by distinctions based on *intensive* or *extensive* patterns of credit accumulation.

The maintenance of two general levels of funding

705. **We recommend** that there should be two principal categories of funding: undergraduate and postgraduate teaching; and research. A case might be made for a further separation of programmes into three undergraduate teaching levels, based on the claim that higher level undergraduate teaching is more costly than lower level teaching. Whilst this may be the case for many programmes, the prevailing funding arrangements smooth out these variations and further complications do not seem to bestow compensating advantages.

A reduction of academic subject categories to the minimum necessary number

706. Currently there are eleven academic subject categories. It is doubtful whether student numbers attributed to these categories are that reliable in a more flexible and mixed programme environment of some institutions. Accounting for students by academic subject category may not be the most effective way of determining the distribution of funding resources. In any arrangement the objective must be to provide the funding council with the best means of *accounting for* the

allocation of funds whilst ensuring that institutions have the greatest possible discretion in their internal distribution. These means that a distinction may need to be drawn between the relative freedom of institutions to distribute funds within broad cost categories and the specific requirement for institutions to report the results of this distribution by some more or less refined subject classification. Accepting that funding councils have a responsibility to control numbers specifically in Medicine and Initial Teacher Training, **we recommend** a simplified set of categories be developed for future funding allocations:

Clinical
Laboratory (high-cost)
Laboratory (low-cost)
Non-laboratory (high-cost)
Non-laboratory (low-cost)
ITT.

707.   Indeed, it might be possible to go further and reduce the categories to three: *laboratory*, *non-laboratory*, and *other (eg studio, semi-lab,* and *languages etc)*. In any event, **we recommend** that such a reapportionment exercise be negotiated with institutions who would be able to describe their costs in various subject areas, supporting claims for appropriate apportionment and allowing some precision in definitions of 'laboratory' volume and similar matters.

708.   The overall effects of the model proposed above would be: a reduction of funding 'cells' from 44 to 12 (six subject categories x two levels x one 'mode'); no less control over the steerage to be exercised by funding councils in the pursuit of general policy, but considerably more freedom for institutions to operate within more flexible and broader categories. There may be somewhat less direct control by funding council over the development of part-time (extensive) programmes which, in a credit-based learning environment, may be promoted anyway by changes to student finance arrangements or personal learning contract decisions. There would be a need to reconsider the distinction between funding allocations by general categories and the monitoring of specific subject volumes. Funding councils could allocate

resources by the proposed general categories but still require statistical monitoring returns to reflect the disaggregation of student programmes by credit and subject. Current monitoring arrangements tend to be insufficiently fine-tuned to discern the range of mixed subject patterns that are now undertaken in many institutions and further consideration will need to be given to the development of methodologies which encourage institutional reporting based on actual student behaviour in modular and credit-based schemes.

709.   If the preceding discussion concerned arrangements for the funding of institutions using credit-based formulae, we turn next to the proposals for similar principles to apply to individual students. This involves a consideration of arrangements for the payment of both student fees and maintenance.

The management of student fees

Differential fee-banding

710.   There is one aspect of the current arrangements defining student fees which needs further attention. The existence of *fee-banding* has some inhibiting effects on student mobility, particularly within institutions, and may have consequences for how institutions choose to structure and to report student behaviour on institutional academic programmes. Firstly, differential fee bands do not recognise the composite character of many individual student programmes. For example, many students enroling for higher fee-banded subjects elect to earn credit in modules from low fee-banded areas. We gave an example from Engineering earlier. In comprehensive modular schemes, the internal transfer between high and low fee-band subjects can be potentially extensive as students studying Science or Engineering choose modules in foreign languages, business administration or similar subjects. In such cases, institutions either report such students wholly in a high fee-band category and make the appropriate claim to local authorities, or they restrict the choice of students to within limited fee-banded options. In either case, the principal variable to which institutions will have regard is financial

advantage rather than the reflection of student choice. The consequences to date have been that, in this respect at least, differential fee-banding is acting contrary both to the promotion of student choice and to the accurate reporting of student behaviour.

711. We recognise that differential fee-banding has been the principal means since 1991 by which Government via the funding councils have achieved two objectives: firstly, the sharpening of market competition via the shift of institutional funding (in varying measure) from recurrent grant to student fees; and secondly, the control of institutional recruitment through (downward) variations in the fee levels. They would be reluctant to relinquish instruments which allow the further pursuit of either objective. Yet we have wondered whether matters need to be so arranged. Accepting that funding councils have a responsibility to the Treasury to maintain control over student demand in line with prevailing policy, do funding councils need to exercise direct control over student demand in specific areas? For example, national policy wishes to ensure that demand for places in science and engineering continues to be stimulated, or at least not to be further depressed. The current means of ensuring this is to steepen the gradient between fee levels. This has the effect of shutting off recruitment (but not demand) in low fee-band subjects whilst retaining relative incentives to recruit students for science and engineering.

Beyond fee-banding?

712. However, there may be another way of achieving some of the same objectives whilst also responding to student demand and student choices within existing resources. Firstly, maintaining a higher fee-band for science and engineering subjects and lower fee-bands for business studies, social science, arts and humanities subjects produces the appropriate recruitment outcomes at an institutional level, but it does little to influence levels of student demand for the subjects concerned. Individual student demand for engineering does not increase because institutions receive a higher fee, and it is also clear that student demand for other subjects does not decrease because of the lower fee level. Matters might change if students were given direct ownership of their fee 'entitlement' but this is not the case at present.

713. The objectives we favour would produce a methodology which is responsive to resource limitations, continues to provide incentives for the recruitment of science and engineering students, but recognises that institutions should also be free to respond to student demand in areas where this is buoyant. This methodology would involve abandoning the policy of differential fees in favour of a model which consolidated the teaching recurrent grant element with the student fee in a formula which reflected both the agreed costs of defined subject categories and the credit-based programmes (and achievements) of students. It might operate in the following way. Firstly, there would be a common fee element of, for example, £1,700 at current prices. Whatever the level, it would need to provide incentives to institutions to recruit students in areas of buoyant demand at marginal rates. Secondly, there could continue to be an element of recurrent grant, required to ensure some institutional stability over time, but in order to provide incentives to institutions to recruit science and engineering students wherever possible, the price gradient offered by funding councils could be steepened across the various cost categories. This could apply absolutely, or once particular recruitment thresholds had been reached. The effect would be to allow institutions to recruit students in low-cost, low price and high demand areas at marginal fee-based rates, whilst providing incentives to recruit students in high-cost, high price but low demand subject areas. Over time, institutions could decide whether they wished to continue to compete in the market for scarcer high priced students, or whether they wished to move (marginally or otherwise) towards meeting the demands of lower priced students. If at any time, Government felt that national objectives were not being met, it could encourage the funding councils further to steepen the price gradient applying to cost categories.

714. We believe the positive effects on access, student choice and individual mobility will be significant. Institutions will be

able to respond to high demand, albeit at marginal rates; incentives are retained for categories of national priority; funding council leverage is retained where necessary; institutional freedom to plan and recruit is enhanced; and internal markets within institutions can be made more operable by the abolition of the differential fee. This will allow institutions to encourage students to construct individual programmes more regularly without the disincentive of fearing that they will incur financial disadvantage.

715.   In keeping with our arguments in respect of institutional funding, we believe there is considerable merit in reconceptualising the 'student' as an aggregation of credits to be achieved over certain periods of study (ie.a term or semester). **We recommend** firstly that the regulations for the payment of student fees be amended to support the changes towards semester-based modular structures across the sector. Certain proposals have already been made to prepare for these changes, including modifications to the *Education (Mandatory Awards) Regulations, 1993,* and others will be contingent upon the outcomes of the Flowers and Irvine Reports on the reform of the academic year.

Responsibility for the payment of student fees

716.   In keeping with changes to patterns of student behaviour and as a reflection of the changing character of higher education generally, it appears difficult any longer to understand the role of local authorities in the payment of student fees and in the adjudication of courses upon which these payments are based. Many students, and particularly mature students, no longer have a connection with a single local authority. They will often have moved from the authority of their initial schooling. If any location is relevant in these matters, it is likely to be the local authority in which they live and pay local taxes. Moreover, the case for retaining responsibility for the payment of fees with local authorities is further weakened by the changes in local responsibility for higher education.

717.   We favour modifications to existing arrangements in line with other proposals in this report. **We recommend** that responsibility for the payment of student fees should no longer reside with local authorities. Instead the funding councils should be invited to take up this role. It is important that this should be so for three reasons: firstly, decisions on the payment of fees, whether banded or otherwise, should be in the hands of a single responsible authority best placed to understand the variables involved. This will more readily be the case if decisions are to be made according to the character of individual programmes based on a credit formula. Secondly, this would allow funding councils to distribute fees according to an achievement element, if this became policy. Thirdly, this arrangement would allow the easier development, if desired, of a consolidation of the tuition fee and recurrent grant element into a composite sum to be distributed by student according to a future credit-based formula. It has been suggested that these arrangements would place in the hands of funding councils too much power and influence over institutional budgets, with material consequences for institutional autonomy. We cannot see how this can be the case. Local authorities have little real discretion. They are very much 'clearing houses' for the payment of fees to higher education courses against criteria advised by the Government. With the development of fee-banding, the Government has developed a yet more definitive role in these matters and they have the power to modify tuition fee levels irrespective of the source of payment. For local authorities, there may be some advantages in continuing to deal with the matter since the infrastructure is in place, and they may be able to make marginal revenue gains through the judicious management of cash flow. On the other hand, institutions may become increasingly frustrated by the variable interpretations some local authorities will place on fee claims, given the complexity of individual programmes with which they will have to deal. It may now be timely to set in place arrangements for the consolidation of student fee payments through the funding councils. Clearly consideration will have to be given to whether funding councils have the means to take on this responsibility and, if accepted, over what period it might be feasible.

The student as purchaser: towards an individual entitlement to learning?

718.   Since the promotion of greater student choice through credit accumulation and transfer is the objective, what is to prevent the development of arrangements which *directly empower the student as a purchaser?* Part-time students are by default already in this position, so why should the same principle not apply to full-time students? In such a model, two different arrangements might be possible. Firstly, the funding council could stand proxy for the individual student by holding the combined teaching resource represented by the recurrent grant and tuition fee and distributing it according to the specificity of a student's programme. Or secondly, the student might be personally responsible for the distribution of a determined sum, represented by an entitlement, voucher or educational credit. In either case, the distribution of the resource represented by the student would be most efficiently achieved by the use of a credit system which enabled the individual units of the individual student programme to be disaggregated.

A managed student market

719.   Could funding councils act as a proxy for the genuine purchasing power of students, by reflecting in some rational manner through the funding distribution system the choices and decisions of students? We describe this as a 'managed market' for students. It would require that funding councils were interested in allocating teaching funds (grant and fees) in line with actual student decisions as far as would be consonant with the rights of institutions to manage their internal affairs, and as would be feasible in terms of planning horizons and the lag in capturing relevant data. To achieve this level of precision and efficiency, funding councils would need to begin with a methodological instrument that could deconstruct or disaggregate all individual learning programmes, by mode, subject, academic level, or length into various categories for the purposes of attributing costs. We believe

this methodological instrument is provided by a credit system.

720.   However, what advantages are there in inviting the funding councils to act as a proxy for individual students in this respect? Firstly, it could be suggested that the current fee-shift policy, mitigated by current Treasury considerations, is already a 'managed market'. Students do not personally see the fee and grant element, but institutions feel the impact of their individual enrolment decisions and funding councils allocate resources accordingly. Secondly, it could be argued that this avoids the difficulties, discussed below, of loading students with the responsibility of distributing large sums of money through a voucher system. On the other hand, by using the funding council as a proxy for student purchasing power, it could be argued that institutional providers are better able to distort the market by encouraging students to 'purchase' a limited and conventional range of courses. This could change if students realised that they had genuine purchasing power in the form of an exchangeable voucher. Under these circumstances, students might exercise a more informed personal choice on the programmes they sought. Moreover, if this approach were pursued, institutions would be effectively required to provide some independent professional guidance support to students to avoid the charge that students were making poorly informed choices. In short, a 'managed market' may encourage institutions to offer a narrow range of courses whereas the direct empowerment of the individual learner might encourage institutions to respond more directly to individual learner needs. To establish whether this latter process could achieve desired objectives – the unification of individual student choice with appropriate learning opportunities – we turn next to the matter of educational vouchers.

Vouchers and training credits

721.   We accept that the principle of an educational 'voucher' system has been proposed on an earlier occasion. It was found to be unwelcome to so many interested parties that colleagues would have good reason to be sceptical whether its reintroduction would be any more warmly received. On the other hand,

times have moved on, and a substantial expansion of higher education has occurred. It is possible that public opinion and relevant interested parties might be now prepared to consider an educational voucher for higher education as an acceptable means of funding further growth and participation in the sector, in the absence of alternative means. Indeed, the idea might be acceptable, for different reasons, across the political spectrum. It clearly remains attractive to those who value the momentum that market mechanisms give to the interactions between individual (student) consumers and corporate (higher education) producers and suppliers. This same dynamic relationship might also appeal to those who are attracted to the prospects of deploying student choices to achieve the modernisation of higher education in the United Kingdom. Furthermore, an educational voucher of this kind might be largely compatible with the aspirations of those who support the principle of a lifelong learning entitlement (Miliband, 1991 for example). Symptomatically, a recent policy paper on adult education (NIACE, 1994) discusses an *individual entitlement to learning* in terms of the financial responsibilities that need to be borne by the individual in the management of learning careers of the future. Such responsibilities include the need to make direct individual purchasing interventions in the market of learning opportunities. Failure to do so may leave many individuals in a condition of permanent educational marginalisation, if conventional institutional arrangements are not challenged in this way.

722.   Some progress has been made in understanding the potential and implications for institutional funding of individual student 'entitlement'. The application of the Youth Credits Scheme, formerly the Training Credits Scheme, to unemployed trainees is one such attempt. Its early operation has attracted a mixed reception and it appears to have been unevenly successful in meeting its objectives. These concerned the belief, strongly supported by the CBI, that young trainees would be 'empowered' by the possession of a personal Training Credit. This would enable them to receive an individual allocation from their local TEC/LEC for tuition and training in a specified occupational area relevant to local labour market needs. The prospective trainee would then be in a better purchasing position to negotiate individually with local training providers (ie. further education colleges in most examples) for relevant training; they would then claim the resource represented by the Training Credit from their local TEC/LEC.

723.   An analogy with higher education is fairly obvious. Students could negotiate entry to a programme of their choice, modify it as appropriate, transfer between programmes and institutions according to their needs, and always retain access to the funding source supplied by the funding council. An educational variant of the Training Credits Scheme would meet most specifications of a portable purchasing capacity for students. But would it work and is it desirable?

724.   The problems with the Training Credits Scheme repay attention. From the perspective of the trainee (student), the voucher represented for many a perceived debt burden which was a disincentive to proceed further with training. Moreover, despite the best intentions, it has not seriously empowered the individual student to overcome the inertia of large organisations (ie. further education colleges). Indeed it may be implausible to believe that an educational establishment will modify its arrangements to attract what is highly marginal individual income; the college would be better placed modifying the learning/training aspirations of prospective students in order to capture their 'income'. This is what has tended to happen in practice. From the perspective of the college and the TEC/LEC, both parties have an interest in stabilising the negotiation environment. The college needs to receive income to match inherent liabilities (ie existing staff and courses); the TEC/LEC needs to meet training targets by achieving successful student training placements in available courses. In short, suppliers and funders become yoked together in the preservation of relatively conventional arrangements. The student as purchaser has difficulty breaking into the relationship.

725.   Would this be different with students of higher education? The case proceeds as follows. The Training Credits Scheme met

difficulties because it addressed the needs of the most dispossessed and under-confident group of prospective students. It is not reasonable to test the merits of such a scheme against the capacity of poorly educated 16-year olds to negotiate their learning needs. More self-possessed and demanding higher education students would be better equipped to conduct the negotiations with institutions for their own benefit. Moreover, funding councils would not be constrained by the same type of targets as TEC/LECs. Therefore, it is suggested, a higher education version of a Training Credits Scheme could be made to work.

726.   On the other hand, higher education students are indeed more mature, skilful and perhaps personally adept at handling negotiations over chosen programmes – or they could become so, with adequate encouragement over time. Indeed, it might be reasonably argued that one of the main purposes of higher education is the development of critical negotiative skills, something which the Enterprise in Higher Education initiative has sought to promote. Moreover, in the United States, some students can earn academic credit directly for the negotiation of personal learning careers. It may not be inconceivable that such an arrangement could prosper in the United Kingdom as well. However, academic staff in universities and colleges are equally very adept at convincing prospective students that they might wish to follow this or that prepared programme, which has of course been constructed in their best interests. Moreover, the higher education institution has conventions, cultures, reputations and resources to protect, modifications to which do not accommodate themselves readily with other than the most persistent, or well-provided, group of 'customers'. Funding councils also are likely to conspire in favour of the maintenance of stability in university provision, at least over the immediate term. In short, the authority relationships of higher education may be no less intimidating to a prospective learner, at least in the short term, than those in a further education college, and they may be more obdurate in many cases. If these concerns are to be overcome, strong quality assurance arrangements, including effective guidance procedures, would need to be established as a minimum security to ensure a fair expression of informed student choice

727.   There is one final objection to this arrangement which needs to be discussed. An educational voucher scheme appears to provide no additional benefits to funding councils in the management of the resources of the sector, and it may detract from existing instruments of control. The problem lies in the fact that a funding council cannot easily regulate access to the 'entitlement', nor how and where the resource would be committed. This may not matter in the theoretically conceivable open market of free competition, where the funding councils would determine the quantum of resource available, leaving its distribution largely to the market. In practice, funding councils have a public duty to ensure that certain policy objectives are met in an efficient and effective manner. This would not be best served by the generation of turbulence and loss of control which could lead to the closure of courses, or even institutions as student choices ebb and flow. A balance would need to be achieved at some point between reasonable oversight and steerage on the one hand, and greater personal freedom on the other. It was considerations of this kind which led the Further Education Funding Council (England) to reject the principle of vouchers or Training Credits as a basis for institutional funding (see *Funding learning*, FEFC, 1993) and the argument may have substantial force in higher education as well.

728.   On balance and despite the difficulties to be overcome, there may be substantial benefits to be derived from the introduction of a voucher system for student fees. This need not be as controversial a proposal as in the past since we do not propose any means-testing of the entitlement to the student fee (or composite fee + recurrent grant element) in any of the models available to us. Some form of payment-by-voucher system exists in Denmark with in-built incentives to encourage persistent attendance and completion of courses. **We recommend** therefore that Government and funding councils consider the introduction of an educational voucher arrangement for the payment of tuition fees for

full-time students, that such a system be based on a credit-led formula. Students would dispose of their fees in proportion to the credit for which they register with the university or college but **we recommend** that further thought should be given to ensuring that the student 'time-to-degree' period does not lengthen overall as a consequence of this flexibility. If an achievement-led element were to be promoted, this may require the funding council to retain a portion of the quantum for payment against recorded outcomes

Would 'top-up' fees impede flexibility?

729. It should be mentioned, not least for the purposes of completeness, that a corollary of the education voucher system is an arrangement involving 'top-up' fees. This model would allow providers (institutions) to offer purchasers (students) the opportunity to pursue chosen programmes at a given institution, subject to the payment of a premium to the university. Universities which felt able to charge a premium would then prosper with additional resources, opening up a division in the sector which could transform the character of British higher education. It would have the effect of establishing a competitive market between institutions and has been widely rejected to date by the representative bodies of institutions. If the charging of 'top-up' fees for full-time students became established practice, the effect on student choice and mobility could be dramatic, with consequences that are difficult to assess. Furthermore, the arrangement would leave institutions open to the charge that they were inviting certain categories of students to buy their academic credit for commercial advantage rather than for sound academic reasons. Under these circumstances, matters of quality assurance would become prominent.

730. Perhaps the most decisive criticism for institutions of the proposal for 'top-up' fees is not that it would be socially and educationally divisive for the immediately obvious reason. It is not for the reason that those in a position to afford such fees could buy their way into a more privileged higher education; arguably they do

Table 41: Finance and flexibility: a ministerial view

One of the Government's key tasks is to develop a funding framework for higher education which helps to ensure that the taxpayer gets the best possible value for money from public investment in the system. We look to competition between institutions to realise the benefits of a market in terms of efficiency and innovation. The shift in the balance of public funding from grants to fees is a fundamental component of the framework. In the 1989-90 academic year the grant-fee ratio was about ten to one. From Autumn 1991 differentiated fees, reflecting cost differences between different subject areas, will reduce it to about two to one. The result will be a much more direct link between an institution's income and its ability to recruit and retain students, and a strong incentive to make full use of marginal capacity.

Institutions are, of course, free to set their own fees. The government has no legal power to prevent them from setting fees above publicly funded rates, or require them to do so. A more market-orientated system can be expected to encourage institutions to consider such options more actively. In making such judgements, they will doubtless take account of all the relevant factors, including the implications for access to higher education.

The higher eduction system has become more diverse, but the traditional nine-term three year specialist degree is still seen by many as the norm. It is worth remembering that the Robbins report, in recommending major expansion, looked to a diversification of degrees which would not simply reproduce on a mass scale an education that had been designed for a small academic elite.

It is not for the Government to determine the structure or content of courses. That would be inimical to academic freedom and indeed would run counter to progress towards a more market-orientated system. Nevertheless, I hope that the expansion of student numbers in the 1990s will continue to be accompanied by innovation in course design, with an emphasis on greater flexibility. It should be for students, employers and institutions to judge whether new modes of provision would suit them better than more traditional courses.

Alan Howarth MP, Higher Education Quarterly, 1991

this already, if not directly. Nor that it might lead to the privatisation of some universities in the American model. The real problem lies with the fact that the additional revenue generated by this process for particular institutions might encourage any Government to subtract it from the quantum available from the public purse for all institutions, thus impoverishing the majority of institutions who may not be in a market position to charge these fees.

731.   The opposition to 'top-up' fees for full-time students has so far been broadly-based, yet it would be disingenuous of us if we did not point to some anomalies in this. As the Ministerial reference makes clear (Table 41), institutions are free to charge their own fees if they wish, and many already do so for certain types of students. For example, many universities charge 'top-up' fees for part-time programmes where they believe they can command the market. The fees charged for MBA programmes often involve supplementary levies above the regular institutional rate. As institutions have become more commercially sensitive, premiums (and some discounts) have been charged on specific modules or clusters of modules. Pricing strategies for short-course programmes have always been managed in this manner. Furthermore, as Continuing Education departments bring their courses into accreditation in order to attract funding council support, and as their institutions turn to them for business plans to support non-fundable programmes, they will have to consider a form of 'top-up' fee for many extra-mural programmes. In other words, the practice of charging 'top-up' fees is already with us. The further development of credit systems will make it even easier to create relatively sophisticated pricing strategies which are sensitive to demands for specific modules. This will have consequences both for external market management, and for internal market relationships.

732.   However, it is apparent that 'top-up' fees and other alternative funding mechanisms do have consequences for access, mobility and flexibility. We have provided a comparison and evaluation of various higher education funding models in Table 42 and Table 43. These have been adapted from the report of the *London Economics* group, commissioned by the

CVCP (1993). As they show, most funding models do involve some element of loan, a practice which is common throughout Europe, America and Australia. Repayment methods vary and default rates are high in many cases. The consequences for course structure, student mobility and credit transfer are unclear. In fact, on this subject, the London Economics report raises more questions than it answers when it observed:

'Credit accumulation and transfer schemes are being considered (and) the implications for funding of higher education must be considered also. With the present system, fees are charged for each year the student attends; lower fees are charged for part-time than for full-time. But with a more flexible course structure, the unit of account may need to change: if different courses are taken at different universities, the universities should then charge for the courses taken. The details of student fee and loan schemes would need to be carefully specified… If a student takes two years off to work in the middle of a degree, does she start paying back the part of the loan she has incurred? Costs of courses would have to be accounted for, as they are incurred at different institutions.'

733.   The picture of student behaviour painted by the *London Economics* report is more mobile and interrupted than we have in mind for the average case, yet it does confirm the pattern outlined in this report. In our opinion, the solution lies in tying a funding policy to a credit system. The currency of credit provides a unique instrument for coping with precisely the diversity of provision that is being anticipated in both reports. We turn now to proposals for flexibility in student maintenance.

Flexibility in student maintenance and attendance

Full-time student grants and loans

734.   The principal form of maintenance is the student mandatory award, providing a grant to all full-time students registered on a designated course leading to a higher education qualification. This system was proposed by the Anderson Committee (1962) when it anticipated that a maximum of

Scheme	Graduate Tax	Fees + Income Contingent Loan	Maintenance + Income Contingent Loan	'Top–up' fees + Fees + Income Contingent Loan
Who pays for HE?	Graduates pay, proportional to income; Government pays some	Graduate pays fraction; Government pays rest	Graduate pays fraction; Government pays rest	All students pay a fraction; some students pay 'top–up' fee
Any subsidies?	High–earning graduates subsidise low earners	Low-earning graduates subsidised by Government	Low-earning graduates subsidised by Government	Low-earning graduates subsidised by Government
Maintenance, tuition, or both?	Generally tuition only, but could cover both	Part of tuition fees	Part or all of maintenance	Part of tuition fees only
Loans: who provides?	Not a loan	Government, or private (banking) sector	Government, or private (banking) sector	Government, or private (banking) sector
Loans: repaid?	Not a loan	Income Tax, or NICs	Income Tax, or NICs	Income Tax, or NICs
Must student repay all loan?	Additional tax is permanent	Yes, if salary passes threshold	Yes, if salary passes threshold	Yes, if salary passes threshold
Insurance and sanctions against default?	Not a loan; no default on tax possible	Government; default = lose degree?	Government; default = lose degree?	Government; default = lose degree?
Where do funds go?	To Government	To universities as part of fee	To Government	To universities as part of fee
Who sets fees?	Government	Government	Government	Government sets basic fee; universities set 'top-up' premiums
Implications for access, student choice and mobility	Would be neutral on access; might stimulate course diversity; could impede transfer between different types of course	Positive for access, but perceived debt burden; good for diversity; and arrangements transferable between courses	Positive for access, but perceived debt burden; neutral for course diversity; positive for student transfer	Negative for access to some institutions; positive on course diversity; positive on transferability

Source: Adapted from the 'London Economics' report, A Review of Options for the Additional Funding of Higher Education, (CVCP, 1993)

	Graduate Tax	Fees + Income Contingent Loan	Maintenance + Income Contingent Loan	'Top–up' Fees + Fees + Income Contingent Loan
Table 43: An assessment of funding schemes against selected criteria				
Revenue	****	***	**	***
Access	**	***	***	**
Equity	**	***	**	**
Flexibility	*	***	***	***
Compatibility across course types	*	***	****	***
Diversity of provision of courses	***	***	**	****
Acceptability to parents	***	***	****	**
Acceptability to students	*	**	**	*
Administration costs = low	****	***	***	***
Transparency	*	***	**	**
Compatibility with European practice	*	***	***	***

Poor =   *   Fair =   **   Good =   ***   Very Good = ****

Source: 'London Economics' report, A Review of Options for the Additional Funding of Higher Education, (CVCP, 1993)

223

175,000 students would be eligible for the grant. By 1992, the number of mandatory award holders had risen to nearly 600,000, representing a 73% increase during the last decade alone. There were a further 200,000 discretionary award holders, representing a similar % increase over the period (DFE, 1993). The value of this award has been frozen since 1990 at £2,265 (with London allowance, £2,980 in 1993). Since that time, full-time students have been invited to take out a 'top-up' loan of a maximum £800 (£945 in London). The total cost to the Exchequer of mandatory student maintenance in 1992 was £860 million, with a further £541 million forthcoming from parental assessed contributions. There was a cost of £150 million for non-mandatory and discretionary awards. Throughout the 1980s, the value of the student grant fell well behind the Retail Price Index. By 1993 the student grant and loan combined had recovered to 98% of RPI although the grant element alone had declined to 75% of RPI. This does not tell the whole story, of course. Firstly, many students do not receive the full parental contribution to their grant. Up to 40% of students fall into this category, experiencing an average 14% shortfall (Barr & Low, 1988). Secondly, the withdrawal of eligibility for housing benefit and Income Support has continued to produce a net deterioration in the financial position of most full-time students.

735.   Since 1990, full-time students have been eligible to take out 'top-up' loans. The number of students choosing to take out a loan has doubled between 1990 and 1993 from 180,300 to 345,300; the % of eligible students taking out the loan has risen from 28% to 41%. The average loan has risen from £388 in 1990 to £656 in 1993. Total expenditure on loans is currently £226.5 million. Female students remain significantly less likely to take out a loan (at 75% of the male rate), and older students (aged 40+) are the least likely of all to take advantage of the facility. The propensity to take out a loan does not appear to be influenced by social class (DFE, 1994). We estimate that some £300 million of loan payments remains unclaimed by eligible students. At a current APR of 3.9%, this represents a substantial neglected resource which might be put to better use.

736.   We are also aware that fundamental modification to the principles and practice of student loans is not currently a subject for policy discussion. Indeed there are signs that a consensus is beginning to emerge in support of 'top-up' loans, which are in any event common throughout Europe and North America (Farrell & Tapper, 1992). Whatever the merit or otherwise of a Graduate Tax or similar scheme, Government appears not to be persuaded and has indicated its intentions to continue with a loan arrangement for student maintenance. Moreover the CVCP itself has been unsettled by the unreliability of hypothecated taxation to deliver additional net resources to higher education.

737.   The lessons that are beginning to emerge from the experience of student loans suggests that students are becoming familiar with the need to manage a more diverse range of funding sources. The advantages and disadvantages of student loans, and their consequences for access, participation and choice, have been understood since the Robbins Report (1963). In favour are the arguments that, firstly, loans distribute the burden of payment for higher education from those who do not participate but pay through taxation to those who do participate and can repay subsequently through higher earnings; secondly, loans provide an incentive for students to take greater individual responsibility for their time in higher education, making it clearer to them that they should get the most out of what they are buying. On the other hand, the arguments against loans suggest, firstly, that the commercial advantages to the individual of higher education may be overstated: not all forms of higher education produce significant earnings differentials; and secondly, that students would be burdened with debt at the end of their programme, providing a disincentive for some to embark on higher education in the first place. Indeed the Robbins Report was particularly concerned at the possible effect of the loan system on female participation. With the chivalry of its time, the report commented:

'Where women are concerned, the effect might be either that British parents would be strengthened in *their age-long disinclination to consider their daughters to be as deserving of higher education as their sons, or that the eligibility for marriage of the more educated would be diminished by the addition to their charms of what would be in effect a negative dowry.'*

Extending the availability of loans to part-time students

738.	In the event, Robbins considered it untimely to recommend a loan system. This was almost certainly the correct decision at the time. An expansion of participation in higher education had yet to be achieved, and female participation significantly lagged behind that of males. Since then both general participation and the participation of women have increased substantially to the extent that Government has judged it possible to introduce a loan system by 1990. If 'top-up' loans are to continue as the principal source of supplementary support for student maintenance, then we have to consider whether their availability might be extended to categories other than full-time students. If our assessment is correct that £300 million of loan payments currently remains unclaimed, and accepting that the take-up rate amongst full-time students will increase still further over the next few years, there is still likely to be a substantial (notional) sum unclaimed which could be made available to other students. The most obvious candidates for the extended availability of loans are **part-time** students, and the process of opening up loans to part-time students might begin here. This should of course be without prejudice to the rights of full-time students for whom the arrangement currently provides in the first instance.

739.	Currently part-time students are expected to bear the full cost of their tuition fees, personal maintenance and educational materials. They may be able to take out personal loans in the conventional manner through the commercial banks but they would then be subject to commercial interest premiums. Under certain circumstances they have access to Career Development Loans, and the '21-hour Rule' exists as a discretionary concession to enable the pursuit of limited educational opportunities, subject to the unemployed student being available for work at any time. One of the problems in these circumstances is that the unemployed student remains liable for course fees (which may be discounted by many institutions) and cannot commit to the completion of the course if an offer of work is made. In short, the '21 hour Rule' assists access and participation for some unemployed students, but inhibits achievement and progression. It also provides no incentive, and possibly some disincentives, to institutions wishing to expand their part-time provision since students have no means of paying fees. Moreover, if funding council allocations are linked, as we have proposed, to some element of outcome-led formula, then the recruitment of part-time students from amongst the unemployed will suffer further.

740.	It is clear that, from the perspective of the Exchequer, part-time students are cheap; yet it is equally clear that little has been done to stimulate the growth of part-time higher education or to eliminate the disadvantages part-time students experience in terms of access to personal support and maintenance. The growth of credit systems, and the predicted assault on the hegemony of the full-time continuous course caused by likely student hardship, makes it timely to consider the best means to modify arrangements for the support of part-time students. Credit systems progressively blur the distinction between full-time and part-time programmes; **it is not the course itself, but the individual student, who is full-time or part-time.** Furthermore, as students move in and out of programmes over a period of time, financing their progress through the university, the distinctions begin to break down again.

741.	We are also convinced that it is timely to consider policy on the further promotion of part-time study opportunities. Recent constraints on the recruitment of full-time students suggest that some institutions would benefit by shifting their attention to the relatively neglected part-time market where no such recruitment restrictions have been imposed. This market is without any obvious form of stimulation at present. There are too few incentives to encourage student participation and too many financial barriers to overcome. Institutions are generally unable to generate a commercially viable market in areas outside management and some professions because of downward market pressure on fees. To assist progress in these matters, and for reasons of equity, **we recommend** that consideration be given as a matter of urgency to extending the availability of the student loan scheme to part-time students. **We recommend** also that this policy also be extended to the improperly named 'access' funds. The designation of this source of funding as an 'Access' fund is misleading; the alternative 'hardship' fund is stigmatising. **We recommend** instead that the fund should be known more suitably as a *Supplementary Support Fund*.

742.   We are aware that the implication of these recommendations is that a further 250,000 students will become eligible for student loans, many of them studying with the Open University. A further 740,000 continuing education students could possibly be drawn in as well. To avoid overburdening the administrative and financial resources available, **we recommend** that the loan scheme should be extended only to those students registered on programmes leading to a designated higher education qualification and **we recommend** that further thought be given to circumscribing the length of eligible course to exclude, in the first instance, short-cycle accredited programmes. **We recommend** that a credit-based formula could be used to define eligibility for participation in a student loan scheme; students contracting for programmes over a certain volume of credit would become eligible.

Incentives for short-course students

743.   It has been suggested for some time that incentives might be provided through the taxation system to stimulate participation in short-cycle retraining and updating. We have no original proposals to make here and reinforce the view that a system of tax credits or similar instruments would be one way of providing incentives for voluntary individual retraining. Similar arrangements are in place to stimulate participation on programmes leading to NVQs

and **we recommend** that such tax incentives should be extended generally to accredited short-cycle programmes in higher education, with a minimum agreed academic credit threshold consonant with a coherent academic or training programme. We believe that such a measure could be provided at modest cost, not merely to stimulate vocational retraining, but also to stimulate enhanced aspirations for lifelong learning through personal educational development.

Incentives to encourage individual initiatives in work-based learning for higher education

744.   We have pointed out in Chapter VII that some 30,000 'students' are pursuing higher education in the 'independent sector', including through programmes offered by corporate employers and public authorities. It is impossible to assess the actual volume of corporate learners engaged in unaccredited higher education-level training and development. The capacity for the accreditation of this experiential learning undertaken through employment is considerable and **we recommend** that appropriate individual incentives should be developed. These may take the form of taxation incentives of the type referred to above. In any event, there appears to be a cost-effective opportunity for stimulating an individual engagement with higher education through work which should not be passed up.

Transferability of student maintenance awards

745.   We return to the problems of flexibility for full-time students. We accept that it would be wholly unrealistic to call for the extension of mandatory awards to part-time students, and equally unrealistic to compromise the basic mandatory grant for full-time students who have no other apparent means of support. This type of levelling out of financial support arrangements would produce unacceptable disturbance to working relationships and is not justified by circumstances. Full-time students are likely to require styles of financial support which are different and relatively privileged compared with part-time students. Our task has been to remove some of the more glaring anomalies.

746.   To this effect, we regard it as both anomalous and anachronistic that an entitlement to a mandatory student award should be circumscribed by the Education Act (1962) as applying to continuous attendance at an institution. The regulation in the Act is sufficiently flexible to permit a student one change of mind over a chosen course, provided that a change of course is registered within fifteen months of the initial registration. This arrangement appears to be helpful to students if one begins from a perspective which assumes that a student naturally commits to one institution of higher education, *and should be expected to remain there continuously* except in unusual circumstances. We believe this is out of keeping with the reasonable expression of informed student choice and flexibility through credit transfer, and that the Education Act (1962) should be modified. We assess the matter as follows.

747.   There may be two good arguments why it is reasonable to maintain the legislation unamended. Firstly, it can be proposed on pragmatic grounds that continuous attendance at one institution is what students wish for, and expect. Their behaviour generally reflects the desire to complete what they begin at a single institution in the company of their friends and peers. Secondly, there are good academic and educational reasons why this should be the case. It is argued that a course of higher education should involve a sustained and disciplined engagement with a profound body of knowledge. Proficiency is acquired steadily over time and is achieved in some measure by wider interactions with the university community. The benefits of a course in higher education are derived from a regular engagement with functional competence combined with an essential cultural accumulation; this might not be so readily achieved through disrupted patterns of study over time, or at more than one institution. Therefore, it is suggested, the terms of the Act merely confirm professional judgements of natural and desirable academic behaviour.

748.   On the other hand, whilst 85% of full-time students currently do continue at a single institution, 15% do not; they may discontinue for a time, transfer intra-institutionally, or leave altogether. We have no way of knowing how many thousands of students embark on the wrong course, but continue sub-optimally because they cannot change for whatever reason. Secondly, there may be convincing academic and educational reasons why students should be encouraged to maintain a continuous relationship with one academic environment; we do not deny the appropriateness of this. However we can find no reason why this argument requires the buttress of regulatory impediment. If the academic argument is so compelling, let it be made to students and let them be the judge. Forcing students to remain at an institution because the mandatory award regulations require this seems to be no good reason at all.

749.   We can think of a number of circumstances in which existing regulations on this matter make a nonsense of flexibility and student choice. Firstly, a full-time student may successfully complete two years at one university but, because of changed circumstances, need to transfer to another to complete a qualification. It cannot be guaranteed that the maintenance award would transfer with her, even if the receiving institution were prepared to accept the transfer into a final year. Secondly, in the future, we may anticipate that students will follow a more interrupted pattern of study, exploiting the flexibility of modular and semester-based structures to negotiate their way through a chosen programme. A 'full-time' student might accumulate credit towards a degree by successfully completing six semesters during a period of eight semesters. If this pattern of study were undertaken at one institution, the regulations might accommodate it; if the programme involved a semester at another university for whatever reason, the regulations would not. Thirdly, in Chapter VII we recommended the development of pilot inter-institutional programmes to exploit local expertise efficiently. The regulations on student maintenance could cope with inter-institutional mobility if the student remains registered with the initial institution; if the registration for qualification changes, these conditions do not meet the regulations.

750.   Accordingly, **we recommend** that the Education Act (1962) be amended with respect to the regulations concerning student mandatory awards to permit the transferability of the student grant with the individual student, irrespective of single or initial institutional registration, and in a manner tolerant of limited interrupted study. The sole measure of a student programme, against which a mandatory award is offered, should be the degree to which any institution is able to satisfy itself that the academic quality of the student programme is assured and is leading to a designated higher education qualification. We accept that certain restrictions must apply, for example, to the duration of eligibility for the award. It would not be helpful at the same time to recommend any weakening of the restrictions on entitlement to a mandatory award. Whilst we wish to see the regulations facilitate and promote the credit transfer of students from lower to higher qualifications, we would not wish to encourage an exploitation of the flexibility our recommendations should achieve by increasing the net burden on the Exchequer of additional maintenance payments. The purpose of the recommendation is to remove unnecessary barriers to the expression of informed student choice, thus aiding credit transfer where this is desired, rather than implying greater cost.

751.   The benefits of this amendment to the legislation may be substantial. It is possible that over time students will become more familiar with the potential for credit transfer between institutions. This may assist students in settling on the programme that is right for them. It may also encourage institutions to pay greater attention to ensuring that students are provided with programmes which suit their needs. At the moment mandatory award regulations lock students into institutions. This benefits institutions by stabilising their student numbers but it may also make them complacent about providing the best possible service to their students. By removing the regulatory restrictions, universities could find themselves competing for the retention of students in ways which might have productive benefit for quality improvement in the sector. Moreover, students would be more able to assert their requirements for relevant high quality programmes because they would be free

of the constraints imposed by existing regulations. The recommendation proposes in effect an end to one aspect of restrictive practice in higher education.

Requirements on institutional residence and attendance

752.   There is one matter expressly in the gift of individual institutions to which we wish to draw attention. Universities and colleges retain within their statutes and ordinances various regulations concerning the requirements of students to be *in residence* at the institution for a defined period in order to qualify for its qualifications. This is most noticeable in the case of some ancient universities and is evident in all institutions as far as we are aware. There may be good reasons why these ordinances are constructed in this way. We have suggested earlier that universities often make a reasonable assumption that continuity of residence is the most effective means of ensuring consistency of intellectual progression within a disciplined scholarly environment. This is not the place to debate the monastic origins of the concept, nor to challenge outright the premises upon which it is based. Rather, we wish to draw attention to the restrictive practice which may be involved and to suggest that not all universities may need to subscribe to the restrictions in the same way. Many institutions may find it advantageous to define more liberally their residential requirements in order to encourage the credit transfer of students.

753.   **We recommend** therefore that institutions, individually, consider appropriate modifications to their statutes, ordinances or other regulations to permit the greatest possible flexibility in the residential requirements necessary to qualify for an institutional qualification. We are aware that institutions have it in their power to *interpret* their regulations as sympathetically as they may wish in this regard, and for many this should remain the case. However, this practice does little for the general capacity of students to know what is available to them. If all institutions interpret their regulations on a case-by-case basis, it will be effectively impossible for students to plan a career of learning

opportunities. We are proposing that institutions should move, wherever possible, beyond the benign interpretation of regulations on these matters to state explicitly their requirements for a minimum period of institutional residence in order to meet the requirements for a qualification. We are sure that matters of quality assurance will feature prominently in these deliberations and we would welcome a wider discussion of a suitable minimum residential requirement.

Student maintenance, home-based institutional attendance and credit transfer

754.   As resources for student support tighten and individual students are forced into greater self-reliance to finance their progress through university or college, many more students may choose to attend their local university whilst remaining in the parental home. This is already the pattern generally established for large numbers of older students with children or with local family ties. Clearly, the savings to the Exchequer in the costs of maintenance awards and capital investment in student accommodation would be enormous. We would anticipate that the gradual effects of student hardship may result in some pressure on students to modify their aspirations for residential higher education. This might happen in either of two directions. Firstly, students may embark on a university course based on residential attendance, successfully complete their academic programme over the first year or two, but incur unacceptable financial difficulties which perhaps necessitate their return to the parental home. It would be hugely advantageous to the student in these circumstances if they were then able to transfer academic credit and complete their qualification at their 'home' university. Secondly, other students may initially be more cautious and begin at their local institution. After a year or so, their financial position and personal aspirations may be such that they would welcome the opportunity to leave the parental home for a period of study elsewhere in the United Kingdom. Again credit transfer, flexible institutional regulations and a more responsive student maintenance system would enormously assist such students.

755.   Despite our observations that student hardship may force changes in the way in which students choose their university place, we would not wish to jettison one of the most valuable experiences a student can receive in higher education in the United Kingdom. The decision to leave the parental home, usually at 18+, and negotiate life in a distant town or city is for many students an enduring experience which they will value throughout their lives. It would be difficult to over-estimate the skills of independence and self-discovery that students acquire as a result of this, and we would not wish to constrain the rights of students in this respect. However, circumstances will vary for individuals and it would be our hope that opportunities for credit transfer and improved administrative flexibility amongst institutions will create an environment in which students can exercise choices and take decisions appropriate to their individual needs. If for no other reason, **we recommend** on principle that all regulations governing student mobility, attendance and maintenance be inspected to establish whether they encourage flexibility or unnecessarily impede prospects for inter-institutional credit transfer and informed student choice.

Full-time courses or full-time students?

756.   We cannot leave this section of the discussion without raising one further significant matter. We made reference earlier to the distinction to be drawn between full-time courses and full-time students. Current legislation covering the entitlement to a mandatory grant requires a student to be registered on a *full-time course leading to a higher education qualification*. In modular and credit-based institutional programmes, it is becoming increasingly unclear how the identity of 'the course' may be defined. Full-time and part-time variants become intertwined with work-based internships, professional placements and periods of independent study or open learning opportunities. It has become archaic to describe 'the course' as full-time; the student's contract of attendance is now important.

757.   The situation is made less clear by the absence of any adequate definition of a full-time student. The Department of the

Environment has a definition for the purposes of Council Tax legislation and the Department of Social Security works with one to define entitlement to welfare benefit. However the Department for Education does not possess a definition, and would not intend to develop one for fear of disturbing the rights of institutions to decide what is or is not 'full-time'. In short, a 'full-time student' is a student registered on a 'full-time course', and a 'full-time course' is whatever a university claims it to be, providing the funding council agrees to fund it as such. For its part, the HEFCE defines full-time mode of study as an attendance requirement of *more than 18 weeks for an average of at least 21 hours a week* in a consecutive 12 month period (HEFCE HESES Circular, Annex F, 1993). At a minimum attendance level of under 400 hours, this requirement would fall below the attendance levels registered by many part-time degree students in some universities.

758.   We do not find this particularly helpful and anticipate that it may lead to complications in the future, especially if students do engage in systematic interrupted, or mixed mode study. **We recommend** that the Education Act (1962) and the Education (Mandatory Awards) Regulations (1993) and other relevant legislation be amended to define more closely what is meant by a full-time student. Currently this is described in terms of a minimum period of continuous attendance, but we would favour a credit-based and a semester-based definition. For example, in the credit framework model we are recommending elsewhere in this report (see Chapter IX), a full-time student would undertaken 30 credits per annum (CNAA = 120). To allow some latitude and flexibility, **we recommend** that a full-time student be defined as one registered to undertake 24 credits or more (CNAA = 96) in a year, or 12 credits or more in a semester (CNAA = 48). From this definition, a 'full-time' student would need to receive tuition equal to 24 hours or more each week for a minimum 30-week academic year. In practice, this tuition will be distributed more or less evenly across the period, but for the sake of flexibility and student choice in a modular and semester-based environment, some imbalance could be tolerated. We accept that this approach gives an expectation of 'attendance' for full-time

students well in excess of the current HEFCE minimum requirements. Moreover, **we recommend** that the legislation be amended to permit limited interrupted study without prejudice to the full-time status of the student. **We recommend** that students be permitted to complete a typical three-year honours degree (of six semesters) over a period of eight continuous semesters. Pro rata arrangements should also be made for designated shorter qualifications.

Conclusions

759.   The proposals we make in this chapter are far-reaching, but necessary, if we are to make student choice the centrepiece of higher education in the United Kingdom. The recommendations are not beyond our means. Those which concern the funding councils may be implemented without prejudice to the desire of institutions to arrange their academic programmes more traditionally. We have no doubt that many students will be happy with conventional specialist degrees and will continue to prosper in the labour market. On the other hand, the development of credit-based and modular programmes is now so well advanced that we may justly anticipate that they will become the norm across the sector over the next few years. Funding councils will need to consider their response to these proposals in the light of this observation.

760.   Secondly, credit-led solutions for the distribution of sector resources seem to be the most appropriate means of achieving a fair and rational funding model. We remain disappointed that we cannot formally resolve the allegiances to different definitions of credit. We have however made it clear that we favour a simple and educationally credible system of credit, with a unit of account based on the 30-hour unit, and yielding a 30-credit full-time year. We emphasise that decisions on these matters by funding councils will be heavily influential in determining the outcome of this problem.

761.   Finally, we are keen to recommend the proposals concerning increased student financial flexibility. Some of these will require

primary legislation and we recognise that this will not be easily or quickly forthcoming. However, it will not be possible to make significant further progress in promoting student choice and flexibility unless some modifications are made to existing regulations. Moreover, some decisions will need to be made about the balance to be struck between the rights of full-time students and the needs of part-time students. Currently we feel that circumstances so favour full-time students that a review of support for part-time students would not prejudice their overall entitlements in a period of limited resources.

Recommendations and guidance for future policy

On a credit-based funding methodology

To funding councils in higher education, HESA and Government

63   In the light of the need to introduce greater precision, efficiency and accountability into funding allocation and distribution decisions, **we recommend** that funding councils in higher education and beyond develop a common credit tariff system in line with the proposals for a common credit currency outlined in this report. Such a credit tariff arrangement would introduce greater evenness and equity into the funding arrangements for full-time and part-time programmes, and allow both institutions and funding bodies to develop helpful performance indicators.

64   **We recommend** that the development of a credit tariff basis for funding allocation be the opportunity to assess the merits of an achievement-related element in the formula. Further consultations with institutions should include consideration of this matter.

65   The distinction between full-time and part-time programmes is becoming less meaningful with the further development of credit systems, and will become more unclear as patterns of student attendance change. **We recommend** that, for the purposes of funding council decisions, the emphasis should change from the funding of students on full-time courses to the funding of students according to their credit-based learning agreements. Students' programmes may need to be distinguished by credit volume over time as *intensive* or *extensive* programmes.

66   To increase the discretion available to institutions in the management of allocated funds, and to discourage the use of internal cost centres as barriers to student mobility, **we recommend** that the funding councils reduce the number of Academic Subject Categories and other funding categories to a minimum, in line with the proposals in this report, and undertake a reapportionment exercise accordingly.

67   The existence of tuition fee bands acts as a considerable impediment to the ability of institutions to encourage internal mobility for students. **We recommend** that further consideration be given to how the objectives delivered by fee-banding might be delivered through other means, without prejudice to improved student flexibility.

68   **We recommend** that the Higher Education Statistics Agency and the funding councils develop methodologies for the monitoring of student numbers which are compatible with the use of credit-based formulae for the recording of student programmes.

69   **We recommend** that both HESA and funding councils monitor student behaviour in academic programmes, encouraging institutions wherever possible to report student numbers in a way which reflects actual student behaviour. **We recommend** furthermore that institutions which are capable of this detailed reporting should in no way be disadvantaged by funding methodologies as a consequence of this.

On improving flexibility for student fees and maintenance

To Government

70 **We recommend** that further consideration be given, in the light of observations in this report, to how students might be directly empowered as purchasers of higher education through a system of credit-based educational vouchers or a similar managed arrangement in the form of an educational variant of the Training Credits Scheme.

71 To improve opportunities for students and create more equitable access, **we recommend** that legislation concerning the availability of student loans should be amended to include provision for part-time students registered for higher education awards as specified in this report.

72 For similar reasons **we recommend** that 'Access' funds be renamed as Supplementary Support Funds and made available to part-time students as well.

73 To improve prospects and incentives for personal retraining and upskilling, **we recommend** that income tax arrangements should be modified to permit tax relief from fees for students registered for accredited short-course programmes as part of a personal programme of work-related education or training. **We recommend** that similar discretion should also be used to provide incentives to engage in accredited in-company training at a higher education level.

74 To end arrangements which appear to be inappropriate and anachronistic, **we recommend** that the Education Act (1962) be amended to provide for the transferability of the student mandatory award with the individual student, permitting credit transfer between institutions over time. **We recommend** that the Act be further amended to allow students limited interrupted study without prejudice to their entitlement to a mandatory award.

75 To clarify eligibility to entitlements, **we recommend** that the Education Act (1962) and the Education (Mandatory Awards) Regulations (1993) be amended to include provision for a definition of a full-time student and other relevant categories. **We recommend** that a credit-based formula could prove useful and should be further considered as a basis for defining the obligations of students in these matters.

76 **We recommend** that the payment of tuition fees and maintenance grants should be brought in line with the extensive availability of semesters, amending the relevant legislation as appropriate.

77 **We recommend** that the responsibility for the payment of tuition fees for higher education students should no longer lie with local education authorities, and **we recommend** that the funding councils be invited to discharge this responsibility. Furthermore, **we recommend** that consideration be given to whether it is any longer appropriate for local authorities to be responsible for the payment of student mandatory awards, and whether an alternative authority might be nominated for this purpose.

78 In pursuit of greater flexibility and efficiency in the management of student finance, **we recommend** that all relevant legislation be inspected with a view to ensuring that its provisions are in line with the extension of personal student choice, mobility and flexibility in higher education and beyond.

XII. *Managing flexibility*

Introduction

762.　In many of the preceding chapters, we have considered the further promotion of student choice and flexibility in terms of factors which affect the higher education sector as a whole. In this chapter, attention is directed at the management of flexibility within individual institutions, to intra-institutional choice and mobility. This follows naturally from the earlier discussions. In Chapter VIII we considered the different meanings which colleagues and institutions attach to the terms 'credit' and 'modularity'. From our investigations, we have found that this is reflected in the different ways institutions have responded managerially and organisationally. In Chapters IX and X, we have analysed the development of a credit framework and future quality assurance arrangements on the assumption that individual institutions will be free to determine their individual responses to these proposals. Where institutions wish to work actively with credit systems, this will have consequences for how institutions organise themselves and the student experience. And in Chapter XI, in discussing prospects for credit-based funding strategies, we have made it clear that this will have significant consequences for decisions on the internal distribution of resources in cases where institutions wish to respond to student choices.

763.　Throughout the investigation, we have been made aware by colleagues of the relative lack of information within the sector on how institutions might practically solve the problems they meet in the process of transforming their institutions to a more flexible and student-centred environment. There is very little literature which gives practical guidance relevant to individual institutional circumstances. One of the few helpful sources available in the United Kingdom (Watson, 1989) describes the particular features of one kind of arrangement – the joint honours modular scheme at Oxford Brookes University. Whilst this narrative, and the scheme upon which it is based, have been influential in pointing out some practical problems and their possible solutions, it has not always been possible to generalise from this account to the wide variety of conditions which obtain in other institutions. This has left most institutions with the need to cope independently with changes.

764.　This may not have been so unproductive as may appear at first. In seeking their own solutions, often by building on the lessons of others, institutions may have arrived at solutions which suit their individual circumstances. From our investigations we are aware that the complex developments involved in moving an institution towards greater flexibility, through credit-based and modular systems, usually involves a combination of committed and inventive individuals being drawn together at the right time with appropriate resources. This coalition of forces and resources is often unique to an institution, and the success of the undertaking usually depends both on the skills of individuals in negotiating the 'political' environment of their organisation and on the maintenance of clear and stable authority roles. Where initiatives lose momentum or direction, it is apparent to us that this will often be caused, less by a failure of individuals to understand the complexities of the transformation but by the failure of the organisation collectively to marshal its resources to the desired end.

765.　In this respect, there will be lessons in the management of change that universities can learn from other organisations in the commercial and public sectors. The literature and case study material is more extensive although the problems of translation into the circumstances and cultures of higher education remain. What we propose to offer in this chapter, however, is some guidance on the problems and possible solutions which have been identified as a consequence of our

Table 44: The educational advantages of credit-based modularisation: an assessment		
	The aspirations	**The practice**
Access, flexibility, and choice	Greater flexibility in the combination of subjects and variety of pathways from which students can choose, leading via delayed choice to more individually relevant learning programmes	Accusation of lack of academic coherence leads to disciplinary closure; flexibility often more apparent than real
	An extension of part-time learning for students who cannot currently consider full-time modes of study because of their domestic, work or life circumstances, for whom part-time degree and Associate Student opportunities will be relevant	Few incentives currently exist to expand part-time student numbers; some claims that there is no substantial unmet demand; teaching may involve 'unsocial' hours
	The accreditation and incorporation of continuing education and professional development programmes within the mainstream portfolio of an institution	Does occur, but institutional inertia, defence of professional 'territory' and perceptions of marginality often prevent this
	An improvement in the number of entry points throughout the year as the academic programme moves to accommodate a 'roll-on, roll-off' flexibility	Little evidence of this practice yet, although some examples at Master's level. Reformed academic year largely untested
	An expansion in the range of open learning, distance learning and multi-media learning opportunities	Only in specialist enclaves; general progress slow, and resource expensive
	A growth in the numbers of students gaining credit through APEL and through work-based learning for academic credit via internships and outplacements	Substantial activity and enthusiasm, but no reliable data. Volume probably smaller than proponents would hope
	Closer collaboration between the modular programmes of higher education institutions and the in-house company training programmes of employers	Some significant examples, but practice is not yet widespread; issues of quality assurance remain substantial
Assessment and progression	The creation of an outcomes-led curriculum whereby students may have access to explicit statements about the achievement objectives of every module	Some significant progress, but often thwarted by conceptual issues, and suspicions of intrusion into professional academic autonomy
	A closer connection between assessment and the learning experience, resulting in creative assessment strategies	Conventional assessment practice still dominates; assessment rarely linked specifically to outcomes or objective standards
	An overall improvement in student progress, retention and the quality of final awards as students are able to monitor their achievement through regular assessment and modify their programmes in the light of achievement outcomes	Much asserted but no convincing evidence yet. Could be an arena for further work. Inherent dangers that students will use freedom to make 'tactical' assessment decisions
	An increase in the availability of interim and staged awards: certificates, diploma and CPD awards	Yes, but infrequently taken up as interim awards. Need for strong interim award
	The provision of transcripts and records of achievement for students, improving their visibility in the labour market and giving students regular progress feedback	Some progress on transcripts in a few institutions; need for national model. Also danger that transcript reveals 'islands of knowledge' in a 'sea of ignorance'
For academics and students	Greater independence, enterprise, and purpose amongst students as regular choices encourage students to engage in forward programme planning, independent learning with established learning contracts	The 'cultural and educational dividend'; virtues largely asserted but yet unproven in either labour market success or improved personal development
	An improvement in the quality of teaching as academic staff adopt a more imaginative approach to student learning, to programme construction and curriculum development, to delivery and assessment strategies and to curriculum objectives.	Evidence of this in the USA where process is understood to enhance individual academic autonomy. Slow progress in the UK and an absence of performance and quality indicators with which to support a judgement

Source: Table constructed from D.Robertson (1992), 'Higher Education: Expansion and Reform', IPPR; D.Watson (1989), 'Managing the Modular Course', SRHE; and evidence collected during the project

investigations. We can do no more than indicate the generality of the matter, which inevitably will not include some particular finesses relevant to an individual institution. If this is useful, it may act as a starting point for the development of *Guidelines on modularity* which we recommended in Chapter X, and it may also help institutions position themselves appropriately in these matters.

Institutional objectives in the development of flexible systems

Educational objectives and mission-driven solutions

766.   Before we embark on an assessment of institutional responses to the challenge of credit systems, we need firstly to establish what is being sought after in these matters. We have spent considerable time in earlier chapters emphasising the importance to be attached to the fulfilment of educational and academic objectives in the further pursuit of credit-based modularity. In Chapter VI, the review of progress in higher education reveals a regular commitment through the 1970s and 1980s to solutions driven by the 'Access movement'. Even before 1987, and certainly afterwards, many institutions embraced credit-based and modular systems as a means of supporting wider participation. These principled and 'mission-driven' approaches to institutional change usually involved a meeting of two forces: enthusiasm and commitment from a (small) group of academics, combined with formal sponsorship of initiatives from the strategic apex of the university or college. The outcome was one or more of the structural arrangements which are described later.

767.   In Table 44, we offer a summary of the arguments that have been generally advanced in support of the educational advantages of greater choice and flexibility, with an assessment of the practical outcomes in the light of subsequent experience. In fairness, it must be said that a convincing breakthrough has not yet been made in the creation of institutions adequately organised to cope with

flexibility and increased student choice. Some significant progress has been made towards various educational objectives but there remains substantial scepticism amongst many academic colleagues either that students necessarily welcome more choice and freedom, or that the proposed instruments will deliver this to them. Some of this scepticism may be professional self-serving from academic staff resistant to the erosion of their personal autonomy; others may be eliding their scepticism over the managerial consequences of the changes (see below) with the educational objectives (to which they might otherwise not object). A final group will draw some support from the mixed rate of progress in maintaining the momentum of change. In this, they point to the apparent changes in Government policy since 1992, and to inconsistencies in the Missions of some institutions in post-binary higher education, leading them to believe that the entire enterprise has been a passing phase. We do not take this view ourselves, but we are aware from the results of the investigation from different institutions that the educational objectives need to be constantly reinforced by consistent management action and staff development.

Management objectives and resource-driven solutions

768.   It would be disingenuous of us not to recognise that managerial considerations often feature prominently in institutional decisions to move to structures which allow greater flexibility and student choice. In a funding climate since the late 1980s which encourages greater competition for students between institutions and greater accountability for costs at the individual budget centre, it would be natural for institutions to respond pragmatically to protect themselves in the new marketplace. We have looked at some of these matters in Chapter XI.

769.   Accordingly, the further development of credit-based systems may be approached from the perspective of improved resource efficiency and management control, whether or not a credit-based funding methodology is developed. Institutional strategies have tended to emphasise the

Table 45: An assessment of the advantages for management control of credit-based modularisation		
	The claims	**The practice**
Institutional funding advantages	The management of *resource acquisition* strategies can be achieved with greater sophistication and precision, establishing a rational basis for an internal *resource distribution* strategy; students can be represented in terms of *net credit* full-time equivalents. Resources can be distributed to cost centres according to patterns of student choice. Defining students in terms of credits also allows the distinction between types of student (full-time and part-time) to disappear over time	Whilst this may be the case in due course, no such credit-based funding systems exists, and proposals have to be fully explored before they could apply across the sector. Some models do operate within institutions but they often meet impediments because of the protectionism of internal academic cost centres. Moreover, unless means are agreed for releasing the capacity of students to act as purchasers, academic providers will continue to shape patterns of student behaviour in familiar ways
	Improved financial stability for institutions. Student recruitment is very responsive to multi-choice schemes and in a fee-driven environment, such responsiveness may be crucial. Many institutions will survive only through diversification	No clear evidence yet that students do prefer multi-choice opportunities. Evidence that some modular courses are popular, but if there are many modular courses, where will the advantage lie? Moreover, successful recruitment may be a stabilising force but unsuccessful or uneven recruitment can produce turbulence and instability
Performance indicators and management information	Comprehensive management information systems are required to support the complex academic programme and monitor patterns of student choice, facilitating the development of sensitive performance control systems and performance indicators, in turn informing decisions on quality improvement and the strategic direction of institutions	Certainly true, but complexity of variables and difficulties in implementing solutions has impeded progress (viz. MAC initiative). Also, whilst institutions may value information for their own purposes, they may be less ready to commit to its wider availability to funding councils and others; cf. the problems of publishing 'death rates' in hospitals
Management of academic resources	The management of high SSRs and the deployment of academic staff is made more efficient by the reduction of duplicate teaching; modules may be shared by a number of pathways/routes and made available to larger groups of students	The evidence is mixed. There is some support for the efficiency argument in that modular schemes do attempt to minimise duplication; on the other hand, subject areas generally seek to retain control over their own modules (and thus students), leading to duplication in certain areas (eg IT, mathematics, etc)
	Time spent redesigning entire courses is significantly reduced; it is much easier to replace particular modules within an overall scheme than to replace the entire programme	This appears to be accepted in certain limited cases. However, quality assurance arrangements continue to treat with the unified course rather than the discrete module, making the development of individual modules less possible
	Academic staff time may be directed more efficiently to the core academic functions of teaching, assessment, guidance and research through the development of co-ordinating administrative arrangements	This may be more the case in ex-UFC universities, with their well-established administrative traditions, than in ex-PCFC institutions, where administration as a mature professional activity is less well-developed and academic staff continue to bear routine administrative burdens
Centralisation and devolution of responsibility	Considerable organisational and administrative advantages are achieved by the co-ordination of various functions (timetabling, accommodation, admissions, enrolments, programme information, advice and guidance, assessment, and the issuing of awards/transcripts)	Schemes do tend to centralise efficiently; structures do not necessarily. Institutions which historically and by inclination tend towards devolved responsibility do not naturally embrace centralised procedures. Efficiencies which might otherwise accrue are often negated by the duplication of effort in various 'devolved' and sub-organisational settings. Evidence suggests that current ideological treatments of organisations may be influencing decisions in these matters

Source: Table constructed from D.Robertson (1992), 'Higher Education: Expansion and Reform', IPPR and evidence collected during research for the project (1993)

advantages that modularisation bestows upon the management control system rather than for the expression of student choice and mobility. The driving forces have tended to be administrative rather than academic. They have reflected a concern to manage increased (rather than wider) participation with diminishing resources. Institutional administrators have found common cause with senior institutional managers in the use of curriculum fragmentation to produce rationalisations in the deployment of resources and, arguably, allowing them to break into the 'secret garden' of professional academic control. Again we have taken a more benign and less conspiratorial view of these developments, believing them to be necessary steps in the modernisation of higher education in the United Kingdom; an assessment of the various resource-led advantages is contained in Table 45. Nevertheless, it is easy to

---

Table 46:
A dichotomy of objectives in the pursuit of choice and flexibility

Educational Focus	Managerial Focus
Principled	Pragmatic
Idealist (Values)	Realist (Resources)
Wider Access	Increased Access
Transformation	Rationalisation
Effectiveness	Efficiency
Greater Choice	Greater Flexibility
Greater autonomy for students	Less autonomy for academics
'Bottom-up'	'Top-down'
Tolerant of turbulence	Search for stability
Student-centred	Institution-centred
Negotiative	Directive
Cultures changed	Cultures confirmed

---

understand how these strategies have been interpreted by many academic colleagues as an attempt at professional 'de-skilling' and disempowerment.

770   In Table 46, we have attempted to show how the different forces might be aligned. Inevitably this over-schematises the true picture; educational and managerial approaches are never in reality as mutually exclusive as the table seems to propose. However, our investigations have led us to the conclusion that by no means all universities currently undergoing modular changes share the educational objectives of greater student choice, wider access and more direct student empowerment. It would be tempting to suggest that the 'older' universities remain generally cautious on these matters whilst the 'new' universities have embraced the new cultural conditions enthusiastically and inventively. Unfortunately, it is not nearly so clearly defined as this. Largely, the ex-UFC institutions seek to protect their strengths in research, which tempers their commitment to developments which might compromise this. On the other hand, many ex-PCFC institutions, having led the way in relevant developments, now seem confused about how to define their engagement with further developments.

771.   As the shape of the unified sector unfolds, would a university which commits extensively to diversification, student choice and flexibility be improving or prejudicing its market position in a higher education of the future dominated by concerns over quality, student-centred tuition fees and maintenance, and a greater emphasis upon multiple funding sources? Many institutions look to Government signals and funding council priorities for the answer. Currently the messages appear to be mixed: government reins back recruitment whilst continuing to press more competition for funds; and funding councils emphasise the importance of diverse institutional Missions whilst rewarding conventional teaching and protecting established research centres. Perhaps institutional responses to the development of management structures reflect this general uncertainty. In the next section, we turn to how institutions have chosen to respond.

Institutional solutions to managed flexibility and greater choice

772.   We mentioned earlier the coalition of *forces and resources* that determined the unique response to change of individual institutions. From our investigations, we have identified the following significant factors (see Table 47).

Table 47: Factors influencing the outcomes of institutional change

Leadership commitment	A necessary but not sufficient factor. Without it, change does not begin; with it, change may start, but stall if commitment perceived to be 'on loan'. Change fails if commitment is not identical with support under pressure and attention to detail when needed
Timescale and scope of change	'Do you want it right? Or do you want it Thursday?' The pace of change is crucial and change agents need to be able to vary the pace without incurring loss of leadership support. Evidence favours both incremental and 'Big Bang' approaches: the former for a quieter life
Current developments within institution	Two factors: 1) if institutions already have limited experience of modular structures, this helps; 2) if institutions are undergoing major parallel change, this hinders progress,strains resources
Availability of resources	Scale must be understood and agreed in advance, then delivered on time. Broken promises mean the end of trust and commitment. Unforeseeable claims must be supported *in extremis*
Availability of personnel with expertise	After leadership commitment, the most important factor. Right kind of skills and commitments must be assembled. Expertise must be valued and rewarded with appropriate status and authority
Organisation and support for change agents	Change agents need teams,authority and reliable support, including resources. Institutional leadership needs to prepare the policy environment and support the agreed implementation strategy
Staff development needs	This will involve more than just technical training; academic and administrative staff are affected, no matter what the scale of the changes
Agreement on objectives	Many change strategies start with one set of objectives but end elsewhere due to lack of institutional clarity on the preferred end state. Successful change requires clearly stated goals

Change by sap or by storm?

773.   There appears to be no clear evidence from our investigations on the most effective way to 'take the citadel'. It may be taken 'by sap' or 'by storm' (Kiloh, 1991) and most colleagues assume that the former is the more effective in the longer term. They may be right. The careful negotiation of change runs with the cultural grain of higher education and changes, once agreed, are likely to be enduring. In any event, universities do not yield that readily to change 'by storm', lacking both the propensity to comply in this manner and the managerial instruments with which to effect compliance. On the other hand, sapping the strength of the resistance can take a long time and runs against the grain of a new managerial culture. Moreover some institutions may need to make changes quickly, either to catch up with competitors or to establish themselves in an appropriate market segment. Proceeding 'by storm' can be effective to the extent that enough progress may be made quickly, before the resistance has had time to regroup, securing permanent change in organisational affairs which thereafter become the new norm of operation. The trade-off between negotiated and adversarial forms of change will be determined by the importance an institution attaches to the pace of change and the preparedness of both institutional leaders and individual change agents to tolerate varying degrees of turbulence in the pursuit of agreed objectives.

Impediments to successful change

774.   There is currently a view that some institutions are moving into 'CATS' and modularity without having carefully appraised what this means for them, or reviewed the options, or considered the implications for resources and professional relationships. One of the ramifications of this is that many current developments are seen by institutional colleagues, academic and administrative, as top-down and hasty. This raises the issue of how best to introduce credit and modularity. Like other debates, this has tended to centre around a

series of, sometimes misleading, dichotomies about how change is managed: big-bang vs incremental; top-down vs grass roots; central vs devolved. For example, the introduction of an institutional credit scheme is going to be, by definition, top-down, centralised, and more than likely in the current climate, 'big-bang'. On the other hand, smaller ' CATS' initiatives have often been started in a fairly low-key, minimalist way and introduced as an alternative to the mainstream educational provision, particularly for part-time, mature students. In short, whilst there are general lessons that can be learned about effective models for change, the most definitive element is what works best in local conditions.

775.   Having established that point, are there any common features which tend to prevent the changes agreed and desired by institutions? We have been able to identify several from the investigation. Of those shown in Table 48, our investigation suggests that the most common problems are, firstly, inconsistent attention and support from institutional leadership and secondly, an over-optimistic or over-reliant commitment to information systems. In the former case, problems can arise when institutional leadership treats the process of transformation as just another project to be managed. Under these conditions, it is understandable that the concentration of individuals moves from one 'project' to another. However experience suggests that changes of the kind released by the introduction of credit-based and modular systems are all-consuming, whether they are introduced as departmental, faculty or institutional arrangements. The impact on the organisation tends to reach beyond the immediate matters of academic restructuring. In many cases, the individuals responsible for change leadership (CATS Co-ordinators, course tutors etc) may not have been vested with the authority to follow the chain of consequences that are released by the initial proposals. They are even less likely to be responsible for securing the resources from other parts of the organisation which are needed to bring the strategy to a successful conclusion. In short, the consequences for the way the organisation behaves and presents itself are profound, requiring constant vigilance and support from the strategic centre.

776.   In the second case, complex transformations require complex systems to support them. Modern information systems are capable of supplying this service, if designed to the correct specifications and if developed under the right conditions. We have more to say about these matters later, but for the

Table 48: Factors inhibiting successful institutional change	
Leadership equivocation	The most damaging impediment. When institutional leadership loses interest or concentration, or lacks conviction, or changes strategic direction.
Failure to support under pressure	When change agents are sponsored but not defended at critical periods in the change process. Politicisation of institutional relations will impede progress and undermine initiatives.
Failure to prioritise resources	Embarking on changes without assessing competing calls on resources. 'Abandoning ship for want of a sail'
Absence of an adequate coalition of support	Failure to secure institutional alliances or failure to win academic and professional arguments; too many perceived losers v. too few winners
Gap between responsibility and authority	Common failure. Change agents expected to achieve transformation without adequate authority; blamed for failures
Lack of expertise or professional credibility	Failure to appreciate professional or technical aspects of change. Misjudgment of available resources
Pace of change in advance of institutional capacity to manage	Need to recognise that, however compelling the argument, organisations are people with a capacity to change or resist change. Leadership may possess neither the skills nor the resources required to assist change, and may not be that committed under pressure
Failure of technical systems	Insecure computer systems which lead to data errors encourage view that entire concept of change is flawed. Minor errors can be cumulative and damaging.
Lack of advance notification	Surprisingly frequent neglect of forward information. Students particularly may need a planning horizon over 18 months

moment it should be sufficient to point out that data processing can be the Achilles' heel of any movement towards credit-based systems. The main problems lie in designing and managing systems which accurately record student behaviour and report on it to managers and students themselves; and secondly, which handle data in a manner consistent with the preferred organisational structures of the university or college. Recording student transactions accurately is fundamentally important for purposes of accurate assessment, and can have consequences for the flow of resources as well. This accuracy may be impeded by the special demands of contributing sub-units to the overall process: individual departments may want to be exempted from certain arrangements. Moreover, the quality of the data will vary directly with the quality of the procedures for its capture and input. In the initial stages of developments, many institutions may have to deal with the phenomenon of 'not invented here', as relevant colleagues disown procedures with which they are unfamiliar. This problem points clearly to the need for training, staff development and longer lead-times in introducing changes of this nature.

777.   There is one final impediment to successful change about which it is difficult to generalise. This concerns the extent to which the institution, and its leadership, signal the significance of the proposed changes. In many ways, this may be a function of the personal style of the Vice-Chancellor and close colleagues. We have been told of many examples where there has been a misfit between institutional policy and local interpretations of this. For example, at one university we were informed that modularisation was extremely easy; the institution in question had 'modularised overnight'. At another institution, we were advised that the whole university was now modular 'but you would not notice'. We would offer the following simple guide to possible problems in this direction:

• **change by proclamation:** where the institutional head wills the ends with a visionary sweep, but fails to will the means;

• **change as a 'passing phase'** where the

change to a modular arrangement has been agreed at the strategic apex but where academic staff and others have remained broadly sceptical of the sustained commitment of the institution as a whole;

• **fair weather change:** where there is genuine commitment initially, but any turbulence forces a change of tack;

• **change as presentation:** where the institution is more concerned with the appearance of change, promising but not delivering significant modifications.

778.   From our investigation of a number of institutional strategies for change we are convinced that modularisation cannot be undertaken superficially or without initial investment in resources and goodwill. These essential elements cannot be delivered solely by the individuals or team responsible for the changes; they must be delivered by the co-operation of the entire organisation, whether it be the whole institution or a sub-unit of it. With respect to the problems of implementation outlined above, we accept that matters are in fact more complex than a simple classification implies. For example, the strength of commitment to change must inevitably be adjusted from time to time in the light of changing circumstances. If an institution cannot cope with proposed modifications, or if national funding policy alters direction, then a Chief Executive must be alert to such factors. The principal problem which remains in those circumstances is whether the trust in change can be re-established and the momentum regained in the future.

Models of credit-based modularity

779.   Although it is becoming commonplace among institutions to engage in comprehensive transformations, it is by no means universal that universities and colleges choose to proceed corporately. In some cases, developments may be restricted to departmental or faculty-wide schemes, with no necessary

implications for, or indeed connections with the rest of the institution. We know of one university which has allowed each of its faculties to decide its own arrangements; this university now has four different models of modularity running within it. Although we do not feel we could commend this approach, neither do we feel it should be abjured. Institutions will develop as they choose and in ways which are most comfortable for them. We have not worked with an 'ideal type' of modular and credit-based arrangements, except to the extent that we would welcome arrangements which bring greater quality to both academic staff and students. Nor have we worked with any prescription on the amount of choice or flexibility that should be provided to students. We are aware that choices are available to students in pre-modular and non-modular arrangements, through existing combined studies and joint honours programmes with their subsidiary subjects and so forth. Our principal test of the character of any arrangements is how it makes learning opportunities available to students.

Modular structures and modular schemes

780.   The most important distinction we can make in clarifying approaches to modularisation and internal flexibility is to distinguish between *modular structures, modular schemes* and *CATS units/schemes*:

- **modular structures** imply that all subscribing sub-units of the organisation will agree to work around some general principles of academic structure, usually semesterisation and modularisation, but that this will not have implications for changes to course or qualification regulations, nor necessarily for patterns of student choice, nor for intra-institutional relationships. In short, modular structures imply minimal administrative change and minimal disturbance to the pattern of course provision. Flexibility may be achieved for staff and students alike, but greater student choice, mobility and internal credit transfer are not guaranteed;

- **modular schemes** imply much closer

connections between contributing sub-units, usually cemented by common scheme procedures and protocols, enrolment management and assessment regulations, quality assurance and information systems. Such schemes may be departmental, faculty-wide or whole-institutional, but they always imply greater degrees of cohesion and compliance than modular structures. There are examples of 'weak' schemes (with a multiplicity of special regulations) and 'strong' schemes (achieving general compliance with agreed regulations). Some schemes may be 'courses' in their own right; others may be held together by a common academic and administrative framework. 'Schemes' tend to permit less local discretion than 'structures'. On the other hand, schemes will generally facilitate much greater degrees of internal credit transfer and student choice since barriers between subject groups are generally weakened by the provisions of the scheme. Crucially, in modular schemes, the management of student programmes is handled at the organisational level *above* the delivery of teaching and learning;

- **CATS Units or schemes** tend to be discrete or 'bolt-on' institutional or departmental arrangements designed to negotiate the passage of individual students through the matrix of existing institutional provision. Sometimes the 'unit' will act as a guidance and transfer point of reference, often for students claiming credit for prior experiential learning; on other occasions, it will act for a discrete body of students – 'CATS students' – usually on a formal scheme or course, but with teaching supplied from contributing departments. In these circumstances, students will tend to 'infill' existing modules or courses.

781.   During our investigations, we observed no arrangements in an ex-UFC university which could be called 'modular schemes' although the presence of modular structures is increasingly widespread. This may reflect the stronger traditions of disciplinary

culture and local autonomy in the established universities, but the benefits of retaining these academic traditions may be substantially offset by difficulties in obtaining necessary administrative efficiency gains. In short, a plethora of local departmental arrangements does not help the design and development of integrated management information systems and co-ordinated administration.

782. On the other hand, we have observed a larger number of modular schemes in many of the 'new' universities. These schemes will be more or less efficient at achieving their objectives of greater student choice and improved administrative effectiveness. In some cases, arrangements which claim to be 'schemes' appear to teeter between co-ordinated procedures and loose modular 'structures'. This usually reflects the prevailing balance of forces between the central scheme authority and the contributing sub-units. In a final set of cases, some modular schemes, some recently developed and some of long standing, seem to have decayed back into modular structures, as individual subject groups or departments pull away into quasi-independence. We have found no examples of *modular structures* progressing into *modular schemes*.

783. We have found many examples of *CATS Units or schemes*. We do not include in this the increasingly familiar practice in some institutions where they have moved beyond discrete 'CATS' arrangements to embrace credit and modularity simultaneously for all students. Generally, CATS units are relatively small-scale undertakings which range from staff development units, dedicated APEL centres, through in-company training accreditation units, to combined studies courses. Student numbers may be gained through external funding or 'top-sliced' from institutional allocations. They tend to be 'first generation' phenomena in the language we have used earlier in the report. Although such units have been successful in challenging conventional institutional practice, they tend to do so at the margins. They have provided formal notification that change was occurring, provided some resource, and could act as a focus for interested and enthusiastic individuals within the institution. In particular, if seen as a

short term vehicle for change, they could create a certain level of momentum within an institution which might lead to broader change. Ironically, they were quite often seen as separate from broader processes of modularisation that might be occurring within an institution simultaneously but in parallel. On the other hand, 'CATS students' can become stigmatised and dislocated from a stable institutional 'home' and academic sub-units may never properly 'own' them. Moreover the investment required to track a small minority of students through large institutions may as readily be undertaken for all students, at marginal additional costs. This has led some institutions to move from the supplementary CATS Unit to the comprehensive whole-institutional model of credit-based modularity.

784. In Table 49, we offer a summary of some of the salient differences between the three approaches. As this table shows, the key variable is how different models release or circumscribe student choice. Modular structures are attractive because they appear to promise choice and flexibility without compromising the academic integrity of the unified course. On the other hand, modular schemes and frameworks challenge the hegemony of the unified course by opening up student choice at the point of entry, in-programme and prior to final qualification. Finally, 'CATS' schemes offer a minority of students the prospect of individually negotiated programmes in otherwise less flexible conditions.

Regressive and progressive modular arrangements

785. In Chapter VI, reviewing progress to date, we commented that one of the major problems with the process of modularisation and credit-based learning in the United Kingdom over the years has been the tendency towards *regression* from initial ideals. During the investigation of various institutional arrangements, we were able to notice a number of instances where developments appeared to be exhibiting features of regression. This caused us to contemplate what might be the opposite, *progressive*, conditions to which institutions might aspire. We offer the following description of the two types of arrangement:

	Modular structures	Modular schemes	'CATS' schemes
Locus of authority	Always decentralised to faculty and/or department level; head of department or course tutor	With the scheme itself, unless scale forces sub-divisions in whole-institution scheme; overall scheme Director/Dean	Usually with local scheme, or dedicated unit. Institutional oversight of arrangements; course tutor
Academic control system	Usually devolved to organisational sub-unit (ie department or faculty) with institutional oversight of quality assurance. Planning initially local with institutional co-ordination	Usually held at the level of the scheme itself, to which sub-units contribute modules. Planning usually at the level of the scheme but interlocked with institutional strategies	Dedicated scheme usually operates within a wider local or institutional planning environment. Student numbers negotiated in the manner of an individual 'course'
Academic development	New courses and teaching and learning methods always developed at the local level unless institutional priorities predominate for some reason	New modules and pathways developed at local level but with scheme co-ordination and, usually, approval. Scheme rarely promotes new academic developments	Not usually relevant. Either unit negotiates student progress through available courses, or scheme itself develops as an 'independent' Combined Studies course
Academic programme structure	Usually unmodified from existing arrangements; courses often single honours, or structured joint-subjects; terms common but increasingly semesters being introduced with few implications for defined academic routes	Usually considerable diversity of subject combinations; some schemes formally structured as joint or combined subjects; others more open still to embrace single honours prospects from a wider base of subject combinations at entry. Semesters very common but also trimesters (less common)	If Combined Studies course, usually as the name suggests. Otherwise students fall within academic structure of academic departments. Students permitted more or less freedom to negotiate individual programmes. Structure of academic year outside control of course/scheme.
Enrolment management	Usually locally managed. Individual departments are keen to recruit and induct their 'own' students. Students join conventional departments	Usually at scheme level, or co-ordinated institutionally. Students join scheme via pathways agreed with contributing departments.	Always at scheme level in the manner of a discrete course where appropriate. Otherwise, via conventional departments
Student support and guidance	Academic guidance and personal tutor support always at local level, unless supported by institutional arrangements (rare)	Academic guidance usually at local level with personal support co-ordinated by the scheme, but requires dedicated independent guidance support (rare, but developing)	Within the 'scheme' or course itself. Indeed, the main purpose of the CATS Unit is often to provide precisely the independent guidance required by mobile students
Assessment management	Usually locally managed with individual course regulations. External examiners recommended locally, approved formally by institution	Usually centrally managed with scheme-based assessment regulations; sometimes central regulations but locally managed. External examiners appointed by the scheme	Usually discrete regulations for the course/scheme; otherwise, departmental regulations and locally managed assessment. External examiners appointed to the scheme
Student records	Managed locally, information distributed locally, but co-ordinated centrally through Registry	Assembled locally, managed centrally; information distributed via the scheme, of which the Registry may be a part (in large schemes)	Variable. May be assembled or managed at the scheme, or handled by individual departments. Final information co-ordinated institutionally
Quality assurance	At departmental or faculty level. Monitoring and review institutionally co-ordinated.	Always at scheme level. Monitoring and review of scheme itself.	Scheme treated in same way as any individual course. Review of scheme itself.
Range and scale of model	Any modularised conventional course; some 'schemes' in whole-institution forms	From smaller departmental schemes (250+) to large institutional schemes (8000+)	Usually small dedicated schemes (50-200+ students)

Table 49: The management of credit-based and modular systems: a comparison of models

- **regressive modular arrangements** tend to apply either to older modular schemes in the process of atrophy, or to recent modular schemes that never got beyond the administrative stage. In both cases, student discretion is relatively low; personal student choice is heavily circumscribed by individual 'special case' regulations, *but* academic staff have not yet regained the autonomy which would distinguish the unitary course environment to which they perhaps aspire. The scheme, if it can still be called a scheme, is little more than a series of regulations binding together disgruntled academics with unreleased students in a relatively sterile relationship. The arrangements are 'stuck-in-the-middle', neither particularly productive in academic inventiveness nor fruitful in terms of student choice. The scheme itself is relatively dormant, possessing no centre of gravity or authority, the test of which can be the extent to which new developments fail to permeate the academic programmes of the scheme. When administrative values are the most significant organising principles, academic innovations tend to be observed in the letter of the regulation but not in academic practice. For example, these arrangements may claim formally to offer credit for prior experiential learning or work-based learning, or to accept students by credit transfer, but in practice students have few means of taking advantage of these opportunities. On other occasions, these schemes have been referred to as *phantom schemes* (Watson, 1989; Robertson, 1992) promising the realisation of aspirations for which there is little practical commitment. In short, regressive schemes produce the worst of both worlds, combining low levels of student choice with low levels of professional academic discretion and enthusiasm;

- **progressive modular arrangements,** of which there are very few examples in the United Kingdom that approach the 'ideal type', tend to value student choice and academic innovation as organising

principles in their own right. Administrative arrangements, whilst important, are always subordinate to the pursuit of these two objectives. Student choice is seen as complementary to the manifestation of academic autonomy; student decisions are regarded as an important stimulus to course development; and course/module development is seen as the perfect expression of individual academic autonomy. The 'ideal type' achieves an effective combination of high levels of student choice with high levels of academic discretion. We believe this may be achieved in many institutions in the United States. In Table 50, we offer a matrix which attempts to show the relationship between various stages of development. In many institutions with which we are familiar, developments seem to oscillate between the cells in the matrix representing high and low levels of academic discretion. Only at the margins have institutions broken out into the domain of increased student discretion. If we could advise on a 'progressive' route through the matrix for institutions to consider, it would take the form of a 'U' curve.

Table 50: A relationship between student and academic discretion in modular programmes

		Student discretion	
		Low	High
Academic discretion	**High**	Standard single subject courses and most modular structures	'Regressive' modular schemes and academic frameworks
	Low	'Progressive' modular schemes and academic frameworks	'CATS' schemes and individually negotiated programmes

787. We have not chosen to deal extensively with the other two cells in the matrix. Neither offer sufficient conditions for the formation of an effective coalition of support in pursuit of greater student choice. At best, the

CAT scheme exists as a catalyst to prompt further developments within the institution. At worst, it can lead to the stigmatisation of a certain category of students. Such arrangements may be helpful at certain points in the history of an institution, but at the final account an institution must decide whether they represent the limits of a commitment to student choice and flexibility or whether these arrangements are indeed a step in the direction of broader developments.

The management of student choice and mobility

788.   For the purposes of this part of the discussion, we have assumed that institutions have an interest in encouraging greater student choice within their academic programmes, and therefore have an interest in developing managerial and administrative solutions to achieve this. Our comments here will be less relevant to those for whom greater student choice is not a problem or a priority, or for whom existing conventional arrangements appear to be satisfactory.

Centralisation and decentralisation in the management of student choice

789.   It is impossible to discuss the management of student choice and mobility in higher education without engaging to at least a limited extent with debates about the nature of the modern corporation. This debate usually revolves around the balance to be achieved between corporate control and corporate responsiveness. In higher education, the former tends to refer to the shift from *administration* (doing things as they have always been done) to *management* (doing things as they need to be done in the future). In particular, this has focused upon a closer control of finances and a greater emphasis on strategic direction, leading to the development of Vice-Chancellors as Chief Executives. This shift has perhaps been more apparent to date in the 'new' rather than the 'old' universities. Closely associated with tighter managerial control is the pressure to create greater flexibility and responsiveness. In most modern corporations this has meant the break-up of former patterns of behaviour, challenges to professionalised definitions of performance, the deconstruction of familiar organisation forms and the re-assembly of the corporation into a 'leaner but meaner' competitive operation. This model assumes that operational authority in the organisation needs to be located at the point of delivery, 'close to the customer', with overall control exercised by a small central management team, focusing on corporate policy and strategic direction. In this manner, corporations become decentralised conglomerates with each segment or sub-unit best placed to respond to its market niche, and held accountable for its performance by devolved budgetary management.

790.   Indeed, this model of the modern (or post-modern) corporation fits very easily with the traditional model of the university, at least in structural terms. Universities have always been loosely coupled organisations, with considerable autonomy at the level of faculty or department. Decentralisation has been the defining condition of the ancient universities and is largely repeated in their latter day analogues. However, there is little evidence that universities, as a consequence of their long-standing engagement with decentralisation, have been particularly nimble-footed in their response to change. In fact, this has been a frequent criticism of the university-as-organisation over the past decade. Universities tend to defend themselves by rebutting the general proposition, and by arguing that change should not take place without proper consideration. After all, universities should not be required to respond to every passing fashion, and the production of knowledge cannot be subject to the sort of commercial pressures that affect most entrepreneurial corporations. Universities are public service organisations; they may need to become more 'business-like' but they are not in the same way *businesses*.

791.   Those institutions which have embraced modern management orthodoxy with enthusiasm may therefore be faced with a paradox when it comes to matters of market management and the response to

greater student choice. By adopting the decentralised forms of the modern corporation, and confirming the forms of the conventional university, they may be creating structures which reinforce the authority of professional academic judgements and which restrict the expression of informed student choice. Ironically, the uncritical devolution of responsibility in the university may act against the interests of the student-as-consumer by bolstering the power of academic providers.

792.   Can this be avoided without lapsing into an equal and opposite reaction through unhelpful and unwelcome centralisation? We believe this may be possible by discriminating between what should properly be devolved and what may be helpfully 'centralised'. Firstly, the responsibility for academic delivery and academic development lies unambiguously with professional academic staff. They are properly grouped into disciplinary or subject clusters for good intellectual, as well as managerial, reasons. There may be some loss of innovative capacity incurred by the reinforcement of disciplinary boundaries in this way but this is probably more than offset by the benefits of inter-collegial collaboration and inter-disciplinary arrangements. Secondly, the responsibilities of academic staff extend to the presentation of teaching (and the outcomes of research) to students. In an environment which seeks to encourage informed student choice, it should not fall to academic staff to prioritise which students they are prepared to teach. Academic staff can reasonably expect students to be adequately prepared for their chosen modules, but largely students need to be able to define their learning careers for themselves, advised but unconstrained by the judgements of academic staff alone. If this argument is accepted, it implies either that the management of student learning opportunities must be separated from the delivery of academic programmes, or that students themselves must be directly empowered to choose, construct (and 'purchase'?) their preferred academic programme.

793.   We are aware of only one university in the United Kingdom where this arrangement has approached reality. The Open University has always recruited students to the university itself, rather than to a faculty or other academic sub-unit. Students do indeed purchase their modules from the university in the form of fees and course materials; and they are largely free to exercise informed choice about their progress through the programmes of the university. For many years, students have composed novel and imaginative module combinations without, as far as we are aware, incurring criticisms over quality, coherence or academic proficiency as a result of this. We would be interested to see the effects on student choice if the Open University were to adopt a more faculty-focused student recruitment strategy, tied to an income-led model of budgetary management. We predict from our analysis that local cost centres will be forced to close down student choice in order to maintain stability and security in their income streams.

Centralise to decentralise

794.   We conclude therefore that institutions need to adopt what we have called a 'mixed structure' (see Table 51). In this, academic responsibilities need to be devolved whilst administrative and student management processes need to be co-ordinated, and in some cases centralised. This can be achieved in either (or both) of two complementary ways:

- **an academic scheme or framework** which places responsibility for the management of student programmes at an organisational level above the delivery of academic resources (ie modules, courses etc), to which participating departments contribute in a negotiated internal market of demand and supply;

- **establishing students as direct purchasers of learning through a voucher/credit system** which would place a responsibility on the institution to provide strong and independent guidance and quality assurance arrangements to ensure students were able to enter their chosen programme, possibly through the medium of an integrated modular and credit-based scheme.

	Decentralisation	Centralisation	Mixed structures·
Table 51: Management structures for achieving academic and student flexibility: strengths and weaknesses			
Alternative references	Devolution, delegation, local empowerment, 'get close to the customer'; OR 'downloading responsibility', 'blame-shifting', 'pushing away the burden'; 'getting more from less'	Co-ordination, integration, meritocracy and technocracy, single point of contact; OR 'rule by decree', 'remote management', 'we know best' management; 'less from more'	'Centralise to decentralise'; pragmatic management; partnership forming; OR 'muddling through'; 'stuck in the middle'; 'value added rather than value multiplied'
General objectives	Creativity through new combinations of personnel and functions, achieved by constant change and deconstruction	Creativity through planning and co-ordination, achieved by stable alliances of professional expertise and legitimated authority	Creativity by balancing both the stability of professional alliances and the flexibility of new combinations
General limitations	Churning can exhaust organisation, destroy trust, rupture external and internal networks, and become unproductive and inefficient	Hierarchy can: stultify innovation and prevent rapid response; value position over competence; encourage permission-seeking rather than risk-taking	Seeks to avoid extremes of both other models, but may run risk of achieving neither a planned nor a rapid response. Achieves neither fame nor calamity
Effects on institutional structures in higher education	Department, subject group or course team formally the focus of authority below VC group, although recentralisation often occurs at faculty (or departmental) level. Often leads to duplication of administrative effort and some inefficiencies.	Management team focus of authority (VC group + Deans) with perhaps unitary administrative structure. Can lead to slow response and inefficiencies in innovation and other developments.	Usually decentralised academic structures (to faculty, school or department) with possibly co-ordinated or centrally directed administrative structures. Some combinations of these elements evident in most HEIs
Effects on student management	Students 'owned' by academic sub-unit furthest from centre; admission by subject/course; guidance and assessment discharged at local level; student numbers allocated from centre by 'contract' with subject/course	Students 'owned' by institution or faculty sub-unit, but academic delivery always devolved. Admission may be centrally managed, but guidance and assessment usually devolved. No typical examples of model in HE	Students may be 'owned' by scheme or local course, but administration of student progress often co-ordinated in distributed networks; admission and guidance may be centralised; assessment usually locally delivered but co-ordinated centrally
Effects on student choice and mobility	Can have a limiting effect. Local sub-units may seek to retain 'their' students, especially as 'income units' under devolved budgetary management. Also effective negotiation by students of intra-institutional mobility can be very difficult. Tendency towards course-based students and away from alternative or 'unplanned' combinations. Elective programmes rare and few means of achieving institution-wide response to new developments (eg work-based learning, open learning etc)	Can have enabling effect if 'centralisation' implies a corporate approach to student opportunities. Barriers between subject groups can be overridden by supra-course schemes. Students can be located as genuine focus of institutional behaviour. Elective programmes can be operated and cross-institutional subject combinations supported. New initiatives can be negotiated from a point of central authority	Should have enabling effect by separating devolved responsibility for academic delivery from co-ordinated and corporate responsibility for the management of student programmes. Scheme-based structures seem to work best with student programmes managed at a point above the point of academic delivery. Implies a matrix model of management and may be necessary in conditions defined by credit-led student funding
Effects on academic administration	Considerable and inefficient duplication on many functions, but some benefits in local responsibility for timetabling, space allocation.	Gains in co-ordinated information systems provision, and related functions. Potential gains in timetabling etc. but not yet achieved. Planning benefits	Generally supports centralised functions as means of freeing academic functions to those responsible. Requires professional cadre of adminstrators
Effects on credit transfer	Largely negative for student choice; positive for academic autonomy and control	Potentially positive for student choice but negative for individual academic autonomy	Potentially positive for both student and academic freedom; positive for innovation

The separation of academic and administrative functions

795.   Secondly there should be a clearer separation of academic and administrative functions. This is largely the case already in the 'older' universities where they have developed a stronger professional administrative tradition, separate from the academic career path. In the 'new' universities this arrangement is less well-developed, possibly because of their local authority origins. In many cases, academic staff at all levels are expected to assume considerable administrative loads in additional to those tasks which are professionally contingent on their academic role. With the creation of modular programmes, this often places new and additional burdens on academic staff in these institutions, which detract from their priority academic duties and give further cause for adverse professional reaction to modularisation itself.

A unitary administrative function with a professionalised administrative staff

796.   Thirdly, there is a strong case to be made for the establishment of a unitary administrative structure in the 'new' universities to complement that which exists in many forms in the 'older' institutions. The structure need not be centralised in any over-mechanistic sense; it could operate in a line descendant from a Registrar's Office through a distributive (scheme-based) faculty or departmental network of administrative staff. This could lead to substantial efficiency gains in the management of student choice:

- administrative procedures could be evenly applied across the institution or other collective academic unit;

- policy and the gains of staff development could more easily permeate departmental boundaries;

- the quality of data management could be more readily assured and enhanced;

- administrative staff are relatively neutral on the outcomes of student decisions;

- the professional standing of administrative staff could be properly recognised, and their contribution valued by the rest of the academic community.

797.   Many of the 'new' universities have not yet established a high calibre administrative cohort, with status and career scales to match, in the manner of the 'old' universities. Not only do local authority traditions still prevail but there has been no developed tradition of research funding with which to support a more extensive administrative complement. Nevertheless, the introduction of arrangements for the management of greater student choice does create the need for better quality professional administration. We are aware that investment in administrative staff is often not welcomed by academic staff, who see it as a form of taxation on their teaching and research activities. This perception is sharpened at times of increased student numbers and heavier teaching loads. However, academic colleagues need to be consistent. They cannot complain on the one hand that they are required to take on too much administration and then object to the employment of professional staff to carry it out for them. Moreover, they cannot seek to have 'their own' administrative staff, and then complain at the volume of administration when so many functions are being duplicated in a decentralised administrative structure. We place considerable importance on the attention that needs to be given to the role and management co-ordination of professional administrative staff in the management of student choice and flexibility.

Administrative functions and institutional organisation

798.   We do not have the capacity to comment extensively on the variety of issues which have emerged from our investigation on these matters. Institutional examples are so rich in the information they provide on special circumstances and particular ways of operating that we have been cautious about making generalisations which can be useful. However, we have been asked more

often on these matters than on any other our views on the preferred or possible solutions to the management of administrative functions with respect to modular and credit-based programmes. We offer therefore our best judgement on some ways forward. These may not be acceptable to individual institutions whose conditions make them inappropriate. Our proposals are, nevertheless, offered as a means of simplifying and rationalising the complex administration of greater student choice.

Enrolment management – the role of staff

799.   Conventionally the admission of students to the university has been a process closely protected by academic staff in their capacity as Admissions Tutors. Their role as 'gate-keepers' has been the subject of specific comment in the past (Fulton & Ellwood, 1989) and efforts have been directed to improving the awareness of these key influential colleagues in the wider developments in further and higher education. Much of the attention has focused on preparing academic colleagues to accept and welcome firstly mature students, then Access course students, and latterly students bearing GNVQs (and NVQ/SVQs). These efforts have tended to confirm the role and importance of the Admissions Tutor in ways which seem to us to reflect previous conditions of entry to higher education rather than current and future conditions.

800.   In our view, extended participation changes dramatically the role of the Admissions Tutor. It is no longer defined principally by selection or rejection. The admissions process has become the **process of inclusion** rather than of exclusion. Indeed, we would go further and recommend that the role of academic staff in the admissions process should be fundamentally changed with most functions being assumed by trained administrative staff. Our reasons for this are straightforward. Academic staff have a crucial role to play in setting the policy environment for the admission of students; they have little useful role to play in the operation of the process. We were impressed by an example from one university, where some Admissions Tutors were reluctant to give up their longstanding role in vetting every

application form. They felt themselves properly concerned to protect the standards of admission to their departments. When we enquired further across this institution, we found that the need of Admissions Tutors to be directly involved with the admissions process varied inversely with demand for the subject and the number of application forms. Those tutors who were most concerned to protect entry standards by personal involvement were located in areas of engineering and science which attracted less than a 3:1 ratio of applications to places. In these circumstances, tutors rejected or made less generous offers to less than 5% of all applicants. On the other hand, in the high demand areas of the humanities and social sciences, with application ratios of 40:1 and above, Admissions Tutors rarely ever saw applications, advising only in marginal cases. This is commonly the case these days.

801.   **We recommend** that this should become the normal pattern and in many institutions it already is the case. For other institutions however, matters have developed less clearly and we propose that a division of labour should be established along the following lines:

- **the role of academic staff** as admissions tutors should be to set policy, identify admissions criteria and determine their relative weighting, set targets for particular groups, conduct interviews and assessment where relevant, and adjudicate in the marginal cases referred to them;

- **the role of administrative staff** should be to discharge admissions policy against agreed criteria and targets, to keep abreast of emerging developments in education and training relevant to university admissions, to make offers to students against agreed criteria and to refer marginal cases to academic staff for adjudication.

Enrolment management – the role of systems

802.   **We recommend** that, where the institution values the general expression of student choice, enrolment management should be centralised through a single institutional *Admissions Centre.*

Applications can be efficiently processed through such an arrangement; UCAS has a single point of contact; corporate policy can be implemented across the institution; student record systems can be co-ordinated with the admission and financial management aspects of the enrolment process; and student guidance services can be organised in a complementary manner. We believe that corporate developments, in electronic enrolment management or staff development for new initiatives, for example, can be more effectively organised by such arrangements. Dedicated staff can be trained to high levels of proficiency and academic staff can address their prime interests of teaching and research.

Management information systems – tracking students

803.   The tracking of individual students as they cross boundaries within the institution and from external learning environments requires a more student-focused system for the collection and analysis of information. There is a lack of predictability, with the theoretical possibility that each student is unique. The notion of a cohort of students passing through the system together within strongly defined course boundaries disappears. The problems this complexity raises are, of course, made more difficult by the fact that, for many institutions, such a change coincides with a greater quantity of students. The student, in information terms, is increasingly constructed from the units s/he takes and the crucial relationship is between the student, the module, and the overall pattern of modules (leading to specific award titles). This is always going to be a difficult issue. Even many institutions in the United States, which have had many more years of experience of such issues, admit to being unable to determine, at any one point in time, the nature of a student's minor combination. However, this might be overcome in UK institutions which retain sufficiently tight control over the availability of modules.

804.   A number of institutions have delivered sophisticated in-house systems. Some have been developed over a long period of time and reflect a complex changing relationship between experience and

technology. More recently, some institutions, in an attempt to achieve state-of-the art effectiveness quickly, have brought in outside firms as consultants to help them develop appropriate systems from first principles. We found one institution which decided to apply the Structured Systems Analysis and Design Methodology (SSADM) in the design of its student records system. This seemed appropriate to them in that SSADM offered a thorough systems analysis of information capacity and capability. However the approach took too long to deliver results, proving unhelpful in this instance. The reasons are instructive. Firstly, SSADM is best at designing computer-based information systems to replace existing paper-based procedures. In other words, if you know what you want to do already, SSADM can deconstruct prevailing procedures and translate them into effective software. Secondly, it is less capable of responding to an environment where information needs are being discovered in the process of the development of a set of procedures. This governs the conditions under which most institutions initiate their flexible programmes. In short, some software program development will require an iterative engagement with the academic and administrative course or scheme designers, learning and implementing in progressive sequence.

805.   Some institutions have developed a commercial relationship with their consultants or in-house designers in order to 'on-sell' the product to other higher education institutions. We have not met many successful examples of this process. Institutions tend to value the customised character of software. 'Off-the-peg' software tends to require institutions to shape their affairs in accordance with the protocols which led to its initial design, producing unwelcome consequences.

806.   There is one point which our investigations have revealed on the design and development of student record software that we must address further. The growth of individual student records is exponential, and systems must be able to cope with the scale of the undertaking. For example, at Liverpool John Moores University, between

the launch of the credit scheme in 1990 and its relatively complete operation in 1992, the number of individual student records grew with the size of the scheme from 25,000 to 65,000 to over 125,000 individual module registrations. This scale is in line, *pro rata*, with that experienced over a longer period at Oxford Brookes University. There will be a number of ways of managing this capacity; indeed the scale can be reduced by reducing student choices. But institutions will need to invest collectively or individually in substantial hardware if the data processing aspects are to be managed effectively.

The MAC initiative – student records

807.   Anticipating this problem to some extent, the UFC established the Management and Administrative Computing (MAC) initiative within the 'old' universities. The MAC initiative, now funded at £18 million by the HEFCE, has as part of a wider brief the development of appropriate student record systems. Since its inception in 1988, the initiative has been formed into four 'families' based around the principal relational database systems – *Oracle, Ingres, Powerhouse* and the smaller *Secqus*. The largest of the 'families', *Oracle*, is being developed by *Delphic Ltd*, a wholly-owned subsidiary of 24 universities. The design specifications of the *Oracle* project, for example, include the requirement for student record systems which can cope with credit-based modularity and interlock student programmes with the admissions and tuition fee collection processes. Although the various 'families' have informed us that they are satisfied with the progress towards objectives, we have not been surprised to learn that the production of software for student records is running significantly behind schedule. In an audit and review of progress on the MAC initiative (April 1993) the HEFCE advised that delays in this area were running at fourteen months (*Oracle*) and sixteen months (*Ingres*) with anticipated delivery of software not expected until mid 1994.

808.   The main problem with the design of software for student records is that most universities require specific variations to accommodate the peculiarities of individual course regulations. This problem is magnified by the association of large numbers of institutions. The search for administrative standardisation is understandable but it cuts across the innate tendency of institutions to prefer autonomous solutions. We were approached by representatives of one of the 'family' groups and asked for advice on experiences of credit-based modularisation in the 'new' universities. When informed that a popular solution was to organise around common institutional assessment regulations as a starting point, this was regarded as a condition that could never be achieved in an 'old' university. Software design appears therefore to follow the contours of institutional conventions and organisational forms. This is understandable in one sense: a university would not wish to organise itself academically merely to facilitate the development of standardised software. On the other hand, the restrictions placed on the development of appropriate software may cause another far-reaching problem. Universities may constrain the ways in which they wish to develop because the software they have commissioned now will prove inadequate for the more flexible arrangements that may be needed in the future.

Student records – a co-ordinated system

809.   However we conclude that on the MAC initiative and other attempts to develop student record and student tracking software, one feature is clear. The closer an institution approaches standardised procedures in these matters, the more easily managed is the information system. Apart from problems at the design stage, existing examples of record systems reveal problems in the quality assurance of data. This concerns the means by which the entire student record information system is managed. In conventional stable cohort arrangements, where students remain in the same subject cluster or course throughout their time in the university or college, the management of individual records was less of a problem. As we have commented earlier, in more flexible arrangements the association of student and course breaks down into a plethora of individual programmes and, therefore, of individually distinct records. This data has to be captured and maintained in unique and pristine condition. It will become visible in

individual assessment records and on personal credit transcripts. Unlike data in the past, this information is overwhelmingly the personal property of the individual student and must therefore be accurate.

810. We have observed the operation of various student record systems which have been designed to track students through complex modular matrices. All share common problems which can be summarised as follows:

- **the 'politics' of information management:** reflecting the difficulties in achieving a settlement on the need for regularisation, standardisation and co-ordination in the capture and recording of relevant data. The local autonomy of individual participants to the process may choose to work to different standards, at a different pace, or to reject the advised procedures altogether.

- **the quality assurance of information:** closely related to the previous point, this concerns the problems caused by 'dirty data' at the point of input, compounding fragile software problems, causing disquiet amongst the recipients of the data (students and staff alike) and calling into question procedures and authority for staff development and training.

- **problems of 'ownership' – whose data?** reflecting the dissonance amongst some academic staff who resent (and distrust) the reliance on remote technology, welcome its outputs when effective, but may make little effort to help the technology help them.

811. A co-ordinated student record system is in our opinion essential under conditions of greater student choice and mobility, yet its success will depend on solutions to quality assurance. There is nothing conceptually or technically difficult about the design and implementation of student record systems which can cater for large numbers of individual records. A banking system is capable of doing this accurately. But a bank is able to train its staff and expect routine compliance with corporate procedures; a branch manager

does not say 'we do not do it that way here'. Moreover, a bank must eliminate corrupt data from its systems. Personal records must be accurate if serious disputes are to be avoided with customers. We have been informed of one institution which successfully developed its own student record systems to cope with its large modular scheme. After the usual initial design problems, the software settled down with a 95% success rate. When the scheme was handling 2,000 students, this level of error was manageable. As the scheme grew beyond 10,000 students, it meant that 500 students on average were complaining about inaccurate records. The advantages of the system for the availability of module class lists, personal credit transcripts, assessment data and performance indicators were overlooked in the efforts to respond to a frustrated 5%. The lesson is clear to us: the quality of the data is crucial to the success of the enterprise, and it is determined by the degree to which student record management is properly co-ordinated. Micro-efficiencies are more important to potential users in many ways than large-scale enterprises. Following our analogy, it matters little to an individual customer that their bank has just underwritten the efforts of a large public corporation if their personal statement contains errors.

Distributive access to information systems

812. Perhaps the corporate model of the bank can help us further. A bank will have corporate procedures but many branches. *Distributive access* is the principle upon which it organises its affairs and **we recommend** this approach. In a university this would require the establishment of distributive information networks based on access in remote sites (ie faculty and departmental offices), staffed by trained personnel, and accountable through a unitary administrative structure to the institution itself. The assurance of systems quality can be addressed through a single chain of command and modifications to information systems can be arranged from a single authority.

Timetabling and space management

813. Within the annual structure of the year, centralised modular/credit institutions require adaptations to their timetabling

structure, if artificial barriers are not to be created that will restrict student choice. This means, at the very least, a common institution-wide timetabling pattern (with all classes beginning and ending at the same time); and greater levels of co-ordination across disciplinary boundaries. In some cases this requires a central timetabling model (possibly computerised) with time slots, blocked by subjects, being allocated to Departments by a central unit. Such timetables should not change substantially year-on-year, so that students can make informed choices well in advance of their programme. A common occurrence within such a structure is the repetition of units throughout the week to widen availability and avoid module capping. The restructuring of both the year and the week are required to increase genuine student choice, but also to allow staff the opportunity to manage and administer the system more effectively.

814.   In practice, we have seen few examples of practice which could be recommended for general application. Scheduling is regarded as 'a nightmare' in the United States and it appears to be little different in the United Kingdom. Computerised systems do not seem to offer stable solutions. The reason is apparently simple. We have been advised that where computerised room-booking and timetabling systems have been used, they quickly break down, not because of any particular flaw in the software, but because people ignore the arrangements. In other words, a computerised system can allocate rooms and times, but individual lecturers and their classes can negotiate together to alter arrangements at their convenience. The cumulative effect of these individual minor modifications quickly causes major disruption.

815.   Yet a stable timetable is essential for the successful operation of flexible systems. Students joining modules as part of their elective programmes need stability; students applying in advance require constant information; and part-time students may have arranged an entire day, including childcare, to attend for one hour. It is little consolation to them that agreed times and rooms have been changed 'by mutual convenience'. We can only propose that this matter is given much greater attention than at present. **We recommend** that the representative bodies of institutions consider supporting a research project to explore what experience of the problem exists and what solutions may be found to establishing a system for timetabling and room allocation. This investigation might take to itself an exploration of the consequences for staff development and institutional culture and practice of what may be perceived by academic staff to be rigidities and inflexibilities in the new arrangements, commenting on how these perceptions might be countered and managed.

The teaching day; the teaching week

816.   We have tried to establish the extent of operation of 12-hour timetables and extend week working practices. We have found many examples of evening activities and some examples of weekend study classes and similar activities. In the latter cases, continuing education programmes may well take place at weekends and there are other examples of block release Master's programmes which involve extended week working. Overall, we have found more support for the principle of 12-hour timetables and extended week working than we have found in practice. In fairness, a limited number of institutions have established operational 12-hour timetables and some programmes take advantage of this. By this we do not mean simply that institutions offer modules or courses in the evening, but rather that modules can be offered to all students across the 12-hour day. In these cases, some groups of full-time students can be expected or more commonly elect to take modules in the evening. This seems to be a practice many would like to encourage and it could be one way of stimulating the development of part-time evening opportunities for some students by allowing modules to be mounted efficiently with a full complement of students.

817.   The operation of the 12-hour day does raise other important considerations. Full-time students do not expect to study in the evenings in this manner; some older students will have family commitments; there are issues of personal security, access to learning

resources and travelling problems to be addressed amongst others. We believe many of these matters can be resolved, with beneficial consequences for flexibility, choice and the deployment of scarce academic resources. Of course full-time students should not be required to study across a full 12-hour day and regulations will need to be designed to cope with this. Moreover, we believe that in the first instance at least, students should be allowed to choose to follow evening modules. Over time perhaps, and with adequate advanced notice so that they can anticipate future study practice, students may be encouraged to take certain parts of their programme in the evening period. **We recommend** that institutions give attention to the systematic introduction of a 12-hour timetable, progressively inviting students to consider modules offered in the evening. We believe that in the longer term this arrangement will assist all students to manage their personal learning careers more successfully, and for some, more conveniently as well.

Reform of the academic year

818.   There has been considerable discussion of the reformed academic year following the establishment of the Committee of Enquiry under the chairmanship of Lord Flowers. Although the origins of this Committee lie in a more general discussion of effective estate management and the introduction of a third (Summer) semester, we have been delighted to see that educational and academic considerations appear finally to have influenced the outcomes of the report. Prior to the setting up of the Committee, it had become clear to many of those running modular/credit schemes that the issue of semesters and terms (or 'trimesters') is crucial to institutions seeking to develop more flexible structures. Trimester-based modules give more potential for choice, and can be organised within the existing academic year structure. They are, however, difficult to manage and administer because they have three assessment points, something that also can lead to over-assessment. Semester structures, on the other hand, whilst giving plenty of scope theoretically for choice, find themselves, the University of Stirling apart, with an inter-semester break that comes early in the Spring

Term and that is too short to ensure both the end-of-semester assessment, and the necessary guidance for students in order to choose their next programme of study.

819.   For this reason many people had concluded that the academic year needed reforming so that the 'phantom' two-semester structure currently operating would be reorganised in such a way as to base the two semesters either side of an extended Christmas break. This would produce a satisfactory basis for staff to deliver the assessment, and students to make an informed choice about their next stage. This model, one of those identified by the Flowers Committee, has received considerable support from a wide range of institutions, irrespective of the nature of their structure and we unreservedly welcome this.

820.   We would however point to problems with enrolment management that may arise as a consequence of the failure to persuade the 'A' level examination boards to adjust their result reporting period. Some institutions which would otherwise wish to adopt the reformed semester structure may be prevented from doing so if they fear their market position will be prejudiced by a contracted period for 'clearing'. A staged start to the first year may not be sufficient to overcome this problem in some quarters. We are sceptical of suggestions that universities will therefore seek to organise their own entry examinations if 'A' level boards do not co-operate. Most 'A' level boards were established by universities in the first place to manage entry requirements; it can make little sense for universities, separately or in concert, to take on the burden of entrance examinations when it would be simpler to continue to urge change on the 'A' level boards themselves. Therefore, **we recommend** the widespread adoption of the reformed 15-week semester model proposed by the Flowers Report as the model most consistent with effective student choice and the efficient management of modular arrangements. **We recommend** also that the representative bodies of institutions continue to press upon 'A' level boards the need to adjust their period of reporting to allow students and institutions prudently to adopt the reformed academic year.

Quality assurance and assessment management

The organisation of quality assurance

821.   Quality assurance is a particular problem in flexible academic programmes. The module is usually the starting point in the process. This is especially true for modular *schemes* although modular *structures*, which are little more than modularised courses, may be subject to conventional treatment in the manner of unified courses. Clusters of modules focused around a particular subject/discipline provide a second order level of scrutiny. Many of the quality assurance functions can be carried out at these two levels. These include standards of delivery; assessment; consistency across modules; subject quality.

Table 52: An evaluation of quality assurance in a modular scheme at one institution

Whilst all acknowledged the value of peer group evaluation, many felt that they had been or were in the process of becoming victims of overkill. In the 1970s and 1980s the common experience was of validations and quinquennial reviews; the recent experience has been of biennial and even annual reviews. Bringing programmes into the scheme, increasing student choice by developing new programmes, franchising programmes to other institutions, preparing for semesterisation, and reviewing programmes in the wake of structural reorganisation have each contributed to the frequency of validation events. That frequency and the associated burden of work is in danger of bringing the process into disrepute. In the context of rapidly increasing student numbers and deteriorating SSRs, the time and energy spent on successive validations has to be at the expense of time devoted to the actual delivery of programmes. After a point, the time and energy spent in searching for quality assurance may be contributing to the erosion of quality in the delivery of programmes.

Evidence to the Project, 1994

---

822.   From our investigation we have found expressions of concern in many institutions that the process of quality assurance in modular and credit-based programmes can be cumbersome and time-consuming. This is particularly true as institutions move their programmes into modular mode, requiring lengthy processes of revalidation, critical appraisal and annual monitoring of extensive subject combinations. Institutions appear to find more or less satisfactory ways of coping with the problem, some of which appear to save on time at the expense of due process. There is a fine balance between expeditious procedures for quality assurance and processes which imply that academic staff cannot be trusted in programme design. In Table 52 we offer representative comments from an evaluation of procedures for one institutional scheme.

823.   We believe there is a pressing need to find out more about institutional quality assurance procedures in the context of modular programmes. Practice is so varied that good practice is difficult to identify. We have not been able to explore these matters as extensively as we would have wished, and **we recommend** that this is an area for further work by the HEQC with a view to advising on appropriate practices and procedures.

Quality assurance and assessment

824.   Assessment Boards and external examiners can serve their required functions of assessing the quality of the work produced by students; students can provide feedback on the quality of what is being offered. The problem arises in relation to overall student performance, and the totality of the student experience. Two-tier Assessment Boards commonly resolve one of the issues by looking initially through one board at performance at the module level, and then through a second one at the overall profile of the students. More difficult is capturing the elements of the student experience that cannot be defined simply by an evaluation of the experience on individual modules.

825.   We have found some disquiet over the role of external examiners in modular programmes. Two contrasting views predom-

inate. Firstly there are those who hold that the external examiner system is the centre of the quality assurance process and this must not be compromised in modular schemes. Secondly, there are those who claim that the external examiner system is an honourable fiction, the conditions of which cannot be met in the real world of modularity. In any event, it is claimed, there is no need for regular and intensive oversight of progression by external examiners; they should be retained, if at all, as a court of last resort in the adjudication of final qualifications. On balance, we favour this latter view but **we recommend** that there is substantial further work that should be undertaken to explore opinion and practice on this matter

826.   Furthermore, many institutions have found considerable difficulty in maintaining an effective personal tutor system, once a standard for obtaining and dealing with student feedback, though this is as much a consequence of large numbers as flexibility *per se*. Alternative techniques are available, including a variety of staff and student-based meetings. Some institutions have sought ways of formally gaining student feedback by bringing 'slice-groups' together, for example within a specific level or subject area, to discuss non-module related issues. Whatever the resolution, the issue is one of balancing the tendency to see the student as the sum of the parts (the modules), and the obvious fact that the student experience is something greater than the sum of these parts.

827.   We have not been able to form an effective assessment of commendable arrangements in these matters. Practice is varied and it is still insufficiently broadly based for us to exercise a judgement. There are certainly important matters at stake however. In Chapter XIII we discuss aspects of the student guidance environment and we are aware that concerns have been expressed over the consequences for student support of increased student choice. Experience to date suggests that isolation and disorientation can result from under-managed arrangements. Institutions will wish to know best how to proceed. **We recommend** therefore that this is an area for further work by the HEQC, from which *Guidelines on modularity* would be one possible outcome (see also Chapter X).

Institutional planning and performance indicators in flexible programmes

828.   Finally in this chapter, we turn to issues which have been raised frequently during the investigation. These concern, firstly, the effects on institutional planning of increased student choice, and secondly, the consequences for the development of performance indicators in the service of corporate objectives. Both of these matters flow from the consideration of managerial efficiency and the quality assurance of institutional behaviour, and they have material impact on the funding and further development of academic programmes.

Planning and the management of turbulence

829.   Greater student choice invariably creates greater institutional turbulence and makes predictability in organisational development less easy to achieve. At its simplest, student choice can disturb at the margins the distribution of planned student numbers. Further on, in income-led (or credit-led) models of budgetary distribution, it can lead to shifts in the balance of funds between academic cost centres over time; some areas will grow in this way, and others will decline relatively. Finally, student choice can lead an institution to re-examine its priorities in a fundamental way, deciding over time to reposition its resources in a different way.

830.   In practice, institutions can never tolerate the unfettered expression of informed student choice, even where quality assurance dimensions are satisfied. The deployment of human and physical assets constrains the exercise of choice in one direction; the desire for continuity and stability limits student options in another. Institutions therefore operate with varying models for the management of student choice, tolerating different degrees of choice and mobility and justifying this in a number of ways. Of the various approaches to controlling mobility, those involving *rationed access* according to defined academic criteria appear to be the most commendable. Institutions will make more or

less strenuous efforts to accommodate student choices, depending on their Mission and on their commitment to greater flexibility. These approaches are summarised in Table 53.

Table 53: Models for the control of turbulence generated by student choice and mobility	
Closed market	Student choice constrained by initial choice of course; some variation allowed within defined course environment; no shift of emphasis from chosen course
Restricted market	Student choice allowed within confined academic 'space' (ie within a department or faculty); mobility restricted principally by academic pre-requisite conditions; sometimes restricted by formal limits on module capacity, lack of geographical proximity or limited academic resources
Competitive restricted market	General student choice encouraged but constraint of physical capacity or academic resources. Students required to compete for *rationed places* according to defined priorities. Preferences on modules may be awarded on the basis of academic continuity, prime need, competitive grade performance, or first choice
Open restricted market	General student choice widely encouraged and institution attempts to meet all possible demands. It may run repeat modules, supply open learning support, overcome physical and travel problems, and employ extra staff. BUT it will be unable to guarantee that all choices are met
Open market	No examples approaching this 'ideal type' amongst taught courses. OU and other purchased open learning programmes could be exceptions. For taught programmes, institution would need to make available all learning opportunities within the physical limitations of timetable and geography.

831.   Institutions may still find that they feel less than fully confident in the management of student choice, if those choices threaten to distort planned student numbers negotiated with funding councils. There can be no good reason why funding methodologies should unnecessarily inhibit the freer movement of students within an institution and for this reason, we have made the proposals relevant to these matters in Chapter XI. If these recommendations are taken as the basis for future methodologies, then it is likely that institutions will have more incentive to allow the liberal movement of students around academic programmes with less fear of 'ring-fencing' or competitive disadvantage through funding.

832.   In the last resort, institutions developing modular schemes will have to rely on the experience of others. This suggests that patterns of student choice establish a degree of regularity and predictability in time. A certain latitude is always necessary, and contingency funds can be established to manage uneven resource requirements. However, certain problems remain unsolved. Firstly, it is not always clear how student choice is best managed in a modular matrix at the point of entry. If students are invited to make interesting combinations of subjects at entry, how are admissions to be managed if applications come forward for combinations of subjects in areas of high and low demand? It could be very commendable for an institution to invite applications for combinations involving, say, chemistry and German, but might some students take advantage of this flexibility as a means of switching to the high demand subject (for example, German) once they have been admitted? Secondly, what are the academic and planning considerations to be addressed in an environment where student choice may respond to subjective elements from time to time? It is not clear what rules of institutional conduct could be described to ensure the reasonable expression of informed student choice consonant with quality assurance and overall institutional stability.

Performance indicators and student choice

833.   We have already made it clear in the earlier discussion on information systems that modular arrangements, by requiring a greater specificity of information on individual programmes and performance, deliver the opportunity for the development of very sophisticated performance indicators. Although great care would need to be exercised

in the interpretation and use of the information, existing arrangements on some modular programmes do allow the exposure of fine-tuned but sensitive data on student and academic staff behaviour. It is possible to use credit-based systems and relational databases to indicate, for example (see also Table 54):

- the entry, progress and performance criteria of any category or cohort of students by any chosen variable or combination of variables;

- the mean assessment mark of any category of students compared with any other;

- the mean assessment mark of students on a particular module over time;

- the distribution of assessment performance by module, subject and route over time;

- the mean marks awarded by individual lecturers, by module, over time;

- the 'added value' to individual students of specific modules, routes or qualifications;

- institutional performance against a full range of recruitment, achievement and academically-related targets.

834.   Much of this information may be useful to students, but unwelcome to institutions and their staff. As with all statistical data, the quality of its interpretation is as important as the reliability of the information itself. Moreover, it would be most unfortunate, and counter-productive to the achievement of increased flexibility and choice for students, if the confidence of academic staff was undermined by insecurities over the fair interpretation of available institutional data. For our part, we can only observe what is currently possible and argue its merits in terms of the constructive use to which such information might be put. We would welcome the improved availability of reliable data if it led to the establishment of better institutional performance targets, the enhancement of

quality, the meeting of equal opportunities objectives and the improvement of information to students and employers. We are sure Government and funding councils would also welcome better performance information to ensure that national resources are being purposefully deployed and national objectives realised. Further work will need to be undertaken by the institutions themselves, and their representative bodies, to ensure that they are satisfied that information and performance indicators of the type indicated are consistent with the continued expression of institutional academic autonomy.

Conclusion

835.   We offer one conclusion with confidence. The management of flexibility will depend entirely on the extent to which an institution is committed to the promotion of flexibility both as an educational objective and an organisational objective. We do not expect every institution to value flexibility in the same way. Indeed, some institutions will wish to preserve the conventions and practices which have served them well over the years and will eschew the proposals that emerge from our discussions in this chapter. It is beyond the scope of this report to encourage any other development.

836.   However, for those institutions which need to engage with increased flexibility and student choice for whatever reason, certain core developments appear to be necessary. In some cases, some of these elements will be in place; in others they may require substantial changes to academic structures, cultural attitudes and investment priorities. For example, as far as we are able to establish, the 'old' universities have largely in place the type of unitary and professionalised administrative cohort that we recommend as the standard model. They lack generally the modular schemes that this style of administrative structure would readily support. Overall, this is the reverse of the situation in the 'new' universities where the development of modularisation may have moved in advance of the infrastructural administrative arrangements necessary for its successful operation.

Table 54: Performance targets in the management of student choice and flexibility: some tests		
	'Test can be met'	'Test could be met under certain conditions' ·
Test 1	'Students receive full details of their academic opportunities in advance and plan their individual programmes prior to registration'	
	No known examples in UK, apart from distance learning opportunities, OU possibly	Institutions would need to produce detailed programme catalogues with details of modules, by credit value, level, time, location, qualifying conditions; thereafter to provide guidance and negotiation environment for the authentication of individual learning contracts
Test 2	'Students plan their academic programme up to three years in advance and combine it with other career and domestic commitments'	
	No significant examples, with possible exception of the Open University	Institutions would need to formalise and stabilise over time the availability of modules against time and location. This would involve an acceptance of fixed timetable and space allocation arrangements. Essential if students are to anticipate part-time or interrupted study. Particularly helpful for women returners and mature students
Test 3	'Students register electronically, by telephone, or by credit card for their chosen academic programme'	
	No known examples yet in UK	Technology exists to make this possible. 'Swipe-card' technology could enable students to choose personal programmes against an electronic voucher-credit system. Centralised enrolment management probably essential together with fixed catalogue and time arrangements (see above)
Test 4	'Students receive sessional assessment feedback, take advice, and modify their initial academic programmes accordingly'	
	Already possible in UK. More advanced modular schemes have the technology to make this possible and can issue *personalised credit transcripts*	Institutions require modular and credit-based programmes supported by dedicated information systems. Reformed academic year (semesters) will assist this development. Quality assurance arrangements can be designed to cope. In-programme guidance service essential. Interactive guidance programmes would be helpful (eg PC-based, or CD-ROM)
Test 5	'Academic staff receive student module registration details (class lists) within two days of enrolment'	
	Already possible within UK in well-established modular schemes, although two days might be a target for some	Institutions would need to invest in sophisticated information systems. Modern relational databases provide the technological base for producing the required data. Processing capacity and scheduling arrangements can be problems, but can be managed
Test 6	'Institutions show individual academic programme registration data by social and educational background, by module and qualification'	
	Already possible in UK amongst advanced modular schemes	Capacity follows from use of modern relational databases. Technology is not a problem; institutions need to be encouraged to make use of the data
Test 7	'Institutions show individual academic performance by social and educational background, by module and qualification'	
	Already possible in UK amongst advanced modular schemes	Performance indicators particularly helpful in academic programmes with common assessment regulations. Ability to compare performance across subject groups, social and educational categories is very revealing. Would be assisted by use of Student Personal Identification Number (SPIN)
Test 8	'Institutions report detailed patterns of student behaviour, in-programme, by qualification and by destination'	
	Already possible in UK amongst advanced modular schemes	Institutions can develop the systems indicated above to supply this level of detail; destination is more problematic but data assisted by SPIN

837.   As we say this, we are aware that it is most difficult to generalise about these matters. For every argument that can be advanced for a particular solution to organisational arrangements, based on experience or management theory, there is a counter-case to be made for some alternative. In the end, we have had to exercise a judgement in favour of certain features which we believe merit further consideration over the longer term, if institutions wish to position themselves productively in the management of student choice and flexibility. Of these judgements, the most significant is the support we give, not to the archetypes of centralised or decentralised structures, but to pragmatic 'mixed' structures. Despite the tendency to pursue decentralisation and devolution in the model of the modern corporation, it may be that this is mistaken if taken to its furthest ideological conclusion. Indeed, we have argued that it can lead paradoxically to structures which inhibit the mobility and choice of students. Instead, **we recommend** that institutions should adopt the principle: *centralise to decentralise* as a way of promoting the view that, in our judgement, some things must be centralised if other elements are to be successfully decentralised. Simplistic nostrums from commercial entrepreneurial practice are unlikely to work in the professionalised world of higher and further education, whatever the objectives of individual institutions may be.

838.   We have taken a firm position on two other matters of strategic importance. Firstly, it is apparent to us that changes contingent on the introduction of choice and flexibility have far-reaching consequences for the generation of corporate information. The capacity of modern information systems appears not to be sufficiently well appreciated by institutional managers. Either they seem to take too limited a view of the investment requirements in both hardware and software design, or they take too optimistic a view of the capabilities of the technology. We have no doubt on this matter. Modern information systems make possible the management of complex academic programmes in ways which were barely thinkable a decade ago. They provide cost-effective ways of processing large amounts of inter-related data to the benefit of institutions, their staff and their students. Investment in good quality information technology and related staff expertise is essential. However, there are limits to the technology. There does not yet appear to be software on scheduling and space allocation which can run with the contours of many organisations. Moreover, software works best with standard procedures; modifications to meet every special case impairs its efficiency. This may run counter to the practices of many universities. We cannot emphasise strongly enough that, where institutions set out to design software, they should agree the specification clearly and expect to work iteratively with the program designers.

839.   Secondly, the management of modular systems requires a professional administrative staff with career status and authority. Systems cannot operate on the basis of routine clerical activities. Administrative staff should be capable of exercising independent professional judgement on all matters of academic administration. Their contributions need to be seen as different from those of academic colleagues, but no less important to the success of the university.

Recommendations and guidance for future policy

On organisational structures

To institutions and their representative bodies

79 In the management of student choice, flexibility and increased personal mobility, institutions will need to give consideration to the balance they wish to achieve between centralised and co-ordinated functions, on the one hand, and decentralised functions on the other. **We recommend** that institutions should consider eschewing both centralised and decentralised approaches to management structure in favour of a pragmatic, 'mixed' model in which many administrative functions would be co-ordinated within a unitary administrative structure.

80 In further pursuit of a 'mixed' model strategy, **we recommend** that academic and administrative functions in the management of student programmes should be separated and clearly defined, with the responsibility for policy matters on admissions, progression, assessment and academic quality assurance remaining with academic staff, but the operational management of the process being left largely to qualified administrative staff.

81 **We recommend** that institutions should seek to establish a highly professional administrative staff, properly trained in matters related to academic policy and educational developments, whose contribution is valued by academic colleagues in the discharge of responsibilities towards student admissions, guidance, assessment, record maintenance and the quality assurance of administrative procedures.

82 In the organisation of institutional academic structures and attendant budget centres, **we recommend** that institutions give close attention to the influence of academic structures on the propensity or ability of students to exercise informed choice. In this, we believe it will be necessary to take into account means of encouraging the freer movement of resources between budget centres as a consequence of internal student mobility, and of ways to encourage academic colleagues to gain confidence in the judgements of students.

83 **We recommend** that higher education institution generally adopt the reformed academic year of two 15-week semesters, as advised by the Flowers Report. We believe this is by far the best solution to the management of modular programmes. **We recommend** furthermore that colleges of further education consider adopting a similar, or closely compatible academic year structure within the near future. **We recommend** that further efforts be made to press upon the 'A' level Examining Boards the need to adjust their processes in order to facilitate the operation of the proposed reformed academic year.

On infrastructural systems

To institutions and their representative bodies

84 **We recommend** that, if this is not otherwise in hand through the MAC initiative or by alternative means, institutions give close attention to the capacity and capability of information systems to provide sophisticated infrastuctural support to flexible academic programmes. As part of this process, **we recommend** that institutions review their information needs with a view to co-ordinating the data available from student academic record systems with that required for institutional monitoring and the creation of reliable performance indicators.

85   To assist the development of reliable academic performance indicators, **we recommend** that institutions should work towards the establishment of common institutional assessment criteria and regulations, permitting performance characteristics to be compared across subject, departmental and faculty boundaries.

86   In particular, **we recommend** that the exercise of initial student choice, the meeting of equal opportunity objectives and the response to relevant national educational developments will be best met by the establishment of a centralised institutional Admissions Centre. Furthermore, **we recommend** that the co-ordinated student records system should be organised on the basis of access to a distributed network with a central authority for the quality control of data.

On staff development

To HEQC, individual institutions and their representative bodies

87   There is a continuing need, at an institutional level and more widely, for programmes of staff development in matters concerning the further extension of student choice and flexibility. In particular, **we recommend** that staff development programmes should concentrate in the first instance on:

- the development of strategies for teaching and learning in an environment of greater individual student choice;

- the assessment of students in modular programmes, emphasising assessment techniques, the need to identify performance criteria and the need to align assessment strategies with stated learning outcomes;

- personal support for students.

On further work

To HEQC, individual institutions and their representative bodies

88   We have been unable to make secure recommendations on common procedures for the quality assurance of modular programmes. The diversity of practice is extensive and we have not been able to determine good practice. **We recommend** that this is an area for further work by the HEQC in conjunction with institutions with a view to producing guidelines for quality assurance in modular programmes. In particular, **we recommend** that attention be paid to:

- procedures for the validation of specific routes;

- arrangements for student support through the personal tutor or alternative system;

- the role of external examiners;

- and the value of the classified honours degree system.

XIII.   *Guiding students*

Introduction

840.   The successful operation of credit
         systems in higher education and
beyond implies, as we have argued in the
preceding chapters, that students are able to
exercise greater individual autonomy over the
choices they make in the construction of their
programmes. However, greater individual
choice will be an empty vessel if it does not lead
students to improved personal success on their
chosen course, measured in terms of
programme retention rates, individual academic
performance and future labour market
placement. Indeed most of the antipathy to the
extension of student choice is advanced by
academic colleagues and others in terms of the
fitness of individual learners to make wise and
beneficial choices with these matters in mind.
These concerns cannot be set aside by assertions
of the intrinsic maturity of students or by claims
that any constructed academic programme is as
useful as any other. If student choice is to be
granted greater authority, it cannot be granted
sovereignty over considerations of academic
quality or the prospects of subsequent
employment, and we do not believe students
would wish this.

The principles of educational guidance for personal choice

841.   For extended choice to be successful, it
         needs to be *informed choice*. This is the
first principle of educational guidance and one
which is honoured in the following discussion.
For students to benefit from the greater
freedoms bestowed upon them by the
development of credit systems, they need to be
provided with the means to meet their personal
responsibilities. Discharging students unguided
into a morass of learning opportunities is likely
to produce an alienation and dislocation from
the productive benefits of learning which may
be just as constraining to the fulfilment of
individual potential as former arrangements
may have been. During the investigation, we
have received opinion from students and others
which suggests that there are fundamental
matters to be addressed here. For example,
within more traditional course-based provision,
learners appear to gain a sense of identity and a
great deal of information and support through
being members of a 'course'; as such they are
members of a coherent group following a
specified programme and thus learning
together. Learners following more flexible
programmes have at times expressed feelings of
marginalisation and a sense that they do not fit
into the existing structures of institutions. It is
clear to us that these concerns require close
attention in the development of credit systems.
The guidance and support infrastructure
appears to lie at the core of successfully
managed flexible systems and this may require
authoritative responses from institutions in the
future.

842.   The main challenge for guidance and
         support arrangements in credit-based
systems is to enable learners to gain greater
control over many aspects of their learning.
Guidance is fundamentally important to any
serious attempt to empower learners. This issue
can best be understood as an attempt to shift
definitions of coherence towards the learner, so
learners will integrate the topics they study into
a whole that is coherent for themselves. This
requires the establishment of quality assurance
arrangements which allow individual claims for
academic coherence to be adjudicated in a
framework of organising principles (see Table 55).

Table 55: Principles of educational guidance

- Client-centredness
- Impartiality
- Confidentiality
- Availability
- Accessibility
- Extensive publicity
- Influence on curriculum development

Source: UDACE, 1986

---

843. The necessary interactions between guidance, student decisions and academic judgements can produce a tension which invites careful management. Different professional interests are often at stake within a hierarchy of perceptions and values that is deeply rooted in the culture of organisations. We do not wish to overburden this point beyond making it clear that, in our judgement, a commitment to greater personal student empowerment cannot be fulfilled without a recognition of what this may mean for the balance of power and authority within educational institutions themselves.

Benefits of educational guidance

844. We have found it necessary during the investigation to try and give some measure to the benefits that may accrue from systematic investment in better educational guidance. For the purposes of this discussion, we have treated *educational guidance* and *careers guidance* as a continuum. On other occasions, it may be important to remember that the professional focus of these activities is indeed different and we comment on this later. Of the benefits that follow from educational guidance arrangements, we distinguish two forms: *material benefits* and *quality benefits* to individuals, institutions and the public interest.

845. Firstly, educational guidance seeks to ensure that individuals find their way to the most appropriate programme of learning, assisting them to modify this programme as institutional structures permit. The expectation is that this process will assist in **improving the student retention rate** on modules and courses. Unfortunately, this remains an assertion. We have not been able to find an information base in higher education from which to test this proposition empirically and **we recommend** that this is an area for further research. However, in further education, the report of the National Audit Office, *Unfinished business* (1993), concluded that investment in guidance was important in securing the correct course placement of 16-19 year olds and recommended the establishment of a stable data platform upon which to make further comparisons.

846. Secondly, a successful guidance system can provide helpful **feedback to inform institutional policies.** At a time when Student Charters are seen as sources of important information, it will be necessary for institutions to consider how they can marshal the intelligence on student needs to best effect. Currently, we have seen very few examples of guidance feedback data having material impact on institutional development in ways which we believe possible. Thirdly, guidance provides important information and support for **future career placement.** In general this appears to be better developed in institutions. Careers Services and graduate surveys are part of the landscape of institutional life in a way that is not yet the case for educational guidance.

847. Then there are the benefits for quality assurance. Firstly, guidance can **improve the student experience** by ensuring that students are placed on programmes as close to their interests, commitments and abilities as possible. Secondly, it encourages students to take responsibilities and **develop control over learning careers.** The self-confidence which can flow from a successfully negotiated guidance interview is recognised widely by professional colleagues. Next, this can be further supported by the fact that students can learn to have **confidence in their own definitions of academic coherence.** Academic staff can come to be seen as essential resources upon which a student needs to draw, but they are no longer the sole defining condition of a successful learning experience. Finally, successful educational guidance can **end feelings of isolation and marginalisation** which may otherwise occur for students in complex choice environments. Students can come to understand that they do have some control over decisions which appear to affect them and that institutional structures can be negotiated, if support and guidance is offered.

848. We have considered the principles and benefits of educational guidance for undergraduate higher education. We are aware that there are aspects of postgraduate guidance which may need attention, but we have not been able to cover them here.

National and institutional dimensions of educational guidance

849. On a national level learners need guidance about the opportunities generally available; when and how to apply for them; the possibilities for transferring between institutions; what credit is available and where it is recognised. We have made recommendations already in Chapter X for the development of a national Credit Register within which institutions and others should be invited to place their negotiated credit ratings and we believe it would be helpful if this Credit Register were to include the conditions for bilateral transfer that individual institutions were happy to encourage. Moreover, we have also indicated earlier that there is a rapidly expanding commitment to credit systems in further education as well. Much of this is unrecorded and poorly co-ordinated. When coupled with the development of vocational qualifications from the NCVQ, national information on credit-based learning opportunities has expanded enormously since the initial assessment of demand for ECCTIS.

850. We are aware that not all developments in each sector assume the same characteristics. There may be a greater need for a national guidance and information network for higher education and for vocational qualifications than for the more locally-based further education. Furthermore, there may be 'local national' dimensions to consider. The Scottish and Welsh arrangements (and possibly future developments in Northern Ireland) may need individual treatment on a national-regional basis. This would need further consideration beyond this report.

851. At an institutional level, learners need guidance about modes of study, entry and exit points, including entry with credit; guidance about credit, including what it is given for and the conditions under which it can be used; guidance about the extent and boundaries of choice, including the units available; teaching, learning and assessment methods; the implications of choices for future learning and career options; how and when choices may be made; the possibilities for changing choices; and what to do if they fail. The elements of guidance provision should be clearly defined, well-publicised and closely co-ordinated, with mechanisms for referring learners within and outside the institutions. Institutions should seek to utilise guidance to enrol students on the programmes most appropriate for them, thus improving retention rates. As credit systems permeate through institutions, on-programme guidance should aim to be unit-based rather than course-based. Appropriate staff development programmes are essential and guidance provision must be given adequate priority in resource allocation decisions.

National policy in advance of institutional developments

852. It is apparent to us from the investigative work undertaken for the project that national developments in the promotion of educational guidance significantly exceed the developments in most institutions. At the national level, from the establishment of ECCTIS through to the National Educational Guidance Initiative (NEGI) and various projects funded by the DFE and the Employment Department, it is clear that student guidance is held to be very important at the level of national policy. Yet it is our impression that progress on the implementation of lessons learned from this work has been slow in the majority of higher education institutions. There have been notable exceptions, where institutions have invested directly in educational guidance initiatives. At the University of Coventry, for example, significant resources have been directed to the establishment of a professional education and guidance service. The University of Wolverhampton has for some years operated a town centre *Higher Education Shop*; and Sheffield Hallam University has established a major new department directed explicitly to guidance and information. Elsewhere, some universities have tended to link closely with local community and local authority arrangements; this would be the case, for example, with arrangements at the University of North London.

853.   On balance, however, it has been clear to us that these and other similar arrangements are exceptions to the rule. Universities and colleges are generally well-disposed towards the principles of educational guidance but this is not widely reflected in either the resources or the status awarded to the activity. We believe this may be explained in a number of ways. Firstly, **national policy priorities have not yet been defined as institutional priorities;** in short, the foresight that has been shown in national policy-making has not been reflected in significant institutional development. This is less clearly the case in further education, where the need may be greater currently, than in higher education. In these latter institutions, existing instruments of guidance are present (ECCTIS CD-ROMs for example) but they do not receive the prominence they deserve.

854.   Secondly, **guidance and recruitment remain confused;** some institutions, having invested extensively in improved marketing and recruitment, neglect to distinguish between this and the creation of an independent professional educational guidance function, or mistakenly believe they are the same thing. Thirdly, **guidance is often regarded as a 'casualty service';** since the majority of students arrive at university from school, they have few demands to make on the system. Many institutions therefore feel little pressure from 'students-as-consumers' to offer a generalised educational guidance service. A limited service may be available for the small minority of particular students who may have special difficulties. Under these conditions, mature students and overseas students are often regarded as focus groups, which reflects a reasonable concern by institutions but also leads to a possible neglect of other categories of student.

855.   Next, **credit-based systems of choice are not yet well-developed;** many institutions have not yet made sufficient progress towards greater internal academic flexibility for them to feel it necessary to put in place guidance infrastructures. This may help to explain the relative absence of guidance arrangements in the 'old' universities, with the notable exception of the Open University. It

may also explain the uneven development of such arrangements in the 'new' universities as well. And finally, there is a belief that **existing arrangements can cope adequately;** this will usually be the case where institutions see little external or internal pressure from students for better course information, possibly in conditions where academic staff are able to supply the minimum guidance necessary for student progression.

The ECCTIS database

856.   The principal database on credit systems and credit transfer in the United Kingdom is the ECCTIS database. Its origins have been described in Chapter VI. After a slower beginning than might have been anticipated ten years ago, the ECCTIS database has now begun to establish a network of institutional users. In 1990, there were 150 subscribers to its CD-ROM database and 1000 on-line users. By 1993, over 3200 subscribers were gaining access to the database via CD-ROM. This included 50% of all secondary schools, nearly 500 further education and sixth-form colleges, 100 TEC/LECs and Training Access Points (TAPs), 100 users subscribing through the British Council, and most higher education institutions. The database is also a principal point of contact for international enquiries and is closely engaged with developments in Europe.

The effectiveness of ECCTIS as a national database

857.   A comprehensive evaluation of the effectiveness of ECCTIS has not been possible within the scope of this investigation. However, we have considered whether any alternative arrangements were appropriate for the effective marketing and dissemination of credit-based learning opportunities. These could include charging other higher education agencies, including the HEQC, with the responsibility; inviting private agencies to contract for the work; or contracting with an individual institution, such as the Open University. On the balance of evidence, and from an assessment of the alternatives, we have come to the following conclusions.

858. Firstly, the HEQC, or another similar agency, could not fulfil the functions of ECCTIS without taking over its assets and arrangements, at substantial cost to the institutions which support the Council. Thereafter, no significant advantages would accrue over existing arrangements and we can find few good reasons why this approach should be commended. Secondly, extending an invitation to provide the service to another commercial agency would serve little purpose at this stage. The database is already provided by a commercially viable company, ECCTIS 2000, and we see no advantages in disturbing this. For the same reason, we can see no advantage in cost or quality from inviting tenders from other institutions or similar bodies. Accordingly, **we recommend** that ECCTIS should continue to be the national credit transfer information service and continue to fulfil the functions for which it has been established by the DFE. The information service should be modified and developed to reflect the new context in which students can benefit from credit transfer opportunities. The form of the information service should be directed at the needs of the consumer to enable well-informed participation in further and higher education.

Improving ECCTIS

859. It is important to note that the penetration by ECCTIS of higher education institutions has been slower than in other sectors. This is largely because most institutional users perceive the database as relevant for higher education entry requirements rather than for in-programme progression. Moreover, students themselves appear to be infrequent users of the database and do not appear to be referred to it in any systematic manner. In many cases, institutions do not make available publicity on the services of ECCTIS, and ECCTIS does not usually provide detailed in-programme information that might be useful to them. This has important consequences for the role of databases for credit systems, and for ECCTIS in particular. We believe that the service ECCTIS offers can be improved in anticipation of an increase in the opportunities for credit transfer and student mobility over the next decade. These improvements are indicated in Table 56 and **we**

recommend that steps be taken to ensure their implementation by institutions and other relevant bodies.

860. In order to implement these proposals cost-effectively, certain steps will need to be taken to ease the transfer of data from institutions to ECCTIS databases. Arrangements currently exist with funding councils for the electronic transfer of data and **we recommend** that pilot projects be established with a restricted range of institutions in the first instance to explore the characteristics of information systems and the form of data that will be necessary for the systematic transfer of relevant data to the ECCTIS databases.

861. There is one suggestion contained in Table 56 to which we attach particular importance. This concerns the proposal that ECCTIS should develop inter-active CD-ROM information and guidance facilities to encourage student use. This points to one of the major weaknesses of the entire ECCTIS project. Electronic databases tend to be passive, non-interactive and, above all else, impersonal; they lack a human interface. For many students, this will be an impediment to systematic guidance. Accordingly, **we recommend** that further consideration be given to closer working relationships between ECCTIS and individual institutions in the management of individual enquiries. We have not been able to explore the implications fully but it could be possible that the network of regional offices, and the established professional experience provided by the Open University, could be a starting point for a human complement to the interactive electronic environment that might otherwise develop.

862. It is apparent to us as well that institutions generally need to develop a more active engagement with the provisions of the ECCTIS database. This may arise as a consequence of steps ECCTIS may take itself in its efforts to improve the quality of information on the databases by closer institutional liaison. If these proposals are implemented by ECCTIS, institutions may find advantage in establishing a professional point of contact for these liaisons in the future. This will also be necessary if institutions are to meet the terms of the

Table 56: Proposals for improvement to the service provided by ECCTIS

As part of the recommendations in Chapter X to develop a National Credit Register, the following proposals are offered to improve the service provided by ECCTIS in keeping with this objective.

1. Institutional liaison and data collection

The range and quality of data held on the ECCTIS database could be improved by closer institutional liaison, involving a case-by-case approach to institutional data. This would be expensive in the first instance but could be handled by trained temporary staff, employing former students as research assistants perhaps, or by other means. The purpose of the exercise would be to assist institutions with extensive or complex credit-based arrangements in defining these for the ECCTIS database, and establishing a basis from which future data collection exercises might be mounted.

2. Strengthening information on credit transfer in modular programmes

As a national credit framework begins to evolve and be established, ECCTIS will need to support a wider range of credit transfer activity. It could do this by:

- strengthening the information which is already provided on entry requirements for courses and named pathways through modular systems so that this could be used more in a credit transfer context as well as in a traditional context;

- providing more information on exit possibilities from courses and pathways (cf. if new interim awards are approved);

- strengthening the information on modular and credit scheme details to reflect credit transfer as well as traditional entry opportunities;

- including detailed entry and exit information at the modular level as and when institutions are able to provide it, and when resources become available to develop the appropriate software, in order to prepare for the development of a *national electronic catalogue;*

- providing specific information, where available, on work-based learning for academic credit and similar institutional internships;

- identifying dual accreditation arrangements between institutions of higher education and NCVQ;

- including tariff information from institutional programmes within a national credit framework;

- developing a specific service with respect to the credit-based provision of the Open University and to provide information for potential centrally-registered students.

3. Extending the service to include credit for 'off-campus' learning

ECCTIS should be invited to hold responsibility for collecting and disseminating appropriate information on 'off-campus' learning opportunities. ECCTIS should collect information from providing institutions, and provide a service to explain their opportunities and promote them to prospective users. This service could also be extended to provide a database of credit from courses in the responsibility of professional bodies, employers and other subscribing agencies or corporate bodies.

4. Publicising ECCTIS in universities and colleges

It would be considerably helpful to the further development of information on credit-based learning if universities and colleges were to include specific reference and guidance on ECCTIS in institutional prospectuses and other similar materials.

5. Providing a service on credit systems in further education and beyond

A comprehensive national database on credit will need to anticipate the rapid development of credit systems in further education. Work within credit-awarding Open College Networks is now percolating more extensively throughout further education, and this is supplemented by the expansion of interest prompted by the FEU Credit Network. A number of related databases need to be developed, with resource implications which will have to be assessed:

- data on links between further and higher education, including 'franchising' arrangements and other bilateral programmes. This data could also include information on exit from further education and on entry to higher education programmes;

- continued information on access courses, but with data to specify single or multiple exit opportunities, and whether any articulation or 'guaranteed places' agreements exist;

- data on the developing credit systems in further education colleges;

- data on credit-bearing programmes of Open College Networks.

6. Fulfilling its role with respect to other agencies

ECCTIS should continue to fulfil its role in the collection and dissemination of information on credit transfer through formal liaison and co-operation with appropriate national agencies, including UCAS, NCVQ, further education agencies and the Open University Central Registry. ECCTIS may need to anticipate a further expansion of its role if the NCVQ agrees to work with a common credit currency for the purposes of credit transfer into higher education academic qualifications and elsewhere.

7. An international role for ECCTIS

ECCTIS should continue to supply the European Higher Education database with information on credit systems in the United Kingdom. It should act as principal conduit for information on European credit transfer opportunities to the United Kingdom. Wherever possible, information should cover national qualification systems, institutional characteristics and provision, qualifications and courses.

8. Improvements in student access to ECCTIS databases

Much information is currently ahead of the needs of students. Yet this may not remain so for much longer although students may need to be 'trained' to use ECCTIS regularly. The present ECCTIS service should be developed to integrate the information already present on qualification systems with the course information to make it more accessible and usable in the credit transfer context. In this respect the ECCTIS database should be:

- designed for interactive interrogation by users, to guide an individual through the information according to his/her circumstances;

- developed as hard copy publications to encourage and direct consumers towards credit transfer opportunities, using electronic services as their main source of information;

- developed as an on-line *national electronic catalogue* with a suitable programme of training for students.

recommendations contained in Chapter X which refer to the expectation that institutions will place on public record, through a *National Credit Register*, their credit rating agreements with various parties.

863.	Furthermore, the extension of the scope of ECCTIS to provide data *at the level of the module* appears at first inspection to be an enormous undertaking. Indeed this would be the case if the exercise remained paper-based. However, we are aware that some institutions are already capable of supplying detailed disk-based information on their modular and credit-based programmes and other institutions are likely to follow in this manner. We have considered the question: is this level of detailed information helpful to students and other users? One answer would suggest that it is not, and could be counter-productive to effective student choice by providing a baffling array of detail that could not be negotiated by students and their advisers. Furthermore, some of the data would change annually and the effort of up-dating information would be considerable. On the other hand, if the data is being captured, formatted and renewed electronically, ECCTIS could build an *electronic catalogue* of learning opportunities which could be accessed on-line as well as provided via interactive CD-ROM.

A national electronic catalogue for higher education

864.	Although we are aware that there will be some well-judged scepticism directed at this concept, we do not think it is so fanciful to imagine students gaining on-line access to an *electronic catalogue* of higher education opportunities. Within five years, nearly 80% of 16-year olds will have significant proficiency in information technology, enabling them to use electronic media in ways which current generations of students do not. We are not suggesting that conventional prospectuses will be replaced, but it is imaginable that ECCTIS could be the organising agency for the co-ordination of institutional course and modular databases. Indeed, it may be possible to develop a division of labour between

- **a national credit register:** containing the general credit rating and credit transfer

arrangements of institutions, employers and professional bodies; published as a hardcopy public reference document;

- **a national electronic catalogue:** containing detailed specifications of institutional programmes, credit-rated *or otherwise,* which would be accessible on-line and via CD-ROM but which would be held as softcopy to allay the costs of physical reproduction. Accessing the *electronic catalogue* would be little different from engaging in a computer-based search of a library catalogue or citations index.

865.	Accordingly, **we recommend** that a pilot study be undertaken to assess the feasibility of establishing a *national electronic catalogue.* Interested parties might be the Department for Education and the Employment Department on the one hand, the individual institutions themselves on the other, and additionally the NCVQ and the further education sector may also have an interest.

A strategy for information on higher education

866.	During our enquiries we have found some confusion amongst students and academic colleagues about where to look for authoritative information on higher education. The problem appears to occur when interested individuals have to decide, on the one hand, between the 'official' sources of information and those which are produced by private companies largely for commercial gain, and on the other hand between the competing claims of individual institutions.

867.	In the first case, 'official' sources of information include the ECCTIS databases, the publications of the Universities' Central Admissions Service (UCAS) and those of the Association of Graduate Careers Advisory Services (AGCAS) as well as the publications of individual institutions and national agencies. Other sources of information include materials from HEIST, CRAC and CSD. However, students are aware that there are alternative sources of information and 'graduate guides' published by commercial companies which will contain varying assessments of the merits of institutions. To this may be added the current trend towards the publication of listings and 'league tables' based on diverse performance criteria.

868.   We understand very clearly that, with 350,000 students annually seeking information on higher education learning opportunities, there are enormous commercial attractions in being able to penetrate such an influential market. Furthermore, in choosing the most appropriate course at the right university, individuals will often be making the most important decision of their personal careers and it is important that this is based on sound information. The significance of this will be enhanced if institutions do begin competitive recruitment by encouraging credit transfer. The combination of commercial opportunity and public interest will need to be carefully balanced if the quality of information is to be assured.

A code of practice and 'kitemark' on information quality

869.   One way to assure the quality of information would be to develop a regulatory code of conduct. However, it is not clear to whom this would apply and who would enforce it. Furthermore, it could unproductively diminish the diversity of information sources available to students and restrict the development of others. We see no possibility of regulation in these matters, nor of restrictions on the pursuit of commercial opportunities.

870.   Instead we recommend the development of a professional *code of practice* on the quality of information to students. This would identify the minimum conditions that an information source would need to satisfy; it would distinguish between products designed for marketing and recruitment on the one hand, and products designed to provide high quality and objective information on the other. The representative bodies of the institutions might define the code of practice themselves, or more probably delegate the matter to the HEQC. Thereafter, **we recommend** that information products which

subscribe to the code of practice and pass the threshold criteria for information quality could bear the 'kitemark' of approval from the HEQC or other designated body.

871.   We believe the effect of this approach will be to secure the confidence of students, professional bodies, employers and the institutions themselves in the quality of available information. It will encourage institutions to decide what they intend for their existing prospectuses and other educational publications. In short, it will allow institutions to develop their prospectuses as marketing and recruitment tools without necessarily giving students the impression that this is the same as reliable information on the academic programme. For that information, students will have to turn to the *course catalogues, electronic databases* or similar products that institutions will need to develop in the future.

872.   For commercial companies, they will be free to prepare publications to inform the student market but if they see advantage in an *information quality 'kitemark'*, they will be able to apply for it from the appropriate higher education agency. We do not believe this will impede the production of listings, 'league tables' or other unofficial information sources, nor do we believe a quality 'kitemark' will deliver to the institutions the power to inhibit the availability of unwelcome assessments. We do strongly believe, however, that such an arrangement will make a significant contribution to securing greater confidence in the objectivity and *independence of information* that is sought by prospective students and others.

Guidance and information within higher education institutions

873.   One of the most noticeable effects of the pressure to increase student recruitment over the past few years has been the attention which institutions have paid to the preparation of the market. Large sums of money have been spent by some institutions in an effort to establish their identity amongst prospective students. We have seen new institutional

products, ranging from videos to expensively redesigned prospectuses, which have been developed to attract students. However, we have not seen a commensurate improvement in the quality of information available to students. Institutional course prospectuses are often better presented and many universities look more inviting, but as academic guidance products they are no more informative than in the past. Our impression is that this initial phase in the transformation of higher education to a system based on democratic participation has been successful in the development of institutional marketing skills. It may now be necessary for institutions to make the same commitment in the second phase to improvements in the quality of the institutional information and student guidance.

874.   The guidance cycle for students follows the progress of their personal learning career. This can be grouped into four stages:

- **guidance for application and admission;** focusing on comparative information for institutional and programme choice;

- **pre-entry guidance;** 'post-acceptance' information on specific programme planning requirements, or the initial negotiation of 'learning agreements';

- **in-programme guidance;** for students who are 'moving on', or modifying initial programmes and learning agreements, or changing course or institution;

- **exit guidance;** usually careers guidance for employment opportunities, postgraduate careers and similar developments.

Guidance and the admissions process

875.   The admissions system enables multiple application to institutions and is primarily based upon the predicted performance of learners. Decisions about offers are strongly influenced by teachers' predictions of learners' eventual performances (usually at 'A' level). These predictions are notoriously inaccurate. A PCAS survey of predictions of 'A' level grades in academic references of

applicants for 1991 entry found that overall 64.4% of grades were incorrectly predicted, with most of the predictions involving over-assessment. Such predictions influence applicants' aspirations and are often used by admission tutors to select for interview or offer and to determine the conditions of the offers they make. Due to pressure of numbers and time, for an increasing majority of applicants the admission process is based upon a paper exercise backed up by attendance at open days after choices have been made. Other methods, including interviews, are also used, particularly for those applying for entry with credit.

876.   Under the existing admissions system, many applicants initially receive conditional offers. While it is straightforward to make an offer conditional on 'A' level points, recent developments, particularly GNVQs, Records of Achievement and the planned introduction of a modular 'A' level, will make it difficult for institutions to phrase conditional offers, as admissions tutors will have to take a wider range of factors into account.

877.   The existing admissions system appears in some respects to work against informed learner choice. In particular, the length of the lead time can push applicants into premature decision-making. Applicants make their choices about higher education courses approximately a year before they begin their preferred programmes, and an applicant of any age can develop considerably during this time. A learner who, after a period out of education, starts a one year Access course in late September will rarely be able to make a properly informed decision about higher education by early December. Equally, teenagers in a sixth form are at one of the most developmental periods of their lives.

878.   Applicants who have not secured a place and courses with places remaining can enter the Clearing system. Clearing starts in the last week of August, after the publication of 'A' level results, and runs until the start of term. Courses often move in and out of Clearing rapidly. The timing of the Clearing system thus forces applicants to make snap decisions, under considerable pressure, about institutions and learning programmes.

The problems this causes are intensified for applicants to credit-based programmes, given the more complex decisions they have to make. The tension that is created between applicants who are keen to get a place and tutors who want to fill courses can lead to poor decisions being made. As a result, learners who have been recruited through Clearing are more likely to subsequently withdraw from their programmes.

879. Universities and colleges provide information individually and collectively through national organisations about the educational opportunities they offer. The majority of this information is produced around eighteen months in advance of learners entering higher education and is primarily aimed at learners entering the first year of undergraduate programmes, often to the neglect of information on BTEC or SCOTVEC diplomas and certificates. The course information upon which applicants base their decisions may not be entirely up-to-date, as it is produced so far in advance and is often in a printed form which cannot be quickly modified. Typically, the information provided is a mix of general background to the institution with some detail about particular courses designed and delivered by the institution.

880. Increasing financial pressures, including the fall in value of the student grant, the withdrawal from students of state benefits and the need to borrow to study full time, will encourage learners to study part-time and to move in and out of higher education as they attempt to pay their way through it. Such developments will also give financial advice a much higher priority for learners than was previously the case. Institutions will increasingly need to provide guidance about financial self-management and about alternative sources of funding such as trusts, charities and access funds. Some groups, including students with disabilities, may be eligible for additional state support, and institutions should be able to guide them on this issue.

881. Under existing methods of student funding, learners can be financially penalised for taking advantage of the flexibility available in credit based systems. As we have argued in Chapter XI, the system of mandatory awards, which was designed for learners following a full-time course, causes particular problems for learners who wish to study in a more flexible manner. They may not be eligible for awards or may run the risk of losing all or part of their entitlement. This can affect learners who move in and out of higher education, transfer between institutions or wish to move between part-time and full-time study during a programme. Part time learners are not eligible for mandatory awards. All of this places practical financial constraints on the flexibility which is theoretically available.

From prospectus to catalogue

882. From this we conclude that institutions may need to consider improving and expanding the information they make available to students *at the point of initial choice* and thereafter. This might be achieved in a number of ways. Firstly, **we recommend** that institutions consider separating conceptually, and then practically, their recruitment from their guidance strategies. In other words, they should decide, in the first instance, whether their prospectus is an instrument for marketing or for student assistance in making the right choice of academic programme. We are disturbed by the possibility that some students may be ensnared by the blandishments of an attractive prospectus and register for a course which does not suit them.

883. To prevent this possibility, we would encourage institutions to consider the following case. For institutions with traditional linear, or single-subject programmes, the conventional prospectus might be able to serve both functions adequately. It can present the environment of the university and its cultural amenities as attractively as possible while recording the courses on offer. Where students wish to exercise no greater choice than that of institution and initial subject, this strategy will continue to work, as it has done in the past. On the other hand, as many institutions adopt more or less extensive credit-based and modular programmes, the needs of students change. Under these conditions, they may be assisted by a more detailed presentation of the individual modules that make up the total programme. This may be required even where there are

modular structures rather than modular schemes (see Chapters VIII and XII). To achieve this, institutions will need to move from the course-based prospectus to a module-based catalogue, in which there may be a marketing product *in addition* to the student catalogue.

884.   A small number of universities and colleges with modular programmes and greater internal choice have begun to move in this direction. Well-established schemes, such as that at Oxford Brookes University, have always been supported by extensive module catalogues, but we have been very impressed by the *Guide and Catalogue* of Middlesex University. It appears to be a good example of its type. It is comprehensive and informative on the details of each module in the academic programme of the university. The module data is grouped by subject and records the credit rating, semester and geographical location, brief content, assessment requirements and eligibility restrictions. The catalogue is itself simply but professionally designed, without pictures or colour, but accessible and attractive. It is clearly a product designed for guidance and information rather than for marketing and recruitment.

885.   In commending the catalogue of Middlesex University as the style which certain other universities may imitate with advantage, we are aware that some other institutions have produced hybrid solutions. These usually involve investment in an expensively designed prospectus which, purporting to promote a modular or credit-based programme, in fact presents the programme as a series of traditional subject-courses. Students are presented with the 'rhetoric' of modularity but cannot grasp its reality, and therefore its suitability for them, from the prospectus itself. *Hybrid solutions* therefore require students to commit to modular programmes on the promise that further detail and explanation will follow at entry. In the absence of a general culture of choice and flexibility, this can prove disturbing for some students. Therefore, we welcome with enthusiasm the efforts by some institutions to publish *Programme catalogues* in addition to their marketing prospectuses, and **we recommend** this as the way forward.

Rolling admissions arrangements

886.   We have received strong representations, particularly from colleagues at UCAS and elsewhere, that more thought should be given to repositioning the start of the academic year until January (or possibly November) in order to give applicants time to make informed choices. We do not intend to reopen the debates that have taken place during the production of the Flowers and Irvine Reports on reform of the academic year. We have supported the principal proposals for reform in Chapter XII as the best means of managing credit-based flexibility. In our judgement, there is an inadequate case for repositioning the entire academic year for a January (or November) start. Whatever the merits for informed student choice, these would be massively offset by the disturbance to most patterns of institutional behaviour, to the conventional rhythms of student life and to prospects for international harmonisation.

887.   However, we do believe there would be merit, for some students, in promoting the development of an admissions cycle starting in January (and/or, say, May). It is with this in mind that we have proposed the establishment of a new interim qualification, the *Associate degree,* as defined in Chapter IX. With its mix of academic knowledge and core skills at the early stages, it could make an ideal candidate for a January admission cycle, particularly when coupled with a Summer semester.

Pre-entry guidance in higher education

888.   As students move from initial selection to application and then acceptance, institutions offering multiple choice opportunities need to ensure that guidance is available from this stage onwards and reaches all potential applicants. The very flexibility and choice available in a credit-based system means that applicants have more complex guidance needs at the pre-entry stage. They may have questions about modes of study and entry and exit points. They need detailed information about the units/modules available if they are to benefit fully from the choices offered. Such information should include content, pre- and co-requisites, teaching, learning and assessment

methods and ideally feedback from previous learners. The needs of students can be increased where institutions provide any sort of elective programme. Pre-planning these programmes can be essential if effective student choice is to be managed.

889.   Students also need information to clarify the implications of their choices, in terms of, for example, future learning and career options. Applicants to modular programmes have a right to know the title of the awards available to them. They also have the right to receive impartial support in the process of making their choices. Ideally institutions need to aim for the following arrangements:

- **pre-entry programme construction,** whereby prospective entrants receive sufficient information and pro forma guidance to be able to propose an initial construction of a personal learning programme. They would need to receive the range of eligible modules, the rules of engagement and combination and the possible routes and qualifications implied by different module combinations;

- **programme negotiation,** where students, on arrival at the university, receive an opportunity for further guidance before having their personal learning programme finally negotiated with, and authenticated by, an appropriate academic authority.

In-programme guidance for moving-on

890.   Credit-based systems create a need for continuous guidance. Institutions need to move from a reactive 'emergency' culture where guidance is often seen simply as the provision of basic information and support for students with problems, to one that is proactive, where learners have consistent access to guidance services from application to moving-on from an institution.

891.   We have been disappointed in our investigations not to have found good examples of institutional practice for *in-programme guidance*. We should be sure to exempt the Open University from this charge

although that institution has developed arrangements in response to a unique mission. At one extreme, 'guidance' appears to take the form of a 'Progress Committee' in cases where a student appears to be failing. In our opinion, whilst it is reasonable to expect students to take personal responsibility for their performance and progress through the university, it is in no way an effective expression of educational guidance for students in difficulty to be asked to attend what amounts to a quasi-disciplinary hearing before the Dean or other authority. Examples of this nature have led us to believe that, in many institutions, the rationale for guidance does not appear to have been fully understood by management. There is considerable room for improvement in most institutions in order to establish educational guidance as a normal part of institutional life.

892.   With the exception of circumstances where guidance is closely related to the management of specific 'CAT Schemes', or to the Open University which we have mentioned earlier, guidance services are often fragmented, with poor communication links between central services and department or school staff. There may be confusion or lack of awareness among both academic staff and learners about what guidance services are available, where they are located and what their function is. Indeed where staff are employed in professional guidance work, they often had to negotiate their way across some sensitive professional boundaries.

Improving in-programme guidance

893.   There may be several practical ways in which this marginalisation and confusion may be replaced by more constructive arrangements. Firstly, institutions could define the educational guidance function as an essential part of learning support activities. It could rank with libraries and learning resources, or with academic computing support, as a professional para-academic service with a definitive staff establishment. This would be costly for institutions, but less costly than the investments they often make in marketing and image consultants. **We recommend** the development of a **professional para-academic service** dedicated to the provision of educational guidance and support.

894. Secondly, we believe there may be advantages for students in defining personal programme negotiation through educational guidance as an accreditable academic activity. In our opinion, it could easily pass the academic quality thresholds which have been established for introductory modules in information technology, for example. Moreover, the Enterprise in Higher Education initiative has attempted to encourage institutions to build into student programmes aspects of personal competence. By offering credit for *personal educational planning and development*, there may be further opportunities to embed personal enterprise skills into the curriculum. If some institutions were to offer credit for modules in the planning of careers for learning and employment, this might have the effect of increasing the standing of personal guidance initiatives. Moreover, in an environment where an institution chooses to operate on the basis of credit-led income distribution, the module could quickly become self-financing. For example, if students were invited to earn 10% of their Level 1 credit for such work, it would involve the enrolment of under 200 students during the year to maintain a full-time professional member of staff. In some institutions in the United States, over 2,000 students per annum can earn credit in this way, rising to over 7,000 students per annum in some community colleges. **We recommend** therefore that institutions which operate credit-based modular programmes consider developing credit-bearing modules at undergraduate level in *personal planning for learning and employment*. This could also link with the core skills element which we have proposed for the Associate Degree (see Chapter IX).

895. Finally, academic staff themselves may need much greater support and development if they are to manage their role in the process. The personal tutor system has long been the mainstay of on-course guidance in many English institutions, but is increasingly coming under pressure. Firstly, the personal tutor system has traditionally been based in departments. The shift to flexible learning programmes has meant that learners are likely to be studying across departmental boundaries, to be studying part-time, or to be moving in and out of institutions, making the allocation of learners to tutors and the building of relationships between them more difficult. It may also mean that tutors lack the necessary information to advise learners about units available in other departments. The increase in student numbers is perhaps an even greater source of pressure, as many personal tutors may feel that they simply do not have the time to fulfil their role. However, an accessible point of reference remains important for learners especially since there may be a lack of cohesive group identities within flexible programmes.

896. In the light of the above, there is a need to examine appropriate developments and alternatives. Firstly, it does not appear to be clear what is expected of the academic 'personal tutor' system. It offers both generalised personal counselling and support whilst purporting to offer curriculum guidance as well. Academic staff can argue with some justification that they are not professionally competent to offer either service adequately, unless the academic guidance is largely limited to subject discipline advice. Members of academic staff may also lack appreciation and awareness of flexible programmes, or even be hostile to them. They may see credit-based systems as undermining traditional academic values and professional expertise or as a manifestation of increased managerial power. Institutional traditions of lateral integration and vertical progression in course planning and teaching conflict with the need for flexibility of credit-based systems and lead to stress among staff. Furthermore, ineffective inter-subject or inter-departmental communication can be frustrating for staff, making it difficult for them to develop and maintain a positive attitude to credit-based systems.

897. This will be of no consolation to learners who may in some cases have strong feelings of isolation and marginalisation, sensing in the frustrations of academic staff that they lack a 'home' within the institution. This seriously affects the quality of their experience and can lead to high levels of dissatisfaction with a programme and/or institution. This kind of mutual alienation can lead to administrative confusion. Important details about a learner's progress or personal circumstances may thus not be registered by the institution, or may be

held in different locations without being properly collated.

Encouraging peer group self-activity

898.   Matters may not be as bleak as these difficulties would suggest. The transition from course-based to programme-based academic support is bound to create a hiatus in familiar relationships. Some of these interruptions may be dealt with by other means. Firstly, learners currently acquire a significant amount of guidance from other learners. Some institutions have made initial efforts to encourage the development of **peer group networks.** These can play an important role, acting as learning aids, information exchanges and sources of informal support and feedback. Institutions have often taken a *laissez-faire* approach to such provision. However, the introduction of credit-based systems and the increasing size and heterogeneity of the learner body means that it can no longer be left to chance. **We recommend** that institutions should take responsibility for the promotion of peer group networks and examine ways of establishing structures to support them.

899.   Secondly, a number of institutions have developed programmes where Level 2 or Level 3 learners act as **student mentors** to groups of Level 1 learners, often as an accredited unit of their study programmes. Mentoring programmes may also be developed for specific groups such as mature and overseas students. Such schemes help build a sense of identity and ensure peer-group support. In addition, the level one learners as well as the mentors can develop valuable personal transferable skills through such programmes. In particular, group work can develop decision-making skills. Institutions have also developed systems of 'core units', which can assist in the development of a mutually supportive student group by providing a meeting point for learners on flexible programmes, irrespective of the particular units that they are taking, and again can develop personal skills.

Exit guidance

900.   It does not fall within our terms of reference to comment on the many

important aspects of careers guidance, and the investigation did not explore practice in this field to any significant extent. We have made reference to the need to address matters related to careers guidance throughout this chapter, but would make three points in conclusion. Firstly, careers guidance and its related services (employer visits, recruitment events, the PROSPECT system, monitoring and feedback arrangements, and others) are much better established in institutions than educational guidance. Secondly, educational guidance and careers guidance are related but distinct domains of professional practice. The former cannot be collapsed into the latter in credit-based systems. Thirdly, and respecting these points, institutions may find it more efficient to organise their guidance arrangements as a continuum, encouraging students to access different parts of that continuum at different stages of their career in the university. We believe strongly that institutions would serve their students well in conditions of expanded student choice if they were to invest in the same sort of para-academic professional establishment for *educational* guidance as they have done for careers guidance.

The practice of guidance in institutions

901.   We have found it an unavoidable and unwelcome conclusion of our investigation that educational guidance is generally poorly developed in almost all institutions we have observed. The Open University is an honourable exception to this. It alone has invested systematically in educational guidance and has made it a natural part of the professional role of many academic staff the University employs. Moreover, it has treated educational guidance as an accessible and familiar part of the curriculum for *all* students rather than a stigmatised minority. In so many ways, it acts as a model for others to imitate.

902.   There are other commendable institutional examples. At Coventry University, for instance, they have re-organised the structure of the guidance provision developing an integrated approach. *Guidance*

Services provides educational and vocational guidance from pre-entry through on-programme to moving-on. It comprises:

- information team

- educational liaison

- education and careers advice

- community education development

- the Study Advice Centre.

The Study Advice Centre is located in the city centre, but the other elements share a common base in the University. Within the Information Team, a former careers library has been developed to address needs from pre-entry onwards, a process which has included the development of computerised guidance packages. The Education and Careers Advisers also have a broadened remit to provide guidance from pre-entry onwards, as well as retaining responsibility for specialist areas. *Guidance Services* offers a more closely co-ordinated service for users than was previously available. It provides a publicised and accessible service for applicants and learners at all stages of their learning careers. It is also well placed to deal with monitoring and feedback, for example assessing the quality of guidance and analysing the needs of enquirers.

903.   At the University of Central Lancashire, with the introduction of a university-wide credit accumulation and transfer scheme, Academic Advising has replaced Personal Tutoring. The Academic Advisers aid learners in designing their study programmes, and record their choices. They therefore need a thorough knowledge of the CAT scheme. They also provide learners with help and advice on other issues, referring as necessary. The University has also appointed an Academic Programmes Adviser, whose responsibility it is to co-ordinate academic advice across the entire institution, working with both staff and learners. The Programmes Adviser is involved with the provision of relevant staff development for all staff involved in advising and supporting learners, and in providing the information and support such staff need to carry out their roles.

The Programmes Adviser also provides independent advice to learners whose guidance needs have not been met elsewhere in the institution.

904.   Sheffield Hallam University has adopted a phased introduction of a more flexible curriculum through piloting a broad Combined Studies Programme and school-based programmes, prior to the development of wide-ranging Level 1 programmes. A number of methods of providing learner support and guidance are being utilised during the initial pilot. These include the development of core 'skills units' at Level 1, which develop personal and curriculum-related skills. These are part of the assessed curriculum and are designed to support learners through Level 1 and to prepare them for making choices at Level 2. Such units are also used within the Combined Studies Programme to facilitate peer group development. There is also a system of academic advisers, who evaluate a learner's work at Level 1 across all units and give feedback and advice to learners. The University is also committed to the promotion of Personal Development Portfolios that enable learners to evaluate their own progress, design action plans, review strengths and weaknesses and have structured discussions with their Portfolio Tutors. This encourages the integration of personal skills as outcomes in units of study.

905.   We could call on other commendable individual efforts from other institutions but they would not yet add up to a convincing system of educational guidance in support of student choice. We have summarised our assessment of the general state of provision in higher education against the criteria identified by the UDACE projects (see Table 57). On balance there is some progress which does not constitute a movement in favour of increased support.

Do students need educational guidance in higher education?

906.   We cannot leave this matter without considering whether universities would be well-advised in practice to undertake investment in educational guidance for which,

Table 57: The practice of educational guidance and progress in higher education: an assessment

	Definition of activities	Progress in higher education
Informing	Providing information about learning opportunities and related support facilities available, without any discussion of the relative merits of options for particular clients. Since most published educational information is produced for promotional purposes, 'pure' information is rare.	Nationally, ECCTIS database developing well but under–used by individual students. Institutionally, information is extensive on general aspects but poor on specific details of programmes (some exceptions). Prospectuses are strong on marketing and recruitment but weak on academic information.
Advising	Helping clients to interpret information and choose the most appropriate option. To benefit from advice clients must already have a fairly clear idea of what their needs are.	Generally slow development. Few independent arrangements in most institutions, where 'course culture' still dominates. Advice tends to be given in context of professionally–defined preferences rather than that which best suits the individual learner.
Counselling	Working with clients to help them to discover, clarify, assess and understand their learning needs and the various ways of meeting them. Clients requiring counselling are likely to be unclear about their needs and require time to explore their feelings about the options, and counselling is therefore more likely to involve a series of contacts with a single client.	Very poorly developed in higher education. Dominant assumption in institutions remains that students should know their own business, choose their course at entry and stay with it. Educational counselling usually offered as a 'casualty service' for students who are not coping. In the absence of a 'culture of choice', this service has not yet developed.
Assessing	Helping clients, by formal or informal means, to obtain an adequate understanding of their personal, educational and vocational development, in order to enable them to make sound judgements about the appropriateness of particular learning opportunities.	Assessment of individual educational needs is largely undeveloped in higher education. In the absence of an independent guidance service, academic staff assume the role in a more or less competent manner. Other duties usually intrude to prevent development of consistent relationship.
Enabling	Supporting the client in dealing with the agencies providing education or training, or in meeting the demands of particular courses. This may involve simple advice on completing application forms, advice on ways of negotiating changes in course content or arrangements, or assistance to independent learners.	Some encouraging institutional examples, but still very few. Most 'CATS and APEL Units' are in practice guidance services; some 'Education Shops' fulfil similar functions. Much support work takes place prior to arrival in HE through specific preparatory programmes (Access courses etc).
Advocating	Negotiating directly with institutions or agencies on behalf of individuals or groups for whom there may be additional barriers to access or to learning (eg negotiating exceptional entry arrangements or modifications to courses).	Main function of CATS Units. Otherwise there is no generally available institutional mechanism by which students can have their interests represented. Academic tutors usually have neither the time nor the training to play this role, and institutional structures tend to impede successful advocacy outcomes.
Feeding back	Gathering and collating information on unmet, or inappropriately met, needs, and encouraging providers of learning opportunities to respond by developing their provision. This may involve practical changes (eg changing the presentation of course information or changing timetables) or curricular ones (eg designing new courses for new client groups, or changing the way in which existing courses are taught to make them more appropriate for adult learners).	This is widely accepted in principle, but more weakly followed in practice. HE institutions have been slow to respond to student definitions of unmet need, whether in modifying programmes, their delivery or assessment. Some data may be collected by some institutions with which to inform future developments, but this is not as widespread as it might be.

Source: M. Oakeshott, 'Educational Guidance & Curriculum Change', FEU &UDACE, 1990; also evidence to the Project

in the light of events, there may be little student demand. The dilemma is quite simple. Universities in the United Kingdom have traditionally been course-based and prospective students have traditionally arrived directly from secondary school. In the past there has been no apparent need to provide pre-entry or in-programme guidance; students arrived largely 'oven-ready', having being prepared by the narrow 'A' level curriculum for single subject courses with limited choices. As the dominance of the conventional entry cohort has been challenged by rising numbers of students with different ages and backgrounds, universities appear to have adjusted by encouraging the assimilation of these 'new' types of student into the prevailing academic culture. This has largely been distinguished by academic self-reliance, a *laissez-faire* approach to individual progression and the deployment of guidance support as a 'casualty service'. This pattern has been as familiar in many of the 'new' universities as it has been in the established institutions.

907.   Under these conditions, students either have had no need of educational guidance (decisions were being made for them), or found their 'needs' discouraged by cultural and organisational constraints. In short, any demand for educational guidance will be suppressed if students do not find a service to respond when they need it. It becomes part of the accepted way of institutional life not to seek what is not available. So, in one sense, universities have not failed to provide a service in response to demand; they have simply denied expression to any demand.

908.   Matters could continue in this manner, and may do so in many institutions, if greater student choice and flexibility are not promoted. However, the introduction of modular and credit-based learning programmes changes fundamentally the balance of institutional forces. Coupled with the large increase in students who are older and with educationally diverse backgrounds, these changes to the academic structure make it nearly impossible for institutions to resist the claims of those who urge greater investment in educational guidance. Under these conditions, students not only need guidance, they should be actively encouraged to seek it as a general part

of their learning careers. In short, the suppression of demand for guidance by cultural or organisational means could lead to a deterioration in the quality of the student learning experience. This may come to be reflected in a worsening of the retention rate, or a decline in academic performance, or a general diminution in the relevance of higher education for personal enjoyment and success. Whether students 'need' educational guidance or not, universities in the future will *need* to make it available as a matter of course.

Would guidance vouchers be a solution?

909.   One way of stimulating investment in educational guidance might be to issue guidance vouchers to all students. This model is currently being explored by some TECs and is further encouraged in further education by FEFC funding methodologies. We have given this idea considerable thought and believe that in the longer term it may be a way forward in higher education. However, at this stage we do not believe it is an appropriate solution to the problem of under-investment in guidance in higher education for several reasons. Firstly, as we have argued above, the case for improved guidance has yet to be made in higher education and demand from most students is muted. Secondly, most academic programmes in higher education remain very prescriptive and most students generally do not exercise extended choice. Thirdly, guidance vouchers would certainly encourage institutions to invest in guidance services, but the exercise could become very cynical. There would be no guarantee that institutions would increase the choices in their academic programmes, yet they would be keen to 'earn' the income from the vouchers. Sources of guidance which were independent of institutions would also be eager to earn income from vouchers but they would have no purchase on academic structures. Fourthly, institutions would rightly resent and resist efforts to cajole them to change their academic course structures in order to legitimate student guidance vouchers. For these reasons, we do not believe guidance vouchers can precede the decisions by institutions voluntarily to introduce greater choice into their academic programmes.

A code of practice for educational guidance in higher education

910.   In conclusion, we have recognised that the need for a sophisticated educational guidance service will vary with the character of the institutional mission. Individual universities and colleges will therefore make different commitments to this service or develop it over a number of years. Every institution does not need to aspire to the level of provision of the Open University in these matters, but many institutions may need to move purposefully in that direction. In Table 58, we have provided a *Code of Practice* by which institutions may choose to be guided. This code complements many of the recommendations we proposed in Chapter XII and augments the recommendations we make in this particular discussion. If the *Code of Practice* has any value, it will be because it encourages institutions to focus attention on the importance of educational guidance as a necessary condition for choice and flexibility in higher education. The code emphasises the targets and practical conditions that an institution may need to meet in the provision of a guidance service. It does not stress the strategic importance of doing so. Throughout the preceding discussion we have been concerned to show how *informed* student choice carries benefits for individuals and institutions. We have perhaps understated the importance of this for the efficient deployment of national resources.

911.   We may look back in 20 years' time to review the progress we have made in higher education towards a more open and flexible system. In our judgement, it is likely that the rate of progress will be a direct reflection of the confidence with which future generations of students are able to negotiate the opportunities that are opening up before them. If they feel intimidated or confused by the freedoms and choices, this may fuel the efforts of those for whom greater individual choice represents a challenge to their priorities in the world. The effect will be to slow down the rate of change towards modular and credit-based academic programmes on the specious grounds that they are unpopular with students, or that they produce fragmented and poor-quality outcomes. In short, a failure to invest in adequate guidance arrangements at this stage may well lead to the undermining of confidence in academic structures which encourage student choice in the future. On the other hand, if institutions make the appropriate investment in educational guidance now, they may succeed in preparing students for a culture of choice and flexibility in years to come. For these reasons, it is important that investment in educational guidance needs to occupy the strategic centre of policy development in higher education institutions in a way that has not been the case hitherto.

Table 58: Principles and a code of practice for educational guidance in higher education

Learner entitlements

1. Potential learners should be entitled to accurate information and advice on the national opportunities available through higher education, on student financial support and on career/professional opportunities. This service should be accessible nationally and internationally.

2. Learners should be entitled to have any appropriate prior learning considered for entry with credit and to advice and information on the necessary procedures, which should be published by ECCTIS 2000.

3. Learners are entitled to comprehensive impartial guidance in respect of curriculum choices within the institution, the consequences of those choices, and the scope for and implications of changes.

4. In order to enable informed decision making, learners should be entitled to feedback and guidance on performance, progression and choice at the end of each semester or academic year, prior to progression.

5. Learners should be entitled to careers information and guidance throughout their time in the institution.

Institutional responsibilities

1. Institutions should provide comprehensive information about educational opportunities, admissions policies, entry criteria, learning methods, levels of entry and careers. Information about entry criteria should be in respect of knowledge, skills and experience as well as qualifications.

2. Information should be student centred, user friendly and preferably computerised. It should be directed at learners and in some cases at targeted groups.

3. Institutions should provide an appropriate, accessible and publicised initial contact point able to give impartial advice to all enquirers.

4. Institutions should collaborate with other educational guidance providers, employers of graduates, LEAs and TECs, through networks, consortia and federations.

5. Institutions should aspire to make available to learners at the earliest possible opportunity in their application and enrolment cycle the best possible information on programme options to assist personal programme planning and development.

6. Institutions should provide for all new entrants (whatever level/mode), a comprehensive induction programme which includes information about: modules, learning methods, assessment methods and regulations, learner support, guidance network/provision, financial support and provision, personal welfare and careers.

7. Institutions should provide all learners with detailed transcripts identifying performance at the end of each assessment period, in order to assist credit accumulation and transfer. The transcripts should include a clear statement of the credit and level achieved within the context of the national credit accumulation and transfer framework.

8. Institutions should ensure that feedback gathered from guidance is fully included within their curriculum review and development process.

9. Institutions should include within their corporate staff training programmes, appropriate and comprehensive staff development activities for all staff, on the advice, support and guidance of learners and potential learners.

Recommendations and guidance for future policy

On the strategic importance of investment in educational guidance

To individual institutions and their representative bodies, HEQC and funding councils

89. For institutions actively committed to extending student choice and flexibility, and to institutions anticipating progress in this direction, **we recommend** that they incorporate a commitment to educational guidance in their institutional mission statements and take steps to secure improved investment in educational guidance through the appointment of an *independent professional para-academic staff* of educational guidance advisers.

90. **We recommend** that institutions consider adopting a *Code of Practice* for educational guidance, based on the principles and targets identified in Table 57 of this report.

91. **We recommend** that individual institutions give early consideration at a strategic level to the conclusions of the *National Educational Guidance Initiative* with a view to implementing its recommendations.

On the future role of ECCTIS

To DFE, ECCTIS 2000, HEQC, individual institutions and their representative bodies

92. **We recommend** that ECCTIS be confirmed and supported as the principal source of information on credit systems, student flexibility and mobility in the United Kingdom in line with the proposals in Table 56 of this report and that its role be expanded to provide data on:

- credit transfer and student choice within modular programmes

- the credit ratings of 'off-campus' learning, including programmes from employers and professional bodies

- credit-bearing programmes in post-secondary and further education, including Access courses and the courses accredited by Open College Networks.

93. **We recommend** that ECCTIS be responsible for the development and production of:

- the *National Credit Register* (including CD-ROM and hardcopy versions)

- a *National Electronic Catalogue* on credit-bearing opportunities in higher education (on-line access only).

94. **We recommend** that further consideration be given by appropriate parties to arrangements for the provision of a national educational guidance and counselling service, complementing the database service provided by ECCTIS, but providing personal interaction between students and professional guidance advisers.

On improving educational guidance for students in higher education

To individual institutions and their representative bodies

95 As part of a strategy to build on existing practice and improve the quality of information and guidance to students in higher education institutions, **we recommend** that individual institutions work towards the following:

- the production of a comprehensive *Programme Catalogue* in addition to their institutional prospectus

- the preparation and dissemination to prospective students, in advance of registration, of programme information which offers guidance on the construction of personal learning programmes, the academic authenticity of which may be negotiated and confirmed at entry

- the development of modules for the award of academic credit in *Personal Planning for Learning and Employment*

- the development of *networks for peer group support* and for in-programme student mentoring.

On a quality 'kitemark' for information on higher education

To the representative bodies of institutions and the HEQC

96 To assure confidence amongst students, employers and the general public in the quality of documentary information published about higher education, **we recommend** that appropriate parties representing the institutions consider the award of a quality 'kitemark' to products and publications which conform to agreed standards and a negotiated code of practice.

XIV.   *International transfer*

Introduction

912.   Prospects for the further development of international credit transfer have rarely been better. Credit systems are in place, or more usually under development, in most industrial countries and in large numbers of developing countries as well. As nations come to expect more from the educational capacity of their citizens, an expansion of participation in higher education appears to be the global response. In most cases this has taken the form of increased diversity and flexibility, mediated by the introduction of credit-based and modular systems.

Credit systems – a global phenomenon

913.   This tendency appears to be most pronounced amongst those nations which do not themselves have a particular higher education culture, or which seek to set aside the culture they may have inherited from a colonial past. To this extent some of the most vigorous developments in the further promotion of credit systems are emerging in New Zealand and Australia, in Thailand and the Philippines, in India and Senegal. In this process, the influence of the American model features prominently. Most if not all credit systems find at some stage that they have to engage with the practices developed in the United States since the mid-19th century. For many countries this involves the production of a synthesis of American ideas with their indigenous structures and cultures. A good example of this approach would be the development of the credit system in Sweden.

914.   Closer to home, 66% of countries in the European Union (EU) and the European Free Trade Association (EFTA) now have some sort of credit system either working or in the process of development. We discuss these developments more extensively below. It is also apparent that credit systems are beginning to develop in Eastern Europe. A number of the Baltic Republics are discussing these developments and Russia has made preliminary explorations. Elsewhere, Vietnam, Singapore, India, South Korea, Japan and Malaysia appear to be in the initial stages of development. We would not suggest that all these nations are yet able to call upon fully operational and comprehensive credit systems, nor that all higher education institutions in a particular country subscribe to the developments. It is clear however that they have been persuaded that a credit system can deliver advantages which may not be attained as readily by other means.

915.   A number of regions of the world have not yet chosen to engage with credit systems. Firstly, in Europe there is no great involvement by nations which subscribe to either the German or the French higher education traditions. We are not sure why this should be the case. It may have something to do with the principal objectives of these systems. The German system has traditionally emphasised *research formation* whilst the French have favoured *professional formation*. This may be compared with the English tradition of *elite formation* from which expansion forces a departure. New developments of credit systems throughout the world appear to be in countries which are seeking to escape from *elite formation* models, or do not wish to develop such models in the first place, or which are otherwise influenced by American practice. In this process, the French and German traditions remain specific (continental) European contributions to global higher education and it remains to be seen whether they will be influenced by the wider developments in modularity and credit-based learning. Secondly, there appears to be little active engagement with credit systems in Latin America. It has been suggested to us that this may be explained by the strength of the independence of the universities of the region. Thirdly, developments in the universities of Africa and the Middle East also appear to be non-existent (with individual exceptions, such as the University of Dakar). There may be good

Table 59: Studying in Great Britain: full-time students from abroad, by volume and selected countries, 1991

Country	Ex-UFC institutions			Ex-PCFC institutions			All HE
	Post Graduate	Under Graduate	Total	Post Graduate	Under Graduate	Total	
European Union	6454	11055	17509	1012	9456	10468	27977
Commonwealth	9195	13970	23165	746	8736	9482	32647
Other countries	12135	8170	20305	956	3861	4817	25122
TOTAL	**27772**	**33097**	**60869**	**2707**	**21898**	**24605**	85474
of which							
Malaysia	1245	3514	4759	161	2586	2747	**7506**
Hong Kong	1182	3125	4307	127	2208	2335	**6642**
Germany	969	3067	4036	189	1542	1731	**5767**
France	794	1811	2605	281	2636	2917	**5522**
Greece	2233	1621	3854	153	1037	1190	**5044**
United States	1489	2864	4353	46	602	648	**5001**
Ireland	516	938	1454	94	2105	2199	**3653**
Singapore	471	2103	2574	21	225	246	**2820**
Spain	499	883	1382	120	821	941	**2323**
Japan (10th)	745	777	1522	38	301	339	**1861**
India (17th)	702	207	909	44	203	247	**1156**
Australia (35th)	365	125	490	25	53	78	**568**
Kuwait (48th)	146	156	302	3	55	58	**360**

Source: DFE Statistical Bulletin, 21/93; October 1993

reasons for this but we have not been able to explore them.

International credit transfer – slow progress

916.   However exciting the prospects for the further development of credit systems appear to be, we need to keep in mind a number of cautions. Firstly, genuine international *credit transfer* is undeveloped and its potential to facilitate different types of international academic relationships is at present unrealised. Outside Europe, trans-national systems are rare and in their infancy. In Europe, most activities are confined to promoting limited forms of undergraduate student mobility. It must be recognised that most UK HEIs want to encourage *credit accumulation* but not international *transfer* if it should lead to any haemorrhage of students. For example, trans-Atlantic student credit transfer between the developed credit system of the United States and the growing arrangements in the United Kingdom is very limited. Approximately 5,000 students come to the UK each year from the United States, of which 3,500 are undergraduates. Of these only 600 students join ex-PCFC institutions within which only a small minority would have systems capable of formally recognising the transfer of credit from the USA to courses in the United Kingdom. We have assumed for the sake of this argument that ex-UFC institutions could cope with the generality of credit transfer but, lacking formal credit-based programmes, do not yet have infrastructures for dealing with the transfer of specific credit points.

917.   Secondly, current European experience exemplifies the political and legal realities that inhibit sophisticated use of international credit transfer. Without an agreed definition of credit, *a priori* credit transfer cannot exist. This problem is compounded by differences in the length of the academic year, the level of awards, the overall study period for a qualification and in the legal authority of institutions to use and recognise the output of credit systems.

918.   Thirdly, the UK is continuing to develop a national credit system (as are many other countries) in response to the demands of domestic priorities that are not necessarily replicated elsewhere. We need to guard against promoting UK solutions to problems that overseas nations with mass open-access, flexible education systems do not experience. Systems and practices associated with the development of international credit transfer need to be capable of application in all international settings and not just within the European context. In the United Kingdom, as in the rest of Europe, non-European students play a significant role in university finances. This raises question about whether policy development should emphasise international *credit transfer* or international *student recruitment*. As Table 59 reveals, significant numbers of overseas students (outside the EU) come to British universities each year with considerable consequences for the financial position of many institutions. It is not clear to us whether institutions are keen to promote genuine credit transfer or whether they would regard this potentially as a source of lost revenue. In short, we may need to distinguish further between *student credit transfer* and *student mobility*, where the latter may not imply the former.

919.   Fourthly, it is important to remember that, although credit systems are best established in the United States, arrangements which obtain in that country may not translate naturally to another cultural setting. Attempts to produce a *synthesis* could turn out as *hybridisation* in which unsuitable elements of different cultures are grafted together in an effort to respond to new conditions. The consequences could be as unsatisfactory for some countries as attempts were to impose the English model of higher education as *elite formation* on former British colonies. Therefore, although we remain throughout this report impressed by the higher education system in the United States, we are aware that its salient features cannot uncritically be commended for adoption in Europe and elsewhere. We have more to say on this matter in Chapter XV.

International credit transfer – a review of progress

920.   The evidence provided later in this chapter of the massive increase in interest and use of credits across Europe and the

Table 60: Academic credit systems and modularisation in Europe, North America and rest of world

	Credit systems and credit transfer						Modularity and structure of academic year							Quality assurance	
	National system	HEI system	Load or contact	Credit transfer	State of develpmt[1]	ECTS	National support[2]	Number of HEIs	Semester	Term	Start date	Wk/year length	Who[3] decides?	National authority for qualifications/quality[4]	Accept UK Bachelor degree as equivalent[5]
Belgium (NL)	yes	yes	load	yes	emergent	yes	no	none	sem		16/9		HEI	At Ministry level	No; Master's only
Denmark	no	yes	load	yes	in place	yes	yes	most	sem		1/9		HEI	At Ministry level	No; Master's only
France	no	no		yes	emergent	yes	no	few	sem	term	16/9	25+	HEI	HEI autonomy	No; Master's only
Germany	no	no				yes	no	some	sem		1/10	28–40	State	Mostly HEI autonomy	No; Master's only
Greece	no	no				yes	yes	most	sem		1/9	30+	State	HEI autonomy	No; Master's only
Ireland	no	yes	load	yes	emergent	yes	no	few	sem	term	16/9	28–30	HEI	HEA; NCEA	Yes
Italy	no	yes	load	yes	in place	yes	yes	most	sem		1/11		HEI	At Ministry level	No; Master's only
Netherlands	yes	yes	load	yes	working	yes	no	some	(sem)	term	1/9	42	HEI	VSNU; HBO–Raad	No; Master's only
Portugal	yes	yes	contact	yes	in place	yes	no		sem		1/10	30–42	HEI	HEI autonomy	Yes
Spain	yes	yes	contact	yes	working	yes	no		sem	term	1/10	30–36	State	HEI autonomy	No; Master's only
UK	yes	yes	(load)	yes	working	yes	yes	many	sem[6]	term	1/10[6]	30–33	HEI	HEQC; (NCVQ[7])	No; Master's only
Austria	no	no				yes	no	none			1/10				
Finland	yes	yes	load	yes	working	yes	yes	many	sem		1/9	30–33	HEI		
Norway	yes	yes		yes	in place	yes	no	few	sem	term	1/9	30–35	HEI		
Sweden	yes	yes	load	yes	working	yes	no		sem		1/9	32–36	HEI		No; Master's only
United States	yes	yes	load	yes	working	(yes)	yes	most	sem	(term)	1/9	30–34	HEI	HEI autonomy[8]	Yes; usually
Australia	yes	yes	load	yes	in place	(yes)	yes	many	sem	term		30–35	HEI	HEI autonomy	Yes
New Zealand	yes	yes	load	yes	working	(yes)	yes	many	sem	term		30–36	HEI	NZQA; HEI autonomy	Yes
Thailand	yes	yes	load	yes	working	(yes)	yes	most	sem			30–34	HEI		
India	no	yes	load	yes	emergent	(yes)	no	some	sem	term			HEI	HEI autonomy	Yes

Notes: (1) 'in place' = not fully functional; 'working' = functional but not necessarily comprehensive; (2) ie moving in direction of modularity; (3) Autonomy often circumscribed; (4) oversight arrangements; (5) UK degree = final host award?; (6) in process of review; (7) HEQC = HEI body; NCVQ = vocational qualifications only; (8) oversight through regional accreditation associations

Sources: European Commission, Academic Credit Systems and Modularisation, draft rpt. 1993; NUFFIC Rpt for U of Amsterdam, 1992; World Bank rpt on Academic Credit Systems in Developing Countries (Regel, 1992); Coopers & Lybrand rpt on ECTS/ERASMUS, 1993; Kouwenaar & Dalichow, Academic Recognition in the EC, 1993; HE in the EC, 1990; publications of NZQA (1991–92); and other sources

rest of the globe gives weight to the view that a world 'credit culture' is gradually beginning to emerge. This will probably not cause the harmonisation or dilution of national systems, rather it will just allow them to co-exist and interact more effectively.

Credit systems in other countries

921.   Credit approaches are not new. The American system dates from the early 19th century and approaches worldwide range from fully-developed **established** (USA) systems, to what has been described as **provisional** (ECTS) and **emergent** frameworks (New Zealand) (Robertson, 1993). Whatever type of classification is used it is undeniable that the past five years have seen major advances in credit systems and credit transfer across the globe. We have attempted to provide a comprehensive survey of the main developments in Table 60. This shows how modularity and credit systems are emerging in tandem throughout Europe and other countries (with the exceptions noted above). Notwithstanding this, there remains an enormous range of different practice, which should not really surprise us. There is no clear reason why higher education arrangements should converge more rapidly than other aspects of international cultural life.

Some convergence and differences

922.   In the data, certain common themes are apparent and there may be a settlement in sight over certain key elements:

- credit systems and modularity are usually seen as part of the same process;

- definitions of *credit*, while varied, tend to accept *student workload time* rather than *class contact time* as the starting point;

- most countries favour an academic year based on *two semesters* of 15-16 weeks and in the more advanced credit systems, at least in the Northern hemisphere, this involves an early September start to the first semester which is completed before Christmas;

- few countries impose solutions on the higher education sector, by national law: for example, subscription is voluntary;

- most credit systems encourage credit transfer between institutions within the same country, and all credit systems maintain some degree of numerical compatibility with each other.

923.   There are also notable international differences. We have already commented on distinctions which can be drawn between higher education in various national settings and between the levels of autonomy and State intervention in the sector. It remains clear that institutions in the United Kingdom remain amongst the most autonomous in the world in a sector which is amongst the most decentralised. Other differences can be identified between national arrangements:

- there is no apparent agreement on appropriate arrangements for quality assurance. These vary from total institutional autonomy (in many developing countries), to self-regulation (UK), to 'light' external accreditation (USA), to 'balanced autonomy' (France), to state legislation (eg Italy and some others);

- there is limited agreement on the standard of qualifications. The undergraduate honours degree of the UK is not widely accepted as equivalent to baccalaureate qualifications in other countries in Europe;

- where credit systems exist, there is little agreement on what 'workload' a credit represents. This can range from 1800 hours of study (Belgium), 40 hours/week (Finland), 30 hours/week (UK and possibly USA), 10 hours (Spain, New Zealand) or variable amounts by subject.

Credit systems in the USA

924.   The USA has the oldest, most extensive and well-established system of credits and credit transfer. It is one of the distinguishing features of American higher education and is

often the one many others seek to imitate as they move their national systems towards expanded participation. The origins of the system lie in the 19th century but the present situation owes much to the adoption during the 1920s of the 'Carnegie Hour' definition of a national unit of credit. This provided the bonding element which tied together the disparate practices in post-secondary and higher education. We have commented on this definition in Chapter VIII and Chapter IX. Modules which require three hours of learning time per week for a semester are three-credit hour modules. Students on degree programmes typically achieve a minimum of 30 credits per year; 120 credits to complete a four-year degree programme. Most colleges and universities have a semester-based year.

925.   Students accumulate credits towards their awards and the grading of the credits indicates the quality of the student learning. Academic programmes are modular, with a combination of core and elective modules. They are not, as is sometimes thought, a completely free 'pick and mix' style. Transcripts, and not Diplomas, are the primary evidence considered by graduate and professional schools in deciding whether to admit transfer students. Transcripts tend to follow a standard approach and grading system, indicating a core of essential information. The codes used in transcripts show the level of the credits taken; this is also true for postgraduate level studies. The assessment of Prior Learning (APL) and the granting of advanced standing is offered by many institutions. Students admitted to a university with less than one year's credit are usually designated 'Advanced Placement Students'. If they are admitted with one year or over, they are called 'Transfer' students. Credit transfer is an almost universally accepted practice. Usually there is automatic transfer of associated degree credits earned at one institution to bachelor degree programmes elsewhere but the quality points associated with the credits do not always count when they have been earned elsewhere. Also, you cannot transfer automatically to a highly competitive institution. The usual time to transfer is after two years, in the middle of a degree. Many universities also assess Prior Experiential Learning (APEL) and give credits for learning and skills gained in work by mature students.

926.   The USA internal model is well worth examination as it offers the 'only example of a mass higher education system at work'. This credit approach suits the USA high schools which have a broad curriculum. Following this, the first two years of higher education (freshman and sophomore years) are also general in character. Then, in the third and fourth years (junior and senior) students 'major' in specific subjects. In this four-year higher education system organised on a 2+2 pattern, the freedom of choice is more carefully circumscribed in the final two years.

927.   The distinctive features of the American system lie in its diverse nature, flexibility, size and above all in its cohesion that comes from having a universally accepted set of common credit definitions. Although much can be learned from it, it must be remembered that it has grown up in response to the pressures and needs of the USA. Individual mobility, both physical and social, is much more ingrained in American culture than would be the case in European or British experience. Credit transfer is therefore often seen as an extension of personal development, 'moving on' and making progress. In addition, credit transfer in the USA is not always a paragon of student choice and mobility; it is becoming increasingly inhibited by funding shortages and inequality of opportunity.

928.   Accrediting bodies play an important role, providing information on institutions and the acceptability of their credits. Accreditation is a voluntary process intended to guarantee standards. Both institutional and subject accreditation take place. The former is accomplished by the six regional accrediting agencies. Most institutions accept, without question, work completed at similar colleges carrying regional accreditation. The level of trust between institutions varies considerably and in a system where anyone can establish a university, it is understandable that these agencies play an important role, but one that is unlikely to transfer to Europe. In addition, the National Association of Credential Evaluation Services (NACES), is a group of private organisations that helps applicants determine the USA equivalent of their education. Similarly this may not transfer to Europe in that a comparable role is already played by the EU-funded National Academic

Recognition Information Centre (NARIC). However, we have made recommendations in Chapter X for the establishment of a credential evaluation service in the United Kingdom, based perhaps on ECCTIS or another body.

929.   The USA system accommodates students frequently interrupting their studies and switching between full-time and part-time mode. This is a flexible system that still has many lessons for others. It has often been copied and certainly functions well but it may be difficult to get European nations to agree an American-style workable definition of a credit. As we have shown in Chapter IX, it is currently proving difficult within the United Kingdom and we have made proposals on this point.

930.   Two further developments are worth mentioning. The USA, Mexico and Canada are implementing a small-scale international credit transfer agreement mimicking the ECTS model. It is to include five institutions from each country and is to be established in 1993-94. The USA has no previous experience of international, multilateral credit networks and is doing this in the light of the success of ECTS. To this initiative, can be added the European Union/US Co-operation in Higher Education initiative. This has been designed to increase cooperation in higher education, develop an EU dimension to the Fulbright Programme and lead to an exchange of views on vocational training and skill needs. More links are envisaged, including staff and student exchanges, the development of joint curricula and credit transfer. The co-operation will draw on ERASMUS, COMETT and LINGUA experience. The call for proposals from institutions indicates that:

'Particular attention should be paid to the academic recognition of study periods spent abroad. Consortia are therefore encouraged to draw from the rich US experience in credit transfer and from developments in the European Community, notably the European Community Course Credit Transfer System (ECTS).'

Credit systems in New Zealand and Australia

931.   Since 1990 the New Zealand Qualifications Authority (NZQA) has been developing a national credit framework that encompasses further and higher education. This is an ambitious scheme that seeks to unify vocational and non-vocational education. The draft framework covers eight levels from basic education to postgraduate studies. A credit tariff is established, based on a time definition of credit and all modules are defined in terms of learning outcomes. They also intend to establish a national information database and student record system. The New Zealand approach appears to be imaginative and it is well worth observing its development. Some of its work has derived from the influence of the NCVQ in the United Kingdom, but by extending its role to include academic as well as vocational programmes, the NZQA has been able to move beyond the NCVQ's role. It is not yet clear, however, that the universities in New Zealand are prepared to embrace the credit framework as readily as its proposals suggest.

932.   Australia created the 'Unified National System' which amalgamated 19 universities and 60 colleges to create just 35 universities. Simultaneously it has been moving towards the creation of a national credit-based system. A majority of Australian universities have credit transfer policies in place. Most transfer activities have, until now, concentrated on transfer between colleges of technical and further education (TAFE) and universities. The final system will link FE and HE and provide APEL, Access and a range of credit transfer opportunities.

933.   The Australian Vice-Chancellors' Committee (AVCC) is the prime force developing the system. The first stage is focusing on principles. These have been identified as the need to mount a 'controlled experiment' based on a framework of mutual trust, emphasising:

- the importance of publishing information on credits in recognised handbooks and prospectuses;

- that credit should be awarded at the highest level consistent with the students' chances of success on the course;

- that decisions on credit transfer should normally be based on published information.

934. A credit-point is used as an indicator of the amount of work required in a unit/module and represents a workload of about four hours throughout a semester. A full-time student will normally undertake a 12-credit point workload per 15-week semester. Credit points are also used in the calculation of the amount of HECS (Higher Education Contribution Scheme or student contribution towards the cost of their education) for which a student is liable. Institutions in the system are usually modular and advanced standing can be given in terms of recognition of credit.

935. Interestingly, it appears that the credit system is used more widely as a basis for funding than it may be for credit transfer. Transfer usually takes place within bilateral institutional arrangements, using blocks of credit in the form of completed courses or years of courses. This style of credit transfer is similar to the pattern sometimes practised in the United Kingdom in conditions which have not required the comprehensive credit-point system to which this report is working.

Credit systems in the developing world

936. There is not a lot of published data on developments elsewhere in the world (outside Europe, and the countries discussed already). The World Bank commissioned one survey on the relevance of academic credit systems for developing countries (Regel, 1992). Assessing progress at the system level (Thailand), institution level (India) and departmental level (Senegal), the report concluded:

'The credit system can only be usefully exported to developing countries if higher education systems in those countries share similar goals: high degrees of flexibility, wide access, inter-faculty and inter-institutional transfer, curricular choice, the integration of recurrent education with the degree system, student orientated higher education, and the application of external experiences toward a degree.'

937. Citing the need for strong support for change from national authorities, the support of academic and administrative staff and the operation of good management information systems, the report goes on to

caution against the uncritical adoption of American practice, and expectations from too rapid change. It comments, in terms which could be readily applied elsewhere:

> The effective transitional period from one model to another may take a decade or more, and time is vital for the credit system to become fully workable and for the support mechanisms to develop. However, while undergoing this period, countries should strongly avoid combining models of higher education. At the National University of Lesotho, for example, initial efforts to combine aspects of British academic requirements with a modified American academic credit system have created a complex and fragmented hybrid programme, making it difficult for students to undertake a coherent programme of studies. Excessive faculty time has also been absorbed in administration and paperwork at the expense of teaching and research. It is important to recognise that the development of the credit system in America took place over a long period of time, and the system continuously responded to other factors which helped form contemporary American universities.
>
> *Omporn Regel, (1992), World Bank Education and Employment Division*

Credit systems, credit transfer and student mobility in Europe

938. Despite the progress on credit systems in countries of the Commonwealth and in North America and Asia, most interest in the United Kingdom focuses naturally upon European developments. If for no other reason than geographical proximity, it is likely that most future international credit transfer (as distinct from student mobility and recruitment) will occur between the United Kingdom, members of an expanded European Union and, in due course, countries of Eastern Europe.

939. In Europe, some type of credit system or credit usage now exists in Belgium (the Flemish part), Holland, Spain, Italy, Denmark, Ireland, Portugal, Norway, Finland,

Iceland and Sweden. In a number of these countries the systems of credit are based on the enactment of a national law. A few countries have undertaken some measure of modularisation of their curricula (Germany, Denmark, France, Greece, Italy, Holland, and Norway). However, there are wide differences in level and extent (see again Table 60). This move to modularity often complements the introduction of credit systems, but it is not always seen as a prerequisite of a credit approach. Nowhere in Europe, with the possible exception of Sweden, has the development of credit and modularity assumed such importance and advanced as far as in the United Kingdom.

940. Planned national credit systems are evolving in a number of countries. In the Flemish part of Belgium, in both the university and non-university sectors, credit points are used and legal decrees give institutions the opportunity to accept credits from other universities. Credit systems are also part of the GENT-Agreement between the Dutch and Flemish HEIs. In Spain, credits are successively being introduced as part of the ongoing reform of their educational system. The national law of 1987 requests universities to introduce the credit system. The Netherlands has also introduced by law a national credit system for universities that is also used by the non-higher education sector. In Italy, a national law of 1990 prepares for the general introduction of *didattica complessiva*, units based on 50 hours of class contact. Finally, in Sweden the higher education system is also nationally credit-based.

941. Most of those countries introducing credit systems (institutional or national) have adopted various descriptions of credits based on some notion of the total average student work load/course load definition (the total number of lecture hours, practical and homework needed to complete a programme unit). The credit point is then the value assigned to a unit that reflects the relative time and effort required to pass it. Learning outcomes are never used. Whatever subtle variations of definition are employed, it has been observed that all can be made compatible with the ECTS system.

942. This picture of Europe, then, is one of relatively rapid introduction of credits, either by law (often involving the creation of a national system) or by encouraging autonomous institutions to implement the type of credit system and approach they desire. The latter can lead to fragmented systems such as in the UK at present, or in the case of Portugal, where the credit system is optional but standardised – a situation where the majority of universities has in fact adopted the same system. The motivations for the introduction of credit systems are diverse but familiar. For instance, countries may wish to change educational philosophies; increase workload transparency; improve access; increase choice within and between institutions; facilitate academic recognition and student international mobility; regulate choice; or reduce non-completion rates. In some cases the spur to adopt a credit approach has come through membership of the ECTS pilot scheme. The existence of these (and many other) different national motives for adopting credit solutions lends weight to the argument that each country will continue to evolve a system that suits its own needs and problems. This diversity may well inhibit the production of a single unified European system but it will not prevent credit transfer.

943. The overall picture across Europe is one of change and development, where closed hostile educational systems are giving way to the new economic and political pressures. Nevertheless, big increases in student mass mobility across Europe appear unlikely in the short or medium term. The aim of achieving 10% mobility of EU higher education students by 1992 has proved unrealistic. The number who can benefit at the moment is about 5% and the Commission appears reluctant to fund more; rather it is passing the obligation back to member states. The Commission is now well aware that it is cheaper to move courses than students, and it is becoming more aware of the benefits of Open/Distance Learning (ODL). The latter is being encouraged by the European Association of Distance Teaching Universities (EADTU) who are committed to promoting co-operation in course and credit transfer.

944.   In this new Europe it is unlikely that a generally acceptable European definition of credit will emerge in the short or medium term. It must also be recognised that many European countries have educational systems of sufficient flexibility to make it unnecessary to replicate a UK-type approach, or one from any other single country. Given these realities it may be better to acknowledge the differences between systems and work with them, by concentrating efforts to ensure that they are compatible. One approach to compatibility is that of the ECTS pilot.

European Community Course Credit Transfer System (ECTS)

945.   The first point we need to remember about the European Community Course Credit Transfer System (ECTS) is that it is not a credit *scheme*. It is a limited and provisional set of prescriptions to encourage small amounts of cross-border student exchange within the European Union. The pilot arrangements have their roots in the 1970s and grew from discussions held then about the possible application of the American credit approach to Europe. The system has been introduced for a six-year pilot phase 1989/90 to 1994/5, under Action 3 of the ERASMUS Programme. Its central objective is:

'to develop credit transfer as an effective currency of academic recognition by providing universities (any HEI) admitting students from other member states with a straightforward and reliable means of assessing such students' previous performance in order to insert them at appropriate points in the host institutions' array of courses, regardless of whether or not an integrated exchange programme exists in the areas concerned.'

946.   ECTS seeks to provide an effective means of improving academic recognition and thus student mobility between EU member countries. It is an embryonic European CAT Scheme, with five disciplines covered in the pilot: business administration, chemistry, history, mechanical engineering and medicine. Currently, 144 institutions from 18 EFTA and EC countries are involved. Each subject group or network is comprised of between 27 and 31 departments from various

institutions. The main features of the scheme are:

Main features of ECTS

- a decentralised system based on mutual trust and confidence.

- academic credits are allocated on the basis of 60 credits per full-time year of study or 30 per semester.

- all units of study are taken from existing mainstream courses.

- all participating ECTS departments agree to break down the description of their own courses into small units to facilitate the allocation of ECTS credits.

- studies completed abroad must be recognised by the home institution.

- students pay no additional fees to the host institution but continue to pay fees at the home institution. They can also receive ERASMUS student grants.

947.   The pilot project has successfully begun to introduce a pan-European credit approach, but it is one that is at present severely limited in nature and application. The strengths, shortcomings and potential of ECTS are now clear and have been well documented by a recent evaluation (Coopers and Lybrand, 1993), which is outlined later. ECTS, as it is currently constituted, remains a voluntary, decentralised scheme designed to suit the political realities of Europe. It remains at heart a limited mobility and recognition scheme that concentrates on allowing full-time students the opportunity to study (usually in one-year blocks) at another institution. These studies often closely match what they would have studied at home. The scheme lacks an exact definition of a credit, using the loose approximation of 60 credits being equal to a full-time year of study. In so doing it can mask equivalence problems by just assuming that work is of an equal nature. This does not solve all recognition problems and can just hide them temporarily. We have also been advised that there are indications that some UK

programmes are proving to be less than adequate compared to those in other countries, at least when measured in comparable student performance. We have not been able to quantify this and we believe this might be a matter for further explicit attention.

948.   ECTS is not particularly flexible and does not accommodate part-time students, experiential learning, further education, non-standard programmes, continuing education etc. Despite this, its principles could be applied in these areas. The pilot was clearly designed to promote the mobility of traditional 'standard' students and has certainly pioneered some important good practice including: a developed grade transfer (translation) scale; a transcript; guidance about what needs to be contained in institutional 'information packages' that then allow informed choice; the coexistence of the ECTS tariff with other credit tariff systems.

949.   A cautious attitude to ECTS has been adopted by a report from the Liaison Committee of Rectors' Conferences. It recognises the positive experiences and good practice generated by the pilot, but suggests that it has not realised automatic *a priori* recognition. The report further states that ECTS study-points only express the relative weight of the courses (or units of study) within the global programme of the study year. There is no clear definition of a credit. The report concludes that this failure and the relative youth of the scheme make the broader use of ECTS 'in its present form… not feasible nor desirable'. Despite the strength of these points there is little to be gained by waiting for what may not be possible. Automatic academic recognition can develop piecemeal and further testing and delay will just halt the evolution of something that appears to work within reasonable limits.

Mobility within ECTS, ERASMUS/LINGUA and similar programmes – UK dimensions

950.   It has been difficult to assess the extent of mobility generated by the ECTS and ERASMUS programmes. In one survey of 1988-89 ERASMUS students (Maiworm, Steube, & Teichler, 1991), it found that the UK 'hosted' 30% of all mobile students in the scheme (France

26%). It also noted that the United Kingdom experienced a significant 'trade imbalance', hosting students at a ratio of 3:2 compared with Germany at 1:2. Student flows between the three 'major' countries accounted for 48% of all mobility (a reduction from 62% in 1987-88). By 1991-92, the proportion had dropped further to 42%.

951.   In further reports from the Commission for Mobility, 1991-93, the United Kingdom has remained a net supporter of EU student mobility programmes, generally participating in co-operative programmes more extensively and importing more students than it sends abroad. Furthermore, the UK is generally more active than others in support for Inter-university Co-operation Programmes (ICPs). For example:

- UK incoming and ongoing students represent 22% and 19% of all ERASMUS and LINGUA exchanges, but the ratio of importation has declined to 20%, from 50%;

- UK institutions are involved in 1400 ICPs, representing 70% of all ICPs. In 1993-94, UK institutions would be co-ordinators for 31% of ERASMUS ICPs and 43% of LINGUA programmes;

- 57% of UK ERASMUS mobility is to France or Germany.

952.   In Table 61 and Table 62, we have shown the flow patterns between countries within the ECTS pilot programmes (flows in Medicine are not included here). From this data it can be seen that mobility to and from the United Kingdom remains the most popular combination for students throughout Europe. Students flows are relatively comprehensive in business administration but less so in mechanical engineering. Smaller member states of the EU appear to be less attractive than the larger countries, possibly reflecting the influence of language in student exchange decisions.

953.   In any event, the United Kingdom appears to be centrally and influentially placed in the mobility programmes of the EU. It

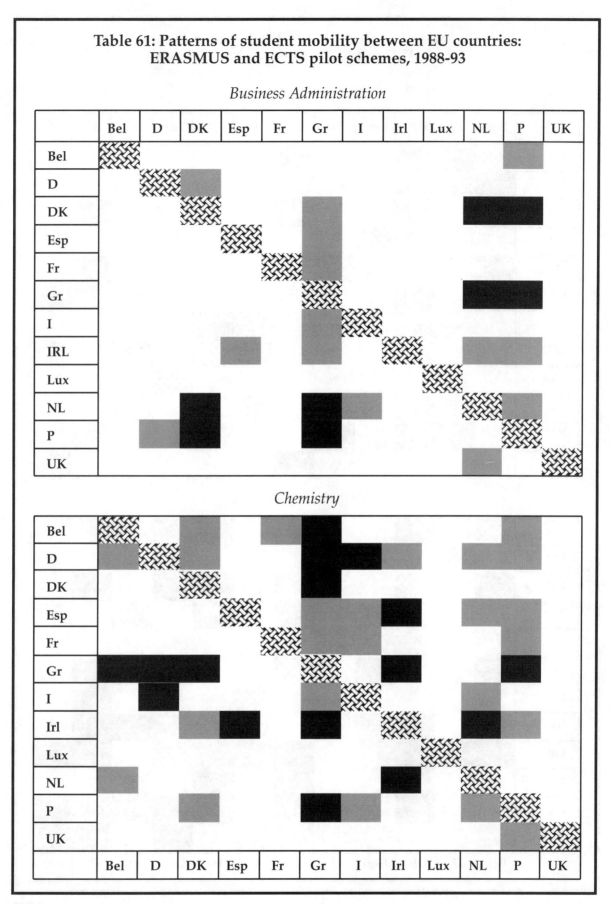

Table 61: Patterns of student mobility between EU countries:
ERASMUS and ECTS pilot schemes, 1988-93

Business Administration

Chemistry

KEY:

dark shade = no student mobility in either direction; light shade = no student mobility from left hand column

Source: Coopers & Lybrand, Evaluation of the pilot phase of the ECTS/ERASMUS programme, February 1993

297

Table 62: Patterns of student mobility between EU countries: ERASMUS and ECTS pilot schemes, 1988-93

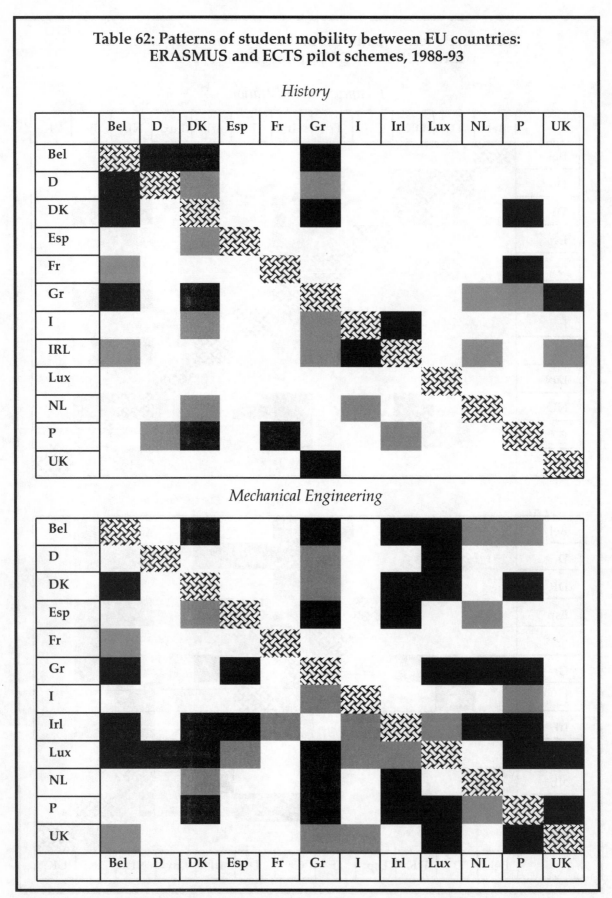

History

Mechanical Engineering

KEY:

dark shade = no student mobility in either direction; light shade = no student mobility from left hand column

Source: Coopers & Lybrand, Evaluation of the pilot phase of the ECTS/ERASMUS programme, February 1993

participates fully and appears to receive inadequate proportional funding for the support it gives. This is likely to have consequences for the future development of ICPs and other mobility programmes, suggesting for this reason, and others, that a review of arrangements for student mobility in the EU is timely.

Changes to ECTS and ICPs

954.   ECTS is acknowledged to be at a turning point in its development and plans for its wider use are currently being explored. The impact of this for the UK is likely to be significant. This is now clear from the publication of a Commission working document on *Guidelines for Community Action in the Field of Education and Training* . This outlines the possible future for all the EU Action Programmes and highlights the importance of ERASMUS. The existing action programmes (COMETT, ERASMUS, PETRA, IRIS, EUROTECNET, LINGUA, TEMPUS and FORCE) all come to an end in 1994 and their current evaluation is timed to allow them to be adjusted for their next phase of development under the new policy objectives of Maastricht (Articles 126, see Appendix v). The working paper states (section 3):

'Amongst the different issues of concern in the Member States, particular attention should be paid to the following key points:

- *clear possibilities for the individual to progress, from vocational and technical studies into higher education;*

- *continuity between initial and adult education and training, through credit transfer and accumulation;*

- *greater parity of treatment between students in technical training and those in general or academic education, and improved possibilities for an attractive career for students who have pursued technical and/or vocation training.'*

955.   What is clear from this and other sections is that the completion of the Internal Market requires the completion of a European training and qualifications market. This in turn is leading to considerable interest in the idea of credit transfer as a device to facilitate such developments. The specific proposals for each EU programme were published late in 1993 and ERASMUS is expected to be 'consolidated and reinforced'. Also, higher education activities are to be regrouped into a single framework including ERASMUS ICPs, ERASMUS ECTS, LINGUA, COMETT, and Open and Distance learning. There is also an intention to explore ways to ensure, at Community level, the effective right of students to carry their grants or subsidies with them wherever they wish to study in the Community.

956.   Finally, it is worth noting two other aspects of the ERASMUS initiative. Firstly, the Inter-university Co-operation Programmes (ICPs) are another part of ERASMUS. These are not usually credit-based and are funded to further a range of academic activities including staff and student mobility and joint curriculum developments. Secondly, the National Academic Recognition Information Centres (NARIC) are also established under the auspices of ERASMUS. They provide a European-wide network and are dedicated to providing information on the recognition and equivalence of overseas qualifications. The UK NARIC is run by The British Council and also provides information on academic qualifications gained worldwide.

957.   It is significant that the UK has no 'official' recognition of overseas qualifications, leaving this to autonomous HEIs and professional bodies. The UK is bound by the multilateral EU *First General Directive on the Mutual Recognition of Professional Qualifications* (89/48/EC), which gives EC-wide recognition of HE diplomas awarded on completion of professional education and training of at least three years' duration. This directive enables fully-qualified professionals from one member state to practise in another member state without re-qualifying. The UK Government, unlike many others in Europe, has never signed any bilateral equivalence agreements. This does lead to a great deal of uncertainty and lack of uniformity of practice. Certainly if a credit-based approach was adopted by NARIC and UK institutions, the realm of qualification

equivalences would be simplified, leading to greater equity of treatment and continuity of practice.

958.	With specific reference to ECTS, there can be little doubt that it needs to change. **We recommend** that the following steps might be appropriate:

- the inclusion of other subject disciplines and institutions, opening up participation to all European universities;

- its adoption as a framework for other EU initiatives including those covering Continuing Professional Development, vocational and further education areas;

- a refinement of the way it defines a credit, and of the principles of guidance used to allocate credit to programmes;

- the introduction of binding 'learning contracts' that guarantee that credits earned are recognised.

959.	The Danish government used its 1993 Presidency of the European Community to press for further development of ERASMUS and 'portable' grants and tuition fees. They suggested that every EU student should have the right to take abroad both maintenance grants covering living expenses and a large proportion of the exchequer costs of their tuition. Ministers shrank from the rapid development of an educational open market in Europe and reaffirmed a gradualist approach. Despite this, ECTS will increasingly provide the basic, loose, regulatory framework and general tariff system for credit transfer across Europe. As previously mentioned, it is unlikely soon to establish an exact definition of credit. Even should it do so it could not be imposed on governments.

NORDPLUS – The Nordic Programme for the Mobility of University Students and Teachers

960.	There is one other cross-border programme in Europe which seeks to promote inter-State student mobility. NORDPLUS was launched by the Nordic Council of Ministers in the Autumn of 1988 as part of an action plan for Nordic cultural co-operation. The aim of this programme is to contribute to the creation of a close-knit Nordic educational community and to counterbalance the ERASMUS programme of the EU, as well as to prepare for future Nordic participation in such European programmes. The ultimate aim is the virtual elimination of national borders with regard to access to higher education. The scheme is credit based and promotes student and staff mobility in a range of more than 15 subjects including agriculture, architecture, fine arts, natural sciences, law and education.

961.	A review of NORDPLUS in 1992 revealed that it has fulfilled its functions in accordance with its general objectives. This evaluation also recommended that NORDPLUS should continue as a co-operative programme. The review also made numerous specific recommendations to help refine the scheme, including a stress on the absolute need for recognition of learning achieved on the scheme. The most interesting features of the scheme are that it is very flexible and encourages unusual programmes and covers a much larger range of subjects than ECTS. There is a clear intention to place it at the core of an even more diverse, intensified and powerful network of co-operation and mobility. However, its success and expansion are clearly linked to its level of funding. Currently, it is a relatively small programme, moving under 900 students in 1989, and organised in a decentralised way like ECTS.

962.	One of the main criticisms of NORDPLUS concerned lack of 'recognition of the time spent abroad as counting towards the final degree or towards any intermediary form of credit units'. Too often the mutual recognition of courses and examinations has not been established by the subject group 'framework agreements'. The participation by Nordic countries in ECTS is expected by the NORDPLUS evaluators to help solve some of these problems and lead to greater co-ordination of curriculum development and harmonisation of study patterns. Although little new can be learnt form NORDPLUS as a credit system, it is important to note the expectation that its problems will be helped by strengthening its credit approach and membership of ECTS. Membership is also expected to act as a powerful lever on domestic national higher education policy.

Memorandum on Higher Education in the European Community, 1991

963.   It would not be appropriate to leave this discussion on credit transfer in Europe without paying some attention to the *Memorandum* and its consequences for international credit transfer, student mobility and institutional co-operation. The *Memorandum* gave considerable prominence to student mobility and credit transfer as a means of promoting further cross-border co-operation but identified a number of impediments to further progress:

- **access restrictions:** where access to certain courses is limited by volume;

- **language problems:** where there is an absence of adequate competence in the host language;

- **recognition problems:** lack of clarity over the recognition of qualifications and previous study;

- **problems of accommodation:** and other practical problems of administration;

- **financial problems:** where the portability of grants and loans has not been achieved, to the disadvantage of poorer students;

- **inadequate information:** absence of purposeful cross-border information on courses, study opportunities.

964.   The *Memorandum* proposed a number of remedies for some of these barriers. Among them were proposals for a Euro-loan to offset financial hardship and an electronic database for course information; encouragement to include students with basic language proficiency and support them with language classes; 'harmonisation' of academic years and other structures; and further steps to ensure the mutual recognition of qualifications.

The response of the British government to the *Memorandum*

965.   In its response, the British Government largely rejected an increased role for the Commission or its programmes, arguing that the Commission should act as a catalyst to inspire further collaboration between willing member states and, in the case of higher education, within the academic community itself. The response pointed out in particular the imbalance of student flow that was occurring in the UK. It was keen to ensure further discussion on steps that might be taken to ensure that funds were available to support imbalances of inward over outward student mobility. Moreover, the Government was concerned to promote a review of arrangements for support where a course was being taken wholly in another member state, and that sending countries should generally be responsible for student maintenance and tuition costs. The response pointed out that the British Government was supporting its students to the extent of 19 million ECUs compared with a receipt from the Commission of 6 million ECUs, thereby underlining its general commitment to European student mobility and credit transfer.

Potential and problems in international credit transfer

966.   General considerations of international credit transfer often become confused with the cultural advantages of study in another country. There is no doubt that students enjoy studying abroad. One study provides unsurprising results on the motives of students for studying abroad. These motives emphasise the desire to learn or improve a foreign language, the desire to live in another country, and to improve career prospects. Matters concerned with academic programmes, their subject matter and assessment, rated very much lower as student motivating factors (Burn, Cerych & Smith, 1990). We would not wish to draw too many conclusions from this material, particularly since it was based on students for whom international credit transfer was not yet a reality. However, we do not doubt that it will

take many years before students look to study abroad principally for a source of academic credit.

Advantages of international credit transfer

967.   Firstly, all areas of educational mobility can potentially benefit from credit approaches which encourage the detailed consideration of recognition issues. This requires the use of a common denominator or credit currency to act as a means of exchange of academic units or programmes. Using credits, different national credit systems can begin to articulate with each other.

968.   Secondly, the use of credit-based learning has been stimulated by the requirements of a changing economic and political environment. It provides a way to increase participation rates (particularly in the UK); encourage part-time study; deliver new programmes in different modes to suit new types of learner. Within the European Community, the use of credits has been acknowledged as a powerful way to promote student/learner mobility; increase academic recognition and create a better educated and trained workforce.

969.   Next, credits have a potential, but unrealised, role in the transnational recognition of professional qualifications. Existing EC Directives cover the recognition of academic qualifications for professional purposes but these regulations do not acknowledge part-completed qualifications and the need to complete programmes in other countries. Credits systems can aid this. Fourthly, they can make it easier for institutions to recognise learning acquired overseas and accurately make judgements about its quality and quantity. An unintended consequence of this is to promote equality and confidence between institutions building international peer recognition.

970.   Finally, credit systems put inter-university relationships on a serious footing and avoid the frivolity of 'academic tourism'. They can help to denote a level of relationship that legitimises close links between institutions, where a foreign programme or individual unit is fully acknowledged as part of a home student's studies.

Problems of international transfer

971.   Firstly, there may a danger of a devaluation of credits where they are given too easily to visiting students on exchange programmes. Some academic staff can over-compensate for the difficulties facing foreign students. Some students are also allowed to study units too similar to ones they have completed at their home institution. Not enough creative use of study opportunities is made. Issues of quality assurance feature prominently in international credit transfer. Secondly, credit transfer can easily lead to the movement of elite groups who can afford the process. Any mass system that employs credits needs to guard against this by being introduced simultaneously with proper funding, distance learning, course transfer and staff exchanges.

972.   Thirdly, it must be recognised that substantive differences exist between national and international credit transfer. National credit systems usually provide common volume measures or bench marks, but in the international sphere these are still ill-formed. Mutual trust and confidence are therefore more strongly provided by national systems where common knowledge is shared, but in international circles, suspicion can usually only be overcome by personal contact and the creation of mutual trust. Any failure fully to recognise appropriately negotiated credit destroys the will and confidence of students to participate in such programmes.

Institutional responses to international credit transfer

973.   In common with the distinction made earlier, institutions often organise themselves with respect to the overseas student market in terms of recruitment as much as genuine credit transfer. It is difficult to prescribe internal strategies and practical arrangements for institutions in the United Kingdom when faced with this dichotomy. A

recent study does usefully explore their specific experience of introducing a CATS strategy for European relationships (Hodgkinson, 1992). Amongst the general lessons that may be passed on, we identify the following matters.

974. **Centralised co-ordination:** no discernible pattern has emerged yet in terms of strategies or internal arrangements. Some evidence exists that centripetal forces unleashed by modular credit systems do lead to some centralisation of administrative functions, but in the area of international arrangements little can be concluded. It is likely that the Commission of European Communities' Task Force for Human Resources, Education, Training and Youth (TFHR) will in future seek to deal with institutions and not departments. Centralised procedures often are more cost effective and provide consistency of treatment. They may make the management of student programmes more efficient.

975. **International offices:** where international offices exist, they are often responsible for induction, counselling, housing and the general management of students. Sometimes these roles are accomplished by departments or faculties. Larger institutions with many overseas links tend to have international offices and European offices. Most of those consulted who had such offices, indicated that they saw considerable benefits in them, not least in the way they helped embed international activities and maintain the focus on student needs. Institutions who seek to introduce credit-based (or any other sort) international links should introduce them sensitively. A 'bottom-up' approach has the advantage of 'embedding' new initiatives and securing staff-commitment at course/programme level.

976. **International policy:** insufficient evidence exists to say whether there is a correlation between the existence of a strong institutional policy and successful development of links based on credit transfer. In our opinion, however, there would be considerable advantages, not least for quality assurance, if institutions were to state their policy towards both overseas student recruitment and international credit transfer. As we have stated in earlier discussion, confusion on these matters clouds the ways in which institutions may be encouraged to develop.

977. **Focused partnerships:** most institutions involved in international credit transfer appear to favour links with a limited number of overseas institutions. This seems to be the most cost effective approach that can lead to quite sophisticated 'academic twinning' arrangements.

An institutional code of practice

978. To address some of these problems, and others concerning quality assurance, **we recommend** that institutions adopt a voluntary code of practice to inform the academic community and promote good practice in international credit relationships (see Table 63). This code is put forward in the knowledge that there are many different ways of achieving the same end and that practice in the international credit sphere is subject to rapid change. It is designed to be as non-invasive as possible, acknowledging the right of institutions to develop their own practice in credit dealings. This code should be used in conjunction with the British Council code of practice for *Educational Institutions and Overseas Students*. It should be viewed as a natural extension of that which should be available for UK students. Many institutions will need to adapt their existing administrative arrangements to encompass international credit transfer. However, if they are already credit-based organisations their home mechanisms will require little change. Most institutions have positive views about overseas links and students, but these are rarely couched in credit terms. Institutions will need to have in place full credit-rating, transcription and assessment mechanisms, management information systems, staff-development programmes etc. These allow full, easy transfer to take place. It must not be left to students to solve problems, or to be guinea pigs. There is a duty of care owed by the institution. We strongly advise against treating international credit transfer activities as bolt-on activities at the academic margins of institutional life.

Table 63: An institutional code of practice for international credit transfer

On policy and the institutional mission

1. Institutions should clearly state why they seek to have credit-based relationships with overseas institutions. This should be incorporated in their mission statement and should become the starting point of existing and future relationships with non-UK institutions.

2. Institutions should publish information indicating their policy towards international credit transfer. This should include details on the recognition of credit, together with possibilities for exemptions, with and without credit, in relation to specific courses. Procedures and grounds for appeal against credit transfer decisions should be explained. All decisions about credit equivalence and value must be the responsibility of the institution, working within a framework of international exchange.

3. Where appropriate, institutions should explain credit-based relationships within Memoranda of Co-operation.

On information for students

4. Institutions should make full data available (electronically or hard-copy) giving details of all units, modules and programmes available for transfer purposes. This should include information on their levels, credit-rating, co-requisites and pre-requisites and mode of delivery. Particulars of the grading systems used and the assessment of each unit should be explained. Institutions should also provide full details of all the qualifications and awards available to incoming credit transfer students and any specific regulations that affect them and their potential registration for awards. Regulations concerning incoming credit transfer students' right to gain UK professional recognition/ accreditation should be fully explained along with their significance.

5. Institutions should provide an induction programme which includes information about the academic culture, credit-system, modules, assessment methods, regulations, learner support, guidance networks, financial support, personal welfare and progression. A parallel process should be provided for outgoing students on credit-based mobility schemes, to prepare them for their overseas studies. In addition, intensive language preparation, plus briefings with students who have previously undertaken similar experiences is desirable. In all cases a contact member of staff should be identified to act as emergency help and mentor.

6. Institutions should periodically re-examine their systems of mandatory pre-requisites and co-requisites. Where possible alternative mechanisms to overcome or ameliorate any barriers should be put in place. Where large non-negotiable sequences of study are prescribed, credit transfer is severely inhibited. A sensitive approach to degree classification should be adopted when significant proportions of study have been completed overseas. Regulations pertaining to credit transfer need to be cast in a flexible manner.

7. Institutions should provide for students a guarantee that any credit-rated studies undertaken in an overseas institution will be fully recognised as part of their home programme, providing they are satisfactorily completed and formally negotiated. This can be achieved by the use of learning contracts. They should advise students of credits offered and any units of study exempted, at the earliest opportunity.

8. Institutions should make available information on all fees, costs and financial implications likely to face incoming and outgoing students. This should include details of bursaries and indications of the general cost of living, including accommodation.

On grade transfer and credit transcripts

9. Institutions should develop and implement a system for the translation of overseas grades and credits. They should issue transcripts for all students on completion of units of study. These form the official record of the programme studied, giving past student performance, and act as a basis for future student choice and programme planning. Transcripts should also be issued in a standard format that is recognisable and usable in other countries. Although it is often not possible to provide all the required information on a transcript to make a decision to admit students with credits, transcripts should clearly indicate where further information can be obtained. Transcripts cannot necessarily be used alone as the basis for accepting a student or giving exemptions with credit. They should be used in conjunction with records of achievement that give the full profile of attempts and attainments. In addition to indicating the credits obtained, transcripts should, where possible express those credits in terms of the ECTS grading scale and/or other international grading scales.

10. Has the institution assured itself about the quality of learning leading to credits in an overseas institution? Has the institution satisfied itself as to the quality, level and content of the students' previous credited learning, whether certificated or uncertificated? How does an institution propose to guarantee the quality of domestic and foreign credits in a situation of competitive market pressure?

11. How does an institution in the UK propose to monitor standards in autonomous overseas institutions (and vice-versa) when there is no control over their quality mechanisms? What level of information and processes are required for a UK institution to make a judgement about the quality procedures and the contents and level of overseas units of study? To what extent should overseas colleagues be involved in UK quality mechanisms, validation and review?

12. Should a student studying credits at two institutions in different countries have them credited towards similar qualifications and in effect receive two awards for the price of one?

13. How can the student experience of international credit transfer be monitored effectively?

14. What is the role of UK External Examiners, Examination and Conferment Boards when dealing with international credit transfer? How can award classifications be decided?

15. How can appeals procedures encompass the international credit transfer dimension?

16. What can national quality bodies do to establish coherence and consistency in the international credit market? Is there a role for international accrediting organisation(s)? What form may these take? What other alternative may evolve? Otherwise, how can credit-ratings be given international recognition and what mechanism might adjudicate conflict in ratings?

Impediments to the extension of international credit transfer

Problems of mutual confidence

979.   The main barrier to the extension of international credit transfer and exchange is the scepticism, inexperience and uncertainty that surrounds it. There is an absence of trust and familiarity between countries. How can confidence be created? Only limited activities have taken place to date and these, in the case of ECTS, have received little publicity or explanation. Activities have not reached the threshold level that would allow significant development and there is no obvious imperative which would make progress any swifter.

980.   Progress on mutual recognition might be made easier if there were agreement on the definition of a credit. Credit systems cannot work without credits and the clear delineation of bench marks and tariffs. Once credits have been defined (preferably in terms of teaching/learning time and outcomes), they will need to function as a valid and acceptable international academic currency. In order for this to happen, confidence must exist between different national education systems. This might be engendered by links between national quality mechanisms or by a piecemeal approach involving individual institutions.

Poor quality information

981.   Moreover, lack of detailed course, module, and programme information prevents informed choices being made. Without this information, students and lecturers cannot plan programmes; assess modules for level and utility; decide prior credits; acknowledge exemptions from pre-requisites, etc. Flexible credit-based systems are inoperable without informed choice. Much valuable good practice has been learnt by the ECTS pilot. This type of data is essential if accurate decisions are to be made about the level and type of units used in credit transfer and recognition. At the general level, more information is needed about classification scales, national evaluation practices and pass rates. Such information is also necessary for making recognition decisions that do not involve credits. The role of ECCTIS 2000 and the proposed development of a 'European Higher Education Database' will be significant determining factors to the widening of credit transfer activities across Europe.

Differences in statutory frameworks

982. Differences between national education structures and the legal licence given to academic institutions prevent the wholesale adoption of credit frameworks. In Europe, academic institutions have differing legal freedom to conduct their affairs. This problem is compounded by the existence of deeply-rooted views on academic autonomy. Some institutions see credit systems as a big challenge to their independence. In Europe, article 126 of the Maastricht treaty reinforces subsidiarity by:

'...fully respecting the responsibility of the member states for the content of teaching and the organisation of education systems and their cultural and linguistic diversity.'

983. Clearly, no pan-European credit system can be imposed, but legal and political barriers between countries do need to be ameliorated. People need to be convinced that credit systems and approaches are not about to destroy their autonomy or diversity. A more open discussion of these issues is necessary.

Differences in academic structure and qualifications

984. The big differences in the length and organisation of the academic year inhibit international credit transfer. Currently in Europe, the academic year starts anywhere between 1 September in Denmark and 5 November in Italy. In the USA the semester can start as early as 20 August. Some unification of the European academic and eventually the world academic year is needed if incompatible semester and term dates are not to prevent some credit and non-credit based student transfers. We believe that the main recommendation of the Flowers and Irvine Reports for an early September start to the academic year represents the best possible contribution we can make from the United Kingdom to this process of convergence.

985. Furthermore, it would be helpful if academic programmes could be designed in smaller blocks of study; year-long programmes constrain their use for credit transfer purposes. If smaller units are used these provide more flexibility for transfer, especially when coupled with a harmonised academic year.

986. Conventionally, the UK three-year full-time honours degree is seen, in the UK, as equivalent to a French *Licence,* German *Diplom* or an Italian *Laurea.* However, evidence is accumulating that in some cases such equivalences are inaccurate and viewed very differently on the Continent. This is confirmed by the recent introduction in the UK of four-year physics and mathematics degrees. Also analysis of the ECTS student flows gives further evidence for disquiet. The ECTS system recognises 60 credits = a full-time year of study, but in practice this recognition is not always provided. We need to establish self-critically why it is that (discounting language problems) so few UK students are capable of academically successful ECTS exchanges. Credit systems must not mask such problems, and clear information and agreed criteria must exist to ascertain levels of study. The different entry criteria, teaching approaches, academic cultures, length and expected output of programmes all need to be very carefully considered in credit transfer and exchange.

987. However, we also need to keep in mind the comments of one survey on academic recognition in the European Community (Kouwenaar & Dalichow, 1993), which concluded:

'There seems to be a deep cleft between the UK and Ireland on the one hand and the continental European countries on the other. In terms of final qualification, the continental countries almost unanimously accept the Master's degree, but not the Bachelor, as equivalent in value to their own qualification. Juxtaposed to this continental agreement is the view of the British and Irish who (with the exception of the French Maitrise in the United Kingdom) grant unconditional recognition at Master's level to none of the continental qualifications... Qualifications of Southern European countries tend to be ranked lower than those of North-West ones... Comparative analysis shows that there are still strong tendencies of national chauvinism in the assessment of foreign qualifications. This chauvinism will wear down only gradually as the systems of higher education come to know and respect each other.'

Cultural and status obstacles

988.	There is evidence that elite institutions across the world are either antithetical to credit approaches, or seek to develop relationships only with those they consider their peers. Examples of this can be found in Europe and the USA. This type of behaviour may not be preventable, but certainly deters the development of a unified open system. Universities in all countries tend to be cautious in their approach to the recognition they give to credits gained overseas. This caution can impede student progress and devalue the worth of a period of study in another institution. Certainly, recognition of the full 'value added' of overseas study is difficult when ways of measuring it are undeveloped. Some students feel credit obtained overseas might prejudice the gaining of a first-class award in the United Kingdom. This problem is compounded by lack of conviction that overseas experience will be positively regarded in the employment market. Evidence of this type of insular behaviour is not confined to the United Kingdom.

Attitudes of professional bodies

989.	In the United Kingdom and elsewhere, professional bodies may insert in the terms of their accreditation of degrees, restrictions on credit earned overseas. This prevents the professional recognition of incoming overseas students seeking UK awards (eg in engineering). It would be helpful if professional bodies were to re-examine such restrictions.

Financial barriers

990.	Several financial barriers exist to inhibit credit transfer. In Europe, the current system allows national governments to shelve the problem of enlarging the system by allowing national status to EC students for grant and fee purposes. But within the United Kingdom, generally institutions make a loss on every ICP and ECTS student on fees alone, due to the imbalance in student flows. This funding issue is a real problem and the UK government has declared its interest in addressing it in its response to the *Memorandum on Higher Education in the European Community*. When EU students are seen as a cost, it is difficult to set targets and

expand credit-based opportunities within an institutional system that is increasingly cost driven.

991.	Personal financial constraints serve to inhibit international credit transfer and access programmes designed to widen opportunities rather than just increasing them. There is a real danger that international credit initiatives will stay elitist. Adults, women, ethnic minorities, people with disabilities, working class students will become more marginalised if ways are not found to include them in new opportunities.

Language barriers

992.	Inadequate foreign language provision in the UK severely inhibits the numbers of outgoing students on credit-based and other traditional exchange programmes. UK university language departments are often overloaded and cannot prepare *ab-initio* students in science and social science areas for units studied overseas in a foreign language. This is a deep-seated and well recognised problem that can only be overcome when adequate second (and third) language teaching is made compulsory in schools from the earliest age. If students cannot be assessed in units taken at other institutions they will have restricted opportunity to be involved in credit transfer at the international level, other than the less frequent opportunities confined to the USA, Commonwealth and other English speaking nations.

Conclusions

993.	We are aware that this survey and assessment of international credit transfer arrangements may appear to pose intractable problems of ethnocentricity, national defensiveness, international divergence and confusion. We are bound to reflect that we do not have to look to Europe for evidence of these matters: many of these problems can be found within the United Kingdom itself. It is salutary for us to recall that it is proving complex to achieve a comprehensive national credit framework in the United Kingdom. This may in itself be enough to calm the enthusiasm of those who aspire to early progress in Europe, or in the Commonwealth and internationally.

994.   On balance, we conclude that the United Kingdom is well advanced in Europe in the implementation of instruments for the promotion and management of international credit transfer. It is widely developing the modular and credit-based arrangements that will facilitate this. Its universities are already vastly experienced in receiving overseas students from the Commonwealth and from North America and it remains the most popular choice for inward mobility of students in the EU. As English becomes further entrenched as the principal language of international exchange, we would expect that pressure on inward mobility will increase.

995.   Government and the universities are rightly concerned about the funding consequences of this imbalance. What could otherwise be an opportunity for marginal financial gain *and* further international co-operation might become an impediment to further progress if the demand for inward transfer yields a net burden on higher education finances. Ways will need to be explored by the European Commission in the first place if the credit transfer programmes are to be sustained in an enlarged European Union.

996.   Finally, we have not been convinced, despite our national state of advancement, that institutions are themselves particularly well-prepared for international credit transfer. Many institutions have 'international offices' but these are usually directed at recruitment initiatives in the Far East. As Table 59 has shown earlier, over 17,000 students from Malaysia, Hong Kong and Singapore are studying in the United Kingdom. This is the equivalent of one large university (with a Graduate School of 3,000 students!) and these students alone contribute some £100 million in fees to higher education in the United Kingdom. With fees from all overseas students and EU nationals added together, the benefit to higher education may be in the order of £350 million. This is substantial business and dwarfs consideration of the social and cultural benefits of educational credit transfer.

997.   The prize may be to unite the objectives of business and credit transfer by further promoting the specific advantages of the latter. If students from Asia and North America, as well as from Europe, knew that they could gain credit which would count towards their home qualifications, or if their previous learning was fully recognised by our universities, then there could be a possibility of opening up previously unexplored markets. To achieve this, universities and colleges in the UK would need to embrace a credit culture more fully than they have done to date. Furthermore, they may need to demonstrate greater versatility in the recognition of forms of learning other than course-based performance. Open and Distance Learning, work-based learning and APEL could become sources of credit-bearing potential for new markets of students in the future.

Recommendations and guidance for future policy

To Government and the Department for Education

97   **We recommend** that the British Government represents to the European Commission the benefits of credit-based approaches to higher education and beyond as a means of facilitating the next phase of community initiatives in education and training by arrangements consonant with institutional autonomy and national interests.

98   **We recommend** that steps continue to be taken by Government with the European Commission:

- to resolve the imbalances to institutional funds caused by the exemption of non–UK EC nationals from fee payments;

- to provide adequate funding for international credit transfer students by rectifying the distortions to funding arrangements caused by net inward mobility of students to the United Kingdom;

- to explore ways in which maintenance grants and the Exchequer cost of tuition could be made more internationally 'portable';

- to support European Commission efforts to encourage institutions in the rationalisation of the academic year within Europe.

99   **We recommend** that, in recognition of the importance of international student mobility and its impact on future careers, Government ensures that the teaching of a second (and a third) language is a regular part of school education from an early age, and consistently available to students throughout their school life.

To the European Community 'Task Force Human Resources, Education, Training and Youth' (TFHR):

100 **We recommend** that the TFHR take the following steps to improve prospects for international credit transfer within the European Union:

- employ credit-based solutions in their future education and training initiatives and widely publicise their experience of ECTS;

- refine the definition of credit employed in the ECTS scheme and introduce a 'learning contract' approach to guarantee the recognition of credits earned. As a priority they should investigate the benefits of a definition of credit using 'learning outcomes' linked to notional time and workload;

- encourage a sharing of knowledge and, where possible, the adoption of common approaches, embraced in agreed voluntary guidelines, towards the allocation of credits to units and programmes;

- speed up the creation of the proposed 'European Higher Education Database', designed to act at a course, institutional and national systems level;

- support a comprehensive mapping exercise (with UNESCO) to create a matrix of national and international credit definitions for comparative purposes;

- host more events and commission projects aimed at researching and expanding the understanding of international credit transfer.

To the Higher Education Quality Council

101 **We recommend** that the HEQC instigates with the institutions a programme of development for international credit transfer, to include:

- a national and international debate to promote more open discussion and appreciation of the potential of credit approaches. This would reduce the apparent threat it presents to institutional and national autonomy. This debate should focus on all applications of credit approaches including Access and CPD and might be launched internationally using this report as a starting point;

- organise workshops with institutions designed to share international credit transfer, good practice and experience;

- explore the consequences of quality assurance issues raised by international credit transfer activities. Further investigation is required of alternative ways to secure confidence in overseas credits by, for example, the creation of an International Accrediting Agency(s); reciprocal accreditation arrangements; linking existing national bodies responsible for quality;

- explore the compatibility between credit practices and systems in the UK and those of the ECTS pilot scheme, with a view to removing any obstacles to prevent positive inter–linking and co-operation;

- promote research into ways to use credit to take account of the full student experience, the value–added dimension of overseas study (including off–campus learning);

- urgently research (with institutional representative bodies and NARIC), using output measures, the apparent mismatch between UK initial awards and their European counterparts, identifying and explaining the comparative academic performance of UK outwardly mobile students and EU inwardly mobile equivalents.

To the representative bodies of institutions, and individual institutions

102 **We recommend** that individual institutions should assist the further development of international credit transfer by taking the following measures:

- adopt the international credit transfer code of practice, as outlined in Table 63 of this report;

- consider their regulations to ensure they are cast in a fashion that promotes national and international credit transfer;

- reconsider the use of large blocks of study that inhibit credit transfer and recognition activities;

- use the ECTS credit scale alongside their existing scale;

- publicise international credit transfer opportunities in prospectuses and other institutional literature;

- prepare institutional, module, and programme information in electronic database form and accessible to overseas institutions, in anticipation of the planned development of the 'European Higher Education Database.'

To professional bodies

103 **We recommend** that professional bodies:

- re–examine restrictions on the recognition of overseas earned credits which may be used to gain UK accredited awards;

- consider the use of credits in the frameworks they are devising for compulsory/advisory periods of CPD that sustain professional status.

On future work

104 **We recommend** that interested parties, including Government departments, HEQC, individual institutions and the academic community find ways of establishing a programme of research and development on the following matters of interest. An important agenda exists for the development of international credit–based relationships. In many areas it remains an under–researched field: the accurate mapping of credit systems is needed; information on different practical approaches to credit relationships is required; the equivalence problems between UK and other European degrees must be researched, as well as the classification and types of award structure most appropriate to a credit culture; and some analysis should be undertaken of the comparative grading, and mark distribution, of students experiencing international credit transfer. To this can be added the following questions for investigation:

- how can Europe be encouraged to agree a definition of a unit of credit (preferably based on teaching and learning time and outcome approaches)?

- how can the rest of Europe be encouraged to recognise UK credits from APEL and off–campus learning?

- how can the general adoption of codes of good practice, related to international credit transfer, be encouraged both domestically and abroad?

- how, and by whom, can the resolution of obstacles to the further extension of international credit transfer be monitored?

- how can international credit transfer/access opportunities become open to the marginal groups of learners (adults, women, ethnic minorities, disabled, poor etc.) in society and not remain an activity for the elite?

- is there a future for a reciprocal multi–accreditation system where one programme or institution is accredited by several other foreign institutions?

- how can domestic UK credit transfer experience and practice be promoted most effectively, in order to influence the emerging European credit framework?

- how can cross–sector credit frameworks articulate between countries with quite different post–primary education systems?

- how can the UK guidelines/codes of good practice be best promoted? To what use should they be put?

XV.   *A credit culture*

Introduction

998.   In this final chapter, we attempt to come to terms with the impact of the proposals contained within this report for professional life within universities and colleges. Throughout the investigation, we have been faced with examples of varying kinds which have suggested to us that institutions are struggling to adapt to fundamental change. This is producing an uncomfortable and sometimes traumatic experience for some institutions, but a refreshing opportunity for others. Academic staff and their colleagues in institutional administration inevitably lie at the centre of this process. We have considered some funding aspects of fundamental change in Chapter XI, the structural issues contingent on modularisation in Chapter XII and the need for a strong para-academic cohort in Chapter XIII. We now turn to aspects of change which concern culture, attitudes and the professional orientations of individuals and their institutions.

Essential change

999.   How far is it fair to suggest that universities and colleges are really faced with fundamental change? We have been interested to establish whether this is merely 'pop-management' hyperbole derived from the nostrums of management 'gurus' or whether it accurately reflects the modern condition of higher education. A case can be heard, of course, which proposes that institutions have a long history, deeply rooted values and a respected social position which, whilst challenged by contemporary ideologies and economies, are sufficiently robust to ride out short-term waves of fashion. Indeed, the case continues, it will be ever more important to defend traditional values in order to protect the university from the encroachment of the State, commerce or other forces intent on compromising its historic purpose. This purpose is founded on the unhindered pursuit of knowledge, supported by academic freedom and sustained by a culture of critique and introspection.

1000.   On the other hand, it is equally apparent that universities, in the United Kingdom and internationally, are being faced with unprecedented demands. Governments no longer appear prepared to spend significant proportions of their GDP on a relatively privileged sector; the accountability of institutions and their members is being emphasised by Governments and the general public; students continue to demand places in universities as the best means of securing lifetime benefits; and higher education is expected to continue to improve the well-being of individuals, society and the State. In short, universities and colleges are being transformed from sheltered institutions of the pre-modern world to public service organisations in a modern (or, some would suggest, post-modern) world.

1001.   This transformation does seem to require fundamental change. The changes to role, structure and purpose of the higher education institution are essential. They are both *essentially necessary* for the survival of institutions in a more competitive world, and they involve changes *in the essence* of the institution as it defines itself. This latter point is true for universities in the United Kingdom, which have been slower than others internationally in being required to respond to greater participation, diversified funding sources, and more market competition, but also for institutions internationally.

1002.   It has been the contention of this report that *essential change* will alter the balance of familiar relationships between institutions, students, employers and the State. The needs of students and employers, as consumers, will become more important in the future, and institutions (and the State) as suppliers of services, will need to become more responsive. Under these conditions, the further development of credit systems becomes one important means by which institutions can deal with their new environment. Credit systems may become proxies for the wide range of initiatives which universities and colleges must undertake if they are to prosper in the future. And as they prosper, universities may experience changes to familiar cultural forms. We explore the ingredients of this *credit culture* in later discussion.

Learning organisations and academic communities

1003.   One of the other aspects of a *credit culture* that we have tried to consider is the impact upon the character of academic communities and the dispositions of academic staff and students. We have not found it helpful to pretend that the changes which are currently underway in the institutions of higher and further education in the United Kingdom are being welcomed by all academic colleagues. What has intrigued us, and this may be an area for further enquiry, is the extent to which unwelcome changes to the management of professional life are being conflated in the minds of many colleagues with changes consequent on the introduction of new forms of educational practice, including credit systems. From our investigation, we have found four groups of academic staff, with different orientations to the introduction of a *credit culture*:

- **enthusiasts,** whose commitment to the introduction of credit systems is driven by a 'crusade' for access, democratic participation and institutional reform, but some of whom may be unaware of alternative ideological positions in play;

- **pragmatists,** for whom the introduction of credit systems seems to offer plausible solutions to sectoral and environmental changes, and who may or may not be informed by particular ideologies or educational objectives;

- **sceptics,** who are open to persuasion on the need for changes, question the appropriateness of many proposals, doubt the permanence of changes, and many of whom remain evenly balanced between their support for educational

change and their desire to retain familiar academic practice;

- **antagonists,** who largely reject the entire enterprise for a number of different reasons, ranging from expressions of vested interest through to expressions of deep-seated intellectual disquiet.

1004.   For obvious reasons to do with the effectiveness of change and support for the proposals in this report, we have been more · interested in the views expressed by the 'sceptics' and the 'antagonists'. We have declined to hear the reservations of such colleagues as merely the pleading of self-interest or of retrenched individuals. This approach is too frequently observed in justifications for ignoring voices hostile to change. Instead, we have tried to understand why there should be considerable scepticism and hostility to changes which should otherwise command widespread support. Who in higher education could possibly support limited participation, restricted opportunities for students and a set of archaic professional conventions if they could be modified in ways consonant with academic priorities?

1005.   There is a considerable body of literature on the management of organisational change, little of it having much direct bearing on change in universities. Much of the contemporary material emphasises the need to produce *cultural change* rather than merely structural change (Beckhard and Pritchard, 1992, for example). This involves committing the organisation to attitudinal readjustment, which in universities might normally be expected following success in an argument. Furthermore, institutional leaders are encouraged to 'lead by example' in order to commit others to their vision, explaining why changes need to take place and staking their personal credibility on that assessment. As Duke has claimed for the university as a 'learning organisation' (1992), it needs to produce a *paradigm shift* in values and attitudes if change is to be seen through successfully and convincingly. That shift is largely led by cultural change, which itself depends on an institutional commitment to 'doing things differently'. In turn, this requires more than a rearrangement of the furniture of institutional life, the careless restructuring of functions and roles in a manner disconnected from a common vision or purposeful educational direction. In short, our investigation has convinced us that strategic change is cultural change, and cultural change is related to institutional mission.

1006. This approach to change seldom appears to be the experience of academic staff. Indeed, we have been repeatedly advised that the more common experience is for institutional leadership to announce changes, leave others to carry them forward and then to create distance between themselves and the change agents in the event that change may not succeed – precisely the pattern of behaviour most likely to signal shallow commitment and poor personal investment in cultural change. Perhaps institutional leaders are wiser than we allow. It has been suggested to us that it is imprudent to attempt change in universities because the majority of academic staff will be against the proposals. Since they are generally highly intelligent, mischievously inclined and with time on their hands, they will have all the resources necessary to make life difficult for change agents. Moreover, it has been argued, universities are organisations like no other; that they are institutions where the principle product is *dissent*, or opposition to received wisdom. Managing dissent by directive means is likely to cut across the central purpose of the institution.

1007. There is not time here to unravel these aspects of the problem. Some sources of literature argue that resistance is most likely to occur amongst 'middle managers' (heads of department in a university perhaps) where the propensity to change is offset by an incredulity towards perceived benefits. This may be true but we fondly believe that academic colleagues usually behave for good reasons rather than otherwise. 'Name-calling' one's critics should not be part of a scholarly enterprise.

Towards a credit culture

1008. To establish what is being proposed and what is being opposed, we need to define a *credit culture*. This may be achieved by considering its principles, its objective manifestations and its consequences for

professional behaviour. It is far more than the prosaic application of a system of academic 'currency', although that is often its most socially visible form. In working towards an understanding of the main ingredients of a credit culture, the following discussion draws on the work of Scott for the investigative project, who in turn builds on the image of (paradigm) *shift* proposed by Duke (1992). This sense of movement from one (inherited) position to another (aspirant) position captures the journey that needs to be negotiated if we are to arrive at an outline of a credit culture.

Principles of a credit culture

1009. We have argued consistently throughout this report that the use of credit and the introduction of modular and credit-based systems have to be approached, conceptually and in practical institutional implementation, from the perspective of chosen purpose. What is being sought by higher and further education in the introduction of flexibility and greater student choice? Do institutions seek to achieve 'first' or 'second' and 'third' generation commitment to the develop of credit systems (see Chapter VIII)? This refers to the *extrinsic* or *intrinsic* goals that are being pursued. Credit systems may be primarily administrative arrangements with secondary academic reverberations in which student choice and access are managed largely with limited implications for academic life. Or they may require an intellectual reconfiguration of institutional practice, with profound consequences.

1010. In describing the principles of a credit culture, we would offer the following summary:

Table 64: Principles of a *credit culture*	
From	**To**
Exclusion	*Inclusion*
Teacher	*Learner*
Process	*Outcome*
Direction	*Guidance*
Failure	*Achievement*
Margins	*Mainstream*
Profession control	*Individual choice*
Structures	*Cultures*

1011. These broad principles underpin some fundamental shifts in institutional culture. The first involves a shift in *taxonomies of knowledge.* Institutions may need to rethink the means by which academic subjects are combined, deconstructed and recombined within the university. This will involve an interaction between: professional academics in the normal course of their work as they interact with the ideas of other disciplines; students, as they exercise choices within academic programmes; and external stakeholders, as they express demands on the service they receive from higher education and beyond. This in turn implies the need to re-consider the process of higher education in the context of outcomes and learning achievement. One does not need to adopt a particularly instru-mental approach to the nature of learning in order to accept that higher education must be concerned with more than just process and the socialisation of individuals into disciplinary norms. More students require different learning experiences, with explicit performance criteria, before they will feel confident of their chances in a future labour market.

1012. Secondly, it may involve the *rewriting of the undergraduate curriculum* (and arguably the postgraduate curriculum). By this, we refer to the curriculum in the broadest sense, embracing the instruments of learning and achievement. Credit transcripts, learning outcome statements, individual learning packages and work-based internships are relevant not only to the construction of specific credit schemes but to wider curricular reform. This rewriting may need to be seen in the larger context of changes in schools and further education, most notably perhaps NVQs, and in the skills demanded of a post-industrial economy. Such a fundamental challenge to conventional curriculum practice in higher education is not something to which all institutions will be readily attracted, nor which they will be able to embrace overnight. Nevertheless, at the frontiers of institutional development, these changes are becoming commonplace.

1013. Thirdly, the *evolution of the academic profession* is a poorly recognised consequence of these changes, as greater attention is attached to the contribution of para-academic and administrative staff. This should be seen as a broadening of the profession rather than as the deskilling of traditional lecturers or as the creation of a twin-track profession: an inner core of full-time academics and guidance and systems people and a periphery of instructors and assessors. Institutions may need to give greater attention to staffing policies and staff development, both in terms of the balance to be achieved between different groups of staff, but also to the contribution these groups make to the wider whole. Quality improvement programmes, such as *Investors in People,* may have a role to play in assisting institutions to create the attitudinal changes necessary for all sections of the higher education community to respect the contribution made by each other to the common good.

1014. The fourth shift involves the *reconstruction of the institution* itself. Credit systems may work less effectively in an institution that defines itself as a loose congeries of quasi-autonomous academic units unless such academic units are de-coupled from control over the individual student programme. We have discussed these matters extensively and have made proposals on student finance (Chapter XI) and academic structures (Chapter XII) which address these matters. In short, as long as institutions continue to pursue greater student choice without reinventing themselves organisa-tionally in ways consistent with this, then it is likely that prevailing cultural habits of profession-al control will assert themselves over new cultural aspirations for individual student choice. This 're-invention' is likely to necessitate the creation of a new balance of power between managers and academic faculty, the erosion of traditional demarcations between higher and other forms of post secondary education, the blurring of disciplinary boundaries and the deconstruction of absolute forms of professional control over the curriculum and its meaning for students.

Structural features of a credit culture

Levels of operation

1015. Credit systems operate at three different levels. The first is the *single course,* or *family of courses within a single department*. The purpose may be to encourage a little more access flexibility, some managed choice and a little more variety of optional choice through, for example, work-based learning or perhaps a specific elective programme. None of these aims is offensive to traditional academic values, nor do they undermine conventional patterns of loyalty, to subject, to department or to external relationships, including research beyond the institution.

1016.   The second level is the *institution scheme* or a large institutional segment like a multi-faculty modular course. The purposes are more radical. First, they may seek to empower students as customers, so introducing the principle of the market into the organisation of courses. Students are no longer attached exclusively to a particular department but are (fairly) free to choose courses across the institution. However, the operation of this choice principle cannot be confined to course organisation. It also influences patterns of assessment, because students no longer have a standard cumulative experience. Secondly, the more comprehensive credit systems become, the more they erode the integrity of disciplines. Within departments, credit systems encourage a voluntary inter-disciplinarity; across whole institutions, top-down credit systems seem to threaten disciplinary identities. Thirdly, institution-wide schemes require institutions to be restructured. This restructuring may first be expressed mechanistically, by establishing a compatible and probably centralised timetable, shared assessment regulations and compliance with an institutional information system. Departments (or schools or faculties) defined in terms of intrinsic academic criteria have to be replaced as effective operating units by much broader organisations defined in terms of extrinsic administrative criteria.

1017.   The third level is the *national framework*. In one sense this represents the next stage, the culmination of institution-wide credit systems and consequently an even sharper threat to traditional academic values. Before institutions can join the national framework, they have to establish clear and effective institutional policies on credit accumulation and transfer. A rag-bag of unco-ordinated

departmental policies clearly will serve less well. But in another sense it is possible to regard a national credit framework as a corrective to over-directive institutional policies. National credit systems have to be freely negotiated between academically autonomous institutions. This may help to reproduce the habits and patterns of voluntary exchange typical of smaller-scale developments within institutions. It should be added, if only for emphasis, that we have not anticipated that a national framework would involve a subscription to homogenous academic structures. *A national framework implies unity rather than uniformity.*

Structural shifts of emphasis

1018.   The development of credit systems involves four shifts of emphasis, each of which has important consequences for cultural and professional life: from courses to credit systems; from departments to frameworks; from subject-based teaching to student-centred learning; and from knowledge to performance. Each shift commits an institution to a 'trade-off' of one set of advantages for another. In practice, however, we have found that colleagues on either side of the argument tend to respect the advantages of their own proposals as if they implied counterweight disadvantages in any alternative arrangement. For example, we have heard it suggested that because credit systems can allow students to choose modules on a Wednesday afternoon, they will lead irreversibly to the destruction of university (and national) sporting excellence. We have taken a less dramatic view in the assessment offered below.

1019.   **From courses to credits:** the shift from the familiar and pre-prepared 'course' to a system based on the accumulation of 'credits' involves changes of both a structural and a cultural nature. The Honours degree in the United Kingdom is not simply an organisational pattern; it is the concrete expression of deep-rooted values. It embodies academic assumptions about the need for sustained academic commitment; intellectual assumptions about the nature of 'knowledge'; and social assumptions about the need to initiate students into particular disciplinary and professional cultures. The case for 'courses' is that they provide for students indispensable ingredients which cannot be easily replaced:

- **intellectual integrity,** a sense of intellectual unity supported by a sustained *conversation with the past*, as students engage with the protocols of a subject-discipline;

- **intellectual rigour,** as students are required to be assessed in the totality of what they have learned rather than in sub-units; a sense of 'completeness';

- **intellectual identity,** by which students come to describe and locate themselves within the academic community as medical, physics or history students;

- **public trust;** the extent to which people generally, and employers specifically, 'know what they are getting' with a 'course'.

1020.   The difficulty of stimulating informal associations of group learning is potentially one of the gravest weaknesses of credit systems. Managing the occasional intellectual associations that occur for students within the context of the 'course' is one of the most difficult aspects to replicate in the more dispersed associations of credit systems. Secondly, if students pursue diverse academic trajectories or individual learning packages, broad generic norm-referenced assessments may have to be replaced by detailed criterion-referenced credit transcripts. There is likely to be a period of uncertainty, confusion and disquiet before that transition is completed satisfactorily.

1021.   Credit systems, it is argued, embody different and even contrary values to those which have held sway in the elite segment of British higher education. In place of grand organic interpretations of 'knowledge' they offer a much less formidable framework for academic progression in which connections, between topics and levels, are pragmatically derived rather than cognitively prescribed. In place of socially exclusive accounts of disciplinary and professional cultures, they offer wider, indeed wide-open, entry into a much

more diffuse 'college culture', possession and enjoyment of broadly based intellectual attributes produced by exposure to higher education itself rather than to particular subjects.

1022.   Credit systems also rarely result in the radical disaggregation of academic programmes and subject clusters. They usually involve more modest attempts to combine *core*, *optional* and *elective* into structured programmes. Students are rarely, if ever, left to wander the matrix of opportunities without significant direction in the combination of credit that would be necessary to sustain specific qualification outcomes. In practice, credit systems usually build into their arrangements supporting mechanisms which encourage student informal association. This may be achieved through *self-study groups, extra-mural guest lectures, special social events* and other similar 'identity-building' activities. Conventionally, credit systems are better than courses at delivering:

- **access:** in that they tolerate a broader range of criteria for entry at a number of stages of entry;

- **achievement:** in that they encourage credit for success to date rather than the prospect of terminal failure;

- **flexibility:** students might vary their choices within and between programmes rather than find themselves trapped in programmes to which they are unsuited or uncommitted;

- **inter-disciplinarity:** as students 'grow their own programmes' by making inventive combinations;

- **self-reliance:** when students are encouraged and expected to negotiate their individual learning programmes rather than simply receive their programme ready packaged.

1023.   On balance, institutions may need to choose what type of experience they are offering students, based on the anticipated destination of their graduates. 'Courses' in the conventional mode appear to prepare students more effectively for entry into conventional academic life; they develop the student as a 'scholarship apprentice' through an intensive induction in the certainties of a single subject discipline. Although credit systems do not require students to exercise choices beyond a single discipline, by making it possible they encourage students to reach beyond the internal world of academic scholarship to consider what components of achievement need to be assembled for success in the labour market outside the university.

1024.   **From departments to frameworks:** a shift from the department, where the 'private world' of knowledge and the 'public world' of institutions and systems collide, to credit and/or modular frameworks, where students are freer to travel across departmental boundaries without deference to the particular conventions of groups of academic staff.

1025.   Departments represent disciplines and embody professional codes as well as forming part of institutional structures. Here the values and practices of these different worlds must be harmonised. They are the natural home of like-minded academics and, as we argued in Chapter XII, they may be indispensable elements in any institutional structure. However, students do not need departments in the same way as academic staff. Where they choose to study across boundaries, credit frameworks encourage this level of mobility. Students need coherent programmes which are meaningful for them; they need centres of support for their personal and academic consolations; and they need sources to turn to for academic and other services. Within frameworks, these may be delivered in a number of different contexts.

1026.   However, it must be admitted that the shift from departments to frameworks produces the most significant cultural challenge. At this point, credit systems become deeply enmeshed in battles over the balance of power in institutions. Frameworks are often seen to be agents of managerial power, standing as they must outside departmental culture. Moreover, credit systems can be viewed by departmental academic staff as devices to intensify academic

labour control. This suspicion may be further aroused by efforts to produce the corporate conformity and compliance that integrated frameworks require. Academic staff may come to interpret the extension of greater choice to students as a threat to their own professional freedoms. On the other hand, this freedom is frequently asserted at the expense of student choice.

1027.   During the investigation, we found the battle between departments (or as often entire faculties) and institutional frameworks to have been the most serious source of disquiet in the introduction of more flexible arrangements. Where institutions manage to break through the membrane of departmental resistance, they usually succeed in establishing the basic features of a more open, and more effective, arrangement. Under these conditions, academic staff quickly appear to realise that their prime activities, teaching and research, are not in fact compromised by credit frameworks. There may be a shift in the balance of power between Deans and the framework Director, with the former group finding their sovereignty constrained, but academic staff themselves can continue their business unimpeded. On the other hand, where institutions succumb to pressure from faculties and departments, they rarely appear to create the cultural conditions for more open student mobility. Departmental boundaries re-form and a 'Balkanised culture' re-establishes itself. The fissures between departments become difficult for students to negotiate and institutions sometimes find themselves seeking to maintain a residual commitment to credit-based opportunities through the establishment of special 'CATS Units' or weak and nominal 'framework managers'. We have described these problems in terms of 'phantom' and regressive arrangements in Chapter XII.

1028.   **From subject-based teaching to student-centred learning:** in credit systems, 'ownership' of students' academic programmes is transferred under carefully defined conditions to students themselves. They must negotiate their own customised packages, which in itself demands the development of useful learning skills. And, during their progress through higher education they must work out for themselves the academic or vocational coherence of the packages they have chosen, which again puts much greater emphasis on learning than teaching.

1029.　On the other hand, critics argue that there are real problems of quality and coherence with this approach. Firstly, by chopping up courses into bits and pieces, students may find it becomes more difficult to challenge disciplinary and professional orthodoxies. Knowledge may be reduced to unproblematical sound-bites. Secondly, credit systems can produce unintended academic effects. They can encourage mechanical, even passive, learning as students cynically accumulate the requisite credits with less regard for the substance of the material studied. Thirdly, the very openness of credit systems, embracing APL and APEL, Access and franchised-course students, multiple entry and exit points, may lead to demands for a much tighter structure of academic programmes, within and between units, more explicit descriptions of aims and objectives, and a more prescriptive quality assurance (and assessment) regime. We have seen numerous examples where institutions appear to offer considerable choice but then hedge around student opportunities with a plethora of conditions, in the name of quality and coherence.

1030.　There is one final aspect of the shift from subject-based to student-centred learning that must be addressed: *the authority of the teacher*. We wish to make it clear that, although this report is required to inform the further development of credit systems in higher and further education, we do not imagine that this should occur at the expense of the professional authority of academic staff in the provision of teaching and research for students. However, credit systems do place greater emphasis upon the student-as-consumer and challenge the sovereignty of academic staff in the judgements over programme construction. We take some comfort from the fact that the century-long experience of credit systems in the United States does not appear to have eroded the authority of the scholar. Where it has encouraged a critical scepticism which is subversive of tradition, then this is probably a desirable outcome. We think it is better that the authority of the teacher should be asserted in the domain of democratic participation than buttressed by the restrictions of the conventional course.

1031.　**From knowledge to performance:** at its most simple, the view that higher education in democratic participation mode needs to shift from the pursuit of knowledge for its own sake for an elite to the pursuit of performance and achievement for future career purpose for the majority of students. Even if matters were as simple as this, it is by no means clear that the prevailing cultural conditions in higher education could absorb the transformation of values implied by this. Many argue that what distinguishes higher education from other levels of education is that the knowledge towards which students aspire is necessarily provisional, half-formed, and so problematical. 'End-stopping' of any kind is seen as incompatible with the essential openness of higher education. We have referred to this problem in the discussion of *competence* earlier in this report (see Chapter VIII).

1032.　On the other hand, the argument that knowledge and skills must always be regarded as provisional and problematical suggests a rather romantic view of the intellectual possibilities of higher education, and one which may be skewed by an orientation towards social science and the humanities, genuflecting perhaps to the provisionality of scientific knowledge in general. Put bluntly, in medium-ranked institutions in a mass system and among students with limited vocational ambitions, the view may be very different from that which obtains in elite and research-led institutions.

1033.　This debate is important for an understanding of the cultural conditions under which credit systems may prosper. Some argue that credit systems should not be applied to elite forms of undergraduate education or to 'core' academic work in general, and are only appropriate for mass forms or in 'peripheral' areas of work (which explains why credit systems are more widespread in the former polytechnics and colleges of higher education and in continuing education). Moreover, the growing popularity of credit systems in the traditional universities and the undergraduate mainstream is a symptom of their drift away from elite roles. However, such arguments are undermined by the experience of taught postgraduate courses where credit-based systems have been readily accepted, partly because of the growing prominence of part-time students. The experience of the United States also suggests that credit systems and elite undergraduate education can comfortably coexist.

1034.   We would be disappointed if this report encouraged the view that flexibility and student choice were properties of a learning experience that was not of the highest standing. Whilst we have no reason to expect all institutions to adopt credit systems uniformly or for the same purpose, we have not subscribed to the view that credit systems compromise the pursuit of knowledge for its own sake, where that is held to be desirable. Indeed, we would be alarmed if a higher education system developed which repeated the academic-vocational schisms that have divided further education to date. The further development of credit systems seeks to avoid precisely those types of unproductive demarcation. In the market of higher education in the future, as now, there may be some institutions which seek to promote 'Mandarin education'. If this is the case, we do not think the development of credit systems would be responsible for divisions between the pursuit of knowledge as inquisitiveness and knowledge as operational competence. Rather, we anticipate that students will be able to position themselves more readily on the spectrum of learning opportunities that runs between these polarities.

Credit culture and the impact on disciplines

1035.   Subject disciplines remain the primary focus of loyalty of most university and college teachers. They are usually the reason why colleagues teach in the university in the first place; they define and justify the professional position of academic staff; and they constitute the intellectual preoccupations, professional routines and socio-economic

linkages of academic colleagues within and between institutions. In both 'cosmopolitan' and 'local' dispositions towards the institution, subject disciplines condition the professional orientation and culture of academic staff in influential ways. Indeed, the loyalties to disciplines can be so intensive and clearly defined that they become 'tribal' in character. As Becher (1989) has explained, the anthropology of academic structures requires us to understand the role of the discipline in producing the personal hierarchies, initiation rites and socialising events which are common throughout universities, yet which can divide disciplines into incommensurable worlds. Disciplines can generate their special languages and codes of communication. It can be more important for students to succeed in adopting the internal codes of the discipline than in meeting formally its assessment requirements, and the former will often condition success in the latter.

1036.   In this sense, disciplines operate as agents of closure, sealing into themselves the specific symbols and signifiers that define their unique view of the world. Conversations within a disciplinary boundary can resemble a tribal indaba, complete with linguistic ritual and deference to appropriate conceptual totems and individual High Priests. The analogy is rich in symmetry. In principle, and also in practice, this can act contrary to the practice of student mobility and the combination of different elements from various subject groups. Indeed, the failure of a student to join the initiation ceremonies at the start of the process can influence the readiness of a discipline group to accept her into the community thereafter. The student, it will be claimed, does not know the rules of engagement, has not been properly prepared, and cannot learn in time the secrets that need to be known. The effect is to exclude members who wish to join the 'tribe' other than on the first possible occasion.

1037.   Although the anthropological metaphor is potent and helpful, we do not wish to take it too far. Disciplines have their own internal divisions (social and physical geographers, mechanical and electrical engineers, for example) but they must also be combined in various ways to form courses. Only single-subject, single Honours degrees might be an exception to this. Becher and Kogan (1992) have suggested a general taxonomy of course types (see Table 65). Where credit schemes should be positioned in this scheme is unclear. This may partly be due to the fact that their book was initially written in 1980 and unmodified in this respect in the second edition.

1038.　　Technically credit systems could apply to any of the cells, but in principle they would not expect to be described as closed-cohesive. Cases could be made for any of the remaining three cells – closed-discrete, permeable-cohesive or permeable-discrete. In fact, in practice, credit systems apply to the conditions described in all the cells of the model. Some modular and credit-based frameworks now allow single subject choices to emerge from the matrix of opportunities and we appear to be moving beyond the time when 'modular' meant anything other than single subject programmes. The principle of deferred choice has encouraged some schemes to allow students a broader initial experience followed by a narrowing down of subject choices towards final qualification. At certain ratios of credit by subject, students may still achieve a single Honours award if they wish.

1039.　　In some ways, the model provided by Becher and Kogan has been overtaken by events. Inter-disciplinary courses are as likely to be multi-disciplinary modular aggregates, such as business studies, as they are to be in the form they propose. Moreover, many modular schemes are now more permeable than closed. If we were to offer an assessment of the direction of drift of developments in higher education institutions, we would suggest that it is generally from 'cohesive' to 'discrete'. In 'old' universities it appears to be from closed-cohesive to permeable-cohesive, or to closed-discrete. In 'new' universities the move towards permeable-discrete is the most noticeable, with some evidence of regression towards all other cells. Single Honours degrees still occupy an important part of the portfolio of most institutions.

Unity and fragmentation in courses

1040.　　In some subjects, largely the humanities, the sum of a course worthy of higher education, and especially of an

Table 65: Some varieties of curricular pattern: Becher and Kogan		
	Boundaries	
	Closed	**Permeable**
Cohesive	Single subject specialist degrees	Inter-disciplinary courses which are area-based or problem-based rather than related to conventional disciplines. Considerable effort is made to develop a sense of unity between the disciplinary components but the boundaries remain permeable to (relevant) new elements
Content **Discrete**	A fairly common species of curricular pattern, namely, that in which a number of separate and self-contained thematic topics are pursued simultaneously but with no special attempt to relate them to one another. Broadly based 'foundation courses', joint honours programmes and unit or modular degree schemes all fit into this pattern	It implies an ability for the student to select individual items of curricular content at will, but not to be subject to the discipline-based restrictions that characterise modular degree programmes. It depends on the notion of cumulative and transferable credit, negotiated in relation to approved pieces of work over a relatively unrestricted time-span

Honours degree, is regarded as more than a mere collection of its parts. Because the intention has traditionally been to initiate students into a particular intellectual tradition, it is the whole that matters. This interpretation of academic purposes is also reflected in the widespread conviction that a categorical distinction can be drawn between 'higher' and other forms of post-secondary education and, if this interpretation is accepted, credit systems may appear to undermine the integrity of courses by over-emphasising their detailed components at the expense of their vitalising whole. So it is argued, credit systems can safely be applied to peripheral courses, like part-time degrees, but if the principle is extended to mainstream courses something of real intellectual value is lost. This is an argument which enthusiasts for credit accumulation and transfer must confront.

1041.   On the other hand, critics of this view can challenge the assumptions upon which it is based. If a full-time Honours degree provides a uniquely excellent learning experience, is this revealed in the quality of the graduate outcomes? It is by no means clear that single honours graduates are better equipped for career development compared with their combined subjects or part-time equivalents. Any evidence is at best inconclusive and at worst insubstantial. Moreover, it is not at all clear that the alleged superiority of the English Honours systems delivers a graduate output that can compete with European equivalents. Whatever its merits in elite formation, buttressed by a selective secondary school system, and for the production of a research cadre, the single Honours course may not be the vehicle which commends itself for future success in a labour market characterised by flexibility and increased competition.

1042.   A further potent problem concerns the extent to which the single Honours degree deserves to be defended as a centre of excellence when it excludes from entry many students with qualifications other than specialist 'A' levels. How are students with GNVQs Level 3 or similar to negotiate entry to degrees which have been habituated to an 'A' level intake?

1043.   Perhaps a more significant and sensible contrast can be drawn between different patterns of knowledge, what Becher (1989) has called *'areas of contextual imperative'* and *'areas of contextual association'*. The former offer closely patterned sequences of explanation, with each new finding fitting neatly into place as the whole picture is steadily pieced together; the latter loosely knit clusters of ideas, with no clearly articulated framework of development. Credit systems that mainly embrace 'areas of contextual imperative' are likely to be different from those operating largely in 'areas of contextual association'.

1044.   In the case of other subjects, a different obstacle is encountered. Here it is not so much that the whole is greater than the sum of its parts but that the nature of knowledge imposes a strict linear sequence on how courses must be organised. We are relatively familiar with claims from engineering and natural science that prospective students need to be equipped with relevant technical competence before they can embark on a programme of study. The same claims are applied to initial entry to French, German and to a lesser extent Spanish language degrees. Moreover we have heard similar arguments in favour of limited entry to programmes in art and design. In these cases, it is argued that the discourse and the practical applications of the discipline act as restraints on the openness of entry that can be tolerated, both at an initial stage and subsequently. Finally, the argument also emerges in the humanities and social sciences. In philosophy, for example, academic colleagues maintain that students need a strong basis in conceptual competence. This can be developed at initial entry, but thereafter students who lack the shared language of the discipline are likely to find internal transfer more difficult.

Categories of disciplinary flexibility

1045.   We believe it may be possible to group disciplines into the following (provisional) categories, which distinguish between the propensity of disciplines to be made available to in-coming students (see Table 66). As with most taxonomies, an overlap between categories can be anticipated for many disciplines and their sub-elements.

Table 66: Categories of disciplinary flexibility

Linear-technical: such as natural sciences and engineering, which require technical competence upon which to build subsequent progression, but which can tolerate limited engagement with sub-elements of disciplines

Linear-cumulative: such as languages, mathematics, which involve progressive improvement throughout the course, and which may have difficulty making later stages available to non-disciplinary students

Linear-practical: such as art and design, which cannot easily be sub-divided for the purposes of intermediate entry within a credit system (ie. a student cannot do 'a bit of sculpture')

Discourse-dependent: such as philosophy, some social science, some humanities, which require the development of a shared discourse to vitalise the discipline, but which may make sub-elements available to 'outsiders'

Discourse-tolerant: such as some social science, some humanities, some business and law, which can tolerate some lack of comprehensive engagement with internal discourses

1046.   Those who support credit systems are faced with a difficult choice. They can either succumb to this linear or discourse imperative, in full knowledge that its effect may be to reduce the flexibility which credit systems aim to produce (although all credit arrangements, even the most radical schemes, incorporate notions of progression); or choose to question at least some of the more restrictive assumptions about fixed progression, in order to preserve as much flexibility as possible. Students in the mid-stream of credit-based programmes are likely to lack the consistent and ordered experience that uniform disciplinary engagement brings.

Changing the culture of disciplines

1047.   The long-term potential of credit systems, therefore, is to dissolve conventional intellectual as well as institutional conventions which limit the mobility of students excessively. We would not wish to propose developments which would weaken the intellectual basis of disciplines. There is little purpose in making modules freely available if the quality of intellectual activity has to be determined by the lowest common denominator. Moreover, students themselves should be expected to make informed judgements of their capacity to earn credit in a particular subject. Flexible systems cannot legislate for insistent but poor student judgement. However, certain new developments might be attempted to encourage greater internal mobility.

1048.   This is likely to require significant changes to the cultural environment of disciplines and their teaching in universities. Firstly, the teaching of disciplinary material may need to anticipate that not all students in a module will have the same conceptual or technical background. Secondly, the module will have varying degrees of importance to different groups of students. Thirdly, the assessment of the module might be separated from its delivery (in the manner described in Chapter VIII). Fourthly, institutions and academic staff may need to obey the principle: *A Right to Fail* by which students have the right to undertake a specific programme of study, *and not be denied reasonable access to it*, provided they have received appropriate guidance on the material involved and understand the consequences of their decision.

1049.   The most significant cultural change is likely to require the adjustment of many academic staff to an element of mixed ability teaching. This will involve two further fundamental shifts of professional attitude. Firstly, within credit systems, the teacher has a responsibility to teach those students who choose a particular module or other learning experience. Secondly, a teacher does not enjoy the right to select which students to teach and cannot discriminate amongst them. This does not mean that a teacher is obliged to make students learn successfully, nor to teach only those elements which all students can comfortably manage. As we have argued earlier, students have a responsibility to exercise informed judgement and to assess the consequences of failure. Ultimately, credit systems do not appear to compromise the authority of the academic teacher but they do require that the teacher takes into account the needs of a more disparate group of students than those who wish to reproduce themselves in the image of the teacher.

Markets, professions and a credit culture

1050.	It is not possible to develop our analysis much further without addressing those aspects of the development of credit systems which relate to the operation of markets in higher education. We have touched on some of these matters in Chapter XI. From the analysis and proposals presented there, it is clear that credit systems seek overtly to change the conventional relationship between academic providers and their customers, particularly students.

Scepticism amongst academics towards markets in higher education

1051.	The main outcome of our investigation on this point suggests that most academic staff within institutions at all levels below senior management, and some senior managers as well, view the operation of markets within higher education with deep suspicion. We have not been able to distinguish between suspicion of competition in general or of markets in particular. Since credit systems are seen as one manifestation of 'market forces' and competition for students(within and between institutions), they often suffer by association. There may be at least four substantial reasons for this scepticism towards markets.

1052.	Firstly, many academics appear to adopt a sceptical attitude in principle to the operation of markets in public service organisations. They are confirmed in this view where they have been unconvinced by market-led reforms in the Health Service, Civil Service, transport and the public utilities. For them, the concept of public service is hostile to the concept of markets. Efficiency and value-for-money can be achieved by sound management but not by inefficient and artificial 'markets'.

1053.	Secondly, at a more sophisticated level, some academics regard the operation of markets as liable to introduce new hierarchies into the education service, dividing groups of individuals from each other in terms of their different capacities to gain access to services, and opening up hierarchies between institutions (Ball S, 1993). Their objection to credit systems, and particularly to funding methodologies based on credit tariffs, educational vouchers and similar instruments, is founded on the belief that markets distribute resources inefficiently – producing a flow of funds from poor areas of provision to centres of established wealth. In higher education, they fear this would strengthen traditional institutions at the expense of the 'new' universities, a resource gradient that would be further steepened by the application of 'top-up' tuition fees.

1054.	A third group questions whether the transaction costs of operating markets in public service institutions have been properly assessed. It appears to them that internal market arrangements result in the establishment of substantial bureaucracies to administer transactions with no clear efficiency gain. In terms of credit systems, they view the new administrative cadre that underpins such arrangements as a tax on 'front-line' academic teaching and research. Furthermore, they remain doubtful whether much is gained from the turbulence and threat of instability that market-inspired fluidity can generate. Unless universities are to be allowed to go out of business (which they see as politically unlikely), competitive pressure has an enervating rather than a stimulating effect on institutional responses.

1055.	Perhaps the largest group of objectors in higher education express the familiar hostility of most professional groups to markets and competitive pressure. Professions abhor markets, and the academic profession may be no different in this respect. Markets challenge deeply rooted professional values of personal service, control over professional knowledge, standards of professional performance and relationships with clients. For professional academics, the most serious (and for some, offensive) challenge is to the professional-client relationship between teacher and student. In market models, of which credit systems are seen as visible evidence, a relationship based on scholarly authority appears at its worst to be reduced to a quasi-commercial transaction. Most teachers, whatever their personal dispositions and priorities, believe that professional practice involves doing their best by 'their' students. It is a service they offer in good faith, which may be compromised and soiled by the overlay of commercial advantage.

1056.   In fact the association of credit systems with market rhetoric may be a political accident. A more comfortable, and more accurate, association may be with the rather different discourses of wider access and social equity. Nor is it right to regard the application of market principles as a recent phenomenon, although until the 1980s it was mediated through habits of political consensuality and professional deference which no longer apply. Yet a mass higher education system, regardless of its political context, is inevitably a 'market' system. As credit systems are a necessary component of such a system, the relationship between credit systems and the market cannot be glossed over.

1057.   It would be disingenuous of us not to accept that the effective operation of credit systems does indeed imply a challenge to professional academic sovereignty through the release of student choice. Institutions which commit to the development of credit systems commit to a shift in the balance of institutional power towards individual students and their decisions. If institutions are not ready to manage the cultural changes this implies, they may need to reconsider their overall strategic direction with respect to the promotion of greater student choice.

Markets and the American model

1058.   It is widely acknowledged that the American system of higher education is the most market-led in the world. It is also the most extensive, and arguably the most successful higher education system. It resonates happily with American values of individualism, self-motivation, success through individual effort and enterprise, competition as a stimulus to success

and personal mobility in time and place. This has led one influential American commentator to talk of 'American exceptionalism' (Trow, 1991).

1059.   Whether the American model is 'exceptional' and can only be reproduced under American cultural conditions remains an open question for the moment. We are more interested here to distinguish what does not translate to United Kingdom conditions, and what may otherwise be learned with advantage.

Discontinuities with the American model

1060.   In considering American higher education, and in commending the further development of credit systems in the United Kingdom, we do not seek to propose an uncritical adoption of American higher education. Its origins lie in large measure in the freedoms enjoyed by early pioneers to establish universities and higher education colleges in an unconstrained manner. It is worth noting the scale of the early investment by the American people in higher education. By 1880, England had a population of 23 million and four universities; at the same stage, the state of Ohio had a population of three million and 37 universities. By 1910, the United States had 1,000 higher education institutions and 330,000 students while France had sixteen universities and 40,000 students. By 1990, the United States possessed 3,500 HEIs and 14 million enrolled students representing over 50% of the 18 year-old age group (Trow, 1991).

1061.   Secondly, investment in higher education, through universities and community colleges, is in some measure an act of compensation for the relatively poor secondary school education received by many Americans. The Freshman and Sophomore years of the American degree programme are based principally on general education; students choose their 'Major' by the start of their Junior (ie third) year. There is no selective secondary school curriculum, such as the 'A' level upon which to build a more intensive initial cycle of higher education. Indeed, the heart of the American university lies not as in the United Kingdom in the honours degree, but in the Graduate School. The development of such schools has been slow in the United Kingdom, but mass undergraduate participation may propel their subsequent evolution as students look towards Master's degrees as the premium terminal qualifications.

American 'exceptionalism'?

1062.   In Table 67 below, we identify the ten reasons given by Martin Trow for American 'exceptionalism'. While he is cautious about encouraging any careless imitation, Trow does believe that in the United States *'we have a precocious system, without many of the problems and weak solutions that mark contemporary European higher education.'* Amongst the most significant causes of this 'exceptionalism', Trow accepts that an open market of fee-driven and unfettered expansion has played the most influential role.

Table 67: Ten reasons for American 'exceptionalism'

1   *Belief in education for its own sake*

2   *Development of public and private institutions; eg 80% of students are in public sector, but 8/10 and 15/20 leading research universities are private; public institutions get 45% from state governments, private institutions receive 2%*

3   *Commitment to general and liberal education; Qualified Leaver Index = 75% (in France = 30% and in United Kingdom = 20%)*

4   *Credit system, elective programme and modular courses*

5   *More egalitarian academic profession*

6   *Little government involvement in higher education*

7   *Strong college President*

8   *Lay Board of representatives for local and regional accountability*

9   *Strong Continuing Education and community colleges system*

10 *Service to society and state; in UK 44% graduates enter public service and 45% continue academic careers. In the USA, far more enter commercial organisations as well as agencies of the state*

Source: Martin Trow, 1991

1063.   He cites the example of Continuing Education provision in Grand Rapids, Michigan, a city of 250,000 with 400,000 in the immediate metropolitan area. In the United Kingdom, this might be the equivalent of Sheffield. In Grand Rapids, however there are ten higher education institutions offering Continuing Education programmes. Nobody plans this; there are no regulations or private concordats between institutions. There is competition but there is demand to meet the supply of places available. The vast majority of the provision is sustained by individual tuition fees paid by students. As Trow points out:

'Continuing education is yet another service that engenders support in the broader community for the provider (in addition to fees). Thus the providers are all highly motivated to recruit students, that is, to create a learning society, and they are all highly sensitive to the consumers' interests. Above all, behind all this lies the assumption that "supply creates demand".'

The benign consequences of the market

1064.   For Trow, and for others, the relatively unregulated expansion of American higher education has had a general benign effect on American society. It has allowed the establishment of enormous institutional diversity, resulting in a large private sector, an extensive public sector, small religious colleges and large community colleges. The appetite of the American people for higher education in one form or another has been met to the extent that higher education enjoys a place in the affections and aspirations of most Americans in a way that is still unimaginable in the United Kingdom and much of Europe. This has consequences both for the political support the sector can call upon and for the willingness of individuals to support their colleges and universities.

1065.   Perhaps the most well-known and heavily explored higher education system in the United States is that operated under the California Master Plan. Access to higher education in California is guaranteed under the Master Plan to all eligible citizens but the market is 'managed' by the creation of a stratified structure of institutions. In California, this involves managed access to one of the nine campuses of the University of California; or to one of the 19 campuses of the California State University; or to one of the 120 community colleges. Access is controlled largely by academic performance, supplemented by equal opportunity policies, and adjusted by flexible inter-institutional credit transfer arrangements. Although fiscal pressure and demographic growth over the past few years have begun to pose major problems for the survival of the Master Plan, its place as an example of a managed market in higher education provision remains assured. It should be added that students also have access to a large number of private universities in California, including Stanford and the University of Southern California.

1066.   Mobility within California and elsewhere depends crucially upon a common credit transfer system. This allows individuals to negotiate their passage from community college to State University and beyond. It is possible to move after two years from a downtown college in Oakland to the University of California at Berkeley. Credit transfer arrangements cannot of themselves compensate for steep inequalities of class and ethnicity but they can help to create the cultural conditions whereby individuals can see a way ahead from their present circumstances.

Quality assurance in markets

1067.   If the American system is any guide, quality assurance is achieved by the establishment of minimum thresholds. Thereafter 'the market' sorts out differences. At its simplest, little effort is expended in assuring the *common* quality of all provision; attention (and resources) are directed at maintaining the *basic* threshold. Few appear to worry about quality differentials between institutions. It is generally understood that Stanford is different from UC Berkeley and they are both different from a local State University, or a Baptist College, or a community college. Students, and their parents, choose the institution which is appropriate for them. The outcomes are assessed in the market. If such a model were to develop in the United Kingdom, it would represent another significant cultural departure

from recent practice. This may be inevitable and it would at least avoid maintaining the pretence that all institutions called 'University' deliver the same quality outcomes. Judgements of that character would need to be left to students themselves, their parents and their employers.

Markets and individual responsibility

1068.   But, as markets can bestow benefits to consumers in the form of diverse products and services, they can also bestow responsibilities. Firstly, individuals are much more likely to pay tuition fees and maintenance in the United States. There is an extensive range of 'market support' facilities in the form of loans, grants and endowments for individual students who require them, but it remains the case that students and their families expect to bear some responsibility for the 'personal good' that a higher education qualification may bring.

1069.   In this respect, a similar development in the United Kingdom would have profound cultural consequences. Some students in the United States are able to proceed through college, not because of parental support but because of grandparental and other ancestral bequests and endowments. In some cases, 19th century immigrants established the habit of family endowments and it continues as a cultural form throughout the country today.

Personal education plans

1070.   This would be an unusual expectation in the United Kingdom, but which may need stimulating in the near future. If higher education can no longer count on support from any political party for continued expenditure on tuition fees and maintenance, and as the maintenance award is steadily replaced by student loans, individual families will need to attend to the long term prospects of their children. It falls outside our ability to predict the course and pace of these developments, but prudence suggests that families with young children might well be encouraged, through the taxation system or otherwise, to invest in bonds, annuities, endowments or similar instruments. If personal investment in equities can be stimulated through tax-efficient Personal Equity Plans, with similar arrangements for personal pensions, could Government introduce an equivalent for education in the form of a *Personal Education Plan* to anticipate a future where individuals will need to contribute to the advantages that higher education bestows?

Mercantilism of knowledge – a critique of markets in higher education

1071.   We are aware that the foregoing analysis is likely to be deeply disquieting in some quarters. It cuts against the grain of traditional forms of provision in higher education in the United Kingdom. It presents a case for market forces at a time when their unregulated application in public service is being severely questioned throughout the country. The analysis runs the risk that critics will suggest that it invites the conditions it describes.

1072.   Opposition in its simplest form comes from those who believe that markets establish *the price of everything, but the value of nothing*. In higher education this is held to be anathema to the core principles of scholarship which do not define themselves in commercial terms. Moreover, if students are invited to make their academic decisions according to the distribution of, for example, education vouchers, this might introduce into the academic relationship distorting elements which would distract students from the disciplined and principled pursuit of knowledge. Knowledge becomes something that can be bought and sold, a mercantile transaction of little moral purpose. The consequences of this will be a moral apocalypse as society disintegrates into individualism, sectionalism and philistinism.

1073.   Indeed, for others, democratic participation in higher education is a contradiction in terms. Universities cannot function effectively as centres of intellectual production if they are overrun by students. Some colleagues draw parallels with the effects of mass tourism on National Parks and similar amenities. For them, increased student numbers and the pursuit of diverse income sources are leading to the *industrialisation of education*, where the mass production of graduates and credentials is replacing the carefully hand-crafted scholar of a former era.

1074.   We are not so sure that this is the natural consequence of improved student choice. Unregulated markets can leave individuals free to choose but without the means to make informed choices. In practice, markets fail if they do not provide some internal structure to stabilise relationships and decisions. This appears to be likely in higher education. However driven by market forces American higher education may be, it still provides a far superior guidance and information service to students, some of which students pay for themselves. It still manages to increase participation rates for all social groups beyond the horizons currently anticipated in the United Kingdom. Markets do not appear to have limited access to any social group. For example, the rate of participation and completion of doctorates by black students in the United States, whilst less pro rata than for white students, is still far in excess of the doctoral participation and completion rate for black students in the United Kingdom, pro rata to population. In some significant measure therefore, the American system delivers to all sections of society levels of access which the British model has never remotely approached. This is one aspect of the 'market model' which its critics must confront.

Pre-modern and modern perspectives

1075.   Furthermore, the rejection of markets and mass participation evokes something of the romantic affection expressed for the feudal era by an aristocracy displaced by industrialisation. Analogies may not provide a sound basis for argument, but we have been interested to observe the parallels between the arguments advanced for preserving the status quo in higher education and those advanced in the 19th century which lamented the loss of village community, intimacy and personal identity. The debate between pre-modern and modern forms of social organisation has dominated social science over the last 150 years, emerging variously as a contrast between *gemeinschaft* and *gesellschaft*, feudalism and capitalism, pre-rational and rational social formations and ideologies.

1076.   We make these points here because they are relevant for the final part of our analysis. Over the last decade or more, intellectual debate in certain parts of the university has been dominated by a new tension – a debate between modernism and *post-modernism*, between expressions of modernity and those of *post-modernity*. In order to understand how certain influential groups of academic colleagues understand and theorise the current changes to higher education, often opposing them, it is necessary to untangle some aspects of these debates. In doing so, we can give only a synopsised version of a highly complex and contentious series of arguments, many aspects of which are still being fought out in the social sciences, the humanities, art and design, cultural studies, architecture, and latterly, in the study of organisational theory.

Credit culture – an expression of the post-modern condition?

1077. The importance of this part of the discussion for an understanding of difference of opinion over the introduction of credit systems cannot be overstated. Nowhere is the issue more fiercely contested than in the theoretical, and therefore the practical, implications of these changes. We have been interested to establish why it should be that opposition to credit systems and modularity should be more vocal in the social sciences and related disciplines than elsewhere in the university, particularly when the social sciences have been so receptive generally to wider access. The answer may lie in the extent to which colleagues in the social sciences believe they perceive in the application of credit systems a threat to the very purpose of the University, vitiated by a combination of market forces, managerial control and an assault on objectivity and reason itself. We believe these concerns cannot be dismissed lightly and, in any event, need to be explored in order to inform progress in the future.

1078. The problem begins with attempts largely by social science but also within the humanities to comprehend developments in the modern world. The ascendancy of free market ideologies and the collapse of the Marxist model of economic distribution in Eastern Europe have combined with uncertainties over the general direction of industrial societies to produce within social science and elsewhere something approaching a theoretical void. Disciplines had difficulty explaining the nature of social conflict and its political expression; people were unequal but still voted for the political Right. Moreover, nations appeared to be less influential than transnational corporations in determining the social purposes of production, and information technology and media systems appeared to be changing the ways in which cultures were being shaped, re-formed and transmitted. In short, and for many other reasons, the global restructuring of economic and national relationships led some commentators in the 1980s to talk of a need to explain *'New Times'*.

1079. There have been many earlier attempts to come to terms with developments in the global socio-economic order. Over the past thirty years, American sociologists, and particularly Daniel Bell, have attempted to theorise these changing conditions in modern industrial society. Bell coined the term *post-industrial society* and went on to explain that the central question of post-industrialisation was *'the relationship of technocratic decisions to politics'* in which society had to decide how to satisfy *'a revolution of rising entitlements'*. While hostilities continued between West and East, it was not fashionable to accept the corollaries of this analysis, that modern societies were now converging around common forms, that we lived in a *post-ideological* age in which disputes over social class would be replaced by different social fissures (eg ethnicity, nationality, religion, gender). Nor was it commonplace to accept that markets, however managed, would be one of the principal organising features of society and its institutions.

1080. However, the collapse of the Soviet economies and the critique of the role of the State offered by the political Right in the United Kingdom and the United States has changed the balance of interest in these matters. No longer could it be claimed that former 'Grand Theories' of social development provided the explanation of human progress. Indeed, there was some doubt whether science itself could do much to combat the threats of environmental damage, poverty and disease throughout the world. In short, there were no ideological solutions, only technocratic and pragmatic solutions. But, critics have argued, this is a counsel of despair, a *fin de siecle* frivolity in which there are no certainties, no principles, no moral codes, merely individual behaviour. For many, the concept of *post-industrial society* and its emergent conceptual amanuensis *post-modernity*, was represented by the shallow individualism of the 1980s, by the shift from manufacturing production to financial services, and by the shift from public service to private avarice.

1081.   The debate between modernism and post-modernism begins here, in the neo-ideological shallows of the ocean of global change and the 'New World Order'. For some in the United Kingdom at least, the introduction of modularity and credit systems appears as part of this debate.

Modernity and the university

1082.   To understand post-modernism in summary form and in ways relevant to this discussion, it is necessary to understand what is meant by *modernism* and *modernity*. Modernity is the term used in this context to describe the contemporary condition – the social structures, organisational forms, values and cultural references which define contemporary (Western) society. Modernity has been described as *the triumph of Occidental rationality*, deriving its strength from the Enlightenment and its commitment to open, critical, rational and therefore *scientific* thought. The Enlightenment has been presented for 200 years or more as the triumph of Reason (and Freedom) over Myth (and intellectual slavery) – the victory of science over religion. In this struggle, the University has represented the one social institution that has moved quintessentially with the Enlightenment from religion as the basis of knowledge to science.

1083.   The establishment of the modern condition is something which the University can claim for itself. The University defines its purpose as the centre for the pursuit of Reason and Truth. Moreover, the University pursues the truth under conditions of

collegiality, the freedom to disagree and respect for the views of others. At all times, the University seeks to make the world coherent, create connections, look behind the surface appearance of things, emancipating society from mystery, myth and intellectual closure. The University is thus presented as an oppositional social institution. It cannot fulfil its purpose if it is subject to the caprices of politicians or the constraints of commerce. The Kantian instruction: *Aude sapere* (Dare to Know) informs its social role and provides the institution with its moral strength.

1084.   Nor can the University fulfil its purpose if it is subject to disruption, fragmentation and irrationality. What unites practically engaged natural scientists and engineers with theoretically inventive social scientists and philosophers is the belief that they are following the same principles in seeking the truth and that seeking the truth is morally preferable to any other purpose to which scholarship might be put. This will therefore involve patient investigation, dispassionate analysis, objective detachment wherever possible, and a steadfast belief in the forward progress of science in all its forms (ie Reason itself) for the improvement of society generally. If any of these values and practices can be passed on to students, then a substantial part of the moral purpose of the University is fulfilled.

Post-modernist critique of modernity

1085.   Post-modernism is usually presented as the conservative reaction to modernity. In its most superficial (and publicly visible) form, it has been presented initially in architecture as a rejection of modern forms of design in favour of historic pastiche or similar alternatives. Later it has emerged in critiques of art, literature and film, but more recently post-modernism has been adopted by those in social science and elsewhere who have sought new theories to explain developments in national and global economies and their social impact. At the same time, others in social science and elsewhere have developed an equally trenchant critique of post-modernism. The dispute centres around the nature of the intellectual project itself: *what is to be known?*

1086.   For post-modernists, previous theories have largely failed to explain the world. The reason for this is relatively simple, they argue. 'Grand Theories' or *meta-narratives*, such as Marxism, rationalism or even theories of scientific progress itself, attempt to get behind the appearance of things but there are no deep structures of meaning lying there. Everything is broadly as it appears to be; we can only know the surface appearance. Post-modernism is therefore defined as an *'incredulity towards meta-narratives and the grand narrative of emancipation in particular'*. Put bluntly, the promise of modernity to free humanity from poverty, ignorance and the absence of enjoyment no longer seems possible. We are left therefore with the search for knowledge revealed, not by the struggle for emancipation from ignorance, but by techno-economic measures of (individual) performance.

1087.   Moreover, in the post-modernist canon, there are no unified discourses. All discourses, theoretical analyses, ways of seeing, ideologies and such like are *fragmented discourses*, often eclectic aggregations of pragmatic elements, valued for their *performativity* (ie for their performance optimality). More outrageously for the 'modernists', post-modernists claim that there has been a social shift from respecting the intrinsic value of knowledge in terms of human goals and conduct towards knowledge related to the optimisation of systems performance. This is held to represent the victory of consumer-centred capitalism over social forms which emphasised the nature and relations of production. In this new world, the individual-as-consumer is cast adrift in an ocean of appearances, each as 'real' as the next, consuming images and other cultural representations. The individual is a *de-centred subject through which discourses flow*. In other words, individuals are passive recipients of whatever fragmented set of messages is propelled in their direction, unable to make connections between them for themselves because they can never be aware of the global totality of things. Messages and images may be mediated for them by various agencies but the effect is to increase the power of information owners and decrease the power of information receivers.

1088.   Control of information is a key property of the post-modern condition. Moreover, the basic principles of organisation become (process) *standardisation*, (performance) *synchronisation*, (organisational) *centralisation* and (output) *maximisation*. This is not to imply that organisations are structurally centralised. On the contrary, they may be locally or globally heavily decentralised and dispersed. They may be organised on the principle of *flexible accumulation* in which no one organisation or sub-element possesses a monopoly of product output or process control. But organisations are held together by information systems which produce information control at the small but powerful strategic centre.

Credit systems and the post-modernism

1089.   Following this analysis, it may be clearer why some informed opinion in universities remains suspicious of the introduction of credit systems and modularity. Their concerns go beyond a superficial antipathy to markets or a collectivist opposition to the individualisation of the curriculum in higher education. They believe that what is at stake is the place and purpose of the University in the modern world. Is it to retain its principal purpose as a centre of intellectual rationality, coherence and moral integrity? Or is it to join other organisations of the 'post-modern' world in intellectual fragmentation, 'consumerist' superficiality and moral relativism?

1090.   Some accounts see in the introduction of credit systems a purposeful shift in the direction of absolute control of academic labour and a de-skilling of the academic labour process through the standardisation of knowledge and the devaluing of disciplines. Others see the fragmentation of the curriculum as a shift in power in four directions: towards the State, the labour market, the student as consumer, and the institutional managers. Of these, the most assertive is held to be that of institutional managers. Moreover, credit systems produce a double fragmentation: in the mind of the student and in the structure of the curriculum (Barnett, 1994).

1091.   Elsewhere, Barnett (1993) remains sceptical whether modularity and credit systems might actually introduce an element of openness into the curriculum by providing as many opportunities for the free expression of ideas by academic staff and learning opportunities for students as there is a market for them. Nonetheless, the prospect of this remains.

1092.   To the charge that credit systems represent a post-modernist retreat from the principles of modernity, one must search for an answer in either of two directions. Firstly, if this is the case, then the American system was the first example of a post-modern higher education co-existing with the modern world at a time when other countries, including the United Kingdom, were seeking to drag their institutions into modernity from the pre-modern world. As Trow commented earlier, a 'precocious system' indeed.

1093.   Secondly, it will probably come as something of a surprise to those who have been most active in the introduction of modularity and credit systems that their modest efforts to open up access and student choice

should now be described in terms which imply an assault on the Enlightenment, the scientific method and all its works. Our investigation has not revealed this intention amongst colleagues. Perhaps they are guileless dupes of other agents; perhaps their efforts are producing unintended effects; perhaps indeed it would be helpful to theorise more fully the purposes behind these changes to higher education.

1094.   On the other hand, before one group of enthusiasts is accused of *trahison des clercs*, it might be better to reconsider whether the post-modern critique of modernity is actually contributing anything new, or whether it is simply a fatal distraction. It is not possible here to unwrap the complexities of that debate. However, it must be recognised that the modern-postmodern debate may be nothing more than a passing intellectual fashion, to be supplanted by other theoretical debates as conditions change.

1095.   We have taken time over this matter because we would be concerned not to promote the further development of credit

Table 68: Orientations towards the strategic role of higher education in national regeneration		
Source: adapted by author from a classification originally developed by Guy Neave (1992) to describe vocational education in higher education	Ideological	
	Right	Left
Technocratic — **Optimistic**	National performance related to level of skills development; distribution of vocational skills to be matched to student preferences and more widely distributed throughout the population; assumed 'natural' division between practical working class and academic middle class students; provision to be combined but not to dilute academic standards of elite group	National skills distribution related to national economic performance, but valued skills unfairly weighted towards academic middle-class; vocational and practical skills should be given parity of esteem with academic qualifications; work-based knowledge should be legitimated; in some models, separate institutions for working-class students (viz argument for former Polytechnics)
Pessimistic	National performance not clearly related to skills development; managed decline inevitable; diminish university monopoly of higher education since it has proved impossible to erode professional power of academics; preserve traditions of academic HE for specific cohort for elite formation; possibly expand places for the rest of the qualified population, but shift investment centre downwards to further education	National decline needs to be arrested; invest in general skills development by challenging institutional power bases; use leverage to change HE; reform/break power of academic profession; parity of esteem between academic and vocational programmes; improve flexibility for students; emphasise further education as centre of democratic education; democratic participation in HE desirable, not priority

systems without accepting that this will take place against a background of considerable theoretical complexity. The confluence of these developments is largely accidental; modularity was being promoted long before the emergence of the post-modernist critique and it will be sustained long after this debate has subsided. However, institutional managers and others may need to be advised that at least one section of the academic community is intellectually animated by the conviction that 'CATS' and credit systems represent the conceptual (and political) fragmentation of knowledge in precisely the same way that the global production of material goods and services has been de-centred and dispersed. The effect, they argue, is to increase the power, not of professional academics in the University, but of the overall controllers of institutional processes and cultures.

Conclusion

1096.   There is one matter to complete before we close. Despite the arcane considerations of the debate on modernity and post-modernity, there is a more fundamental and familiar set of issues lying within it. These concern the conventional polarities of the political spectrum and the way ideological positions inform strategic thinking. In Table 68, we show how different political positions line up on prospects for the role of higher education in national regeneration. The model is based on the work of Neave (1991) who used the categories of Optimistic/Pessimistic and Left/Right to try and distinguish between the ideological positions of various segments of the political spectrum. It has interested us during the investigation to notice how frequently Left and Right perspectives overlap on many points concerned with the reform and modernisation of higher education. We make this point, not to argue for an end to ideology, but to suggest that on these matters if no others, differences of political opinion are no longer so clear cut.

1097.   Political positions of both Left and Right share a similar diagnosis of the problems of the British economy and, in respect of higher education, they appear to share similar prescriptions for how this might develop in the future. Credit systems feature prominently in all accounts. Also there appears to be agreement on the remedies that need to be sought for funding continued expansion, implying a shift towards individual responsibility.

1098.   Political differences *between* Left and Right seem to be less significant than differences *within* the various segments between 'radicals' and 'romantics'. We mean by this that there appears to be more unity of purpose between radicals of the Left and Right on the need for change, and between romantics of the Left and the Right opposing it, than there is between the radicals and the romantics of either Left or Right. In other words, there appears to be a common radical agenda across the political spectrum to introduce greater flexibility and student choice, to encourage markets within higher education and to expand access. This is likely to embrace student loans, a personal commitment to learning and an acceptance that professional academic sovereignty should not remain a barrier to the achievement of these objectives.

1099.   On the other hand, romantics of the Left and the Right appear to be united in their search for an earlier 'Golden Age' of higher education, before mass expansion, modularisation and credit systems, when academics had time to engage their preferences and when everyone knew that standards were being maintained. Romantics appear to fear the consequences of radical solutions to any aspect of higher education transformation.

1100.   We make these observations because they may help us understand the type of coalitions that can be assembled to pursue the further development of credit accumulation and transfer in British higher education, both in national policy-making and for institutional implementation.

Cultural change, resistance and progress – towards a policy and a strategy

1101.   Finally, we end on a more practical note. What can be done to produce cultural change in the face of professional resistance? There can of course be no simple answer. From our investigation, however, we are convinced that neither rational argument alone nor *dirigiste* management styles are effective in academic communities. The former appear to be relatively ineffective in these matters in challenging vested professional interests or confirmed ideological positions; the latter are ineffective in winning the 'hearts and minds' of sceptical colleagues. A balance of approaches is probably more effective, but there is nothing more effective than demonstrating the benefits of change to all parties over time. This requires persistence in both argument and management commitment.

1102.   In the end, it may take some considerable period before institutions are able to claim that they have produced the necessary cultural change. Two personnel factors at least will impede this; a third may assist progress. Firstly, institutions generally possess an academic staff cohort the age profile of which does not encourage prospects for new and radical ways of doing things. This may be an unfair assessment of the majority of colleagues approaching middle age in universities, but inevitably their careers have been constructed around one set of arrangements and they may not obviously benefit from changes contingent on credit systems.

1103.   Secondly, most academic staff in higher education have been educated in conventional academic programmes and this will continue to be the case for some years yet. It will take several decades of continuous progress in universities towards modular and credit-based systems before we are able to create a new generation of academic colleagues who have themselves been prepared academically through flexible courses. Indeed, one pessimistic but realistic account suggests that these developments are contradictory. Those academic staff members whom universities seek to attract, for their professional expertise and research potential, are just the academic staff who are *least likely* to have been academically prepared in the choice-centred and flexible academic programmes which many universities may seek to promote in the future. In short, prospective academic colleagues in universities may always be less personally committed to student choice, flexibility and mobility, by nature of their academic experience, than institutions, employers or most students themselves.

1104.   However, in this period of transition to a more open and democratic system of higher education provision, those universities which are committed to these developments could take advantage of their limited academic staff turnover to attract good quality young academic staff who might be committed to the values and cultural conditions offered by innovative institutions. This would require some institutions to adopt a courageous academic staffing policy. This would retain the expectation that an institution would always wish to attract the most suitably qualified and capable candidate for a post, but it might require the institution to state clearly at all relevant points in the application process that the university or college is committed to modular and credit-based developments *and successful candidates will be expected to contribute to the further academic development of such arrangements*. We believe this would make it clear to candidates what type of academic environment they were applying to enter, allowing institutions the freedom to select candidates who may be well-qualified but more or less committed to the corporate direction. At least this style of staffing policy would make it clear to all parties where they stood and no party could then claim to have been misled.

1105.   If this approach were widely adopted by relevant institutions, we believe that in time some institutions will develop a professional academic cohort which is culturally and attitudinally committed to student choice and flexibility. We are optimistic that some institutions, if they maintain their poise and continue to receive encouragement from Government, funding councils, professional bodies, employers and students, will be able to achieve the high levels of academic discretion *and* the high levels of student choice that we referred to in Chapter XII. Perhaps then we shall be able to speak of the natural partnership between freely acting scholars and students that distinguishes a *credit culture.*

Part Four

Bibliographic sources

We have been approached during the investigation by colleagues expressing the need for a source of reference on publications relevant to the development of modularity and credit systems in further and higher education in the United Kingdom. The main report, by its nature, has not been overburdened with references, but those which have been included may be found here. The following does not propose to be an exhaustive list of references on the subject, but it does indicate the international as well as the national dimensions of the investigation. The sources have all informed the thinking in the report. We have listed the items alphabetically rather than by category because we hope that colleagues will enjoy the opportunity over time of making connections for themselves between the wide-ranging matters that are dealt with by these publications. Almost all the references are in the public domain, but a small number remain in unpublished form and have been made available to the author of the report. This reflects the emerging character of much of the work on modularity, credit systems and the growing interest in student choice and mobility in higher education and beyond. We would hope that in years to come this list will be extended by further influential contributions from the United Kingdom.

Sources and references

Abramson M *Five years of Franchising: an analysis of the profile, performance and progression of LINCS students, 1985-90*, University of Central Lancashire, 1993

Absalom R 'Practical rather than Declamatory Co-operation: ERASMUS in 1990 – an appraisal', *European Journal of Education*, Vol 25 No 1, 1990

Adelman C and Silver H *Accreditation: the American experience*, CNAA, London 1990

AGCAS *What Do Graduates Do?*, report of the Graduate Careers Advisory Services, 1993

Allen R *Development of Credit Accumulation and Transfer in Non-Modular Schemes: an overview*, University of Greenwich occasional paper, 1988

Alloway J and Opie *Understanding Educational Guidance – A Project Report* , UDACE/NIACE, 1988

Anglia Polytechnic University, *The ASSET Programme*, final report, 1992

Armstrong M and Raban C *CATS and the Post-Qualifying Framework*, report for CCETSW Northern region, University of Northumbria, 1992

Ashworth PD and Saxton J 'On Competence', *Journal of Further and Higher Education*, Vol 14 No 2, 1990

Association of Graduate Recruiters *Roles for Graduates in the Twenty-First Century* (Goodman Report), Cambridge, 1993

Atkins MJ, Beattie J and Dockrell WB *Assessment Issues in Higher Education*, University of Newcastle and Employment Department, 1993

Atkinson GBJ 'Student Loans?', *Journal of Further and Higher Education*, Vol 7 No 1, 1983

Audit Office/OFSTED *Unfinished Business*, HMSO, 1993

Australian Education Council *National Qualifications Framework*, proposals for a national credit framework, AEC, 1993

Avent C and Ellis D ed *A European Framework for Flexible Education and Training – Report of a SEEC Conference*, London, 1989

Ball, Sir Christopher *Aiming Higher: Widening Access to Higher Education*, London, RSA, 1989

Ball, Sir Christopher *More Means Different: Widening Access to Higher Education*, London, RSA, 1990

Ball, Sir Christopher *Learning Pays: the Role of Post-Compulsory Education and Training*, London, RSA, 1991

Ball, Sir Christopher *Profitable Learning*, London, RSA, 1992

Ball, Sir Christopher 'Prerequisites for the discussion of an international framework of qualifications', public lecture mimeo, New Zealand Qualifications Authority conference: International Qualifications for the 21st Century, 1992

Ball SJ 'Education Markets, Choice and Social Class: the market as a class strategy in the UK and the USA', *British Journal of the Sociology of Education*, Vol 14 No 1, 1993

Barden L, Barr N and Higginson G *An Analysis of Student Loan Options*, Occasional Paper, CVCP, London, 1991

Barnett R *The Idea of Higher Education*, SRHE/OU, London, 1990

Barnett R *Improving Higher Education – Total Quality Care*, SRHE, London, 1992

Barnett R ed *Learning to Effect*, SRHE/OU, London, 1992

Barnett R 'Knowledge, Higher Education and Society: a postmodern problem', *Oxford Review of Education*, Vol 19 No 1, 1993

Barnett R *The Limits of Competence*, SRHE/OU, London, 1994

Barr N 'Alternative Funding Resources for Higher Education', *Economic Journal*, Vol 103, 1993

Barr N and Falkingham J *Paying for Learning*, London School of Economics, 1993

Barr N, Falkingham J and Glennerster H *Funding Higher Education*, BP/London School of Economics, 1994

Barr N and Low W *Student Grants and Student Poverty*, Paper 28, Welfare State programme, LSE, 1988

Barrett J *Educational Guidance Services for Adults UK Directory 1992/93*, FEU, 1992

Becher T *Academic Tribes and Territories: Intellectual Enquiry and the Cultures of Disciplines*, Milton Keynes, SRHE, 1989

Becher T ed *Governments and Professional Education*, SRHE/OU, 1994

Becher T and Kogan M *Process and Structure in Higher Education*, London, Routledge, 1992

Beckhard R and Pritchard W *Changing the Essence: the art of creating and leading fundamental change in organisations*, San Francisco, Jossey-Bass, 1992

Benn R and Fieldhouse R 'Government Policies on University Expansion and Wider Access, 1945-51 and 1985-91 Compared', *Studies in Higher Education*, Vol 18 No 3, 1993

Bennett R, Glennerster H and Nevison D *Learning Should Pay*, London, BP Educational Services, 1992

Berdahl RO, Moodie GC and Spitzberg IJ ed *Quality and Access in Higher Education*, SRHE/OU, 1991

Bines H and Watson D *Developing Professional Education*, SRHE/OU, 1992

Bird J, Crawley G and Sheibani A *Franchising and Access to Higher Education: a study of HE/FE collaboration*, Employment Department, 1993

Black H and Wolf A *Knowledge and Competence: Current Issues in Training and Education*, Sheffield, Employment Dept

Bligh D ed *Professionalism and Flexibility in Learning*, Guildford, SRHE, 1982

Bourner T et al *Part-time Students and their Experience of Higher Education*, SRHE/OU, 1991

Bourner T and Barlow J *The Student Induction Handbook*, Kogan Page, 1991

Boyer E Public Lecture on the Place of Teaching in Higher Education, Royal Society, 1993

Boys CJ, Brennan J, Henkel M, Kirkland J, Kogan M, and Youll P *Higher Education and the Preparation for Work*, London, Jessica Kingsley, 1988

Boys CJ and Kirkland J *Degrees of Success*, London, Jessica Kingsley, 1988

Brandstrom D et al *Evaluation of NORDPLUS – the Nordic programme for the mobility of university students and teachers*, Vol 1/2, Nordic Council of Ministers, 1992.

Brennan JL, Lyons ES, McGeevor PA and Murray K *Students, Courses and Jobs*, London, Jessica Kingsley, 1993

Bridgwood, A ' Someone to talk to – developing a mentor system', *Journal of Access Studies*, Vol 7 No 2, 1992

British Council *Educational Institutions and Overseas Students*, Education Counselling Service, British Council, London

Browning D 'Are Open Colleges too bureaucratic?', *Journal of Access Studies*, Vol 6 No 1, 1991

Burke J ed *Competency Based Education and Training*, Falmer Press, 1993

Burke J ed *Outcomes, Learning and the Curriculum*, Falmer Press, 1994

Burn B 'The American Academic Credit System', in OECD *Structure of Studies and Place of Research in Mass Higher Education*, OECD, Paris, 1974

Burn B 'Opening Opportunities: Educational Exchanges between the United States and USSR/CIS', *Higher Education Policy*, Vol 6 No 1, 1993

Burn B, Cerych L and Smith A *Study Programmes Abroad*, London, Jessica Kingsley, 1988

Calder J ed *Disaffection and Diversity*, Falmer Press, 1993

California Legislature *California Faces...California's Future: Education for Citizenship in a Multicultural Democracy*, final report of the Joint Committee for the Review of the Master Plan for Higher Education, Sacramento, 1989

California Post-secondary Education Commission *Higher Education at the Crossroads: Planning for the 21st Century*, report of the CPEC, Sacramento, California, 1989

Carley M *Performance and Monitoring in a Professional Public Service: the case of the Careers Service* Policy Studies Unit, London 1988

Carter J and Webb SP *Professional Education in the Finance Sector – Open to All?*, London, City University, 1993

Cassells, Sir John *Britain's Real Skill Shortage*, London, Policy Studies Institute, 1990

Cassells, Sir John 'The Competence of the British Workforce', *Policy Studies*, Vol 11 No 1, 1990

CBI *Towards a Skills Revolution*, London: CBI, 1989

CBI *World Class Targets* London: CBI, 1991

CBI *Routes for Success*, London: CBI, 1993

CBI *Ensuring the Expansion of Higher Education*, London: CBI, 1994 (forthcoming)

Chaplin T and Drake K *American Experience of Accreditation of Employer-Provided Training*, CONTACT Paper No 4, Manchester, 1987

Chapman B *Austudy: towards a more flexible approach* Canberra: Australian National University

Christensen L 'Academic Tourism, a redundant or fruitful study abroad – tracks and wrong tracks to credit transfer', *Higher Education Management*, Vol 6 No 1, 1994

Church C 'Modular Courses in British higher education: a critical assessment', *Higher Education Bulletin*, Vol 3 No 3, 1975

CIHE *Towards a Partnership: Higher Education-Government-Industry*, CIHE, London, 1987

CIHE *The Company Response*, London, CIHE, London, 1989

CIHE *Collaborative Courses in Higher Education*, CIHE, London, 1990

CIHE *The Business Contribution to Higher Education*, CIHE, London, 1991

CIHE *Investing in Diversity*, CIHE, London, 1992

CIHE *Investing in Talent: a view from employers*, CIHE, London, 1992

CIHE *Changing Colleges*, CIHE, London, 1993

CNAA *Minutes of the Committee on Academic Policy, 1984-87*, CNAA, London

CNAA *Minutes of the CATS Committee, 1987-92*, CNAA, London

CNAA *CATS: a Guide for Students Registered Centrally with the Scheme*, CNAA, London, 1989

CNAA *Credits for Change: the CNAA Credit Accumulation and Transfer Scheme and the Universities*, London, 1989

CNAA *Going Modular*, Information Services Discussion Paper 2, London, 1989

CNAA *The Modular Option*, CNAA, London, 1989

CNAA *The Credit Accumulation and Transfer Scheme: Regulations*, CNAA, London, 1989

CNAA *Practising CATS: a report of the Telford conference*, London, CNAA, London, 1992

CNAA 'Quality Assurance – an agenda for the future', internal discussion paper, 1992

CNAA *Progress and Performance in Higher Education*, CNAA, London, 1992

CNAA *Scottish Credit Accumulation and Transfer Scheme – a flexible framework for higher education courses in Scotland*, London, 1992

CNAA *Guidelines on Credit Rating* (draft), London, 1992

CNAA/CVCP *Access Courses in Higher Education*, London, 1992

CNAA/UDACE/FEU *Guidance in HE – South Yorkshire and North Derbyshire Final Report*, 1991

Coffield F 'Training and Enterprise Councils: the last throw of voluntarism?', *Policy Studies* Vol 13 No 4, 1992

Coopers & Lybrand *Evaluation of the Pilot Phase of the European Community Course Credit Transfer System, (ERASMUS ECTS)*, Report to Task Force Human Resources, Education, Training and Youth, Brussels, February 1993

Coldstream P 'Higher Education and Business' *European Journal of Education* Vol 27 No 4 1992

Crawford RL and Skinner AS *Credit Transfer in the USA*, Study Visit report, Universities in Scotland, September 1990.

Crouch C 'The Dilemmas of Vocational Training Policy: some comparative lessons' *Policy Studies* Vol 13 No 4, 1992

CSUP *Teaching and Learning in an Expanding Higher Education System (MacFarlane Report)*, Edinburgh, 1992

CVCP *Financing Expansion*, discussion paper, CVCP, 1992

CVCP *A Code of Practice for Overseas Students*, London, 1992

CVCP 'Survey of Universities' attitudes to reform of the academic year', London, CVCP, 1992

CVCP *Report of the Working Group on Vocational Higher Education*, London, 1994

CVCP/UFC *University Management Statistics and Performance Indicators in the UK*, CVCP, London, 1992

Dalichow F 'European Community Course Credit Transfer System ECTS – History, present State, selected National and International Reactions', paper to TEXT annual conference, Derby, 1992

Daniel J 'Part-time Higher Education: the next stage', *Adults Learning* Vol 3 No 6, 1992

Daniel J 'The Challenge of Mass Higher Education' *Studies in Higher Education* Vol 18 No 2, 1993

Davidson G 'Credit Accumulation and Transfer and the Student Experience' in Barnett R *Learning to Effect*, SRHE, 1992

Davidson G *Credit Accumulation and Transfer in the British Universities, 1990-93*, the report of the 'CATS and Continuing Education' project, UACE and the University of Kent at Canterbury, 1994

Davidson G and Deere M ed *Modular Curriculum and Structure*, seminar papers, Canterbury, UCACE/UKC, 1991

Davidson G and Power B ed *Semesterisation, Modularity, Credit Accumulation and Transfer: Harmony and Development*, papers from the 4th CVCP seminar, Open University, 1992

Davies D and Robertson D 'Open College – towards a new view of Adult Education' *Adult Education* Vol 59 No 2, 1986

Davies P 'Participation of Access Course Students in Higher Education', *Journal of Access Studies*, forthcoming, 1994

Davies P and Parry G *Recognising Access*, NIACE, Leicester, 1993

De Jonge JF and Dillo IG *Access to Higher Education in the European Community*, Synthesis Report, Vol 1, Task Force Human Resources Education, Training and Youth, July 1992

De Jonge JF and Dillo IG *Student Mobility in Higher Education in the European Community* Synthesis Report, Vol 1, Task Force Human Resources Education, Training and Youth, July 1992

DES *Teacher Education and Training* (James Report), HMSO, 1972

DES *Education: a framework for expansion*, HMSO, 1972

DES *Adult Education: a plan for development* (Russell Report), HMSO, 1973

DES *Higher Education into the 1990s: a discussion document*, HMSO, 1978

DES *Higher Education: Meeting the Challenge*, Cmnd 114, London, HMSO, 1987

DES 'Shifting the Balance of Public Funding to Fees', a consultation paper, DES, 1989

DES *Aspects of Higher Education in the United States of America*, HMSO, London, 1989

DES *Vocational and Continuing Education* (USA series), London, HMSO, 1990

DES *Access Courses to Higher Education*, HMI report, HMSO, 1990

DES *Quality and its Assurance in Higher Education* (USA series), London, HMSO, 1991

DES *Indicators in Educational Monitoring* (USA series), London, HMSO, 1991

DES *Education and Training for the 21st Century*, Vol I & II, Cmnd 1536, London, HMSO, 1991

DES *Higher Education: a New Framework*, Cmnd 1541, London, HMSO, 1991

DES *Higher Education in Further Education Colleges*, HMI Report on Franchising, DES, 1991

DFE *Statistics of Further and Higher Education in Polytechnics and Colleges, 1991-92*, DFE 1992

DFE *Statistics of Further and Higher Education: Student-Staff ratios and Unit Costs 1990-91 (England)*, DFE 1992

DFE *Statistics of Education: Student Awards (England & Wales), 1988-91*, DFE 1993

DFE *UK Government Response to the 'Memorandum on Higher Education in the European Community'*, DFE 1993

DFE *Charter for Higher Education* (consultation draft), 1993

DFE 'Examination Results and First Destinations of Higher Education Graduates 1983-91', *Statistical Bulletin 7/93*

DFE 'Student Loans 1992-93' *Statistical Bulletin 2/94*

DFE 'Student Numbers in Higher Education in Great Britain 1981-82 – 1991-92' *Statistical Bulletin 17/93*

DFE 'Students from Abroad in Great Britain 1981-91' *Statistical Bulletin 21/93*

DFE 'Participation in Independent Sector of Further and Higher Education' *Statistical Bulletin 25/93*

DFE 'Women in Post-Compulsory Education' *Statistical Bulletin 26/93*

DFE 'Student Loans 1992-93' *Statistical Bulletin 2/94*

DTI *The Single Market – Europe Open for the Professions*, 1991

DTI/CIHE *Policy and Strategy for Companies*, DTI, London,1989

DTI/CIHE *Policy and Strategy for Higher Education*, DTI, London,1989

DTI/CIHE *Getting Good Graduates*, DTI, London, 1990

DTI/CIHE *Organisation and Management in Higher Education*, DTI, London, 1990

DTI/CIHE *Continuing Education and Training*, DTI, London, 1990

Droge JF *Survey and Proceedings of the Seminar on Flexible Systems in Higher Education*, Van Hall Instituut, Groningen, 1992

Duffin L and Woods M *Lifelong Learning: Britain's Future*, a report of the conference, University of Oxford, 1990

Duke C *The Learning University: towards a new paradigm*, SRHE, 1992

Earwaker J *Helping and Supporting Students*, SRHE/OU, 1992

ECCTIS *Educational Credit Transfer Directory*, London 1991

Ellis D and Portwood D ed *Flexible Education and Training*, report of the conference, SEEC, London, 1988

Employment Department *Labour Market and Skills Trends, 1993-94, ED, 1992*

Employment Department 'Credit Accumulation and Transfer Schemes in Higher Education' paper to *Learning without Walls* conference, Oxford, 1991

Employment Department *Learning through Work*, Sheffield, ED, 1992

Employment Department *The Skills Link*, Sheffield, ED, 1990

Engineering Council *Engineering Futures: new audiences and arrangements for Engineering Higher Education*, EC, 1990

Engineering Council *National System – Continuing Professional Development – Framework for Action*, EC, 1991

Engineering Council *Review of Engineering Formation*, London, Engineering Council, 1993

European Commission *Higher Education in the European Community: the Student Handbook*, Brussels, Kogan Page, 1990

European Commission *A Guide to Higher Education Systems and Qualifications in the European Community*, NUFFIC/Brussels, Kogan Page, 1991

European Commission *Memorandum on Higher Education in the European Community*, Brussels, 1991

European Commission *Memorandum on Open and Distance Learning in the European Community*, Task Force Human Resources, Education, Training and Youth, Brussels, November 1991

European Commission *Report from the Commission on Open and Distance Higher Education in the European Community*, Task Force Human Resources, Education, Training and Youth, Brussels, May 1991

European Commission *Annual Reports from the Commission – ERASMUS Programme 1990/92*, Brussels, 1991-1993

European Commission *Maastricht Treaty of European Union*, Chapter 3, Brussels, 1992

European Commission *Options for the Future Generalisation of ECTS: Generalization Scenarios,* Brussels, 1992

European Commission 'Concerning the Development of EC/US Cooperation in the Field of Education and Training', briefing paper, Brussels, May 1992

European Commission *Academic Recognition of Higher Education entrance, intermediate and final Qualifications in the European Community – Multilateral and Bilateral Conventions, Unilateral Decisions* NARIC, 1992

European Commission *Responses to the Memorandum on Higher Education in the European Community,* Synthesis Report, Task Force Human Resources, Education, Training and Youth, Brussels, February 1993

European Commission *Academic Credit Systems and Modularisation in EC and EFTA Countries: Comparability with ECTS,* Synthesis report, Brussels, January 1993

European Commission *Guidelines for Community Action in the Field of Education and Training,* Working Paper, May 1993

Evans N *The Assessment of Prior Experiential Learning*, London, CNAA, 1988

Evans N *Experiential Learning: its assessment and accreditation*, London, Routledge, 1992

Evans N and Turner A *The Potential of the Assessment of Experiential Learning in Universities*, Learning from Experience Trust and Employment Department, 1993

Farley M et al *Modularisation and the New Curricula*, Coombe Lodge Report 19, Bristol, FESC, 1986

Farrell S and Tapper E 'Student Loans: The Failure to Consolidate an Emerging Political Consensus', *Higher Education Quarterly* Vol 46 No 3, 1992

FEFC *Funding Learning*, FEFC, 1993

FEFC *Recurrent Funding Methodology: Tariff Values for 1994-95*, Circular 93/32, FEFC, 1993

FEFCW *Funding Further Education in Wales*, FEFCW, 1993

FEU *A Basis for Choice*, FEU, London, 1979

FEU *Towards a Personal Guidance Base*, FEU, London 1983

FEU *Support Staff in Further Education Staff Development Needs*, FEU, London 1987

FEU *Two-Year Youth Training Schemes: an evaluation of LEA modular programmes* Vol 1-6, FEU, London, 1987-89

FEU *Performance Indicators in the Education and Training of Adults*, FEU, London, 1990

FEU *Educational Guidance for Adults: identifying competence*, FEU, London, 1991

FEU *A Basis for Credit?*, FEU London, 1992

FEU *A Basis for Credit? Feedback and Developments*, FEU, London, 1993

FEU *Discussing Credit*, FEU, London 1993

FEU *Learner Support Services in Further Education*, FEU, London, 1993

FEU *Open College Networks: Participation and Progress*, FEU, London, 1993

FEU *CAT Network Directory*, FEU, London, 1994

Finegold D and Soskice, D 'The Failure of Training in Britain: Analysis and Prescription', *Oxford Review of Economic Policy*, Vol 2, No 2, 1988

Finegold D 'Breaking Out of the Low-Skill Equilibrium', Paper No 5, National Commission on Education in *Education Economics*, Vol 1 No 1, 1992

Finegold D 'Student Finance: Equity and Expansion' in IPPR *Higher Education: Expansion and Reform*, London, 1992

Flowers, Lord *The Review of the Academic Year*, a report for CVCP, DENI, HEFCE, HEFCW and SCOP, London, 1993

Fulton O ed *Access to Higher Education*, Guildford, SRHE, 1981

Fulton O ed *Access and Institutional Change*, SRHE/OU, 1989

Fulton O 'Modular Systems in Britain' in Berdahl et al *Quality and Access in Higher Education*, SRHE/OU, 1991

Fulton O and Ellwood S *Admissions to Higher Education: Policy and Practice*, Department of Employment/Training Agency, Sheffield, 1989

Gallacher J and Osborne M 'Differing national models of Access provision: a comparison between Scotland and England', *Journal of Access Studies*, Vol 6 No 2, 1991

Gallie D and White M *Employee Commitment and the Skills Revolution: first findings from the Employment in Britain survey*, Policy Studies Institute, 1993

Gibbs G and Jenkins A ed *Teaching Larger Classes in Higher Education*, London, Kogan Page, 1992

Glennerster H, Merrett S and Wilson G 'A Graduate Tax' *Higher Education Review* Vol 1 No 1, 1968

Goodchild RE 'The Northern Universities Working Party on CAT – a report', paper to 4th CVCP Seminar on Modularisation, Open University, June 1992

Green A and Steedman H *Educational Provision, Educational Attainment and the Needs of Industry: a review of research for Germany, France, Japan and Britain*, NIESR, London, 1993

Harrison M 'The Importance of Student Loan Programmes in the United States' *Higher Education Policy* Vol 6 No 3 1993

Harvey H and Norton B *Survey of Credit Accumulation and Transfer Schemes*, IEHO and University of Ulster, 1993

Haslam E 'Analysis of the pattern, incidence and extent of student withdrawals, 1990-92', mimeo to Liverpool John Moores University, 1993

Hassard J and Parker M ed *Postmodernism and Organisations*, London, Sage, 1993

Hawthorn R Allaway J and Naftalin I *Evaluating Educational Guidance* UDACE, 1988

Hawthorn R and Butcher V *Guidance Workers in the UK: Their Work and Training* NICEC, 1992

Healey N *Britain's Economic Miracle: Myth or Reality?*, London, Routledge, 1993

HEFCE *Academic Subject Categories*, Circular 2/92, Bristol, 1992

HEFCE *The Management and Administrative Computing Initiative*, audit report, HEFCE, Bristol, 1993

HEFCE *Continuing Education*, Circular 18/93, Bristol, 1993

HEFCE *Length of HE Courses*, Circular 1/94, Bristol, 1994

HEFCE *Funding for 1994-95: Council Decisions*, Circular 2/94, Bristol, 1994

HEFCE *Funding of part-time students*, letter to institutions from the Council, 6 January 1994

HEFCE *Continuing Education*, Circular 3/94, Bristol, 1994

Heffernan JM 'The Credibility of the Credit Hour: The History, Use and Shortcomings of the Credit System', *Journal of Higher Education*, Vol 44 No 1, 1973

HEQC *Guideline on Quality Assurance*, London, 1993

HEQC *Some Aspects of Higher Education Programmes in Further Education Institutions*, London, 1993

HEQC *Checklist for Quality Assurance Systems*, London, 1994

HEQC/HEFCE *Joint Statement on Quality Assurance*, January 1994

Herrington M and Rivis V *Guidance in Higher Education*, Report of the Project, HEQC, 1994

Higgins MA 'Admissions to Higher Education: Visions of the Future', public lecture, Admissions in Higher Education Project Conference, University of Sussex, 1993

Higginson G 'A Levels and the Future' in Parry G and Wake C ed, *Access and Alternative Futures*, London, Hodder, 1990

Hills, Sir Graham *The Funding of Higher Education in Britain*, Occasional Paper, CVCP, London, 1992

Hilton A and Ellis D ed *Learning without walls,* Report of the Conference, Oxford, July 1991

Hodgkinson M *A Higher Education Credit Accumulation and Transfer Strategy for Europe,* Project report, Department of Employment and University of Teesside, 1992

Honzik, Jan M 'Credit Accumulation and Transfer', unpublished paper to TEXT conference (Budapest), 1993

Howarth A 'Market Forces in Higher Education', *Higher Education Quarterly* Vol 45 No 1, 1991

Howieson C 'Parity of Vocational and Academic Awards: the experience of modularisation in Scotland' *European Journal of Education* Vol 28 No 2, 1993

Institute for Public Policy Research *A British Baccalaureat,* IPPR, London, 1990

Institute for Public Policy Research *Higher Education: Expansion and Reform,* IPPR, London, 1992

Institute of Careers Guidance and National Association for Educational Guidance for Adults *A Guidance Entitlement for Adults,* 1993

Institute of Manpower Studies *How Many Graduates in the 21st Century? The Choice is Yours,* Report 177, Brighton, 1989

Institute of Physics *The Future Pattern of Higher Education in Physics,* London, IoP, 1990

Jallade JP and Schink G *Participation and Access to Higher Education,* Report on Responses to the Memorandum on Higher Education in the European Community, Task Force Human Resources, Education, Training and Youth, February 1993

Jessup G *Outcomes: NVQs and the Emerging Model of Education and Training,* Falmer Press, 1991

Jessup G 'Developing a Coherent National Framework of Qualifications', *Education and Training Technology International,* Vol 29 No 3, 1992

Johnes G 'Performance Indicators in Higher Education: a survey of recent work', *Oxford Review of Economic Policy* Vol 8 No 2, 1993

Johnes J 'Determinants of Student Wastage in Higher Education', *Studies in Higher Education* Vol 15 No 1, 1990

Johnes J and Taylor J 'Undergraduate non-completion rates: differences between UK universities', *Higher Education* Vol 18 No 2, 1989

Johns D and Field J 'HE Perspectives: institutional and system level', paper to conference on Credit Accumulation Post-16: towards a national framework, Sheffield College, AUT/NATFHE, 1993

Karabel J *Freshman Admissions at Berkeley: a Policy for the 1990s and Beyond,* report by the Committee on Admissions and Enrollment, Academic Senate, University of California, Berkeley, 1989

Keen C and Higgins T *Adults' Knowledge of Higher Education,* HEIST, 1992

Kelly T *Developing Wider Access to Universities,* London, DES, 1991

Kerr E 'Credit rating and Awards', paper to the *Learning without Walls* conference, University of Oxford, 1991

Kiloh G 'Modularity at the University of Sussex', in Davidson G and Deere M ed *Modular Curriculum and Structure,* University of Kent, 1991

Kouwenaar K and Dalichow F 'The Situation of Academic Recognition in the European Community', *Higher Education Policy* Vol 6, No 1. 1993

Lamoure J and Lamoure Rontopoulou J 'The Vocationalisation of Higher Education in France: continuity and change', *European Journal of Education,* Vol 27 No 1/2, 1992

Layer G 'Credit Accumulation and Credit Transfer' in Calder J ed *Disaffection and Diversity,* Falmer Press, London, 1993

Layer G, Lyne J and McManus M *CATS for Post-Registration Courses for Nurses and Professions Allied to Medicine,* CNAA, London, 1989

Layer G and Booth J *Guidance in Higher Education,* report of project, CNAA/UDACE, 1991

Layer G, Moore R and Booth J 'Guidance, Adult Learners and HE' *Journal of Access Studies,* 1994 forthcoming

Leadbeater C and Mulgan G *The End of Unemployment: Bringing Work to Life,* DEMOS, London, 1994

Liaison Committee of Rectors' Conferences. 'The Pilot-Project for a European Community Course Credit Transfer System (ECTS): Experiences and Recommendations', June 1993

Lindley R ed *Higher Eduication and the Labour Market,* Guildford, SRHE, 1981

Liverpool John Moores University (Liverpool Polytechnic) *Integrated Credit Scheme: a Modular Credit Accumulation and Transfer Scheme*, Liverpool 1990

London Economics *Review of Options for the Additional Funding of Higher Education – a report for the CVCP*, London, 1993

London Together *A Prototype Credit Framework for London*, joint London TECs, 1994

MacDonald-Ross M 'Behavioural Objectives – a Critical Review', *Instructional Science*, No 2, 1973

McGivney V ed *Opening Colleges to Adult Learners*, NIACE, 1991

McNair S *Trends and Issues in Education and Training for Adults*, UDACE, Leicester, 1989

McNair S *Open College Networks, Credit Transfer, and the Future of Further Education*, UDACE, Leicester, 1992

McNay I ed *Visions of Post-Compulsory Education*, SRHE/OU, 1992

Mager RF *Preparing Instructional Objectives*, California, Fearon, 1965

Maguire M, Maguire S and Felstead A *Factors Influencing Individual Commitment to Lifetime Learning*, Department of Employment Research Series No 20, Centre for Labour Market Studies, University of Leicester, 1993

Maiworm F, Steube W and Teichler U *Learning in Europe: the ERASMUS Experience*, Jessica Kingsley, 1991

Marks R *Implications of National Vocational Qualifications for the Polytechnic Sector*, Project Report for the Committee of Directors of Polytechnics, CDP, 1991

Maynard A *The Finance of Higher Education by a System of Student Loans*, memorandum to House of Commons Committee on Education, Science and Art, 21 May 1980, HC 787/11

Metcalf H *Non-traditional Students' Experience of Higher Education*, CVCP, London 1993

Metcalfe L and Richards S *Improving Public Management*

Miliband D *Learning by Right: an entitlement to paid education and training*, IPPR, London, 1990

Mintzberg H *Power in and Around Organisations*, New Jersey, Prentice-Hall, 1983

Mills R and Sykes S 'Do credit tariff models reflect reality?', paper to *Learning without walls* conference, Oxford, 1991

Mitchell L 'NVQs/SVQs at Higher Levels', *Competence and Assessment*, Briefing Series No 8, Employment Dept, 1993

Mohammed N 'Access to Higher Education (European and International Dimension)', unpublished paper, October 1992

Murray DJ and Van Deventer CW *Report on Course and Credit Transfer*, EADTU, Brussels, 1988

NAB *Report of the Continuing Education Group*, London, NAB, 1984

NAB *Report of the Consortia and Regional Structures Group*, NAB, London, 1988

NAB *Action for Access: widening opportunities in higher education*, NAB, London, 1988

NAB/UGC *Report on the Study of Credit Transfer/Accumulation and Qualification Structures*, London, NAB/UGC, 1987

NAB/UGC *Credit Where Credit's Due*, London, 1988

NAEGA *A Code of Practice for Members*, London, 1990

NATFHE *The Community College: a model for the future*, London, 1992

NATFHE *Credit Limits: a critical assessment of the Training Credits pilot scheme*, NATFHE, London, 1993

National Academic Recognition Information Centre, *International Guide to Qualifications in Education*, The British Council, 1992

National Commission on Education *Learning to Succeed*, Heinemann, 1993

National Institute for Careers Education and Counselling *Who Offers Guidance?*, London 1991

National Training Task Force *National Targets for Education and Training*, London, 1992

NCVQ *Accreditation Procedures*, NCVQ, London, 1988

NCVQ *Guide to National Vocational Qualifications*, London, 1991

NCVQ *General National Vocational Qualifications: a consultation paper*, NCVQ, London, 1991

NCVQ *National Standards for Assessment and Verification*, Report 13, NCVQ, London, 1991

NCVQ 'Towards a national system of credit accumulation, a discussion paper', May 1993

NCVQ *GNVQ Information Note,* September 1993

NCVQ *GNVQs at Higher Levels,* draft consultation paper, December 1993

NCVQ 'Credit accumulation and transfer between (G)NVQs and academic programmes', draft mimeo, December 1993

Neave G 'On Instantly Consumable Knowledge and Snake Oil' *European Journal of Education* Vol 27 No1/2, 1992

Neave M *Models of Quality Assurance in Europe,* CNAA, 1991

Newcastle Polytechnic *Polytechnic Association Student Scheme (PASS) Handbook,* Newcastle, 1988

New Zealand Qualification Authority *A Qualification Framework for New Zealand: An introduction to the Framework,* Wellington, 1992

NIACE *The '21 hour Rule' and Support for Adult Learners,* NIACE, Leicester, 1990

NIACE *An Adult Higher Education: a vision,* NIACE, Leicester, 1993

NIACE *The Learning Imperative: a discussion paper on National Education and Training Targets and adult learners,* NIACE, Leicester, 1993

Nicholson, Sir Brian 'An Employer's View – Education and Training: strategy and delivery' in Hilton A and Ellis D *Learning without walls,* 1991

NOCN *The National Open College Network: a position statement,* UDACE, London, 1991

NOCN *Quality Assurance: National Arrangements,* UDACE, London, 1991

Noel L et al *Increasing Student Retention: Effective Programmes for Reducing the Dropout Rate,* Jossey-Bass, 1985

NUS *Student Charter,* London, 1993

NUS *Learner Agreements,* London, 1993

Oakeshott M *Educational Guidance and Curriculum Change,* FEU/UDACE, 1990

Oakeshott M *Educational Guidance for Adults: Identifying Competences* FEU/UCACE, 1991

OECD *Policies for Higher Education in the 1980s,* OECD, Paris, 1983

OECD *Employment Outlook,* OECD, Paris, 1993

OECD *Education at a Glance,* OECD, Paris, 1993

Opper S, Teichler U and Carlson J *Impacts of Study Abroad Programmes on Students and Graduates,* London, Jessica Kingsley, 1990

Otter S *Learning Outcomes and Higher Education,* Leicester, UDACE, 1992

Parry G 'Marking and Mediating the Higher Education Boundary' in Fulton O ed *Access and Institutional Change,* 1989

Parry G and Davies P *Kitemarking Access,* FEU, 1992

Parry G and Wake C ed *Access and Alternative Futures,* Hodder & Stoughton, London, 1990

PCAS *Statistical Supplement to the Annual Report, 1991-92,* PCAS, Cheltenham, 1993

PCFC *Widening Participation in Higher Education,* Bristol, 1992

PCFC *Funding and Enrolments 1991-92,* PCFC Bristol, 1992

Pearson R and Pike G *Supply and Demand in the 1990s,* IMS Graduate Review, Report 192, Brighton, 1990

Porter M *The Competitive Advantage of Nations,* London, Macmillan, 1990

Portwood D 'Institutional Models of CATS', *SEEC News* No 5, 1990

Powell B *Measuring Performance in the Education of Adults,* UDACE/NIACE, 1991

Raban, C ed *Accreditation: Principles and Practice,* Sheffield Hallam University, 1992

Race P and Portwood D 'CATS – Bringing Education and Training Together', *Education and Training Technology International,* Vol 27 No 4, 1990

Raffe D 'Participation of 16-18 year olds in Education and Training', *Briefing Paper No. 3,* National Commission on Education, 1992

Raggart P and Unwin L ed *Change and Intervention*, Falmer Press, 1991

Raggatt P 'The Development of Credit Transfer – a review', unpublished paper

Regel O *The Academic Credit System in Higher Education: effectiveness and relevance in developing countries*, World Bank, 1992

Ricketts, Sir Raymond 'CATS and a Vision for Higher Education', in Hilton A and Ellis D *Learning without walls*, 1991

Rickwood PW *The Experience of Transfer*, Open University mimeo, 1993

Risvig Henriksen H and Haug G *Survey of Academic Recognition within the framework of ICPs in the field of Mechanical Engineering*, Erasmus Monograph No 5, Brussels, 1989

Rivis V ed *Delivering Educational Guidance for Adults: a handbook for policy-makers, managers and practitioners*, Leicester, NIACE, 1989

Rivis V and Sadler J *The Quest for Quality in Educational Guidance for Adults*, UDACE/NEGI, 1991

Robbins D 'The opportunities for credit transfer', *Higher Education Review*, Vol 12 No 3

Robbins, Lord *Report of the Committee on Higher Education*, Cmnd 2154, HMSO, 1963

Robertson C 'Accreditation of Company Training Programmes', in Bines H and Watson D *Developing Professional Education*, 1992

Robertson D *The Unit of Credit and Statements of Competence*, report, Merseyside Open College Federation, 1988

Robertson D 'Credit Systems, Learning Outcomes and the Unit of Credit', paper to CNAA Seminar on credit systems, Sheffield City Polytechnic, 1989

Robertson D 'Credit Systems, Outcomes and the NCVQ', *Annual Report and Proceedings of the National Open Learning Federation*, 1990

Robertson D 'Can Credit be earned and spent? The use of credit systems as academic and resource management instruments', internal mimeo, Liverpool John Moores University, 1991

Robertson D 'Terms of No Endearment: reforming the academic year', *The Guardian*, 17 December 1991

Robertson D 'Modularisation, Semesters and CATS – lessons from the 'new' Universities', in Davidson G and Power B *Semesterisation, Modularity, Credit Accumulation and Transfer: Harmony and Development*, papers from the 4th CVCP seminar, Open University, 1992

Robertson D *Learning Outcomes and Curriculum Change: accountability and relevance in the HE curriculum*, Enterprise Conference, public lecture, University of Northumbria, 1992

Robertson D 'Courses, Qualifications and the Empowerment of Learners', in IPPR *Higher Education: Expansion and Reform*, London, 1992

Robertson D 'The National CATS Task Force: an Agenda for Action', *Adults Learning*, Vol 4 No 2, 1992

Robertson D 'Credit Frameworks – An International Comparison', *Discussing Credit*, FEU, 1993

Robertson D 'Towards a Credit Culture', *NATFHE Journal*, Spring 1993

Robertson D 'Flexibility and Mobility in Further and Higher Education: Policy Continuity and Progress', *Journal of Further and Higher Education*, Vol 17 No 1, 1993

Robertson D 'The credit you spend as you learn', *Times Higher Education Supplement*, 18 June 1993

Robertson D 'Aspiration, Achievement and Progression in Post-Secondary and Higher Education', in Burke J ed *Outcomes, Learning and the Curriculum*, Falmer Press, 1994

Roff A 'Franchising: assuring the quality of the student experience', *Coombe Lodge Reports 22*, Bristol, FESC, 1992

Rothblatt S 'The American Modular System', in Berdahl R et al *Quality and Access in Higher Education*, SRHE, 1991

Rothblatt S and Wittrock B ed *The European and American University since 1800*, Cambridge, CUP, 1993

Royal Society *Beyond GCSE*, London, 1991

Royal Society *Higher Education Futures*, London, 1993

Sadler J and Rivis V *National Educational Guidance Helpline and Referral Network: A Feasibility Study*, NEGI, 1993

Saunders D ed *The New Agenda for Further and Higher Education in Wales*, University of Glamorgan and Welsh Office, Cardiff, 1992

Schuller T 'The Exploding Community? The University Idea and the Smashing of the Academic Atom', *Oxford Review of Education* Vol 16 No 1, 1990

Schuller T et al 'How Two-Year Degrees Help to Widen Student Opportunities', *The Times Higher Education Supplement*, 30 November 1990

Schuller T ed *The Future of Higher Education*, SRHE/OUP, 1991

Scott P 'Post-binary Access and Learning', in Parry G and Wake C *Access and Alternative Futures*, Hodder & Stoughton, London, 1990

Scott P 'Access: an Overview', in Schuller T ed *The Future of Higher Education*, SRHE/OUP, 1991

Scott P 'The Idea of the University in the 21st Century: a British Perspective', *British Journal of Educational Studies*, Vol 41 No 1, 1993

Scott P and Watson D 'Roles and Responsibilities', conference paper: *Managing the University Curriculum in the Year 2000*, London, October 1992

Scottish Education Department *16-18s in Scotland: an Action Plan*, SED, 1983

Scottish Office Education Department *Staying the Course*, Research Paper No 13, SOED Edinburgh, 1992

Scottish Office Education Department *Upper Secondary Education in Scotland* (Howie Report), HMSO, Edinburgh, 1992

Scottish Office *Access and Opportunity: a strategy for education and training*, Cmnd 1530, HMSO, Edinburgh, 1991

SEEC *SEEC Handbook, 1986-87*, SEEC, London, 1986

Shackleton JR 'Investing in Training: Questioning the Conventional Wisdom', *Policy Studies*, Vol 14 No 3, 1993

SHEFC/COSHEP *Review of the Academic Year: interim report* (Irvine Report), SHEFC, 1993

Sheffield Hallam University *Final Report of the Advice and Guidance in a Flexible Institution Working Party*, 1993

Sizer J 'Can a Funding Council be a Proxy for Price Competition in a Competitive Market?', *Higher Education Policy*, Vol 5 No 3, 1992

Smith G and Bailey V *Staying the Course*, BTEC, 1993

Smith DM and Saunders MR *Other Routes: Part-time Higher Education Policy*, SRHE/OU, 1991

Smithers A and Robinson P *Increasing Participation in Higher Education*, London, BP Educational Services, 1989

Smithers A and Robinson P *Beyond Compulsory Schooling*, Council for Industry and Higher Education, London, 1991

SRHE *Excellence in Diversity*, SRHE, 1983

Squires G *Modularisation*, CONTACT Paper No 1, Manchester, 1986

Squires G 'Interdisciplinarity in HE in the United Kingdom', *European Journal of Education*, Vol 27 No 3, 1993

Steedman H 'Improvement in Workforce Qualifications: Britain and France 1979-88', in Raggart P and Unwin L ed *Change and Intervention*, Falmer Press, 1991

Stephenson J and Weil S ed *Quality in Learning: a capability approach to higher education*, London, Kogan Page, 1992

Stern MR *The New Majority: Impact of Older Students upon the University Today*, keynote address to OECD Programme on Institutional Management of Higher Education, 29th Session, mimeo, December 1990

Stoddart J *Developments in Continuing Education – the next ten years*, 10th Anniversary Lecture of the Polytechnic Association for Continuing Education, Nottingham, PACE and Employment Department, 1990

Storan J *Making Experience Count*, London, Learning from Experience Trust, 1988

Storan J 'Credit Accumulation and Transfer for the Diploma in Social Work: Guidance Notes for Programme Planners', CCETSW, London, 1991

Taylor FJ *Report of the Project on Credit Transfer Policies and Practices*, Open University, 1990

Teichler U *Changing Patterns of the Higher Education System: the experience of three decades*, Jessica Kingsley, 1988

Teichler U *Experiences of ERASMUS Students – select findings of the 1988/89 Survey* ERASMUS Monograph No 13, Brussels, 1991

TEXT *Guidelines for Good Practice in Credit Accumulation and Transfer*, University of Derby, 1990

TEXT *Credit Accumulation and Transfer in Europe*, papers from conference at University of Cambridge, 1991

Theodossin E *The Modular Market*, Further Education Staff College, Bristol, 1986

Thompson G, Frances J, Levacic R and Mitchell J ed *Markets, Hierarchies and Networks*, London, Sage/OU, 1991

Tight M *Higher Education: a part-time perspective*, SRHE/OU, 1990

Tight M 'Part-time Higher Education in Western Developed Countries', *European Journal of Education*, Vol 26 No 1, 1991

Toyne P *Educational Credit Transfer: feasibility study*, DES, 1979

Trow M 'Reflections on the transition from mass to universal higher education', *Daedalus*, No 90, 1970

Trow, M 'Problems in the transition from elite to mass higher education', in OECD (ed), *Policies for Higher Education*, Paris, OECD, 1974

Trow M 'Comparative Perspectives on Access', in Fulton, O (ed), *Access to Higher Education*, SRHE/Leverhulme, 1981

Trow M 'The Exceptionalism of American Higher Education', in Trow M and Nyborn T ed *University and Society*, 1991

Trow M and Nyborn T ed *University and Society*, London, Jessica Kingsley, 1991

Tuck R, Lee BS and Benett Y *A Self-Assessment Model for the Integration of Work-Based Learning with Academic Assessment*, report of the project, University of Huddersfield and Employment Department, 1992

Tuckett A *Towards a Learning Workforce: a discussion paper on adult learners at work*, NIACE, 1992

UDACE *The Challenge of Change*, NIACE, Leicester, 1986

UDACE *Performance Indicators and the Education of Adults*, NIACE, Leicester, 1989

UDACE *Understanding Competence*, NIACE, Leicester, 1989

UDACE *Understanding Learning Outcomes*, NIACE, Leicester, 1989

UDACE *Open College Networks: current developments and practice*, NIACE, Leicester, 1989

UDACE *An Agenda for Access*, NIACE, Leicester, 1990

UDACE *Open College Networks and National Vocational Qualifications*, NIACE, Leicester, 1990

UDACE *What Can Graduates Do? – a consultative document*, NIACE, Leicester, 1991

UDACE *Understanding Accreditation*, NIACE, Leicester, 1992

Uden, T *The Will to Learn: individual commitment and adult learning*, NIACE, Leicester, 1994

UFC/PCFC *A Funding Methodology for Teaching in Higher Education*, UFC and PCFC, Bristol, 1992

UFC/PCFC *Capital Funding and Estate Management in Higher Education* (Pearce Report), UFC/PCFC, 1992

University of Cambridge Board of Continuing Education *Towards a Credit Framework*, feasibility study, 1994

University of Central Lancashire *MODCATS – a report on a credit accumulation and transfer scheme*, Preston, 1993

University of East London *Assessment of APL and APEL*, Institutional Handbook, London, UEL, 1993

University of Massachusetts at Boston *CPCS College Handbook – 'The Red Book'*, Boston, 1990

University of Middlesex *Guide and Catalogue*, Middlesex, 1993

University of Portsmouth *Partnership Programme for work-based learning*, University of Portsmouth, 1993

Unwin L 'Meeting the Needs of a 'Global Society': Vocational Education and Training in the United States of America', in Raggart P and Unwin L ed *Change and Intervention*, Falmer Press, 1991

USR *University Statistics 1991-92: students and staff*, USR, Cheltenham, 1993

USR *University Statistics 1991-92: first destinations of university graduates*, USR, Cheltenham, 1993

USR *University Statistics 1990-91: finance*, USR, Cheltenham, 1993

Van Eijl PJ 'Modular Programming of Curricula', *Higher Education*, Vol 15 No 5, 1986

Van Vught FA and Westerheijden DF *Quality Assessment in European University Higher Education: A Report on Methods and Mechanisms and Policy Recommendations to the European Community*, European Rectors' Conference, 1992

Vaughan P *Maintaining Professional Competence*, University of Hull, 1991

Wagner L ed *Agenda for Institutional Change in Higher Education*, Guildford, SRHE, 1982

Wagner L 'National Policy and Institutional Development' in Fulton O ed *Access and Institutional Change*, 1989

Wagner L 'The Teaching Quality Debate', *Higher Education Quarterly*, Vol 47 No 3, 1993

Warren J and Weir AC *Survey of Modular First Degree Schemes in the United Kingdom*, Hatfield Polytechnic, 1973

Waterhouse R 'Modularisation and Further Education', unpublished mimeo, 1987

Waterhouse R *The Educational Potential of Credit Systems*, TEXT, Derby, 1992

Waterhouse R *EUROCATS – The Concept, A Higher Education System for Europe*, 1992

Watson D *Managing the Modular Course*, SRHE/OUP, 1989

Watts AG and Hawthorn R *Careers Education and the Curriculum in Higher Education*, NICEC/CRAC, 1992

Welsh Higher Education CATS Forum *Welsh CATS Project: Interim Report*, Cardiff, 1993

Williams G *Changing Patterns of Finance in Higher Education*, SRHE, 1992

Williams G and Blackstone T *Response to Adversity*, SRHE, 1983

Williams M *Credit Transfer: In-Course Credit Recognition*, CONTACT Paper No 5, Manchester, 1988

Wilson P 'Access and quality: the debate re-opened?', *Journal of Access Studies*, Vol 6 No 1, 1991

Wilson P *Beyond 'A Basis for Credit?' – developing technical specifications for a national credit framework*, draft consultation paper, FEU, unpublished, 1993

Wilson P 'Developing a Post-16 CAT Framework: the technical specifications', in FEU *Discussing Credit*, London, 1993

Winter R 'The Problem of Education Levels: conceptualising a framework for credit accumulation and transfer – Part I', *Journal of Further and Higher Education*, Vol 17 No 3

Winter R 'The Problem of Education Levels: conceptualising a framework for credit accumulation and transfer – Part II', *Journal of Further and Higher Education*, Vol 18 No 1

Winter R 'Education or Grading? Arguments for a Non-Subdivided Honours Degree', *Studies in Higher Education*, Vol 18 No 3, 1993

Wisher P *Open College Networks: participation and progress*, London, FEU, 1993

Woodhall M ed *Financial Support for Students: Grants, Loans or Graduate Tax?*, London, Kogan, 1989

Woodley A, Thompson M and Cowan J *Factors Affecting Non-Completion Rates in Scottish Universities*, a report to SOED, Milton Keynes: Open University, 1992

Woodrow M 'Franchising: the Quiet Revolution', *Higher Education Quarterly*, Vol 47 No 3, 1993

Wright PWG 'Who defines quality in higher education? Reflections on the role of professional power in determining conceptions of quality in English higher education', *Higher Education*, Vol 18 No 2, 1989

Wright PWG 'Access or accessibility?', *Journal of Access Studies*, Vol 6 No 1, 1991

Yorke M 'Quality Assurance for Higher Education Franchising', *Higher Education*, Vol 26 No 2, 1993

Appendix 1. *Membership*

HEQC, Credit and Access Advisory Group

Professor Peter Toyne	Vice-Chancellor, Liverpool John Moores University, (Chair)
Dr Roger Brown	Chief Executive, HEQC
David Browning	Director, Manchester Open College Federation
Professor Peter Bush	Pro Vice-Chancellor, Glasgow Caledonian University
Professor Chris Duke	Pro Vice-Chancellor, University of Warwick
Dr Peter Easy	Deputy Director, Cheltenham and Gloucester College of HE
Colin Flint	Principal, Solihull College
John Hillier	Chief Executive, NCVQ
Dr Edwin Kerr	Education Consultant
Richard Lewis	Pro Vice-Chancellor, Open University
Professor James Lusty	Head of Academic Programmes, University of Central Lancashire
Ted Nakhle	Planning Officer, University of Sussex
Dr Derek Pollard	Director of Open University Validation Services
Dr David Scurry	Director of Modular Scheme, Oxford Brookes University
Professor Maria Slowey	Head of Continuing Education, University of Glasgow
Anthony Webb	Head of Policy, CBI
Ros Seyd	Department of Employment
Anthony Woollard	Department for Education

Project Management Sub-Group

Richard Lewis	Pro Vice-Chancellor, Open University, (Chair)
Professor David Robertson	Project Director
Professor Peter Bush	Pro Vice-Chancellor, Glasgow Caledonian University
Dr Edwin Kerr	Education Consultant
Alan Callaghan	Department for Education
Ros Seyd	Department of Employment

Research Team

Professor David Robertson	Executive Director for Policy Development, Liverpool John Moores University (Project Director)
Stephen Adam	University of Westminster
Dr Robert Allen	Director of Education and Training Development, University of Greenwich
Norman Evans	Director, Learning from Experience Trust
Professor Anne Hilton	Anglia Polytechnic University
Geoff Layer	Director of Access and Guidance, Sheffield Hallam University
Gareth Parry	Visiting Lecturer, University of Warwick
Professor Peter Scott	Professor of Education, University of Leeds

Project Consultants

Dr John Ashworth	Director, London School of Economics and Political Science
Professor Laing Barden	Vice-Chancellor, University of Northumbria at Newcastle
Professor Tony Becher	Head of Quality, University of Sussex
Janet Clark	Principal, City and East London College
Patrick Coldstream	Director, Council for Industry and Higher Education
Dr John Daniel	Vice-Chancellor, Open University
Dr Gaie Davidson	UACE CATS Project, University of Kent
Professor Chris Duke	Pro Vice-Chancellor, University of Warwick
Lorna Fitzsimmons	President, National Union of Students
Professor Hywel Francis	Professor of Continuing Education, University College of Swansea
Ruth Gee	Chief Executive, Association for Colleges
Margaret Jack	Director of Quality Assurance and Control, BTEC
Dr Gilbert Jessup	Deputy Chief Executive, NCVQ
Professor David Johns	Vice-Chancellor, University of Bradford
Dr Edwin Kerr	Education Consultant
Stephen McNair	Associate Director, NIACE
Sally Neocosmos	University Secretary, Sheffield Hallam University
Sue Otter	Higher Education Consultant, Employment Department
Rachel Pierce	Assistant Director, CCETSW
Dr Derek Pollard	Director of Institutions and Programmes, Open University
Geoff Stanton	Chief Officer, Further Education Unit
Professor Leslie Wagner	Vice-Chancellor, Leeds Metropolitan University
Professor Roger Waterhouse	Vice-Chancellor, University of Derby
Peter Wilson	National Open College Network

Project Advisory Group Members

PAG 1   Taxonomy of CAT systems

Gareth Parry	University of Warwick; Project Officer

PAG 2   Quality Assurance in Institutional and 'Off-Campus' Learning

Norman Evans	Director, The Learning from Experience Trust; Project Officer
Jeff Donovan	Group Training Manager, Lucas Industries
Mike Hanson	Chief Executive, South Thames TEC
Dr Len Moore	Pro Vice-Chancellor, University of Wolverhampton
Margaret Murray	Head of Educational Policy, CBI
Rachel Pierce	Assistant Director, CCETSW
Michael Pitt	Assistant Registrar, University of Nottingham
Dr Derek Pollard	Director of Programmes and Institutions, Open University
Madeleine Swords	NCVQ

PAG 3   National Credit Framework

Dr Anne Hilton	Anglia Polytechnic University; Project Officer
Chris Boys	Development Officer, NCVQ
Dr Andrew Brooks	Senior Assistant Registrar, University of Leeds
Janet Clark	Principal, City and East London College
Sandy Coleman	Development Officer, BTEC
Dr Alan Crispin	Assistant Director, HEQC
Malcolm Deere	Standing Conference on University Entrance
Di Ellis	Senior Officer, SEEC
Dr Peter Johnston	Director of Access, University of Essex
Andrew Morris	Unified Curriculum Project, Institute of Education
Sue Pedder	National Open College Network
Jonathan Slack	Chief Officer, Association of Business Schools
Tony Tait	Development Officer, Further Education Unit

PAG 4   Institutional Management Structures

Dr Rob Allen	University of Greenwich; Project Officer
Dr Gaie Davidson	Project Officer, University of Kent
Dr Peter Easy	Deputy Principal, Cheltenham and Gloucester College of HE
Keith Elliott	Project Director, Welsh Access Unit
Dr Dennis Farrington	Deputy Secretary and Registrar, University of Stirling
Joel Gladstone	Head of Modular Scheme, Middlesex University
Reg Goodchild	Academic Registrar, University of Sheffield
Dr John Piper	Validation and Review, Manchester Metropolitan University
Freda Tallantyre	Head of Unilink, University of Northumbria at Newcastle
Anne Tate	Enterprise Manager, University of Ulster
Mollie Temple	Pro Vice-Chancellor, University of Sunderland

PAG 5 Educational Guidance and Student Information

Geoff Layer	Sheffield Hallam University; Project Officer
Jeanne Booth	Educational Guidance Unit, Coventry University
Jackie Booth	Educational Guidance, Sheffield Hallam University
Sheila Cross	Association of Graduate Careers Advisory Services
Lorna Fitzsimmons	President, National Union of Students
Tony Higgins	Chief Executive, Universities and Colleges Admissions Service
Phoebe Lambert	Director, Guidance and Progression, Liverpool John Moores University
Viv Rivis	Assistant Director, Higher Education Quality Council
Chris West	Chief Executive, ECCTIS 2000

PAG 6 Credit-led Resourcing and Student Finance

Professor David Robertson	Liverpool John Moores University, Project Officer
Jon Baldwin	Director of Modular Scheme, Queen Margaret College, Edinburgh
Chris Batten	Academic Registrar, Open University
Malcolm Christie	Corporate Planning Officer, Leeds Metropolitan University
Dr Hywel Davies	Assistant Registrar, University College Aberystwyth
Paul Ellis	Development Officer, NCVQ
Dr Philip Jones	Assistant Director, HEQC
Ted Nakhle	Planning Officer, University of Sussex
Dr Shekhar Nandy	Head of Analytical Services, HEFCE
Sally Neocosmos	University Secretary, Sheffield Hallam University
Dr Adrian Seville	Academic Registrar, City University
Antoinette Titchener-Hooker	CVCP
Valerie Wilson	Planning Support Officer, University of Northumbria at Newcastle
Anthony Woollard	Quality Division, Department for Education

PAG 7 International Credit Transfer Arrangements

Stephen Adam	University of Westminster
Carolyn Campbell	Assistant Director, HEQC
Dr Leni Oglesby	University of Lancaster
Dr Derek Pollard	Open University
Professor Maria Slowey	Head of Continuing Education, University of Glasgow
Mike Vaughan	University of Wolverhampton

PAG 8 Academic Values and Institutional Culture

Professor Peter Scott	University of Leeds; Project Officer
Dr Ron Barnett	Institute of Education, University of London
Professor Tony Becher	University of Sussex
Jean Bocock	Assistant Secretary (Higher Education), NATFHE
Professor Chris Duke	Pro Vice-Chancellor, University of Warwick
Professor Hywel Francis	Head of Continuing Education, University College Swansea
Monica Shaw	Dean of Social Science, University of Northumbria at Newcastle

Appendix 2. *Consultations*

Universities visited and representatives consulted

Anglia Polytechnic University
City University
Coventry University
Glasgow Caledonian University
Leeds Metropolitan University
Liverpool John Moores University
London Guildhall University
London School of Economics and Political Science
Manchester Metropolitan University
Middlesex University
Open University
Paisley University
Sheffield Hallam University
Thames Valley University
University of Bradford
University of Central England
University of Central Lancashire
University of Derby
University of East London
University of Glasgow
University of Greenwich
University of Huddersfield
University of Kent at Canterbury
University of Lancaster
University of Leeds
University of Liverpool
University of Luton
University of Northumbria at Newcastle
University of Nottingham
University of Sheffield
University of Sussex
University of Ulster
University of Wales, Cardiff
University of Wales, Swansea
University of Warwick
University of Westminster
University of Wolverhampton

Colleges of higher education visited and representatives consulted

Bath College of Higher Education
Bolton Institute of Higher Education
Cheltenham and Gloucester College of Higher Education
Chester College of Higher Education
Edge Hill College of Higher Education

National bodies consulted

Association for Colleges
Association for Data Systems in Education and Training
Association for Part–time Higher Education
Association of Business Schools
Association of Graduate Careers Advisory Services
Association of University Administrators
Association of University Teachers
Business and Technology Education Council
Committee of Vice–Chancellors and Principals
Confederation of British Industry
Council for Industry and Higher Education
Council for International Education Exchange
Department for Education
Department of Employment
ECCTIS 2000 Ltd
Economic and Social Research Council
ERASMUS Bureau
European Commission
Forum for Access Studies
Further Education Funding Council
Further Education Statistical Record
Further Education Unit
Higher Education Funding Council for England
Higher Education Quality Council
Higher Education Statistics Agency
Learning from Experience Trust
London Together
Management Charter Initiative
National Association of Health Care Professions
National Association of Teachers in Further and Higher Education
National Council for Vocational Qualifications
National Institute of Adult Continuing Education
National Open College Network
National Post–16 Network
National Union of Students
Northern Federation for CATS
Public Management Foundation
Society for Research into Higher Education

South–East England Consortium
Standing Conference of Authorised Validating Agencies
Standing Conference on University Entrance
Trans–European Exchange and Transfer
Universities and Colleges Information Systems Association
Universities Corporate Planning Network
Universities Association of Continuing Education
Universities and Colleges Admissions Service
Universities Statistical Record

Professional bodies consulted

Association of Science Education
British Computer Society
British Dental Association
British Dietetic Association
British Institute of Administrative Management
British Institute of Management
British Medical Association
British Orthoptic Society
British Psychological Society
Central Council for Education and Training in Social Work
Chartered Association of Certified Accountants
Chartered Building Societies Institute
Chartered Institute of Bankers
Chartered Institute of Bankers in Scotland
Chartered Institute of Building
Chartered Institute of Management Accountants
Chartered Institute of Marketing
Chartered Institute of Public Finance and Accountancy
Chartered Institute of Transport
Chartered Insurance Institute
Chartered Society of Designers
Chartered Society of Physiotherapy
College of Occupational Therapists
College of Preceptors
College of Radiographers
College of Speech and Language Therapists
Construction Industry Council
Engineering Council
English National Board for Nursing, Midwifery and Health Visiting
General Dental Council
General Medical Council
Hotel Catering and Institutional Management Association
Institute of Biology
Institute of Building Control
Institute of Chartered Accountants in England and Wales

Institute of Chartered Accountants of Scotland
Institute of Chartered Secretaries and Administrators
Institute of Export
Institute of Financial Accountants
Institute of Health Services Management
Institute of Housing
Institute of Incorporated Executive Engineers
Institute of Linguists
Institute of Marine Engineers
Institute of Personnel Management
Institute of Physics
Institute of Quality Assurance
Institute of Taxation
Institution of Chemical Engineers
Institution of Civil Engineers
Institution of Electrical Engineers
Institution of Electronics and Electrical Incorporated Engineers
Institution of Environmental Health Officers
Institution of Industrial Managers
Institution of Mechanical Engineers
Institution of Mechanical Incorporated Engineers
International Association of Book-keepers
Law Society
Library Association
Royal College of Nursing
Royal College of Veterinary Surgeons
Royal Institute of British Architects
Royal Institution of Chartered Surveyors
Royal Pharmaceutical Society of Great Britain
Royal Society of Chemistry
Royal Town Planning Institute
Society of Chiropodists
UK Inter–Professional Group
UKCC for Nursing, Midwifery and Health Visiting

Employers consulted

Allied–Lyons
British Telecom
Ford UK
Grand Metropolitan
NHS Training Directorate
Rover Group
Yorkshire Regional Health Authority

Training and Enterprise Councils consulted

Joint London TECs (9)
SOLOTEC
South Thames TEC

Appendix 3. *Glossary*

ABS	Association of Business Schools
ACRG	Access Courses Recognition Group (until 1993)
ADSET	Association for Data Systems in Education and Training
AFC	Association for Colleges
AGCAS	Association of Graduate Careers Advisory Services
AGR	Association of Graduate Recruitment
APEL	Accreditation of Prior Experiential Learning (uncertificated)
APHE	Association for Part-time Higher Education
APL	Accreditation of Prior Learning (certificated)
AUA	Association of University Administrators
AUT	Association of University Teachers
AVCC	Australian Vice-Chancellors' Committee
BTEC	Business and Technology Education Council
CATS	Credit Accumulation and Transfer Scheme
CBI	Confederation of British Industry
CDP	Committee of Directors of Polytechnics (until 1992)
CIEE	Council for International Education Exchange
CIHE	Council for Industry and Higher Education
CNAA	Council for National Academic Awards (until 1992)
COMETT	Community action programme in Education and Training for Technology (EU)
COSHEP	Committee of Scottish Higher Education Principals
CPD	Continuing Professional Development
CSCFC	Committee of Scottish Centrally Funded Colleges
CSUP	Committee of Scottish University Principals
CVCP	Committee of Vice-Chancellors and Principals
DENI	Department of Education (Northern Ireland)
DES	Department of Education and Science (until 1992)
DFE	Department for Education (from 1992)
DTI	Department of Trade and Industry
EADTU	European Association of Distance Teaching Universities
EC	European Commission
ECCTIS	Educational Counselling and Credit Transfer Information Service

ECTS	European Credit Transfer System
ED	Employment Department (Department of Employment)
EDAP	Employee Development Assistance Programme (Ford)
EFTA	European Free Trade Association
EHE	Enterprise in Higher Education
ERASMUS	European Scheme for the Mobility of University Students
ESRC	Economic and Social Research Council
EU	European Union (formerly the European Community)
EUROTECHNET	European Community action programme in the field of vocational training and technological change
FAST	Forum for Access Studies
FEFC	Further Education Funding Council
FESR	Further Education Statistical Record
FEU	Further Education Unit
FORCE	Action programme for the development of continuing vocational training (EU)
GNVQ	General National Vocational Qualification
HEFCE	Higher Education Funding Council for England
HEFCW	Higher Education Funding Council for Wales
HEQC	Higher Education Quality Council
HESA	Higher Education Statistics Agency
HMI	Her Majesty's Inspectorate
ICP	Inter-university Co-operation Programmes (Europe)
IIP	Investors in People initiative
ILB	Industry Lead Body
LEC	Local Enterprise Council (Scotland)
LET	Learning from Experience Trust
LINCS	Lancashire Integrated Colleges Scheme
LINGUA	Programme to promote foreign language competence in the European Community
MAC	Management and Administrative Computing initiative
MCI	Management Charter Initiative
NAB	National Advisory Body (for HE)(until 1988)
NACES	National Association of Credential Evaluation Services (USA)
NAEGA	National Adult Educational Guidance Association
NAEGS	National Association of Education Guidance Services
NARIC	National Academic Recognition Information Centre
NATCAT	National Association for Credit Accumulation and Transfer
NATFHE	National Association of Teachers in Further and Higher Education

NCVQ	National Council for Vocational Qualifications
NEGI	National Education Guidance Initiative
NIACE	National Institute of Adult Continuing Education
NOCN	National Open College Network
NORDPLUS	Nordic Programme for the Mobility of University Students and Teachers
NTET	National Targets for Education and Training
NUFFIC	Netherlands Organisation for International Co-operation in Higher Education
NUS	National Union of Students
NVQ	National Vocational Qualification
NZQA	New Zealand Qualifications Authority
OCF (OCN)	Open College Federation (Network)
ODL	Open and Distance Learning
OECD	Organisation of Economic Co-operation and Development
PCAS	Polytechnics Central Admission Service (until 1993)
PCFC	Polytechnics and Colleges Funding Council (until 1992)
SCAVA	Standing Conference of Authorised Validating Agencies
SCOP	Standing Conference of Principals
SCOTCAT	Scottish Credit Accumulation and Transfer Scheme
SCOTVEC	Scottish Vocational Education Council
SCUE	Standing Conference on University Entrance
SEEC	South-East England Consortium
SHEFC	Scottish Higher Education Funding Council
SOED	Scottish Office Education Department (also SED)
SRHE	Society for Research into Higher Education
TEC	Training and Enterprise Council
TEMPUS	Trans-European Mobility Scheme for University Studies
TEXT	Trans-European Exchange and Transfer Consortium
UACE	Universities Association of Continuing Education (formerly UCACE)
UCAS	Universities and Colleges Admissions Service (from 1993)
UCCA	Universities Central Council for Admissions (until 1993)
UCISA	Universities and Colleges Information Systems Association
UDACE	Unit for the Development of Adult Continuing Education (until 1992)
UFC	Universities Funding Council (until 1992)
UGC	University Grants Committee (until 1988)
USR	Universities Statistical Record (until 1994, then HESA)
WBL	Work-Based Learning